CW01369130

AIRBORNE TO ARNHEM

Personal Reminiscences of the Battle of Arnhem, Operation Market, 17–26 September 1944

Volume 1

Grant R. Newell

Helion & Company

This volume is dedicated to the memory of all those that participated in the Arnhem operation, particularly members of the 1st Airborne Division and the Polish 1st Independent Parachute Brigade Group.

Helion & Company Limited
Unit 8 Amherst Business Centre
Budbrooke Road
Warwick
CV34 5WE
England
Tel. 01926 499 619
Email: info@helion.co.uk
Website: www.helion.co.uk
Twitter: @helionbooks
Visit our blog at blog.helion.co.uk

Published by Helion & Company 2023
Designed and typeset by Mach 3 Solutions (www.mach3solutions.co.uk)
Cover designed by Paul Hewitt, Battlefield Design (www.battlefield-design.co.uk)
Printed by Gutenberg Press Ltd, Tarxien, Malta

Text © Grant R. Newell 2023
Images and maps © as individually credited

Front cover: Arnhem, Tuesday 19 September. After the abortive advance towards the bridge, a number of British prisoners of war from 1st and 3rd Parachute Battalions were taken to the Arnhem Musis Sacrum for processing. This unidentified paratrooper, probably from the 1st Parachute Battalion, was one of a group photographed by Kriegsberichter E.Wenzel outside the Music Hall. (Photo: Courtesy Bundesarchiv, Bild BA 101I-497-3526-12A). Rear cover: 6 September 1944. Photo Reconnaissance Spitfire RM644, of 541 Squadron RAF, based at RAF Benson, flown by Flight Lieutenant L J Scargill, RAF, took a series of low level oblique photographs in preparation for Operation COMET, later to be replaced by Operation MARKET. (Photo: Courtesy Gelders Archive).

Every reasonable effort has been made to trace copyright holders and to obtain their permission for the use of copyright material. The author and publisher apologize for any errors or omissions in this work and would be grateful if notified of any corrections that should be incorporated in future reprints or editions of this book.

ISBN 9-7-81804510-39-1

British Library Cataloguing-in-Publication Data.
A catalogue record for this book is available from the British Library.

All rights reserved. No part of this publication may be reproduced, stored in a retrieval system, or transmitted, in any form, or by any means, electronic, mechanical, photocopying, recording or otherwise, without the express written consent of Helion & Company Limited.

For details of other military history titles published by Helion & Company Limited contact the above address or visit our website: http://www.helion.co.uk.

We always welcome receipt of book proposals from prospective authors.

Contents

List of Maps		iv
List of Abbreviations		v
Acknowledgements		x
Preface		xi
Introduction		xv
1	3rd Parachute Battalion, 1st Parachute Brigade	35
2	1st Parachute Battalion, 1st Parachute Brigade. Attached elements 1st Airlanding Anti-Tank Battery, RA, attached elements 1st Airlanding Light Regiment, RA. 2nd Parachute Battalion, 1st Parachute Brigade, 16th Parachute Field Ambulance	154
3	1st Airborne Division Ordnance Field Park, RAOC, 1st Airlanding Light Regiment, RA.1st Parachute Squadron, RE	242
4	261 Field Park Company, RE. Defence Platoon, Headquarters 1st Airborne Division. Advance Workshop Detachment, REME	314
5	1st Airlanding Anti-Tank Battery, RA, Polish 1st Independent Parachute Brigade Anti-Tank Battery, 'B' Squadron, The Glider Pilot Regiment	367
Appendix: Tigers and Snipers		434
Veteran Acknowledgements		435
Primary Contributory Account Sources		438
Bibliography		447
Index		455

List of Maps

German Defensive Positions, Arnhem area, 11th September 1944.
    (Courtesy P.G. Atherall, Maps Division, MCE)   xxx
Sketch map by Private Fred 'Rad' Radley. He writes: 'Sketch map which although not accurate (as far as I can make it) regarding route across field and afterwards and where various things etc. were or happened. After we got across Utrechtseweg it was one mad fight from one street to another and across back gardens – can't trace true route – was up near the railway, then near the prison – then down a long straight road. Also I have a stupid faint recollection of actually being up on the railway following the lines along? I can recall looking down at a small hut watching for enemy in it, eventually I came back down Klingelbeekseweg to position just on L after going under *(low)* railway bridge.'   63
Lombok, Situated between St Elizabeth Hospital and Den Brink/KEMA.
    Map: SGW Designs.   132
Lance Sergeant Mervyn J. Potter, 261 Field Park Company, Royal Engineers – his sketch of his Oosterbeek positions. The small cottage or gate lodge was, and still is, on the eastern corner of Sonnenberglaan. Kasteel de Sonnenberg, the 'château' top left of sketch.   331
Lance Corporal Ken L. Underwood, No. 3 Detachment, 261 Field Park Company, Royal Engineers' sketch map of positions in the Utrechtseweg/Sonnenberglaan area.   333

In Colour Section

Operation Market Garden, the plan. (SGW Designs)   i
Operational map: DZs, LZs and SDPs with 'Leopard', 'Lion' and 'Tiger' routes into Arnhem.
    (SGW Designs)   ii
Wartime operational map enabling coordinate referencing. (SGW Designs)   iv
Pre-war street map of Oosterbeek. (Courtesy Gelders Archive)   vi

List of Abbreviations

AA	Anti-Aircraft
AA	Assistant Adjutant
AA & QMG	Assistant Adjutant and Quartermaster General
AB	Airborne
ABM	Airborne Museum Hartenstein
AB/BA	Air Bomber/Bomb Aimer
ACPO	Assistant Command Post Officer
ADMS	Assistant Director of Medical Services
ADC	Aide-de-Camp
ADOS	Assistant Director of Ordnance Services
Adj	Adjutant
AFPU	Army Film and Photographic Unit
AFV	Armoured Fighting Vehicle
AGRA	Army Group Royal Artillery
A/G	Air Gunner
A/L	Airlanding
Amb	Ambulance, (as in 16th Para Fd Amb, RAMC)
AP	Armour-Piercing
APCBC	Armour-Piercing Capped Ballistic Cap
APDS	Armour-Piercing Discarding Sabot
ATL	Assistant Troop Leader
APM	Assistant Provost Marshall
AWOL	Absent Without Leave
A/Tk	Anti-Tank
Bde	Brigade
Bdr	Bombardier
Bn/Btn	Battalion
Borders	1st Battalion The Border Regiment
Borderers	7th (Galloway) Battalion The King's Own Scottish Borderers
BQMS	Battery Quartermaster Sergeant
BRASCO	Brigade Royal Army Service Corps Officer
Bren	British Light Machine Gun, calibre .303
Brig	Brigadier
Bty	Battery
Canloan	Canadian Officer on Loan to the British Army

Capt	Captain
Cdn	Canadian
Cfn	Craftsman
CO	Commanding Officer
Col	Colonel
Coy	Company
Cpl	Corporal
CGP	Commander Glider Pilots
CPO	Command Post Officer
CRA	Commander Royal Artillery
CRE	Commander Royal Engineers
CSM	Company Sergeant Major
CQMS	Company Quartermaster Sergeant
CRASC	Commander Royal Army Service Corps
CW	Continuous Wave transmission
DAAG	Deputy Assistant Adjutant General
DADMS	Deputy Assistant Director of Medical Services
DAAG	Deputy Assistant Adjutant General
Dak	Dakota (C-47)
DFC	Distinguished Flying Cross
DFM	Distinguished Flying Medal
Div	Division
Div HQ	Divisional Headquarters
DMA	Divisional Maintenance Area
DoW	Died of Wounds
DS	Dressing Station
DUKW	American-made Amphibious Vehicle
DAQMG	Deputy Assistant Quartermaster General
Dvr	Driver
DZ	Drop Zone
Fd	Field, (as in Fd Pk Company RE or Fd Amb)
F/E	Flight Engineer
FO	Forward Observation
F/O	Flying Officer
FOO	Forward Observation Officer
FOU	Forward Observation Unit
Flak	German Anti-Aircraft (*Flugzeugabwehrkanone*)
F/Lt	Flight Lieutenant
F/Sgt	Flight Sergeant
Gammon Bomb	No. 82 Grenade
GHQ	General Headquarters
Gnr	Gunner
GOC	General Officer In Command
GPO	Gun Position Officer
Gp	Group

LIST OF ABBREVIATIONS vii

GPR	Glider Pilot Regiment
GSO	General Staff Officer
Hamilcar	Large British vehicle carrying glider, e.g.17-pdr A/T gun & Morris Towing Truck or Bren Gun Carrier
Hawkins Grenade	British No. 75 grenade. Small anti-tank mine
HE	High Explosive
Horsa	Standard British glider carrying troops or Jeep 6-pdr A/T gun
HMG	Heavy machine gun
HQ	Headquarters
HQRA	Headquarters Royal Artillery
Hrs	Hours
i/c	In Command
2i/c	Second-in-Command
IO	Intelligence Officer
KEMA	Keuring van Elektrotechnische Materialen te Arnhem
KG	Kampfgruppe: German battle group
KIA	Killed in Action
KOSB	7th (Galloway) Battalion King's Own Scottish Borderers
L/Cpl	Lance Corporal
LO	Liaison Officer
L/Sgt	Lance Sergeant
Lt	Lieutenant
Lt Col	Lieutenant Colonel
Lt Regt	Light Regiment
1st A/L	1st Airlanding Light Regiment, Royal Artillery
LZ	Landing Zone
Maj	Major
Maj Gen	Major-General
MC	Military Cross
MDS	Main Dressing Station
Mills Bomb	British No. 36 Fragmentation Grenade
MM	Military Medal
MG/mg	Machine gun
MMG	Medium machine gun
MP	Military Police
MT	Motor Transport
MT Pl	Motor Transport Platoon
MO	Medical Officer
NAAFI	Navy, Army and Air Force Institutes
N Africa	North Africa
Nav	Navigator
NCO	Non-Commissioned Officer
OC	Officer Commanding
O.C.T.U.	Officer Cadet Training Unit
'O' Group	Orders Group

OKW	Oberkommando der Wehrmacht
OP	Observation Post
OPA	Observation Post Assistant
Para	Paratrooper/Parachute
Para Brigade	Parachute Brigade
Para Bn/Btn	Parachute Battalion
PBI	Poor Bloody Infantry
Pdr	Pounder
6-pdr A/T gun	British 6-pounder anti-tank gun
17-pdr A/T gun	British 17-pounder anti-tank gun
PFA	Parachute Field Ambulance
PIAT	Projectile Infantry Anti-Tank
Pk	Park, (as in Fd Pk Company RE or Fd Amb
Pl/Pltn	Platoon
PO	Pilot Officer
POW	Prisoner of War
Pte	Private
PzJgAbt	Panzerjäger-Abteilung: German anti-tank battalion
PzKp	Panzer-Kompanie: German armoured company
PzKpfw.	Panzerkampfwagen: German generic name for a tank
QM	Quartermaster
QMS	Quartermaster Sergeant
QMG	Quartermaster General
RA	Royal Artillery
RAF	Royal Air Force
RAP	Regimental Aid Post
RAAF	Royal Australian Air Force
RAMC	Royal Army Medical Corps
RAOC	Royal Army Ordnance Corps
RCAF	Royal Canadian Air Force
RASC	Royal Army Service Corps
RCE	Royal Canadian Engineers
RE	Royal Engineers
REME	Royal Electrical Mechanical Engineers
Rev	Reverend
RHQ	Regimental Headquarters
RMP	Regimental Military Police
RSM	Regimental Sergeant Major
RQMS	Regimental Quartermaster Sergeant Major
RT	Radio Transmitter
RV	Rendezvous
SA	Small arms
Schmeisser	MP40, German 9mm sub-machine gun
SDP	Supply Dropping Point
S Coy	Support Company

LIST OF ABBREVIATIONS

Sgt	Sergeant
Schiffsstammabteilung	Naval Infantry Battalion
Sigm	Signalman/ Signaller
Smoke Bomb	British No. 77 phosphorous grenade
Spandau	German 7.92mm machine gun MG34–MG42
Sp	Support, (as in Div Sp)
SP	self-propelled (gun)
Spr	Sapper
Sqdn	Squadron
Sqdn/Ldr	Squadron Leader
South Staffs	2nd Battalion The South Staffordshire Regiment
Stalag	Prisoner of War Camp (Stammlager)
Sten	British 9mm sub-machine gun
Stick	Designation of plane load of paratroopers
StuG	Sturmgeschütz: German self-propelled assault gun
TAF	Tactical Air Force
TC	Transport Command
TC	Troop Commander
TCG	Troop Carrier Group
TL	Troop Leader
Tp	Troop
Tpr	Trooper
UK	United Kingdom
US	United States
USA	United States of America
USAAF	United States Army Air Force
VC	Victoria Cross
VMG	Vickers machine gun, water-cooled, calibre .303
Waffen SS	Armed wing of the Nazi Party's SS
Waco	Standard American glider carrying troops or vehicle and gun
WIA	Wounded In Action
W/Ldr	Wing Leader
WOII	Warrant Officer (II)

Acknowledgements

First and foremost, I must thank my family, particularly my wife Linda for her patience and support over the years and our now grown-up children, Samuel, Jemma and Benjamin. Samuel's help and guidance regarding computer literacy made my task easier for which I am eternally grateful. My sincere thanks and appreciation to past and present members and families of the Luton Branch of the Parachute Regimental Association without whose help my research would have proved far more difficult, they adopted me into their family and gave me great encouragement. In particular: Vic Wyles, Anne and Tex Banwell BEM, Jack Jennings, Arthur Allen, Ted Shaw MC, Dave Morris MBE, Dave Cosgrove, Sandy Masterdon, George Aldred, Roger Blake, Harry and Ginette Blake, Dave Kerr, Tommy Schaffer, Jim Dowse, Ken Scott-Phillips, George Hill, Charles and Anne Rushton and Bert and Dot Orrell.

Special mention must be made of Mike Stimson RAF, for making available not only his own personal account but for giving permission to use the accounts and photographs of other members of 196 Squadron which he had accumulated. In some cases widows of veterans provided me with accounts. One in particular I would like to give special mention to is Mrs Evelyn Kent, widow of BSM T.W. Kent, RA, who painstakingly wrote her late husband's entire wartime diary out for me by hand in 1989. My thanks also to James Jordan, Hon. Secretary, 64th Medium Regt RA (London) T.A. Regimental Association for making available the account by Colonel H.S. Hunt, CO, 64th Medium Regiment, Royal Artillery, XXX Corps.

Without doubt, my mentor and inspiration for my research, was the late Dr Adrian Groeneweg, OBE, Vice-Chairman of the Trustees of the Airborne Museum, Hartenstein, Oosterbeek, whose untimely death in July 2010 denied the museum and researchers of his meticulous understanding and knowledge of the battle. Adrian generously offered his advice and knowledge providing a great deal of background material along with many of the images for this work from the museum archives for which I am extremely grateful. Last and not least, I must also record my thanks to Robert Voskuil for his help regarding photographic material.

A percentage of any profits from sales of this book will be donated to 'Support Our Paras', previously the Airborne Forces Security Fund.

Preface

The main raison d'etre for this volume was to record the reminiscences of participants in the British 1st Airborne Division and to include the roles of RAF aircrew involved in the delivery and resupply to the battlefield. In addition, there are accounts from members of XXX Corps, including 4th Battalion Dorset Regiment, 43rd Wessex Division and the Royal Engineers tasked with the relief and evacuation of the Airborne perimeter. It is beyond the remit of this book, and was never the intention, to analyse the overall Market Garden operation in depth which has been covered by countless other books. Only the basic context of the operation has been adopted in order to concentrate on the individuals involved.

In order to place the actual personal accounts in context relating to the British and Polish participants, a brief outline of the units involved, almost in the form of a war diary, precedes each chapter. I have attempted to provide timings where possible. This has been straightforward in some unit cases where the official war diary has been methodically detailed, but in other cases, unit war diaries were lost or written later by non-participants. Reference to published unit histories and official reports fill in any gaps.

There are probably more books written on the Battle of Arnhem than any other battle of the Second World War. Yet the subject still captivates historians; what is the continuing fascination? The battle, perhaps on a personal level, epitomises the characteristics and tenacity of the British soldier in adversity. Ordered to hold on for 48 hours, they held on for nine days. Often devoid of leadership due to casualties, eventually fighting in small and at times uncoordinated actions, armed with very few heavy weapons and against overwhelming odds, the Airborne soldier carried on regardless, fuelled by bloodymindedness, determination and a survival instinct.

What I initially attempted to do is simply record and attempt to tell individual accounts of the battle from a personal point of view. The sequence of the battle and how it unfolded is in many cases actually told by the participants themselves in revealing ways. Many accounts corroborate each other with various individual perspectives of the same action, which is revealing in its human perception of events, often in traumatic circumstances.

One must try and put oneself 'in the slit trench', with a limited field of fire, short of ammunition, thirsty, hungry, excessively tired and with a diminishing sense of hope. Expectations of the arrival of the overdue relief force, a sense of hope eroding by the hours and days as the 2nd Army failed to arrive. Almost constant shelling and mortaring, waiting for the incoming barrage to impact; yet most men never gave up hope, determined to hold on despite whatever the enemy threw at them. Eventually, when relieving elements of XXX Corps arrived close enough to provide artillery support, morale lifted. The sound of friendly artillery fire as far away as Nijmegen registering on German positions close by, sometimes only yards from their own trenches, made a terrific difference. Still they tenaciously hung on within an ever-decreasing perimeter, until Monday, 25th

September. Nine days after they had landed, the order came to pull out during the night, back across the Neder Rijn or Lower Rhine, ironically codenamed Operation Berlin. It was only then, with a subdued, numbed sense, mixed at first with anger and then relief, that they thought they just maybe might make it out alive.

There were countless instances of individual heroics which the participants themselves witnessed. Far too many acts of courage went officially unrecognised; the circumstances needed for a superior to recommend any instances of valour simply did not exist in many cases. Acts of heroism are described here in the participants' own words. Five VCs were awarded for Arnhem, four of them posthumously.

A large number of Arnhem veterans remembered witnessing the heroic exploits of the RAF Stirling and Dakota crews of 38 and 46 Groups attempting to resupply them. The aircraft flew low and slow into an ever-increasing barrage of concentrated anti-aircraft fire, which strengthened daily as additional enemy flak guns were brought into action around the perimeter. Predator German fighter aircraft were encountered on occasions circling above the drop zones. The RAF aircrew and Royal Army Service Corps despatchers did their utmost to get their containers and panniers onto the drop zones and supply dropping points that were often, unbeknown to them, outside of the airborne zone of control. Only 7.4 percent of dropped supplies are thought to have reached the beleaguered Airborne.[1] Resupply aircraft and aircrew losses increased as the operation progressed. For example, during drops on D+6, Saturday, 23rd September, 58 percent of the resupply force was lost or damaged.[2] Through no fault of their own, the RAF crews kept to the predetermined resupply zones, and the airborne forces, for much of the battle, were unable to communicate where to drop the supplies into their dwindling perimeter. Only after wireless contact with XXX Corps was established on Thursday 21st through Royal Artillery channels were alternative supply dropping points communicated. As the week went by, RAF aircrew began to view the resupply missions with trepidation. What began as a simple fly-in and drop at the beginning of the operation turned out to be a nightmare for the resupply crews within a very short space of time.

One of the posthumous VCs awarded at Arnhem went to Flight Lieutenant David Lord, of 271 Squadron, RAF. On Tuesday, 19th September, Lord continued to fly his burning C-47 Dakota aircraft until all the supplies had been released before his aircraft crashed. 38 and 46 Groups RAF, along with the United States 52nd Troop Carrier Wing, flew 1,339 sorties during the operation and in the process lost 68 aircraft and 258 killed including RASC despatchers.[3]

A Personal Perspective

My interest in the battle began in 1973 when I read *Arnhem* by Major General R.E. Urquhart, GOC, 1st Airborne Division and the following year *A Bridge Too Far* by Cornelius Ryan. Both books in my opinion are still essential fundamental reading for anyone interested in the battle. One book that I still hold in high regard was published four years later; John Fairley's book *Remember Arnhem*, concentrating on the 1st Airborne Reconnaissance Squadron, still a classic in its own

---

1   1st Airborne Division Report on Operation Market Garden; TNA WO 171/393.
2   Luuk Buist, Philip Reinders and Geert Maassen, *The Royal Air Force at Arnhem* (Oosterbeek: Society of Friends of the Airborne Museum, 2005), p.97.
3   Martin Middlebrook, *Arnhem 1944, The Airborne Battle* (London: Viking, Penguin Group, 1994), p.441.

right. I came to the conclusion that I needed to find out more about the battle. I contacted my then local Parachute Regimental Association (PRA) in Luton and through their chairman, Ken Scott-Phillips (ex-156 Parachute Battalion, Arnhem) I was invited along to one of their monthly meetings. It was then that I first met veterans who could personally relate their experiences at Arnhem and Normandy. The Luton Branch of the PRA could not have been more welcoming; I felt somewhat overwhelmed in such illustrious company, they made me feel comfortable and were generous in passing on not only their experiences but their contacts within the Airborne fraternity. I was offered an Honorary Membership and with that I continued to expand my research with help from the branch members. Subsequently, I was fortunate to be invited to various regimental dinners and made further contacts. I quickly realised that there were a lot more facets to the Battle of Arnhem than I had previously realised and it dawned on me that these marvellous stories of the battle and personal experiences should be recorded before it was too late. By then I had joined the Society of Friends of the Airborne Museum, Hartenstein, Oosterbeek, still in its infancy. The late vice-chairman of the Airborne Museum, Dr Adrian Groeneweg OBE and I became firm friends. Soon I was visiting Holland covering the battlefield with one of the most knowledgeable individuals one could possibly wish to meet with a positively encyclopaedic knowledge of the battle. On one occasion, Adrian introduced me to John Fairley who was inspirational with advice, having published his own work on the subject; Adrian also introduced me to other Dutch experts, including Robert Voskuil, Robert Sigmond and the late Chris van Roekel whose expertise is much respected. On asking Adrian's advice on how I should proceed with my research, he simply advised me to follow his lead. Along with W.J.M. Duyts, he had published *The Harvest of Ten Years* in 1988, an edited collection of diaries and photographs of the Battle of Arnhem acquired by the Airborne Museum between 1978 and 1988. 'Just put them all together,' he said, and that is what I intended to do.

Years passed and I continued to systematically correspond with veterans all over the world as far as Australia, New Zealand, Norway, Canada and the United States, and personally visit veterans in their homes in the UK to record their reminiscences. During this time I married and started to raise a family and also began my own business, all of which consumed much of my spare time previously occupied with research on the battle. Pressure to finish my research and publish before the fiftieth anniversary of the battle in 1994 increased and it was around then that I decided that I could no longer devote the amount of time to my research that it demanded. My active research declined to a manageable level and I finally decided to wait until I had enough time to devote to compiling all the stories together as Adrian Groeneweg all those years ago had advised. Then in 2017 I finally retired and at last I had the time to devote to working on what was now a very long overdue enterprise. In the intervening years, many more books have appeared on the battle, some with contributions from veterans whose accounts I had already received. However, most authors have drawn only extracts from these accounts. It was always my intention to publish as complete a personal account as possible from each individual, and here I have achieved what I set out to do over 30 years ago.

I have amassed a large number of accounts, having been in contact with over 300 veterans. Unfortunately, not all that I received are presented here, as it would simply have proven to be too large an exercise. Therefore I have restricted the work to around 150 accounts which will be spread over three volumes. Regrettably there are one or two unit omissions. These omissions in no way reflect on the unit's contribution to the battle and for which I apologise. Along with the chapter introductions, I have attempted with each account to provide as accurate a time line as possible so that the reader has the necessary information to relate various unit actions on a comparative day to day, hour by hour basis. This is not as easy as it sounds; most veterans recalled the preliminary stages of the battle, the take-off, flight and the landings. The next two days of advance towards Arnhem sometimes become confused geographically and chronologically, particularly the hectic fighting around the St Elizabeth Hospital in the attempt to reach the Airborne troops that had reached and secured the north end of the Arnhem bridge on the evening of Sunday 17th September. The days that followed, up until the withdrawal, began to take up a pattern of semi-static defence within an ever-decreasing perimeter at Oosterbeek. Those participants that fought at the Arnhem bridge on the whole have memories which reflect the intensity of the action around the bridge and the violent German efforts to evict them.

So all of these accounts are published in full, as supplied to me by the participants, family or friends in either written or audio format. As editor, I have endeavoured to leave everything as original as possible; corrections have been kept to an absolute minimum and each story provides individual continuity. I have, in places, added details relevant to or enlarging on the circumstances surrounding the death of various individuals. I hope that these details enhance rather than distract from the content of the account. I must at this point give recognition to the superlative work by the late J.A. Hey in his book, *Roll of Honour, Battle of Arnhem, September 1944,* detailing each serviceman involved in the operation that lost his life. This comprehensive work, which at the time of writing is now in its 5th edition, has been constantly updated, of late by Geert Maassen and Philip Reinders and I thank all those involved with this invaluable source of information on those that gave their lives during the battle. I have cross-referenced this work throughout and in many cases have been able to throw more light on individuals mentioned in the accounts. Some of the accounts actually expand on the circumstances of the deaths of those mentioned in J.A. Hey's original work.

As for the validity and authenticity of the actions described within the accounts, I leave that up to the reader. Many accounts cross reference with others, whilst those of a singularly personal nature sometimes have to be taken at face value. Where doubts may exist, I have attempted to correct or offer an alternative explanation. One must remember that many of these accounts were recalled years after the event, whilst others were written in prisoner of war camps soon after the battle or upon return home. Few of us can claim an infallible memory. Ask any two witnesses of a traffic accident and you will understand. If glaring inaccuracies are to be found, I can only apologise.

Personally, I have a tremendous admiration for the men of the 1st Airborne Division, the RAF and the USAF crews that delivered them and the RAF aircrews that attempted to resupply them. I consider myself fortunate to have had the honour of meeting and becoming friends with many of them. Their views contained within their accounts, often blunt and sometimes critical, must I feel, be respected. Many felt let down by poor operational planning, leadership and lack of communication and as a result they were left to fend for themselves, driven by loyalty to each other, their unit, and their own survival instincts.

Grant R. Newell
Bedford, England
2021

Introduction

Operation Market

1st Airborne Division and the Polish 1st Independent Parachute Brigade

There follows a brief introduction to the planning and execution of the operation from the point of view of the 1st Airborne Division and the Polish 1st Independent Parachute Brigade. A more detailed examination of individual units precedes the personal accounts and reminiscences of unit members.

Preparation and Planning
Following the successful Allied invasion of Normandy on D-Day, 6th June 1944, American, Canadian, Polish and British forces finally broke out of their beachhead at the beginning of August 1944. The British Second Army under General M.C. Dempsey, MC, pushed through the German defences, drawing in German reinforcements which in turn relieved pressure on adjacent American forces. The American Third Army under the legendary General 'Blood and Guts' Patton swept into the German rear. British, Canadian and Polish forces under the British Army Group Commander, Lieutenant General Bernard Montgomery, 'Monty', pushed slowly forward, with the American Third Army forming the southern arm trapping much of the German Army Group B at Falaise, Chambois; by 21st August the lid had been closed on the trap. The encirclement captured or killed some 70,000 Germans, however, many Germans did escape, as estimated by Feldmarschall Model in his report to OKW dated 29 August: 'Five decimated divisions returned to Germany. The remains of eleven infantry divisions allowed us to regroup four units each with a handful of field guns and other minor equipment. All that remained of eleven armoured divisions when replenished with personnel and material amounted to eleven regiments each with five or six tanks and a few artillery batteries.'[1]

After Falaise, the British and American armies were able to follow up the German retreat from Normandy and pushed hard on the heels of the German Army across France, finally liberating Paris on 25th August. By the end of August, the remnants of German Army Group B had withdrawn across the Seine. The allied pursuit of the enemy was renewed after crossing the Seine preventing the Germans from forming any firm resistance towards Belgium and the Dutch border.

Montgomery had utilised the 6th Airborne Division in Normandy to secure vital bridges and now had his 1st Airborne Division available, but with few opportunities to commit the division due to the rapid advance across France. With supplies still being transported vast distances to the

---

1   Eddy Florentin, *The Battle of the Falaise Gap* (London: Elek Books, 1965), p.304.

American and British forces from Normandy, the securing of workable ports with which to supply the advancing forces became increasing important. Sharing supplies, vital to keep American and British vehicles and tanks running, became an issue. Demand on transport aircraft to supply the American and British advance remained even after Antwerp was captured on 4th September. The port of Antwerp remained unusable because the German 15th Army still retained the 50 miles of approaches along the Scheldt estuary. The German High Command was determined to delay the Allied advance as much as possible from reaching German soil. The advancing Allied forces began to prioritise the limited resources and the need to open up the channel ports of Brest and Le Havre.

The 1st Allied Airborne Army was commanded by American Lieutenant General Lewis H. Brereton with Lieutenant General Sir Frederick A.M. 'Boy' Browning his deputy as commander of the 1st Airborne Corps. However, Brereton's HQ was predominately controlled by Americans who held key positions. (Before the cancellation of proposed Operations Linnet and Comet, as early as 1 September, Brereton voiced his reservations about launching a crossing of the Rhine from bases in England; Brereton favoured moving the 1st Allied Airborne Army to bases east of Paris to facilitate easier access; they had similar weather patterns, an increase in aircraft range and would have closer proximity to the various Army Headquarters involved.)[2] Numerous airborne operations were planned and then cancelled, and Operation Linnet was one such operation. Due to be launched on 3rd September with the objective being to seize a firm base in the vicinity of Tournai to secure a bridgehead over the River Escaut so as to take control of major roads leading north-east from the front through Tournai–Lille–Coutrai. The operation was cancelled like many preceding it due to the rapid Allied advance. An alternative, Linnet 2 was to be mounted on 4th September or shortly after to secure a crossing over the Meuse north of Liege. Browning, unhappy with the plan, threatened Brereton with his resignation. Brereton considered the threat as tantamount to disobeying an order and Browning was forced to withdraw his threat of resignation. Their relationship as a consequence suffered.[3] On 5th September Linnet 2 was cancelled. General Bradley, influential commander of the American 12th US Army Group, was not in favour of Linnet 2, insisting that efforts to maintain the advance should be prioritised with all available transport aircraft.

Montgomery formed a plan to utilise and prioritise what supplies were available to provide his 21st Army Group with enough materials, particularly fuel, to drive a single thrust north-eastwards into the heart of the German Ruhr and eventually Berlin. Browning was instructed to begin planning Operation Comet on 3rd September. Monty's plan was to advance 2nd Army Group in line with Brussels–Antwerp on 6th September or the morning of the 7th, directed on securing bridges between Wesel and Arnhem. Operation Comet would involve delegating the capture of all objectives to the British 1st Airborne Division and the Polish 1st Independent Parachute Brigade with Arnhem the main objective. 1st Parachute Brigade would be tasked with capturing the Arnhem road and rail bridges; 4th Parachute Brigade,1st Airlanding Brigade and the Polish 1st Independent Parachute Brigade would capture bridges across the Waal at Nijmegen and the Maas at Grave. Each objective would be secured by a pre-dawn initial glider-borne coup de main party close to the various bridges until the arrival of the main brigade units in two daylight lifts on suitable drop zones (DZs) and landing zones (LZs).

Meanwhile German opposition was increasing in the proposed operational areas with the 2nd Army meeting stronger resistance on the Albert Canal line. With logistical supply problems

---

2   WO219/2186, Correspondence Brereton to Eisenhower, 1st September 1944.
3   Richard Mead, *General Boy: The Life of Lieutenant General Sir Frederick Browning, GCVO, KBE, CB. DSO, DL* (Barnsley: Pen and Sword 2010), pp.108–11.

(Montgomery was only in receipt of around 75 percent of resupply tonnage needed with supply lines stretching back to Bayeux), Montgomery postponed Comet on 9th September. On the 10th, Montgomery and Dempsey had a meeting at 21st Army Tactical HQ and concluded that one airborne division was insufficient for the proposed Comet objectives. Montgomery then gained agreement to use three airborne divisions utilising the American 101st and 82nd Airborne Divisions with the 1st Airborne Division and the Polish 1st Independent Parachute Brigade as an enlarged version of Comet. Montgomery was set on the Rhine crossing at Arnhem. It suited his planned drive to the north-east, as the Wesel alternative would involve the Americans (which in fact Browning and Dempsey preferred) plus there were reports of more flak around Wesel. Aware of the supply problems and the need to clear the Scheldt estuary, Montgomery asked General Brereton if airborne troops could take the island of Walcheren. On the 10th, Montgomery received a reply from Brereton that the terrain was not suitable, too much flak in the area, plus there were no airborne troops available. On 13th September, Montgomery ordered the Canadian Army to make (some may say unrealistic) plans for capturing Boulogne, Dunkirk, Calais and simultaneously start planning amphibious landings on the Scheldt, codenamed Operation Infatuate.[4] Montgomery would not transfer the British 53rd Division in the Antwerp area to assist the Canadians as they were needed for Market Garden flank security.

Initially set for 14th–16th September, Brereton had little time to plan the operation despite much of the preliminary preparation for Comet (1st Airborne Division Operational Orders issued in some cases still contained headed references to Comet), and there would be no time for exercises or rehearsals. Unlike Comet there would be no coup de main landings near the objectives, leaving 1st Airborne Division to assign Jeeps of the 1st Airborne Reconnaissance Squadron as a coup de main to secure the bridges at Arnhem.

Proposed Airborne Operations June–September 1944

1st Allied Airborne Army planned 16 or so operations between June and September 1944. Only one actually took place, which was Arnhem–Nijmegen–Grave. Later, the airborne River Rhine crossings, Operation Varsity, involving the British 6th Airborne Division and the American 17th Airborne Division would take place in March 1945.

1. Operation Tuxedo. Normandy, 6th June onwards, involving 4th Parachute Brigade in a 'fire brigade' role if the D-Day landings did not go well.
2. Operate Wastage. Same as above involving entire 1st Airborne Division.
3. Reinforcement of 82nd Airborne Division by 1st Airborne Division, 7th–10th June, Carentan Peninsula.
4. Operation Wild Oats. 1st Airborne Division Caen, Carpiquet airfield, overrun before launch.
5. Operation Beneficiary. 22nd June–3rd July. 1st Airborne Division, Polish 1st Independent Parachute Brigade, 504 US Parachute Regiment Combat Team, 878 US Airborne Engineer Battalion. One SAS Squadron. Assist capture of St. Malo.
6. To assist in breakout of Normandy Bridgehead. Mid July. 1st Airborne Division, Bretville area.
7. Operation Swordhilt. 1st Airborne Division. Destroy Morlaix Viaduct.

---

4 Nigel Hamilton, *Monty. The Field Marshal 1944–1976* (London: Hamish Hamilton, 1986), p.57.

8. Operation Hands-up. 15th July–15th August, 1st Airborne Division, Polish 1st Independent Parachute Brigade. Quiberon Bay, Brittany Peninsula.
9. Operation Transfigure. 7th August–17th August. 1st Airborne Division, Polish 1st Independent Parachute Brigade, 52nd (Lowland) Division, 878 US Airborne Engineer Battalion plus additional units. Rambouillet.
10. Operation Boxer. 17th August–26th August. 1st Airborne Division, Polish 1st Independent Parachute Brigade, 52nd (Lowland) Division, 878 US Airborne Engineer Battalion plus additional units. Capture of Boulogne.
11. Operation Axehead. 15th August–25th August.1st Airborne Division, Polish 1st Independent Parachute Brigade. Securing River Seine bridgehead or on the general line of Les Andelys–Villerest–Douville sur Andelle–Anfreville sous les Montes.
12. Operation Linnet. 3rd September. 1st Airborne Division, Polish 1st Independent Parachute Brigade, 52nd (Lowland) Division, 878 US Airborne Engineer Battalion, US 82nd and 101 Airborne Divisions, plus additional units. Tournai area, high ground at Mont de L'Enclus. Seize Courtrai, airfield and Bisseghem. Bridgehead over River Escaut.
13. Operation Linnet 2. 4th September. 1st Airborne Division, Polish 1st Independent Parachute Brigade, 52nd (Lowland) Division, 878 US Airborne Engineer Battalion plus additional units. Aachen–Maastricht.
14. Operation Infatuate. 6th September. Walcheren Islands. Insufficient Airborne available.
15. Operation Clover. 7th September.
16. Operation Comet. 10th September. 1st Airborne Division, Polish 1st Independent Parachute Brigade. Grave, Nijmegen, Arnhem Bridge s.
17. Operation Sixteen. 15th September. 1st Airborne Division, Polish 1st Independent Parachute Brigade, US 82nd and 101 Airborne Divisions and SAS element.[5] Grave, Nijmegen, Arnhem Bridges.
18. Operation Market. 17th September. 1st Airborne Division, Polish 1st Independent Parachute Brigade, US 82nd and 101 Airborne Divisions. Grave, Nijmegen, Arnhem Bridges.[6]

Operation Market Garden

The code name given for the entire air and ground operation was Market Garden: 'Market' for the Airborne side and 'Garden' for the XXX Corps ground forces intended to link up with the 'Airborne carpet' dropped on or around the major objectives en route. The Airborne would form the carpet, consisting of 1st British Airborne Division, Polish 1st Independent Parachute Brigade, 101st US Airborne Division and the 82nd US Airborne Division.

Finally launched on 17th September, 1944, the American 101st Airborne Division under Major General Maxwell Taylor would jump around the canal bridges at Zon and Veghel, whilst further ahead the American 82nd Airborne Division led by Major General James Gavin would be dropped to secure the bridges over the Maas at Grave and the Waal at Nijmegen. The British 1st Airborne Division under Major General Roy Urquhart along with the Polish 1st Independent Parachute Brigade under Major General Stanislaw Sosabowski were assigned the task of capturing and holding the Arnhem Bridge for an anticipated 48 hours. This was the prize and the objective

---

5 Nigel Simpson, Secander Raisani, Philip Reinders, *Battery C Troop, The First Airlanding Anti-Tank Battery at Arnhem* (NL Books, 2021), p.32.
6 Lieutenant Colonel T.B.H. Otway, *Airborne Forces* (London: IWM, 1990), p.206.

of the uncharacteristically audacious plan of Field Marshal Montgomery who believed if it were successful, could end the war by Christmas 1944. (Allied Intelligence considered that 21st Army Group would be unable to advance beyond Arnhem until the Channel ports were captured and opened. This view was confirmed by XXX Corps Commander General Horrocks.)[7]

To reach the 1st Airborne Division and their ultimate objective, the ground forces had to cross numerous river obstacles; the Wilhelmina Canal around 30 yards wide, the Mass River at Grave, 270 yards wide, the Maas–Waal Canal, 67 yards wide, the Waal at Nijmegen, 283 yards wide and the Neder Rijn at Arnhem at around 100 yards.[8] The distance the ground forces were expected to travel from Bareel, south of Valkenswaard to Arnhem was no less than 68 miles. All travel and resupply was to be along a single exposed road, often raised high above the surrounding low-level polder country. The start line was south of Eindhoven, along the Meuse–Escaut Canal. The ultimate aim of the entire operation was to force a path, 20,000 vehicles strong, 99 miles from Eindhoven through Holland to the Ijsselmeer, effectively outflanking German defences and cutting off the German Industrial Ruhr and striking into the heart of Germany and ending the war.

Heading east from the Belgium border, spearheaded by the Guards Armoured Division, the British XXX Corps under General Brian Horrocks began to advance after confirming the arrival of the Airborne armada overhead at 1435 hours on 17th September, 1944. Supported on the flanks by XII Corps on his left and VIII Corps on his right, Horrocks began the advance towards Arnhem.

1st Airborne Division

General Roy Urquhart and his 1st Airborne Division had been waiting since D-Day in June 1944 to get into battle. Elements of the division had already been in action during the North African Campaign, Sicily and in Italy, but it was a while since they had been in battle; replacements from losses in North Africa and Sicily were yet to be battle hardened. The British 6th Airborne Division, under the experienced Major General R.N. 'Windy' Gale, had performed well during the Normandy landings and 1st Airborne were eager for their turn to get to grips with the Germans. Numerous operations had been planned and aircraft and gliders prepared only to be cancelled often at the last minute before take-off simply because the planners could not keep up with the rapid advance of allied forces across France after the Normandy breakout. The men of 1st Airborne Division were becoming restless. The planning for Arnhem from the perspective of the 1st Airborne Division had some serious and profound implications on how efficiently the division could perform its task. The division could not be flown and delivered in its entirety on the first day. Aircraft availability, turnaround and maintenance times and the fact that all the bases were in England would dictate lifts and delivery. Lifts would also have to be staggered to daylight hours over successive days due to the night-flying limitations of the US Troop Carrier Command. Available glider numbers and men on the ground during the critical first few hours of the landing would also be reduced due to General Browning's ambition to take his entire corps HQ to Holland in the Nijmegen area alongside Gavin's 82nd Airborne Division which would cost Urquhart 38

---

7 Sir Brian Horrocks, *Corps Commander* (London: Sidgwick and Jackson,1978) p.125.
8 Major L.F. Ellis, *Victory in the West* (UK:HMSO, 1962).

glider-loads of troops on the first day. The RAF, responsible for the safe delivery of the Airborne, had insisted on the landing zones and drop zones be well away (between seven to eight miles) from the main objective of the operation due to the proximity of heavy concentrations of German flak defences around the Arnhem road and rail bridges and to the north at Deelen Airfield. Urquhart acknowledged the RAF concerns in the planning stage even though the element of surprise, crucial in airborne operations, would rapidly be lost and the objective of the Airborne troops would very quickly become apparent to any German forces in the area. Nevertheless, by 2000 hours on 17th September, Frost's 2nd Parachute Battalion, albeit incomplete due to supplementary company tasks, would be occupying the north end of the bridge.

The 21st Independent Parachute Company would fly in as pathfinders for the 1st Airborne Division and mark out drop and landing zones close to Wolfheze for the first lift; LZ 'S' at Reijerscamp, with LZ 'Z' and DZ 'X' at Renkum Heath. Divisional glider units including the 1st Airlanding Brigade, Artillery and Anti-Tank units transported in Horsa and the larger Hamilcar gliders would then land on LZ 'S' and LZ 'Z'. 1st Parachute Brigade under Brigadier Gerald Lathbury, consisting of 2nd Parachute Battalion under Lieutenant Colonel John Frost, 3rd Parachute Battalion under Lieutenant Colonel John Fitch and the 1st Parachute Battalion under Lieutenant Colonel David Dobie, would then descend onto DZ 'X' and make their way to their pre-assigned positions, deploying in and around Arnhem by three routes through enemy-occupied territory. The routes were codenamed: Leopard, the 1st Parachute Battalion's furthest northern route along the Ede/Arnhem road; Lion, the 2nd Parachute Battalion's southern route which ran parallel to the River Rhine, seizing the Railway and Pontoon Bridges and then into Arnhem; and finally Tiger, the 3rd Parachute Battalion's middle route along the Utrecht/Arnhem road. Urquhart's plan was for the 1st Airborne Reconnaissance Squadron with their lightly armoured Jeeps to rush ahead and carry out a coup de main and seize the Arnhem bridge before the 1st Parachute Brigade arrived.

The 1st Airlanding Brigade comprised 2nd Battalion The South Staffordshire Regiment (South Staffs) under Lieutenant Colonel W.D.H. McCardie, 1st Battalion The Border Regiment commanded by Lieutenant Colonel T.H. Haddon and finally, 7th (Galloway) Battalion, The King's Own Scottish Borderers (KOSB) under Lieutenant Colonel R. Payton-Reid. The Airlanding Brigade were given the preliminary role of landing and drop zone defence. The Border Regiment were responsible for safeguarding Renkum Heath whilst the South Staffordshires defended LZ 'S' at Reijerscamp. 7th (Galloway) Battalion, The King's Own Scottish Borderers were to make their way north-west towards the following day's DZ 'Y', at Ginkel Heath, intended for the 4th Parachute Brigade under Brigadier John 'Shan' Hackett.

Sunday, 17th September 1944
The division began the landings in the early afternoon on 17th September after a comparatively quiet flight across the channel. Enemy opposition was negligible and for many it seemed like an exercise. After forming up at their respective DZ rendezvous points, the battalions moved off the drop zones. After a short delay, 1st Parachute Battalion headed north-east towards the Leopard route, 2nd Parachute Battalion rapidly moved on the Lion route heading south and south-east through Heelsum and through Oosterbeek, whilst the 3rd Parachute Battalion made their way along the Utrechtseweg, the Tiger route. Whilst the Parachute Battalions began their advance towards Arnhem, the Airlanding Brigade deployed to their appointed locations to defend and protect the LZs and DZs for the next day; B Company of the Border Regiment made for the

village of Renkum along the western divisional perimeter to cover the southern flank along the Rhine. Artillery and anti-tank units deployed around the DZs for local protection and to provide fire support to any unit should the need arise.

Apart from difficulties in radio communication between units, at the beginning the operation seemed to be going according to plan; however, it was all about to change. German forces in the area began to react with their customary speed and efficiency. The main primary German force training in the immediate area when the landings took place was the SS Panzergrenadier-Ausbildungs und Ersatz-Bataillon 16, under SS Sturmbannführer Sepp Krafft. Characteristically, Krafft reacted swiftly and threw together one of the initial blocking lines which in the following days would be repeated in depth and reinforced with greater numbers of German units. Kraft's troops ambushed C Troop of the Reconnaissance Squadron's coup de main party close to the Wolfheze railway crossing just east of the landing zones on the Johannahoeve Weg. They also hindered the 3rd Parachute Battalion advance along the Utrechtseweg. The 2nd Parachute Battalion's progress to the bridge was held up temporarily at Oosterbeek Laag Station by a small ad hoc group of Germans under the command of SS Sturmmann Helmut Buttlar of the 10th SS Panzer Division *Frundsberg*. C Company 2nd Parachute Battalion's attempt to capture the Arnhem to Nijmegen railway bridge over the Rhine was thwarted by the enemy who blew the railway bridge before it could be captured.

The 1st Parachute Battalion did not fare any better when they approached the Ede/Arnhem road, running initially into Kampfgruppe Von Allwörden with elements from the 9th SS Panzer Division, SS Panzerjäger-Abteilung Bataillon 9. The movements of two depleted SS Panzer Divisions, 9th and 10th, had been tracked by 'Ultra' intercepts at Bletchley Park and on 4th September the two divisions had been ordered to rest and refit in the Venlo–Arnhem–'s-Hertogenbosch area, both arrived in the Arnhem area on 7th September. Their arrival was confirmed by the Dutch Underground. 1st Parachute Battalion were some of the 1st Airborne Division units to come into contact with the quick reaction force put together by the 9th SS Hohenstaufen Panzer Division.

By nightfall, 2nd Parachute Battalion less one company (C), had reached the Arnhem bridge along with elements of 1st Parachute Squadron Royal Engineers, 1st Airlanding Anti-Tank Battery RA and other divisional troops and captured the northern end of the bridge. C Company, 3rd Parachute Battalion had also evaded German forces and elements managed to reach the Arnhem bridge via the railway line into Arnhem. (Had the rest of 3rd Parachute Battalion followed C Company along the railway line, it would have considerably strengthened Frost's force at the bridge although it may have only delayed the eventual outcome.) During the night, 1st Parachute Battalion decided that progress could not be made any further along the Ede/Arnhem road and sidestepped the German blocking force on the Dreijenseweg, beginning to move south-east towards the Tiger and Lion routes into Arnhem. 3rd Parachute Battalion, after C Company's departure, rather inexplicably halted for the night in Oosterbeek. Delays in the Airborne advance caused by the underestimated German resistance played heavily upon General Urquhart's mind. The breakdown in communications was beginning to have a negative impact on the whole of the division. Due to heavily wooded terrain and built up areas, not all wireless sets were functioning as they should have for many operators, resulting in units moving independently and in a somewhat uncoordinated manner. Urquhart, along with Brigadier Lathbury, 1st Parachute Brigade CO, stayed with the 3rd Parachute Battalion when the battalion resumed its advance on the Monday to the outskirts of Arnhem in an attempt to find out what was going on; becoming separated from friendly troops, Urquhart and his small party became trapped in the maze of houses in an area known as Lombok, immediately west of the St Elizabeth Hospital in Arnhem, and was forced to remain there until the area was retaken. With the divisional commander no longer at his HQ at Oosterbeek, those left at HQ were now beginning to wonder what had happened to the divisional commander.

Monday, 18th September

Back in England on the morning of Monday 18th September, poor weather conditions were such that the second lift was delayed by five hours to later in the day (a decision made the day before based on the weather forecast). Meanwhile, 1st and 3rd Parachute Battalions fought their way into the western edges of Arnhem bumping into increasingly hostile and strengthening German forces along the way. In Urquhart's absence at Divisional HQ, Brigadier 'Pip' Hicks, CO 1st Airlanding Brigade, took over command of the 1st Airborne Division. The 2nd Battalion South Staffordshire Regiment (South Staffs) were ordered by Hicks to leave their LZ and make their way into Arnhem as quickly as possible to try and reinforce Lieutenant Colonel John Frost's 2nd Parachute Battalion and C Company, 3rd Parachute Battalion at the bridge. The understrength South Staffs were still awaiting their full complement of rifle companies which would arrive with the second lift. When the delayed second lift did eventually arrive around 1500 hours, the reception was far more hostile than the previous day's first lift. German units were pressurising the periphery of DZ 'Y' and the King's Own Scottish Borderers defending the DZ were being hard pressed. Brigadier Hackett's 4th Parachute Brigade were composed of 10th Parachute Battalion, under Lieutenant Colonel Kenneth Smyth; the 11th Parachute Battalion was commanded by Lieutenant Colonel George Lea, and 156 Parachute Battalion was under Lieutenant Colonel Sir Richard des Voeux. All three parachute battalions took casualties on the DZ which, covered with dry under-brush, caught alight in places from incoming German mortar fire. Brigadier Hicks, now in Divisional HQ at the Hartenstein Hotel in Oosterbeek, took the decision to order Lea's 11th Parachute Battalion directly into Arnhem to support the South Staffs.

The late arrival of the second lift necessitated the 1st Battalion Border Regiment delaying their move off the landing zones which prevented their early move towards Arnhem. Their southern-most company (B) in Renkum came under considerable pressure at the Renkum riverside brick-works and made a hasty withdrawal eastwards via the Rhine tow-path to their phase two positions in the area of high ground at Westerbouwing, Oosterbeek. Once the second lift had landed, the remaining companies of the battalion moved off late in the day towards Oosterbeek to form the eastern boundary of the division stretching from close to the river at Heveadorp/Westerbouwing, up to the area of Kasteel de Sonnenberg on the north side of the Utrechtseweg running through Oosterbeek. The battalion were responsible for a considerably extended frontage interspersed with thick woodland which in places made mutually supporting defensive fire impossible.

4th Parachute Brigade formed up and moved off with 7th (Galloway) Battalion The King's Own Scottish Borderers (KOSB) now temporarily attached, replacing the 11th Parachute Battalion now heading to Divisional HQ in Oosterbeek for further instructions. After a three and a half hour delay at Divisional HQ awaiting orders, 11th Battalion finally began to move towards Arnhem. 10th Parachute Battalion only made a short distance before it was ordered by Hackett to halt for the night near the Wolfheze railway line and then begin its move northeast towards the Ede/Arnhem road the following morning. 156 Parachute Battalion moved parallel to the railway line past the Wolfheze railway crossing due east towards their first objective, the Koepel high ground east of the Johannahoeve farm just north of Oosterbeek. The KOSB also made their way in the same direction to form defensive positions for the next day's lift of the glider elements of the Polish 1st Independent Parachute Brigade due in the afternoon of Tuesday 19th on LZ 'L'. By late Monday evening German resistance was being encountered by 156 Parachute Battalion and a halt was called in the woods south of the Johannahoeve farm. German infantry and armoured units were being rapidly deployed in front of 4th Parachute Brigade's line of advance. Sperrlinie Spindler, composed of units from the 9th SS Panzer Division, were reinforcing positions primarily on the Dreijenseweg, a road running north out of Oosterbeek linking up with Krafft's battalion to the north of the Ede/Arnhem road the Amsterdamseweg, along which the northern most unit, 10th Parachute Battalion, would need to advance. Immediately southeast of the 10th Battalion, the 156 Parachute Battalion would be heading directly towards the Dreijenseweg and the Koepel feature beyond.

By Monday evening, the South Staffs had linked up with 1st Parachute Battalion on the outskirts of Arnhem. The 3rd Parachute Battalion were also fighting in the area of Lombok to the west of the St Elizabeth Hospital, a maze of narrow streets. By midnight the remaining South Staffs companies from the second lift had arrived along with the 11th Parachute Battalion and plans were made for a final push towards the Arnhem Bridge in the early hours of the following morning, Tuesday, 19th September.

Tuesday, 19th September: The Turning Point

Events were now approaching something of a climax in the attempts to reach the Arnhem bridge. Frost's mixed force at the north end of the bridge had been fighting since Sunday evening to retain control of the northern approaches and had successfully dealt with German attempts at crossing the bridge from the south and attacks from the north and east. They were still holding on, despite increasing enemy pressure including armoured and infantry probes and direct artillery and mortar fire; Frost needed reinforcements urgently and with this in mind plans were made for an all-out attack by the 1st Parachute Battalion in conjunction with the South Staffs and the 11th Parachute Battalion for the early hours of the Tuesday morning. The 3rd Parachute Battalion further ahead were already making unilateral attempts to get through and had limited success. The 3rd Parachute Battalion dropped back and then met up with Dobie's 1st Battalion going forward.

The main weakness of the whole Arnhem operation was one of geography. Not only were the distances from the landing and drop zones great, the areas of woodland and heavily built-up residential areas that the lightly equipped troops had to negotiate were ideal for defence where a small determined force could effectively prevent or delay any forward movement. Once in Arnhem, the advance was funnelled through a very restricted residential area with the fast-flowing Rhine immediately on the right flank and the railway cutting into Arnhem on the left flank. In between ran two roads, west to east, the Utrechtseweg along the left flank parallel to the railway, then a steep tree and bush covered embankment down to the river road, the Onderlangs. It was through this bottleneck, heavily defended by German flak guns, armour and infantry both to the immediate front and flanks, that the relieving force, intending to reach Frost at the bridge, would have to travel.

Despite confusion and contradictory orders from Divisional HQ units eventually began to move forward in the direction of the bridge in the early hours just before dawn of Tuesday morning. By 0730 hours they had past the area of St Elizabeth Hospital and had overrun the house at No. 14 Zwarteweg, in which General Urquhart and his group were hiding. Urquhart made his way back to Oosterbeek and his HQ at the Hartenstein, leaving Brigadier Lathbury in the care of Dutch civilians having been wounded the day before. The 1st Parachute Battalion made some headway along the Onderlangs but at an appalling cost and managed to pass below the Gemeentemusuem (Municipal Museum) high up above them to their left on the embankment. The 3rd Parachute Battalion, already depleted from an earlier failed attempt along the Onderlangs, were deployed along the river and the embankment between the two roads in support of the 1st Parachute Battalion and fared no better. The valiant attempts at breaking through the German defences were grinding to a halt. At the Gemeentemuseum on the high ground, the remaining South Staffordshires advancing along the Utrechtseweg ran into Sturmgeschütz self-propelled guns of Sturmgeschütz-Brigade 280 and infantry of Kampfgruppe *Möller*. Whilst along the lower Onderlangs, Kampfgruppe *Harder* with the other half of Sturmgeschütz-Brigade 280 began to advance westwards in a counter-attack. The British effort to relieve the Airborne force at the bridge had literally ground to a halt; gradual attrition over the eight or more miles from the landing zones and the final costly attack had taken its toll. The 11th Parachute Battalion were still spread out along the Utrechtseweg from their start line during the attack and later received orders to move northwards to capture high ground for the proposed 4th Brigade advance. By early afternoon, this move had been thwarted by the Germans and the 11th Parachute Battalion, despite assistance from remnants of the South Staffs to provide a pivot by capturing the high ground of KEMA/Den Brink, and had been caught by the swift advance of German armour which forced the remaining South Staffs and the 11th Parachute Battalion to withdraw. As the day progressed, all the units involved in the morning attack, 1st and 3rd Parachute Battalions, the South Staffs and 11th Parachute Battalion and their support units were forced back towards Oosterbeek either along the Utrechtseweg or predominately via Hulkesteinseweg, Klingelbeekseweg and then the Benedendorpsweg lower road.

Whilst all the heavy early morning fighting had been taking place in Arnhem, the 10th and 156 Parachute Battalions of the 4th Parachute Brigade were finding their own advance to be blocked. 156 Parachute Battalion moved off in the early hours along the axis of the railway line north of Oosterbeek. After some initial headway it soon discovered the German defence line set up along the Dreijenseweg. With the 10th Parachute Battalion advancing on its left flank along the axis of the Ede/Arnhem road, both battalions met stiff resistance which included mobile flak guns, armour and infantry, and appalling losses were suffered. It became apparent to Brigadier Hackett when the advance was stalled, that with increasing German pressure from his rear against the Border Regiment, his 4th Parachute Brigade rear was in danger of being cut off from Oosterbeek and the rest of the division by the steep railway embankment to his right flank. Despite a plan to advance along the railway to Oosterbeek Hoog railway station which never materialised and with only the Wolfheze crossing capable of taking wheeled transport, Hackett, with Urquhart's agreement, withdraw his brigade.

A withdrawal whilst under fire is one of the most difficult manoeuvres to carry out and as the 10th Parachute Battalion began their withdrawal, the Germans intuitively chose the moment to launch a counter-attack. It was at this time, around 1600 hours in the afternoon, that the glider element of the Polish Independent Parachute Brigade came in to land carrying Jeeps and anti-tank guns. Matters became quite chaotic with the KOSB still trying to defend LZ 'L', with Polish gliders engaged by the Germans, and meanwhile the 10th Parachute Battalion under fire trying to cross the LZ to get to Wolfheze as ordered. A brick-built culvert provided an additional route under the railway embankment which was just wide enough to take a Jeep. The KOSB followed the withdrawing troops towards the railway embankment and either crossed it or moved to rendezvous at Wolfheze before the majority made their way to Divisional HQ, being allocated positions to the north of the forming perimeter. Fighting around the Wolfheze railway crossing erupted and continued into the night, by which time the majority of remaining personnel of 156 and 10th Parachute Battalions and KOSB had crossed over the railway and into the woods between the railway and Oosterbeek.

The 4th Parachute Brigade had become somewhat fragmented. Small groups worked their way back to Oosterbeek and the perimeter being set up there. One of the larger groups with 4th Brigade HQ set up on the south side of the railway embankment to harbour for the night and many other such groups did the same. The surviving elements of 4th Parachute Brigade, along with remaining elements of the KOSB would, in the early hours of the following day, begin the fight through thick woodland to join the core of the division set up around the HQ at the Hartenstein.

Down in Lower Oosterbeek as the afternoon of the Tuesday progressed, parties of troops from the morning's abortive attack into Arnhem began to filter through along the Benedendorpsweg under the lower road rail viaduct at Oosterbeek Laag station. The first troops to arrive at Oosterbeek were met by Lieutenant Colonel 'Sheriff' Thompson, CO of the 1st Airlanding Light Regiment, RA, whose 75mm gun batteries were dug in around the lower Oosterbeek church (Oude Kerk). Thompson took control of the situation and began organising troops under their officers around the houses close to the lower road rail viaduct commanding the railway embankment to the east. Elements of South Staffs, 11th Parachute Battalion, and the 1st and 3rd Parachute Battalions were initially deployed in and around these houses. With the coming of the night on 19th September, any realistic hopes of reaching the Arnhem bridge had evaporated. The following day the German forces out of Arnhem would begin probing attacks along the lower road and railway embankment and further north in a flanking move. The battle for the British had turned from one of an offensive operation to one of a defensive nature.

Wednesday, 20th September

For the remaining units of the division, Wednesday, 20th September was to be a day of re-establishing contact with the Divisional HQ at Oosterbeek. Hackett's force, along with the separated KOSB elements, spent the best part of the Wednesday fighting their way in various sized groups through German-occupied woodland from the railway crossing area at Wolfheze towards Oosterbeek. Some succeeded but many of the KOSB did not, including a company-sized unit that were taken prisoner. Hackett's 4th Brigade and HQ group fragmented, resulting in the 10th Parachute Battalion element breaking through to Oosterbeek leaving Hackett's group cut off. Hackett's party finally broke through with a bayonet charge to the northwestern most positions of the Border Regiment late on Wednesday. The divisional area, centred around the Hartenstein Hotel and the residential area of Oosterbeek, slowly formed into a perimeter to which the units of 4th Parachute Brigade and remnants of the previous day's fighting in Arnhem were drawn. The 1st Airlanding Light Regiment RA around the lower Oosterbeek church formed the base of the perimeter and the south-easterly portion initially was known as 'Thompson Force'. The mixed force of South Staffs, 11th, 1st and 3rd Parachute Battalions had held off repeated German attacks successfully but were under pressure from the north and east. During one such attack, German infantry of Kampfgruppe *Hardor* supported by self-propelled guns of Sturmgeschütz-Brigade 280 had advanced in a pincer movement under the rail viaduct bridge along Benedendorpsweg at Oosterbeek Laag station and from further north, advancing in a south westerly direction down Acacialaan only to be halted by 6-pounder anti-tank gunfire from the South Staffs Support Company. In this action, Lance Sergeant John Daniel Baskeyfield, S Company, South Staffs, won a posthumous VC.

Late afternoon on the Wednesday, whilst having repelled determined enemy probes in the area, the force around the lower rail viaduct across the Benedendorpsweg were steadily withdrawn back to the area around Oosterbeek Laag church and the 1st Airlanding Light Regiment RA positions. This was carried out to avoid possible envelopment; contraction of the evolving perimeter was deemed necessary.

The day finished as one of consolidation and regrouping and the acceptance that every effort had been made to reach the beleaguered force at the Arnhem road bridge. For the men at the Arnhem bridge it also became apparent that the attempts by the rest of the 1st Airborne Division to reach them had failed, although hope of relief by XXX Corps had not diminished; they were, however, on their last legs with many of the buildings around Arnhem bridge burning down around them. Apart from small scattered groups, by the end of the day effective resistance at the bridge had ended. Overnight, many went into hiding in cellars and the burnt-out remains of buildings. The following morning, Thursday, 21st September, German forces finally mopped up the remnants of Frost's force at the bridge. Replenished on Tuesday 19th with heavy armour of Schwere Panzer-Kompanie *Hummel,* the Germans could now concentrate on Oosterbeek and use the recaptured Arnhem Bridge to send reinforcements south to engage the advancing XXX Corps at Nijmegen.

Thursday, 21st September–Sunday 24th September
Thursday morning in Oosterbeek heralded an early morning mortar bombardment followed by an all-out assault on the 1st Battalion Border Regiment, particularly B Company positions atop the tactically important high ground at Westerbouwing. The attack consisted of four tanks from Panzer-Kompanie 224, and infantry of the Worrowski Battalion of the Hermann Goering Training Regiment. After initial success, the enemy suffered heavy casualties with B Company destroying three of the four tanks. In the confusion that followed, B Company were pulled back off the high ground. Subsequent limited counter-attacks failed to retake it. The importance of this loss, overlooking the hardstanding approaches to the Driel ferry, cannot be over emphasised, the significance of which would become all too apparent as the battle progressed. Meanwhile, further German probing from the west by SS battalions *Schulz, Eberwein* and *Helle* began to exert pressure on the extended company positions of the Border Regiment. Down by the Oosterbeek church, Lieutenant Colonel Thompson, RA, was wounded by mortar fire and command of Thompson Force was passed to Major R. Lonsdale, 2i/c 11th Parachute Battalion. The group defending the south-eastern base of the perimeter was renamed Lonsdale Force.

To the north of the Oosterbeek perimeter, the KOSB held the line just south of the railway, centred around the Hotel Dreijeroord (often referred to as 'The White House') on Graaf van Rechterenweg, supported on their flanks and rear by glider pilots and the remnants of 156 Parachute Battalion and for a while the 21st Independent Parachute Company. Through the centre of the divisional perimeter from east to west ran the Utrechtseweg main road which essentially divided the northern sector from the southernmost sector with Divisional HQ at the Hartenstein Hotel in the middle. With the Border Regiment astride this road to the west, to the east sat the medical dressing stations of the Vreewik, Schoonoord and Tafelberg Hotels around the crossroads of Stationsweg and Pietersbergseweg. To the east of the crossroads, protecting the dressing stations, were elements of the 10th Parachute Battalion, later replaced by the 21st Independent Parachute Company. Immediately to the north of the dressing station crossroads ran Stationsweg. In the large houses along the western side of Stationsweg units of the 156 Parachute Battalion and Glider Pilot Regiment held off German attacks from the east through the Dennenkamp Park and from the area of the railway to the north. The constant shelling and mortar bombardments preceding the infantry and armoured probes and the resulting airborne casualties forced the periphery of the perimeter to shrink over the next five days. This resulted in a contraction, in particular at the northern aspect of the perimeter, with the KOSB dropping back to houses and gardens on Paul Krugerstraat and Nassaulaan.

One positive piece of news on Thursday 21st was the establishing of wireless contact with the Royal Artillery of XXX Corps. This vital contact enabled artillery support to begin from the 64th Medium Regiment Royal Artillery. With Hackett responsible for the eastern half of the perimeter and Hicks in charge of the western half, both could now call in artillery fire support from XXX Corps.

Because of the continuing deteriorating situation, the Polish 1st Independent Parachute Brigade were forced to delay their participation in the operation until the Thursday and were finally dropped south of the Rhine at the village of Driel with a view to crossing the river at the Driel/Heveadorp ferry below Westerbouwing. By the time they landed, the heights of the Westerbouwing were in the hands of the Germans. Subsequent Polish attempts to cross the river on the Friday night in rubber boats were only moderately successful with 52 Polish crossing into the perimeter, and these attempts were again repeated on the Saturday night with another 153 men across. Whilst temporarily giving local support, it did not alter the situation of a shrinking perimeter and an ever-increasingly serious situation with food, water and ammunition running low. Dressing stations were already overflowing with medical facilities overstretched.

Sunday, 24th September

Plans were made to launch an assault by the remainder of the Polish Brigade at Driel and the 4th Battalion Dorset Regiment who had arrived with the leading units of XXX Corps at the southern bank of the Rhine. The plan was for the Dorsets to form a bridgehead for possible expansion and breakout by XXX Corps. On the night of Sunday 24th September. the Dorsets gallantly crossed the Rhine in assault boats below the German-held Westerbouwing and despite brave efforts the majority were taken prisoner, and few made it through to 1st Airborne.

Monday, 25th September: Holding on For a Withdrawal

At 0808 hours on Monday morning, 25th September, General Urquhart agreed over the radio link with 43rd Division, XXX Corps, to withdraw the 1st Airborne Division from north of the Rhine that evening, codenamed Operation Berlin. 1st Airborne Division would have to hold on for one more day. German forces in Arnhem had just received armoured reinforcements arriving in Zevenaar overnight on 23rd–24th September. Two companies of Schwere Panzer-Abteilung 506, each comprised of 15 King Tiger IIs, went to Arnhem; one went on to Elst to fight the advancing XXX Corps whilst the other, 3 Panzer-Kompanie 506 went immediately to Oosterbeek under command of 9th SS Panzer Division. The arrival of the huge 68-ton tanks in Oosterbeek not only had a tactical impact but a psychological one too, when a number of them supported an attack on the Monday along the Weverstraat axis from the north-east of the perimeter towards the Oosterbeek church. Despite their size and restrictions on movement through the narrow Oosterbeek roads, deep penetrations were made into the gun and wagon lines of the 1st Airlanding Light Regiment RA overrunning several troops of 75mm guns. The German advance along the base of the perimeter close to the Rhine jeopardised the entire 1st Airborne Division's proposed withdrawal route for that night. The German advance was only brought to a halt by concentrated artillery fire from supporting units of 43rd Wessex Division of XXX Corps south of the river. Fortunately for 1st Airborne, the Germans did not pursue their attack. It was only a short distance from the church to the western boundary of the perimeter which would have had catastrophic consequences.

When evening came on Monday, 25 September, under cover of an XXX Corps artillery bombardment, units began to prepare for their move towards the river. Wounded that could not walk were ordered to be left behind. Troops the furthest away from the river on the northern periphery of the perimeter began to leave first. They moved silently south past the Hartenstein Divisional HQ into the woods and across the lower road, past the church, to reach the flat open polder land leading to the fast-flowing Rhine where engineers of the 23rd Field Company Royal Canadian Engineers and 260th Field Company Royal Engineers were waiting with storm boats and assault boats to ferry the evacuating troops back across the river to the comparative safely of the south bank. Further to the west below the German held Westerbouwing, 553rd Field Company RE and the Canadian 20th Field Company, RCE, would attempt to evacuate the 4th Battalion Dorset Regiment, unaware of their fate; few Dorsets were rescued. All night long the main evacuation carried on, ordered to avoid making contact with the enemy; lines of troops often lost their way in the woodland and stumbled past German positions. Torrential rain masked the withdrawal; German forces in the area eventually suspected movement as an indication of further attempts to reinforce the perimeter.

By dawn, the Germans had fully realised what was going on before their eyes and brought down mortar and sustained direct fire from machineguns on the Westerbouwing and surrounding areas. Once the boats ceased to cross the river in daylight those airborne troops remaining had little choice but to swim or surrender, or try and hide in the hope of evading long enough to eventually make it back across the river.

Casualties in the 1st Airborne Division were considerable. Dressing stations were overflowing with wounded; dead were piled up outside and in adjacent buildings. Walking wounded were marched off into Arnhem and captivity, whilst stretcher cases were transported to St Elizabeth Hospital for treatment and then moved to Apeldoorn for further care. When considered fit enough by their captors to travel, and many certainly were not, they were then loaded into overcrowded cattle trucks and taken on circuitous journeys often with little food or water to prisoner of war camps.

Casualties amongst the senior officers of the division were indicative of the intensity of the fighting. Lieutenant Colonel John Frost 2nd Parachute Battalion was wounded by mortar fragments and was now a prisoner along with the majority of his surviving force at the Arnhem Bridge. Brigadier Hackett, 4th Parachute Brigade, lay badly wounded in St Elizabeth Hospital; Brigadier Lathbury, 1st Parachute Brigade, was wounded and a prisoner of war; Lieutenant Colonel Fitch, 3rd Parachute Battalion lay dead close to the Rhine Pavilion in Arnhem. Lieutenant Colonel Dobie, 1st Parachute Battalion, was a prisoner of war as was Lieutenant Colonel Lea of the 11th Parachute Battalion. Lieutenant Colonel 'Sheriff' Thompson, 1st Airlanding Light Regiment was wounded; Lieutenant Colonel Sir Richard des Voeux, 156 Parachute Battalion, lay dead in the woods between Oosterbeek and Wolfheze and Lieutenant Colonel Smyth, 10th Parachute Battalion, died of wounds in captivity. Lieutenant Colonel McCardie, 2nd Battalion South Staffordshire Regiment and Lieutenant Colonel Hadden, 1st Battalion, Border Regiment were both prisoners.[9] Lieutenant Colonel Payton-Reid, 7th Battalion (Galloway) The King's Own

---

9   Phillip J. Shears, *The Story of The Border Regiment* (London: Nisbet & Co. Ltd, 1948), p.25. Haddon's first lift glider had a tow rope failure and had to wait for the second lift when his glider was forced to land south

Scottish Borderers, was the only Battalion Commanding Officer to make it out across the Rhine along with Brigadier Hicks, 1st Airlanding Brigade and the General Officer Commanding 1st Airborne Division, Major General R.E. Urquhart.

Urquhart's 1st Airborne Division and the Polish 1st Independent Parachute Brigade, initially nearly 12,000 strong, was reduced to just 3,910 evacuated (or withdrawn, as in the case of the Poles), leaving over 1,485 dead and over 6,525 as prisoners of war, 2,000–2,500 of whom were wounded.[10] The remnants of the 1st Airborne Division that made it back across the Rhine to Nijmegen were flown back to the UK from Brussels. The Polish 1st Independent Parachute Brigade remained in positions a little longer south of the Rhine and eventually returned to England in October. The population of Oosterbeek and Arnhem faced a horrendous winter after they were forcibly removed from their homes, which were in turn looted by the Germans with the contents being sent back to Germany. The Germans then proceeded to convert the Dutch homes into strongpoints along the northern bank of the Rhine.

The frontline along the Rhine between Nijmegen and Arnhem still under XXX Corps retained the services of the US 82nd and 101st Airborne Divisions until November due to British manpower shortages. Following the withdrawal from Arnhem all thoughts of reaching the German Ruhr in 1944 were put aside amid a realisation that the war was not nearly over as many had thought.

Soldiers usually win battles and generals get the credit for them.
Napoleon Bonaparte

---

of the Rhine. In his absence the battalion was commanded by its 2i/c, Major S. Cousens. Haddon eventually crossed the river with the 4th Dorsets and was then taken prisoner.

10 Martin Middlebrook, *Arnhem, 1944* (Barnsley: Pen and Sword, 2009), p.439. Although figures vary from one source to another, I have used these figures from Martin Middlebrook's excellent work on the subject.

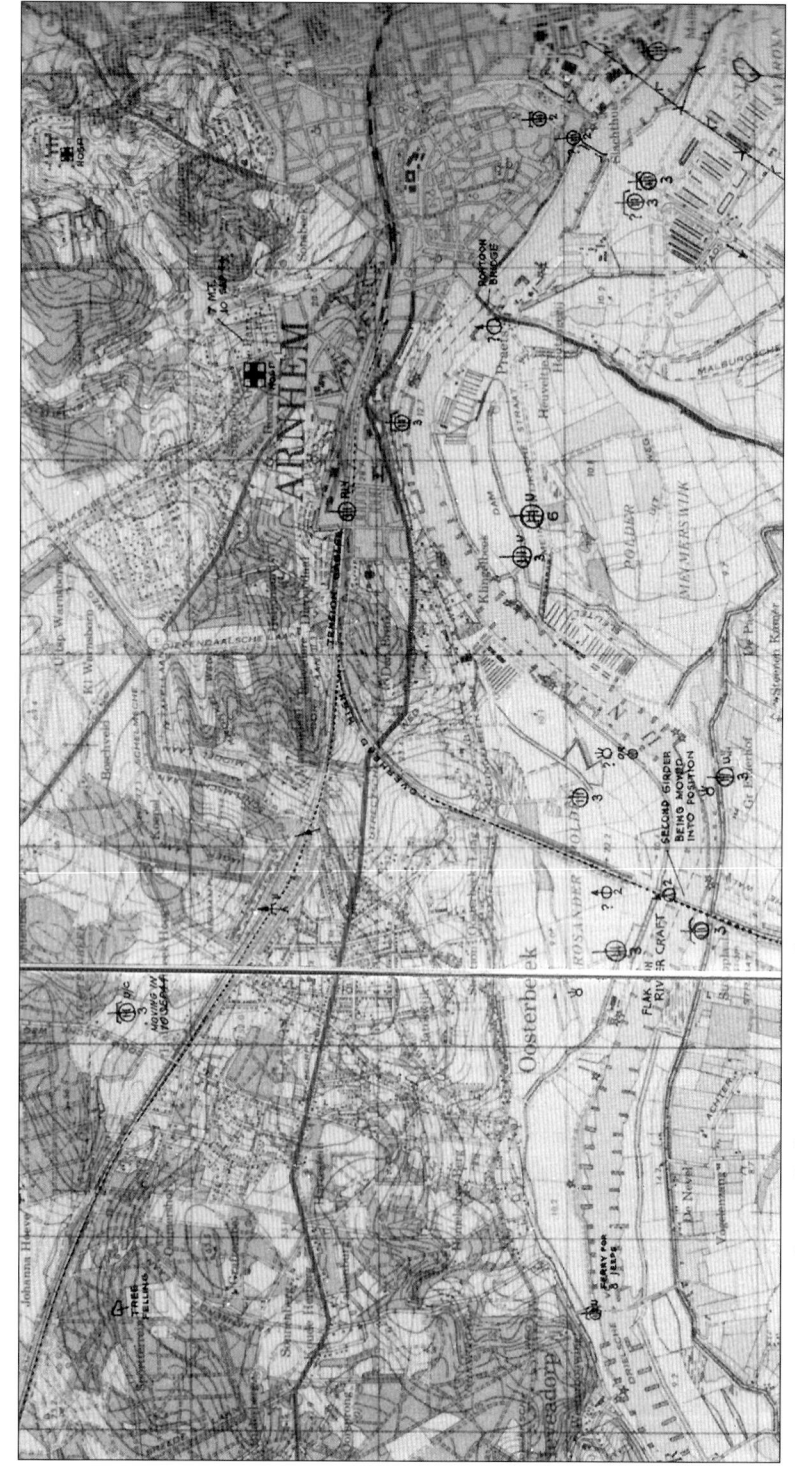

German Defensive Positions, Arnhem area, 11th September 1944. (Courtesy P.G. Atherall, Maps Division, MCE)

DEFENCE LEGEND

Based on F.S.P.B. Pamphlet Nº 6A, 1943 and Conventional Symbols for use by Photographic Interpreters.

1. General

Unconfirmed	(on left of symbol)	?
Unoccupied		u
Dummy	(on left of symbol)	!
Under Construction		u/c.
Constructional Activity		WK

2. Defence Works

(a) Field Defences

Strongpoint		✻	(C)
Gun-emplacement	(see also under Weapons)		
Weapon-pit	(see also under Weapons)		
Observation Post		△	(CT)
Artillery O.P.			(CT)
Fire-trench			
Communication trench			
Dug-out shelter			

(b) Concrete Defences

Strongpoint in concrete		(C)
Concrete shelter (type-number shown on left of symbol, e.g. 302)		(C)
Concrete shelter (under construction)		(C)
Concrete shelter with cupola		(C)
Gun-casemate (see also under Weapons)		(MB)
Pillbox for infantry weapon (see also under Weapons)		(MB)
Concrete shelter with emplacement on roof (weapon-sign on top of symbol; see also under Weapons)		(C)
Concrete O.P.		(C)
Concrete Artillery O.P.		(C)

(c) Railway Artillery

Railway-gun turntable	(C)
Railway-gun spur	

3. Weapons

(a) Artillery

Artillery Weapon (unspecified)   (MB)

	Lt.	Med.	Hy.	In open position	In concrete or armoured turret	
Fixed coast gun						(MB)
Fixed coast How.						(CO)
Mobile gun or gun-how	Up to 105mm	105 – 175mm	Over 175mm			(MB)
Mobile How	Up to 120mm	120 – 175mm	Over 175mm			(CO)
AA Gun	less than 50mm	50 – 75mm	Over 75mm			(MB)
A Tk Gun	less than 50mm	50 – 75mm	Over 75mm			(MB)

Note: 105mm coast guns (fixed) are light.
105mm mobile gun-hows are light.
105mm mobile guns are medium.

Calibres will always be annotated in millimetres

Number of guns written below symbol, calibre written on left of symbol, e.g. 150 = "four 150mm howitzers".

The gun-emplacement symbol (⎴) alone indicates "unoccupied", e.g. 4 = "four unoccupied emplacements".

Railway guns in position are shown thus

(b) Infantry

Infantry Weapon (unspecified)

	Lt.	Med.	In open position	In turret or concrete	
M.G.					(MB)
Mortar	Up to 80mm	80 – 120mm			(CO)
AA MG					(MB)
Flamethrower					(MB)

The weapon-pit symbol (⊓) used alone indicates "unoccupied".

Note: On this map the symbol ↑ is used to indicate a weapon-pit whether occupied or unoccupied.

(c) Searchlights

Searchlight		(C)
Beachlight		(MB)

Arnhem Defence Legend (Courtesy of Gp Cpt RAF (Rtd) Steve Lloyd)

xxxii AIRBORNE TO ARNHEM

Arnhem Defence Legend (Courtesy of Gp Cpt RAF (Rtd) Steve Lloyd)

17th September, 2nd Parachute Battalion begin their drop on D 'X' around 1350 hours.
(Photo: Sergeant Dennis Smith AFPU, Courtesy IWM, BU1161)

1

3rd Parachute Battalion, 1st Parachute Brigade

Introduction[1]

On 22nd June 1940, Prime Minister Winston Churchill wrote to General Sir Hastings Ismay, head of the Military Wing of the War Cabinet Secretariat, asking for 5,000 parachute troops to be trained for the formation of British Airborne Forces. The RAF had shortly before set up a parachute training centre at Ringway, Manchester, known as the Central Landing School. It was there that Major John Rock, RE, was given the task of organising British Airborne Forces. A call for parachutist volunteers went out, and a newly formed No. 2 Commando of 500 ranks was converted to an airborne role. By September 1940, the school became the Central Landing Establishment which incorporated glider training as well as parachuting. No. 2 Commando was redesignated the 11th Special Air Service (SAS) Battalion in November 1940, incorporating parachute and glider wings. After Dunkirk, the need was felt to 'strike back' and at the same time test the effectiveness of the newly formed airborne forces and its equipment. Operation Colossus was planned to send a small airborne party, designated 'X' Troop, to blow up an aqueduct at Tragino in Italy, which supplied water for the province of Apulia. The raid was launched on 10 February, 1941, from ageing Whitley bombers converted to an airborne role flying out from Malta, containing 38 men from 11th SAS, including seven RE sappers. Despite drop dispersion and equipment failure the raid was a success, although all those that took part were subsequently made POW. The outcome of the raid was a great morale boost to the newly established airborne forces and important lessons were learned for future airborne operations.

In May 1941, the Chiefs of Staff issued a memorandum directing the formation of a parachute brigade based around the 11th Special Air Service Battalion. A brigade HQ, four parachute

---

1   Sources: USAAF, Operation MARKET, September 1944, Headquarters 52nd Troop Carrier Wing.
    Air Movement Table. Operation MARKET. First Lift. British – Parachute. Sheet 8. AIR 37/1217.
    War Diary 3rd Parachute Battalion
    War Diary 1st Parachute Battalion
    Operation Market; Diary of Events: 1st Parachute Brigade HQ :WO171/393 :Annexure 'N'
    Operation Instructions 1st Airborne Division: WO171/393:Annexure 'C'
    Operation Instructions 1st Parachute Brigade: WO171/393: Annexure 'D'
    Operation Instructions Royal Engineers, 1st Airborne Division: Annexure 'J'
    Report by CRA, 1st Airborne Division: WO171/393:Annexure 'R'
    Report by CRE, 1st Airborne Division: WO171/393:Annexure 'S'
    War Diary 1st Parachute Brigade HQ: WO171/592.

battalions and an RE airborne troop were initiated in July 1941 with a recruitment drive within the army for volunteers. By September 1941, HQ, 1st Parachute Brigade along with a signals section and an RE troop was assembled at Hardwick Hall, Derbyshire, under command of Brigadier Richard Gale; at the same time, the 11th Special Air Service Battalion was redesignated as the 1st Parachute Battalion. It was decided that two, rather than three, further parachute battalions were to be created initially. The 2nd Parachute Battalion was formed under command of Lieutenant Colonel Edward Flavell and the 3rd Parachute Battalion under command of Lieutenant Colonel Gerald Lathbury. In January 1942, the 4th Parachute Battalion was created and would provide the basis for the 2nd Parachute Brigade formed in July 1942. On 17th July, Lieutenant Colonel Eric Down, CO, 1st Parachute Battalion, was promoted to brigadier to take command of the new brigade.

Bruneval Raid

During 1941, the RAF had suffered losses due to German radar interception. One of the enemy radar installations was situated right on the French coast at Bruneval. Of importance was the acquisition of equipment used by the Germans to guide their night fighters to intercept RAF bombers. With a seaborne assault deemed potentially too costly, an airborne alternative was planned. 2nd Parachute Battalion were chosen to carry out the raid, and Lieutenant Colonel Flavell chose Major Johnny Frost's C Company to carry out the mission. On the night of 27th February 1942, at around 2230 hours, C Company, supported by a party of Airborne REs, took off in 12 Whitleys for the snow-covered French coast. The parachute landings were a success and the radar equipment was dismantled by 0215 hours despite enemy opposition. Six Royal Navy landing craft arrived somewhat late and at 0330 hours transferred Frost's force to motor gunboats offshore. By dawn on 28th February, Frost and his men, along with the prized German radar equipment, were safely back in Portsmouth.

Towards the end of 1941 the War Office required a glider-borne airlanding brigade in addition to the 1st Parachute Brigade. The 31st Independent Infantry Brigade was chosen to change over to an airlanding role, becoming the 1st Airlanding Brigade, under Brigadier G.F. Hopkinson, as of 31st October 1941. The HQ, 1st Airborne Division, was formed at the same time with Brigadier Frederick 'Boy' Browning promoted to Major General, Commander of Paratroops and Airborne Troops. On a War Office directive, the newly formed parachute battalions would come under the umbrella of the Army Air Corps along with the fledgling Glider Pilot Regiment. On 24 February 1942, both were added to the Army Order of Battle. Several command changes now took place, leading to Brigadier Richard Gale being transferred to the position of Director of Air at the War Office, with Brigadier Edward Flavell taking over from Gale. Flavell, as CO of 2nd Parachute Battalion, was replaced by Major Johnny Frost and Lieutenant Colonel Gerald Lathbury moved from the 3rd Parachute Battalion to the War Office. The command of the 3rd Parachute Battalion then passed from Lieutenant Colonel R. Webb to Lieutenant Colonel Geoffrey Pine-Coffin. On the 1st August, 1942, the Parachute Regiment was formed, and along with the Glider Pilot Regiment, officially became part of the Army Air Corps.

In early November 1942, the Allied seaborne landings took place in North Africa. The 1st Parachute Brigade were destined to participate but beforehand, during October, they had to familiarise themselves with jumping out of the side door of American C-47 Dakota aircraft instead of out of a hole in the fuselage of a converted Whitley bomber. The 1st Parachute Brigade distinguished themselves during five months of intense fighting, incurring 1,700 casualties whilst capturing over 3,500 prisoners and inflicting around 5,000 enemy casualties.[2] It was during the heavy fighting in North Africa that the members of the 1st Parachute Brigade earned the respect of their German adversaries who bestowed the title *Rote Teufel* or Red Devils; the Red Beret had indeed created a reputation which would command respect and admiration to this day.

On 23rd April 1943, the War Office issued instructions for the formation of another Airborne Division. In order to confuse the enemy, it would be named the 6th Airborne Division and would be headquartered at Syrencot House near Netheravon.

In May 1943, the 1st Parachute Brigade rejoined elements of the 1st Airborne Division at Mascara in North Africa. The division was now under intense training for the next operation, the invasion of Sicily. In July the division moved to its new operational base at Kairouan, near Sousse. The division had three objectives: the Ponte Grande bridge near Syracuse, the port of Augusta and the Primasole bridge across the River Simeto, and the Gornalunga Canal. 1st Parachute Brigade were tasked with capturing the Primasole bridge.

On 9th July 1943 at 1900 hours, Operation Ladbrooke was launched with 144 Horsa and American-made Waco CG-4 gliders carrying the 1st Airlanding Brigade with its objective being the Ponte Grande bridge. With very poor weather and inexperienced USAAF air crews, the gliders were released too far offshore with 73 ditching in the sea. One Horsa landed on its LZ with two others nearby enabling the capture of the bridge; although initially lost, it was retaken shortly after by British seaborne forces.

Just days later, on 13th July, at 1901 hours, the aircraft carrying the 1st Parachute Brigade took off as part of Operation Fustian, consisting of 113 paratrooper aircraft and eight Waco and 11 Horsa glider combinations heading for Sicily. En route, the aircraft were met by friendly naval fire and then enemy anti-aircraft fire. Eleven aircraft were shot down; eight managed to drop their sticks, although in the event, just 39 aircraft dropped on the DZs, some 48 dropped wide and 17 returned to base with a full load. Four gliders arrived on their objective with three 6-pounder anti-tank guns and Jeeps. Nevertheless, with just 295 men out of the brigade of 1,856, they managed to at first capture their objective at 0430 hours before being forced back. The Primasole bridge was retaken on 16th July with the arrival of the 4th Armoured Brigade and the 9th Battalion Durham Light Infantry. 1st Parachute Brigade losses were 27 KIA and 78 wounded. The brigade then returned to Sousse, received reinforcements and retrained for the up and coming invasion of Italy.

The 1st Airborne Division sailed for Taranto which they reached on 9th September 1943. 1st Parachute Brigade were allocated a reserve role and took up positions around Taranto. It was during the fighting at Castellaneta involving the 10th Parachute Battalion, 4th Parachute Brigade, that the divisional commander, Major General Hopkinson was killed by German machine gun fire. The division was taken over by Brigadier Eric Down, CO, 2nd Parachute Brigade. In November 1943, the 1st Airborne Division sailed from Taranto back to the UK, while the 2nd Parachute Brigade remained in Italy as an independent brigade unit. 1st Airborne Division arrived home to discover that a new airborne division had been formed; the 6th Airborne Division would be commanded by Major General Richard Gale, late of the 1st Parachute Brigade and deputy Director of Air at the War Office. The new division would grow rapidly between May and September 1943 under a concentrated training programme under the control of Gale. The division was put on standby at the end of the year in preparation for operational deployment in early 1944. Gale was very much an

---

2   Harclerode, Peter, *Para! Fifty Years of the Parachute Regiment*, BCA, 1992, p.51.

airborne 'soldiers' general' and a great inspiration to his men within the division. It is no surprise that he was chosen to spearhead the airborne assault on D-Day, 6 June with his 6th Airborne Division. Gale's division fought through Normandy with great determination, fulfilling all its tasks. After nearly three months of fighting, in which time it advanced 45 miles, it had suffered 4,457 casualties, of which 821 were killed.[3] The division returned to England in early September, shortly before the 1st Airborne Division would leave for Arnhem on Operation Market.

Operation Market

For Operation Market, the 2nd Parachute Battalion under Lieutenant Colonel J.D. Frost would be tasked with four roles. The priority task was to seize the main Arnhem road bridge; secondly to clear the town within the battalion perimeter and establish defensive positions facing north-west and west. The third and equally important task was to secure the Arnhem to Nijmegen railway bridge and exploit this capture by advancing on the main road bridge from south of the river and secure the Arnhem pontoon bridge en route. Its final role upon completing these tasks was to push out covering patrols. The 1st Parachute Battalion, under the command of Lieutenant Colonel D.A. Dobie, was tasked with capturing high ground to the north of Arnhem town, thereby denying the enemy direct observation on to Arnhem. Secondly, it was required to cover northern approaches to the town through its battalion boundaries and finally to keep one company as brigade reserve. The 1st Airborne Division Operational Order for the 3rd Parachute Battalion under their Commanding Officer, Lieutenant Colonel J.A.C. Fitch, was to assist the 2nd Parachute Battalion in capturing the main Arnhem road bridge. On capturing the bridge and establishing a secure bridgehead, the battalion was to then set up defensive positions in Arnhem facing northeast and east of the bridge. Once this had been done, covering patrols were to be sent out.

These then were the plans set out for the spearhead of the 1st Airborne Division in attempting to secure the Arnhem bridge.

Pathfinders

Sunday, 17th September

The 1st Parachute Brigade group drop on 17th September was preceded by the pathfinder force of 186 officers and men of the 21st Independent Parachute Company under command of Major B.A. 'Boy' Wilson. The unit took off in 12 Short Stirling aircraft Chalk Nos. 1–12, from 38 Group based at RAF Fairford at approximately 1015–1030 hours. At 1240 hours, the pathfinders dropped onto LZ 'S' and DZ 'X' and set up Company HQ at Reijerscamp farm on LZ 'S'. The company deployed, and immediately went about marking the DZs and LZs for the main force of paratroops and glider-borne infantry and equipment. DZ ground identification consisted of marker strips in the form of the designated DZ letter along with wind direction panels and smoke indicators. To aid approaching aircraft, transmitter Eureka beacons emitting eight watts of power were switched on to guide the incoming aircraft equipped with receiver Rebecca units inside the lead aircraft sending out 214 megacycles, to which the Eureka replied on 219 megacycles. LZ 'S' was allocated

---

3   Otway, Lt Col T.B.H., *Airborne Forces*, IWM, 1990, p.191.

to the gliders of the 1st Airlanding Brigade, whilst the 1st Parachute Brigade group would jump onto DZ 'X'. LZ 'Z' was allocated to gliders containing the 1st Parachute Brigade vehicles along with the divisional troops and the Jeeps of the 1st Airborne Reconnaissance Squadron.

1st Parachute Brigade: Glider Element Allocation[4]

First Lift, 17th September
RAF Keevil. 299 and 196 Squadrons, RAF. LZ 'Z'
299 Squadron take-off time approximately 1015 hours+. Returned to base 1535 hours+.
196 Squadron take-off time 1040 hours+. Returned to base 1600 hours+.
Chalk Nos. 459–478. Twenty Stirling tug/Horsa glider combinations flown by 'D' Squadron glider pilots, GPR, towed by 196 Squadron, RAF, Serial No. B19. Chalk Nos. 459–478 (462, 468, 474, 478 aborted).

Load
Chalk Nos. 459–470, 1st Parachute Brigade, 24 Jeeps.
Chalk Nos. 473–478, 1st Parachute Brigade HQ signal personnel. 16th Parachute Field Ambulance including 12 Jeeps. Chalk Nos. 479–480, two Parachute Platoon Jeep Sections (2 Jeeps and 2 trailers).

RAF Keevil. Abortive Sorties
Chalk No. 474. Containing two Jeeps, two personnel of 1st Parachute Brigade HQ. Tow rope failure, landed at RAF Gosfield, near Braintree, Essex.
Chalk No. 462. Containing three 1st Parachute Battalion personnel under command of CQMS Cook, DCM, two Jeeps and two motorcycles. The glider experienced a tow rope failure due to slip stream turbulence off the Dutch coast at Walcheren. All onboard were rescued by an air/sea rescue launch.
Chalk No. 468. Containing three 3rd Parachute Battalion personnel, two Jeeps. The Horsa had a tow rope failure over Holland landing near Dinteloord; all on board were made POW.
Chalk No. 478. Containing two Jeeps and four personnel from 1st Parachute Brigade HQ, two RASC personnel, Dutch Lieutenant Luitwieler, No. 2 (Dutch) Troop No. 10 Interallied Commando and Lieutenant Szegda, IO, Independent Polish Parachute Brigade attached to 1st Parachute Brigade HQ. Horsa No. 478 had a tow rope failure and landed near Biezenmortel, Holland. All onboard evaded capture and made contact with allied forces in October.[5]

---

[4] Sources: Air Movement Table. Operation 'MARKET'. First Lift – British Gliders. Sheet 9. AIR37/1217
Air Movement Table. Operation 'MARKET'. First Lift – British Gliders. Sheet 10. AIR37/1217
Air Movement Table. Operation 'MARKET'. Second Lift – British Gliders. Sheet 12 & 13. AIR37/1217
Air Movement Table. Operation 'MARKET'. Second Lift – British Gliders & Resupply. Sheet 14. AIR37/1217
Operatierapporten RAF Operatie 'MARKET GARDEN' Headquarters Group 2.
[5] Hees, Arie-Jan, *Tugs and Gliders To Arnhem*, A.J. van Hees, 2000, p.79.

RAF Tarrant Rushton. 298 and 644 Squadrons, RAF. LZ 'Z'
1st Parachute Brigade. Three Halifax tug/Hamilcar combinations flown by 'C' Squadron, glider pilots, GPR, towed by 298(2) and 644(1) Squadrons, RAF. Serial No. B14. Chalk Nos.322–324.
Load
Six Bren Gun Carriers allocated to 1st, 2nd and 3rd Parachute Battalions, 1st Parachute Brigade.

Second Lift, 18th September
RAF Broadwell. 512 and 575 Squadrons, RAF. LZ 'X'
1st Parachute Brigade. One Dakota tug/Horsa combination towed by 575 Squadron, 46 Group, RAF. Serial No. B26. Chalk No. 834.
Load
Chalk No. 834 containing two Jeeps and HQ 1st Parachute Brigade personnel.
RAF Fairford.190 and 620 Squadrons, RAF. LZ 'X'
1st Parachute Brigade. Five Stirling tug/Horsa glider combinations Chalk Nos.945–949, towed by 620 Squadron, 38 Group, RAF, Serial No. B31.
Load
Chalk Nos. 945–949, five Jeeps and four trailers of 16th Parachute Field Ambulance attached to 1st Parachute Brigade.
1st Parachute Brigade. Fourteen Stirling tug/Horsa glider combinations Chalk Nos. 990–1003, towed by 190 Squadron, 38 Group, RAF. Serial No. B34. (Chalk Nos. 994, 996 aborted).
Load
Chalk Nos.990–993, each containing one 1st Parachute Battalion Jeep, trailer, two motorcycles and personnel.
Chalk Nos. 994–997, each containing one 2nd Parachute Battalion Jeep, trailer, two motorcycles and personnel.
Chalk Nos. 998–1001, each containing one 3rd Parachute Battalion Jeep, trailer, two motorcycles and personnel.
Chalk Nos. 1002–1003, each containing Jeep and trailer of 1st Parachute Squadron, RE, and RE personnel attached 1st Parachute Brigade.
RAF Fairford. Abortive Sorties
Chalk No. 994, mission aborted due to tug engine problems. Both tug and glider landed at RAF South Cerney, Cirencester, Gloucestershire and reallocated to Third Lift.
Chalk No. 996, experienced problems with broken tow rope, both tug and glider landed at RAF Woodbridge, Suffolk. Load allocated to Third Lift.
RAF Keevil. Aborted Sorties from 1st Lift. DZ 'Z'
1st Parachute Brigade. Chalk No. 474. One Tug/Horsa glider combination towed by 196 Squadron, 38 Group, RAF. Serial No. B19.
Load
Chalk No. 474. Containing two Jeeps and two personnel of 1st Parachute Brigade HQ.

Third Lift, 19th September
RAF Fairford. 190 and 620 Squadrons. LZ 'L'
> 1st Parachute Brigade. Chalk Nos. 994, 996. Two tug/Horsa glider combinations towed by 190 Squadron, 38 Group. RAF. Serial Nos. B34 (994 aborted again).
>
> Chalk No. 994, containing a 2nd Parachute Battalion Jeep, two trailers, two motorcycles and five 2nd Parachute Battalion personnel experienced difficulties in poor visibility off the Belgian coast. The Horsa was forced to cast off, and ditched into the sea. One of the glider pilots was drowned; the remaining glider pilot and passengers made land but were taken POW.[6]

3rd Parachute Battalion, 1st Parachute Brigade

RAF Saltby
Both the 3rd and 2nd Parachute Battalions would take off from Saltby. Take-off time would be around 1126 hours for the 3rd and 1121 hours for the 2nd Parachute Battalion.

The US 314th Troop would carry 520 airborne personnel of the 3rd Parachute Battalion, Chalk Nos. 49–82, the 16th Parachute Field Ambulance, Chalk No. 83 and the attached No. 1 Parachute Platoon RASC in 36 aircraft, consisting of 33 C-47s and 3 C-53s. The aircraft carried 128 parapacks (containers) weighing 29,500lbs. Fourteen containers failed to drop due to mechanical failure; all aircraft made successful drops although one aircraft had to make a second pass for one paratrooper, and there were two refusals. White DZ 'X' identification panels and blue marker smoke was reported as effective and there were no losses of aircraft.

The first battalion to drop onto Drop Zone 'X' around Jonkershoeve were the 2nd Parachute Battalion around 1350 hours, followed minutes later at around 1356 hours by 3rd Parachute Battalion and the 1st Parachute Battalion. Having landed successfully, the 3rd Battalion rendezvoused under a red smoke marker and then formed up with its Jeeps and Bren Carriers that had landed earlier by glider on Landing Zone 'Z' at around 1330 hours. It was to then advance into Arnhem along Utrechtseweg, the main Utrecht/Arnhem road (codenamed Tiger), which was the middle route of the three-pronged thrust of the 1st Parachute Brigade tasked with capturing the Arnhem road bridge. Attached to the 3rd Parachute Battalion was a troop of four 6-pounder anti-tank guns belonging to C Troop, 1st Airlanding Anti-Tank Battery, Royal Artillery, less one gun relegated to the second lift due to towing difficulties, plus half of C Troop of the 1st Parachute Squadron, Royal Engineers under Captain L.G. Cox (the remaining half were left to assist on the DZ under Captain S. George, 2 i/c). Medical support would be provided by a section of 16 Parachute Field Ambulance, Royal Army Medical Corps.

By 1500 hours, 3rd Parachute Battalion headed off the DZ onto the Utrechtseweg towards Oosterbeek with B Company in the lead under Major Peter Waddy with rifle platoons advancing either side of the road. Behind B Company followed Battalion HQ, then C Company with HQ Company with its three-inch mortars and Vickers machine guns and lastly A Company as rear guard.

Following at intervals along the column were two of the 6-pounder anti-tank guns under Lieutenant E.E. Shaw Commanding Officer of C Troop, 1st Airlanding Anti-Tank Battery.

---

6   Hees, Arie-Jan, *Tugs and Gliders to Arnhem*, A.J. van Hees, 2000, p.186.

Sergeant Garnsworthy's No. 1 gun was in close support of B Company, whilst further back down the column Sergeant Shaw followed with his No. 4 gun. Of the two remaining troop guns, No. 3, under Sergeant Robson was ordered by the battery commanding officer, Major W.F. Arnold, to follow B Troop 1st Airlanding Anti-Tank Battery, Battery HQ, 1st Parachute Brigade HQ and 2nd Parachute Battalion to the Arnhem bridge along the Lion lower road route. The remaining C Troop gun, No. 2 under Sergeant Proctor, would join the battery later having been detailed to join the second lift to land on the Monday having cast off from his tug during the first lift.

The 3rd Parachute Battalion moved steadily along the Utrechtseweg with B Company's No. 5 Platoon under Lieutenant James Cleminson on point. Around two hours after moving off, the battalion point element was alerted to the sound of a car approaching from its left towards the Wolfhezerweg/Utrechtseweg road junction. The car was a German Citroen staff car which attempted to turn left onto the Utrechtseweg towards Oosterbeek. The immediate reaction of the forward platoon was to open fire on the car as it slowed to turn the corner. The car came to a halt with all four occupants dead. It was only later that the B Company men learnt that they had killed General Major Friedrich Kussin, Feldkommandantur 642 Arnhem. Kussin was attempting to return to Arnhem having visited the HQ of SS Panzergrenadier-Ausbildungs und Ersatz-Bataillon 16 under the command of SS Obersturmbannführer Sepp Krafft at the Hotel Wolfheze on the Wolfhezerweg. Krafft at the time was in the process of rapidly deploying his battalion in order to slow the progress of the airborne troops towards Arnhem. Kussin had just updated Krafft on the latest developments and was warned by Krafft before his departure of the proximity of the advancing airborne forces. Kussin ignored Krafft's advice to take a different route and proceeded to drive straight into 3rd Parachute Battalion's B Company.

At around 1630 hours, Brigadier Lathbury joined the 3rd Parachute Battalion concerned at the slow speed of the advance. The battalion moved forward only to be halted at 1700 hours with the appearance of an armoured car supported by infantry which appeared from a side road just past the Wolfhezerweg junction. The lead elements of the 3rd Parachute Battalion melted swiftly into the shrubbery and houses at the sides of the road whilst under fire from the armoured car. This 'parting of the waves' revealed a 1st Airlanding Anti-Tank Battery, C Troop Jeep under command of Sergeant Garnsworthy, towing its No. 1 6-pounder anti-tank gun directly in front of the German armour. Hitched in the towing position, the Jeep and its gun and crew were fully exposed to the advancing armoured car which opened fire, immobilising the Jeep, wounding Gunner Fail and killing driver Bombardier Robson. The airborne infantry PIATs could not be deployed or were put out of action and whilst the German infantry were engaged, the armoured vehicle turned off the road and disappeared, having placed the wounded Gunner Fail on the bonnet of the armoured car. Fortunately the C Troop 6-pounder anti-tank gun remained serviceable and another Jeep was found to tow the gun.

By 1730 hours, Krafft's battalion had intensified their efforts to occupy the Utrechtseweg/Wolfhezerweg crossroads firstly mortaring the area and pushing infantry from his 9 Kompanie to the left flank of the advancing 3rd Parachute Battalion. Fitch's battalion was now strung out over approximately 800 yards from the Wolfhezerweg crossroads to the Koude Herberg crossroads and was encountering flanking fire from the woods to the north of the Utrechtseweg. A Company, at the rear of the 3rd Battalion column, was ordered to clear the woods in the Bilderberg area of German infantry and by 1830 hours two platoons under Major Dennison returned to the column, having temporarily forced the Germans back. German mortaring of the crossroads continued and Brigadier Lathbury ordered the battalion tail of A Company to tighten up the column and move forward at all speed to vacate the intense mortar bombardment of the crossroads area. Major General Urquhart had by this time also joined Lathbury and the 3rd Parachute Battalion and was concerned at the 'unsettling accuracy' of the mortar fire. Whilst dismounted from his Jeep and discussing the deteriorating situation with Lathbury, Urquhart's Jeep received fragments from the mortar fire, wounding his signaller.

The 3rd Parachute Battalion suffered a number of casualties from mortar fire and forays into the woods in an attempt to clear them of German infantry along the Utrechtseweg between Wolfhezerweg and Koude Herberg crossroads. At least 18 men were wounded including the 2i/c of A Company, Captain Thessiger, with a stomach wound, along with Lieutenant Baxter, CO 2 Platoon, A Company, and Lieutenant Bussell, CO 1 Platoon, A Company. A number of men were killed: amongst those were Sergeant Hildyard-Todd, A Company; Lance Corporal William Bamsey; and Privates Benstead, Mathews and Chennell.

As it began to get dusk around 1930 hours, Lieutenant Colonel Fitch, along with Brigadier Lathbury, ordered C Company under Major R.P.C. Lewis to sidestep the line of advance in a north-easterly direction away from the Koude Herberg crossroads up the Valkenberglaan towards the railway, in order to bypass the German opposition along the Utrechtseweg. C Company then passed through B Company. Meanwhile, it was decided by Lathbury, after a discussion with Fitch (and in the background General Urquhart) that the remainder of the battalion should consolidate and take up all-round positions in the area of Hartenstein. This decision lost valuable time. Had the whole battalion followed C Company along the railway line into Arnhem, the numbers at the bridge would have been increased, as elements of C Company successfully reached the bridge and fought there until finally overrun on the night of Wednesday 20th and the early morning of Thursday 21st. This inexplicable delay created serious concern within the ranks of the experienced veterans of 3rd Parachute Battalion, considering that they had only recently landed only to find themselves coming to a halt rather than pushing on under the cover of darkness.

Monday, 18th September

During the night of the 17th–18th, it was decided by Urquhart and Lathbury to move Fitch's 3rd Parachute Battalion off the Tiger route and follow in the footsteps of Frost's 2nd Parachute Battalion along the lower Lion route. Frost had successfully reached the Arnhem Bridge around 2000 hours on the 17th and established his battalion on the northern end of the bridge, and had been joined by elements of 3rd Parachute Battalion's C Company during the night.

So in the dark before dawn of Monday 18th, at around 0430 hours, the 3rd Parachute Battalion slowly moved off. The order of march was B Company along with Sergeant Garnsworthy's 6-pounder anti-tank gun, Battalion HQ, Royal Engineers, and HQ Company was followed at the rear by A Company and Sergeant Shaw's 6-pounder anti-tank gun. So slow was the advance that by the time rear elements of A Company reached the Hartenstein, it was beginning to get light. The route taken was to the Oosterbeek crossroads, a sharp right-hand turn down Pietersbergseweg and another turn down Paasbergseweg eventually joining Benedendorpsweg close to Oosterbeek Laag Church. The initial progress of B Company in the dark was promising but by the time the rear of the column reached the area of Oosterbeek Laag railway station, German machine gun and small arms fire cut off parts of the battalion tail with HQ Company, its heavy weapons and A Company encountering heavy fire on the Benedendorpsweg railway viaduct slowing down any forward movement.

By 0630 hours, B Company had reached within 300 yards west of the St Elizabeth Hospital and were halted by fire from German flak guns south of the river and German armour on the road ahead. To counter the German fire from across the river, the C Troop 6-pounder anti-tank gun of Sergeant Garnsworthy which was supporting B Company was brought into action by Lieutenant Shaw, the troop commander. Sergeant Garnsworthy successfully dealt with the offending enemy gun but incurred retribution. German retaliation was swift, with intense mortar fire being brought down on the gun position resulting in the gun being abandoned.[7] With this temporary halt came a quick reappraisal of the situation which revealed that the rear of the battalion had become separated from the main body. No. 5 Platoon, which was on point, under Lieutenant James Cleminson continued to make progress until approximately 0830 hours when it pulled back, having made contact with a small group of C Company, 2nd Parachute Battalion under Lieutenant David Russell on Onderlangs, some 400 yards east of the St Elizabeth Hospital on Utrechtseweg.

Having consolidated just west of the St Elizabeth Hospital, 3rd Parachute Battalion consisting of Battalion HQ, B Company and a troop of Royal Engineers, were still without any wireless contact with A Company and HQ Company. They then came under a German counter attack from armour and infantry along the Utrechtseweg at around 0900 hours. The German attack was supported by mortar fire, and the 3rd Parachute Battalion immediately took cover in the substantial Dutch houses along the Utrechtseweg. By 0900 hours, A Company had finally passed the railway viaduct and embankment at Oosterbeek Laag and were now about a mile from the main part of the battalion, although still coming under fire along the way. Wireless contact was established with A Company who were still struggling to break through opposition and an urgent request for support was made for ammunition to be rushed forward in the battalion Bren gun carriers. By 1430 hours, a group of A Company under Lieutenant B. Burwash, HQ Company, CO Assault Platoon, finally made contact with the rest of the battalion and brought with them a Bren gun carrier full of the much-needed ammunition. Fitch immediately ordered the ammunition to be distributed to the various houses locally that were occupied by the battalion. It was at this time that German mortaring started up again and Major P. Waddy, CO B Company, was killed making his way to unload the carrier.

Lieutenant Colonel Fitch, still accompanied by General Urquhart and Brigadier Lathbury, decided that as the 3rd Parachute Battalion was pinned down it needed to move out of its current position and move north towards the railway line which ran into Arnhem. From there, they could pivot eastwards and follow the line of the railway into the town and hopefully make it to the bridge, which in fact was exactly what C Company had done the previous evening, moving through the railway station itself into the town. Therefore at 1600 hours, the battalion moved through the back gardens negotiating the high garden walls and fencing towards the railway. Leading the breakout were A Company, Battalion HQ, and B Company followed by the Royal Engineers. At this time, moving through what is known as the Lombok area, General Urquhart and Brigadier Lathbury left Fitch to make their own way back through the myriad of closely-packed houses and alleyways. Lathbury was shot and wounded shortly after in Alexanderstraat and was dragged into No. 135 for cover. Urquhart moved on, accompanied by Lieutenant Cleminson, B Company and Captain W.E. Taylor, who was the Intelligence Officer of Brigade HQ. Very soon, General Urquhart's group found themselves cut off and took shelter in a house at No. 14 Zwarteweg opposite St Elizabeth Hospital, the area now swarming with German infantry. Shortly afterwards, a Sturmgeschütz SP

---

7   Peter Wilkinson, *The Gunners at Arnhem* (Northampton: Spurwing Publishing, 1999), p.60.

Utrechtseweg immediately west of St Elizabeth Hospital. Buildings occupied by 3rd Parachute Battalion, Monday 18th September while pinned down before moving north out the back gardens through the Lombok area. Photo taken in 1980 with visible repairs to the battle-damaged brickwork. (Photo: Author, 1980)

Tuesday, 19th September, Utrechtseweg, immediately west of St Elizabeth Hospital. German StuG.III facing back towards the hospital whilst the gun commander cuts low hanging cables. A StuH.42G on the left faces the lower Onderlangs road where houses are still being cleared by the German infantry. (Photo: Courtesy Gelders Archive)

Utrechtseweg immediately west of St Elizabeth Hospital. Buildings occupied by 3rd Parachute Battalion. 1945 photo taken from Zwarteweg looking west along Utrechtseweg. (Photo: Courtesy Gelders Archive)

gun pulled up outside the house, Urquhart was trapped and was therefore effectively out of the battle until relieved by advancing forces.

In all, the 3rd Battalion and attached units had a combined strength at this time of around 130–140 men. There were still small groups of the battalion attempting to link up. The Lombok area of densely-packed houses with narrow passages and large rectangular cobbled squares proved difficult to negotiate as a large unit and the battalion quickly fragmented into small sections of individuals often led by NCOs. The Germans had infiltrated the area and had set up fixed-line machine guns facing down the streets, alleyways and passageways, making traversing the area hazardous; every street potentially had a machine gun trained down it, as Urquhart and Lathbury had found out. Great care had to be taken, which slowed the battalion down and made command and control extremely difficult. A Company reached the railway line but were prevented from moving any further; not only were there Germans ahead but they were occupying houses on the northern side of the railway on Noordelijke Parallelweg and engaging A Company from the flank. The company became divided; half under command of Fitch, the other half under Captain Dorrien-Smith 2i/c B Company, each group made up of around 70 men. It was now beginning to get dark, and any attempt to get forward via the railway was stalled.

Lombok looking south down Oranje Straat. Utrechtseweg runs east to west at the bottom of the road. (Photo: Author, 1979)

Lombok, looking east along Zuidelijke Parallelweg. Having reached the railway (on the left) the 3rd Battalion advance stalled on Monday 18th September. (Photo: Author, 1979)

48 AIRBORNE TO ARNHEM

Looking north across the railway to German positions in the houses on Noordelijke Parallelweg from Zuidelijke Parallelweg. (Photo: Author, 1979)

Lombok, looking west along the northern boundary of the 3rd Parachute Battalion, Monday advance. Maurits Straat on the left. Zwarteweg behind the camera next turning to the left. 3rd Battalion did not reach this far on the Monday to release General Urquhart trapped in No. 14 Zwarteweg. A Sturmgeschütz sat outside parked in the street until early morning. (Photo: Author, 1979)

Lombok, Zwarteweg No. 14 middle of photo; it was here that General Urquhart, Lieutenant Cleminson and Captain Taylor were forced to hold up until relieved by troops from 2nd Battalion South Staffs in the early hours on Tuesday 19th. Cleminson returned to his unit and Urquhart and Taylor were driven back to Div HQ at the Hartenstein by Lieutenant E.E. Clapham, CO of A Troop, 1st Airlanding Anti-Tank Battery RA, arriving at around 0725 hours. Clapham then returned to his battery. (Photo: Author, 1979)

Pre-war view from Utrechtseweg near the St Elizabeth hospital looking down the steep embankment to the Onderlangs below along which the 3rd and 1st Parachute Battalions advanced. On the extreme left, high up overlooking the Onderlangs can be seen the houses on the Utrechtseweg/ Utrechtsestraat. Further down the river, the pontoon bridge can clearly be seen. This was around the extent of the advance for both battalions. Just beyond the pontoon bridge sits the objective, the Arnhem road bridge. To the right, across the river, is the brickworks from where German flak engaged the advance. (Photo: Courtesy Gelders Archive)

Corporal Alex Whitelaw, HQ Company, 3rd Parachute Battalion, 1st Parachute Brigade

Tuesday, 19th September

'We again moved off. This time it appeared we were moving faster, maybe it was my imagination! The first attack had taken us just to the Pontoon Bridge. How far would we get this time? Hopefully to the bridge, but with lack of support from the rear, I just could not see it. It appeared the Germans had been slower opening up, but this had only been because they had been fetching more shit up to throw at us. Every foot of space seemed to be covered with some sort of weapon or other.'

Having resisted German attacks the previous evening which ceased around nightfall, Fitch held an 'O' Group and informed his company commanders that he had decided on a change of route, an advance along the railway no longer remaining viable. The battalion was to move south towards the Utrechtseweg (down the axis of Oranjestraat) and then head due east past the Rhine Pavilion along the riverbank towards the bridge.

By now other reinforcements were arriving in the western approaches to Arnhem. 1st Parachute Battalion under Lieutenant Colonel Dobie had arrived in the area at around 2000 hours the evening before, along with elements of A Company and HQ Company 3rd Parachute Battalion which had become detached from the main body during the advance into Arnhem. During the night, despite conflicting orders from Divisional HQ, Dobie, unaware of the actions of Fitch and his battalion, held an 'O' Group with the recently arrived Lieutenant Colonel McCardie, CO, 2nd South Staffs and Lieutenant Colonel Lea, 11th Parachute Battalion was also in attendance. 2nd Battalion South Staffs, having been earlier relieved of their DZ guard duties, followed them, with the 11th Parachute Battalion freshly arrived with the second lift on DZ 'Y'. Dobie's plan was to push his 1st Parachute Battalion along the river embankment with support on his left flank along the Utrechtseweg provided by the South Staffs. It was intended that the 11th Parachute Battalion should follow up behind in reserve.

At around 0230 hours of the Tuesday morning under the cover of darkness, the 3rd Parachute Battalion moved off to launch their attack, unaware that Dobie was not far behind. The advance initially went well until engaged by two German machine guns, likely firing in a sustained fire role along fixed lines in the dark, but the battalion managed to avoid any casualties. As the battalion moved along the riverbank towards the Arnhem pontoon bridge in the Oude Kraan area, it came under increasingly heavy machine gun and mortar fire and began to take casualties to its already depleted force; these included RSM Lord and Lieutenant Dean, with over a dozen men wounded. Fitch decided to withdraw back to the Rhine Pavilion, reform and attempt another advance in daylight.

On the way back to the Rhine Pavilion, the battalion came into contact with advance elements of S Company under Major Stark of 1st Parachute Battalion. Whilst Fitch and his battalion had been advancing along the river bank, the 1st Parachute Battalion had fought their way into the area and they too began moving towards the bridge. A Company, 3rd Parachute Battalion under Captain Dorrien-Smith were moving back towards the Rhine Pavilion when they encountered Dobie and warned him that the route ahead was impenetrable. Dobie was emphatic that his advance along the riverbank road to the bridge should continue. Fitch therefore offered to provide fire support for Dobie in his attack with the remains of his already reduced 3rd Parachute Battalion. Dobie's 1st Parachute Battalion moved off, with little room for manoeuvre along the axis of the Onderlangs. The intensity of German fire increased with the early morning light. Despite the tenacious efforts of the 1st Parachute Battalion with grenade and bayonet, by 0500 hours the Germans had deployed armour as well as infantry and Dobie's battalion attack ground to a halt. The same was happening on the Utrechtseweg above them, with the South Staffs advance halted around the museum due to heavy opposition. The situation around the museum quietened down around 0600–0630 hours. Dobie had noted that there were little signs of action to his left flank; however, this temporary lull was ended by an intense mortar bombardment on the South Staffs positions. By 0800 hours, the Germans of Kampfgruppe *Harder* had cleared enough of the lower Onderlangs road to launch an attack up the slope towards the South Staffs around the museum, which was repulsed. The 1st Parachute Battalion had burnt itself out in its brave attempts to break through to Frost at the bridge. The 3rd Parachute Battalion fared no better with little opportunity to provide fire support to Dobie and began to take increasingly heavy fire, particularly from German 20mm flak guns and captured French 75mm artillery situated on the south side of the Rhine around the brickworks.

3rd Parachute Battalion found itself advancing across the open ground by the river and only found light cover amongst the undergrowth of the embankment which soon resembled advancing across the butts on a rifle range. With little cover from sight and fire, casualties multiplied as the German flak gunners poured devastating 20mm and 75mm fire into Fitch's battalion headed by A Company under Lieutenant Burwash MC. Battalion HQ along with their RE support under Captain Cox were followed by B Company under Captain Dorrien-Smith. Fitch decided to withdraw once again towards the Rhine Pavilion and form defensive positions in the houses in the area. Now under intense mortar fire, the battalion began its uncoordinated withdrawal, and it was a case of every man for himself. On arriving at the pavilion it was discovered that Lieutenant Colonel Fitch had been killed by mortar fire during the withdrawal. The 3rd Parachute Battalion 2i/c, Major Alan Bush, took over and began to organise defensive positions in the houses along the Utrechtseweg before going forward to the pavilion area to confirm that Fitch had indeed been killed; in doing so, Bush got cut off and only managed to return to the battalion two days later on the Thursday afternoon. By now the battalion was very depleted and spread out in small groups occupying fortified houses in the area. The battalion actually received some reinforcements at this point by the arrival of Lieutenant William A. Fraser, CanLoan, Liaison Officer, 3rd Parachute Battalion HQ, with a party of stragglers from various battalions which were then employed in the defence.

By 1600 hours, what remained of units involved in the morning attack began a withdrawal to Oosterbeek. This included the 11th Parachute Battalion and the South Staffs who fought their way back through the Lombok/KEMA area but were then outflanked by German armour and infantry from the north of the railway that had crossed over a railway bridge to the north of Oranjestraat. In effect, the Germans were now advancing westwards along the Utrechtseweg and outflanking the airborne from the north either side of the Arnhem Prison. A full-scale withdrawal of the four battalions involved in the push to the bridge now began. The routes used in the main were down Hulkesteinseweg and Klingelbeekseweg although some units used the Utrechtseweg. Once the various units passed under the railway viaduct at Oosterbeek Laag on the Benedendorpsweg the majority were halted and deployed to prevent German infiltration under the viaduct and across the railway embankment. The 3rd Parachute Battalion now commanded by Captain Dorrien-Smith occupied houses and gardens on the Benedendorpsweg along with the remnants of 1st Parachute Battalion. A number of South Staffs set up around the Acacialaan area supported by their three 6-pounder anti-tank guns. Three Vickers machine guns were trained on the railway embankment. The 11th Parachute Battalion, now very much reduced as a battalion took up positions just north of Benedendorpsweg around the Acacialaan/Hogeweg junction with its HQ on the south side of Benedendorpsweg on the junction of Acacialaan. Initial German patrols were repulsed in the 3rd Parachute Battalion area. A degree of stability was regained and the night passed relatively calmly.

Post-war view looking north taken from the railway embankment over the Rosande Polder at Oosterbeek. The electric train had been moved from Arnhem sidings to avoid Allied bombing of German military railway traffic in Arnhem. During the battle the abandoned train provided cover for German infantry and in response was fired upon by airborne Vickers machine guns from first of all, the initial Thompson Force positions around Acacialaan, and later from the Vickers guns in front of Oosterbeek Laag Church. Further damage to the train was incurred from Allied shelling during and after the battle. During the filming of *Theirs is the Glory* after the war, the train was set alight causing further damage. Of interest to the left of the train can be seen the houses along Benedendorpsweg to the west of the railway viaduct. Around these houses were the positions of 1st and 3rd Parachute Battalions on the eastern end of the Thompson Force positions prior to withdrawing to the church area and becoming Lonsdale Force. (Photo: Courtesy Utrecht Archives)

Wednesday, 20th September

In the early morning of the Wednesday, German infantry began seriously probing the airborne positions to the west of the Oosterbeek Laag railway viaduct, but these initial fighting patrols were easily repelled. The intensity increased as the morning wore on, with infantry now supported by armour moving through the viaduct. At least one German SP was knocked out and several damaged by the 6-pounder guns of the South Staffs and it was during this phase of the battle that Lance Sergeant John Baskeyfield of the South Staffs Support Company was killed and subsequently awarded a posthumous Victoria Cross for his actions as a gun commander. Around midday, Major Lonsdale, 11th Parachute Battalion, arrived and took command of the units in the area whilst still under overall command of Lieutenant Colonel Thompson, RA; the group became known as 'Thompson Force'. When Thompson was wounded the following day it subsequently came under control of Major Lonsdale and became known as 'Lonsdale Force'.

As the day progressed, the Germans began to outflank the airborne positions from the north of Acacialaan and north-east across Steennen Kruis. Despite feeling confident of holding their positions, the 3rd Parachute Battalion had to fall back before being cut off along with the 1st and 11th Parachute Battalions who were all under increasing pressure from German armour and infantry from the railway viaduct and particularly from the north. The rifle companies of the 2nd Battalion South Staffs under Major Cain had been pulled back to the Van Hofwegen Laundry during the morning. By 1845 hours, having held off repeated German attacks throughout the day, all the units now made their way back to the area of Oosterbeek Laag church. The 11th Parachute Battalion took up positions in the area of Oosterbeek Laag church, some to the north and others to the west. The remaining South Staffs were deployed around the Van Hofwegen Laundry and the church perimeter on the meadowland facing due east to the railway embankment and to the blown railway bridge over the Rhine. 3rd Parachute Battalion, now reduced to around 60 men along with the remnants of 1st Parachute Battalion, received orders to proceed south-east down Polderweg onto the area of the Rosande Polder and to take up positions on the open ground facing east forward of the guns of 3 Battery, 1st Airlanding Light Regiment, RA, situated around the Oosterbeek Laag church. The Rosande Polder force was under command of Captain Dorrien-Smith, B Company, 3rd Parachute Battalion.

As night drew in and mist settled over the polder, men of 1st and 3rd Parachute Battalions, accompanied by a handful of South Staffs, dug in on the saturated ground. They tentatively awaited the inevitable German reaction to their very visible and vulnerable positions the following day. The choice and sighting of the polder positions created a great deal of anger amongst the experienced North African campaign 1st Parachute Brigade veterans who quite correctly predicted the consequences of choosing such a defenceless position, but their vocal concerns were met by at least one threat of disciplinary action.

Thursday, 21st September

The damp early morning mist gradually cleared over the polder revealing the freshly dug trenches of 1st and 3rd Parachute Battalions. The Germans continued their previous day's westward advance along the Benedendorpsweg and immediately began to engage the exposed airborne positions on the polder with mortar, StuG and 20mm flak gun fire. By the afternoon, the airborne casualties had mounted, including 3rd Parachute Battalion's Lance Corporal Walter H. Stanley, Sergeant David J. Davies, Lieutenant William A. Fraser and 1st Parachute Battalion's Lieutenant A.D. Clarkson who were killed during the intense shelling. 1st and 3rd Parachute Battalions and the few South Staffs were forced out of their trenches, and under very heavy fire managed to extricate themselves along the Beek Leigraaf, a stagnant water-filled ditch that ran behind their positions westwards parallel to Polderweg and back to the church where they were received by Major Lonsdale. It was during this withdrawal to the church that Captain Dorrien-Smith was mortally wounded. Many troops had fallen back to the church and after a morale-raising speech by Lonsdale, the men were sent to their new positions around the church area.

The 3rd Parachute Battalion, with a strength of around 40–50 men now under the command of the reunited Major Bush, moved to houses and gardens around 117–119 Benedendorpsweg along with the 100 or so men of the 1st Parachute Battalion and a handful of glider pilots. Elements of the 3rd Parachute Battalion also occupied positions alongside Lonsdale's HQ close to the corner of Bildersweg and Van Delden Pad. By nightfall, trenches had been dug in the gardens facing north towards Ploegseweg and the open ground to the north and east along the Benedendorpsweg. Lonsdale Force consisted of 1st, 3rd and 11th Parachute Battalions along with the 2nd Battalion South Staffs, glider pilots and remaining attached anti-tank guns. All these units were not only part of the Oosterbeek perimeter but served to provide and incorporate protection for the 75mm guns of the 1st Airlanding Light Regiment RA, dug in around the church area with their RAP a short distance from the church in the home of the Ter Horst family.

All resistance by 2nd Parachute Battalion and units at the bridge had finally ceased by the Thursday and the Germans could now concentrate on eliminating the remaining elements of the 1st Airborne Division at Oosterbeek where the division had consolidated forming a bridgehead should XXX Corps cross the Rhine.

Friday, 22nd September
Just as it was getting light on Friday morning, after a preliminary mortar bombardment, the Germans launched attacks on the 3rd and 1st Parachute Battalion positions on the Benedendorpsweg from the Bato's Wijk area in the north-east under cover from the smoke of a burning building and east along the Benedendorpsweg; both attacks were repelled. The enemy regrouped and attacked the 1st Parachute Battalion positions again later that morning, supported by two tanks. The attack was repulsed with PIATs and good use was made of the remaining 1st Parachute Battalion 3-inch mortar under Sergeant Whittingham situated at the rear doorstep of 119 Benedendorpsweg. Although missing its baseplate, the mortar proved effective against the advancing German infantry. The 1st Parachute Battalion were situated in and around the houses on the northern side of the road along with a small number of glider pilots in the back gardens. The Germans infiltrated and probed through the houses along the south side road and this necessitated sorties across the road to clear the Germans from the buildings. This threat persisted until the end of the battle as there simply were not enough British troops in the area to indefinitely occupy every house. German mortar fire continued from the area of the Bato's Wijk and beyond in degrees of intensity until the end of the battle, all the while causing increasing casualties.

Saturday, 23rd September and Sunday, 24th September
The Lonsdale Force around the Oosterbeek Laag church came under pressure from infantry supported by armour and when not under direct attack were subjected to mortar and sniper fire. At night, both sides sent out patrols which from the point of view of 1st and 3rd Parachute Battalions enabled intelligence to be gathered regarding the proximity of German positions in the locality and also gave them the chance to silence troublesome snipers. German patrols took the opportunity of darkness to infiltrate and take up new positions. Since Thursday 21st September, the 1st Airborne Division could take advantage of artillery support from the advancing XXX Corps now proceeding northwards from Nijmegen. This artillery support proved invaluable right up until the evacuation, halting enemy attacks or troop concentrations. (See Chapter 15, Volume Three.) Local artillery support was provided by the 1st Airlanding Light Regiment, RA, often firing in a direct fire mode in and around the Lonsdale Force area over open sights against houses occupied by German snipers or infantry. Airborne 17-pounder anti-tank guns, apart from engaging German armour, were also employed to remove unwanted attention by German snipers particularly on the south side of Benedendorpsweg.

Monday, 25th September
German activity in the Lonsdale Force area increased as the morning went by and by 1100 hours, with support from a mortar bombardment, a determined German attack developed from the north and north-east on the axis of Weverstraat towards the Oosterbeek Laag Church. Heavy

German armour in the form of SdKfz 182 PzKpfw VI Tiger II tanks of the 2/Schwere Panzer-Abteilung 506, supported by Sturmgeschütz self-propelled guns of StuG Brigade 280 and infantry of Kampfgruppe *Harder* and *Von Allwörden* pushed south-west and overran many of the 75mm gun positions of the 1st Airlanding Light Regiment RA. At least 3 Troops – A, C and D – were overrun, despite a valiant defence by the gunners. Fortunately, a massive artillery concentration by the guns of the 64th Medium Regiment RA, XXX Corps, avoided the total penetration of the base of the airborne perimeter and the German tanks and infantry withdrew. Had a more determined attack pushed on another several hundred yards it would have completely cut off the 1st Airborne Division from its only escape route across the Rhine.

During the night of the 25 and 26 September, the British 1st Airborne Division along with elements of the Polish 1st Independent Parachute Brigade withdrew across the Rhine south of the Oosterbeek Laag church. According to the 3rd Parachute Battalion War Diary, 27 members of the battalion were evacuated along with 104 men from the 1st Parachute Battalion.

RAF Station Harwell, 17th September, prior to take off. General Browning (left); Air Chief Marshal Sir Arthur Tedder, Deputy Supreme Commander; Brigadier General Floyd F. Parks, Chief of Staff, First Allied Airborne Army. Tedder and Parks had both come to see Browning and his 1st Airborne Corps HQ off to Nijmegen. (Photo: Courtesy IWM CH13856)

Major Martin Willcock, Parachute Regiment, Airborne Control Officer, RAF Station Harwell

I was the go-between for the Army and the RAF and all the Inter-Service communication went through me. I was given full details of all the units departing from the station and the seating requirements for each glider (no paras at Harwell) and I also found an office for General Browning. He used mine and turfed me out! I seemed to be at everyone's beck and call, I had a staff of one army sergeant, two privates and four RAF provost NCOs, a truck and a Jeep. 38 Group RAF carried an army staff of one lieutenant colonel, one captain and two privates. All my orders came from them. Most of which had to be passed onto the RAF or Army as necessary and so on!

Sunday, 17th September

My main memories of the operation were of General Browning standing at the door of his Horsa glider as it hurtled down the runway, waving at Tedder (Air Chief Marshal Sir Arthur W. Tedder) another top brass, just as if he was going on leave! He was immaculate as ever. (Take-off time approximately 1108 hours.) Lieutenant Colonel Thompson, R.A. was misinformed (not by me!) about the take-off time and nearly missed the show, no one knew where he was (less than an hour before take-off). I rushed to the Officers' Mess in my Jeep and got him to his aircraft (Nigel Mansell would have been proud of the way we went around the perimeter track!) The Glider Marshalling Area was on the far side of the airfield from the station buildings.

All, I think, of our aircraft returned, but on the succeeding re-supply days a lot of the aircraft had been hit by flak and the landings were distinctly hairy but I have no recollection of any crashes or casualties.

RAF Station Harwell, 17th September 1944. Stirling IV LK115 (8Z-S) of 295 Squadron towing Horsa glider, Chalk No. 410, containing 1st Airborne Corps HQ personnel, takes off for Groesbeek, Nijmegen. (Photo: IWM CH3857)

Private Fred 'Rad' Radley, Signaller, A Coy, 3rd Parachute Battalion, 1st Parachute Brigade

Sunday, 17th September 1944

The flight out was incident-free as far as 3rd Parachute Battalion was concerned; a glider was seen ditched in the Channel and flak was seen, but it was about two miles or more distant. I was number three in the stick. The 'drop' was better than any manoeuvre, spot on the Drop Zone (DZ), a sunny day with no wind (nothing like Sicily, where you could almost walk down the ack-ack, and where the sweat ran off you in buckets). 3rd Parachute Battalion were the second wave of paras to drop, and as we descended we could see our pals of 2nd Parachute Battalion, who had dropped just prior to us, quitting the DZ and heading for their RV. We had a very easy landing, no opposition anywhere; we collected our equipment and left the DZ for our own RV, a small wood, that we had been able to identify on the way down, and that was marked by red smoke as an identification signal, red being the same colour as the (then) 3rd Battalion lanyard. Apart from my personal weapon (a MkV Sten in two pieces, secured through the parachute harness; six 36 grenades; two Gammon bombs and 8 spare magazines for my Sten), I jumped with a kitbag strapped to my leg which contained one of A Company Signal Section's wireless sets, two headsets, two mikes, one remote, aerials etc. (The set was a WS18, standard issue among the various battalions, and used for communication by the various companies, up to battalion level. It weighed approximately 35lbs, had an output of 0.5 watts, a frequency range band of 6.0 to 9.0 megacycles (mc/s) and an operating range of two miles on voice, six miles on morse (CW) when mobile, and five miles on voice, eight miles on CW when stationary. Although a good signaller could easily double or even treble this distance if he was efficient and knew how to use or improvise his aerials.)

Private Fred 'Rad' Radley, Signaller, A Coy, 3rd Parachute Battalion, 1st Parachute Brigade. (Photo: Courtesy F.R. Radley)

The standard Signal Section of 3rd Parachute Battalion consisted of: one NCO and four ORs, and carried two WS18s; the operational one that I had, plus a spare that was carried by one of the other members of the section. For any operation the section split up. The NCO and two men, with the operational set, would go in the same aircraft as the OC of the company/unit they were attached to, and the other two would drop with the spare set, and go in the aircraft with the 2 i/c of the company/unit (that way you did not have all your 'Sigs' in one basket). The OC would always jump No. 1, followed by his bat-man, followed by his Sigs (in our case it was Major Dennison who was OC, A Company).The Signal Section of A Coy at Arnhem consisted of Lance Corporal Bert French and Privates 'Jock' Jones, Geoff Marsh, Dennis Collins, and myself, at that time known as 'Rad' Radley. We were very lucky in our compliment, as apart from Dennis Collins we had all been with the battalion throughout North Africa, Sicily and Italy, and knew each other well. Dennis was a replacement who had joined us after we got back to the UK, and by the time Arnhem finished, he had bruises all over his body, where one or the other of us had hit him at one time or another when he was not quick enough to either 'Move' – 'Down' – 'Quiet' etc. He was a good pupil; he got back across the River Rhine.

As I left the DZ, Jock Jones joined me. As we moved quickly to the RV, we kept a sharp lookout sky-wards, because we were clearing the DZ so the lads of the 1st Parachute Battalion (the remainder of our brigade) were dropping overhead, and it was not unknown for a kitbag to break loose and hurtle down among the unwary. As we were looking up, we noticed that one of the 1st Battalion had a 'Roman Candle' – his chute streamed behind him all the way to the ground.[8] We reached the RV and opened the set (switched on and listened for the control station, Battalion HQ). Control was 'on – the – air' within about 10 minutes; within about another 15 minutes the stations were 'on net' (all talking and hearing each other) apart from one set. (This was a spare set that was used by Battalion HQ, when a second set was needed elsewhere. When a new set-up was used, such as an officer needing a set to himself to keep in touch with Battalion HQ, or a patrol etc., needing to communicate with Battalion HQ.) But about six or seven WS18s of 3rd Parachute Battalion were functioning properly, and were working to each other. Why those at Brigade were not working is a mystery, as they were using a more powerful set than the battalions were and in most cases were operated not by a regimental signaller, but by a member of The Royal Corps of Signals; they were good operators who knew their job. (Personally, I can't believe that there was a complete breakdown of communication on their part; it is not possible. Probably a set here and there, but not all of them as claimed. Much more plausible is the theory that senior officers were apt to 'wander' to wherever they chose, sometimes getting caught out, and used the excuse of lack of communication, and having to seek information as an excuse, for their not being where they should have been.)

At the RV there was *no* excuse, it was after we left the RV that difficulties occurred; in fact, after we left the RV, I never heard another message passed over the 3rd Battalion net. I forgot who was the operator on our Battalion HQ set, but he never had a proper hold over his net; a good control officer will ensure that his net is operating at all times. If there has been a silent period for more than five minutes, he should call up all stations for a report of signals, to ensure they are still there. Ours did not, and by the time he did, it was too late. Sets were either screened, shot up, out of range, or the Sigs (as in some cases) were killed or wounded (whether the control station called the group or not I don't know, I don't think so – at Arnhem on Monday I was in touch with B Company, and he had not heard Control since leaving the RV. After the war I met some of the C Company Sigs, and they did not hear Control either) so none of the companies heard Control after we left the RV.

When we left the RV, we followed a farm track until we reached the road, turned left on it and headed for Arnhem. It was still quiet with no firing; the Dutch people were either standing on their doorsteps waving, or were standing in their gateways, saying (more often than not), 'Welcome to Holland, we are glad to see you, have you an English cigarette?' all in one breath. We followed the Utrecht–Arnhem road. It was a cobbled road, tall trees either side that met overhead, very few houses, once we left Renkum. A cycle track ran along one side of the road, and at the edge of the track it was sandy, heavy with loose sand, almost red in colour; wherever possible we walked on this. We had barely left Renkum when a burst of mortars exploded in the tree-tops above us. It was bloody good shooting, and among those hit was Captain 'Roddy' Thesiger, the 2 i/c of A Coy who was standing almost next to me (he was probably one of the first casualties of 3rd Parachute Battalion at Arnhem, a repeat of his North Africa performance).

It was very difficult to move all that fast. There were thick woods either side of the road, and you became conscious of being fired upon as bullets whistled over or past your head, but you could

---

8   This was Private John Towhey, 7046990, R Company, 1st Parachute Battalion, age 24. Initial burial near Ginkel Heath, Verlengde Arnhemseweg.

not pin down where the firing was coming from, only the general direction, as the woods were too thick to see through. Occasionally it would be a machine gun that opened up on you. This was a bit disconcerting as we of A Coy were in reserve, and about 300 others (at least) had passed that spot where the machine gun was firing from before we got there; patrols were often dispatched off into the woods to deal either with the machine guns, the snipers or, as in one case, to a tall tower to flush out a possible OP (observation post) for the mortars. Not the best of jobs, as the enemy, more often than not, apart from being hidden, had decamped by the time his position had been reached.

There were numerous halts. Seldom was it possible to travel more than 500 yards before you had to halt, on each occasion diving into a ditch, or seeking cover in the roadside curb, any low-lying ground, or behind a tree. On one of these occasions I was in a ditch, when a member of the 'I' (Intelligence) Section came walking back along the road, prodding a member of the German Luftwaffe along with his .45 automatic. The German was aged about 19 to 20, had very blond hair, blue eyes, and was actually wearing make-up (rouge and lipstick). In the ditch near to me was one of the 'old' members of 3rd Parachute Battalion, 'Don' Hardman, and as the Jerry passed us, Don said, 'Cor, look at him, I could f**k him!' Even if the Jerry did not understand English, he must have had a good idea of what Don meant as his pace visibly quickened, and we burst out laughing.[9]

We reached a junction where a minor road joined ours on the left; there was a small German staff car there. It was slewed across part of the road, and had several bullet holes in it, the front doors were open and a body of a dead German was lying part in the car with his head and shoulders laying on the road. He was an officer and like the driver, he was quite dead. We later learned that it had been shot-up by a section of B Company who were in the lead at that point.[10]

Heavy mortaring occurred as we reached a crossroad and caused several casualties. Everyone went to ground, but as the mortaring continued, we got the idea that they were not so much firing at any particular target, but were merely firing on the crossroads, which was an obvious target if troops were using the road. We moved on with the mortar bombs bursting in the tops of the trees (similar to air bursts) and were soon away from the flying shrapnel. During all this time I had been carrying/operating the WS18, with Jock at the side of me. (When operating the set, the headset was worn only half over the ears, but on occasions it was necessary to pull the headset fully over the ears in order to hear the signals properly. When this happened you were oblivious to what was happening around you, so your mate or 'oppo' used to be close to you, and warn you if necessary.)

I had been calling Control since leaving the RV but had got no reply. I knew that my own set was working correctly, as I was getting plenty of 'side-tone' through the head set as I transmitted, and also Jock had checked that we had an aerial reading and that it was fluctuating when I was on 'send'.

---

9   One German female was taken POW. *Luftnachrichtenhelferinnen* (Luftwaffe female telephonist) Irene Reimann was taken prisoner on the 17th September in Wolfheze where she occupied billets in one of the buildings of the psychiatric institution, Neder-Veluwe, near where she was captured. Alan Wood, the war correspondent, described her as 'half cheeky, half in tears, extremely ugly'.

10 The officer was Wehrmacht Feldkommandantur 642, Generalmajor Friedrich Kussin; with him was his driver Gefreiter Josef Willeke and his aides, Unteroffizier Max Koster and Unteroffizier Willi Haupt. Kussin's identity was confirmed by his signature on a court of inquiry report on the death of a sentry killed by a train on Nijmegen bridge. Source: 1st Airborne Division Intelligence Summary, 22nd September 1944. Upon Kussin's death the CO 9 SS Panzer Division, Obersturmbannführer Walter Harzer, moved his HQ into Kussin's HQ because of its centralised position for telephone communications using the Dutch telephone network with German switchboards.

Major Dennison was a first-class company commander, with plenty of experience behind him, and was always in the thick of things, often telling us Sigs to 'wait here', and then he would dash off to see what any particular firing or hold-up was. With a great deal of responsibility, he often forgot to tell us he was moving on, and consequently we would ask each other, 'Where's Dennison?' to find that he was moving some distance ahead of us, which meant a fair old trot in order to catch him up again.

We had not reached Oosterbeek when it began to get dark; Major Dennison came back to us Sigs (from one of his sorties) and said to us, 'We have been ordered to halt for the night. Company HQ will be at the rear of this house.' He was pointing to a house that was set back from in the trees. 'Go around to the rear and set up your wireless there. I will join you shortly.' He then moved to tell the others of the company. The house was surrounded at the front by a strong wire-mesh fence about four feet high, too high to clamber over very easily, ladened as we were with our equipment, and too strong to push or pull over, so we entered by the front gate and proceeded up to the front drive towards the house. As we did so we were moaning and groaning about the order to 'halt for the night'. Collins was listening to us as we were saying such things as, 'It's the best time to move when it's dark' and 'We never packed in at bloody night before, let's bloody well hurry up and get there' and 'What silly sod gave that order, we'll never get there at this rate.' (I still wonder who gave that order?)

We reached the front of the house; we could not get around to the right-hand side of it, so followed the path that went around the left of it. It was a gravel path that crunched as we walked on it, so we walked on the grass verge at the side of it. We got to the rear of the house. In the dim light, we could make out a large French window (no lights anywhere) and a fairly large patio surrounded by a low wall, with the garden disappearing into the darkness. I slipped the WS18 off my back, and rested it on the low wall. Then I knelt beside the set, and was about to call Control again, when from the far end of the garden came, *'Engländer, Hände hoch!'* – this was immediately followed by a burst of firing from an MG34, and tracer whipped across the bottom of the garden from left to right. Bert, Jock, Geoff and I immediately 'dropped' as soon as we heard the word *'Engländer'*, but Collins was not so fast and was still standing, until one of us hit him behind his knees: 'Down!' I had a 36 grenade fixed to the webbing on top of each of my pouches. I pulled one free, yanked out the pin, released the lever, then hurled it towards the bottom of the garden. As I did so, I had the terrible thought: *what if there is an overhanging branch and it drops on us?* There was a lot of yelling from the bottom of the garden, then a crash of the grenade, followed by more yelling and the sound of footsteps as someone ran through the leaves under the trees, then it was all silent.

A few moments later, Major Dennison came running round to join us, crunching on the gravel as he did so. 'What the hell is going on?' he asked. We were still laying down and Geoff looked up and said, 'It's ok now Sir; we had a few Jerries at the bottom of the garden!' He did not question us about it, and we did wonder if he believed us, as we were almost the end of the battalion, and these Jerries had suddenly appeared in among us. I reckon Dennison had really been on his way to us, heard the shooting, and was all prepared to 'tear-us-off-a-strip' for making a noise, probably thinking that the firing had been an accident or similar. We stayed in that position approximately two and a half to three hours; nobody visited us (Major Dennison had left almost as soon as he arrived, probably to Battalion HQ, somewhere further along the road). We kept a good listening watch on the wireless, but heard nothing. We also we kept a very good ear cocked for any noise of movement at the bottom of the garden, but after that first burst it remained quiet, which seemed to be pretty much the same everywhere, as the mortaring/firing that we had been hearing earlier had also ceased.

Monday, 18th September
Sometime during the early hours of Monday (the 18th) it was still dark, not quite dawn, and Major Dennison appeared at the back of the house we had stopped at, and told us (Sigs) that we were moving off (it was the first time we had seen anyone since being shot at by the Jerry machine gun). We had spent our time in a defensive position, all wide awake in case we had a return visit from those who had fired at us. Also, several times during the night we had attempted to make contact via the WS18 with other 3rd Parachute Battalion Sets, but each time we heard nothing. (I was not unduly worried, as since leaving the RV, nobody at any time had asked me to use the WS, for passing any messages etc.; also as it was night/early morning, it was a very common occurrence for communications to be on the blink. This happened every night when the ionosphere came down lower to the earth, and leaving you listening to 'heavy mush' in your headphones, making voice communication practically impossible, irrespective of where you were.)

We moved off. Once again we made many stops; it was a slow advance and by the time we had reached the Hartenstein Hotel, it was practically first light. It was fairly misty, the grass and the trees were heavy with dew, and you could easily notice the strong fresh smell of the woods. (At no time during the advance from the RV had any information as to what was happening ahead been passed back, and it was very hard for any of us behind to understand why we kept stopping so many times. Also it was very dangerous, as the previous day, the advance stopped whilst whatever was in front had been dealt with – it was AFVs. We did not know what it was; all we knew was that the 'Halt' came as we reached a road junction. We were halted, just as Jerry mortared the junction, and we had to take cover and wait, not only for the mortars, but to advance, which if it was not quick enough, would find us still at the junction when the next 'stonk' came down.) We finally reached Oosterbeek crossroads. It was littered with large branches and leaves off trees that had been blown down by mortars/shells; there were holes in the cobbled road, and the wires of the electric tramway were hanging down in several places. We left our intended route, and turned right at the crossroads into Pietersbergse Weg. On the left was a shop a little way down, and we tried to decipher what it sold, without success; we then forked left onto Paas Berg and passed a school that was surrounded by a wall approximately eight feet high.

As we came to the end of the wall, we came under fire from some snipers that seemed to be firing at us from across some open ground on our left. It was approximately 100 yards of ground edged by fairly dense trees, from which the firing was coming. We were unable to see who or what was firing, and could only double sharply across the open space between the school and the next house, shouting a warning to those following behind us. The road twisted and turned downhill and in places it was a job to stop sliding on the cobbles with the studs in the army boots. (We endlessly cursed these, and were forever asking why we were no longer issued with 'Jumping Boots' as we had been when we first joined the Paras in 1941/2, as they had a thick rubber sole. I have no doubt that the regulation ammo boot with its noise was responsible for several soldiers losing their lives.) We had seen no civilians in the town (probably still abed) and Jock and I were quite surprised when an elderly man came out of a side-way between two of the houses and beckoned to us. We went with him and he pointed to the rear garden of the house, jabbering away in Dutch. We looked at him puzzled, and then he imitated a machine gun, and we heard the word 'Deutsche'. I said, 'Deutsche machine gun. There?' He nodded: 'Yah-yah, Deutsche!'

I turned to the rest of the Sigs Section who were nearby. 'Hey! This bloke says there's a Jerry machine gun out the back.' They came across to us, then Jock and I moved cautiously towards the rear garden whilst Bert and Colly covered us. I was surprised to see that the old man walked ahead of us, straight to the bottom of the garden. Jock and I looked at each other; the old man had stopped at the end of the garden and was beckoning for us to join him. We walked toward him. We were both trying to watch him, the trees at the end of the garden, the adjoining gardens, and to where he was pointing. We didn't know if it was some kind of ambush or not, and we didn't trust anyone. As we got level with the old man, we could see a slit trench, empty, dug in the garden. Finally with a mixture of English, French, Italian and a little German, plus a lot of theatricals, we were able to understand what he was trying to tell us. The previous evening, three Germans had gone into the garden and dug the trench, and they had a machine gun with them. They had stayed the night and as soon as it had got light, had left. We could not understand why, as like the machine gun that had fired on us the previous evening, this also had an extremely limited field of fire and as a position was useless. It was an unexpected position, and with the trees behind it, was easy to get away from, but that was all it had in its favour. It puzzled us to what the Jerries had seen in occupying that position.

We went back to the road and rejoined the rest of the battalion (with the slowness of the advance, it was very easy to do such things like this, and still keep up with where you were in the line of march.) We eventually reached the bottom of the road, turned left (Benedendorpsweg) and soon walked past a church (the Old Church) that was on our right. Further along the road as we looked across the fields on that side we could see the demolished railway bridge with its middle span collapsed. There was no sign of any movement in the fields, but we could see up on the railway embankment, that was quite high (approximately 30 feet) that there was a train, stationary on the line. It was about four or five coaches long, painted in yellow and blue and about 300 to 400 yards from the blown bridge. After a short distance, there were house on both sides of the road, and occasionally we had to run across gaps between them. We were warned that snipers or machine guns were firing from between them. When the road reached the top of a slope, the houses ceased on the right, giving way to a slightly wooded embankment that was dense with undergrowth. We hoped that there were no Jerries there as we would have been like ducks in a shooting gallery on the top where we were.

We heard machine guns firing up ahead and the battalion stopped again. Strangely there were some Dutch civilians standing at the front doors of some of the houses. It was here that I had the sudden urge to go to the toilet. I spoke to a woman who was at her door and was very surprised that she answered me in excellent English. I asked her if I could use her toilet and she said, 'Certainly,' and took me in and showed me where it was. All the time I was being stared at by her two young children. Thinking of it as nothing out of the ordinary, I stripped off my webbing, went into the WC, still with my Sten, and for the next ten minutes or so, called my own Cease Fire whilst I answered the call of nature. As I was washing my hands before leaving, the woman told me that she was a school teacher. I undid my 'small pack' and took out two bars of chocolate that I offered to her children. They looked at me and backed away, and the mother explained that neither of the children had ever seen any chocolate. I got out another bar, broke a piece off and put it into my mouth, but the children were unimpressed – so I gave all the chocolate to the mother who said she would give it to them later. I thanked the woman for a glass of lemonade that she had given me, and was about to leave when she gave me a map, explaining that it was a street guide of the local area. I took this with me when I left, and later gave it to either a sergeant or an officer. Before I had left the house, I advised the woman that if she had a cellar she should take her children and go into it. (Little did I know that two days later I would be back, fighting on the embankment opposite her house, and wondering if she had taken my advice, and how she and her children were).

When we got moving again, I had taken over the carrying of the WS18. We had no sooner started to move than we stopped, I unshouldered the WS and checked it for battery/aerial reading (this was slightly low, so I retuned it). I also checked the meter needle was oscillating when I went to 'send'. The WS was operating OK, in fact from the amount of 'side-tone' in the head set, it had never been better. I pressed the 'mike' and started off once again with the endless call we had been making since we had left the RV: 'Hello Romeo one, report my signals, I say again report my signals, Romeo one over,' then, 'Hello Romeo one, nothing heard, I say again nothing heard, report my signals, Romeo one over.' Then – surprise surprise – I heard, 'Hello Romeo two for Romeo one, loud and clear, report my signals over!'

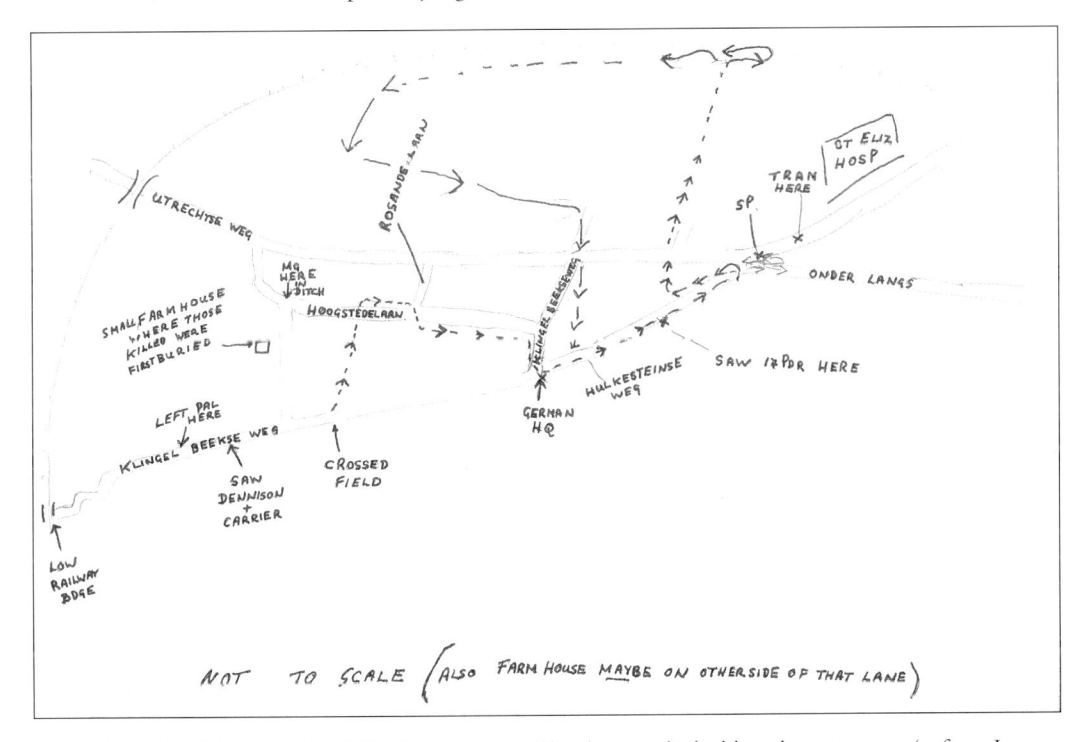

Sketch map by Private Fred 'Rad' Radley. He writes: 'Sketch map which although not accurate (as far as I can make it) regarding route across field and afterwards and where various things etc. were or happened. After we got across Utrechtseweg it was one mad fight from one street to another and across back gardens – can't trace true route – was up near the railway, then near the prison – then down a long straight road. Also I have a stupid faint recollection of actually being up on the railway following the lines along? I can recall looking down at a small hut watching for enemy in it, eventually I came back down Klingelbeekseweg to position just on L after going under (low) railway bridge.'

I immediately recognised the voice of 'Aub' Rowthorn (Corporal, i/c of B Company Sigs). I said, 'Hello Romeo two for Romeo one, loud and clear, it's nice to hear your friendly voice, have you heard anything from Control, over?'

'Hello Romeo two for one, nothing heard from Control for past 24 hours, we appear to be the only two stations on the net, over.'

'Hello Romeo one for two, roger. How are things over your way, over?'

'Hello two for one, it's busy right now … how about this…' (I heard machine gun and rifle fire, plus explosions, coming over the air). 'The natives are rather restless, over.'

I said, 'Hello one for two, it's about the same this end, get a load of this…' (I then held up the 'open' mike and broadcast the sound of a machine gun and rifle fire, plus mortars that were firing at us). 'How are the Section, over?'

'Hello two for one, all OK, am moving off, will call you every three zero minutes, over.'

'Hello one for two, roger – be seeing you, take it easy, out.'

And that was the only transmission that was ever passed over the 3rd Battalion net after they had left the RV. Aub was not able to keep the appointment for any more transmissions, and A Company's set was the last on-the-air, talking to itself.

There was a further transmission, sometime later, about one hour after speaking to Aub. I was trying to contact Control. As I released the pressel switch of the mike, I heard a voice in the headphones, about strength three (readable with difficulty). I said, 'Hello Romeo one, hearing you strength three, say again, over.' All I heard was, 'Romeo one close down, over.' I had clamped the headset tight to my ears, and was able to hear it quite clearly. I immediately said, 'Hello square head, f***k off before me and my pals get up to you, OUT.' The Sigs had worked together for some time, we knew each other's voices instantly; this was a stranger, and he was using the wrong procedure for closing down a wireless net – I have no doubt that it was Jerry on the 3rd Parachute Battalion frequency.

As we moved along Benedendorpsweg, we came to the low railway bridge where the Nijmegen–Arnhem line crossed over it. We were again held up there by a couple of machine guns and some infantry; as we finally moved on under the bridge and followed on toward Arnhem, it was stop-start-stop-start all the way. About 400 yards past the bridge there was a Para laying wounded upon the pavement. He was alone, with the column moving slowly passed him. As I got to him, I was upset to recognise him as being one of the old hands of 3rd Parachute Battalion. (It was the only time I was affected by any casualties). I thought, *Oh Christ, it's 'Harry'*. (I forget his name, but knew him well, so we will refer to him as Harry). *Poor sod, all the bloody way through North Africa, Sicily, Italy and here he is laying wounded on a pavement in bloody Holland.*

I said, 'Look Jock, it's Harry so and so.'

We stopped and knelt beside him. I said, 'Oh blimey, Harry. What did you want to go and do a bloody silly thing like this for, after all this time?'

He said, 'Wasn't my fault, Rad, it was our own bloody guns. We were after Jerry who was in that hut in the field over there and just got to the door and about to go in, when our own guns dropped one on us, caught me in the guts.'

I believe him; it would not have been the first time that had happened, and Harry had seen enough action to know the difference. I got his ground sheet out of his small pack and covered him with it, then placed the pack underneath his head.

He said, 'Thanks mate, have you got a cigarette?' I got out a packet of twenty Players, lit one, gave it to him, then lit one for myself and gave another to Jock.

I said, 'Here, you keep 'em, mate, and the matches,' and put them in his smock pocket. We stayed with him for about five minutes, talking and smoking. He had been given a shot of morphine by a medic earlier on; there was nothing we could do for him.

I said, 'We have got to push on, mate, we will find someone and send him back to you, don't worry, you'll be okay.'

He said, 'Thanks, mind how you go, mate, and watch out for those bloody guns.'

We didn't like leaving him, but we had to. We moved off, and had only gone about 300 yards when we were surprised to see a Bren gun carrier coming down the road towards us. (We did not even know that our own carriers were there, and this one had definitely not passed us on the road going up). It was loaded full of wounded, so full that they were all over the outside of the carrier. One of those on the front was Major Dennison (OC of A Coy). He was wounded in both hands. We hailed it, and as it slowed by us we shouted, '300 yards up the road on this side, Harry so & so is on the pavement wounded in the guts. Pick him up will yah?' The driver nodded and moved off. Whenever I think of Arnhem or the lads, I can't help but think about poor old Harry and feeling so bloody upset and helpless. I dearly hope that he survived Arnhem and lived to tell the tale.

We caught up with the other 'bods'; it was easy enough as the stops were becoming more frequent and longer. We were following the road, when suddenly those in front of us turned left and started to cross a large field. Jock, Bert, Colly and myself were fairly close to each other. (Geoff Marsh had disappeared earlier as we had not seen him for some hours. We were not worried about that, as he had a bit of a habit of doing this and appearing later.) We turned into the field and started to cross. It was very uneasy, the field was quite large, about 400 yards across, and not an ounce of cover anywhere; it was completely flat and bare, the type of place that would normally be given a very wide berth by any troops, especially in broad daylight.

The usual sniping was going on, and though we had got acclimatised to it again, we broke into a 'double'. Suddenly, mortar bombs began landing in the field. The earth was soft which deadened their impact a little, and then at least one machine gun started to fire at us. By this time it had become one mad dash for the other side. As we ran you could see the earth erupt as the mortar bombs landed. Bullets and tracer were humming and flashing past us, you dared not stop and several times you had to leap over bodies that had been hit and fallen in front of you. Eventually, we reached the far side and flung ourselves into the first available ditch, gasping for breath. As we lay there panting, I tapped Bert on his leg (he was just in front of me).

He turned. 'What, Rad?'

I said, 'I bet you wish you'd stayed in bed.'

He grinned, saying, 'Piss off!' (A favourite saying of mine, and what I felt like in those types of situations.)

As we got our breath back, Bert said, 'Hey, look at this, I thought I felt that bastard go past my ear.' His left epaulette was neatly cut across.

Jock said, 'I thought I felt something too, look at this.' He had a bullet hole through his right pouch. I knew the aerial on the WS had gone, so I took the set off to look at it and found that not only the aerial had copped it, but there were also four bullet holes in the set itself, so I was glad to dump it. (The spare set was with Geoff Marsh, and we never did get it. When we separated he tried to use it and eventually flattened the battery.) We moved off again, through gardens and streets; at one point we crossed over Utrechtseweg and got involved in running fights among a mass of turnings. It was just one long mess of firing, running, climbing garden walls and everything else that stood in the way.

Tom Davis, 3rd Parachute Battalion, on a later visit to Arnhem came across a place he recognised. He said, 'I was just here when an armoured car came around that corner there; I threw my Bren gun over this wall and followed it so bloody fast I almost caught it before it landed on the other side.' He then went close to the wall and scrutinised it. When asked what he was looking for, he said, 'Claw marks. This wall is about ten feet high and there is just no way could I have jumped it, I must have gone up it like a bloody cat.' That is something of what it was like and what we were capable of. Where we went to I can only guess; the action was far too hectic and prolonged to pay attention to any place that was not threatening you.

We must have crossed back over Utrechtseweg again, because I distinctly remember the firing died down a bit and I was able to notice we were back among some houses that we had passed a long time earlier, near to where we had come out of the field. It was a side street and we were moving along it, intending to join the road we had been on before we entered the field. We found the road and carried on (strange as it may seem) to where it emerged onto Utrechtseweg, but before we could get there, we were held up by two armoured cars and some troops in the corner houses at the crossroads. It was a sort of stalemate for a time, for with the AFVs, the Jerries had as much, if not more, firepower than our group had. Also they must have had some sort of high velocity rifle with them, as a couple of times bullets actually penetrated the wall of a window that I was firing from, coming through with quite a bit of force behind them, and striking the opposite wall, giving me quite a surprise.

We worked our way around the crossroads (or so it seemed at the time, but looking back, Jerry may have decided to pull out whilst we were doing it). Later, during the evening, we still had still not got onto Utrechtseweg, when we were fired on by a persistent sniper. (This one was a proper sniper; most of the times when anyone said a 'sniper' was firing at them, what really happened was that they were being 'sniped' at by an ordinary infantryman with a rifle or machine gun on single shots. Otherwise, if all the shots fired at you *were* from snipers then the whole German Army would have consisted of hardly anyone but snipers). A sniper seldom wasted his shots. If you were *not* moving when he fired, he hit more often than he missed. This one had hit two chaps and everyone had gone to ground. Jock and I were on the same side of the road as the house he was firing from, and out of his view. It was a large white house, a semi-circular drive at the front, with a striped sentry box at the entrance. It was situated in Klingelbeekseweg where it changes its name to Hulkesteinseweg at the junction of Diepenweg. It is on the righthand side of the road when you approach it from the direction of Oosterbeek. It must have been an HQ of some sort, otherwise why the sentry box at the entrance to the drive? We entered the garden of the house two doors from it, and then crossed the gardens of them. We then ran across the lawn of the large house and got to the front of it, where the large front door was open. I dived in low down with Jock covering me from the door. I covered the stairs facing us and Jock came in. Covering each other, and holding our breath, we crept up the stairs (or tried to – there was no lino, carpet or furniture in the house apart from a couple of large desks and our ammo boots made a hell of a clatter).

We made a careful search of the house and found nothing. All that was there were some empty cases by a front window, and a back window was open, leading onto a low roof with easy access to the ground. It was from this window that we saw the Arnhem bridge for the first (and last) time. It was about three quarters of a mile away. Downstairs there was a huge room with an open fireplace, which had a life-size picture of Hitler hanging over it; there was also a large desk in the room with its drawers open and empty of any papers, etc. It soon became dark, and we (the four Sigs) took up a position in a house, not far from where we had encountered the sniper. After making a brew, we decided to stay outside the house, and chose to stay in the garden as we thought it was less obvious if Jerry made a night attack. As it happened, it was a quiet night, and the morning found us stiff and cold.

Tuesday, 19th September

Tuesday the 19th started off with a bang! Some mortars at the back, and a self-propelled gun (SP), saying 'I'll huff and I'll puff and I'll blow your house down,' at least he had a good try; he turned up at the corner and *wham!* He put one shell through the top of the house, which caused us no worry at all, as we were not in it at the time. It disappeared as quick as it came, and apart from that start to the day I can't recall much of the morning. We had been trying to get forward and not having a lot of success, being met at every junction by machine gun fire. Near a square off Alexanderstraat, we were belting through a small passageway and turned left at the end of it and found ourselves on cobbles (in ammo boots, going downhill, without brakes, with Bert French beside me) straight towards a German machine gun at the corner of the square. Luckily the Jerries were as surprised as we were and thought we were deliberately attacking them. Bert blasted them with his Sten and I tossed them a 36 grenade for good luck, both of us going so bloody fast we couldn't stop. We actually jumped the railings and went across the square like rockets, leaving the Jerries hanging over the railings. It was a habit of Jerry to leave one or two machine guns at every road junction and almost every alleyway and open space, and it took hell of a time to either overcome them, or work around them. It seemed that we had not been fighting long (it was all morning actually), more or less a repeat of the previous day, when we noticed that troops were moving back through us. At first it was not too many, then some were running – about a dozen had run past, so we went out into the road to see if we could find out what was happening. A fair chap, helmet-less, was running towards us and as he got closer he shouted, 'The Germans are coming! The Germans are coming!' and he ran on past us. All we could see were paras and *no* Germans. We stopped another and he said he was 2nd Battalion: 'The whole bloody lot of the brigade had been wiped out, the tanks are coming.' And then he ran on.

We could still see nothing, but we were getting a bit edgy and beginning to wonder. I imagine my ears at that moment were swivelling like radar dishes. About five to ten minutes later, we saw a chap of 1st Parachute Battalion who Bert knew; he was not running, but walking back, not even glancing over his shoulder, and he was looking depressed. We spoke to him and got more of the picture. Tanks had broken the attack, there was nothing they could do against them, and finally they had been ordered to get back. Then they had been told to take up a position at the railway line. (Whoever had given this order, or was responsible for it, could not have known that the railway line was about three quarters of a mile behind the ground we had fought so hard to take.)

Where we were, there were only about just over 25 of 3rd Parachute Battalion left. There were no officers; if there were, I did not see any. In fact the only officer I had seen since Oosterbeek on the Monday morning had been Major Dennison, and he had been wounded at the time, on the carrier. We withdrew along with the chap from 1st Parachute Battalion. At times we were overtaken by others running past us, with good old Bert yelling at them, but they took no notice, they just carried on running. Probably all the bodies that we passed, laying in the road, were not all hit on the occasion when we went up the road, as some Jerries had got behind us, and in places they were firing at us from the houses as we passed.

The worst place for this was where there were some terraced houses, they had hardly any front gardens, and I assumed that they were empty as all of them had their windows boarded up (which I thought strange at the time). These were a bugger, as firing would suddenly come at you from behind the boards, either that or a machine gun would try to catch you on the hop if you were stupid enough to walk past an alleyway. It was along this stretch that I became rather adept at firing my Sten on its side, this being the only way I could get the bloody thing to keep firing. It was a deadly weapon when it was working, but it was so bloody unpredictable and could not be trusted.

We eventually reached the low railway bridge and Benedendorpsweg, and was looking for someone to report to, when an officer (not 3rd Parachute Battalion) came up to us. We told him that as far as we knew we had to report there somewhere.

He said, 'Good lads, I want you to go down the road, and dig in just past the last house. I'll send some others to join you when they arrive.'

As we walked down the road, Bert said, 'I'm glad that some fucker knows what he's doing!' We got to the last house on the left hand side of the road, about 300 yards or so past the railway bridge and dug in on a kind of embankment that was covered with a thick growth of trees and undergrowth. At the bottom of this embankment was a very large field, and when we looked across it, a distance of about 800 yards or thereabouts, we could clearly see the blown railway bridge that was lying in the Rhine. We could not see the Rhine itself. As we looked across the field to our right, the Rhine disappeared in the distance toward Oosterbeek. On the left side was the railway embankment that we had seen on the Monday as we passed that way (ages earlier, or so it seemed). The embankment was about 25 to 30 feet high with the main railway on top, and about 400–500 yards from us (about halfway between the low railway bridge over Benedendorpsweg, and the blown bridge over the Rhine), there was this stationary train of about 5 or 6 coaches.

The original idea had been for us to dig-in and cover this field against any attack from that flank, but it was so open that we decided, if anyone was foolish enough to come across the field, we would see them long before they got anywhere near us; whilst if they came from the direction of the houses, we would be in big trouble, with our slit trenches taking a flank attack. There was an officer with us. Who he was I don't know, but he was a good officer, who did not try to impress us with his authority and who listened to us. He agreed at once that the field was nothing to worry about; there was no hesitation and we dug in facing the fence of the last house, with one trench on the edge of the field, in the cover of the trees, and as the trenches were dug in on the sloping embankment, they were all able to fire on the field should it become necessary. The fence of the last house was of wood. It ran from the house almost down to the field. Jock and I dug in about 50 yards from it, close to the top of the fence, so that we covered a gap between it and the house. There was also a gate that was about 10 yards down from the house. We were ready to take them on again.

We waited but no attack came. It got dark, and still no attack. All that night we waited, saw and heard nothing, except a cow in the field at the bottom of the embankment that was crying and mooing all night with hardly a break. It carried on the whole night long. It was standing over its calf that had been killed at some time by a mortar bomb. By morning it had got on our nerves and several times we had threatened to shoot it. (We didn't. Nobody had the heart to, and it carried on crying and mooing all the time we were in that position, so eventually we got used to it.)

Wednesday, 20th September

All quiet in the woods with no 'dawn chorus', not even from the birds. (Strange, but apart from a chicken that someone was chasing with his fighting knife, I can't recall seeing any birds of the feathered variety at all at Arnhem.) We had a quiet night (perhaps we could have gone home?) with no flares, no shooting, no nothing apart from the cow in the field next door kicking up a racket all night. During the night, we could see in the distance the 'glow' of fires on the clouds, over where XXX Corps was supposed to be. They were still a bloody long way off, and a bloody site further when you remembered that they should have been with us sometime yesterday.

The night (apart from our bovine friend) was a very quiet night, and the expected attacks by hordes of tanks etc., did not take place. Dawn broke and it was still very quiet all round, so Jock got a brew going (marvellous thing that tea/sugar/milk mixture, made quite a good brew). It was not until about 0700 hours when Jerry made his first move in our area, when we saw some of them coming through the gate in the fence. They didn't seem very alert, as though they were out for a morning stroll. Jock and I were content to let as many as possible get through the gate, and we were set up lovely with five through and waiting for the tail end of them when *bang* – some stupid git opened up with a rifle, and they scattered. We also fired, but it was too late, and if it had not been for three of them trying to get back through the gate together, we would have missed them altogether. We only hit two of them and they managed to stagger through the gate, so we sprayed that area of the fence with some well-placed shots.

About half an hour later, we found some more coming up the embankment from the field. We waited, but once again, someone fired too bloody early, and they all went to ground. We opened fire at the area and also tossed a couple of 36 grenades in their direction. (I personally did not toss any grenades whilst in the wood. I tossed a couple over the fence later, as I had the horrible feeling that I might hit a tree or a branch, and have the grenade rebound in my lap, the same feeling I had on the Sunday night after I had thrown a grenade at those in the garden.)

Germans again came through the gate. This time for some reason (I forget why), Jock and I were not in our slit trench. We were about 20 feet in front of everyone else, about 15 feet apart, each lying behind a tree. We saw the Jerries coming through the gate, straight in front of us, at about 40 yards range. We couldn't miss, surely? We were in a perfect position, and we actually counted them as they came through the gate: one, two, three, four … *lovely* … five … *keep coming* … six … then: '*Ach, Engländer!*' and they turned and were off. We fired and got four of them, but two of these got through the gate. Jock and I were really mad. I turned and shouted, 'What silly fucker moved?' straight into the ear of an officer who had crept up beside me. He looked, said nothing and neither did any of the others behind us. So I said, 'Someone keeps fucking it up! Next time wait, we want 'em all.' (I often laugh at the expression on that officer's face when I shouted in his ear. I didn't know he was there; in fact he had made me jump. I don't think it was him who was firing too early, but I was convinced that it was he who had moved that time; probably he thought we needed help, or he was a bit too eager.)

The next time we repulsed an attack, we left our slit trenches and followed after them. Grenades were thrown over the fence (I did throw one) and when they exploded we followed, firing as we ran into the garden. On the other side of the fence, close to the house, it was a mass of broken slates and bricks. The slates cracked as we ran over them and we chased the Germans through three houses before we stopped. Jock and I were lying on the grass of the garden of the third house and an MG42 was hammering away (it fired at such a fast rate it was capable of actually cutting down small trees). He may have been firing at us, we were not sure. We were not overlooked by any windows that we considered dangerous to us and also we were fairly close to a low wall, and it was this wall that the bullets were coming over, probably firing from a ground position as the bullets were well over our heads. Suddenly I felt something quite heavy hit me in the middle of my back. I turned over quickly as I thought it was a grenade or something similar and I was going to attempt to throw it before it exploded. There it was, an apple! We were under an apple tree and as I looked at the apple, others fell down. It was the MG42, and the bullets were knocking the apples off the tree. I said, 'Jock, catch,' and threw one to him. They were delicious; lovely, sweet and juicy. We ate as we lay there, and picked up others that we stuffed into the front of our smocks. Every time the machine gun fired, down would come more apples, *B-B-R-R-R-P*. 'Thanks, mate.' *B-B-R-R-R-P*. 'Through the top, mate.' When we moved back to our position we shared the apples out among the others, as we were quite hungry.

On another occasion, I went to the front of the house we had reached. I crawled up at the side of the house, and at pavement level I looked along the street. I saw two tanks and about 20 German infantry about 80 yards further along the street. Opposite me on the other side of the street were four Paras who waved across to me; they too were at the side of a house. I also noticed on the pavement about 10 yards along on the other side of the road, a WS18 set, of all things. It did cross my mind to dash out and get it, but I did not chance it. I thought that probably it would not work, and even if it did work, there was either nobody to talk to, or with the lack of use of the last set, there was nobody who would want to use it anyway. I also noticed that I was not far from where the school teacher lived. I hoped that she had taken my advice and was in her cellar with the two children. (Also, it was in this area, I later learnt, that Lance Sergeant Baskeyfield met tanks, possibly those I saw, and won the VC.)

Jock and I left our slit trench several times, because we thought it was possible that Jerry could remember seeing us in it, thus placing us for any attack. On one occasion, Jock and I were lying in the wood and our theory worked in reverse. Suddenly there was a terrific *bang!* It was the loudest bang we had ever heard. I was a 'tater-masher' (German stick grenade) that landed almost on top of us. Luckily, we were both lying down, and it was not as deadly as our own 36 grenades, or both of us would now be pushing up daises in Oosterbeek Cemetery. All we saw and knew was this *bang*. Then an eruption of leaves, a sudden blast and we were left with our ears ringing and covered in dead leaves and dirt. (I am now almost deaf in my left ear, and have my front teeth chipped as a result of it.)

On one occasion a Jerry got into the downstairs toilet of the end house and was firing at us from out of the side window. One of the chaps of 3rd Parachute Battalion HQ Company (I now forget his name), a short North Country chap, ran to the wall, got to the window, pulled the pin from a grenade, released the lever, and then tossed it inside. There was a yell (we could hear him) and then the grenade went off. We were attacking again at the time and as we got into to the garden, there was this Jerry stone dead, lying on the toilet door that had been blown off of its hinges, and he still had an unlit cigarette in his mouth. The chap who had thrown the grenade said, 'He won't be needing this,' took the cigarette out of his mouth and lit it up. (It may sound unbelievable, but it is gospel.) We had some real rough and tough sods at that position, and strange as it may seem, we did not have one casualty there, 'twas a sort of 'happy hunting ground' for us.

Whenever we pushed Jerry back, it was always only three or four houses. We were careful not to go any further, and we never held the houses, etc. We always retired after a few minutes and went back to our positions beyond the houses. Someone (I don't know who, may have been the officer; he got to be quite good. In fact, we had become attached to him and was sorry when he left us later) but anyway, someone had an idea – why not go back only to the second house and wait? This we did and took up firing positions. Along came Jerry, crunch, crunch, crunch over the slates and rubble, it was impossible to move quietly over that lot. They came over the wall of the garden we were covering (by this time we were all used to waiting … bloody experts). To put it bluntly, we shot Jerry from arsehole to breakfast. There was one hell of a shout from them, but it was too late, and only a few got back over into the next garden. It was quite a day; there were about 30 of us at that position, mainly 3rd Parachute Battalion with a few odds-n-sods. There was also a Vickers machine gun detachment there, just a little way behind us. We were getting pestered by firing coming from our right flank. We decided that it was not coming from the field and that it was coming from the stationary train. So we got the Vickers machine gun to fire on it. (A lovely gun, the Vickers, a lovely sound when going flat out). They fired at the train, a 30-second burst at intervals of about a minute. The officer loaned us his binoculars and when the VMG fired you could see pieces flying off the train and actually see the wood etc. flying around inside the carriages. It was like a sieve. We got no more problems from there.

During the late afternoon and early evening, although there had been no impression made upon our position (we were happily enjoying ourselves) we were ordered to withdraw. We were actually told that a 'perimeter' had been formed and we were to go in and join it. Nothing could get through the wood where we were but maybe there was the danger that we would be cut off, being bypassed on the road above.

Behind us where the wood thinned as it came to the end, there was a very narrow lane. There was a Jeep there with the driver sitting in the driving seat. There was nothing of any danger to worry about there, it was well concealed and well down in a sort of cutting, hidden by overhanging trees and shrubs. We were just walking past all unconcerned, when a bullet did about three ricochets and killed the driver. (I always said, if one has your number on it, you'll get it, never mind what you were doing or where you were).

After we left that position, I don't remember walking back to Oosterbeek, I have a feeling that something or other happened during the move back, but I can't remember. I doubt if we went along the road somehow, as it was a bit lively at the time, on that road.

Polderweg–Rosande Polder Positions

At Oosterbeek we were told to dig in, in a field at the other side of Polderweg. It was about 300 yards or so east of the church, and about 400 to 500 yards away from Benedendorpsweg going towards the Rhine. (It was an absolutely stupid position, and everyone must have said so at one time or another.) We were slightly east of the lane (or track) itself. The track and the field at that place are as flat as a pancake. There were about a half dozen willow trees there, and we were dug in just by them. (They were not in a group, just a line of trees about 20 feet apart.) To our front, the field stretched off in the distance and eventually joined up with the field at the position we had been at earlier. Way off to our right we could see the blown railway bridge over the Rhine. To our left was this track (Polderweg, just behind us about 30 yards away) that went back to Benedendorpsweg which was, as I said, 400 to 500 yards away, which then ran along our left flank up to the low railway bridge. This, as far as I was concerned, was our main threat, because about 600 yards or so up Benedendorpsweg, from where Polderweg joined it, the road went uphill, and at the brow of it there was a gap between the houses there, and the ground there was easily 30 feet higher than the field we were in, and only about 800 yards away. There we were, dug in, in an open flat field, of lush green grass, and where we were dug in, a blind man would have had no trouble seeing us. The earth in that area is a sandy soil, red in colour, so we stood out like sore thumb – whoever had chosen it was absolutely bloody stupid – but that is what we were told, and that is what we did. It would not have been so bad if that was the only place from which you could cover that approach, but it was not.

About 30 yards behind us, on the side of Polderweg, was a fairly wide ditch, a sort of dyke. It was about eight feet deep with sloping sides that at the top were about three feet above ground level. If we had been placed there, we would have had a better field of fire and been more or less out of sight and had room to manoeuvre around if necessary, and if we ever needed it, a way out. I was far from happy with the position and was glad when it got dark. There was nothing of much interest that night. We could still see the glow from the fires over where XXX Corps were supposed to be, and they did not seem any nearer than they had before.

Thursday, 21st September
There was heavy dew during the night, and as it got to first light we saw that there was also a thick mist. Until the mist cleared, our eyes were hanging out like organ stops, our ears twitching like radar and at the same time we were holding our breath to listen for any sound that would warn us of an attack. If you stared at one place for too long, it moved, or seemed to. Also everyone spoke in whispers, or not much louder. Eventually the mist cleared, *hooray*, then I saw the high ground to our flank and wished the mist would come back and hide us again.

I was a born worrier; on the other hand, after North Africa, Sicily, and Italy, to say nothing of the past few days, I just knew that the high ground was trouble. I was sharing a slit trench with Dennis Collins this time. It was his first time in action – Arnhem, what a place to kick off with. I was with Dennis because we were 'older' hands. (I was *old;* 19 years and 1 month – but according to Army Records, 20 years and 4 months and I had been a para for the past two years or so.) Anyway, us 'older' hands sort of looked after him, and he had the bruises to prove it.

We managed to improve the slit trench (dug it a bit deeper). Some water had come up from somewhere or other, so I filled my water bottle and then we got the usual brew on the go. (Don't know where the water came from, couldn't have been the ditch as that was thick with green slime and smelt awful; I can't even remember what sort of container it was in, but there was definitely some water going.) There was a bit of walking about going on, as I remember seeing Sergeant Major Harry Callaghan (3rd Parachute Battalion) and Captain G.R. Dorrien-Smith (2i/c B Coy, 3rd Parachute Battalion) roaming around – first time I had seen them since Spalding. We found out that Captain Dorrien-Smith was i/c of our little lot. I don't know where the other officer had gone. We had our brew and sometime later there was a shout of 'Signaller!' and probably because we were the nearest, Dennis and I went across to 'Dolly' Smith (Dorrien-Smith's nick-name we had for him).

He said to me, 'You see that White House over there? Well, I want you and him to go across to it and when you see the tanks coming, I want you to signal to me with this torch!' I thought this was bloody stark raving mad. The house he had indicted was on Benedendorpsweg, near to where Polderweg joined it. I knew from having been there a couple of times earlier (Monday and the day before, that is, Wednesday) that there was a bend in the road there that looked onto another bend further up, and the house was set back a bit which made it awkward, plus it did not have any bay windows. So the only way of seeing up the bloody road was to lean out and I was not that stupid.

So I said, 'You will know when those tanks come along soon enough, Sir, they won't get to that house, and they'll stop on that high ground over there and shell fuck out of us out here. We should be in that ditch behind us.'

When he was nervous or excited, Dolly used to stutter like hell. He said, 'You will d-d-d-do as you are f-f-f-f-fucking well t-t-t-told, get t-t-t-to that house.'

I said, 'I am sorry, Sir, but I don't know Morse.'

He looked at me then said, 'Call yourself a f-f-f-fucking s-s-signaller, f-f-f-fuck-off back to your p-p-p-position.' (And that is Gospel.)

I went back to my slit trench with Colly (Dennis Collins) and he said, 'I thought you knew Morse, Rad?'

I said, 'I do, but I'm fucked if I'm going over there!'

What I did not know, until visiting Arnhem with Jock Jones some years later, was that he went over to the house. Dolly asked him, and Jock went. We were talking and Jock said, 'If that man Dorrien-Smith was here now, I'd buy him a pint. As when we were in that field that time, he got me to go across to a white house to signal back to him when I saw tanks coming. I never did because they set the bloody house on fire and I only just managed to get out of the back window when someone put a ladder up. But he (Dorrien-Smith) saved my life by sending me, because while I was away, a mortar bomb landed in my slit trench and killed the bloke I had left in there.' When I told Jock about Dolly having asked me to go, Jock bought *me* a pint!

It was sometime later, Colly and I were talking about Southend, his home town, when suddenly *bang-bang-bang-bang-bang*, followed by *crack-bang, crack-bang, crack-bang* – a burst of cannon shells, followed by 88s. The cannon shells whipped along the tops of our trenches and the 88s hit each trench in line. I shouted to Colly, 'Get down, we're next!' and we both dived for the bottom of the trench. There was a *crack-bang* and I felt something hit me on my legs and when I looked, I found that a willow tree had been blown out of the ground onto the top of us (or the best part of it). About the top two-thirds of the tree fell on top of us, covering us in leaves, branches and a load of dirt. There were yells for 'Medic' going on all around us as most of the 88s had hit the trenches. We had been lucky. I looked out from under the branches of the tree and saw a self-propelled gun and a flak cannon firing from the high ground that I had pointed out to Dolly earlier on. By this time a mortar and at least one machine gun had also joined in, and with their usual accuracy, the mortar bombs were falling on and around us. I looked to the front of our position (and for a few seconds in a bit of a panic) about 500–600 yards away and coming towards us was a tank. Around it and firing as they came were about 15 to 20 infantry – Christ Almighty!

Bullets were whistling everywhere; cannon shells still cracked as they hit and exploded. The 88mm had dropped off a bit but the mortar bombs were still coming and to make matters worse, a small pack on the top of the slit trench next to ours must have had some smoke grenades or something in it, because it was belching forth clouds of yellow smoke. All this added to the cries of the wounded and the shouts for 'Medic', it was a pretty hectic place and what is more, it was obviously time we got out of it, before we joined those that were already lying around the position either wounded or dead.

I shouted, 'Hey, Bert, are you OK?' He said, 'Yeah, let's get the fuck out of here.' (My sentiments exactly.) It was a hopeless position and there was not a chance of survival if we stayed there. I knew that about two trenches down was 'Ginger', a Bren gunner of B Coy. I shouted 'Ginger! Are you OK?' He shouted back that he was, and others were also shouting. I shouted to Ginger, 'Ginger, we are going to make a dash for the ditch, give us some covering fire, in front, 12 o'clock.' (They were the nearest Germans to us.)

The Bren opened up and there was one mad dash for the ditch. Others had heard us and they also dashed for the ditch when Ginger opened up. Bert, Colly and I did not run directly back; there was a very slight dip in the ground to our rear flank. And we went across this like scalded cats. We hit the ditch, took up firing positions and yelled 'Come on, Ginger!' and all three of us opened up across our front. I had not been firing long when I felt something hit me on my boot. It was not hard, just a tapping. I looked down and was surprised to see three chaps in the ditch. They were dug in, deep in the side of the ditch. (I remember thinking, *How the bloody hell can they see what is coming from down there?*) They were shouting at us, 'Cease firing! Cease firing! You'll get us all killed, cease firing!' I was amazed; one of them had a handkerchief or a white cloth on the end of his rifle, and he was saying, 'Surrender! Surrender, you'll get us all killed!' He made to climb up higher in the ditch. Bert (a Scot from Edinburgh), grabbed him, and punched him at the side of his face, saying, 'We are the 1st Parachute Brigade, and *we never surrender!*' Another went to climb out of his trench and I lashed out with my boot, knocked him back in again. 'Stay there!'

All this time the bloody firing was still belting away at us. Bert turned his Sten on them: 'Wave that fucking flag and we'll shoot you our fucking selves!'

They then shouted, 'The officer told us to surrender.'

'Officer, what bloody officer?'

They said, 'Him, there.'

I looked, and there was an officer, he was in a slit trench on the other side of the ditch. (Christ knows why, it put him with his back toward Jerry.) I went across. He was covered in a greyish powder from blast; his ears, nose and eyes were bleeding, his mouth was hanging open with spittle running from it, and his head was rolling from side to side. I shouted 'Hey!' and he took no notice. I turned and said, 'He's bomb happy, and he can't hear you.'

They said, 'We wrote it down on a piece of paper, "Shall we surrender?" and he nodded *yes*. Look, here it is,' and they pushed forward a piece of paper.

Bert said, 'He doesn't even know what fucking day it is! Now fuck off out of the way.' All this happened a lot quicker than it takes to explain it.

The three of us Sigs got back to the top of the bank and commenced firing again. We fired a few rounds, changed position, and fired again etc., as the cannon shells were still very much around. (That is the worst gun I have ever had fired at me, they made such a sodding great *bang* when they hit, like an exploding machine gun, all the time.) We were moving backwards and forwards along the ditch, firing from everywhere we could (all the time with my Sten on its side). We did not see anyone else, although we could hear them at times.

I don't know how long we were dodging about in that ditch, but eventually we noticed that it had gone a bit quiet, not as regards the stuff that was being thrown at us – that was still like a mad house. Mortars were dropping in the ditch by now but they did not do a lot, just sent up a load of water and little else. It was Bert who said, 'I think we are on our fucking own out here.' We had not seen anyone else since we had got there, apart from the three scared sods. We decided that nobody had gone up the ditch past us, and that all there was up past us was the Rhine. So everyone must be down from us, so we decided to move, down the ditch. We went to where the officer was. He was still the same. It was impossible to carry or drag him as the water in the ditch was about three feet deep covered in green slime and there was about one foot of grey mud at the bottom. We said to the three blokes, 'We are moving. If you stay, look after him.' We then went off and left them to it – probably they surrendered as soon as we had gone, I wouldn't wonder.

With everything except the kitchen sink flying around, we dodged along the ditch and what a stink came up from the water. After about 150–200 yards, we came to where a sort of bridge went over the ditch. It was brick-built and bullets were ricocheting off the brickwork (they don't all whine like they do in the films!) I was leading at this point and as it was impossible to leave the ditch, I went *through* the bridge, through because the water passed under it via a pipe, about three feet in diameter and about 18 feet long. I slid along it and found the other end was blocked by a sort of sluice gate that went down to within two inches of the top of the water.

I felt in the water and decided it was deep enough for me to get under the gate, so I took a deep breath and then ducked under the water and under the gate, coming up on the other side covered in water, slime and stinking to high heaven. I put my face close to the water and called into the pipe, 'It's OK, Colly, come on.' Collins came up, covered, I then pushed him forward saying, 'Carry on along the ditch, Colly.'

I went to shout to Bert, when I heard a yell. I turned, and found Colly had disappeared. The ditch had opened out to form a pool about 30 feet round with the ditch continuing on the far side. It was also about 10 feet deep and Colly was underneath the water. I grabbed hold of his webbing and pulled him back up, spluttering like hell. I said, 'Grab hold of the grass at the side and pull yourself round,' but what with the past few days, the flak cannon, the 88s, those three in the ditch, it was a little too much when this happened. He was shouting at the top of his voice, 'I don't want to drown, I can't swim. I'm not scared, I don't want to drown. I'll stay here cover you and Bert.'

I said, 'Move, fuck yah!'

He said, 'Don't make me, I don't want to die, I'll stay here.'

Again I shouted, 'Move!'

He said, 'Don't make me, I don't want to die.'

I said, 'You'll die if you don't, and so will we, now fucking move!'

Just at that point, there was a splash in the water beside Colly and a voice said, 'Grab hold of this and I'll pull you across.' It was a parachute container set of rigging lines and on the opposite bank was Captain Dolly Dorrien-Smith.

Colly grabbed it, I shouted to Bert, 'Come on, Bert,' and through he came. He said, 'What the fuck's going on?'

I said, 'It's OK now. Colly can't swim, so watch it, it's deep in the middle there.' We then got across the pool and carried on along the ditch, saying to Colly, 'Keep going Colly, you stick with us and you'll see Southend again.'

Mortar bombs, 88s, cannon shells, shrapnel, branches, stones, dirt – everything was falling around us as we moved along. Colly, in front, stopped. His way was blocked by a dead body, and it was floating on top of the water. Some of its clothes were burnt off of it and its right leg was at a grotesque angle, with its broken bones protruding. Bert and I moved forward, and as we got to the body it waved to us. It was lying upon a telephone line which our feet had snagged. We pushed it to one side. Further along were other bodies. We had seen others earlier on, but they were not in our way, being mostly outside the ditch, or along the bank. Two were lying on the bank and a third was lying half on the bank with its head in the water. The two on the bank were dead (somehow you got the 'feel' and knew just by looking). We pulled the other out of the water, and he was also dead. Colly was staring at them. Bert said, 'Move! Before you join them!'

We encountered several dead bodies, none of which we recognised, although we were not really looking to see who they were, but looking to see that they were not lying out there wounded. As we neared the rear of Oosterbeek church there was a sergeant, standing on the top of the bank of the ditch. The firing was still going on, but in this area it was not so intense and the mortar bombs were not falling here any longer. Compared with what had gone on further up it was a picnic.

He said, 'Good lads, any more behind you?'

We said, 'No, not from where we've come from, only seen some dead 'uns.'

He said, 'Right, come on, get in the church.'

We got out of the ditch, soaked from head to toe, stinking, and our boots squelching water as we made our way to the church. We entered via a small side door; about the first person I saw who I recognised was a chap from 1st Parachute Battalion. He too was soaked and covered in mud.

I said, 'Hi there, Nobby. How's it going?'

He grinned. 'Hello mate, bit of a fuck up, ain't it.'

I turned to Bert French. 'That was a bit hot out there, mate.'

He said, 'Aye, 'twas a bit warm while it lasted.'

I then saw Harry Callaghan. I said to him, 'Where's Captain Dorrien-Smith?'

He said, 'Dead, got a bullet through the neck, had to leave him out there.' I don't know why I asked about Dolly Smith, it may have been to thank him for his help, or it may have been to have said, 'I bloody well told you so,' or both.

Regarding the whole incident of our previous position out in the open and the courageous act on the part of Captain Dorrien-Smith, it *was* courageous, but at the same time, we should not have been in that predicament in the first place. Whether Dolly Smith was responsible or not for the sighting of those trenches or whether he had been given a direct order to place us there, I don't know and I don't suppose it will ever be known. But he *was* the officer on the spot. It was pointed out to him, the stupidity of it. It was so bloody obvious what was going to happen. He should have had a bit more sense. Instead of which, he dismissed it out of hand, was bloody rude and told us to 'fuck off'. Maybe he was trying to make amends later, but by then it was too late – several had been either killed or wounded out there. I don't say we would not have taken casualties had he moved us to the ditch before the attack. But they definitely would not have been so many. We would not have stuck out like a sore thumb. We would have had room to manoeuvre, been in a more commanding position, not disorganised, had better cover and possibly in this state have given more than we received. Jerry may also have had second thoughts about attacking the better position.

I must mention this with that above, that Captain Dorrien-Smith was quite a popular officer among the men, in particular among those of B Coy. This was mainly because of his rough and ready way of talking at times or expressing himself. He was not with 3rd Parachute Battalion in North Africa; in fact I am sure I am correct in saying, he joined us at Spalding, being posted as 2i/c of B Coy under Major Peter Waddy (a real character, *very* well liked and well known by almost everyone in 1st Parachute Brigade). Waddy also had a pronounced stutter like Dorrien-Smith and quite often it led to some amusing incidents between them.[11]

---

11   On Wednesday morning at meeting at Div HQ at the Hartenstein Hotel, Lieutenant Colonel W.F.K. 'Sheriff' Thompson, OC of 1st Airlanding Light Regiment, RA, asked Brigadier Hicks, then in control of the area, if he could be allowed to keep the assortment of troops he had accumulated at the church. These were the remnants of 11th Parachute Battalion, 2nd South Staffs and 1st and 3rd Parachute Battalions. Thompson was given the immediate task of forming what was to become the lower part of the Oosterbeek Perimeter encompassing Oosterbeek church and it was named 'Thompson Force'. Just before Thompson was wounded by a mortar burst on Thursday 21st, command of the infantry under Thompson came under Major 'Dickie' Lonsdale, 2i/c, 11th Parachute Battalion, and was subsequently re-named 'Lonsdale Force'.

The initial 'Thompson Force' troop deployment was chosen by Lieutenant Colonel Thompson RA. Regarding the positions he allocated to 1 and 3 Parachute Battalions, Thompson said, 'There was a lot of criticism of the positions taken up by 1 and 3 (Parachute) Battalions, on the battlefield tour. I accept full responsibility for these positions. There was in fact, little alternative. Several of the houses alongside the road had been shot up by direct SP fire and to have then put men in them would only have led to a repetition of Wednesday's battle, moreover, after their previous experiences the majority of the men would only be able to recover their morale in the open.' Ref. WO 171/1016.

It would seem from the survivors accounts of the Polderweg deployment that positioning troops out in the open Rosande Polder did little for 'recovering morale'; quite the opposite in fact. Lieutenant Colonel Thompson, as an artilleryman, quite understandably wanted an infantry screen for his gun positions at the church. It could be argued that his choice of deploying troops in an exposed forward position achieved little. Captain Dorrien-Smith carried out his orders to deploy his men on the polder much to the consternation of

Inside the church, we stripped off our wet clothes, wrung them out (all in the 'buff') and then put our clothes back on again. Then in came Major Dickie Lonsdale. (Books say he spoke to everyone there, but they are wrong. He included everyone, but he was speaking to those of 1st Parachute Brigade, such as we were, 30–40 of us. There were others of the brigade already in and around the perimeter, but there were only about 30–40 in the church at that time who were actually of 1st Parachute Brigade.)

He started off by saying, 'All 1st Parachute Brigade, over here.' He meant some pews on the righthand side, while he was standing in the pulpit. He then explained what was happening, and what we were going to do. He told us to get as good a meal as we could, and to have a rest, etc. The books on Arnhem are more or less correct regarding what he said, *but* they omitted the words '1st Parachute Brigade' when he came to the part about going out again. If you remember, the 1st Parachute Brigade, were the only paras at Arnhem who were in North Africa. As Lonsdale came to the end of his pep talk, he said, 'We have fought them in North Africa, in Sicily and in Italy, they didn't beat us then and they won't beat us now. So go outside and show those bastards that the 1st Parachute Brigade will never be beat, and good luck to you all.' (He would not have said, 'You have met him in North Africa' had he *not* been talking to 1st Parachute Brigade. He himself was of the 1st Parachute Brigade before he went to 4th Parachute Brigade, and knew us well, as we did him.)

When we came out of the church after hearing that, we were at least ten feet tall. We were taken and shown the new position we were to occupy during the afternoon. We went to the right as we left the church, along Benedendorpsweg until we got to Polderweg. We were then shown to a position in the gardens at the rear of some houses opposite Polderweg. The position overlooked a large field. As we looked to our front it was about 300 yards across, and immediately opposite us was a road that came downhill and finished at the other side of the field (as though uncompleted, and just leading to the field.)[12] There were houses on either side of this road, and as the road met the field there was a knocked-out Tiger tank that was facing us. To the left of this road was the fence of the end house that eventually ran into some woods. The field extended to about 400–500 yards on our left, whilst on our right it extended towards Arnhem for about 1,000 yards or more, with trees of the wood all the way along the other side. Dotted about the field were several small sheds, similar to tool sheds.

This time, Jock and I dug in together, and Bert had Colly for company. (Also with us was a Sig, Sergeant Jimmy Chandler who originally had been with Battalion HQ. For some reason or other, he never once mentioned the *other* Sigs, what happened to them, etc. It even struck me as odd at the time. Personally I did not care too much for this sergeant, and had known him for some time,

---

his North African and Sicily campaign veterans of 1st Parachute Brigade who could foresee the consequences of digging-in in such a highly visible and vulnerable position. Captain Dorrien-Smith's heroic actions in extracting his men through the sluice whilst under fire indicates his sense of loyalty and responsibility for the predicament in which they found themselves. Dorrien-Smith at the time came under criticism from the men under his command and whilst his exact positioning of the trenches could, according to veterans, have been improved by digging in behind the stream bank, it would seem that this experienced officer was simply following orders.

Lieutenant Colonel William Francis Kynaston 'Sheriff' Thompson was commissioned into the Royal Artillery and joined the 21st Mountain Brigade in India in 1934. Following his return to the UK he served in staff appointments until in 1943 he became 2i/c of the 1st Airlanding Light Regiment RA, taking over fully as CO in July of that year.

12   Ploegseweg.

prior to his being made an NCO. I don't know what it was about him that I didn't like, he was not 'regimental' and I had very little to do with him.) The slit trench of ours was directly opposite the Tiger tank, with a very good view of the road and the houses, probably the best of all the others. Behind our position were the gardens of the houses, about six or seven in all. These were fairly long and sloped down towards the houses, where most of them finished with three or four steps down to the rear of the house. Between us and the houses were about three more slit trenches, but why these were here I have no idea. I think they there even before we got there. They were definitely not for defence, as behind them were the houses occupied by some of 1st Parachute Battalion. (I saw Nobby there; he was a signaller also, and we often bumped into each other – Nobby Clark, it was.) To the front of these three trenches was where we were dug in. They could not see to their left or right because of trees and higher ground, so like I said, they were occupied but not for defence. One of them had an officer in it, either a captain or a major of the RA. I think he was a captain, probably i/c of some 75mm guns that Jock and I found. To the left of our trench, about 30 feet away, was a 6-pounder anti-tank gun, manned by a Polish crew, and sited to fire up the road opposite (the one who was i/c could just about understand English). Further down on the left, about 30 yards beyond the gun, was a barn. Major Alan Bush (2i/c of 3rd Parachute Battalion) was in there, along with CSM Harry Callaghan, 3rd Parachute Battalion. Then further down beyond the barn, the field finished where it met some trees. To our right there were four slit trenches spaced out at intervals of about 20 feet between each and there was a thin hedge running along behind us. The only bit that worried me was on our right. The ground fell away a bit and the last trench was, to my idea, not far enough along. It was not able to bring fire or to observe the ground at the bottom of the slope, where it met the field. Had it been my position, or had I been responsible for the sighting, I would have put it closer to the slope, so that it was possible to see it. As it was, they had some dead ground there. (Jock and I were called to this position a couple of days later, for that very reason.)

We had not been in position long when Harry Callaghan arrived, to see that all was OK. He also had a Bren gun with him and a load of filled mags for it. Apparently he had assembled this Bren by cannibalising a couple of others that were useless. He got into our trench, loosed off some rounds of tracer on automatic and single shot, said, 'That's OK, you use it,' and then he left us. I said to Jock, 'I wonder where it is firing?' I got behind the Bren, put it on single shot and aimed about five rounds at one of the huts in the field. It was very slightly 'high left', I told Jock.

During the late afternoon there was a dull thud of guns coming from behind us, way back. Some few moments later a salvo of shells landed in the wood on the other side of the field (it was the guns of the 64th Medium Regiment RA, attached to XXX Corps) and after the events of the past few days they were a sight for sore eyes. 'Hey, it's our own guns,' everyone was saying. 'That'll show the bastards. Pick the bones out of that little lot.' They were smack on the wood, trees were heaving all over the place, a beautiful sight. As it got dusk the guns ceased firing. It got dark, was quiet, and we could still see the glow of fires in the distance behind us. Also, opposite us a house was burning – it was the end one on the right-hand side of the road opposite, burning fairly well and giving off a fair amount of smoke.

Friday, 22nd September
In the early hours, Jerry attacked our position. They came at us from across the field, probably planning to use the smoke from the burning house as a screen. The only flaw being the smoke did not reach our position, it was blowing across our front and as the Germans emerged from the smoke they were silhouetted against the background of the burning house.

We opened up on them with the Bren and others joined in with their rifles and Stens, at about 250 yards. None of them made it, and those that were able dashed back into the smoke as I let the Bren chase after them. No further attacks came in before it got light. As it got light, I was standing leaning back on the wall of our slit trench, I was in fact looking at the tank and wondering who had knocked it out, then in the distance behind me I heard the guns of XXX Corps open up again.

'There go our guns again,' I said to Jock, and then stood watching the wood across the field, to see the 'fall of shot'. Some moments later I was brought out of my carefree state by a shell that landed with a crash about 30 yards in front of me, which actually made me bounce up in the slit trench. This was closely followed by its mates that proceeded to drop all around us, far too close for comfort. 'Tell those silly bastards to get up 200,' was the unanimous yell.

Major Bush came up to see what all the noise was about. Jock and I said, 'Tell those sodding guns to get up 200 will you, Sir,' and off he went to the barn, and after a little while the guns ceased firing. Up we all popped like gophers – sod this for a game of soldiers! – and in spite of the last few days we were in quite good spirits. Mortars as usual had been firing at us all the time. They never seemed to stop. It was just one endless crescendo of sound, and eventually you got more or less used to it and tended to ignore it. In fact when it stopped, I thought at first that I had gone deaf; that was on the following Tuesday, which I'll mention later.

The mortars were a bloody nuisance in more ways than one. One way, although we did not know it, Jock and I were about to find out. We were amusing ourselves trying to decide where a sniper was, by shooting up a couple of small sheds, when there was a shout of, 'Signaller!' from the direction of the barn. I said to Jock, 'Fancy stretching your legs?'

'Yeah,' he replied, so we got out of our slit trench. Bert was about to get out of his, and we said, 'It's okay Bert, we'll go,' and we went along to the barn, but not before the sniper had taken a 'pot' at us as we left the trench. As we were walking along, I said, 'I wonder where that bastard is?' and we were looking across the field for any signs of him as we walked to the barn. (If a sniper hit you there was nothing you could do about it, but if he missed, which really was quite normal, you would hear it go past, and ignored it. This is actually a lot easier than it sounds, once you know what you are doing and why and by this time we were quite used to being fired at. If you ducked, it was too late, the bullet had gone anyway, *but* if you ducked you were letting the sniper *know* that he was not that far off. Whereas, if you ignored it, he had no idea of where his shot had gone. He could have been firing blanks as far as the response he got. So that is what you did – mind you, the morning he almost took my ear off, I did jump then.)

We got to the barn and Major Bush said, 'My line to Major Lonsdale is dead. Will you have a look and see what you can do for me?' It was the first we had heard of any line as we had not laid it. It had probably been in before we arrived. Where it went, or where Lonsdale was, we hadn't the foggiest.

'Yes, Sir,' we said (he was a nice chap, one of our 'old' officers). So out we went tracing this line. Luckily we had pliers on our belts, some insulating tape on us, and also a couple of 'teeing-in' leads in one of our packs that we went and got before starting off, and also a spare phone. Teeing-in leads were two lengths of cable, each about two feet long. At one end of each cable is connected a safety pin, making contact with the wire in the cable. The other ends of the two cables are bared. The idea being you would go out with these leads and the spare phone, and every so often you would stop, pierce the cable with the safety pins, one or both depending upon whether it was two wires or just one on an earth return, and then you would connect the spare phone to the bared ends of the two wires. Then you'd give the handle of the phone a whirl, and if the line between you and the position you had left was OK, you could speak to them. You would carry on and test again further along the line; more often than not you found the 'break' as you went along, but sometimes the covering of the cable was intact with the wire broken inside and the only way you could find this type of break was with the teeing-in leads. Usually the hidden break occurred because some dozy sod had walked over the line, not noticed it and walked on with it tangled to his foot, until he stretched it and broke the wire inside the insulation. We were clever little sods, us Sigs, no end to our talents.

We first checked out the phone to ensure this was working (and got a dirty look), then we went outside to the cable. I picked it up and gave it a flick to see where it went. I wished I hadn't because it went straight out into the field! What was over there? We thought Jerry was over there!

I said, 'Blimey! Look where it goes. Well, I'll take the first 100 yards, Jock, and you cover me.' And off I went at a smart double. As this line was a stranger to us, we had decided that the best way to do it was for one of us to run in front following it for about 100 yards, whilst the other one covered him, then the one in front would stop, and cover the other one as he ran up. Then we would leap-frog past the first one, each covering each other, and so on and so on. This line went out into the field and as I ran, I wondered what I was going to do when I got to the other side, because I knew that somewhere over there was Jerry. I stopped and waited whilst Jock came up, then he passed me and a few yards further on turned left. He stopped, I ran up to him by cutting across, and sure enough the line was going to the left. I followed it along and found that I was going between some guns, Airborne 75mm howitzers. There were four of them, all neatly surveyed in. There was nobody with them or anywhere nearby either. They were 75mm M1A1 Pack Howitzers, which fired a 3.76lb shell a range of 9,760 yards. We were in that position until the withdrawal, and we were to pass these guns at least six times a day. During the whole of that time, we never once saw any activity at this gun position or saw or heard them fire. There may have been another gun position in that area of Oosterbeek church, as various books quote the A/B Artillery as still firing after this day. If there was another, it must have been west of the church as we covered the areas to the north, east and south of the church during our travels and did not see any other gun positions.

We wondered if there was another gun position, as one day whilst listening in on the line, we heard Major Lonsdale talking to an RA officer. Apparently the officer was having trouble with his line to his OP. We heard Lonsdale say, 'My communications are fine. I have two signallers from 1st Parachute Brigade, I'll see if I can send them along.' At the time, Jock and I thought it was an OP at the gun position, but it could have also been the line to the OP for the guns of XXX Corps. I don't know, as we never went. We were extremely busy and had enough to occupy us, so we 'cocked a-deaf-un'. We knew that there were at least six other signallers in that particular area, with probably others around, and Jock and I had been on the go continuously. We thought, *If there is another line, let some of those who have* not *been out of their slit trenches since the time we got here get off their arses and mend it.* We knew that we had been lucky in not being hit, so let some other sods take a few chances, like we were doing. We *had* offered to show some of them the route the line took etc, but we got no volunteers.[13] From the gun position the line entered the small wood

---

13   By the 19th September, all three batteries of 75mm guns of the 1st Airlanding Light Regiment, RA, were deployed in action in various gun positions around the Oosterbeek church. Most likely the guns that Fred Radley saw were those of B Troop, 1 Battery, situated in the field east of Weverstraat. The Troop Command Post (CP) was slightly north of the guns with the Battery HQ a few yards further north at the back of the Van Hofwegen Laundry. 3 Battery were in action beside Oosterbeek church on the 18th September. The

at the end of the field, then made a right turn and eventually went between some buildings which we searched before looking at the line there. It was a small school set among the trees,[14] and it was empty, and gutted in several places, with rubble everywhere and no water supply (that is, no water then). The line at this spot was broken in three places by mortar fire and it occurred to me that this was a good area *not* to dally in. We repaired and tested the line; it was still not working properly. From the school, the line followed a narrow footpath that was completely enclosed by the trees. We followed, very aware that the wood could be hiding almost an army. We thought it rather odd that since we had left our position we had *not* seen any of our own troops at all. Anyone could simply walk through that area. At the end of the footpath we found it emerged onto a cobble road. Taking no chances, we got down on our stomachs and peered out, looking up and down the road. To the right, it went uphill, finally disappearing around a bend about 300 yards up, with a few houses on each side but mainly trees. To the left, it went downhill and this too disappeared around a bend about 200 yards down and this end was mainly wooded. I gave the line a flick to see where it went – the line was often covered in leaves and branches that had been blown down by the mortar fire – it went diagonally across the road to a building. We ran across and found that the footpath continued on this side of the road and the line still followed it. We followed it wearily, as it was not unknown for an enemy to cut a telephone line, and lay in wait for the repair party. About 30 yards along was another break caused by mortar fire, so we repaired it and tested it. It was still not complete, and we carried on. We were discussing 'how much bloody further' and 'be alright if Jerry is waiting at the other end', when we saw some troops dug-in in front of us. They were at the side of the footpath and we were approaching them from their right flank, level with them. They did not see us until we emerged from some trees and shrubs about 20 feet from them. They turned when they heard us; we were surprised to see that one of the chaps in the first trench was Don Hardman, an old hand of A Coy, 3rd Parachute Battalion. The other one with him turned to look at us, and we were really surprised, as it was Geoff Marsh (the missing signaller from our section). We said, 'What are you two sods doing here?'

Geoff said, 'Hi, Rad, Jock. Where did you buggers come from?'

We replied, 'Do you know that this side is wide open; there's no sod between you and that bloody road over there? Good job we're not Jerries.'

Geoff said, 'There's another mob over there.'

I replied, 'The nearest mob over there is *ours*, about half a mile away. Where's Lonsdale hiding?'

Lonsdale's HQ was in a small house behind Geoff and Don's position. We went in, saw Dickie, and said to him, 'Sigs, Sir, want to check your phone. We've repaired the line from Major Bush.' I checked the phone, found no 'clicks and blows' (no clicks when pressing the switch, no sound when blowing into the mouthpiece). I checked the phone batteries, found a duff loose connection, put it right, tried the phone, all OK.

I then rung on the line and got Major Bush. 'Line Party here, Sir. Your line to Major Lonsdale is OK now, I'll put him on.'

I gave the phone to Dickie; I then went outside and talked to Geoff. 'You coming back with us? The rest of the boys are over there. Jimmy Chandlers turned up as well, also some more of 3rd Parachute Battalion.'

---

remaining 1 and 2 Batteries and RHQ moved into positions near the church early evening of the 19th September.

14   Klompenschool, Weverstraat.

Geoff replied, 'No, I can't, we have been ordered to guard this gun!'

'OK, we'll see yah,' and off we went. This became a bit of a standing joke between Jock and I. If ever I mentioned Geoff, we would say, 'Was he still guarding that gun?'

There were quite a few slit trenches around the edge, and we were sure that the 6-pounder anti-tank gun that was next to their trench, was easily able to look after itself, after all, they didn't ever carry an armed guard with them?[15] As we walked along the footpath toward the road, Jock said, 'He's a silly sod; he wouldn't take any notice when I told him about this road. If Jerry comes down it, he'll soon find out if we're right or not. There's no bloody unit here.' And there wasn't. Why they had not spread out to cover the road, I don't know. Someone must have known it was there.

We decided not to follow the cable back, but to do a bit of a recce of the area. In the past, we had always found this came in handy, and you never know when you might need to know that particular place, you could be there later on a night patrol or something. We reached the road and instead of crossing over and going back via the footpath etc, we turned right, after making sure it was clear, and went down the road. As we turned the bend further down, we were surprised to see Oosterbeek church. It was on the other side of the t-junction at the bottom of the road (actually, there was another very narrow lane going off to the right just before Benedendorpsweg). It was here that we saw the first of our troops (apart from Geoff, etc.). On the corner opposite the church was a 17-pounder anti-tank gun and crew. The gun was facing to cover anything approaching from the east. Mortar bombs were falling; they had been non-stop for days and by now we were a bit blasé toward them, unless of course they were too close for comfort, in which case we would be down – 'quicker than a ferret down a rabbit hole'.

We turned left along Benedendorpsweg, until we found another footpath that ran parallel to it, through some sort of park, then back onto the road till we came to a gap in the houses opposite Polderweg (this brought back memories of the day before…) It was all quiet, apart from the mortars. We went through the houses and found we were among the houses at the rear of our position. These were mainly occupied by 1st Parachute Battalion. In the cellar of one of the houses – it *may* have been 117, but I think I'm correct in saying 119 – was a Dutch family. That was where I first met the wonderful Bertha Breman; she spoke excellent English, better than myself and several others. Even now [1983] she looks upon us as 'her boys', and all of us who were there at that position, never fail to visit her whenever we return there.

Between the houses and our position was a building, a little apart from the others. Jock and I went in. It was a stable-come-coach-house, and inside it was a lovely old horse-drawn hearse. The rear of it was glass panels all engraved, and inside was a coffin. The coffin was empty (we did look) and in the front on the seat were three very tall top-hats (the original high-hat, I should imagine) with black cockades at the sides. We were not all that interested as we were really on the scrounge for something to eat, which is why we had looked in the coffin in the first place, thinking it might be a good hiding place. Finding nothing of interest we went back to the barn and reported our arrival to Harry Callaghan, and Major Bush told Harry, 'There's a smashing coffin over there in that stable, if you need it anytime!' and went back to our position. On the way we had the life frightened out of us by some of 1st Parachute Battalion when they fired a 3-inch mortar directly over our heads as we were passing. It was firing, we noticed, minus the base plate.[16] We got back to

---

15 The 6-pounder anti-tank gun was a C Troop gun under command of Sergeant Frank Shaw, 1st Airlanding Anti-Tank Battery, RA.
16 Manned by Sgt. Harold 'Dick' Whittingham, Nobby Clarke and Frank McCormic, 1st Parachute Battalion.

our slit trench, and were soon ordered to 'watch your front'. We saw nothing in front, but heard a lot of shooting coming from the road behind. It didn't last for long, and we later learned that Jerry had tried to get along the road, but had beat a hasty retreat when everyone down there let loose with their PIATs, etc.

Had about a twenty-minute 'blow', then: 'Signaller!' It was the bloody line again. We went across to the barn. At the rear of it was a dead officer, killed by a mortar bomb. (Some bugger had already relieved him of his .45, so I was unlucky for that.) This time, knowing the route it took, we ran along the line together and found that it had been cut at the same place by the school. We had wanted to re-route this piece as it was on a solid surface, and more liable to blast, but had not been able to scrounge any cable. I was bending down repairing one break, and Jock was repairing another, when suddenly two Jerries walked around the corner of a building as large as life about twelve feet away. I don't know who was more surprised, them or us. It took us a few seconds to take it all in, and I was bringing up my Sten, when they dived back behind the building. They ran one way and we did a smart exit the other. We didn't go around after them, not the way they do in films, as we thought they would be waiting, so we beat a hasty retreat into the school. We ran across the room to one of the broken windows, expecting to bag the two Jerries from their rear. We looked out, about to squeeze the trigger, when we found there wasn't a sign of them anywhere. We were intending to go back to our own position after we did the breaks in the line (now *very* alert when we did them) as the line was then OK, but we remembered that Geoff, Don and the others were probably unaware of the two Jerries wandering around *behind* them almost. So we went along to them. We had searched, but couldn't find our two wanderers. We saw Geoff and Don, and told them, 'Watch out on your right, there are a couple of Jerries wandering around, we almost bumped into them.' After a bit of a chat we moved off. We went via the line route searching for our two 'friends' but although we had a thorough search, we found no trace of them.

It was not raining during the afternoon for a change and I remember that we were looking up at four 'fighters' that had appeared above us almost. Some said that they were Typhoons and nobody was firing at them, so we said, 'They look like bloody Jerries to us.' The doubts were soon cleared up. About half a mile away or so from us at about nine o'clock, we saw yellow smoke rise above the trees where someone had ignited a smoke recognition signal. The planes got into line and dived on it, letting fly with their cannon and machine guns. They came out of their dive and flew almost directly over us at about 100 feet, their black crosses and swastika clearly visible, as were the pilots – they were FW190s. We made no attempt to fire at them, having learnt long before to adopt the attitude, 'He isn't bothering us, so why bother him.' It paid good dividends regards aircraft. We always left them strictly alone unless being directly attacked, and even then it took a lot of guts. Why the hell anyone should want to signal to fighters with a smoke signal, we wondered. You couldn't do anything even if they were friendly; you had no radio contact with them. If you had aircraft recognition panels, you could only signal 'strike/bomb there' with a large arrow pointing to a house, tank or gun or what have you; that is providing you had the panels and a signaller who knew about them. I would not be surprised if this was not the attack that was reported on the BBC radio broadcast, as it appeared to be in the same direction as the Hartenstein Hotel. I bet someone got a good hefty kick up the rear, or a very red face to say the least.

After the aircraft had gone, I turned my attention back to the Tiger tank that was in front of us, and saw the feet of two Germans who were behind it. I picked up the binoculars that were in the trench (left there by Sergeant Chandler, of the Glider Pilot Regiment), and looked across at the tank. Sure enough, they were German uniform and boots. The two had probably run from the end house and stopped there, thinking they were safely out of sight, like an ostrich, but with our trench at ground level, we had a clear uninterrupted view underneath the tank from front to rear. I said to Jock, 'There are two Jerries hiding behind the Tiger, see their feet. See if you can shift them, I'll wait for them on the Bren.' I thought there are only two, so it won't be a patrol, probably a couple of engineers seeing if they can do anything with it. They'll probably run back when they know we've spotted them, and I lined up the Bren on the gap between the tank and the right-hand house, intending to fire as soon as they moved, so that they would run into it and I would then 'lead' them.

Jock used the sniper rifle we had, minus scope, and as he loosed off the third shot, the Jerries ran to the left of the tank. By the time I had switched my aim and fired, they were fast disappearing behind the fence of the house on that side of the road. I knew the fence was a thin weatherboard, so I hopefully put a burst of six rounds along the fence at where I judged they should be. We were again called on to repair the line and this time, as we reached the school we circled it from the left, hoping our two 'friends' were waiting for us, but though we searched for them we found no sign. We repaired the line and reported to Dickie Lonsdale that it was OK. Then after a few words with Geoff and Don, once again we went back via the church and Benedendorpsweg, entering our position from the houses behind. At the houses we again met some of 1st Parachute Battalion. They were moaning about some Germans that had got into a house on the opposite side of the road and had caused some casualties. The 1st Parachute Battalion bods had cleared them out, but not having enough men to occupy the houses had gone back to their own house, only to have Jerry return and start all over again. They had fired a PIAT at the house, a white flag had been waved, but by the time the 1st Parachute Battalion bods had got across to the house, the Germans had departed via the rear door. They had now returned again and were giving trouble. I asked which house it was and was told it was the 'white one' (shades of 'Dolly Smith). I said, 'Stay here, I know just the thing for them. There's a 17-pounder down at the church.' Jock and I ran through the backs of the houses, onto the footpath and down to the church, saw our 'friend' the sergeant and explained the situation to him. We had no sooner finished than *wham* – a 17-pounder shell went streaking up the road, straight through the top floor of the house.

We never heard that 1st Parachute Battalion got any more trouble from that side again. On our way back, Jock and I were having a bit of a laugh together, something like, 'I bet those Jerries said, "Fuck this, we only fired our rifles at them and they hit us with a sodding great gun."' It was *very* effective; in fact we later did the same with a persistent sniper, using the 6-pounder gun of the Poles, later that afternoon.

As it got dark so the guns of XXX Corps that had been firing on the wood went silent for the night. It was completely dark when three sergeants from the Glider Pilot Regiment passed through our position to take up a listening post about 80 yards out in front of us. This stopped us from carrying out a little job we had planned. We had acquired a few empty tins and (as in North Africa) we were intending to peg these out about 50 yards or so in front of our position, then place a 36 grenade in each of them with the pin removed so that the lever was held in position by the sides of the tins, then place a string onto each grenade, tied to a stick about 10 feet or so from the grenade. With these across the front of your position, it worked better than having tins full of stones to give warning of anyone attacking during the night.

Saturday, 23rd September

It had been raining most of the night and at dawn it was still drizzling. I can't remember when we'd last had any sleep, even then (whenever it was) it could not have been more than an hour or so at the most. With Jock in the bottom of the trench preparing the last of our brew, I had just finished cleaning the Bren, and unloading, cleaning and reloading some of the 30-odd magazines we had acquired when, whilst leaning back in the trench studying the wood opposite for any sign of movement, behind us came the familiar sound of the guns of XXX Corps as they started up their daily support. After yesterday morning's rollickings, they should have been on their toes. *Boom, boom, boom, boom* – we waited for them to fall … Suddenly there was an almighty *crash!* The first round landed almost on top of our laps and smothered us in dirt. I dived for the bottom of the trench before the rest arrived. *Crash, crash, crash, crash,* they almost straddled our positions. I looked up over my shoulder; just in time to see the 6-pounder anti tank gun turning cartwheels about 35 feet up in the air.

I said, 'Hey Jock! They've hit the 6-pounder,'

Jock said, 'Never mind about the fucking gun, they've fucked up our 'char' – half the fucking trench has fallen in.'

Once again, it was, 'Tell those stupid bastards to get up 200.'

We never got an explanation for this. Why the guns should be firing spot on the previous evening and then in the morning be at least 200–300 yards short. It was *not* only our sector that suffered. We were a hell of a lot luckier than some of the Border Regiment, in the vicinity of Lonsdale's HQ; they had quite a number killed and wounded by these guns. Maybe the reason was not known. Later I was serving as Sergeant i/c of Sigs, to 285 Para Field Regt RHA, also with 880 Forward Observation Officers (Para), and it was very evident that when firing at extreme range (as were XXX Corps), that a very early morning shoot would drop short compared with the previous evening's. The explanation I was given was the morning air was colder and denser, giving more resistance to the shell in flight, and causing a variation in its range.

After the guns had made sure we were awake, we set to digging the earth out of our trenches once again, and had not quite finished when the German mortars decided it was time to start their daily barrage. It didn't worry us too much as we had got used to them, and treated them as an everyday occurrence, but it was not long before Jock and I were off repairing the line again; in fact we hardly finished one repair than we were off on another.

It was whilst returning from Lonsdale's HQ via the church about 1100 hours, that I noticed the 17-pounder had gone from the junction there, and just along the road from where it had been we found a knocked out Jeep that had been abandoned. We looked it over, hoping to make some use of it but found it was too far gone, but in the back of it were about four kitbags. We opened them and found they were solid with *new* kit. We stuffed the fronts of our smocks full of shirts, vests, socks, and pants and decided to change our own underwear first before taking the rest of the kit back to share among the others at our position. By now the rain was a steady soaking drizzle, so we thought we would find a dry place where we could strip off and change. We went into the small wood nearby, found a nice dry building, got in out of the rain, stripped off, towelled ourselves off with a couple of towels that we had also found, and put on the nice warm underwear. It was as we were leaving the building that we gave any thought to the building we had chosen. It was a large greenhouse, *and* mortar bombs were falling around and about! After the war, I was at a battalion dinner and was talking to a pal of mine, Al Whitelaw (Mortars) and mentioned the 'Greenhouse' bit to him. I described the Jeep to Al – where it was, when it was, how it looked, what was on it, etc. And he said, 'That was *Hackett's* Jeep!'

I said, 'Hackett's? How do you know?'

'I was up at Divisional HQ. I'd been told to take some ammo down to the church as it was needed urgently. They said to take one of the Jeeps that were outside Divisional HQ. "Any one, it doesn't matter, just get that ammo down there", so I took the nearest Jeep and went off to the church and unloaded the ammo when I got there. Mortar bombs were falling all over the place, and when I got back to the Jeep, it had been hit, so I abandoned it.'[17]

We got back, shared out the kit and got called out again to repair the line. If we had been able to scrounge some more cable, the repairs would easily have been reduced by about two thirds, as the majority of the breaks were in the vicinity of the school.

We had only been back in our trench for about 30 minutes when we were called along to the trench on our far right. We were called to various trenches during our stay there, and looking back, I think that apart from Bert French and Jimmy Chandler, Jock and I were about the only ones who had seen any action before Arnhem. We got called to too many little things where someone had *thought* he had seen something or other, or they just wanted someone to talk to. Jock and I were roaming around quite a bit and not taking a great deal of notice to what was going on. Anyway, we went along to the trench, and I took the Bren with me, as asked, and was told that a 'tall Jerry' had almost stumbled on them, and had gone to ground amongst grass on the slope in front of them. Due to the position of the trench, it was impossible to see the whole of the slope, in fact very little of it was visible, so I moved about 20 feet to the right, where I could see the whole slope. I could see nothing there, as it was covered in high grass, and there were several folds in the ground that could easily hide anyone.

After waiting 'in the aim' for about ten minutes, I began to wonder if maybe the Jerry had gone (unobserved) before I had got there. I said as much to Jock who (as usual) was lying alongside me. We then shouted to the others, 'Where did he drop?'

They shouted back and we couldn't understand them, so I shouted, 'Throw something where he is.' They threw a clod of grass or earth, and no sooner had it landed than the German was up and running. He must have mistaken it for a grenade or something. He was practically in the middle of my sights and running into them, so I did not shift the aim, and fired a short burst with the Bren. It hit him and he fell out of sight in the grass on the slope. We did not go out to check as we did not know if he was alone or not, although we waited, but there was no further movement from him or anyone else, so maybe he was just wandering around alone.

The German was an officer of some kind, could have been SS; he was dressed in a dark blue uniform, long shiny black boots or leggings, long black mac, and a stiff peaked cap. It was a pity that we were unable to go out and find him, as he was probably carrying a bloody good Luger pistol.

We were returning to our slit trench when there was a shout. We looked, and there in one of the gardens behind our positions were two Jerries, the same two that Jock and I had been searching for. At least six different people saw them and simultaneously loosed off shots at them, but they must have had charmed lives, as the last I saw of them they were fast disappearing between two of the houses, apparently unhurt. We returned to our slit trench just in time to get called out on another line repair. We did this without incident. It was at the back of the barn (the dead officer still there and beginning to take on the usual smell of a corpse after a couple of days) when there was a sudden noise near to us. We turned and saw a para chasing a rather scrawny chicken, trying

---

17   Brigadier J.W. 'Shan' Hackett, Commanding Officer, 4th Parachute Brigade.

to bring it down by throwing his 'fighting knife' at it, missing every time. He got so bloody angry that he stormed off to return with his Sten. There was a burst, a cloud of feathers and that was the end of the chicken. I often wondered how much of the chicken was left for the pot.

We were again asked to repair the line and again it gave us no trouble. We got back to the barn and decided to have a scrounge around. In the cellar of a house at the far end (the house was unoccupied), we found quite a number of jars of bottled fruit. We opened them up and dug out apricots with our clasp knives, sampled them and found they were delicious. We ate a jar apiece and then took the others back and shared them out among the others.

The position we occupied was on ground that was higher than the ground where the houses behind us were, and when looking through a gap in between the houses, you could easily see the blown railway bridge over the River Rhine. We were quite used to seeing it and it was a surprise to us when we noticed some troops on the far side of the river. There was about 15 to 20 of them, and they had two vehicles with them. The distance was too far to discern who they were and there was quite a bit of speculation as to whether they were XXX Corps or not. Whoever they were, they were not in a hurry, and neither did they seem to be at all interested in what was going on the Oosterbeek side of the river. They were completely out in the open, making no attempt to hide themselves or to form an all-round defence. They were grouped together, and by the smoke going up, it appeared that they were having a brew-up or similar. Some were certain that they were XXX Corps, but they were well out in the open, making no attempt to hide and were not being fired upon. So Jock, Bert and I reckoned it was pretty certain that they were Germans. There was also some talk of the Poles crossing the river that night. As regards to XXX Corps, *when* they arrived they would be in for a right rollicking – we all felt they need to get a bloody move on. Bert reckoned that they were all 'on passes' in some Paris brothel.

Towards the end of the day we got another call to repair the line (nobody mentioned the OP line). It was getting cut a lot more often and sometimes we had to repair it again on our way *back*. It finally got dark, and the glider pilots once again went out to take up their listening post out in front of our position.

Sunday, 24th September

I was woken up just before first light by being shaken by the shoulder and being told: 'Wakey, wakey!' Having been without sleep, for practically the whole time since we landed seven days ago, the whole of our sector fell asleep during the night, nearly all standing up, slumped over our weapons at the sides of the slit trenches. The officer (RA) in the trench behind us noticed we were asleep. A bloody good bloke, he moved from his trench into one of those in front and kept watch all night. Just before first light, he woke us all up, then said, 'Right, you beggars have had your beauty sleep, now I'm going to have mine,' and he then went off and got his own head down. He was much appreciated by all of us; he never interfered with us during the whole time. He'd probably seen that we knew our job, and let us get on with it without worrying. We were all alert and ready to duck the minute we heard the guns of XXX Corps. We weren't going to get caught – third time lucky this morning – we all intended to be well down this time. We waited and waited, but no guns. Heads popped up and we looked at each other. 'Maybe someone told them we're the same bloody army as they are!' (It may have been the morning that the Border Regiment got hit by them, as they certainly did not fire on us again.) No sooner was it light than we were off repairing the line again. We saw Geoff and Don down by Lonsdale's HQ, and told them about the Jeep and the kit down by the church. They wanted some but were not inclined to go and get it (even though we also mentioned finding a 24-hour ration pack there). We offered to show them the way, but they declined, so we left and went back to our position. After we got back, we were talking to the glider pilot, Sergeant Chandler, who manned our Bren gun whenever we left it, when our 'friendly' sniper almost hit my right ear – the bastard! I had actually felt it go past. I got into the trench and said to Jock, 'Right, let's see if we can get that bastard, he's going to hit one of us before long.' Jock got the binoculars, and I got on the Bren, put it on single shot and with Jock spotting/directing, I put shots into several of the houses, trees, bushes, huts, in fact anywhere and everywhere we thought he could be. Finally, Bert in the next trench said, 'Hey, Rad, Jock, for fuck's sake pack it in, I've got a headache!'

Jock said, 'We're after that poxy sniper.'

'Why worry? He's a rotten shot anyway,' replied Bert.

Jock said, 'Yeah, but he's getting too much bloody practice. He almost had Rad's ear off last time.'

We decided to make a brew from the 24-hour ration pack that we had scrounged and were waiting for the water to come to the boil when there was a shout from Bert.

'Hey, look at this! Look at this!'

We looked, and there was Bert holding up his helmet, and poking his fingers through a hole in the front of it, and another through the back of it. He said, 'I felt that bastard go right across the top of my head.'

Jock said, 'Serve you right, I told you he was getting too much fucking practice.'

I looked at Bert's face and burst out laughing, Jock joined in, and Bert said, 'You silly bastards. Look at it, look at it!'

Jock said, 'What d'ya want, a medal? Tell Major Bush, he might give you one.'

All three of us then played 'hunt the sniper' and during the next twenty minutes or so we must have shot up half of Oosterbeek between us. Major Bush came along from the barn to see what was happening, and we said to him, as he stood looking down on us in our slit trench, 'Don't stand still up there too long, Sir, there's a sniper taken a liking to us.' Then we laughed. 'He's just shot Bert's helmet off, but he's not too good though.'

He said, 'Oh! As long as you are all OK. Those mortars, any idea where they are firing from?'

We said, 'They seem to be coming from behind that house over there in the wood," indicating a house about 500–600 yards away at two o'clock.

Major Bush said, 'We are in touch with the army back there. We'll see if they can do anything for us, may take a little while but we'll see.'

I said to Jock, after Bush had gone, 'I hope to fuck he doesn't ask those guns to fire at the house.' The reason why Major Bush had asked about the mortar was because the mortaring in our sector had increased tremendously. Mortar bombs were falling almost non-stop, at about eight or more a minute. Not only that, they were falling in and around us a lot more often. After he had gone, we went back to hunting the sniper. I had the binoculars, and out of curiosity more than anything else, I focussed on a tall tree that was about 400 yards up the road facing us.[18] Whilst I was looking at it, a dark bulge that I had thought was part of the tree, disappeared, then re–appeared. It was about two-thirds of the way up, at the right-hand side of the tree. I watched it for a little while, and then it moved again. I thought, *Gotcha*, and said to Jock, 'I've got him. See that tree, the tall one

---

18   Ploegseweg.

up the road there?' Jock saw it. I said, 'Just above that big branch poking out on the right, there's a bulge on the right-hand side, that's him!'

'Got it,' replied Jock, and proceeded to fire off three short bursts with the Bren gun. I saw the bulge suddenly move, and thought I could see something fall from the tree.

'I think you got him!' We should have found him earlier, but we were looking for a bad shot close in; we got no more trouble. Whether or not it was *the* sniper I don't know, as we may have hit one or more, earlier on when we were shooting up the town, it was hard to tell.

It was just after this that the first two of our own aircraft we had seen, and the *only* aircraft of ours, as we never saw any more, put in an appearance. Two Typhoons were over the top of us circling, then they suddenly dived and let fly in the wood near to the house we had pointed out. They did not hit the house, and when they had gone there was quite a lot of thick black smoke coming up, so they must have found something. This more than surprised us, and there were plenty of comments like, 'Christ, I'd forgotten we had an air force' etc.

We got called out to repair the line again; the breaks were at the usual place, at the school. We went through to Lonsdale's HQ, told him it was all OK, and then went back to the barn. The line was still OK, so we started back to our old slit trench. As I passed the officer (RA), he said, 'Any news, Signaller?'

I stopped by his trench and said, 'Yes, Sir, the Dorsets are going to have another try to get across the river tonight.' I had just finished speaking when there were two bangs behind us (Jock, as usual was standing next to me). I knew I'd been hit, although I could not feel it, and I had been blown into the trench, on top of the officer. I shook my head, looked down, and saw blood pouring down the front of my smock, from where I had been hit in the neck. I could also feel blood running down my back, my right trouser leg, and my right sleeve was also wet with blood running and dripping off my right hand.

The officer was tearing open his field dressing. I said, 'Jock? Where's Jock?'

The officer said, 'He's alright, keep still, old lad.'

I said again, 'Where's Jock?'

He called out, 'Jock, will you come here!' and Jock came up to us. The officer said, 'There you are, he's alright, now lay still.'

I said, 'Jock, tell Bert I've copped one, ask him to put Colly with you on the Bren.' Turning to the officer, I said, 'It's right what they say, you don't hear the sod that's going to hit you. I never heard that one.'

'Do you smoke?' he said.

'Yes, Sir, but I ran out days ago.'

'Try this,' he said. 'There's not much in it, I'm afraid.' And he placed his pipe in my mouth, so I took a couple of puffs at it – marvellous. He had already shouted for the medics. They appeared and he asked for another dressing as the one he had put on was already soaked and dripping. They put a shell dressing on top of the field dressing, then lifted me out of the trench, onto a stretcher and carried me to the house at the rear of the position, and put me in the cellar. The cellar was a fairly large one, and about seven feet high. I was still conscious, and was *very* surprised to see about 30 others, at least, already in the cellar. At least *half* of them were *not* wounded, and what struck me most was they did *not* look tired and dirty. I was placed on a mattress on the floor just to the left of the stairs. I was feeling a bit groggy, and groaning a bit where my leg and back had begun to sting. They were really beginning to smart, when someone came in with another soldier who had been hit. They placed him on another mattress that was next to me on my left. When they had gone, I looked at him and recognised the glider pilot, Sergeant Chandler. He was grey, and having great difficulty trying to breathe. He struggled for a few moments; I then heard him gurgle and knew that he had died. I then passed out cold.[19]

Monday, 25th September–Tuesday 26th September

I was lying in bed at home and someone kept tickling my nose. I kept brushing them away, but they kept on tickling my nose. I opened my eyes, and there was a very small black and white puppy, licking my face and wagging his tail as I moved: 'What the…?' *Oh, now I remember, I got hit, must have dozed off. Where did you come from, eh? And where is everyone? They've all disappeared, wait a minute … Yes, that Sergeant Chandler is still here. There's something wrong, what is it? I can't hear anything. What's going on, what's happened to all the firing, XXX Corps must have got through and they have all moved on. Why did they leave me here? Maybe the silly bastards thought that I was dead like old Chandler there? Alright boy, alright, I'll get up in a minute, come here, what are you doing down here?* And that was how I finally came to.

I then heard a crash from outside in the street. 'What the fuck's that?' I pushed myself up and my right leg gave away under me, and I started to bleed again. I still had my own field dressing so I put that on tightly, and then looked at Sergeant Chandler, he still had his dressing in his pocket, so I took his, and put that around my leg as well. I then pushed myself on my backside across to the other side of the cellar. It hurt a bit, and I did not know that I had also been hit in the arse by two small pieces. I pushed myself up against the wall and looked out from a grill that was set in the wall. I was looking up the street, Benedendorpsweg. I don't exactly know what I was expecting to see, certainly not what I did see: five Jerries about 30 yards up on the other side of the road, tossing a 'tater masher' into a house or something, and then entering it. They came out and then went to the next place and did the same again.

Fuck this, I thought. *I'd better get out of here before they do the same thing here. Now if I can get out, get through the back of these houses, I should get to that covered path that comes out by the church. It's round a bend there, so they shouldn't see me as I cross the road. I won't be able to move very fast, I won't be able to swim that poxy river either. Maybe there will be a log or a blown-up tree down there somewhere that I can float across on. Right, I've got about two days, and by then I'll have to have my leg seen to or it'll be going bad. Let's make a move. I wish I had some sulphanilamide powder to smother it in.*

I pushed myself up onto my feet, and went to walk across to the window. I nearly fell flat on my face as my right leg almost folded up under me. Christ, did it ache. The foot and ankle were not all that clever either, also my right arm and wrist were smarting a bit, but at least my neck had stopped bleeding, and I wondered where my helmet and Sten gun were. I got to the rear window and looked across the gardens. From the rear of the houses, the gardens went up about four or five steps, to almost eye level, then there were about 75 yards of garden leading up to the field. There was no sign of anyone at the back. With Jerry out the front, wandering around as though he owned the place, I had decided that something must have gone wrong. XXX Corps had *not* gone through, and my own lot must have moved, I had no idea where. All I knew was that somewhere on the other side of the River Rhine were British troops, and going by the fires and smoke that I had seen, they were not all that far off.

---

19 Sergeant Francis J. Chandler, 14650728, B Squadron, Glider Pilot Regiment, aged 18. Found buried in the field behind 119, Benedendorpsweg.

I got out of the house, moved into the next garden, then the next, and was just about to enter the third when I heard voices coming from it. I tried to make out what they were saying, and whether they were German or not, but all I could hear was a murmur with nothing distinct. I got closer to the wall that separated the houses; I was breathing heavily and was certain that they would hear me, if only the mortars and guns were still firing. It was so bloody quiet, it seemed unnatural. I slowly raised my head and looked over the wall, and saw six paras! I thought to myself, *You are in luck, Rad.*

I startled them a bit when I went into the garden. I noticed that none of them were wearing helmets (but then neither was I) and two of them were not wearing smocks; also one of them was a sergeant, a stocky, well-built chap with fairish ginger hair. I had never seen any of them before, and none of them were even slightly wounded. It also struck me as a bit odd that none of them appeared to be carrying a weapon of any kind.

I said, 'Where's everyone gone to?'

'They all went back across the river last night,' the sergeant replied.

I said, 'Last night! What are you still doing here?'

'We were asleep in the cellar and they left us there,' they replied.

I said, 'What day is it?'

'It's Tuesday.'

I thought, *Christ! I didn't doze off; I've been out nearly 48 hours.* I said, 'There are some Jerries at the front, so went can't go out that way. What are you going to do?'

The sergeant said, 'I don't know. We were just talking about it; we are surrounded.'

I said, 'Look, I know how to get down to the church. We can reach a ditch there, and from there get down to the river. We can hide up, cross it when it gets dark, and then meet up with XXX Corps.'

He looked at the others; they all then looked at each other. I said, 'Come on, it's worth a try. You can't stay here.' Just at that moment, I saw five Germans in the field at the rear of the garden. I said, 'Quick, get down, Jerries.'

The sergeant and the others said, 'We think we ought to surrender. It's the best way.'

I said, 'Surrender? Fuck that, they haven't seen us yet, what do you want to surrender for? Let's get down to the river.'

They all started talking together. 'We should surrender. We are surrounded, and we must surrender.' I was about to sod off and leave this lot to get on with it, when two of them jumped up with white handkerchiefs and shouted, '*Kamerad, Kamerad,*' and the five Jerries came across the garden to us. It was at this stage that I blew my top: 'You stupid shower of bastards, call yourselves fucking paratroopers, if my mates were here they'd shoot the fucking lot of you.'

The sergeant said, 'We had to.'

I said, 'Like fuck you did. I've met your kind before. No wonder they fucking left you.'

When the Jerries got to us, I noticed that three of them were armed with Sten guns. I thought, *A lot of good they are!*

One of the Germans, a tall chap with a 'Hermann Göring Regiment' cuff title on his sleeve, said, 'Come, it's over, Tommy,' and the other 'shower' climbed up the steps of the garden. He looked at me. 'Come,' and waived his Schmeisser in the direction he wanted me to go. I limped up the steps one at a time. He helped me up the last one and then shouted to the other 'shower' who were off in front: 'Hey, come, comrade is wounded.'

They turned and came back to me. The sergeant said, 'Get on my back, I'll carry you,' and then bent down for me to climb on his back.

I said, 'Fuck off! I've had all the help I need from you bastards,' and carried on limping across the field. The Jerry said something to me in German. I looked at him and said, *'Non parlez-vous'*. (I thought as they'd been occupying France, he'd know some French.) I then said, 'Non comrades', pointing to the others. 'They're shit houses.' He nodded as though he understood. (He must have understood, as I later learned that 'shit house' in German sounds very similar.) I got across the field, but it was slow going. As I got to the Tiger tank, I saw several dead Jerries lying around the vicinity of it and thought to myself that they must have been some of them that Jock and I hit. I didn't look at them for too long in case the other Jerries got a bit niggly. We went along the road, and after a while the tall Jerry slung his Schmeisser round his neck, said 'Come,' and put his arm around me and helped me along. We went via the back streets and eventually I recognised where we were, Utrechtseweg, not far from Saint Elizabeth Hospital. About 400 yards from the hospital, on the right-hand side of the road as we approached it, I noticed a small grassy dip in the ground at the edge of the road. In it were about 15 or so dead Airborne. All still wearing smocks and they were still wearing their belts or pouches and small packs. Who they were, I didn't know. They must have got caught in this dip and probably shot up by a tank. On the front of each ammo pouch, and on each small pack, was painted a small red dot, about the size of a sixpence. I thought that this was some form of platoon recognition marking. I did not know of any paras who wore these and I assumed that they were probably some of the dead of the South Staffordshire Regiment. Whoever they were, they never had a chance. The whole bloody lot were dead, 15 to 20 or maybe more, all together on this little piece of grass. Probably they all dived into this dip, being the only cover around and a tank found them, had not run over them, and just shot them.

I finally reached the St Elizabeth Hospital. I could feel my foot squelching around inside my boot where my leg had bled and ran down into my boot and I was just about knackered. My German help-mate sat me on the ground and went off into the hospital. The other Jerries went off with the other 'shower'. Soon, my 'mate' came back with a stretcher and a British bloke. I was placed on the stretcher. The German left, the British chap took my particulars, he asked me my unit, and I said, 'You don't need that, do you?' I didn't give it to him. I was then left outside on the stretcher. In fact I was left lying out there all afternoon – I could have done with a smoke. Finally, just before it got dark, I was carried into the hospital, not far, and was left on the floor just inside the door.

The hospital was packed to the seams, and as I lay on the floor looking up, I could see a stairway that seemed to go up to about two floors. As it reached each floor, there was a balcony. I was eventually carried up the stairs and placed still on my stretcher, out in the corridor. Apart from the chap taking my particulars, nobody said a word to me or attended to me. All in all, I had been there for about six or seven hours and not even had a drink of water. As it got dark, I noticed that there were carbon burning lamps lit, and at that point I must have passed out again. Everything was black, and there was this figure bending over me. The figure was dressed completely in white from head to toe.

I shook my head. 'What the … where the hell am I? What's happened, what's this bloody thing all in white?'

'English soldier, you are very dirty.' The figure spoke! Thank Christ! I was beginning to wonder for a minute. It was a Dutch nun, and she was trying to wash my face. She said again, 'English soldier, you are very dirty.' I managed to speak: 'So would you be if you hadn't had a wash or a shave for a week,' and promptly passed out again.

Wednesday, 27th September – Onwards
A couple of days later I was taken to Apeldoorn and stayed a few nights and was finally moved on to Stalag XIB and a whole lot more exploits. And I still maintain that Arnhem was a picnic compared to North Africa).[20]

20 After the war and repatriation, Fred Radley re-visited Oosterbeek and called in at Bertha Breman's house on the Benedendorpsweg where he met ex-sergeant 'Dick' Whittingham.
   Fred Radley: 'Dick Whittingham was 1st Parachute Battalion and it was his 3-inch mortar that was being fired without the base plate, I told him about the "shower", he said, "Them! They were in the cellar the whole time, wouldn't come out. So when the orders came to withdraw, I was badly wounded, so I told my chaps to leave me, had to order them to in the end. I told them don't let those bastards in the cellar know you are going." I said, "Dick, thanks a lot, I met them and they dropped me right in the shit on the Tuesday morning."'
   I did query Fred Radley about the 'Tiger' tank knocked out at the end of Ploegseweg. As already explained, in many accounts, StuGIII, self-propelled guns (SPs) and other types of tank may have been mistaken for a Tiger. Photographic reconnaissance of the area in October 1944 confirms the presence of a knocked-out Sturmgeschütz, self-propelled gun, several hundred yards north from the junction of Ploegseweg and the field opposite Radley's position on Benedendorpsweg. Fred Radley:
   …the aerial photograph may not show a Tiger tank that was knocked out at the end of Ploegseweg, but as this photo was taken in October, then the tank was obviously moved and recovered. Myself and Jock Jones, Harry Callaghan, Major Alan Bush, Bert French, Dennis Collins, Jimmy Chandler, plus about six others whose names I forget, were gazing at a knocked-out Tiger tank at the end of that road and did not confuse it with an SP that was *destroyed*, at about 200–250 yards behind it. The SP may have been there, I cannot recall seeing it, up the road behind the Tiger tank, and this was either because it was completely destroyed and was not a threat, or it was knocked out after I was. The tank was at the end of the road, in the middle, and almost level with the last house on the left hand side of the road (the off side of the tank was more or less level with it). The hatch of the tank was open; in fact Jock and I were of the opinion that it was possibly being used by a sniper or an OP, and if we had not been put hors de combat on the Sunday, we were planning to siphon some petrol from the knocked-out Jeep near to Oosterbeek church, into a Jerry-can and then that night we were going to make a wide flanking move to the tank, throw the Jerry-can into it and then toss a 36 grenade in after it.
   We had studied this tank through the binoculars, and as far as we could see (it was head-on to us, with its 88mm pointing directly over the heads of Jock and I) we could see no damage, the tracks were intact, and it was complete, so if there was any damage, it was either at the rear out of view, a small PIAT hole at the side, or it may merely have broken down, but there was definitely a Tiger tank sitting in the middle of Ploegseweg opposite that position Jock and I were occupying, and there is no way we mistook an SP for a Tiger tank, and neither am I mistaken regards its position, it was a Tiger tank, and it was where I said. It was there on the 21st, 22nd, 23rd and 24th September and it was still there when Jerry took me past it on my way to St Elizabeth Hospital on the morning of the 26th along with six or seven dead Jerries that were lying in the road close to it.
   According to one account, an armoured vehicle (described as a 'Tiger tank') destroyed halfway up Ploegseweg was knocked out by the combined efforts of Lance Corporal Sidney Nunn and an unknown glider pilot who manned the nearby 6-pounder anti-tank gun after its (Polish) crew had been killed. Ref: *A Bridge Too Far*, by C. Ryan, page 398. (This is the 6-pounder gun referred to in Fred Radley's account).
   On Thursday, 21st September, Signaller Monty Faulkner, D Coy, 2 Battalion South Staffs, took part in the repulse of a German infantry attack supported by armour down Ploegseweg. Faulkner witnessed a self-propelled gun knocked out with a PIAT fired by Major Cain, 2 South Staffs. According to Faulkner the vehicle, a Sturmgeschütz III Ausf. G, was brought to a halt halfway up Ploegseweg of which we have photographic evidence. Cain's own account confirms this action along with the elimination of the dismounted crew.

94 AIRBORNE TO ARNHEM

Ploegseweg, Ooosterbeek. Sturmgeschütz III Ausf. G, of *Sturmgeschütz-Brigade 280*, knocked out with a PIAT on 21 September by Major Robert Cain, South Staffs, several hundred yards north opposite Fred Radley's position.
(Photo: Courtesy ABM)

1930–1935 photo of houses on Ploegseweg, the thatched house on the right named 'Rietje'.
(Photo: Courtesy Gelders Archive)

3rd Parachute Battalion Signals, September 1944.

Back row, L to R: Pte Curtiss, Pte Ginger Wood, Sigm Ron Wiles, Bdr Jacobs, Pte Stan Derbyshire, Pte Jack Hunter, Pte Rad Radley, Pte Matt Mathews, Pte Bill Hulme, Pte Slim Moran, Sigm Danny Bastow, Pte Hitch Hitchen, Cpl Reece, Pte Joe Palmer.

Centre row, L to R: Sgt Jimmy Chandler, Pte Ernie Redman, Sigm Geoff Dunning, Pte Jock Jones, Lieut Johnny Pryce. Maj Hoppy Houston, Lieut Douglas, L/Cpl Bert French, Pte Geoff Marsh, Pte Dennis Collins, Sgt Brad Bradley (sitting, end of row).

Front row, L to R: Cpl Aub Rowthorne, Cpl Wilson (MM), Pte Barlow, Pte Reg McCabe, Pte Len Curtis, Pte Grundy, Pte Johnny Johnstone, Pte Alan Watson.

Fred Radley: for information.

The signalmen (Sigm) were attached 1st Parachute Brigade and 1st Airborne Division Signals, as were Cpl Wilson (MM Sicily) and Cpl Reece.

Bdr Jacobs was attached, 1st Airlanding Forward Observation Unit, Royal Artillery.

Maj Hoppy Houston was OC, HQ Company, Lieutenant Johnny Pryce was OC, 3rd Parachute Battalion Signal Platoon, 2nd Lieutenant Douglas, joined 3rd Parachute Battalion approx day of photograph, did not attend Arnhem.

Not in photo, Pte J. 'Soapy' Hope, KIA 20th September 44 aged 34, was looked upon as 'The Old Man', he, like three other 'Battalion Sigs' (also absent from the photo) i.e. Ptes Emery, Rankin, and Channel Islander Pte Toshtavin, had served on the North West Frontier pre-war. The oldest member of 3rd Parachute Battalion (to my knowledge) was Pte Walter 'Pop' Yates, the assistant armourer, aged 46, KIA 18th/25th September 44. Originally Pop was not due to go to Arnhem, but the Sgt Armourer (briefed for the 'OP') was unavailable, so Pop deputised for him and went by glider.

Signalman Ronald C. Wiles, 7889762, age 22, 1st Airborne Divisional Signals, J Section. Believed shot whilst POW.

Signalman Geoffrey C. Dunning, 2328639, age 20, 1st Airborne Divisional Signals, J Section. First buried in the grounds of St Elizabeth Hospital, 18th September 44.

Private Desmond J.J. 'Joe' Palmer, 5783376, age 21, 3rd Parachute Battalion Signals. First buried in the grounds of St Elizabeth Hospital, 19th September 44.

Major James L. 'Hoppy' Houston, 53748, age 32, CO, HQ Company. KIA Oude Krann area Arnhem, 20th September 44.

Private Albert L. 'Hitch' Hitchen, 2082298, age 28. 3rd Parachute Battalion Signals. Died of wounds Apeldoorn, 25th September 44.

Private Hugh C. 'Matt' Mathews, 14205796, age 22. 3rd Parachute Battalion Signals. Died of diphtheria whilst POW.

Returned across the Rhine: Sgt Chandler (awarded MM), L/Cpl French, Pte Jones (awarded Dutch Bronze Cross), Pte Marsh, Pte Collins. Returned later with 'Evaders': Pte Johnstone.

(Photo: F. Radley; author's private collection)

96   AIRBORNE TO ARNHEM

Oosterbeek, looking east along Polderweg with the modern railway bridge over the Rhine in the background. The Rosande Polder positions were off to the left in the distance behind the present day willow trees. Private Fred Radley writes of the Wednesday, 20th September: 'At Oosterbeek we were told to dig in, in a field at the other side of Polderweg. It was about 300 yards or so east of the church, and about 4–500yards away from Benedendorpsweg going towards the Rhine. It was an absolutely stupid position, and everyone must have said so at one time or another. We were slightly east of the lane or track itself. The track and the field at that place are as flat as a pancake. There were about a half dozen willow trees there, and we were dug-in just by them.' (Photo: Author, 1984)

1st and 3rd Parachute Battalion positions were just forward of the slope to the left of the picture on the Rosande Polder in front of a row of willow trees, most of which are no longer there. The trenches faced east to the right of the picture towards the railway embankment some 600–800 yards away. Houses on the Benedendorpsweg are visible in the background. Private Fred Radley writes of the Wednesday, 20th September: 'About 30 yards behind us, on the side of Polderweg, was a fairly wide ditch, a sort of dyke [*Beek Leigraaf*]. It was about eight feet deep with sloping sides that at the top were about three feet above ground level. If we had been placed there, we would have had a better field of fire and been more or less out of sight and had room to manoeuvre around if necessary and if we ever needed it, a way out. I was far from happy with the position and was glad when it got dark.'
(Photo: Author, 1984)

Mrs Bertha Breman photographed on the doorstep of her house on the Benedendorpsweg, around which elements of 1st Parachute Brigade were dug-in during the battle. Private Fred Radley writes: 'The Breman family: there was Bertha, her husband and a little girl. We took them some water, apples etc., when we had them. Also they had a piano there and we encouraged the little girl to play *Chopsticks* on it. She is now grown up, lives next door to her mother (at 117) and has a child of her own.' (Photo: Author, 1984)

Corporal Alex Whitelaw, HQ Company, 3rd Parachute Battalion, 1st Parachute Brigade

Sunday, 17th September

Prior to the operation, I had sustained a knee injury and a few days before the Arnhem Operation I had the job of taking RSM J.C. Lord (3rd Parachute Battalion) down to the MO for clearance to go on Operation Market as he also had a bad leg. It was he who suggested that I try now to pass fitness. They were not very happy at first about this, but owing to the fact that a couple of men had dropped out of HQ Coy I was able to make up the previous numbers. I was unable to get back to my own platoon in mortars/Vickers machine guns, as they had been made up to strength, but it was thought that I would be able to plug any holes within these platoons. Also, I was a trained sniper. But as events were to prove later, I was with most of these men during a lot of the Arnhem battle, so I was happy.

Very early reveille on 17th September and we set off for Folkingham. I still didn't know which stick I was on or number of the plane. After some delays we took off, and as the plane raced down the runway, I wondered if I was quite right in the head, but thought, *What the hell* – the 'powers that be' said this would all be over in four to five days. I should have known better; experience in the past had proved that they sometimes get it wrong. More often wrong than right. Our problems were never within the battalion, they were usually higher up.

We had a very good flight over to the Dutch coast, no problems, saw a bit of flak in the distance, but a long way off. No lack of fighter escorts helped to keep morale up. I remembered Sicily and the hellish reception we got there from flak and a rather hot reception from our own Royal Navy. I noticed the flooded countryside and it was only a few more minutes of flying time until the next point of interest, the River Rhine. Soon it was time to hook up, and we started to look for landmarks, which were no problem. We first noticed the railway line and then looked for the road/rail crossing and knew exactly where we were.

'Red–Green' and we were off. I soon felt that gentle tug at my back as the chute opened. I looked at the ground and noticed parachutes laying all around and quite a few gliders, who had landed before us on the drop zone (DZ). Once again I thought back and remembered Scilly and how lazy the flak appeared to start up at us, and then as it got near, it fairly screamed past. Thank God none of that here. With a gentle bump, I landed on DZ X near Heelsum. Our immediate job was to keep the DZs clear and defended until the rest of the 1st Parachute Brigade landed, then make for our RV which was a farm, Jonkershoeve.

I collected my gear and made off in the direction I thought our RV lay, when I heard a shout: 'Not that way, you silly bugger, not there.' It was 'Dolly' Gray, member of the 21st Independent Parachute Company (21st Ind Para Coy) who had landed before anyone, to mark out the DZs and LZs (landing zones) to guide us in. Soon we arrived at the farm and prepared to take up defensive positions, and within a few minutes 1st and 2nd Parachute Battalions came in. There was some firing but not a lot, coming from the corner of a wood over to the east and there was an awful lot of running around collecting containers, etc. There had been one or two injured on landing, but nothing serious. We soon got settled and the battalion prepared to move off. Our objective was the bridge, no time to piss about round here.

Suddenly I heard a familiar voice shout, 'Corporal Whitelaw, where the hell are you?'

I acknowledged his call, and moved pretty damned quick; I learned a long time ago that when this man shouts, you move, and quickly. (RSM Lord's voice, strange to say, always seemed to give me confidence. In 1942 and 1943 he was always around to give advice and boost morale. I assure you his voice lifted my morale no end on this occasion.) He passed me over to a lieutenant who gave me a written message to pass onto Division HQ (Div HQ), and he said, 'Take a man with you from Sigs and he will explain that we are having problems with our wireless sets. Take a Jeep and be careful; it appears that a few of our recce Jeeps have not arrived and we are short.' Pointing to a map, he said, 'We will be moving away down this road. You can rejoin us at this road junction, Wolfheze/Utrechtseweg.'

The chap from Sigs was called Johnny and after some time Johnny and I found Div HQ. Needless to say, it was not where they had said it would be. We carried on through the grounds that we found out later belonged to a mental home. Moving through the grounds towards the main road, I needed a 'leak'. I told Johnny and we pulled into the side of the road, I grabbed my Sten and dived into the trees. When I had finished, I stopped to listen and could hear various sounds, including voices.

I started to turn round and out of the corner of my eye, I saw this figure step out into the open. I do not know who got the biggest surprise, but did not wait to find out; I just gave a short burst on the Sten, and he fell. We both examined the body, and were rather surprised to find he belonged to an SS Panzer Regiment. That bothered me because we had been told back home that there were no Panzers in this area. We didn't hang about; he probably had mates close at hand. We got back to the Wolfheze road and made for the road junction. I was quite pleased with my reactions – after all, we had not fired a shot in anger for at least ten months.

We pissed off away down the road to the junction with Utrechtseweg and hopefully to join up with our own companies, but owing to very heavy fire up ahead, we were forced to slow down. As we approached the road junction we could see that the lads had been in action; there was a German staff car with four bodies lying around. We also discovered that the area was being heavily mortared. (When coming down Wolfhezerweg towards Utrechtseweg we did notice a bit of activity down the left flank. We were fired on but I think it was mainly one or two snipers.) We reported to Captain Dorrien-Smith what had happened, also about the Panzers, I honestly think we were dreaming. We were told to rejoin our companies and dig in. I realised that what had started off like a pleasant Sunday outing had now turned into something very much more serious.

I found my company, joined my mates and proceeded to dig in – with great haste I might add, because the shelling was bloody awful. I was informed by Ivor Blakely that C Company had shot up the staff car.[21] C Company had now been pushed out across the road junction, through the woods on the left to the railway line towards Arnhem station with instructions to get to Arnhem bridge by any means possible. If I remember correctly, we were held up in this area for some time, I think three to four hours; why, I do not know. Certainly as time went by it became clearer that the mortaring became very much heavier. To me, it appeared that the longer we stayed here in this position, the stronger the opposition got and by now the casualties were getting heavier. We had now lost our chance to push forward.

Monday, 18th September
When we did eventually move, we did not get far. The enemy had gathered in strength and soon the battalion was cut in half. The first half progressed towards the centre of Oosterbeek, and the remainder were held up here. This half consisted of HQ Company and A Company and was getting very heavily attacked. After a while, it was decided some would make an attempt to cut through to the right and try and bypass the crossroads up ahead and make way down to the river and lower road to the bridge. Many of us were feeling rather bitter that owing to the unfortunate delay earlier, we had now lost the best chance to reach the bridge tonight, or at best, our task was now going to be very much harder. I was with a very mixed group that was hurriedly put together, and cut across the road to the right, down a road I now know as Hoofdlaan. Up ahead was a fairly thick wood but before that we were forced to seek shelter in houses, but were winkled out, getting heavily shelled. Air bursts in the trees were now becoming a real menace. Our progress was now confined to the woods. I was at point at this time with another corporal; we could hear heavy firing away to our left, from an area we assumed was below the crossroads, so we started thinking that some of our lads had broken through at the crossroads and had made their way up to the right. Hopefully with luck we may be able to join up with them, if we could get over that way. We were well into the woods by now and moving as fast as we could; we crossed a slight clearing and started to make our way up a slight incline towards a ridge. On reaching the ridge, we came under heavy fire from what appeared to be an old ruin. Our group was split into two and it was decided by our lieutenant to get to grips with the enemy by a pincer movement. We fixed bayonets, and on a whistle signal from, I think, Lieutenant Hill, we struck from both sides. I remember crossing that open hollow shouting and farting with excitement. As we entered the building we saw there were eight men there prepared to fight, but the rest were not, putting up their hands. There was no time to piss about with POWs; they were all knocked out, some with the Sten and others with the bayonet.

Further progress was made through the trees until we reached open ground. I noticed a hotel on the left and tennis courts on the right. We decided to go straight through between those two points and make for the road up ahead. As we were running across this open ground, I felt a tug at my shoulder straps and my equipment came loose. Mortar bombs were coming in thick and fast and I was glad when we reached the road and dived into a house for shelter. I just had time to try and adjust my equipment; I found that my shoulder strap had been sliced through! How lucky can you get? No time for anything else, as shells started to rip into the roofs and walls. We dived out again, turning left and trying again to get south towards the river and lower road area to join our mates.

21   Actually B Coy, 3rd Parachute Battalion.

But it was not to be. As we moved forward, we ran into a hail of bullets and found out we were completely cut off. We had no other choice but to turn back into Pietersbergseweg, but forced yet again to seek cover, this time in the Tafelberg Hotel. It was decided now to make our way back to the crossroads area, but this time using side roads and coming out below the crossroads. Soon we were in the area of the main road with many scenes of heavy fighting, wrecked jeeps and bodies, etc. We met up with some chaps from 1st Parachute Battalion who had also been cut off from their battalion. It had been our intention to make for the railway line further up the street, again using side streets, avoiding crossroads and to try and make for the railway bridge, little knowing that others had tried this before. Going along the railway we soon saw evidence of a heavy battle, with bodies everywhere. We proceeded until we came to a steep rail cutting where we came under very heavy fire from ground on our left. We were led up this embankment on the left which led us into an area known as Mariendaal. This to me seemed bloody stupid as most of the fire was coming from here, and yet, here we were, walking straight into it. My objections were overruled and we proceeded, coming under terrible fire – very confusing. I remember very heavy fire coming from what we took to be a factory, where snipers and heavy machine guns were positioned.

God knows we tried to get through here, casualties were very heavy and I was thankful when our officer called us to stop and get back. Our losses were very great. What was left of us made for the low ground of the railway line to get out of sight of the Germans on the higher ground. We moved quickly up the other banking and down onto the road. We could not go further back and it became obvious that we had been cut off yet again, with no way back to the crossroads. We had no choice now but to take to the main road, which I knew was heavily defended, and I did not see much chance of us getting through, but we could try. A big problem was not being able to get in touch with any other groups. All the bloody radios we had would do nothing but crackle and whistle. After getting on to the main road it was becoming more and more confusing.[22] Which way to go? Going by the mess in the street, many others had come to grief here.

After a lot of ducking and diving and weaving our way around and about in the many side streets and lanes, we eventually found ourselves in the area of the St Elizabeth Hospital, just east of the hospital and south of the Arnhem railway station. (I do not know exactly how we managed to get there. Over the years I have tried to re-trace my footsteps but failed to find the route.) It was around this area that Lieutenant Hill was killed, I think. I do know that he was badly wounded and later died of wounds.[23]

We were glad to finally meet up in this area with another group of 3rd Parachute Battalion, about 50 men in all, under the command of Captain Dorrien-Smith. We joined this group and apparently somewhere in this area there was believed to be another group of around 50 men. We also encountered here a great deal of confusion, mainly again through lack of communications. No one knew where the rest of the battalion was. It was impossible to find out where the main bodies of the division were, only that 2nd Parachute Battalion with C Company, 3rd Parachute Battalion had reached the bridge and were holding, but only just. An attempt had been made from one of the groups in the area to reach Arnhem railway station, but had failed when they reached the railway line, and were forced to turn back.

We soon found out that every street and lane was well and skilfully covered by the enemy. The Germans had much heavier weapons than us and did not require coming to close quarters with us.

---

22   Utrechtseweg.
23   Lieutenant Gordon T. Hill, 182422, aged 26, died 18th September.

We were to find out later that he never was keen to come to close grips with us. He was deadly with his fire and if anyone was silly enough as to poke his head out, it was very often his last. Everyone took up defensive positions in the houses and wherever possible men tried to get some rest.

Tuesday, 19th September

The colonel had made plans for us to move via the lower road, the most direct route along the river towards a building called the pavilion. If the enemy did not attack before first light, we would take the most direct route to the river.

Volunteers were asked for; a patrol was to go out to find the most direct route to the river and to probe for enemy positions. There were about eight men on this patrol and I was one of them. I realised that if we were going to be on the move early in the morning there would be little time for sleep for anyone, and rather than just have a couple of hours rest, I would rather go out on this patrol. I never liked getting up after being knackered and only getting a wee rest, I'd rather go without. The eight of us proceeded down the street carefully, in the general direction of the river area and almost immediately ran into a bit of trouble. We discovered some Germans in a house, but drew back in time and skirted round their place to avoid them and pushed on towards the river. Soon we were in the area of the pavilion and turned left, headed towards a large church with a high spire, which was the place the snipers had been causing a lot of trouble the day before. We listened awhile and could hear sounds from towards the church and also from some houses nearby. It could have been Germans in the houses or some Dutch who had not yet moved out; some had left, but not all.

Sergeant Blakely, who was in charge of the patrol, decided to go back via the houses where we had noticed the enemy on the way out. We found out that they had left, so it appeared that the ground between us and the river was clear. It was then our unpleasant duty to wake everyone up. Some men rose not too badly, others required a touch with the boot. There was one or two four letter words used before we were all ready. I was now glad that I had gone on the patrol.

It had been hoped that we would be able to move out in one body, but this was found not possible, and we moved out in small groups. I for one was happier that way, with less chance in getting found out. The move was quiet and orderly. I was surprised at this; usually a very tired man is a careless man, but all went well. On approaching the pavilion, we were moved out in groups, spread out from the riverbank to the pavilion. We turned left, facing the bridge which was quite a distance away. On moving we found the enemy were not long in ranging in from the high ground on our left. We were advancing in fairly heavy undergrowth, and in some small way it gave us cover from view, but that did not last long. The Germans knew we were there and only needed to give intense fire into the undergrowth to cause many casualties. It was heartbreaking to find that you were on the receiving end. We knew where their fire was coming from but were unable to return fire; our weapons were far too light. Oh for some heavy artillery assistance from the rear. Where in Christ's name was XXX Corps with their artillery? Our heaviest weapon were our Vickers machine guns, but they were not much good in this type of attack as the undergrowth was too high. The German fire was bloody accurate and I was happy indeed when the order came to retire back to the pavilion to re-group. During the first attack we were relieved to see some more of the 'Shiny Third' join us; they had been advancing along the riverbank from much further back. Among them were some well-known faces. One in particular was Sergeant Bill Perryman, but sad to say that Bill was killed later that day, trying like the rest of us to dodge the murderous fire from that high ground.

On re-grouping we found that the order of march was 1st Parachute Battalion, company of South Staffs and what remained of the 3rd Parachute Battalion, along the same route. The thought of that route was enough to turn anyone's guts, but it had to be done, and again no cover from the rear. Could we not get fighter-bomber cover in place of artillery? It was light enough now or soon would be; but no – 'Get stuck in, lads, it's not the first bloody time you have been left on your own.'

We again moved off. This time it appeared we were moving faster, but maybe it was my imagination! The first attack had taken us just to the pontoon bridge. How far would we get this time? Hopefully to the bridge, but with lack of support from the rear, I just could not see it. It appeared the Germans had been slower opening up, but this had only been because they had been fetching more shit up to throw at us. Every foot of space seemed to be covered with some sort of weapon or other.

I thought the first attack had been bad, and the reception we got was bad, but this little lot was something else. It was obvious now that he had more weapons than the first time. Progress was painfully slow and casualties were now coming back in groups. Suddenly it was impossible to move and we were brought to a halt. It appeared to me that every inch of ground was getting plastered. We were forced to take cover where we could in shell holes and so on, as the undergrowth was of no use – this was well covered by heavy machine guns and they were pouring fire into every bit of undergrowth. Calls could be heard from all over for 'medics'. Around me, there were only about seven men that were able to walk; all the others appeared to be either badly wounded or dead. My brain was now becoming numb with the shocks of the explosions, the hellish noise all around us and I slid into a hole and watched the slaughter. The medics were terrific, we could see them dashing from one wounded man to another but noticed that they were getting terrible attention from the snipers, who were completely ignoring the Red Cross arm bands. Dirty bastards, must have been SS men. I didn't think the German paras would have acted that way.

The word came in again to retire, and this time it was 'Everyman for himself'. The colonel had said that owing to the fact that we were unable to defend ourselves, and that we were quickly becoming decimated, we were to get back to the pavilion area quickly.

It was with great relief that I got up to go back. I was with Harry Wren and Pat Welsh at the time. There was going to be no time to try anything fancy or be a hero, just rise and get the hell out of it and pray that none of your friends came to grief. The three of us set out together. For a while we were dodging from hole to hole but really getting nowhere. I could see all around us that others were doing the same and I was horrified to see that some of them were running directly into a hail of bullets or shells. If we continued we would obviously come to the same end if we did not stop.

We came to rest in a shell hole and decided to go straight for the pavilion. All went well at first, when we suddenly heard the horrible wail and howl of the multi-mortars, the 'Sobbing Sisters' of North Africa. They were bloody awful and very deadly, especially if you got caught out in the open. They fired anything up to twelve bombs at a time and the feeling was then, that if the first bastard didn't get you, one of the others would.

I found myself really moving now, tiredness gone for a minute. The first salvo went directly up ahead and landed away up front. I was hoping that they would alter their direction or we would be running at best, directly under their flight path, not a pleasant thought.

We were lying in a shell hole when Harry said, 'There is nothing like the *Sisters* to get the adrenalin going, is there?'

Pat said, 'Well, if the adrenalin smells like shit, I have my adrenalin going: I've shit myself.'

No shame to that, most of us at some time or another had this happen to them. Strange how some men can crack a joke at a bloody time like that. It was a wee bit quieter now, so we took a chance again, but it was not long before we heard that sodding 'wail' again (like a bloody dog in agony). We kept on running and suddenly I felt a hellish explosion – for a few seconds I felt the whole world had come to an end, and remember vaguely being flung high in the air. I must have been knocked out for a while, and when I came too I found that what I thought at first had been muddy water running down my face, was blood. I looked for Harry and Pat. There was no sign of Harry but I saw Pat lying about six yards away, his body like a wet rag-doll. I think every bone in his body was bust. *Christ, another mate gone. Will this slaughter never stop?*[24]

Harry must have been OK as there was no sign of him, thank God for that. I then found that my bloody legs would not carry me. I looked up and saw that it was about 40 yards to the pavilion: I would just have to crawl. It seemed to take a hell of a time to cover those 40 yards. I noticed a lot of action away to my right near some ruined houses, with a few men moving around some of the houses. I may be wrong, but I am sure I saw Sergeant Tommy Battle there with four or five men.[25] A good man, Tommy, I remembered him from way back in the Harwich Camp days. I suddenly found I was wandering a bit in my mind, I was thinking of all sorts of stupid things. I was confused; it must have been the belt on the head. I was thinking about school days. *My God, I'd better get a hold of myself.* I could not even remember what day it was.

Eventually I found myself getting pulled up into a trench. I found out afterwards that a medic came and cleaned up my head and I finished up in the hospital which was not too far away. I had about 15 stitches put into my head and got an anti-tetanus jab. I was asked if I was okay to go back outside, I said yes. Other than being a bit confused and having a rather sore head, I was okay. Anyway, the way things were going outside, Jerry was really mauling us, and still no sign of 2nd Army. It was possible that the enemy could over-run the hospital and we could all end up 'in the bag'. I would rather take my chances outside and there was every chance that there would be more deserving cases needing bed space than I. Not being brave, at that moment, I was just thinking of 'Number One'. I got outside and discovered most of the men had taken up defensive positions in and around the houses and at that moment I discovered that there were very few of my mates from 3rd Parachute Battalion around. I got pushed into a house and discovered one of the 'Old and Bold', Taffy Reece. Thank God there was someone I really knew. The rest were a mixed bag of South Staffs and Air Landing Brigade. Good men, no doubt about that, but the position we were in now, we were all inclined to look for well-known faces, men you had trained with for years and respected, who knew your ways and you knew theirs. It made hell of a difference in a tight corner. No doubt the other chaps thought the same. Right at that moment all I wanted was the company of my own kind. I took a walk outside with Taff, and we saw CSM Harry Callaghan. I asked him if he knew where all the lads were, and he said that the ones he knew were left were in another area close by, but not possible to get to at that moment. I was then informed that we had lost Lieutenant-Colonel Fitch, killed by mortar fire amongst many others either killed or wounded. Among the wounded was CSM Watson, known affectionately as 'C.B.', badly wounded in both legs.

We went back into the house and discovered that there was a real dumb bastard of a sergeant causing trouble for a couple of young lads who were suffering from shellshock. What they required was a bit of sympathy, not abuse from a twit like that. He looked to me like the type that would

---

24 Private Patrick W. Welsh, 3rd Parachute Battalion, 14424229, age 19. Found buried 100 yards west of Hartenstein.
25 3rd Parachute Battalion.

duck and run at the first sign of trouble; I'd met this type before. They could usually be heard, shouting and roaring, mostly to cover their own fear. We tried to get him to ease up, that we were going to need every fit man available, not mental wrecks. He described them as 'useless bastards' and he said there was nothing for them to fear now. What a bloody stupid statement to make. Show me a man that says he has no fear and I will show you a bloody idiot, and a dangerous one at that. I felt it my duty to report this, and the sergeant was removed to another squad. The two young men stayed, but sad to say one of them flipped. He ran out into the street screaming and was shot by a sniper. I just felt that he was pushed by a stupid sergeant to breaking point (by a bastard that should have known better). Before we were to leave that house we found out just how stupid that sergeant was. He had omitted to search the house. Taffy found a rear entrance to the house that led directly through the cellar up into the main part of the house. If Jerry had found that, we would have all been dead meat. Later that afternoon we moved further back to near the railway bridge over the lower road to Oosterbeek. Eventually we settled down for the night, guards posted at various points. Most of us tried to get some sleep or at least a rest. Not easy when you knew that just across the street, Jerry was ready to blow your bloody head off at the first sign of a wrong move on your part.

At dawn, we were standing to, ready to fight off any attack from the enemy. More enemy infantry had crept into our area during the night. Various attacks by tanks supported by infantry were made on our positions that day. One tank was knocked out by a 6-pounder anti-tank gun and 'brewed'; another tank with infantry scuttled away up some side streets. The problem was they left some infantry in nearby houses that were then in a position to fire almost directly into our house, which led us a hell of a dance. On instruction from a warrant officer, we set up a 3-inch mortar in the garden further back and were able, after getting a scratch crew together, to range in on the house opposite and try and flatten the top floors. Sad to say, but also around this time, the enemy were doing the same to us – problem was, he had the weapons, such as tanks, self-propelled guns and 88s and he started to systematically destroy each and every house, floor by floor.

The noise was bloody hideous and this was going on just a couple of doors away from us and coming our way. It was obvious that we would have to move. During a brief quiet period, we dashed out a few at a time down the street about 100 yards. It was a hellish feeling running down that road, waiting for the impact of a sniper's bullet in the back. Over the past few days, we had lost a great deal of men to these snipers. They were crack shots.

Polderweg, Rosande Polder Position, Oosterbeek Church
As the day went on, it was becoming obvious that the situation was becoming more desperate. We were eventually pulled further back, to take up positions near the wee kirk.[26] They had pulled everyone back into a tighter perimeter round the Hartenstein Park (Div HQ). I would say that the move was almost incident-free. However, we were all very tired and also bloody annoyed when we found out the positions they had given us to dig into. Many objections were raised over this and no bloody wonder. We had been told to dig in, away out on the open ground between the lower road, river side, south-east of the church. Where the original orders came from, Christ only knows, but we were all very concerned. Captain Dorrien-Smith issued the orders, where he got them is anyone's guess. There were threats that if we did not obey we would be charged. I could hear 'Rad' Radley's voice raised in anger. He got the same, answer that I got: 'Dig or get charged.' The last

26   Oosterbeek Laag church.

place I had been like this had been in North Africa, but there, there was no bloody choice. Here there was: in the trees, around the road, etc. It was to be proved later that we were right and this could have been done. I was in charge of a small group of men consisting of mainly South Staffs, a couple of 3rd Parachute Battalion and a few odd bods. We were eventually forced to obey orders (I had been told earlier that before he had been wounded, RSM J.C. Lord had made up some promotions and that I had gone up from corporal to sergeant, and I was not very taken with this.) We waited for dawn to break and all that would bring when the enemy saw this stupid bloody place we were in. I was wondering where all my mates were now. The last I had seen of them was away back at the St Elizabeth Hospital area, just prior to us being told to move back. Around that time the hospital and surrounding streets had been overrun and I think they were bunged in the 'bag'. I missed most 'Checkers' Chamberlain, 'Busty' Wiltshire, Frank Eccles, Fred Moughton and many more.

Thursday, 21st September
The inevitable happened. We came under a murderous hail of bullets and shells from the high ground, and it was plain to see now the horrible mess someone had put us in. We could not complain about the men protesting about the so-called defensive position we were now in. 'Defensive Position' – that's a bloody joke. The man that had issued these orders originally, must have done his training with the bloody Girl Guides. This was a fucking death trap, impossible to call it anything else. I was in a trench with Taffy Reece and we were trying to force ourselves down further, but as we lay there another problem came up – the sodding trench was beginning to fill with water, seeping up from the bottom and the sides of the trench. It had been raining heavily and it was now running in from the top.

Taffy said, 'If we don't get killed by a bloody shell, we'll fucking drown!'

The trench was filling up fast when I heard a voice shout, 'Whitelaw, get over here.'

What the hell does that bastard want now, I thought. I shouted, 'If you want me, come and get me.'

He came over and said, 'Can you drive?'

'Yes,' I replied.

'Well get up to Div HQ, collect a Jeep and load it with ammunition and get back down here as quick as you can. We should have collected it last night.'

I said, 'That's your bloody fault, not mine!'

'Any more of that, Whitelaw, and you'll be on a charge.' An awful lot more was said and he told me, 'You are on a charge; I've had enough of you, Whitelaw.' (The man that sent me up to Div HQ was Captain Dorrien-Smith; at that time we were all under the impression that he had stuck us in that impossible position. We should have known better; Dorrien-Smith had always shown good sense in the past. That was the reason there were so many angry words spoken that day.)

I moved off in the direction I thought was Div HQ. The air bursts around me were terrible and then I discovered a couple of sodding snipers were after me, the bullets were humming around like bloody bees. Soon I managed to reach the parkland and dug-out of a WO1 and told him my request.

'Where's your bloody helmet?' he asked. I pulled off my beret and showed him the plaster a medic had put on in place of the bandage. I told him I could not wear the helmet. 'By Christ, Whitelaw, I have heard some fancy excuses from you before, but this beats the lot!'

We loaded up a Jeep at the dump on the other side of the road. On parting, he warned me to be careful of snipers on the way back down. How the hell I ever got back to the kirk I will never know.

All the streets were almost impossible to drive on – rubble, bodies, etc., but after a big detour, and a couple or so bullets bouncing off the Jeep, I arrived at the kirk. I was told to unload the Jeep under a tree and go tell the men to come and collect. This I started to do but fortunately most of the men saw the Jeep arrive and some were on their way up.

I tried to get back to my own trench but after dodging around the side of a hedge and ditch with bullets zipping into the banking beside me, I began to think that they were using my arse as an aiming mark, they were getting so close. I heard a voice say, 'Come over here, mate, room for one more at the inn.' I nipped over the hedge and into a trench, and at the same time a heavy burst of fire came across the area. I looked over and saw a figure lying there near the sluice gates; it was Captain Dorrien-Smith, dead, shot through the throat. The enemy was shelling the area continuously, and we could hear the calls for the medics all the time.

I heard a voice shout out, 'Get the hell out of there! He is picking off each and every trench, and it'll soon be your turn. Go up the ditch and meet in the church. Tell the rest.' I didn't need to as they all heard it, and there was a big cheer. We slid over into the ditch, and as I looked back I saw the trench that we had just left get a direct hit. We made our way up the ditch. What a bloody smell was in there, but with a few bodies in there it was pretty rank. Soon we reached the head of the ditch and were directed into the church. There were a lot of men in there and I noticed Rad Radley and his mate trying to make a brew.

Major Lonsdale came in and there was silence, he was that type of man. Then he started to speak. 'So far we have had battle against good troops. Troops that are not up to our standard. We fought them in North Africa, Sicily and Italy and at times against odds. They were not good enough for us then and I am certain that they are not our match now. I shall expect you all to fight to the last round and above all, you will not give way. Shoot to kill … good luck.'

I looked up at him and thought, *What a man*. I'd first met him in North Africa and again in Sicily where he was in charge of a very unstable situation. In many ways, a situation such as we presently found ourselves. I had every faith in the man and I know every man who was there felt the same. If anyone could get us out of this shit, he could.

After a few minutes' rest, we were taken outside and placed in defensive positions. Lonsdale Force was to defend the south-east corner of the perimeter, and a very important position it was to become. Our positions were directly facing the lower road, where most of the enemy attacks would obviously come from.[27] If he could capture this corner of the perimeter, he would have cut off the whole of what was left of the 1st Airborne Division. Some of us dug in behind a row of houses in the gardens, on a slight rise. It gave us a fairly good all round view with the road to the east and also along in front of the church, etc.

I spotted a couple of guys standing starkers, changing their clothes, and it suddenly dawned on me what had happened. Rad had obviously spotted the kit-bag left in the Jeep I'd 'borrowed' at Div HQ, and decided to change into dry clean clobber. I wished I had used my brains and taken the contents myself. Then I remembered that I was supposed to have taken the Jeep back, with its contents, to Div HQ. I asked Sergeant Ivor Blakely about this and he said, 'Forget it.' (Brigadier Hackett, whose Jeep I'd borrowed, had been wounded around this time and I am sure would not have been bothered about a couple of shirts, etc. I was informed some time later that he had been making enquiries about both his Jeep and gear!) The Jeep, by the way, was now buggered; a direct hit on the arse-end had not improved its looks.

27 Benedendorpsweg.

Prominent among our officers in this area were Major Lonsdale, Major Bush, and a couple of other officers whose names I cannot remember. Another name that comes to mind readily is CSM Harry Callaghan MM, who was a great leader. He had a way with the men. He never seemed to need to roar and shout as some senior NCOs needed to do before they could get a response from the men; they respected him. There were other officers, but those three men seemed to stand out from the others, for their leadership and example they always showed. Harry was sometimes to be seen around the area wearing an old 'Lum-Hat'; it was found near the place we dug in. There was an undertaker's workshop there and in it was a hearse with a coffin and a Lum-Hat. He sometimes walked up and down the road, cheering the men up with his antics, also tempting Jerry to 'have a go'. This Lonsdale Force was made up with men from 1st, 3rd and 11th Parachute Battalions and men from the 2nd Battalion South Staffs, and a few other odd bods. By saying 'odd bods', I do not mean anything against them; they like the rest of us pulled their weight, and were great fighters. By 'odd' I meant that they had become separated from their own regiments and had joined us.

It was quite a job to organise the crews for mortars and Vickers machine guns, but we eventually got organised. Also amongst these, were men who proved themselves to be experts in the use of the PIAT. Thank God for that, because in the next few days there was to be many attacks by the enemy along this section of our perimeter, and frankly speaking, if it had not been for these men armed with PIATs, I doubt if we would have survived. The only other real weapon against the tanks was the 6-pounder anti-tank gun, and they proved to be good but a bit on the light side.[28] Many of the men were badly shellshocked, which was only to be expected. We were all filthy, dirty and very tired. Lack of food had also taken its toll. Unshaven, ashen-faced, with sunken red eyes, not a pretty sight. But it was not a beauty contest; we were there to do a job and most of the men realised that. Our hopes of getting to the bridge had long since gone and our only hope now was if the 2nd Army turned up, we might still be able to make it. But I, like many others, was trying to forget the 2nd Army; they had obviously run into trouble and had been held up. The thoughts of our men when we found out at the start of this operation of the long way they (2nd Army) had to come to get us out, was that the 'powers that be' had asked too much and expected too much from the 1st Airborne Division. The big mistakes were now becoming very clear and we were suffering for it. One thing for sure, the great 1st Parachute Brigade was no longer in existence. Only a handful of that great unit was left.

The day continued with many attacks, tanks, SPs and 88s and infantry. But I think the most demoralising thing was the snipers, they were bloody deadly. We could cope with the terrible shelling, but his sniping was getting us down. We never knew where they were going to strike from, that was the worst part. You never knew if your next move could be your last. Even at night he took lives, with the terrific sights he had on these weapons; in the flickering flames from burning buildings, he could still pick you off. I began to find it impossible to concentrate on other vital things that must be done. You could not even go to the toilet in peace. Many a man lost his life going for a shit. I remembered a few days back when the toilets were still working before Jerry turned off the water; there was this poor sod in the bog at the side of a house. Jerry started shelling this house he was in. The bog was completely demolished, and he was left sitting on the pan, out in the open. It looked very funny for us but not for him. He swore blind that he would never go to the bog again.

---

28 There were also several 17-pounder anti-tank guns in the church area. One from D Troop and two from P Troop.

Anyway, it was decided to do something about this sniping. We drew lots, and Harry and I got the job. There were a couple of fairly high trees in the area and it was thought that the enemy snipers were using them. We would have to go out and try and find them. As soon as darkness fell, we slipped out and crept up to the trees and lay down in the bushes to wait. We were too early, so I turned over on my back, resting and stared at the night skyline through the flickering flames from burning buildings. We could see figures moving around – theirs or ours? It turned out to be a wee bit creepy. But after a while I must have dozed off.

I found Harry shaking me, saying, 'There are a couple of the bastards coming our way.' The two of them went to the other tree and both climbed up. We went to the bottom of the tree and waited. With a sudden crash, one of them dropped down to the ground. We grabbed him and stuck a fighting knife at his throat. Harry went to the bottom of the tree and waited about a minute then fired a burst up through the branches from the Schmeisser he was carrying. A body came crashing down partway, and stuck; he was tied to the tree with a rope. Jerry did this all the time. The guy I held started to struggle and I thought of sticking him with my knife, but did not. Instead, I let him go and as I expected, he took off. I gave him about five yards, and then a couple of shots from the Sten and he fell. We could have taken him prisoner, but no bloody good to us. He was SS, probably one of the gits that had shot up our medics a couple of days ago. We could not have taken him back with us, no food for ourselves, and certainly none for bastards like him. We went back to our lines feeling a bit better, but as a sort of farewell gesture for the night, he sent over a few shells, air bursts, in the trees. Now there are two things you can do. Stand still making yourself a smaller target for the splinters to hit, or hit the deck. I hit the deck. Usually I stood up, and if possible stood near the base of a tree for protection. But this time I was wrong. On the deck, I could feel a hellish stinging around the back of my legs, small of my back and around the arse. I had copped quite a lot of small splinters and they were burning like hell. One of our medics was called, I think, George Thompson. He started digging them out, and got quite a lot out, but owing to very bad light, left about three. I was to feel those pieces, going over the river on the Monday night, they stung like hell. I settled down for the night, very weary and hungry.

As usual, around about dawn, the enemy attacked us with about fifty infantry and again our line held. Amazing when you think that there was now very few men in this part and if I remember correctly we had no casualties. But soon the bloody multi-barrelled mortars, the 'Sobbing Sisters', started along with the 88s. This was to continue for most of the day. We now had quite a few shellshocked cases and some were very bad. One poor sod could not even walk across from one place to another without throwing himself down on the ground; this was when there were no shells landing. He'd walk about eight yards and suddenly just hit the deck. His nervous system was completely gone.

Down on the lower road below us there lived a lady known as Bertha. She was a wonderful person who would do anything for the lads. She gave us food she could ill-afford such as bottled fruit and spuds. We now existed on little more than apples and such like. Some days there was some funny old stuff dished up, but edible. Today one of the lads came back with some spuds; another said they had got hold of some onions. Great, fried spuds and onions! At first we didn't notice the strange taste – anyway a strange taste was nothing new when you remembered the equipment that was used for cooking in, and we were never surprised at this. But I must admit, this was something else, the spuds were good, but oh Christ, the onions! We had a look at the 'onions' that were left. They looked okay, but on closer examination it was discovered that the 'onions' were tulip and daffodil bulbs. Strange to say, they were all eaten and some even came back for more. If I could lay my hands on a cup of tea I wasn't too bad and a fag was always welcome but they were all gone by now, so we had to make our own. When the tea had been used many times, it was dried off. We made it into fags by using toilet paper, bloody awful, but it took the edge off. How we did not die of lung cancer I will never know. What with the bloody awful weather we had to put up with, sodding rain, continually wet, plus those bloody awful fags, some of us had terrible awful coughs which seemed to come from the sole of the boots. With the filthy mess we were in and unshaven, we sometimes could not recognise each other, plus we were all getting very confused. I was at the stage I could not separate one attack from another, it was like the days now appeared to run into the other. Many men were at the end of their tether and some were getting very short-tempered, me included. Most of us just longed for the darkness but that did not always bring peace and quiet; it also had many dangers.

Today men coming in from a patrol found three men in a trench, an officer and two privates, Air Landing Brigade, just sitting in a trench and would not move for anyone. Then some of the men spotted a PIAT plus bombs lying in their trench. They were desperately need at our positions. We had been repeatedly attacked by tanks and the only weapon we had of any use was the PIAT, but now we were getting very short. Pleading for help, they just wanted to give up fighting. An officer back at our positions was informed about this and he went along, pleading, making threats. Eventually he jumped into the trench and got them out. He said the stench was terrible there; they had just obviously lain there and did their bodily functions where they were.

I saw many acts of bravery in this 'cauldron' during the last few days. No sooner was the enemy pushed back, than he came again and again. Many times it resulted in close hand-to-hand with bayonet or fighting knife. Some of the lads became very good with the bayonet. I preferred the knife but used both. We did not have much choice now, as our ammo was almost finished.

Harry gave me some bad news today. He told me that Ivor Blakely had been killed, a direct hit by an 88 shell. Sergeant Ivor Blakely, one of the best friends a man could have, gone! I did not have the guts to go over and look at him. Ivor and I had been in the Territorial KOSB before the war started, called up together, transferred to the Paras together in 1941 and had been together all the time … now he was gone. I was really broken-hearted now.[29] When would this bloody awful slaughter stop? How many more of these great young men were to die before this was to come to an end? The Germans had named this place *Der Hexenkessel*, the 'Witches' Cauldron'. No place on God's earth could have had a more appropriate name.

Saturday, 23rd September–Sunday, 24th September
I do not know how Saturday 23rd and Sunday 24th began or ended; no doubt like all the rest with a hateful shower of shells. All I can remember is that the place was becoming a hellish death trap, with all its hellish noise and the cries of the wounded. How did we survive? I do not know. Except that we had great leadership of Lonsdale, Bush and NCOs like Harry Callaghan to thank.

Monday 25th September
Dawn came and as I looked around all I could see were desperately weary men, tired beyond human endurance. Hungry, but most still full of fight. The first bit of news we got was that we

---

29   Sergeant Ivor Blakely, 3190715, aged 24, no known grave. According to the 5th Edition of the Roll of Honour, Sergeant Blakely was killed by a direct hit on his trench by a German stick grenade and buried in the Breman family garden on Benedendorpsweg 119.

were going to try and get out tonight across the river. At first, I felt a great sense of relief. But then as one we started to think, *Were all those young lives wasted?* Surely not, and yet here we were planning to leave it all behind. A great sorrow came over us, that all our attempts to get through to the bridge had failed. Our only pleasure came from the fact that we had prevented the Panzers from getting through from north to south. They had killed a lot of very fine young men. But by God, they knew they had been in a fight. It had all become a rather hopeless cause.

Some of us could not but help think that many bad mistakes had been made 'up top'. Communications had been very bad; at least that is what we are supposed to believe. I have grave doubts. More support from the RAF would have seen us through to success in most of those battles. If our fighter aircraft had performed like the Transport Supply Crews, we would have had all the support we required. Mistakes had been made, I suppose with hindsight, it is easy to say this, but if those 'up top' had been going into those actions with us, I am sure that there would have been a different set up, with more protection.

Around mid-morning there were heavy attacks pushing into our defences. Once again they were pushed back, this time with the assistance of our artillery from over the river which came to our aid just in time, landing their shells just in front of our positions, and clearing our trenches with nothing to spare. Whoever on our side was observing and directing fire was doing one hell of a job. Once again they were beaten back. Then it went quiet for a spell and even that was unnerving. All that was to be heard was a poor sod whimpering away in his dug-out, his nerve completely gone. From a humane point of view, we were getting out none too soon. The brain can just take so much. I honestly think that some of our heads, living many miles behind the lines, had been thinking of their own futures, when they were living in their caravans.

It had been suspected all morning that the enemy had been building up their forces to the north and east of us. So a couple of patrols were called for. Small patrols were all that was required, to probe and find out exactly what was going on, so all that was required was about four men on each. On ours were two men from 3rd Parachute Battalion and two others from, I think, South Staffs and myself. The 3rd Parachute Battalion men were Harry Wren and Bert and I. I do not know what the other patrol consisted of. The object was to find out the enemy strength, where exactly they were, and return. Our route was to take us directly up towards a line of trees, round a knocked-out Tiger, avoid it and proceed across a small piece of open ground into a housing estate. We got across the open ground when we heard engines up ahead. We reached the end of the street and around a corner we saw three Tigers motionless, just waiting. We moved off to check on the rest of the estate and discovered that this whole area had been very badly shelled, with only a few houses standing here; the rest were just a huge pile of rubble and heaps of bricks. It looked more like an abandoned brickworks. We covered all over the area and there was nothing to be found. We were on our way back, when we found ourselves almost caught out. We rounded a corner, and there in front of us stood two stationary self-propelled guns, one with a flamethrower. We ducked back into the cover of one of the few remaining walls standing. I sent two chaps to keep a look out on the Tigers, and the remaining three of us stayed behind the wall and waited for the SPs to move, hopefully towards our corner.

We sorted ourselves out some hand grenades and some Gammon bombs, etc. None too soon either, because they started up, and moved towards the corner of the street where we were. They moved slowly and reached the corner and stopped. We could hear their voices when they got out of one of them. Harry took a look and said that the crew on one was out and the other vehicle was just standing there.

We three popped up and lobbed most of the grenades over. Some went directly into the SP and others landed amongst the crew. There was a hellish explosion. We should have waited longer, but Bert wanted to be sure that the crew were all dead, and if not, to have a go with his Sten gun. He jumped up, head and shoulders well above the wall. Meantime, the flamethrower was obviously just waiting for such a thing, and he immediately let fly with that awful weapon. Poor Bert had no chance, and took the whole force of that burst of burning oil full in the face, chest and arms. He fell back on top of us, screaming and rolling around in agony. We looked over the wall carefully and saw the second SP scuttle away around the corner. The first one was 'brewing' and all the crew appeared to be dead. We tried to put out the flames with old curtains we found in the houses, but this was found to be impossible. For a while he lay there screaming, his body smouldering. He was in terrible agony, pleading with us to do something, but what? We tried a couple of tubes of morphine in his legs, with nowhere else to put it. But after a while it was obvious that this was not working. Right at this moment, I was praying that he would die, and he would be out of his misery. There was no way we could even think about getting him back to our lines. The shock, I think, would have killed him anyway and moving him would just cause more agony. In his quieter moments, he was pleading to be put out of his misery. But how the hell could you even consider this? I looked at his face, where his eyes had been – there were just holes; same with the nose, all gone, just two holes. The flesh had virtually melted all over his face and chest, and all his clothing had been burned off. The obvious reason this was so bad, was that he had been so close to them when the bloody thing had fired. Men do not as a rule get so close to them when they fire and we had just been very unlucky.

I will see that blackened face for the rest of my life.

I heard the other two saying, 'Do something, for Christ's sake.' But what could I do? No way could I take his life. But on the other hand, we could not leave him in his misery. Die he surely would. I asked the others and was told, 'You are the gaffer, mate; no one here to help you now.' Then I noticed he still had a Colt .45 in his holster; it was about the only thing that had not been touched. I took the .45 and slid it into his hand, said a few words, and we went away around the corner with Harry. After a few seconds we heard a shot, a .45. Harry went and took a look. He came back and said to me, 'It's all over Jock. He is out of his misery now.'

We buried him in a garden, at the corner of the street.

We then carried on with the rest of the patrol, but owing to the fact that we were getting heavily shelled by now, we cut it short. Other than the three Tiger tanks and one SP, there did not appear to be anything else in the area. We were obliged to come back through the positions of 10th Parachute Battalion and 156 Parachute Battalion, before getting back to our own lines very late. The shelling persisted throughout that day. Maybe at times the perimeter bent a little, but it never broke.

I could not get peace of mind, and during a quiet spell, I found my way down to the church. Frankly speaking, I was looking for a way out. It was strangely quiet in there at that moment. Shelling was still going on around the area, but I felt an atmosphere of peace. I tried to come to terms with myself. That was not easy. I asked for forgiveness, but that does not come easy to a man that was never very religious, ever. What I kept asking myself was that, in my tired state of mind and very confused, would I have committed that act if I had been fresh, fit, and thinking straight? Sometimes I think I will never know. I left the wee kirk feeling a bit more sane and calmer.

The rest of the day, as far as I was concerned, was spent staggering from one crisis to another. Never had I wished so much for darkness to come and with the darkness, came the thought that with luck we may get out of this hell-hole.

At around 2200 hours the top part of the perimeter started to move. The first units were KOSB, 10th, 156 Parachute Battalions, followed by the 21st Independent Parachute Company and the others furthest away and so on, until it came to our turn. Meantime, we were very conscious of the fact that it was our prime duty to stem any attack from the enemy through our section. If they got through now, we were all finished. At long last, with our boots wrapped up in old clothes, we tucked in behind the tail of a very long queue, trying to follow a white tape put up earlier by the glider pilots. As usual it was pouring with rain, but for once we did not mind; it helped to deaden the sounds, but did little for morale.

We slowly made our way down through the polder. There was a lot of shelling going on, and there were plenty of halts with men getting wounded. Jerry was belting hell out of this route and we wondered if he had found out we were on the way over the river. Instructions had been given that walking wounded could be helped, but others must be left. I felt a pair of hands grab my leg, and I looked down and on examination of this man, found that his leg was virtually hanging off. I could only make him as comfortable as possible. That was not easy in the rain and mud.

Monday 25th September–Tuesday 26th September
By now it was obvious that Jerry had found the range to both river banks and the river itself and was blowing hell out of anything he saw, and even in this poor light we could see explosions in the middle of the river. Boats were getting swamped, and being reduced in numbers. I was watching closely what was happening. It would soon be time to make a decision. After a very long wait, in which some men panicked and tried to jump the queue and were brought down by rugby tackles and put back in line, I finally reached the river bank. It was about 0430–0530 hours and there were quite a few men still milling around the banks desperately trying to find a way out. What to do? Not many choices to make. Try for a boat, or swim! I had been watching other blokes trying both methods and decided to try and swim. I did not like the look of the terrible current in the middle. I stripped off down to my underpants and slung everything else into the river, including a Mauser sniper rifle, which I had picked up a few days ago. I had used it to good effect, too. I even had the stupid idea of taking it back, but thought that I would hate to be bloody drowned by carrying a ruddy German weapon.

I waited on the bank for the opportunity to judge the time to enter the water, preferably the same time as a boat leaving, and hopefully get a tow. I slid into the river: by Christ, it was cold! And I started swimming. I had just reached the very bad bit in the middle and I felt the terrible current grab me and for a minute thought that I had made a hellish mistake. But just with that, I heard this boat coming alongside me, being paddled by rifle butts. As it passed me I reached the rear of the boat and hung on; I'd made it. But one guy on board had other ideas and thought I was trying to come on board, and belted me over my fingers with his rifle butt; I will always remember that man's face. Naturally, I let go and felt the full force of the current grab me and thought, *This is it*. Fortunately, a sergeant on board saw what had happened and let the boat come alongside, and again I got a hold. The current was hellish and I realised that I could never have swum this bloody river on my own. Maybe under normal circumstances I could have made it. But never after those nine very tiring days.

I was happy when the boat came to a rest near the bank. Many hands helped me through the heavy mud and up the side and onto the grass. The sergeant came over and introduced himself as Donny. I thanked him for saving my life. All the men appeared to be making for Driel, but Donny suggested that owing to the heavy shelling, we bypass Driel and make for the main road. He had a small army map giving basic roads and so on, so I agreed. I didn't fancy getting knocked out at

Driel, after enduring those hellish days on the other side. He pointed out the route he proposed, and we set off. Progress was very slow and we still had some water to get over and the ground was very heavy and marshy. I wasn't sure exactly where the enemy were on this side, so we decided to keep clear of Elst away to our left. After a very long walk, we came to a ridge, and on top of the ridge was the road we had been looking for. We rested awhile and looked back, and away in the distance we could see all the smoke and flames: Oosterbeek and Arnhem were burning.

Across the road was a side road and lying in a hollow were a few black-coloured buildings, so we decided to go there for help. As we approached, we saw an elderly couple standing at the door. We didn't have to explain who or what we were; they knew where we had come from. We got washed and were given lovely black coffee. What little clothing we had was dried for us and we sat down beside a big log fire, drinking big glasses of 'Jenever'. Within a few minutes we were both sound asleep. That would have been around 0700 hours and we did not come to until 1500 hours, feeling very much better. We then had more coffee with bread and stuff that looked like porridge. We thanked them for their kindness and went back to the main road where we soon heard an army three-tonner lorry coming, looking for stragglers. We climbed aboard and were taken to a school in Nijmegen, where, believe it or not, we were asked, 'Where the bloody hell have you two been? You should have been here hours ago.' This from a jumped-up little lieutenant, strutting around like a bloody tailor's dummy.

I told him, 'We've just been for a swim in the Rhine, just for the hell of it.'

We were then taken away and given a meal, our clothing was washed and we had a shave. There were a few others there, some wounded, but no one I knew. Soon we were put on to trucks and sent down the road to Louvain, where we were transported back to the UK.

Post-Arnhem

I got back to Spalding with a very heavy heart. I drew gear from the stores and then went back to our Nissen huts. That for me was one terrible shock, seeing all those empty beds. In my hut there was only six men left. The other hut also had the Mortar Platoon which normally held 35 men, and it was totally empty. It was then that I really broke down and shed quite a few tears. At that moment, everything that had happened felt just like a very bad dream.

How and why I had been spared, and all these great men had been taken?

What was obvious to me now was that every day was to be a bonus. Anyone that came out of that hideous place was living on borrowed time.

Lance Corporal B.J.G. 'Bert' Stidson, B Company, 3rd Parachute Battalion, 1st Parachute Brigade

Sunday, 17th September

Sunday, we arose at a ghastly hour in the morning, queued up for breakfast and then attired ourselves ready for embussing. (During harvesting time I'd injured my arm and had to report to the medical officer and he'd ordered me to hospital. Instead of remaining in the medical inspection room, I went back to the platoon and discussed it, and a plan was formed – I hid. The camp was being searched for me but I was sitting in the Odeon Cinema. I think the film was on three times before I returned at night to the platoon. The camp search had been abandoned, so we all departed to the canteen for a farewell drink.) Having only one useful arm, my mates stowed my

Polderweg–Rosande Polder positions. 20th–21st September 1944. The positions were in the open (a lot more exposed in 1944) facing east, on the other side of the bank in the photograph along the line of the willow tree (which were trees in 1944) in the middle of the picture running north towards the Benedendorpsweg, upon which are the houses in the background. Heavy German fire came from the Benedendorpsweg on the extreme right of the picture. Corporal Alex Whitelaw, HQ Company, 3rd Parachute Battalion, 1st Parachute Brigade, writes: 'We had been told to dig in, away out on the open ground between the lower road, river side, south-east of the church. Where the original orders came from, Christ only knows, but we were all very concerned. Captain Dorrien-Smith issued the orders but where he got them is anyone's guess. There were threats that if we did not obey we would be charged.' (Photo: Author, 1984)

kit in a 'universal' kitbag and I tied it on my leg; a slip knot would allow me to release it during my descent, and let it dangle on a length of rope, just as the issued ones did. Yes, even the platoon officer was in on it and knew I was determined to go. We embussed and arrived at Saltby where all the Dakotas were waiting. We emplaned and then and then took off. We saw part of the vast armada forming up and fighters darting here and there. *Over Holland – red light – GO*. It was 1400 hours, Sunday 17th September and it was a glorious day and I floated gently down to earth amidst hundreds of others. I slipped my kitbag and that was the last I saw of it.

On landing, I went towards the RV and on the way found some spare kit including a Sten gun, and there I met an old Dutch granddad with his two granddaughters. They were very frightened; however, they eventually understood we were friendly and I gave the children some sweets. I then continued to the RV. We formed up, and then we were on our way via the middle road into Arnhem. Dutch people were standing along the roadside and I remember an old lady singing 'Tipperary' with tears of joy streaming down her cheeks. Our advance was uneventful for a while and then some high-ranking German officers in their staff car appeared but were quickly disposed of. We continued onwards and then met some opposition from 88s, I think, astride the road. We eventually deployed and took over a hotel, which was the German officers' mess: tables all set for dinner.[30] Sporadic firing went on all night and a few skirmishes as we probed around the roads etc, but by morning we were all ready to proceed to Arnhem.

30   Park Hotel Hartenstein, German Army Group B, HQ.

Monday, 18th September

We were now doing house to house clearance on our way in. In one house, I remember vividly, there was a wonderful smell of fried breakfast and, making my way to the kitchen, there it was, still cooking on the stove top. I thought, *What a lovely nosh-up*, and just then Sergeant 'Busty' Walker walked in and said, 'Watch out, Bert, the stairs.' Naturally, I took appropriate action and after a few minutes realised that there wasn't anyone there and, neither was the nosh, but Busty looked happy. Just after this incident whilst proceeding further along the road, one side of which were fields with very tall grass growing, I spotted a chap getting away. Along with the platoon CO, Jimmy, we went after him and spotted him crawling through the long grass but his bum was sticking up and so it was at this splendid target I fired. It was a good hit alright but Jimmy was slightly offended; he thought it was a bit off shooting chaps up the bum – *ungentlemanly, what!*[31]

By now we were on the outskirts of Arnhem, near the post office where we met some Dutch Underground men identifiable by their armbands. We took the lower road, beside the river, towards the bridge: on our left flank was a high bank and it was here we were trapped by artillery being fired across the river and we couldn't advance any further. We had to get out of this somehow. It was a slaughter but at moments like this there is always someone who comes to the fore and, in this instance, it was 'Dolly' Smith, B Company second-in-command, and under his orders and bullying, we all got off the lower road, up the bank to the higher road and into the rather elegant houses across from the bank. The house I went in was occupied at the time by an elderly couple and a young girl of about 15 to 16 years old; the elderly couple were composed but the young girl was in a state of panic and I eventually helped her to scale the rear garden wall – no back door there – into a narrow back lane. Thinking back now, she was quite a lovely armful as I lifted her over the wall, and very attractive. Inside the house we took up positions, mainly on the first floor, and in the attic which was above the third floor. A Bren gun was positioned which, after removing some tiles, commanded a view of the rear where other large houses overlooked ours and where there was a very active sniper.

A strange assortment of chaps were inside and this included Major 'Pete' Waddy, OC B Company and believe it or not, General Urquhart with his aide. What he was doing with us, none of us could fathom out; we assumed he would be with his HQ, controlling our little scrap.[32] It wasn't long before German troops came along the road, and to everyone's amazement, they were marching as if on a normal parade. This was too good to miss and having a Bren gun on the front balcony of the first floor we let go at them and scored a big success before they decided to scarper. Now, as if that first time wasn't enough for them, they reformed and came marching down again, so it was decided to change Bren gunners each time to see who got the most hits; strangely enough, they did this several times with consequent losses. At last what we feared happened. Tanks came and began to systematically blast away at the houses. One tank stopped almost below the balcony and Major Pete made up a large gammon bomb, then turned to the general and said, 'Would you like to throw this, Sir?' (He took longer to say it than most because he stammered.)

'No,' replied the general, 'It would be best if you did, Pete.' Pete then threw it and it landed on the rear of the tank. A tremendous explosion followed which blew in the windows and some doors. As for the tank, it turned and trundled up off back up the street. We were getting a lot of bother

---

31 Lieutenant James Arthur Stacey Cleminson, i/c No. 5 Platoon, B Company, 3rd Parachute Battalion.
32 Brigadier G.W. Lathbury, 1st Parachute Brigade, & Captain W.A. Willie Taylor, IO, 1st Parachute Brigade.

from the snipers and machine gun fire at the back. We eventually got one and his body fell forward through the window and hung half out.

Not having heard our Bren in the attic for a while, I went up and found that the gunner (one of our regimental police) had been killed, presumably by the sniper. Pete, our company CO, decided to go out and do something about the sniper. (He was sometimes referred to as 'Cowboy Pete' because he carried two pistols.) He was a great soldier and excellent company commander and one of 'the lads'. (Here I must digress somewhat from the story and relate the fact that when we had a company piss-up, Pete had 'Pete's Party Song', and everyone had to contribute. It went as follows, and he didn't stammer: *Rule Britannia, marmalade and jam, Chinese cracker up yer arsehole, Bang, Bang, Bang.*) Pete didn't return and we carried on sporadic firing until tanks eventually made it impossible, so out the back we went, over the garden wall to find a safer place.[33]

We got out over the back wall into a lane and made our way to some smaller terraced houses, rather like the small rows of houses at home, and on the way, we passed through a small courtyard: it was here that we were mortared. We all ducked into the houses surrounding the yard with the exception of the general. He was running up and down looking bewildered – he did seem rather tired and anxious. His aide eventually got him to safety. One man was wounded; I believe he was a sapper. After the mortaring had ceased, we made further progress, presumably to link up with the brigade. However, again we got into a house and here we waited until nightfall. During the late evening, we lined up through the passageway of the house and the stairs. In the lead was the general and his aide and one of our officers, Cleminson, I think was his name. After waiting what seemed hours, it was discovered that the front part of the queue had scarpered and the remainder of us then decided to wait till daybreak.

Tuesday, 19th September
During the night we had some close calls but came through intact and at last it was daybreak. Most of the houses had cellars and the Dutch people were great ones for pickling all sorts of fruit and veg, so we foraged in the cellar for by now we were hungry. Whilst doing this I peered through a vent which was just above pavement level and flashing by were the bottom legs adorned with ammo boots and 'anklets web'; great stuff, it could only be our lot, polished boots and all. We got out and found it was either the South Staffs or 11th Battalion coming into town. Our job now was to join with the rest of the 3rd and we made our way back to a wood near the edge of the town where they were. Whilst there, under constant fire, it was decided to withdraw into a tighter perimeter, towards Oosterbeek. This was accomplished and again there were lots of little battles taking place in and around the houses.

The position we took up was on the rear lawn of a large house. The back of the lawn was on top of a steep bank; behind us the land flattened out and led towards the river.[34] On the left as you faced it was the partly demolished railway bridge. By this time everybody was practically out of ammunition. We didn't know about the supply drops going astray; however, somehow,

---

33 General Urquhart witnessed Major Waddy's death. 'I saw him go down the steps of the house, wondering what he was about; then, as he was crossing the small square of lawn, a mortar exploded and he fell. He was the only soldier I ever saw killed solely by blast and when they picked him up there was not a single mark on him. He was buried in the garden where he had fallen.' Major General R.E. Urquhart, *Arnhem* (London: White Lion Publishers, 1973) page 62. Major A.P.H. Waddy, 95501, aged 25, was killed by the blast from a mortar bomb outside the house at No. 134, Utrechtseweg around 1430 hours Monday 18th September.
34 Benedendorpsweg station/Oosterbeek Laag viaduct area.

somewhere, somebody got some to us. Here, facing this large lawn, it was decided to withdraw towards the river and so the move was made. 'Smiley' Burnett and I were left with the Bren gun to cover. After some considerable time I said to Smiley, 'I think they've all gone,' and decided to have a look around. The lawn by this time was occupied by the Jerry who we had been constantly firing at. I was right. We were alone and, whilst I was thinking of the next move for me and Smiley, a lone figure appeared as if from nowhere. What more can you expect of a man of God? Yes, it was the padre who led us to the rest of the unit.

Wednesday, 20th September–Thursday, 21st September
Polderweg–Rosande Polder Position

Now here was a situation, on a level plain, a drainage system cutting through it, small stunted trees dotted here and there, and ringed around by high ground with the river at the back. Dig in, yes, but with what? Bayonets and knives? Tom[35] and I, with two others, dug a trench for the four of us just above the ditch. To our right were Jimmy James[36] and Bert and to our left was Harry Whitehead. On the side of the ditch, old Stanley dug a place but it was exposed on one side. Well, there were others around but I can't remember all of them by name. There we were watching tanks set up on the high ground, and we were being constantly mortared but never did their infantry attempt to close with us. The day was spent there and during the morning we saw Harry's helmet go up in the air after a direct hit on his trench; shortly after, Jimmy's trench was hit and after a long wait, he suddenly started shouting out and although we answered, he still kept on.

I said to Tom, 'I'll go over and have a shifty.' I got there and what had happened was that the mortar had landed on top of his trench, stunned him and left him completely deaf. I was able to convey to him what was happening still and he made his way down to the ditch to recce a way out for all of us. Whilst this was going on, Stan had been hit. He was calling out but by now, we couldn't move around much. Tom shouted to him to lie down and said, 'We'll get there soon,' and Stan shouted, 'OK, I know you won't let me down.' His favourite song was 'Paper Doll', and this was what we heard next from him, sung loud and clear, better than he had ever done … and then, silence. When we eventually got to him we saw that he had never stood a chance, even if we could have got him out.[37]

Whilst in this position, for the first time we were able to see the aircraft support. Typhoons were flying up and down the river shooting up, presumably, gun emplacements; the steady old workhorses, Dakotas, came flying in with supplies. What a sight to watch them flying, keeping steadily on their course, getting the hell shot out of them but not deviating one iota. They didn't realise that we weren't where they dropped the supplies and we couldn't understand why they gave it all to the enemy, so arises bitterness at the time, which could only have been resolved if each of us had known that wireless communication was practically non-existent – and on top of that, the Germans were trying out our ground-to-air signal codes on the original DZs. Oh for walkie-talkies that our policemen use nowadays.

The sporadic action continued with us being mortared and shelled, the latter by tanks that were now on the high ground looking down on us. We were more or less impotent at this stage

---

35   Lance Corporal T. Halley-Frame.
36   Lieutenant E.A. James, CO 4 Platoon.
37   Lance Corporal Walter H. Stanley, 5121459; aged 34. No known grave. Probably buried in his trench on the polder.

because their infantry would not close and fight, and who could blame them! Now a strange thing occurred. Jimmy James appeared out of the ditch, still deaf. However, he had been through the ditch and contacted Captain Dorrien-Smith, Dolly as he was affectionately known. He and Dolly had organised the route out of this rather confined 'shooting gallery' area. Through the ditch, duck under the sluice gate, into a type of sink area about six to eight feet deep, and then on down to a part which led up to Oosterbeek church. Gradually we all got out; Tom and I followed with Smiley Burnett, the Bren gunner I mentioned previously. When it came to our turn to duck under the sluice gate, it was difficult to say the least because your kit was enclosed and got hooked up on the top of about three inch gap, so it meant that you had to have sufficient breath or a mouthful of sewage. Smiley and the Bren were stuck, so we freed the gun quickly and he got out. The other side of the gate was some hard concrete standing and then the sink. On the opposite bank was Dolly and Staff Sergeant Callaghan. Dolly and him were throwing a rope across to assist all of us in crossing quickly. Smiley dropped the Bren and as far as I recall it is still there in the sludge at the bottom of the sink. Making our way along the ditch we arrived at the 'dis-em-ditching' spot and then to the church. We entered the church through the side door. Inside, the main door was to the right and the altar to the left, a pulpit in front of the altar and above to the rear, a gallery. Tom and I occupied a pew to the right, facing the pulpit. Being soaking wet and smelling a bit, I decided to go on the scrounge; luckily just outside the church I found some kit which had been dumped, British, and I helped myself. I apologise to anyone who reads this in case it was theirs. DR boots and socks for myself, trousers and some underwear for Tom, into which we both changed whilst the remnants of our division were assembling.

Dickie Lonsdale arrived. He was our new boss and our group of remnants were named the Lonsdale Force. Dickie got into the pulpit and gave us all the latest, split us into fighting groups and assigned positions with a tight perimeter which, on the whole was part of the Hartenstein perimeter. We left the church in our individual groups and took up our position on what was to be a long, drawn-out, bone-wearying fight to the end.

Our particular commander was Lieutenant Cleminson. There was a large open space, rough ground, with terraced houses running to the left as we faced outwards, facing on to a road, and houses the other side. To the right, the road was unmade. The corner house we occupied, and our chef, 'Cordon Bleu' (of course) was Cory who set up his mobile cooking equipment.[38] Trenches were dug on the edge of the rough ground running inwards at a right angle from the house. Tom and I were in one facing a tree and to this spot came a most remarkable and brave man, Major Cain I believe his name was. Lieutenant Cleminson was in the next trench and others spread further around. Their trenches were only protection from mortaring, shelling, etc. The task we had, other than the inevitable skirmishes, was patrolling the houses between ourselves, and to the north, the pilots of the glider units that had been saved. So the three of us, Tom, Cory and I patrolled, two hours out, four hours in, continuously till the finale. Cory, who besides doing what he could as regards scrounging grub and brewing up for all of us, did his share of patrols as well. Same as usual, more shelling and mortaring and now some Polish joined us with an artillery piece, 75mm I think, and it was placed in the rough ground.[39] The Polish paras were stationed in the house on the corner with 'Cory's take-away' downstairs, and I positioned them on the upper floors.

---

38   Lance Corporal Alf 'Cory' Farnfield.
39   6-pounder anti-tank gun.

By now all of us were feeling tired. We had been going now for four days and on no occasion did anyone get to sleep; that is, we catnapped, dozed for a few minutes and then alerted again. Now the armour began to move in, first SPs then tanks. Their approach was from the rear, on the river side and where we were positioned to our rear top-left corner. Here Major Cain excelled. He took them on with a PIAT and knocked some out or drove them off and somehow, he managed to get ammo and then go out stalking them on his own. His outstanding feat, which most of us saw but he undoubtedly did others without an audience, was to gather up some troops to man the 75mm which had been deserted, and have it loaded and fired at an SP. All this was performed whilst the SP was spraying all the open ground with automatic fire; a very brave man indeed. The rest of the day continued with shelling, mortaring, machine gun fire and continuous patrols, and the night was the same.

Thursday, 21st September

Was it? The days and nights were all running into one. It was tiredness that was just as big an enemy as them facing us. Little or no sleep now since the landing and in the midst of skirmishes, quite a few dozed off for a few minutes before coming-to with a start. During one blast of shelling, I got blown into a trench on top of Lieutenant Cleminson. He shouted and had a right to, as he had been wounded. During the lull I helped him out of the trench and he made his way to the RAP and then the church. Rumours were rife that relief was near at hand but the perimeter was being squeezed tighter by the relentless pressure of enemy armour. During this night I almost copped it from the glider pilots who mistook me for a Jerry due to me wearing DR boots. The boots were soon discarded and I found a pair of ammos and felt much safer. Cory during this time had got a rabbit from somewhere and made a magnificent stew in an old tin bath. Not much, but marvellous nevertheless.

Friday, 22nd September–Monday, 25th September

So it went on and on into Saturday and Sunday, the eighth day. Had we really been going that long? Still we were holding out but the numbers were dwindling daily. Some of the Dorsets got across, a company I think, but didn't have much luck and I believe most of them landed 'in the bag'. It was Monday 25th and word had been given for us to pull out – difficult, yes, but 'impossible' was a word that was never used. During the night, a route was marked from our positions to a point on the river by the glider pilot unit using white tape. So, silently carrying our arms but with little ammo, we slowly made or way to the river where XXX Corps had got a couple of assault boats across. It must be understood that although we could swim the river it was wide with a very fast current and all of us were tired, so boats were necessary. Getting to the river took a long time but everyone was orderly and quiet until dawn and then panic by a few who rushed the boat (not British). Order was restored by an officer brandishing his pistol threatening to shoot; however, the boat was sunk. With the light, the order was given for every man for himself and then from there quite a few went to their death or captivity. Was it worth it? Yes.

Arnhem, Never Alone
Tom and I fought side by side but not alone
Remember the battle how bravely men died, they weren't alone
Days and nights, all fought, all tired, never alone
So to the end, how we strived,
They tempted, they tested, oh how they tried
But in the end, we who survived, didn't walk alone.

Polderweg–Rosande Polder positions. Thursday, 21st September. Beek Leigraaf. Sluice gate looking east through which 1st and 3rd Parachute Battalions withdrew from their exposed positions on the polder to avoid the heavy German fire. Moving through the tunnel laden with weapons and equipment necessitated going under the gate and the water. Lance Corporal Bert Stidson, B Company, 3rd Parachute Battalion, 1st Parachute Brigade, writes: 'When it came to our turn to duck under the sluice gate, difficult to say the least because your kit was enclosed and got hooked up on the top of about three-inch gap, so meant that you had to have sufficient breath or a mouthful of sewage, Smiley and the Bren were stuck, so we freed the gun quickly and he got out. The other side of the gate was some hard concrete standing and then the sink. On the opposite bank was Dolly and Staff Sergeant Callaghan. Dolly and him were throwing a rope across to assist all of us in crossing quickly. Smiley dropped the Bren and as far as I recall it is still there in the sludge at the bottom of the sink.'[40] Private Fred Radley, Signaller, A Company, 3rd Parachute Battalion, 1st Parachute Brigade, writes: 'I was leading at this point and as it was impossible to leave the ditch, I went *through* the bridge, through because the water passed under it via a pipe, about three feet in diameter and about eighteen feet long. I slid along it and found the other end was blocked by a sort of sluice gate that went down to within two inches of the top of the water.' (Photo: Author, 1984)

40 Bert Stidson's account of a three-inch gap in the sluice can be explained if one looks closely at the high water mark on the sluice brickwork.

Lance Corporal Tom Halley-Frame, B Company, 3rd Parachute Battalion, 1st Parachute Brigade

Sunday, 17th September

> Having left the Drop Zone 'X', 3rd Parachute Battalion, headed by B Company moved east via Heelsum along the Utrechtseweg.

We were advancing along the road, a cobbled one if I remember, on the left side. On our right we had trees and undergrowth and the kerbside had trees along it at intervals. As we were proceeding at a steady pace, an enemy armoured car came advancing towards us, firing a constant stream of fire. At that moment a Jeep came belting along the road towing a 6-pounder anti-tank gun, from our rear. I was standing behind one of the trees when the Jeep screeched to a halt about ten yards in front of me, but before the crew had time to get out, the armoured car shot up and killed the crew, then the armoured car withdrew and that was when this chap, Private Crowther, came walking along as calm as you like, urging us all on. He seemed immune to any enemy fire. He just kept on his feet urging everybody on. He was cool and calm and I must say he was a tower of strength, and he still wore his red beret. (I'm sure he was a B Company chap; well, he was there, no doubt about it. I knew his name, I believe he was one of the last intakes to join the battalion; he was a North Country chap, I know, but I don't remember seeing him anymore after that.)

Wolfhezerweg/Utrechtseweg Crossroads Junction

I remember the German staff car incident quite well, although I wasn't at the exact spot when it was shot up. I arrived just after to see the car and bodies hanging out of the front doors. Presumably the driver and front passenger were trying to get out in a hurry, and there were a couple of bodies in the back seat.

Monday, 18th September

> During the morning advance just west of St Elizabeth Hospital, B Company and Battalion HQ became separated from the rest of the battalion and moved in to six houses until HQ Company and A Company arrived mid-afternoon.

About the houses occupied by B Company, as far as I can remember – the section I was with occupied a house where we took up positions in an upstairs room and had a Bren gun poking out of the window, which was a long window opening out on to a small balcony with iron railings. We laid up for a while, keeping watch and the next thing we saw were German troops advancing up the road, but we lay dormant. The Dutch occupant of the house told us we were surrounded by Germans; he invited us to go down in the cellar where his family were hiding. We did this, about six of us, and stayed for God knows how long until we decided to creep out and look around and discovered we were with our own troops again, and that's about the only time we occupied any houses until we eventually pulled out to Oosterbeek church. I have no idea what happened to Lieutenant Hill.[41] The only officers I can remember being with us at all times was my own platoon officer, Lieutenant James, and Captain Dolly Smith.

---

41 Lieutenant Gordon T. Hill, 182422, age 26, KIA 18th September 1944.

Tuesday, 19th September
Dawn to Mid-afternoon

Well, to carry on with the advance we passed through the residential area where we had laid up and passed by the St Elizabeth Hospital, eventually coming out on to the road which runs along by the side of the river. We preceded along the road with houses on our right.[42] On our left, there was a bank which had a road running along the top.[43] We came to a stop as the houses ended and we came into view of the river and also enemy troops on the far bank of the Rhine, who immediately fired at us as we attempted to carry on to get to the bridge, but alas that's where our attempt failed. We pulled back and found ourselves somewhere near the railway lines. Here we found a brick building empty – it looked like a stores hut. We, about a dozen of us, were told to man the windows by Sergeant Busty Higgins (who had taken charge of us by then) who kindly told us we were to fight to the last as this seemed to be our lot. We took up defensive positions, when there seemed to be a lull, whereupon Busty shouted out, 'Come on, lads, let's go,' so out we shot and proceeded to pull back. From then on it seemed as if we were pulling back all the while.

Wednesday, 20th September–Thursday, 21st September
Polderweg–Rosande Polder Position

We had to dig in beneath a line of trees which ran along the top of a fairly wide and deep ditch which had sloping sides. In the trench on our right was Lieutenant James, 4 Platoon Commander and his batman, Bert Felton. A tree near their trench was hit by a shell causing the blast to knock Lieutenant James unconscious and I presume his batman, although I'm not certain. Lieutenant James apparently regained consciousness and realising the blast had deafened him, called out that if anyone was about, to throw a stone over towards him, which we did. So the only communication between us was that when we received any orders or questions we had to toss over some stones. I'm glad to say he and his batman managed to pull out with us. (I never saw Lieutenant James afterwards but I know he survived as I saw him after the war in the film, '*Theirs is the Glory*', but his batman, I was told, got killed trying to get across the Rhine.[44] On our left in a trench was a Corporal Harry Whitehead who, as I was told later, was killed by having a mortar bomb land in his trench.[45] One of the lads, Lance Corporal Walter 'Stan' Stanley, dug in on the slope of the opposite side bank, consequently having no cover to his rear. The tanks firing at us blasted at the trees, one of the blasts catching Stan and seriously injuring him. The only communication we had between ourselves was shouting above the din, when we heard a shout to dive into the ditch when it was possible, which we did. Poor Stan started singing (as he always did in the pubs). One of the lads managed to get him on his back to carry him out when another blast caught him (Stan) and finished him off. We proceeded along this ditch until we came to a footbridge which had a sort of sluice gate down. This meant to get to the other side, we had to duck down in the mud and slime to come up on the other side to be faced with what I can only describe as a large cess pit. On the far bank our second-in-command, Captain Dorrien-Smith, sat and warned us not to cross as there was no known depth, whereupon he threw a parachute harness still attached to the rigging

---

42 Utrechtseweg into Onderlangs.
43 Utrechtseweg into Utrechtsestraat.
44 Private Albert Felton, 2082298, aged 24. No known grave.
45 Corporal Harold J. Whitehead, 6468248, aged 27. Found buried in the Ter Horst family garden, Benedendorpsweg.

lines and dragged us over one at a time and getting us all safely across. This was one of the finest actions I ever saw at Arnhem. We proceeded along the ditch until we eventually managed to get into the church all covered in mud, just before Major Lonsdale got up into the pulpit and gave his speech and orders. A little while after, Sergeant Callaghan came over to us with tears in his eyes saying that Dolly (Captain Dorrien-Smith's nickname) had been killed; his own words were that, after seeing us all safely across, Dolly stood up and a sniper caught him in the neck, killing him.

Thursday, 1530 hours
After arriving at the church and cleaning up a little, we were given our defensive positions. The group I was with were all B Company, 3rd Battalion. We occupied a farm house from which we did patrol work to some far houses and which were also patrolled by Jerry. At the farm, there were several tame rabbits in hutches, some loose. In the cellar of the house we found a box of potatoes and several jars of preserved vegetables (beans, peas, etc) – guess what? Rabbit stew. This was left to our capable cook, Lance Corporal Alf 'Cory' Farnfield; he was the chap who knocked off the officer's 'pet' rabbit when ours ran out.[46]

Patrols were carried out with me (Lance Corporal) and my pal Lance Corporal Bert Stidson as patrol commanders, having no senior ranks with us. We took it in turns to take out patrols and do skirmishing, and on one patrol I took out we were approaching some houses when the chap on my left, Private Fred Pirie, came running over to me saying, 'That's it, I've had enough.' I asked him what the trouble was and he said he'd been hit in the back. When we returned to our positions we found that a bullet had cut across his back but not causing any serious damage, he was still mobile. This was a coincidence; in North Africa, myself, Fred and another chap were proceeding up a hill when we were suddenly 'Stuka'd'.[47] We fell flat on our faces, me on the left, Fred in the centre. A piece of shrapnel knocked Fred's helmet flying from his head and a piece cut across his cheek (left one, I believe). Seems he was unlucky when he was with me.

Monday, 25th September–Tuesday, 26th September
Eventually we got the order to pull out down to the river bank at night and to follow the white tape; this we did in pouring rain and when I finally reached the evacuation area and was ready to board one of the boats, we were asked to stand back and let the wounded in first and that turned out to be the last boat we were to see, so I don't know how it can be said the evacuation was 100 percent successful as stated in the 3rd Battalion War Diary. Of us who remained till first light, some decided to swim across, I being one.

Off went one lot but the current was rather fast on the Rhine. Some managed to go with the tide and make their way over, some seemed to just go with the tide and not make it and others were just shot by Jerry, either in the water or going over the river bank the other side. Things seemed grim, so what few of us were left decided to stay and see what would happen. We eventually met up with more lads who had an officer in charge; he said there was nothing we could do but to

---

46 Mention of this is made by an unknown officer in the booklet *By Air to Battle*, by Hilary George Saunders (London: HMSO, 1945) page 126. I quote: 'There just weren't any army rations after the first day, but there were some tame rabbits, one of which I fed. He used to scratch the wire of his hutch as I went by, and I'd give him a leaf of lettuce or cabbage. One day a parachutist on the scrounge walked off with my rabbit, dead. I made him hand it over and left it between my batman's trench and mine, where it got blown to pieces by a shell.'

47 The Junkers Ju87 or *Stuka* was a German dive bomber and ground attack aircraft.

124 AIRBORNE TO ARNHEM

1. POLDERWEG DEFENSIVE POSITIONS, LATE 20TH– EARLY THURSDAY 21ST.
2. POLDERWEG
3. SLUICE
4. CHURCH
5. BENEDENDORPSWEG

Reconnaissance photo taken from 14,500 feet on 19th October 1944. Resupply chutes can still be seen on the Rosande Polder. The exposed positions of 1st and 3rd Parachute Battalions can clearly be seen. (Photo: Courtesy NCAP 4135)

surrender. We ditched what arms we had in the river and the officer stood up with a white flag and was immediately fired on. We remained where we were until German forces arrived and called on us to surrender. We stood up and we were waved on to march. We walked on the river bank until we came to a hillock where we were told to halt. While we were standing there, a machine gun opened up, killing and wounding several of our lads plus some German guards. We eventually marched off through Arnhem to Zutphen where we stayed overnight, then we were put on cattle wagons and moved off. We travelled for five days without food or water, eventually finishing up at Limburg at Stalag XIIA. We were badly treated for the couple of days we were there, and then finally we were moved out, finishing up at Muhlberg on the Elbe, Stalag IV B. There my mates and I finished up until relieved by Russians and handed over to the Americans.

Polderweg–Rosande Polder positions, Thursday 21st September. 3rd and 1st Parachute Battalions under heavy fire were forced out of their vulnerable positions on the open polder, back into the stream and made their way through the sluice gates aided by Staff Sergeant Callaghan and Captain Dorrien-Smith from their position on the far right opposite bank in full view of the Germans. After safely organising the withdrawal of his men towards the Oosterbeek church further west along the stream, Dorrien-Smith received a mortal wound. Lance Corporal Tom Halley-Frame, B Company, 3rd Parachute Battalion, 1st Parachute Brigade, writes: 'On the far bank our second-in-command, Captain Dorrien-Smith, sat and warned us not to cross as there was no known depth, whereupon he threw a parachute harness still attached to the rigging lines and dragged us over one at a time and getting us all safely across. This was one of the finest actions I ever saw at Arnhem.' Sergeant Harry Callaghan, HQ Company, 3rd Parachute Battalion, 1st Parachute Brigade, writes: 'Captain Dorrien-Smith's conduct was beyond 'brave' and even at this late stage if possible, I would like to see him get some form of decoration.' (Photo: Author, 1984)

Private Bill Collard, 5 Platoon, B Company, 3rd Parachute Battalion, 1st Parachute Brigade

Sunday 17th September
Early on the morning of September 17th, the sun shone and peace reigned over Lincolnshire. This peace however, was shattered by the roar of engines as wave upon wave of aircraft flew low over the countryside. A great airborne armada was on its way. People could be seen coming out of their houses into the streets to wave to us. They knew that at last we were on the way to war.

The North Sea presented no difficulties and a great feeling of wellbeing existed. The whole of the 2nd Tactical Air Force was airborne and I doubt if any such air armada will ever be seen again. To me it seemed possible to get out and walk on aircraft. There were heavy bombers on the way home to England. High above us swarms of fighters milling around and, of course, our slow low-flying transport planes. The drop for me was comparatively easy and it seemed that we had caught the Germans on the hop. A few bullets whistled around but I was much too concerned about my landing, heavily laden as I was. How American paratroopers managed with two parachutes, one in reserve, I shall never know. We would never have had room and we had complete confidence in the one with which we were issued.

The rendezvous for the 3rd Battalion was red smoke and we made our way towards this. For the first mile, there was little or no opposition, a few odd bullets but nothing to hold up the advance. B Company were leading 3rd Parachute Battalion's advance along the Utrecht/Arnhem road and my section were leading. We were in single line sections on each side of the road. A German motorcyclist who seemed oblivious of what was happening attempted to ride through our ranks. As I was at the front of the column, I think that I can claim the first positive kill of our advance. A further mile up the road a motor engine was heard coming from a side road, from Wolfheze. A German staff car appeared in front of us just as our section was passing the road and it was our section which riddled it, killing all the occupants. It was later learnt that one of the occupants was General Kussin, German Commander of Arnhem.

A short distance after this incident, we came to the first houses and such was the greeting of the Dutch people that it slowed our advance. They were dispersed somewhat when sniper fire was directed at us. For some reason this sniper fire slowed our advance but it must be remembered that we had been reinforced, and we did have some fellows with us who had never been under fire before. Major Peter Waddy came forward to see what the hold-up was and he called me and was asking me to grab a bicycle at the side of the road when Spandau shells passed between him and me without touching us. These were from a German armoured car just up the road but until then unobserved. We actually moved back about two hundred yards as the armoured car came towards us supported by infantry. Along with several others I moved into a house at the side of the road. Immediately behind our platoon was a Jeep towing a six pounder anti-tank gun. The gun was knocked out as it was being turned. As the armoured car passed our house, we opened fire on it and the German infantry with it. What with our fire and support from the rest of the platoon, the Germans retreated. A couple of prisoners were taken and these were SS. We then moved on slowly again, subject to sniper fire. Thinking back over the years, I am certain that this was where we lost our momentum. If we had taken advantage when the German patrol retreated and pushed on quickly we might have been in Arnhem that night. As it was, we stopped and fortified the house around us and all night were subjected to a devastating mortar attack. The large house that I was in was obviously a German HQ of some kind; it had been hurriedly evacuated and at the end of the night there wasn't a window left, glass everywhere.

Monday, 18th September

It appeared that General Urquhart had been up during the evening, as a result of which our route into Arnhem was changed.[48] Early next morning we backtracked and took a lower route through Oosterbeek. There had been some casualties in the battalion, but not that heavy and although only an ordinary soldier I still feel that the position was not sufficiently exploited. The best way out of a mortar attack is to press on, not stop still and sit it out.

It was whilst moving along this alternative route that armour was heard coming towards us and we moved off the road into houses and gardens. It was while climbing over spiked railings at the side of the road that my trousers became impaled and I hung at the side of the road with my feet in the air and my head on the ground. No one helped and there was no way that I could get off myself. Fortunately, whatever armour it was didn't reach us and it was Peter Waddy who actually helped me off the railings. A medic was asked to put a shell dressing around my shin which had been badly torn and we moved on. A little further on, near a road junction, we came under attack from infantry positioned on open ground to our left and a fierce fight took place. I found myself firing through a hedge at the Germans. Stood up behind me was the platoon commander firing like mad with a pistol. It was at this position that I was hit. I ran into machine gun fire and was knocked over backwards. It felt as though I had been hit over the head but in actual fact a bullet had gone straight through my helmet. It wasn't until I tried to stand up that I realised that I had been shot through the knee. A bullet had also passed through my pack containing phosphorous bombs. The Jeep which the previous evening had been towing the six pounder gun was still with us and someone put me on the bonnet; the attack was beaten off and the battalion moved on. Shortly afterwards, the Jeep was hit near the railway bridge and had to be abandoned. There was little that could be done for me so I was put into someone's front garden behind a hedge, given a couple of extra Sten magazines, and left. I know that there were other casualties in and around the area, both British and German, and some of the German medics were giving them attention. I must have been there for three hours or so and although there was quite a bit of shooting going on, the battle seemed to have moved on with the battalion and from my position I saw nothing. An elderly man and woman came out of the house, a Mr and Mrs Terwindt (the house was Number 2 Rosanderweg) and indicated that I should come into the house. I remember not wanting to move from where I was – firstly my leg was hurting like hell and secondly I didn't feel like putting these two Dutch people in a position where the Germans could say that they were hiding the enemy. I had my own personal capsule of morphine but was reluctant to use it. The problem was solved however when out of the blue, a para medic appeared and he was called over. He gave me a shot of morphine, dressed my wound, stuck up a Red Cross pennant and helped carry me into the house. Weapons had to be left in the garden. The medic left after I had been put in the cellar, saying he would try to get aid, to get me to an aid post.

That evening a young lady, Joti Roelofsen, aged about nineteen came into the cellar to look after me. Joti, a student at Amsterdam University, stayed with me for two nights while the battle raged around. Then the medics came for me and I was moved on a Jeep to an aid post, this being right in the battle area. Joti came with me. The aid post was hit several times by mortar fire and several of the wounded were killed so it was evacuated under fire, and I was taken to another aid post, a school. Within hours this was blasted by mortars and was also evacuated. We then moved to a building adjacent to what I think was the Schoonoord Hotel. Joti Roelofsen came with me

---

48   From Tiger route to Lion route.

and risked her life looking after British wounded. Here she was involved with many wounded and was a very courageous young lady. Her assistance was much in demand by our doctors. The building that I was in was really only a barn and in the 24 hours I was there, it changed hands three times – British, SS, and back to British. From there we were moved to a church and I didn't see Joti again until I went back to Arnhem in 1947. The SS took the wounded from the church to St Elizabeth Hospital. In the hospital itself there were indescribable scenes. Wounded, both German and British everywhere; there just wasn't enough room. German and British doctors worked together on the wounded. An endless stream of wounded men was being carried in. Those that succumbed to their wounds and died were quickly carted outside to make way for the living. For me the war was over, but so too was the battle for Arnhem Bridge.

My memories of Arnhem are many, but some things stick in my mind, such as the hate in the eyes of the SS troops, some of whom were no more than sixteen years old. The courage and bravery of the Dutch population, some of whom had lost everything. The noise; this never stopped, there were bombs, mortar shells, continuously throughout the whole operation. No one could possibly sleep. It was seven months before I returned to England, having been taken to Germany and it was only upon my return I learned that out of the 500-odd men who had left Spalding, only thirty-five returned after the battle.

Private Les Harrison, Intelligence Section, HQ, 3rd Parachute Battalion, 1st Parachute Brigade

Sunday, 17th September 1944

I was in the Intelligence Section of Battalion HQ. I was however not an active member of the section as such but was batman to the Intelligence Officer, Lieutenant Alexis Vedeniapine MM, and was billeted at the Officers' Mess together with other batmen; this was the other side of Spalding to that which the main part of the 3rd Battalion was situated. I never got around to meeting up with members of the section.

The flight over and the landing was quite uneventful. We saw no flak and there was no action when we landed. We formed up at the rendezvous with no trouble and were off within about ten minutes of landing. The first sign that any action had taken place was a German despatch rider lying in the road. A short way forward was a staff car which had been riddled with shots and the occupants all killed; one of the forward companies of 3rd Battalion must have been responsible for this. It was not till we were approaching Oosterbeek before reaching the Hartenstein did the action really start and our progress towards Arnhem was brought to a halt. It was at this time that I first saw Brigadier Lathbury and General Urquhart with our CO.[49] It was evening time by then and starting to get dark. The officers were in the house that night and the rest of us dug in out in the front garden. Who decided to stay there till first light the next day I do not know.

Monday, 18th September

It was first light when we moved out, around 0630–0700 hours (not 0830 hours as stated in the 3rd Battalion War Diary). We formed up and made our way to the lower road across allotments and so on, while encountering fire off the enemy in the upstairs of houses. We did not stay to attend to

---

49 Lieutenant Colonel John A.C. Fitch.

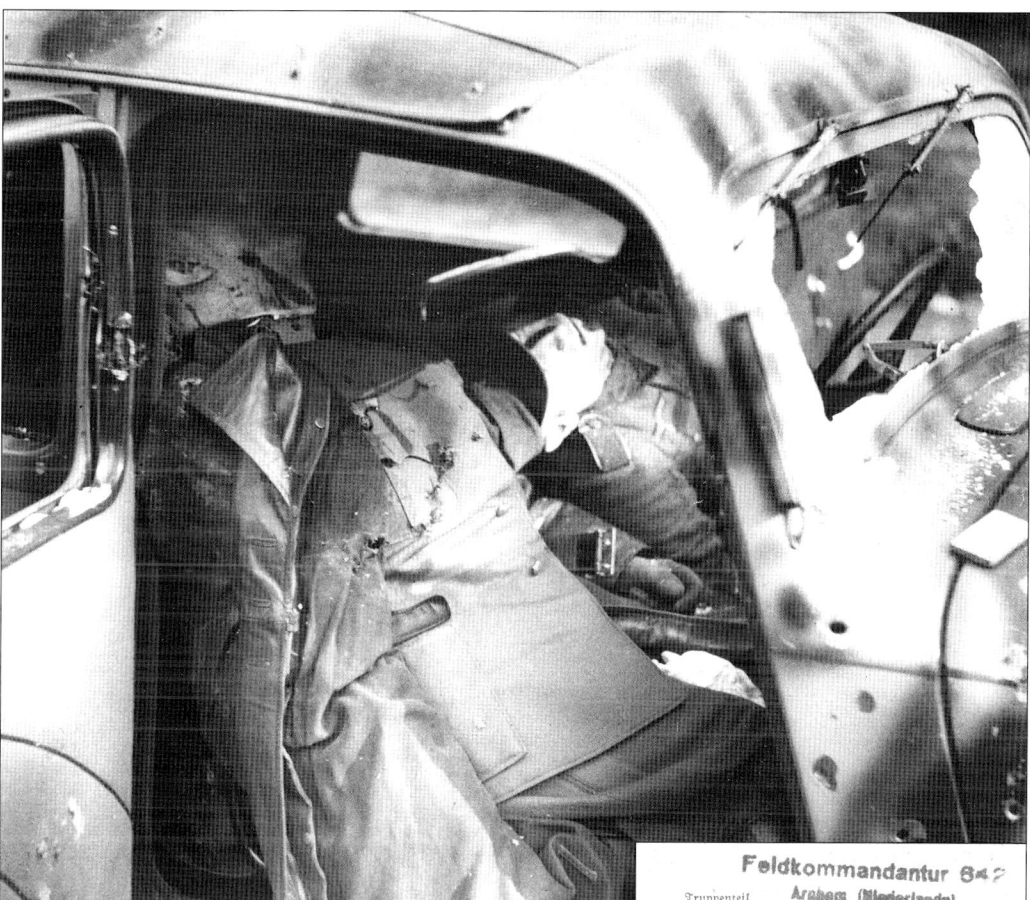

Above: Wehrmacht Feldkommandantur 642, Generalmajor Friedrich Kussin and his driver Gefreiter Josef Willeke shortly after being shot in his staff car. The bodies of his two aides, Unteroffizier Max Koster and Unteroffizier Willi Haupt were in the back of the car. Private Bill Collard, 5 Platoon, B Company, 3rd Parachute Battalion, 1st Parachute Brigade, writes: 'B Company were leading 3rd Parachute Battalion's advance along the Utrecht/Arnhem road and my section were leading. We were in single line sections on each side of the road. A German motorcyclist who seemed oblivious of what was happening attempted to ride through our ranks. As I was at the front of the column I think that I can claim the first positive kill of our advance. A further mile up the road a motor engine was heard coming from a side road, from Wolfheze. A German staff car appeared in front of us just as our section was passing the road and it was our section which riddled it, killing all the occupants. It was later learnt that one of the occupants was General Kussin, German Commander of Arnhem.' (Photo: IWM 1154)

Right: Field Pass removed from the staff car of General Kussin, Feldkommandantur 642 Arnhem. (Author's private collection)

them but kept on heading for the lower road in order to make progress as quickly as possible. We then moved freely along the road and reached Utrechtseweg, crossed the road and got into a couple of large houses. The brigadier and the general, etc., were in one house and I was in the one next to it and was in a cellar. From the back garden there was a grilled opening through which I could see the upper part of the backs of the houses to which we eventually broke out and reached. I was quite alone in that cellar; whether there were others upstairs in the house I could not say. The reason for my staying where I was, is that I could direct fire into the upstairs windows of the houses in the back street. We could not move out of them as we seemed to be completely surrounded and were being mortared. I heard the Bren gun carrier when it arrived and could hear Major P. Waddy directing the unloading. It was while this was going on that the mortaring started. Suddenly it went quite quiet, orders were shouted out that we would have to move out, and when I came up the steps I looked around a corner and saw Major Waddy lying dead. The front of his head was facing into the ground and the wall of the house; anyone in the battalion would recognise him without seeing his face. I did read somewhere that he went out on a recce, but this was not so. It was, I guess, around two or three o'clock when it was decided to break out by way of the back garden across a wall and into the gardens of the houses which ran parallel to Utrechtseweg. There were now about four of us in our house, while the brigadier and the general were in another with the CO. We did not know that they had left to go out to the back street; we did not leave there till around five or six o'clock. We went up the back street and turned left up a court way towards the railway. A machine gun had been placed at the top of the court way which opened fire on us forcing us to dive headlong into the houses on either side. Sometime during the night, we broke out and made our way down toward the river. Machine guns appeared to have been posted at every corner. I can remember turning a corner, or I was about to, when a machine gun on the other side of the road opened up – it was in what I took to be gardens with railings around. It was dark but that is what it appeared to be, Lieutenant Vedeniapine directed us to cross the road to the railings and crawl along beside them so that we were under their line of fire. Once past that point, it was one mad dash to the Rhine Pavilion.

Tuesday, 19th September
I was with Lieutenant Vedeniapine (IO), Colonel Fitch (CO) and Regimental Sergeant Major Lord together with others. Just as it was getting light, we left the pavilion and made our way along a narrow track on the river's edge. We were within sight of the bridge when small arms fire from across the river stopped us. I got a bullet through my foot and decided to make my way up the bank, as there were bushes there for a bit of cover. (They all made their way up the bank to the road; it was not healthy to stay where we were, being fired at from the direction of the bridge also from across the river.) I was pulling myself up by one of these when I felt a thud on my arm and realised it had parted from me, together with my rifle. It was not till later that I learned it was a flak gun in the brickworks across the river which had been the cause. When I got the wound in my arm I managed to crawl up the bank and came across a slit trench about three or four yards from the road. I think the CO had been there prior to my reaching it, so that's the last time I saw the CO, RSM and the IO. When I reached the slit trench I managed to get the 'Pull-Through' of my rifle out to use as a tourniquet. I do not know to this day who the fellow was that stopped and fixed it around the top half of my arm before pulling myself into the slit trench. He really did risk his life, for the fire from across the river was pretty deadly; it was skimming over the trench I was in, not more than a foot above me. As I say, I was no more than three or four yards from the road. A Tiger tank came along from the direction of the bridge; it stopped on the road just above where

I was and started firing down the road toward the Rhine Pavilion.[50] I thought the trench I was in would cave in with the vibration, it shook loads of earth on top of me. I must have looked a pretty sight with it sticking to the sticky mess I was in.

How long it was there before things quietened down I can only hazard a guess, maybe an hour or two hours, then the Jerry medics came along to collect us. I was yanked out of my hole by the collar of my smock and put into an ambulance and taken to a field dressing station. I was in no fit state to know in what direction or how far away it was. From there it was a journey to Apeldoorn where the German doctor operated on me the following Saturday. While in Apeldoorn I met up with a member of 3rd Battalion. We mucked in together for he had also lost his right arm and his name was Les Fuller. It was November before I was moved to Stalag XIB where (as you may know) RSM Lord was. I was repatriated in January, so my stay was not too long.

View east along Onderlangs from the Rhine Pavilion. Private Les Harrison, Intelligence Section, HQ, 3rd Parachute Battalion, 1st Parachute Brigade, writes: 'I was with Lieutenant Vedeniapine (IO), Colonel Fitch (CO) and Regimental Sergeant Major Lord together with others. Just as it was getting light, we left the pavilion and made our way along a narrow track on the river's edge. We were within sight of the bridge when small arms fire from across the river stopped us. I got a bullet through my foot and decided to make my way up the bank, as there were bushes there for a bit of cover. (They all made their way up the bank to the road; it was not healthy to stay where we were, being fired at from the direction of the bridge also from across the river).' (Photo: Author, 1984)

50   Probably a Sd.Kfz.142/1 Sturmgeschütz III Ausf. G of Sturmgeschütz-Brigade 280 (StuG.BriG.280) one of five StuGs assigned to KGr Harder tasked with clearing the lower road, Onderlangs. Another five StuGs, part of KGr Möller, were simultaneously advancing along the higher road, Utrechtsestraat into Utrechtseweg (Bovenover). StuG.BriG.280 was equipped with seven Sturmgeschütz III Ausf.G armed with a 7.5cm gun and three Sturmhaubitze 42G (StuHs) armed with a short barrelled 10.5cm howitzer.

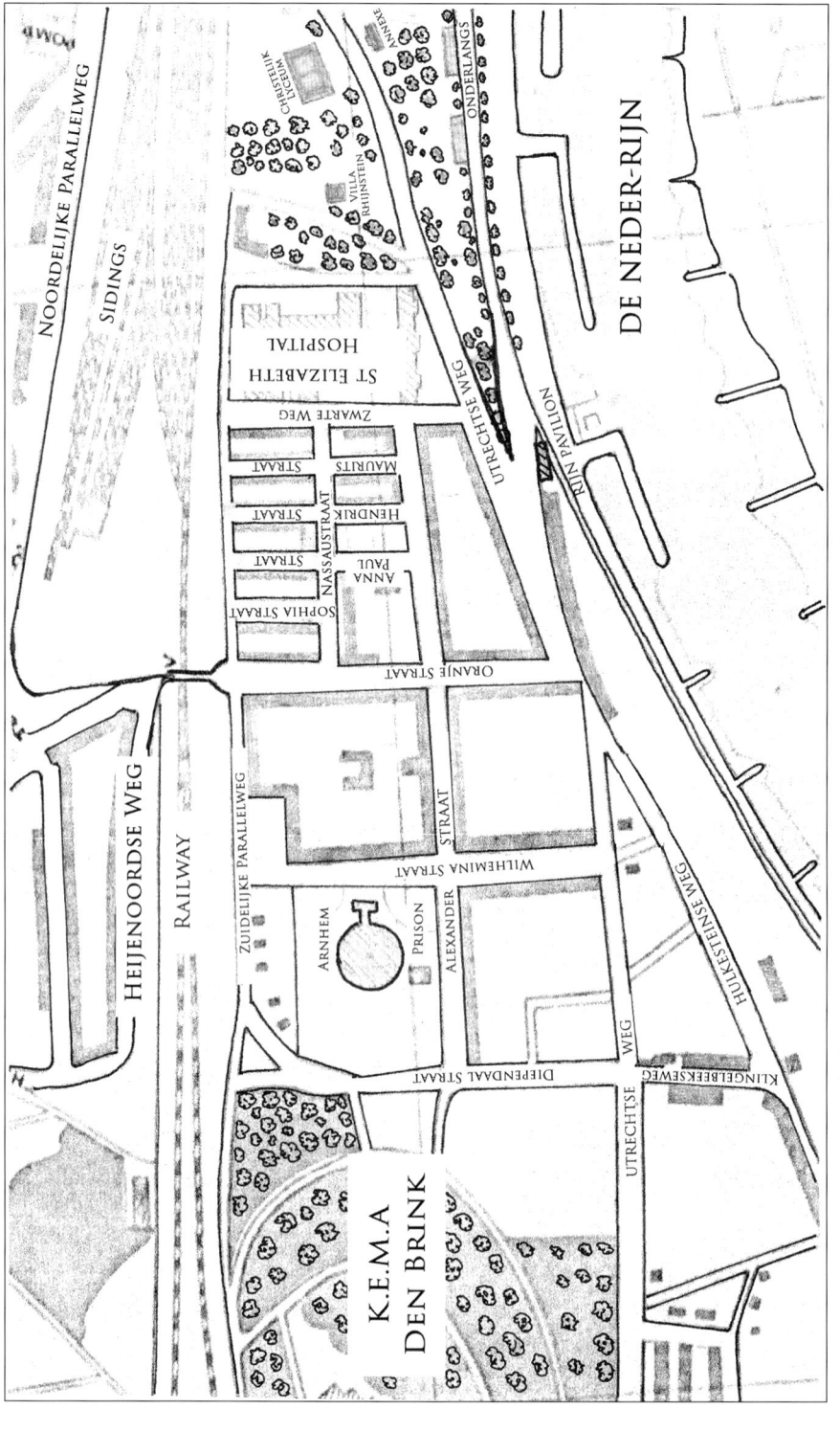

Lombok, Situated between St Elizabeth Hospital and Den Brink/KEMA. Map: SGW Designs.

Utrechtseweg left, Onderlangs right. The Rhine Pavilion (now the Rijnhotel), on the right. (Photo: Author, 1984)

Lieutenant Len Wright, Commanding Officer, 9 Platoon, C Company, 3rd Parachute Battalion, 1st Parachute Brigade

Sunday, 17th September

On the afternoon of Sunday 17th September, 1944, following a quick RV and assembly, 3rd Battalion was led off by B Company to and along the Utrecht/Arnhem road. Increasing opposition forced a halt west of Hartenstein, and the Major R.P.C. 'Pongo' Lewis (Officer Commanding, C Company) was ordered by the brigade commander to circle north and find a route to the main Arnhem bridge with all speed.

Led by 9 Platoon, C Company followed secondary roads northwards through a wooded area before reaching the railway line about dusk.[51] Several incidents en route resulted in some casualties including Lance Sergeant Tom Graham on the way into Arnhem.[52] 9 Platoon continued to lead as we followed the railway line to the station where 8 Platoon took the lead and we moved to the rear.[53]

---

51 Valkenberglaan.
52 Lance Sergeant Thomas E. Graham, 3653653; age 24. Shot whilst ambushing a German lorry in Bilderburglaan, near the junction with Valkenberglaan. No known grave.
53 Lieutenant Infield.

The company marched through the town, demolishing an armoured car and marching past German troops in lorries, arriving at the north end of the ramp road to the bridge around 2300 hours. Officer Commanding C Company contacted 2nd Battalion and was instructed to occupy a schoolhouse which commanded the approach road and the north end of the bridge from its upper floors, and also a building on the opposite corner of the crossroads south of the schoolhouse. 8 Platoon was sent to that building which appeared also to be a school or similar public building. Officer Commanding C Company moved into the schoolhouse and it was intended that 7 Platoon should do so immediately whilst 9 Platoon held the north end of the approach road temporarily whilst the buildings were being fortified.[54]

However, before 7 Platoon could move up the ramp road, they were overrun and 9 Platoon came under increasingly heavy fire during a series of attacks from the front and both flanks. A fighting withdrawal by 9 Platoon resulted in nine men reaching the schoolhouse, five of them being wounded. Sergeant 'Chalky' White was shot by my side on the evening of the 17th on the ramp road leading to the bridge.[55] In addition to HQ C Coy and the remnants of 9 Platoon, the schoolhouse force included two Royal Engineer officers and about 30 sappers, making around 50–60 in all.

The schoolhouse was a large building with a basement, ground floor, first floor and attic. The basement was for wounded, ground floor holding force, first floor main body because it was 10 to 15 yards from the ramp road and about level with it, the attic for observation and sniping. Between the ramp and the schoolhouse was a shrub slope and then a path about two to three yards wide.

Monday, 18th September–Wednesday, 20th September

During Monday 18th, 8 Platoon experienced strong infantry attacks supported by heavy mortaring. Around 1700 hours a German tank fired armour piercing and high explosives into the building, concussing and dazing the occupants. The position was assaulted and captured by SS infantry before 8 Platoon could recover from the shelling.

The schoolhouse force repulsed infantry attacks, experienced mortaring and tank shellfire, inflicted heavy casualties on the enemy and destroyed many vehicles during almost continuous engagements throughout Monday 18th to Wednesday 20th. By midday on the 20th, the building provided little cover although it was still standing. In the afternoon, shellfire from a heavy tank and an SP gun to the south set fire to the upper floors in several places and the building began to collapse.

(As far as I am concerned, Major R.P.C. Lewis, Officer Commanding C Company, was in command of the force within the Van Limburg Stirum Schoolhouse. Only he and Captain W.H. 'Chippy' Robinson gave me orders. I was not aware of the presence of any other officers in the building apart from Lieutenant 'Stiffy' Simpson RE).

Officer Commanding C Company ordered the evacuation of the schoolhouse; the force began moving north but immediately came under mortar and machine gun fire. Six men were killed and many wounded. Surrender was ordered and a white flag was raised, but more casualties occurred before the firing ceased and the majority of the force were taken prisoner. Bob Summerfield was killed just after we were burnt out of the schoolhouse and were trying to escape.[56]

---

54 The Van Limburg Stirum School. 7 Platoon Commanding Officer, Lieutenant Peter L. Hibburt, 243546, age 21, last seen near the northern end of the ramp of the bridge. No known grave.
55 Sergeant Michael White, 6084753, age 32. Found buried in the Moscowa General Cemetery at Arnhem.
56 Corporal Robert H. Summerfield, 3058103, age 26, was one of those taken prisoner. After being taken POW he was shot dead by his German guard for reacting to the guard tearing up a photograph of Summerfield's wife, removed from his wallet by the German.

Lieutenant Len Wright, 9 Platoon, C Company, 3rd Parachute Battalion far left, supports Sapper Charlie Papworth, 1st Parachute Squadron RE from the ruins of the Van Limburg Stirum Schoolhouse. In front of them, more C Company men. On the right is Private Joe 'Slim' Moran, followed by Private A. Stanford, Private N. Gooseman, Private Les Dakin with head wound and Private Joe Spicer. (Photo: Author's private collection)

9 Platoon, C Company, 3rd Parachute Battalion, August, 1944. *Back row, left to right:* 1. Pte J. Bullough; 2.?; 3.?; 4. Pte A.K. Davies; 5. Pte J. Pritchard; 6. Pte D. Madigan; 7. Pte A Stanford; 8.?; 9.?; 10.?. *Centre row, left to right:* 1. Pte D. Colmer; 2. Pte J.Millard; 3. Pte T. Plearin (died in POW camp); 4. Pte H. Sait; 5. Pte P. Talbot; 6. Pte H. Tidy; 7. Pte J. Buglass; 8. Pte D. Mullineux; 9. Pte L. Dakin; 10. Pte J. Spicer; 11.?; 12. Pte N. Goosman; 13. Pte J. Marshall. *Front row, left to right:* 1. L/Cpl W. Stubbings; 2. Cpl R.H. Summerfield, (KIA); 3. Cpl G.Perry; 4. L/Cpl D. Lumb; 5. Sgt B. Conway; 6. Sgt M. White (KIA); 7. Lt L.W. Wright; 8. Sgt R.Mason; 9. L/Sgt T.E. Graham (KIA); 10. Sgt W. Wallis; 11. Cpl Green; 12. L/Cpl A. Swainson. *Unidentified:* Pte A. Gibbs, Pte W. Edwards, Pte. H. Hobbs, Pte A.E. Soffe, Pte J. Welsh. *Not present:* Pte J. Newbury (Photo: Author's private collection)

Top: 8 Platoon, C Company, 3rd Parachute Battalion, August 1944. (Photo: Author's private collection)
Middle: 7 Platoon, C Company, 3rd Parachute Battalion, August 1944. (Photo: Author's private collection)
Bottom: C Company, 3rd Parachute Battalion, August 1944. (Photo: Author's private collection)

Sergeant Tommy Battle, Mortar Platoon, HQ Company, 3rd Parachute Battalion, 1st Parachute Brigade

Sunday, 17th September

We took off about midday on the 17th September and we jumped about 1400 hours. I had a bit of an unfortunate landing because I was Number One in the stick. I was coming down on the leading edge of the DZ and there were trees surrounding the DZ. I drifted into the trees. I had a kitbag suspended from my leg about twenty feet below me. Well, the kitbag hit the trees before I did, and I was drifting, not coming down directly and my kitbag got caught in a fork of the tree. Well, you can imagine, then I carried on drifting, and when I came to the end of the twenty-foot rope it tipped me over and I landed upside down in the tree. The kitbag at one end, me at the other, upside down. However, a bit of a tricky position, upside down, thirty feet up a tree. But I hit my quick release and got out of the harness and managed to get down the tree. I fell down half of it. Luckily when my weight came off the parachute itself it allowed the kitbag to drop itself down on its own weight to a position I could reach from the ground. I got my weapons out of it and made my way with the rest of the lads to the RV. We made pretty good progress right the way through to Oosterbeek. When we got to Oosterbeek, that's when we came into trouble; we were pinned down overnight. I spent the night along with my lads in the garden of a big house, I couldn't tell you exactly where it was but it was Oosterbeek. Now we were subjected to rocket fire. Luckily none of it hit us though it was all around us but we escaped any real injuries or casualties from the rocket fire.

Monday, 18th September

Come morning, we moved out again in daylight and we got into the lower part of Oosterbeek going towards the Rhine. We were going down a street called Benedendorpsweg with the railway bridge going over it. We were going down a narrow street and cobbled road and when we came to the railway bridge we came under fire, not just us but the rest of the battalion who were all making its way down this road. We came under heavy fire from the bridge. It was such heavy fire, we were in such a closed area to get through the bridge which was a stone bridge, only about 15–20 feet wide and about 15 feet high. We had to either go through the bridge or up the railway embankment. The battalion was held up at this particular point. Now, we were stuck there for about an hour and a half planning ways to get around this one. I was platoon sergeant, and my platoon commander and I set off with four mortar detachments. From the bridge, the railway bridge itself, we were cut off, to the right that was going down to the river. We followed the embankment down, hoping to find a place to get through or get over, further down near the river. Luckily we did. The embankment itself petered out, but the railway line was supported on stilts from the river onwards and where the bank petered out near the river, we could cross right there. When we got around the other side of the embankment going towards Arnhem, we came across a long wide stretch, an open field, approximately 400–500 yards of open ground. To the left of us, approximately 600–700 yards away, was the enemy position that was holding us up at the bridge.

However, we set off to cross this stretch and it was a suicidal run. We ran across this hell-for-leather as fast as we possibly could, a lot of us. The thing with mortars and the Vickers machine gun platoons, they were always the heaviest laden of the lot. Each man carried at least three or six mortar bombs, and each one weighed 10lbs apiece. That was all and above all his normal equipment, rifle and ammunition and what have you, plus his pack, etc. I had no bombs but I had a 38 radio set, Sten gun, Sten gun bandolier, pistol, ammunition for the pistol, spare batteries for the

38 radio set I was carrying – so you can imagine how heavily laden I was too. The biggest problem getting across all this open ground was that we could not run all that fast, and with all the stuff we were carrying. It was not exactly smooth ground, it was rough through the grass. It had been ploughed at some time or other but the grass had grown over it and it was still rather rough underneath. So you can imagine trying to run across there with machine gun fire from the left; there were two or three machine guns. It broke the advance up completely at that point. I managed to get through myself along with Mr Gillespie, our platoon commander;[57] alongside us was Lance Sergeant Bill Perryman, one of the section sergeants, and also a private, I forget his name. On the other side of this open patch we came upon a lee, a bank; on the right-hand side was the river about 40 yards or so to the right and this bank, which wasn't very high, it was only about three or four foot high and it led up to the main road going through to Arnhem from Oosterbeek. Along that road were machine gun positions and also small arms fire, plus they also had small mortars, about two inch mortars, firing at us.

So the only thing we could do was to hug this bank to give us cover from the fire on the left and trust there was nothing on the river side, which there wasn't at that particular time. So we went down along this banking along the river side and I should say we got about 500–600 yards when we started to get fire from the other side of the river. However, we carried on, the main trouble to us was the fire coming from our left, the main road into Arnhem and that's where we were getting the small arms fire from, plus small mortars. We managed to get through about a quarter to half of a mile away from where we left the railway embankment, where we again came under heavy fire. We could actually see the Arnhem Bridge at that particular point and we came under very heavy fire from the other bank, small arms fire and an 88mm. We had no alternative but to break out from the cover of the bank on our left and make our way into the houses, which we did.

We lost a private soldier there at that particular time and that's when I first realised that we'd lost all our mortars, everything. Everything was strewn behind us, whether the men had been stopped or what, we didn't know at that particular time. There was three of us left in the party, the private soldier with us; he just got it just as we were moving out, from the other side of the river. When we moved inland we went a couple of streets, not too far because we came under fire from the main Arnhem road, beside the 88mm fire we were getting from the opposite bank, so we dived straight into cover in a house. Sergeant Perryman was a taller bloke than me, but 2nd Lieutenant Gillespie was about the same size as me so he moved at my speed. Sergeant Bill Perryman, being taller with longer legs was in front of us; he was supposed to jump into the house that we made for. Now the house we were moving to, we went to the back open window, the back door was locked so we dived through the window. Now, what we didn't realise at that particular time was, the window at the back of the house, the connecting door to the front of the house and the window in the front of the house – all the doors and windows were in line with each other. Now, around the other side of this house we got into was a kind of a square, houses and buildings all around it, and straight across at the other side of the square about 200 yards, something like that, a machine gun was set up which we didn't know about and that machine gun could see us silhouetted in line with the two windows and the doorway. They let us get in, and then they opened up, and instinctively, as soon as they opened up (we were all in line), I shot to the right and as I shot to the right, Bill Perryman in front of me, took the full burst of the machine gun fire. Lieutenant Gillespie behind me, he shot to the right, and he was alright.

57   Lieutenant Stanley Gillespie.

Bill Perryman stopped the full burst but one of the bullets went right through him and it hit me as I dived to the right for cover. Bill Perryman was killed outright. For the moment we didn't know what to do, so we waited five or ten minutes and then crept out, opened the door, crept out on our hands and knees through the door itself and made our way back down towards the river again.

Going very slowly, we actually managed to get away from the house in which we'd been hit and out of that vicinity, untouched, apart from I had a bullet in my left arm. The bullet had entered the arm just above the elbow midway between the elbow and the shoulder, and it had stopped there in my arm. What had actually happened as I found out afterwards, Sergeant Perryman had taken the full force of the bullet and it had gone through him and hit the bone in my arm and the bullet had broken in two. Now, if he hadn't have taken the full force of the bullet in the first place and it had gone straight into my arm, it would have smashed it completely, so in effect, by Bill Perryman taking the bullet first, it saved my arm, in the long run.[58]

We made our way back down towards the river because it was the only place we could go; to travel on our left along the main Arnhem road was impossible. From this time onwards, I don't know what it was, it could have been loss of blood or shock, I don't know, but from here on, my mind became kind of hazy as to what happened. But I do know we kept trying to get through. We could see the bridge; we kept trying to get through. This period of time, we seemed to have passed through the main defence on the outskirts of Oosterbeek, on the Arnhem side, and the other main line of defence was around the bridge itself and we seemed to be hitting pockets, in between the two. Some places we returned fire and we did this for the rest of the day. Half the time we were hiding, the rest of the time we were trying to move forward.

Tuesday, 19th September

During the night, we found it impossible to move. We tried it, in the dark, but it was impossible because there was too much movement around us and we didn't know if it was us or the enemy – invariably it was the enemy. So the night was wasted as far as the advance and our section was concerned. Our little section now comprised of two: Lieutenant Gillespie and I, as Sergeant Perryman was dead and we'd left him in the house. We were still trying to get through and we couldn't; we were coming under fire from the other side of the river and the main Arnhem road and we eventually dived for cover, to have some rest, get out of the fire and reorganise ourselves again.

There was this disused boat on the riverside, in fact it was a sunken wreck, partly exposed, more exposed than actually sunk, and it had probably been there quite a few years. We dived for that and got inside; at least it was quiet in there, if nothing else. We must have been seen going in. We hadn't been there long before the Germans came upon us, 'Hände hoch!' – 'Hands up!' – I knew that much German anyway. We knew we had no chance, so we came out and that was it. I was a prisoner, much to my regret.

I must have passed out completely with loss of blood; I'd been bleeding all the night since the previous day. I remember coming to in Apeldoorn, on the outskirts of Arnhem. How I got there I don't know, whether I'd been carried there or what. My arm was still very painful and still bleeding.

---

58   Sergeant Dennis W. Perryman, 5189259, HQ Company, age 28. No known grave.

Wednesday, 20th September onwards

Apeldoorn, they moved us, and I was now with the rest of the lads. It was in something like a churchyard, some kind of a yard. The weather at that time was quite warm and we were alright laid out in the open. They packed us all together; this was part of the Divisional HQ of the German troops that were against us, and they moved us into a place called Zutphen, I think about 20 miles away from Arnhem itself. They fed us there, mashed potato with some greens in it and garlic flavouring. That was the first meal I'd had since leaving England. I think that was the Thursday. I must have been out for the best part of a day, I don't know. From there, they moved us down to Frankfurt in Germany itself. I remember going down in cattle trucks, about 20 of us in a truck. In Frankfurt, being a senior NCO of course they thought they were going to get some information off me. They got nothing, of course. They got me off the train and saw that I'd been badly wounded and looking a bit sick and weak, and they put me in solitary confinement for a couple of weeks, trying to get information out of me, which they didn't get and eventually gave it up as a bad job. From there they sent me up to a place called Neubrandenburg, in Germany, about 85 kilometres north of Berlin and that is where I finished my time, the rest of the war.

Looking west towards Benedendorpsweg under the railway viaduct at Oosterbeek Laag railway station from Klingelbeekseweg. The airborne were advancing towards the camera. It was whilst trying to negotiate this narrow bottleneck that many airborne troops were held up. The Germans were firing at the bridge from the extreme right near the station and even today the intensity of their fire can be seen in the pockmarked bridge brickwork to the left side of the bridge exit. Sergeant Tommy Battle, Mortar Platoon, HQ Company, 3rd Parachute Battalion, 1st Parachute Brigade, writes: 'Come morning, we moved out again in daylight and we got into the lower part of Oosterbeek going towards the Rhine. We were going down a street called Benedendorpsweg with the railway bridge going over it. We were going down a narrow street and cobbled road and when we came to the railway bridge we came under fire, not just us but the rest of the battalion who were all making its way down this road. We came under heavy fire from the bridge. It was such heavy fire, we were in such a closed area to get through the bridge which was a stone bridge, only about 15–20 feet wide and about 15 feet high. We had to either go through the bridge or up the railway embankment. The battalion was held up at this particular point.' (Photo: Author, 1979)

Sergeant Tommy Battle, on manoeuvres prior to Arnhem with his 3 inch mortar and crew. (Photo: Author's private collection)

3rd Parachute Battalion, HQ/Support Company, Vickers Machine Gun Platoon, just prior to Arnhem. Front row seated centre is Commanding Officer, Lieutenant M. John P.S. Dickson. (Photo: Author's private collection)

Sergeant Harry Callaghan, HQ Company, 3rd Parachute Battalion, 1st Parachute Brigade

Sunday, 17th September

We dropped about one o'clock on the Sunday 1st September. I was corporal acting sergeant; my appointment was provost sergeant for the battalion, responsible for the defence of Battalion HQ and responsible for the adjutant and the regimental sergeant major. On a film we'd seen of 'D-Day' I'd seen an American sergeant smoking a cigar, saying, 'Well boys, this is our day.' So I thought *well, this is 'our' day, boys, so let me have a cigar and give our boys a boost.* So I had a cigar with the lads in the plane. We dropped on the DZ without any opposition whatsoever and reported to the edge of a forest where we formed up and I reported to the RSM, John Lord, who told me to follow the CO with my crew wherever he went. I followed immediately behind the CO; he was a very forward-looking person, one couldn't keep up with him as he was dashing from company to company, but I maintained the central core from which the CO could report back to from his bursts forward or aft.

We proceeded after a short time along the road to Arnhem and there were some delays and hold ups and eventually we got under way. We proceeded on either side of the road; I was on the left with my detachment behind me with my CO and a company forward moving up front. Brigadier Lathbury caught up with us on our right-hand side walking in the hedge way. We were passed by a Jeep towing an anti-tank gun which had just gone passed us about 20 yards approaching a bend, when around the corner came a German armoured car which fired at the crew and killed them instantly. We all dived for cover, and my cover was behind a tree that was about six inches wide with my boys behind me. This armoured car had stopped and its turret was revolving, not shooting at anyone in particular as probably there was no one to see, because we'd all gone to ground. I called for a PIAT from my crew behind me and they passed it to me and I found out it had not been cocked. The thing with a PIAT is it takes a great deal of physical effort to cock the thing and as I was behind a tree about six inches wide, I thought discretion the better part of valour and just ignored it. I did think about tossing a Mills grenade at the bottom of the vehicle but it was quite a distance away and it was rough old ground, cobbled stones, and I would probably have done more damage to my own people than the armoured car even if I'd got the grenade underneath it directly. After a short time it opened fire, spreading its shot all over the place and we began to disperse quickly left and right, it then withdrew. I was with my crew across the road and over to the right in front of where Brigadier Lathbury was and it disappeared into the forest on the right hand side of the road.

Monday, 18th September–Tuesday, 19th September

We made our way via the lower road; there I met up with the CO and his party making their way towards the bridge. I met up with Major Dennison amongst other people including the CO, Colonel Fitch, and he moved on up ahead and there was some heavy firing and some mortaring.

I was told to fortify a house, to make a strong point out of it, which with my crowd I did. There was a lot of firing going on, a lot of casualties, and the CO was killed and we were ordered to withdraw.[59] I then came under command of Major Dennison who was wounded in both arms and on the right. He pointed out to me that they were under sniper fire off a steep slope which

---

59 Lieutenant-Colonel John A.C. Fitch, 58834, KIA 19th September, afternoon.

was covered by conifer trees and the people were up in that tree. So I led a party of about ten or eleven people forward, two of which got wounded and one killed and I eventually arrived at the top after an exhausting time and we met some opposition. I picked out the sniper and fired a Sten gun burst into him and he didn't come down but his rifle did, on the end of a piece of cord. There was no further opposition from anyone else. We searched around, couldn't find anybody, no more Germans, in fact we didn't find the body of the soldier the weapon belonged to, but we didn't bother looking. We arrived back down the hill and reported to Major Dennison, only to find that there was no one there. There was a great deal of firing going on and mortaring, shelling from the direction of the bridge and we lay up for quite a while overnight. I met up with a Major Brown who was quartermaster of the 1st Battalion near the lower railway bridge. There were three of us leaning up against this armoured carrier and a mortar bomb burst about five yards in front of us and knocked us all flat on our backs and took the right hand off the quartermaster from the 1st Battalion.

Zednesday, 20th September–Thursday, 21st September
Polderweg–Rosande Polder Positions
We made a meal from what rations we had and put out defensive positions, I was still in command. There was no officer in charge and eventually next morning we followed the road over open country, still under fire, trying to find our own people and trying to find cover at the same time. With me was Lance Corporal Roy Munroe, an ex-Loyal; he was carrying a sandbag with all our supplies in it, grenades and ammunition. I had a pistol and a Schmeisser which I'd taken off this dead German and he had a rifle with him. Roy was an old friend of mine from the regimental days with the Loyals; we had lots of fun and chuckles. He had a great sense of humour.

Eventually I caught up with a crowd of people and I said, 'Who's in charge here?' and they said, 'Captain Dorrien-Smith over there.'

We were still under intensive fire from mortars from the direction of the bridge and there were Self-Propelled guns. I reported to Captain Dorrien-Smith. 'Sergeant Callaghan reporting, Sir,' and he said, 'You are now my sergeant major.'

'Thank you very much, Sir.' I was quite chuffed as at that time I was acting sergeant. So we hung on there for a couple of days, but we couldn't dig in properly, we'd not many tools. I don't know who authorised us to stay in that particular position as it was pretty hectic.

Thursday, 21st September
Polderweg–Rosande Polder Positions, Oosterbeek Church Area
We were dominated by enemy fire from enemy positions. We were about 400–500 yards from Oosterbeek itself. Eventually authority came through with permission for us to withdraw. Captain Dorrien-Smith sent someone ahead to collect people and him and I went round these little section posts and arranged for four or five people at a time to withdraw at regular intervals. He and I were the last to leave. When sufficient time had elapsed, we had to leave lots of dead bodies around; it was too late for those and we had to look after the living, and there were one or two quite seriously wounded chaps. We had to win a war and casualties were sustained. Captain Doreen-Smith's conduct was beyond brave and even at this late stage if possible, I would like to see him get some form of decoration. A most unusual man, Captain Dorrien-Smith, a man of many facets; he was a stutterer and he could out-swear the vivid ranker. Yet on this occasion when Fred Radley and his crowd came through the pond (the sluice gate), there he stood,

standing fully under enemy fire, stood erect, threw his arms across and withdrew them from the water without the slightest loss of his voice, setting an outstanding example of courage under fire for the care and safety of his men. He and I were the last to leave the area and were running side by side. We'd run about 150 yards and had had a rest and were running forward again; he was running on the left of me and the fire was coming from the right and although he was shorter than I was by about three or four inches, he got hit in the neck. I consider myself very fortunate it wasn't me. He died instantly. This left me in command of the remnants of the 3rd Parachute Battalion, who survived that horrible event.

When I reported to Oosterbeek church, I found my boys waiting for me. I reorganised them and we took five sections according to dispositions of ammunition, weapons and NCOs. I fell them out and told them to wait until I found out who was in charge. I went to look around and saw Lieutenant Cleminson, and he said it was Major Lonsdale who was in charge of the force. I went inside the church just in time to hear him give his speech. It was a great one and just what we needed at the time, bucked the lads' morale up no end and mine as well. After all, I was an original Red Devil or at least I thought I was, and here we were again in another tight spot and still surviving, against great odds, greater than we'd ever faced.

So I was ordered to a certain place to take up defensive positions.[60] I placed my HQ in a barn and in that barn was a hearse which was used by the local people. Underneath was a top hat and frock coat used by the local undertaker. I went into a cellar with the top hat on and tried to raise the morale of the wounded and told them that I was going to be Hitler's representative at his funeral in Berlin. When I came back up to the top of the cellar stairs they said to me, 'Be careful, Sergeant Major, there's a sniper about.'

I said, 'Don't worry, lads; nothing can hit me under this.' (More for my morale than theirs, as I was shit scared. However, one has to keep up appearances, and the lads responded magnificently.)

Thursday, 21st September–Sunday, 24th September
Benedendorpsweg–Oosterbeek Church Area

Major Alan Bush came to see us. He was one of the 'old' 3rd Battalion; in fact he and I had toured together with the 3rd Battalion in 1941 when it was first formed. He was wounded pretty badly around the head and I told him I considered I was in charge and explained my defensive positions to him. Major Dennison arrived and he was wounded so we put him in a little corner out of the way so we could take care of him. We were being fired at by all kinds of rubbish, and then the padre came along and wanted volunteers to go back to the killing ground where we'd retired from, at dusk at night, to see what he could do for the dead and living there.[61] What he supposed he could do for the dead I don't know, beyond him I suppose. However, I instructed my men when they retired from the place to bring with them as much arms, ammunition, food, medicines and supplies as they could and dump them in my place, so I could dole them out. They did this, and they came back after a night's work and occupied their slit trenches. We had very little food, living on mangel and turnips from cellars. The last of the compo rations were exhausted practically and we had a cellar full of wounded. I managed to brew some food for them and take it out to them. The place was full of them, the wounded, and one could hardly see the far end of the cellar.

60   The houses along Benedendorpsweg based around nos. 117–119.
61   The previous Polderweg positions on the Rosande Polder.

My main job was to command the forward positions; this was the main forward position between Arnhem and the church at Oosterbeek where the command and immediate headquarters were. When time became available, I examined these weapons and cannibalised one or two of them and made up some Bren guns, Sten guns, Schmeissers and even cannibalised a PIAT gun. This was the same PIAT used by Major Cain of the South Staffs, who later became a VC, by disposing of various enemy tanks. I was with him at one time when he tried to lob a PIAT bomb over the top of the stables, and all he succeeded in doing was to bring the roof down on top of us and nearly killing us on the spot. I gave a Bren gun to a certain Private Radley who was magnificent as a signaller; he should have been decorated for bravery, the lad, he was all over the place running the lines and repairing the lines between our HQ near the Oosterbeek church and our positions and Major Bush's position. I gave him this Bren gun and whilst I was away elsewhere, he managed to beat off an enemy attack; they were attacking under the cover of smoke from a house that was on fire and they were mown down, not realising that we had an automatic weapon, because when I tried the weapon out, I'd tried it out on single shot which was very fortunate as it later proved to be. The six-pounder gun: I'd had experience in all kinds of automatic weapons and anti-tank guns, from Dunkirk; I'd been on a six-pounder anti-tank gun course. In fact, I'd done most jobs in the army except signalling. We got a whiff of an armoured car coming along and I put a long lanyard on this thing, not touching the mechanism of the gun; fortunate that I did so, because it just fired the one shot and disintegrated. I don't think we hit it. The gun was far too knackered and the noise frightened me, never mind the Jerries.

Sunday, 24th September–Monday, 25th September

Things quietened down and eventually we got permission to retire from the area one evening. We were out of ammunition, no food for the last few days and morale was very low but spirits were high. They were a good set of lads, they did what they were told and I did my best to lead them to the best of my ability. They responded to my leadership, to my calls, magnificently. Never once did I have occasion to reprimand anyone. On the occasion of the withdrawal, we withdrew all parties across this approach line; the area was denoted by tracer shellfire down a corridor. We were to proceed down the corridor until we came to the Rhine and meet the boats to be evacuated, to take us over to safety. I rounded up my lads and we took our place in the queue. We couldn't see the river, it seemed like miles away, probably a hundred yards. I saw Major Bush struggling along on his own, very much the worst for wear. He had a bandage around his head and he was limping. I left my place in the queue and directed and assisted him to the best of my ability and made sure the major that had so gallantly led us, such a great inspiration to us all, was safely across. I remember with the major falling down a dyke, falling down into a blasted pond of some kind. We had a laugh together, which was good for morale for both of us; we hadn't far to go, the boat was here now and we eventually made it. I put him in a boat and I went back to my position in the queue.

I'd gone past where I'd left when one of the boys shouted out, 'Sergeant major, this is your position here.' I reached in turn the boat and went over the Rhine. As soon as we got over the river there were military police waiting for us. We had some wine of some kind, tots of rum I think it was, after a snifter or two and after no food for three or four days and an empty tummy, up it came. I staggered and fell in a blasted ditch on the side of the road up to my knees in water and one of the military police, not willing to get his feet wet, merely held his hand out to pull me out: 'Thank you very much, sergeant.' We got back to Grave and had a nice kip and eventually we got back to England, to Spalding.

146 AIRBORNE TO ARNHEM

Post-Arnhem
One of the worst times in my memory was the sisters of Captain Dorrien-Smith came along, asking about their brother and I told them he'd died very bravely and did not suffer in death and they were pleased. I was sorry for the family because he was last of the male line of the name of Dorrien-Smith; they'd served for generations in The Buffs Regiment, I believe. It was a very sad occasion, nevertheless.

Communications, Command and Control
There seemed to be constant problems with communications. Our Battalion HQ, the CO, was off dashing to and fro because he was having trouble with links to the forward companies; he kept coming back again trying to raise brigade. Brigade obviously had trouble trying to find us; division probably had trouble trying to find brigade. The brigadier was on top of us when we got first in contact with the enemy, he was across the road from us, and not far behind him was the divisional commander.

Instead of staying in their own blasted positions where they should be so that they could control events, they were all forward; the forward positions were occupied by 'Chiefs', and there weren't enough 'Indians'. They (3rd Parachute Battalion HQ) were inhibited, there was far too much 'brass' on top of them. Instead of leaving the forward soldiers to fight the battle they'd been taught, sending the soldiers forward, giving them orders to do their job, they were being breathed on heavily by the brigadier[62] and by the divisional commander[63] who should have been back at their own positions commanding the battle from a calm and detached situation where they belonged and where they were needed, rather than breathing fire down on the forward companies and forward battalions.

Awards
Harry Callaghan was recommended for the Distinguished Conduct Medal (DCM). However, he received the Dutch Bronze Lion. The citation reads:

> During the entire Airborne Operations at Arnhem 17th/25th September, 1944, this NCO displayed the most outstanding gallantry. He acted as the RSM from the 21st to the 25th September, when the battalion's armament was reduced to grenades only; Sergeant Callaghan collected and distributed vast quantities of German arms and ammunition which he obtained from No Man's Land in front of the forward defended localities. All this work was done in the face of practically continuous mortar and small arms fire. On the evening of the 22nd, his sector was relatively stronger in fire power than it had been immediately after the parachute descent. He also performed throughout invaluable work at the Regimental Aid Post bringing in many wounded under fire. His zeal, enthusiasm and undisputed gallantry all through the operation was magnificent and an inspiration to all ranks.

---

62 Lathbury.
63 General Urquhart.

Sergeant's Mess, 3rd Parachute Battalion, Spalding, June, 1944. (Photo: Author's private collection)

Private Arthur Watson, Signaller, C Company, 3rd Parachute Battalion, 1st Parachute Brigade

Sunday, 17th September 1944
In the morning before taking off, I went to see our sergeant to tell him, 'I've lost my bayonet.'

He said, 'Don't worry about that. There'll be a dead bloke on the ground and you can pick his!'

The silly things you worry about. We had a good drop, didn't meet any opposition; flying over Holland there was the odd tap-tap-tap on the plane but it had no effect on us at all. I was No. 2 out the plane being a signaller. An officer went first, 'Wrighty', I think.[64] I came down and it was like Epsom Racecourse, everyone walking around saying, 'Hello, I haven't seen you since Hardwick or Ringway, it was like a fairground.' I didn't use the radio at all on the way into Arnhem; 'Soapy' Hope was the other signaller. The sets[65] were useless, I carried it on my back and Soapy said, 'I'll carry it for you,' but I said, 'You've got to be joking, if any shrapnel comes about it'll be the radio that gets it, not me!' and I carried the radio. It received until it got hit in the school. I don't know who sent a message out, all I was getting was the BBC, and I couldn't get anybody.[66]

---

64 Lieutenant Len Wright.
65 No. 18 sets.
66 Private James W. Hope, 4341741, age 34. KIA 20th September 1944, Klingelbeekseweg, near the Arnhem-Nijmegen railway line.

148   AIRBORNE TO ARNHEM

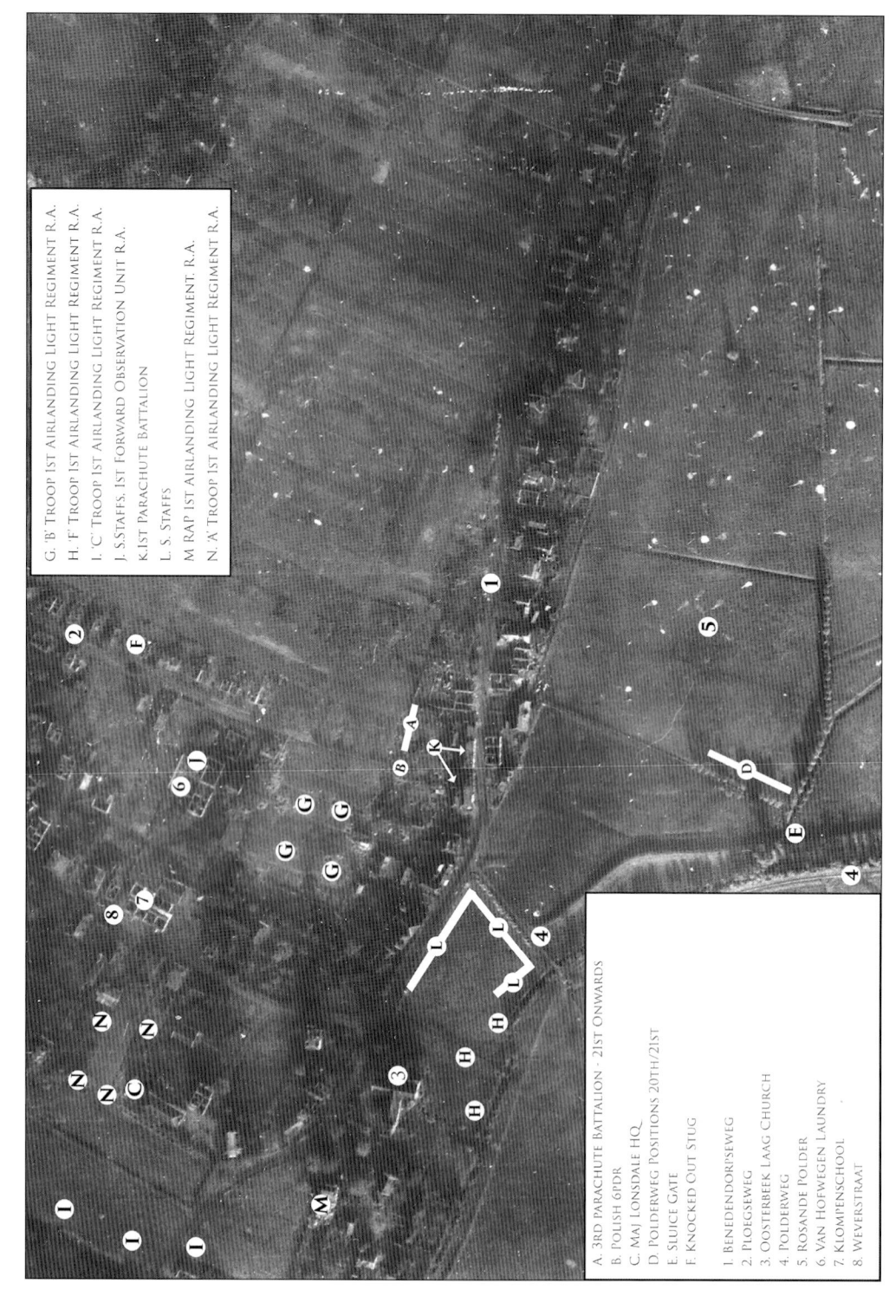

G. 'B' Troop 1st Airlanding Light Regiment R.A.
H. 'F' Troop 1st Airlanding Light Regiment R.A.
I. 'C' Troop 1st Airlanding Light Regiment R.A.
J. S.Staffs. 1st Forward Observation Unit R.A.
K.1st Parachute Battalion
L. S. Staffs
M RAP 1st Airlanding Light Regiment. R.A.
N. 'A' Troop 1st Airlanding Light Regiment R.A.

A. 3rd Parachute Battalion - 21st Onwards
B. Polish 6pdr
C. Maj Lonsdale HQ
D. Polderweg Positions 20th/21st
E. Sluice Gate
F. Knocked Out Stug

1. Benedendorpseweg
2. Ploegseweg
3. Oosterbeek Laag Church
4. Polderweg
5. Rosande Polder
6. Van Hofwegen Laundry
7. Klompenschool
8. Weverstraat

3rd Parachute Battalion positions, part of Lonsdale Force 21st September onwards. (Photo: NCAP 4135, with permission)

I remember us coming down the very wide road (Utrechtseweg). It had some nice bungalows on it. We came down and passed the German general that was shot, and as we went down, there was a string of us, I rubbed this boy's head and said, 'Ginge.'

His mother rushed out and grabbed me and said, 'Trap, trap!'

I said, 'It's alright, we can do it, don't worry,' and we went on and then this German six-wheeler came down the road and it really duffed us up. It didn't get me, and after that we went into the woods and had a bit of a do in the woods. After the woods we got to the railway cutting. We must have been hours walking down the railway cutting; well, it seemed like hours. We were alright in the railway cutting because we couldn't be seen. We went into Arnhem Railway Station, through the ticket office, through the barriers, the company of us. No Jerries about. We got right into the town and then we only met a patrolling tank, which had got a light on it, a searchlight, and we kept away from him by hiding in the shops and then we got into the main square and we ran into a couple of Jerries. We fixed them up good and proper. The road from there led straight down to the bridge. We crawled down there, very cautiously, a load of fighting blokes, up against the wall hoping they wouldn't be seen. A truck came up and we did a Gammon Bomb job on it. I remember getting into the school; we stuck the furniture up against the windows to make it fortress-like. Sunday night was pretty quiet.

Monday, 18th September

On the Monday it really livened up. I was in the attic and I got a lump in the shoulder – they mortared or shelled the roof, it came in and exploded just above the ceiling. It was only a flesh wound, but the point is, it's shock.

I went downstairs, through the rubble and said to Wrighty, 'I've been hit, Sir,' and he said, 'I couldn't care less how many time you've been hit, get back up again!'

So I scrambled back up the stairs which were nothing but rubble and I got back up there and they gave us a right duffing up. After the battle died down I came down again and I was ill, it was shock, and I asked for a rest. I went down to the cellar and I think I passed out, that's where all the wounded were. The thing with going up and down the stairs was that's where we'd laid all the dead out, at the bottom of the stairs. It was a stone floor and every time I went upstairs, there was one more there. I looked at it and thought to myself, *Am I the next down there?*

Tuesday, 19th September

We were upstairs a couple of blokes and me, and the Germans came up outside and said, '*Poleski, Poleski.*' We said, 'They're not bloody Poles,' so we got the old 36s out and dropped them out of the window; it shut the 'Poleski' up completely. In the morning, I think it was 'Greeny', Sergeant Major Green, he had a look out there and he said, 'They're piled up out there like mad.' So I said, 'We must have got some!'

The terrifying thing was when the Tigers and tanks came up. What we'd done was, we'd got mattresses, got furniture, put the mattresses against the furniture and hid behind the mattresses. They wouldn't stop a shell, but it stops blast, and that's how we stopped the blast. These were within the room, because it would soften the blow of the blast. Blast kills a lot more than bullets do.

Tuesday afternoon, I think it was, we'd been scrapping with blokes and we said that these blokes were good, and you know what Pongo or Wrighty said? 'We're up against British Parachute troops.'

I said, 'We're not,' and he said, 'Yes, we are!' and you know what we done in that house? We shouted 'Whahoo Mohammed!' and the blokes outside shouted it back. I don't know whether old

Frosty had sent across a patrol, but we'd fired on each other. It went on, you couldn't help it, and we didn't always know who was who.[67] Just imagine, we're hiding away from the Germans, then all of a sudden you've got 30 or 40 of us, everyone screaming 'Whahoo Mohammed!' The Germans must have thought we were stark raving bonkers. We had to do it as it was the only way to identify ourselves. The Germans wouldn't have known that.

Tuesday night, they said the Germans were in the house and we fought a battle in the house. We shot at anything we could see. I was upstairs on a balcony and anything I saw, I shot at. We had a gun battle inside the house, but there weren't any Germans – it was just panic. We thought they were there, you were jumpy.

I was on the radio, my No. 18 set, and Pongo Lewis said to me, 'Get through to brigade.'

I couldn't get through. I said, 'No one is answering, Sir.'

'Tell them who we are,' he said.

Tell them who we are! You know what I said on the radio? 'This is C Company, 3rd Parachute Battalion on the bridge and we need help. Someone help us!' – and there's Germans all around us! Well, I appealed to everybody for help and no help came, no replies.

Then Pongo said to me, 'Tune into the BBC, one o'clock, and get the news and find out what's happening,' and that's what I did. You could pick the BBC up and we tuned it in every time there was a news bulletin and found out what was going.

I think it was the third day, I was sitting there with the radio on the balcony then suddenly *bang* and it's gone. They'd hit the radio and that was our lot as far as the radio was concerned. Those radios only picked up and we were listening to the BBC to find out how we were getting on. The point is, is when we'd dropped, we dropped them down below us in the bags and it put them 'off tune' and you couldn't re-tune them again under those conditions.

Wednesday, 20th September

During the night, Pongo came to me. We had two big doors and they were wide open. I had a 9mm automatic, and he said to me, 'Look, here's another 9mm and if anything comes through those doors, let them have it.'

I thought to myself, *Christ, I'm standing up, and we've got these big doors.* I was saying to myself that I hoped no one came through; fortunately, no one came through though we thought they might rush it. I think the most dramatic thing that happened to me was, that it is so easy to go to toilet in battle. We had one little room, and that wasn't defended, it was downstairs and it had a 'slit' window, and that was the toilet. I went in there with my 9mm and I undressed with one hand, because I wouldn't take my eyes off that one window. I did what I had to do, and dressed myself again without taking my eyes off the window. I was afraid that someone was going to poke a gun through there.

I was standing at the window with another bloke and the Germans were in the garden and do you know, they were arguing, and we could hear them. We couldn't understand what they were saying, but they were arguing. Well of course, both of them didn't argue much longer. I think one must have been saying he wanted stay and the other must have been saying go, so we settled their problem by solving it for both of them, so they both stayed.

---

67 Major R. Peter 'Pongo' Lewis, Commanding Officer, C Company, 3rd Parachute Battalion. 'Whahoo Mohammed' was a 1st Parachute Brigade battle cry originating from the North African campaign.

One time, we kept losing blokes. We couldn't understand why the Germans were such ruddy good shots, and then we worked it out. There was a girl used to be out across the road from our house. The blokes used to look at her, then she'd disappear and soon after that, we'd lose another bloke. So we decided – I hope I'm right – we decided that she was a spotter, so next time she came up, she was about 15 or 16 ounces heavier. We put her down. She was spotting for the German machine gunners.

Then the house caught alight. The top was alight where I was, and we came down one floor and then that caught alight. Pongo assembled us all downstairs in the big hall. Slim Moran, myself, I forget who the other two were, we carried the wounded Pongo out on a window shutter or door but I had to drop him after a while because I'd got hit a second time, I got hit in the face. I saw stars when it hit me. I said, 'Sorry, Sir, I'm going down,' and another bloke carrying him went down because his hand had gone. It was mortar fragments I suppose, in the gulley.

When we came out of the house finally, we had Pongo in a gulley outside the house, and Pongo said, 'We will go forward to attack.' He said to me to go and look at the road, and about five hundred bullets went across my head.

I said, 'They know we are here, Sir.'

He said, 'I thought they did.' We went along the road to go out in the open and that's when they gave us the works, they really set about us and that's when he said, 'Right, dismantle your guns, every man for himself.' Just before that he'd said, 'Go out and surrender.' One man went out with a white flag and they shot him, dropped him right where he was. That was it. We walked out, waiting for them to bump us off. We expected to be shot and it's surprising how you accept it. I think we were so battle-weary you accept the inevitable. They were in a big white house, it must have been 200 yards away, and they were beckoning us from the house to come. They wouldn't come to us, we went to them, and do you know, they were trembling examining us. I think what they didn't like was our fire bombs, that's what they didn't like, they were supposed to be smoke grenades but we used them on blokes, and it's terrible hearing a bloke dying of phosphorous. You used what you'd got.

I remember the German newsreel cameramen were there and that's when they said 'Up, up!' (meaning our hands). *Bollocks*, I thought … and that was that.

They took us back into the town, into the town itself, a residential area, and put us in a garage, awaiting transport. You ought to have seen all those tanks lined up under the trees, I could have cried to see what we were up against. When we got put into the garage, the Germans said to us that they were Panzer Grenadiers. They were pretty good blokes, soldiers, not Nazis, and they gave us chocolate. What was the make? Cadbury's, they'd got the lot! We were carted off in ambulances and we were in the ambulances for hours, without, I'm sure, any pumped-up tyres. We finally found a hospital that would take us in and they parked us on the lawn and said, 'Right, you are on the top floor.' We dragged ourselves up five floors. Their idea was, if it got bombed, we'd get it. The only treatment we got there was a punch for gangrene, that's all, the first treatment I'd had. After that, we were on trains for about four days, cattle trucks, and we finished up in a town called Minden. They put us into a meat-packing plant, then into a church hall where they were going to do the operations. I was in there with a bloke named Gerry Strachan, RSM (2nd Battalion I believe). They put some white powder on my wounds and tied it up, with toilet roll. They didn't have bandages, they used paper; you can imagine how long that lasted, and a couple of hours, it was gone.

Van Limburg Stirum School, pre-war, looking south-west from Eusebius Buitensingel.
(Photo: Courtesy Gelders Archive)

Van Limburg Stirum School after the battle, looking south-west from Eusebius Buitensingel.
(Photo: Kramer. Courtesy Gelders Archive)

Utrechtseweg/Onderlangs junction looking east. Tuesday, 19th September. The two Kampfgruppen of *Harder* and *Möller* meet up and push westwards following the airborne withdrawal to Oosterbeek.
(Photo: Courtesy Gelders Archive)

2

1st Parachute Battalion, 1st Parachute Brigade Attached elements 1st Airlanding Anti-Tank Battery, RA, attached elements 1st Airlanding Light Regiment, RA. 2nd Parachute Battalion, 1st Parachute Brigade, 16th Parachute Field Ambulance

Introduction[1]

Sunday, 17th September

The 1st Parachute Battalion took off at around 1147 hours from RAF Barkston Heath, Chalk Nos. 85–118, along with one aircraft, Chalk No. 119, carrying 16th Parachute Field Ambulance medical personnel, and another carrying elements of the Headquarters 1st Airborne Division; in all, a total of 559 paratroopers. As with the other two battalions of the 1st Parachute Brigade, they were delivered by the IX United States Troop Carrier Command. The 2nd and 3rd Parachute Battalions both took off from RAF Saltby. All three battalions dropped in quick succession onto

---

1 Sources: USAAF 'Operation MARKET' September 1944, Headquarters 52nd Troop Carrier Wing. Air Movement Table. Operation MARKET. First Lift. British-Parachute. Sheet 8. AIR 37/1217.
Operational Orders 2nd Parachute Battalion WO171/1237
War Diary 3rd Parachute Battalion
Operation "Market"; Diary of Events: 1st Parachute Brigade HQ: WO171/393: Annexure 'N'
Operation Instructions 1st Airborne Division: WO171/393:Annexure 'C'
Operation Instructions 1st Parachute Brigade: WO171/393: Annexure 'D'
Operation Instructions Royal Engineers, 1st Airborne Division: Annexure 'J'
Report by CRA, 1st Airborne Division: WO171/393:Annexure 'R'
Report by CRE, 1st Airborne Division: WO171/393:Annexure 'S'
War Diary 1st Parachute Battalion: WO 171/1236
War Diary 1st Parachute Squadron RE: WO171/1509
War Diary 1st Parachute Brigade HQ: WO171/592
War Diary 9th Field Company RE: WO 171 /1515

DZ 'X' in order of 2nd Battalion, Chalk Nos.13–46, carried by the US 314 Troop Carrier Group, landing around 1350 hours followed by the 3rd Battalion, Chalk Nos.49–82, also carried by the 314 Troop Carrier Group and at just after 1403 hours finally the 1st Parachute Battalion jumping from 36 C-47 aircraft of the US 61st Troop Carrier Group. All the aircraft carrying the 1st Parachute Battalion reached the DZ successfully with only one refusal. Two aircraft were forced to make a second pass over the DZ due to a release malfunction on one container. The American formation leader accompanied the aircraft on the second attempt at release. Two hundred and sixteen containers were carried, weighing 29,610lbs. Despite light flak encountered en route, no aircraft were damaged. Accompanying the 1st Parachute Battalion on the drop was Sergeant Mike Lewis, photographer with the AFPU.

We shall first follow the 1st Parachute Battalion and then the 2nd Parachute Battalion. As mentioned in the previous chapter, the 1st Parachute Battalion under the command of Lieutenant Colonel D.A. Dobie was tasked with capturing high ground to the north of Arnhem town. It was also required to cover northern approaches to the town and to keep one company as brigade reserve.

Upon landing on DZ 'Z' at Renkum Heath, the battalion quickly formed up and after impatiently waiting around for an hour for permission from Brigade HQ to move off, they finally left the DZ along with their transport and attached support at around 1540 hours in the direction of Wolfheze Railway Station, minus two Jeeps from HQ Company which had ditched en route. Dobie began to move the battalion but soon met up with Major Freddie Gough of the 1st Airborne Reconnaissance Squadron who informed Dobie that Jeeps of his coup de main C Troop had been ambushed just east of the railway station along the track Johannahoeveweg, which ran parallel with the railway. Gough was already experiencing communication problems and was in the process of going back to Divisional HQ with Brigadier Hicks, CO of the 1st Airlanding Brigade, to try and establish communications with 1st Parachute Brigade (the CO of 1st Parachute Brigade, Brigadier Lathbury, was at this time with the 3rd Parachute Battalion on the middle Tiger route, the Utrechtseweg). With Dobie's operational task of moving towards his objective of securing ground to the north of Arnhem town and avoiding the Reconnaissance Squadron ambush area, Dobie moved the battalion north from the Wolfheze Station towards the Ede–Arnhem road, the Amsterdamseweg, which ran from west to east towards the north of Oosterbeek and towards Arnhem along the codenamed Leopard route.

R Company took the lead under Major John Timothy supported by No. 2 gun, 17-pounder D Troop anti-tank gun,1st Airlanding Anti-Tank Battery, RA, followed by Tactical HQ, S Company and Battalion HQ. (The 17-pounder No. 2 gun had a damaged buffer recuperator and would only have been capable of firing one round). Behind them came HQ Company along with the three A Troop 6-pounder anti-tank guns with T Company, followed by No. 4 gun, P Troop, 17-pounder anti-tank gun, 1st Airlanding Anti-Tank Battery, RA. The battalion headed northeast to Wolfheze railway station and then headed north along the axis of Wolfhezerweg, east of Reijerscamp, until R Company came under fire from forward German infantry positions aside the Wolfhezerweg in woodland to the south side of Amsterdamseweg. The German troops involved formed part of the hastily-assembled Kampfgruppe *Weber* comprising of 90 men from 'Teerose II', a Luftwaffe company from 213 Nachrichten Regiment based at Deelen airfield to the north. After taking casualties, the German infantry withdrew and Major Timothy pushed his company through to the main Amsterdamseweg where it became heavily engaged by German infantry and armoured vehicles at the junction with the Wolfhezerweg. R Company, still ahead of the battalion, pushed on in an easterly direction along the axis of the Amsterdamseweg, incurring heavy casualties and encountering increasingly strong resistance from infantry and armour. By 1800 hours with daylight fading, Dobie decided to bypass the German opposition ahead and moved the rest of the battalion south of the Amsterdamseweg and then swung left parallel to the main road along a track. At 1900 hours, Dobie was preparing to more north once again towards the Amsterdamseweg/Maasbergseweg junction when German armour reached the junction first, some 400 yards north of Dobie. Dobie halted the battalion and noted that German troops were digging-in east of his current position in the woods. Dobie had come into contact with Kampfgruppe *von Allwörden* formed from dismounted tank destroyer crews of Panzerjäger Abt.9 of the 9 SS Panzer Division *Hohenstaufen* and additional naval personnel supported by self-propelled guns and tanks.

Communications now began to break down with no wireless contact with R Company or 1st Parachute Brigade HQ. With fading light, at 1930 hours Dobie sent Major J.C. Bune, 2i/c Battalion HQ to find R Company and bring the remnants back to the battalion. R Company were heavily engaged and reduced to 50 percent casualties and unable to extricate themselves and their wounded. Around 2000 hours the battalion main group with Major R.L. Stark's S Company, now in the point position, was approached and engaged by German infantry which withdrew after inflicting another six casualties. Dobie took up defensive positions and awaited the return of Major Bune with R Company. Eventually, at 2200 hours, Major Bune returned to Battalion HQ and reported to Dobie that it was impossible at that time to extricate R Company due to the amount of casualties they had incurred and the proximity of the Germans in the area. Dobie then sent all the available battalion Jeeps for the evacuation of the wounded, accompanied by Major Bune, back to the beleaguered R Company with instructions to rejoin the battalion as soon as possible. The wounded made it back to the main dressing station at Wolfheze but the unfortunate Major Bune was killed in the woods. (It was not until the following day that Major Timothy was able to withdraw his diminished company, now down to less than 40 men, and eventually make it to Oosterbeek where he attached his company to the 2nd Battalion South Staffs and finally regained contact with the rest of 1st Parachute Battalion on the outskirts of Arnhem around 2000 hours on Monday 18th September). Dobie, still dug-in in the woods, sent out patrols during the night which probed the German positions and confirmed what Dobie had feared: that the route along the Amsterdamseweg was too heavily defended by not only infantry but also armour.

Monday, 18th September

After calling an 'O' Group in the early hours of Monday morning, Dobie decided that the battalion had to bypass the enemy ensconced on the Amsterdamseweg main road. Without waiting for the arrival of R Company, after optimistically leaving guides for their eventual arrival, at 0100 hours he moved the battalion off in a south-easterly direction under cover of darkness towards Oosterbeek through the woodland between Johanna Hoeve and the Dreijenseweg; T Company under command of Major Chris Perrin-Brown led the way. Little did Dobie know at the time, but the Germans were already in the process of constructing a major defensive blocking line from north to south along the Dreijenseweg which would later prove an impenetrable barrier, north of Oosterbeek, blocking the 4th Parachute Brigade in its efforts to reach the Arnhem road bridge.

Dobie's path took the battalion through thick woodland in the pitch black which proved hard going for both infantry and vehicles including Jeeps and carriers and anti-tank guns. All vehicles that could be manhandled were, to reduce engine noise. At one point, around 0300 hours, the point element ran into a German advanced forward position in front of the Dreijenseweg which was duly engaged, inflicting German casualties before the enemy withdrew. The battalion pushed on until it reached the eastern outskirts of Oosterbeek just north of the Utrechtseweg where at 0430 hours it encountered enemy armoured cars and came under machine gun, mortar and 20mm cannon fire. Dobie had encountered elements of a strong German defensive line around the Den Brink area encompassing the upper railway bridge over the Utrechtseweg. Dobie intended to move along this middle Tiger route but found the German opposition too strong. S Company under Major Stark engaged the Germans on the left flank, causing German casualties whilst also sustaining another further 30 casualties of their own. Before the attack could proceed further, around 0530 hours, Dobie received a message from the 2nd Parachute Battalion via a Royal Artillery Forward Observation Officer at the Arnhem road bridge, informing him that matters were deteriorating at the bridge and reinforcements were urgently needed. Dobie decided to disengage S Company and leave his intended route along the Utrechtseweg whilst outflanking the immediate German opposition by way of the lower road, the Lion route, used successfully earlier by the 2nd Parachute Battalion the previous evening in reaching the Arnhem road bridge.

On reaching the lower road, the Benedendorpsweg, around 0700 hours, Dobie linked up with elements of HQ Company and half of A Company of the 3rd Parachute Battalion which had become detached from the rest of the battalion during the night. Yet again the Germans continued to vigorously defend the area of the Oosterbeek Laag railway viaduct from the high ground of Den Brink, having successfully delayed every unit trying to make its way under the viaduct. Once under the viaduct to the east, the Benedendorpsweg becomes Klingelbeekseweg, and it was around the viaduct and from houses beyond further along the Klingelbeekseweg that Dobie's battalion came under fire. Having negotiated the viaduct, the battalion had to deal with not only incoming fire from the houses further along the Klingelbeekseweg but also a factory area yet further ahead. Meanwhile the battalion was receiving incoming flanking fire from the area of the Utrechtseweg railway bridge on Den Brink where German armoured cars and one tank were observed. It was by now 0800 hours and Dobie needed to gain momentum; German reinforcements in the area were increasing by the hour and he did not need the battalion delayed any longer than was necessary in its efforts to reach Frost at the bridge. Advancing on a very narrow battalion front was a problem encountered over and over again in the advance to the bridge.

Dobie assigned Major Perrin-Brown's T Company to start the advance towards the German-held houses at 0900 hours. This attack was supported by 75mm artillery fire from the 1st Airlanding Light Regiment RA, dug in at Oosterbeek Laag church. Further support was provided from the 3rd Parachute Battalion HQ elements including mortars and machine guns. One of the problems the advance suffered from was enfilade fire from across the river from German 20mm flak guns. These were engaged at 1000 hours by Lieutenant A.V. Driver, E Troop leader and the E Troop CO, Captain C.A. Harrison, of 3 Battery, 1st Airlanding Light Regiment, RA. The battalion advanced, slowly clearing houses, advancing across back gardens for cover and it came under fire from the factory just south of the Klingelbeekseweg. The attack stalled at this point.

Several attempts were made to take the factory area. Eventually Dobie, with his T Company still on point, coordinated his renewed assault on the factory area supported with half of A Company, 3rd Parachute Battalion under Major M.W. Dennison, which had been separated along with its HQ Company from the rest of 3rd Parachute Battalion. A Company, 3rd Parachute Battalion advanced on the high ground on the left side of the road whilst T Company, 1st Parachute Battalion advanced along the axis of the road and to south of the road into the factory area. The battalion should have had two 17-pounder anti-tank guns attached from P Troop, 1st Airlanding Anti-Tank Battery RA, but due to overturned glider losses on the LZ only one D Troop gun under Sergeant Rams accompanied the battalion. It is possible that a substitute P Troop 17 pounder, No 4 gun under Lance Sergeant Meagher followed on the tail of the battalion. Three 6-pounder anti-tank guns of A Troop, 1st Airlanding Anti-Tank Battery, RA were also attached but unfortunately the fourth gun was dropped short at Nijmegen. A 6-pounder anti-tank gun from C Troop, under command of Sergeant F. Shaw attached to the separated half of A Company, 3rd Parachute Battalion under Major M.W.

Dennison was brought into action to successfully deal with a German strongpoint in the factory which was threatening to stall the advance. A German armoured car was also knocked out in the attack. The factory was eventually taken and the Germans forced out. By now the 1st Parachute Battalion, still missing R Company, had been severely reduced in numbers. T Company started the attack on the factory with around 40 men and by the time the factory was taken they were down to 22 men. S Company suffered a further six casualties when attacked in the rear; the attack was repulsed but merely emphasised the vulnerability of fighting in built-up areas where every house had to be painstakingly and methodically cleared, and yet could easily be reoccupied later by the enemy.

The battalion losses were beginning to be felt with a lack of subalterns and Dobie had taken to splitting the remaining manpower between Major Perrin-Brown and his 2i/c, Captain J.A.D. Richey, each with a platoon sergeant. At 1500 hours, the battalion group continued its advance up the rising ground of the Klingelbeekseweg–Hulkensteinseweg until it reached the road junction with Utrechtseweg in the Lombok area some 350 yards west of the St Elizabeth Hospital. Upon reaching the junction, the lead element came under 88mm, mortar and small arms fire. The junction was taken by 1600 hours and the battalion turned right to begin its advance into the outskirts of Arnhem along Utrechtseweg.

As a result of poor communications, unbeknown to Dobie at the time, the 3rd Parachute Battalion were not that far ahead of his battalion and simultaneously fighting their way through the northern Lombok area towards the railway. It became an advance of attrition in both men and munitions, fighting from house to house along the south riverside of Utrechtseweg. Eventually the battalion was halted short of St Elizabeth Hospital by German armour situated further up the road. The battalion was still receiving flanking fire from flak guns across the river to the south. The flak guns were again engaged with 75mm howitzer fire, and the German crews being forced to temporarily abandon the guns due to air bursts provided by the 1st Airlanding Light Regiment, RA at Oosterbeek. Many of the fleeing crews were engaged by the Vickers machine guns of Dobie's HQ/Support Company Medium Machine Gun Platoon.

The afternoon was slipping away and time was of the essence in reaching the bridge, so Dobie decided to switch his attack to the north side of Utrechtseweg. At 1700 hours, under the cover of a smokescreen, Dobie rushed his men across the main road and entered the labyrinth of houses in the Lombok area to the west of St Elizabeth Hospital which the 3rd Parachute Battalion had previously attempted to negotiate. Indicative of the density of housing of the Lombok area was the fact that a battalion could be easily absorbed. The battalion made little headway embroiled in the narrow streets and alleyways and took further casualties of men and materials; in particular a valuable universal Bren gun carrier was lost. The forward elements reached the area of the hospital but drew German fire and had to withdraw. At 1830 hours, wireless contact was established with the force at the bridge who urgently requested assistance and ammunition. Dobie again considered switching his advance back to the riverside but the intense fire along the main road and side streets effectively put an end to the idea for the moment.

At 2000 hours, Dobie made contact with advance elements of 2nd Battalion South Staffordshire Regiment (South Staffs) under Lieutenant Colonel W.D.H. McCardie, accompanied by the remnants of Dobie's R Company which had joined forces earlier in the afternoon in Oosterbeek when the South Staffs were ordered to make all haste to reinforce the 1st Parachute Brigade's advance into Arnhem. Major Timothy and his R Company were down to 40 men. Fresh supplies of ammunition were distributed and when news came through that the force at the bridge had been overrun any immediate thoughts of another attack were briefly adjourned. Earlier in the afternoon around 1515

Paratroops supported by a 6-pounder anti-tank gun and Jeep advance along Rosandelaan off Utrechtseweg about 1000 yards west of St Elizabeth Hospital on Monday 18th in the afternoon. Probably elements of 1st Parachute Brigade, either 1st or 3rd Parachute Battalions. (Photo: Mr van de Sijde. Courtesy ABM)

Hulksteinseweg facing north-east. With forward rifle companies engaged around the St Elizabeth Hospital, battalion transport tails back from the Utrechtseweg in the distance. In the foreground a Bren gun carrier piled high with stores and equipment. (Photo: Lance Corporal Reg McFarlane, RCS. Courtesy ABM)

Hulksteinseweg facing west. The tail of battalion transport, a 6-pounder anti-tank gun unlimbered behind its towing Jeep. German POWs are led back towards Oosterbeek. (Photo: Lance Corporal Reg McFarlane, RCS. Courtesy ABM)

6-pounder anti-tank gun and crew set-up on the corner of Klingelbeekseweg/Utrechtseweg facing north-west towards Den Brink/KEMA. Possibly No. 1 gun of A Troop, 1st Airlanding Anti-Tank Battery, RA. Probably taken on Monday 18th. (Photo: Lance Corporal Reg McFarlane, RCS. Courtesy ABM)

Above: The above 6-pounder anti-tank gun position on the corner. Photo looking south down Klingelbeekseweg. Utrechtseweg running right to left in the foreground. Below: A few yards away the final position of a 6-pounder (the same gun or another) facing east along the Utrechtseweg; the gun finished up at the corner of the hedge, half on the pavement with its right tyre burnt off. (Photos: Author, 1984)

hours, Dobie's Motor Transport Platoon under Lieutenant Turrell, 2i/c HQ/Support Company, had landed by glider during the second lift on LZ 'X' bringing in four Jeeps with trailers full of much needed additional ammunition and supplies, which then made all haste towards Arnhem.

Tuesday, 19th September

At 0100 hours, orders were received from Divisional HQ issued by Brigadier P.H.W. 'Pip' Hicks, acting Divisional Commander for the absent General Urquhart, informing Dobie to withdraw to Oosterbeek. It was around this time that the 11th Parachute Battalion led by Lieutenant Colonel G.H. Lea arrived on the heels of the South Staffs. At 0230 hours, under candlelight in a cellar of the Arnhem Garage on the Utrechtseweg close to the Oranjestraat junction, Dobie held an 'O' Group along with Colonels Lea and McCardie. At that moment a Jeep arrived from Divisional HQ containing a Canadian, Lieutenant Leo J. Heaps. Due to inconsistent wireless communication, Heaps had been given the task of contacting Dobie to inform him of new orders to immediately continue his attack towards the bridge. Upon receiving this counter-order to once again proceed to the bridge, Dobie formulated a plan whereby at 0330 hours, his 1st Parachute Battalion would advance in the dark along the river's edge whilst the South Staffs would simultaneously parallel the advance to his left along the high road Utrechtseweg, supported by Dobie's HQ Company and 1st Parachute Battalion transport. Dobie would be followed by the 11th Parachute Battalion along his axis of advance.

Meanwhile, mutually unaware of Dobie, 3rd Parachute Battalion at 0230 hours had moved forward to begin what was to become their first abortive attack along the river embankment.

The Rhine Pavilion formed a start line as well as a rallying point for 1st and 3rd Parachute Battalions in their attempts to reach the bridge. The river runs immediately behind the hotel. (Photo: Author, 1980)

Despite the attack being planned to start at 0330 hours, the South Staffs arrived half an hour late. It was not until 0400 hours that Dobie's battalion crossed the start line at the Rhine Pavilion. Dobie's battalion point element, S Company, moved cautiously along the river and had not moved far when they met the 2i/c, B Company, 3rd Parachute Battalion, Captain G.R. Dorrien-Smith, coming the other way. Dorrien-Smith informed Dobie that the 3rd Parachute Battalion had already met stiff German resistance and that any further advance would meet the same. 3rd Parachute Battalion moved back to the Rhine Pavilion, consolidated and endeavoured to move forward and support Dobie's advance. By 0430 hours, encountering very heavy opposition, the 1st Parachute Battalion made costly progress some 600 yards to the Boterdijk approaching the Rhine pontoon bridge and the houses on the higher ground to the battalion's left flank. Now beginning to get light, the battalion came under intense 20mm and 75mm fire from the brickworks and flak barges on the south bank of the Rhine. No. 1 gun, A Troop, 1st Airlanding Anti-Tank Battery, RA was deployed near the St Elizabeth Hospital to engage the enemy guns which successfully registered hits using only AP rounds. The barges were also engaged by a 17-pounder No. 1 gun of P Troop, 1st Airlanding Anti-Tank Battery RA situated close to the Rhine Hotel which managed to hit a number of barges before being forced to withdraw due to enemy fire. T Company, under Dobie's orders, moved from the open ground on the bank, now under heavy fire, into the houses on their left flank followed by S Company. With few anti-tank weapons available, now on point, R Company used hand-thrown Gammon bombs at any approaching German armour. By 0630 hours, the advance had stalled. The South Staffs advance on the high road were meeting stiff resistance and Dobie's R Company were down to six men, S Company around 15 men and T Company down to eight men. By 0640 hours, T Company was cut off, and 1st Parachute Battalion HQ was reduced to 10 men. As the morning progressed, the 1st Parachute Battalion that remained tried to hold the houses to their left flank, and house-to-house, room-to-room fighting ensued. The companies became separated and the battalion became reduced to handfuls of men fighting individual battles against overwhelming odds. Dobie was down to six men in his immediate HQ. German StuG SP guns approached Dobie's house and he was taken prisoner, now wounded, by the supporting SS infantry.

Whilst Dobie was putting in his attack in the early hours of Tuesday morning, further west to his rear at the Hulkensteinseweg/Utrechtseweg junction, at around 0200 hours, battalion stragglers and isolated parties along with the recently arrived second lift glider party were consolidating. This group, now around 40–50 strong under Lieutenant J.L. Williams, Motor Transport Officer, formed a firm base. Patrols were sent out endeavouring to make contact with Dobie and the rest of the battalion. By 0900 hours, the bulk of the 1st Parachute Battalion's strength now lay with Lieutenant Williams' reinforced group of around 200 men. The remnants of the battalion, no longer able to continue their advance, fell back westwards past St Elizabeth hospital along with the remains of the 3rd Parachute Battalion, 11th Parachute Battalion and the 2nd Battalion South Staffs. (The simultaneous movements of the 11th Parachute Battalion and the South Staffs will be covered in detail in Chapters 6 and 9 in subsequent volumes.)

After some initial consolidation, new defensive positions were deployed around the A Troop anti-tank screen around the junctions of Klingelbeekseweg Utrechtseweg and Hulkensteinseweg–Utrechtseweg. These positions did however form temporary defensive points to delay the German armour heading west along the Utrechtseweg and south across the railway down Diependalstraat. Meanwhile across the Utrechtseweg, the 11th Parachute Battalion and the South Staffs prepared positions on the western edge of Lombok/KEMA area in preparation for a move north-east of the railway, a plan issued by Divisional HQ which was out of date even before it was launched. Eventually, the 1st and 3rd Parachute Battalions and the other battalions involved in the abortive attempts to reach the Arnhem road bridge were forced to withdraw towards Oosterbeek. The 3rd and 1st Parachute Battalions with their remaining anti-tank guns, including one remaining 17-pounder attached to 1st Parachute Battalion plus 11th Parachute Battalion's attached E Troop of 6-pounder guns, provided anti-tank cover and delayed German armour advancing westwards, albeit only temporarily.

By late afternoon around 1600 hours, as mentioned in the previous chapter introduction, all four battalions took up positions just west of the railway viaduct at Oosterbeek Laag on the Benedendorpsweg. The No. 2 D Troop 17-pounder anti-tank gun accompanying the 1st Parachute Battalion became stuck in roadside soft sand in Arnhem and was abandoned on the way, along with a further six men of the 1st Parachute Battalion killed and another 20 wounded. By 1930 hours, the remnants of the four battalions began digging in and preparing positions for the expected German attack the following day.

Utrechtseweg, looking west, 19th September. German SS Pioneers house clearing enter the Arnhem Garage close to Oranjestraat where Lieutenant Colonel Dobie had earlier held his 'O' Group in the cellar on the night of the 18th/19th September along with Lieutenant Colonels McCardie and Lea. (Photo: Courtesy Gelders Archive)

1 & 2 PARA BNS, 16 PARA FD AMB   165

As they tried to push for the Arnhem bridge, 1st and 3rd Parachute Battalions both received not just frontal but also left-flanking fire from the German occupied positions on the high ground of Utrechtsestraat overlooking Onderlangs. Enfilade machine gun and flak was simultaneously taken from the brickworks across the river. View looking up from Onderlangs. (Photographs: Author, 1979)

Wednesday, 20th September

Early morning of Wednesday, 20th September, German forces of Kampfgruppe *Harder* began probing the airborne defensive positions west of the Oosterbeek Laag station area, infiltrating armour under the railway viaduct with supporting infantry. By 1100 hours, the German pressure increased with several SP guns moving west along the Benedendorpsweg accompanied by infantry and supported by German troops along the railway embankment. At least one SP gun was immobilised by 6-pounder anti-tank gun fire. German infantry occupied what houses they could and kept the defenders under fire, leading to local counter-attacks to clear the troublesome houses. These were led by Lieutenant J. Turrell, 2i/c HQ Company and 2nd Lieutenant L. Curtis, M.M. Curtis was killed during the fighting in the area. German pressure continued throughout the day particularly in the 11th Parachute Battalion positions along Acacialaan and Hogeweg. Despite and valiant resistance by the South Staffs anti-tank gun-crews, the constant mortaring and probing attacks by armour and infantry began to take effect. The Germans were now setting the buildings alight, forcing the occupants to change positions. With the possibility of the airborne positions being outflanked to the north, Lonsdale decided to withdraw the force. To quote the 1st Parachute Battalion's War Diary, 'Positions were becoming untenable'. The withdrawal began covered by a solitary Vickers machine gun and one remaining South Staffs 6-pounder anti-tank gun.

As previously mentioned in Chapter 1, around 1845–1900 hours, the 1st and 3rd Parachute Battalions received orders to proceed west along Benedendorpsweg and turn south down Polderweg onto the open area of the Rosande Polder, to take up positions on the exposed ground facing east forward of Oosterbeek Laag church. The 1st Parachute Battalion with S and R Companies under Lieutenant Quartermaster Brown to be on the left flank, HQ Company under Lieutenant J.L. Williams, Reverend R.T. Watkins and Lieutenant A. Clarkson in the middle, and T Company under Lieutenant J. Turrell on the right. Artillery support was provided by Captain W.S. Caird, No. 1 FOU, RA. The 3rd Parachute Battalion under Captain Dorrien-Smith took up positions next to their fellow 1st Parachute Brigade veterans. It must again be recorded that there were a handful of South Staffs also dug in alongside the 1st Parachute Brigade, although the majority had already been deployed around Oosterbeek Laag church and the Van Hofwegen Laundry.

The extremely tenuous position occupied by the remnants of the 1st Parachute Brigade consisted of a line of trenches in front of a row of willow trees. The trenches faced directly east towards the railway embankment some 1,000 yards to their front with the Benedendorpsweg to their left flank, some 200 yards away at its nearest point, to over 1,200 yards at the Oosterbeek Laag railway viaduct. Owing to the low-lying nature of the polder, which at times was liable to flood, the water table was extremely high and digging trenches in the soft sand soon reached the underlying water table. Before the day was out, the 1st Parachute Battalion had sustained another thirty casualties with three killed.

Thursday, 21st September

The inevitable German reaction to the exposed positioning of the 1st and 3rd Parachute Battalions was not long in arriving. Mortaring and shelling on the trenches preceded a 0900 hours German infantry and armour attack from the direction of the railway and along the Benedendorpsweg which was repulsed. Again, at 1130 hours, the positions were subjected to a Nebelwerfer mortar bombardment, and throughout the morning enemy fire intensified; HE fire from a German 20mm flak gun used in a ground role was particularly devastating along with pinpoint shelling of the trenches. Around 1300 hours, Lieutenant A. Clarkson, 1st Parachute Battalion HQ, was killed in his trench.

1st Airborne Division had earlier that morning established wireless contact on the 64th Medium Regiment RA regimental net, enabling the artillery of XXX Corps in the Nijmegen area to provide much need artillery support from 1035 hours onwards. The support was initially limited due to range but at 1243 hours, Captain W.S. Caird, No. 1 Forward Observation Unit, RA attached to the 1st Parachute Battalion was able to call in a Scale 3 artillery barrage on the German forces 800 yards away along the Benedendorpsweg embankment opposite Acacialaan. This was followed by several additional barrages in the Acacialaan area over the next two and a half hours with a final barrage around 1515 hours. The Germans positioned along the high ground of the Benedendorpsweg nevertheless continued to pour a tremendous amount of fire into the trenches of the two battalions of the 1st Parachute Brigade, and at 1600 hours the decision was made to withdraw the remains of the 1st and 3rd Parachute Battalions to Oosterbeek Laag church (Oude Kerk) via the Beek Leigraaf stream to avoid further casualties. The position was untenable and from the outset served little purpose against German long-range weapons. The 1st Parachute Battalion alone incurred a further eight casualties with two dead during the withdrawal. The dead and wounded of both battalions had to be left where they fell, such was the intensity of fire and the exposed nature of the terrain. Lieutenant J.L. Williams, having earlier been wounded, Captain W.S. Caird, No. 1 Forward Observation Unit, RA thereafter assumed command of the battalion. (The 1st Parachute Battalion War Diary for this period states that the withdrawal was made due to an imminent XXX Corps barrage on the polder. However, apart from the previous barrages above, no mention of any impending allied barrage in the area at that time was recorded in the 64th Medium Regiment RA War Diary).

Events surrounding the reception upon arrival at the Oosterbeek Laag church have already been covered in Chapter 1. After a short rest and reorganisation the men of 1st and 3rd Parachute Battalions, now under the overall command of Major A. Bush, 2i/c HQ, 3rd Parachute Battalion, were sent to take up their new positions in the houses and gardens around 117–119 Benedendorpsweg. 1st Parachute Battalion were primarily responsible for engaging enemy movement along the Benedendorpsweg and preventing enemy infiltration of the houses to the south side of the road, although if necessary the nature of the position enabled them to engage German forces attacking from the north as well. The battalion received anti-tank support from a nearby 17-pounder P Troop No. 2 gun, situated opposite the Ice Factory on Benedendorpsweg with another 17-pounder, D Troop's No. 3 gun, positioned further west outside the church. At least three 6-pounder anti-tank guns were in the area in support, one from C Troop at the garage Klassen and another Polish gun to the rear of 119 Benedendorpsweg facing north, with one further Polish gun next to the church facing north. By nightfall the battalion was ensconced and ready for the defensive role it was now to play. Apart from some shelling and mortaring early on in the evening it was a quiet night. Casualties for the day totalled a further ten wounded and two killed.

Friday, 22nd September
For the next couple of days a pattern developed whereby the Germans mortared the static airborne positions at regular times and intermittently in between with varying intensity. An early morning 'hate' would begin the day followed by probing of positions by infantry, sometimes accompanied by armour. A German infantry assault began between 0700 hours and 0900 hours on the Friday by around 50 infantry in the 3rd Parachute Battalion sector and 30 infantry in the 1st Parachute Battalion sector and both attacks were successfully thwarted, ably assisted by 3-inch mortar fire under the command of Sergeant Harold 'Dick' Whittingham, crewed by Nobby Clarke and

Frank McCormic, 1st Parachute Battalion, firing without a baseplate from the back doorstep of 119 Benedendorpsweg. Further German infantry attacks supported by two armoured vehicles occurred later that morning; additional artillery fire from 64th Medium Regiment RA at Nijmegen was brought to bear at 1031 hours and again at 1245 hours, just 400–500 yards east of the 1st Parachute Battalion on German positions in the Engelenpad/JHR Neder Meyer area. The artillery fire certainly helped disrupt the enemy from forming up for any potential attacks, or indeed was useful for actually breaking up any enemy advances. One important, sometimes overlooked factor, was the effect the supporting fire had on the morale of the airborne troops who drew great comfort knowing that help was on the way and that they had the ability to hit back at the Germans. The day usually finished with an evening incoming 'hate' of mortar or shellfire. Apart from fighting patrols sent out during the night to deter enemy infiltration the night passed relatively quietly.

Saturday, 23rd September
0700 hours was the prelude to the early morning German bombardment followed by probing attacks by armour accompanied by small groups of German infantry. The Germans used the day to infiltrate infantry into houses and sniping positions which made life uncomfortable for the defenders. At 1800 hours the evening 'hate' began. After dark the 1st Parachute Battalion was reinforced with an officer and 20 men from the Glider Pilot Regiment to the east of the 3rd Parachute Battalion positions, to the rear of the 1st Parachute Battalion.

Sunday, 24th September
After the usual early morning 'hate', German pressure intensified as the day progressed. German StuG SP guns of Sturmgeschütz-Brigade 280 and supporting infantry now reinforced with flamethrower-equipped pioneers of the Pionier-Lehr-Bataillon 9 began to penetrate along the northern flank of the Lonsdale Force through the Bato's Wijk area, threatening the guns of the 1st Airlanding Light Regiment RA deployed in the area of the Oosterbeek Laag church. Requests were made once again for artillery support and the artillery of the 64th Medium Regiment RA at Nijmegen were called upon to halt the German advance. Between 1811 hours and 1820 hours, three barrages were called in on the northern end of Ploegseweg into the Bato's Wijk area. Friendly rounds falling short on Lonsdale Force were an ever-present threat. One such round that fell short destroyed a Polish 6-pounder anti-tank gun in the 3rd Parachute Battalion positions facing north up Ploegseweg. Lieutenant J. Turrell, 2i/c HQ Company, 1st Parachute Battalion was detached during the afternoon to take over the adjacent 3rd Parachute Battalion that had lost its officers, either killed or wounded.

Monday, 25th September–Tuesday, 26th September
Determined King Tiger tank and infantry attacks of Kampfgruppe *Allwörden* during the day supported by very heavy mortar fire penetrated the perimeter to the north of the 1st Parachute Brigade through the 1st Airlanding Light Regiment RA gun positions, and threatened to cut the 1st Airborne Division off from the Rhine and XXX Corps on the southern bank. It cannot be overemphasised what a critical role the guns of the Royal Artillery of XXX Corps made in halting this German breakthrough. No less than 55 shoots were carried out during the day and evening by the artillery of the 64th Medium Regiment RA; many of the barrages fell close to friendly forces and many within the airborne perimeter. One barrage at 1335 hours fell almost on top of

1st Parachute Battalion, just 100 yards east along the Benedendorpsweg against advancing enemy forces.

By 2200 hours, the 1st Parachute Battalion received orders for the evacuation that night across the Rhine and by 2300 hours the short move down towards the river began in pouring rain. By 0400 hours on 26 September, the 104 survivors of the 1st Parachute Battalion had reached the south bank of the Rhine where they were transported by DUKWs to Nijmegen.

2nd Parachute Battalion and 1st Parachute Squadron RE

The 2nd Parachute Battalion under Lieutenant Colonel John Frost took off from RAF Saltby at around 1121 hours on 17th September and at 1350 hours were the first battalion to land on DZ 'X'. 36 C-47s would carry 595 paratroopers including an element of 16th Parachute Field Ambulance, Chalk No. 47, and part of No. 1 Parachute Platoon, RASC, Chalk No. 48. Aircraft additionally carried 120 containers weighing 25,110lbs. Five of the containers failed to release over the DZ due to mechanical failure, with one being released 50 miles en route from Saltby due to a mechanical malfunction. The lead aircraft successfully relied on their Rebecca–Eureka homing devices although the GEE navigational equipment onboard was jammed by the enemy shortly after landfall in Holland. Light flak was encountered en route resulting in minor battle damage to three aircraft.

On approaching DZ 'X', yellow smoke indicated the 2nd Parachute Battalion RV which was situated at the intersection of two tracks at the southern end of the DZ close to Klein Zwitserland Hotel on the outskirts of Heelsum. (Some confusion was caused initially as someone released yellow smoke to the north of the RV, but fortunately this was ignored.) Having joined up with B Troop, 1st Airlanding Anti-Tank Battery and their other glider-borne elements, of which battalion transport consisted of five Jeeps and a Bren Gun Carrier (another additional 6-pounder anti-tank gun from C Troop, under Sergeant Robson, was ordered by the Battery CO, Major W.F. Arnold, to follow B Troop). Attached to the 2nd Parachute Battalion were Royal Engineers of B Troop, 1st Parachute Squadron RE, and No. 2 Platoon, 9th Airborne Field Company RE under Captain R.B. O'Callaghan which was tasked with clearing charges from the railway bridge. Medical support was provided by the RAMC under their Medical Officer, Captain J.W. Logan. The 16th Parachute Field Ambulance RAMC surgical teams were destined to establish themselves in St Elizabeth Hospital.

Following the 2nd Parachute Battalion were 1st Parachute Brigade HQ under Brigade Major J.A. Hibbert (minus Brigadier Lathbury who was accompanying 3rd Parachute Battalion on the middle Tiger route) along with 1st Parachute Brigade, HQ Defence Platoon, under Lieutenant J.P. Barnett. Also following the group spearheading the advance to the bridge were around 30 members of a reallocated No. 3 Parachute Platoon Jeep Section of RASC under Captain W.V.A. Gell, along with Jeep transport and trailers full of ammunition supplies. Gell was originally intended to support 1st Airlanding Brigade but due to the late arrival at the RV of No. 1 Parachute Platoon, Gell accompanied 1st Parachute Brigade HQ to the bridge. Attached to 1st Parachute Brigade HQ was a small party of 1st Airborne Ordnance Field Park Company, RAOC under Captain B.V. Manley. Frost's artillery support was provided by an observation party from No. 3 Battery, 1st Airlanding Light Regiment RA accompanied by the Battery Commander, Major Dennis Munford. Also attached to the 1st Parachute Brigade were Forward Observation Officers Captain C.O. Kennedy and Captain H.S. Buchanan from the 1st Forward Observation Unit RA.

Various other smaller units followed 1st Parachute Brigade HQ including the 89th Parachute Field Security Section under Captain J.E. Killick.

The 1st Airborne Reconnaissance Squadron was to precede the 2nd Parachute Battalion and provide a coup de main party to capture the bridge. However at 1545 hours, the squadron's C Troop were ambushed just east of Wolfheze by members of SS Panzergrenadier-Ausbildungs und Ersatz-Bataillon 16 under command of SS Sturmbannführer Sepp Kraft, which effectively blocked the intended route by the squadron's lead troop. Major C.F.H. Gough, the squadron CO, plagued like everyone else in the division by poor communications, was to eventually make his way to the bridge with several Jeeps and join Frost late on Sunday evening.

The 2nd Parachute Battalion had multiple tasks assigned to its companies. A Company's priority was to make all speed to capture the Arnhem road bridge. C Company was allocated the task of following A Company up to Oosterbeek and then make a right flanking move down Polderweg to capture the Arnhem railway bridge. If successful in capturing the railway bridge the company was to move along the south bank parallel to the river and take the southern end of the road bridge. Should the bridge be blown, C Company's other task was to capture the German HQ building in Arnhem. B Company were tasked with capturing and holding the pontoon bridge in Arnhem just west of the road bridge and use the pontoon bridge to cross the Rhine should the railway bridge capture fail.

The battalion moved off at around 1500 hours heading for their Lion route through Heelsum and Heveadorp towards Oosterbeek along the Koninginnelaan and Oude Oosterbeekseweg. A Company, under command of Major Digby Tatham-Warter, led the way off the DZ followed by Major S.C. Panter's Support Company and Major Victor Dover's C Company, then Frost and his Battalion HQ and HQ Company under Major F.R. Tate. Following up the rear were B Company under Major D.E. Crawley. A Company were first to encounter the Germans shortly after leaving the RV. A convoy of lorries and a staff car were ambushed by A Company's 3 Platoon under Lieutenant A. McDermont who took some 30 German prisoners. The battalion moved on and after two miles was held up at around 1530 hours by machine gun and mortar fire. The leading platoon dealt with the German obstruction, and the battalion then moved south slightly to avoid any further interference. On entering the Benedendorpsweg and lower Oosterbeek, the battalion approached the Oosterbeek Laag station railway viaduct and was engaged by a German armoured car which halted the advance. At 1700 hours, Frost ordered his C Company to make the assault on the railway bridge; they then made their way over the open polder towards the bridge. The bridge was defended from the south side and had demolition charges already in situ. With No. 9 Platoon in the lead followed by Company HQ, 8 and 7 Platoons in a support role, the company occupied positions in an abandoned brickworks close to the river and used the buildings as a fire base to provide support to the assault platoon under Lieutenant P. Barry. Under cover of smoke, Barry led his assault section up the embankment and onto the bridge approach. On reaching the first span of the bridge, the Germans blew the bridge, sending the centre span crashing into the water below. Under fire, Barry ordered his men to withdraw although he was wounded and unable to move; several others were hit and one killed by enemy fire. It really wasn't a good start and the opportunity to cross the river via the railway bridge had been lost. Major Dover pulled his company back along the Polderweg and intended to move to his secondary objective, the German HQ in the Nieuwe Plein close to Arnhem railway station.

Whilst C Company were attempting to capture the railway bridge, A Company were involved in dealing with the continued presence of the German armoured car around the railway viaduct on the Benedendorpsweg. Under pressure, the armoured car withdrew but the battalion was then engaged by a small group of 13 German infantry under command of SS Sturmmann Helmut Buttlar of the SS Panzer-Flak-Abteilung 10 from the higher ground around the Oosterbeek Laag railway station. With time very much on his mind, at 1830 hours Frost decided to move B Company up to take on the German troops in the station area whilst outflanking the station with A Company through the gardens to the south of the road, thereby carrying on with his advance to the Arnhem Bridge along the Klingelbeekseweg. B Company sustained a number of casualties and fatalities attempting to clear the station area including twins, Tommy and Claude Gronert of 6 Platoon and the platoon commander, Lieutenant Peter Cane. Whilst the Germans withdrew it was only temporary, and time and again the bottleneck of the railway viaduct was to hamper airborne units moving towards Arnhem.

Post-war photo. Looking north-east, Oosterbeek Laag railway station cleared by B Company. (Photo: Courtesy Gelders Archive)

By 1930 hours, A Company and HQ Company, 2nd Parachute Battalion, were within two miles of their objective with 2 Platoon, A Company under Lieutenant J.H. Grayburn on point. Apart from one or two Germans dealt with along the way, Frost passed the pontoon bridge with its centre section moored on the north bank. Leaving a few men to wait for B Company and the rest of the battalion, Frost pushed on and finally reached the road bridge at 2000 hours. A Company deployed Nos. 1 and 3 Platoons into defensive positions in buildings either side of the northern end of the bridge whilst Frost set up his Battalion HQ in a house overlooking the bridge on the corner of Marktstraat and Eusebius Buitensingel. Lieutenant Grayburn moved No. 2 Platoon up the road embankment in preparation for a move across the bridge. Support Company and the anti-tank guns of the 1st Airlanding Anti-Tank Battery arrived, still accompanied by some of the glider pilots that had flown them in. Support Company under Major S.C. Panter deployed Lieutenant R.B. Woods Mortar Platoon with its two 3-inch mortars on to a grassed traffic island on Marktstraat, and the two Vickers machine guns of the MMG Platoon under Lieutenant J.H.A. Monsell into the upper floor of a building on the corner of Kadestraat and Nieuwekade overlooking the river and the south bank. The 1st Airlanding Anti-Tank Battery 6-pounder guns, four from B Troop and one from C Troop, initially moved into cover under the bridge tunnel. HQ Company set up in a large 'H'-shaped Government Waterways building next door to Frost's HQ and by 2045–2100 hours were joined by Brigade HQ. Major C.F.H. Gough, the Reconnaissance Squadron CO along with two Vickers 'K' gun mounted Jeeps arrived with Brigade HQ and joined Frost. Gough's beleaguered squadron came under command of his 2i/c, Captain David Allsop, and divisional control in the Oosterbeek area until the end of the battle. As the evening wore on, more units began to arrive at the bridge including the No. 3 Parachute Platoon Jeep Section of RASC under Captain W.V.A. Gell, plus elements of RAOC under Captain Manley.

At approximately 2100 hours, Lieutenant Grayburn's platoon began to stealthily move onto the bridge in the dark and began to advance. Within a few yards as they approached a pillbox on the side of the bridge road they came under withering machine gunfire from within and from an armoured car on the south side. The wooden strongpoint, with behind it a concrete pillbox, had in fact a flak tower with a 20mm cannon mounted behind it on a bridge abutment and it presented a formidable emplacement. Grayburn was hit in the shoulder and a number of men were wounded, the attack was called off and Grayburn pulled his men back.

Consideration of how to remove the strongpoint and pillbox was made easier by the arrival of B Troop under Captain T.J. Liversey and A Troop under Captain F.M. Mackay of the 1st Parachute Squadron RE under overall command of Major D.C. Murray, which arrived between 2130 and 2200 hours. The troublesome pillbox had to be eliminated and this was achieved by a combined effort: a B Troop, 1st Airlanding Anti-Tank Battery, RA, 6-pounder anti-tank gun under Sergeant Shelswell was brought up the side ramp and engaged the pillbox at point blank range supported by a Royal Engineer flamethrower team from B Troop, 1st Parachute Squadron, RE, firing from an adjacent building to the bridge. The flamethrower missed its target and hit another wooden hut containing ammunition and signal equipment resulting in the hut catching fire with accompanying secondary explosions. The 6-pounder gun withdrew as did the sappers, the burning hut lighting up the night sky as they departed. Shortly after this episode, a convoy of three or four German lorries approached from the south side and were halted near the pillbox. The resulting fire set alight one of the lorries containing fuel, which burst into flames. The crews were either killed or taken prisoner, and the remaining lorries quickly caught alight and added to the blaze.

Frost decided to deploy the 1st Parachute Squadron RE on the eastern side of the bridge ramp into two of three buildings that ran parallel to the ramp. The nearest to the bridge was the Van Limburg Stirum School which was initially occupied by elements of B Troop. The second building next door in line along the ramp known as the 'Red School' was occupied for a short time Sunday night by part of A Troop until 2315 hours when they were attacked by the enemy. Captain Mackay and the A Troop sappers drove the Germans out of the surrounding garden and then were forced to withdraw to the main Van Limburg Stirum School building due to the vulnerability of their building to further assaults. The Van Limburg Stirum School now contained approximately 18 A Troop sappers under Captain Mackay and 25 B Troop sappers under Lieutenant D.J. Simpson.

Lieutenant D.R. Hindley, CO of HQ Troop, and 10 sappers along with 20 signallers and a group of RAOC under Captain Manley took control of a building 30 yards from the school on the east side of Eusebius Buitensingel on the corner of Westervoortsedijk but found their field of fire restricted.

With the bridge area alight and illuminated there could be little chance of crossing over the bridge to the south side so Frost came up with a plan to utilise any boats that could be found in the area of the pontoon bridge. Frost planned to send B Company and the brigade defence platoon across in boats and take the southern end of the bridge from the south side of the river. Frost delegated the CO of the 1st Parachute Squadron REs, Major George Murray and some of his sappers along with the Brigade Defence Platoon to oversee the crossing. Frost planned at the same time to use C Company (which was still missing in the town) to take on B Company's commitments. The plan was to be of no avail. Captain E. O'Callaghan, 9th Field Company, RE, had arrived at the pontoon bridge around 2130 hours to find the centre section removed and moored to the north bank and immediately had his sappers examine the viability of reassembling the pontoon, which was decided against. No alternative suitable boats or barges could be found, plus the Germans were already becoming very active on the opposite southern bank. After meeting up and discussing the feasibility of the exercise with Major Murray the plan was abandoned, and they both decided at 2300 hours to take their sappers and the Brigade Defence Platoon and head for the road bridge and join Frost.

Meanwhile B Company were making their way towards their original objective, the pontoon bridge, arriving around 0200 hours. They consolidated in buildings around the pontoon and eventually moved off, making their way along the Rijnkade in their efforts to join Frost at the bridge and in the process coming under fire from German armoured fighting vehicles south of the river. Apart from some of its No. 4 Platoon under Lieutenant R.H. Levien, which was the last platoon in B Company to leave the pontoon area, the remnants of B Company, around 84 men, linked up with Frost during the early hours of Monday morning at around 0530 hours and deployed to defensive positions around the western side of the bridge. Levien and around 13 of his men lost contact with the rest of B Company and made an unfortunate move in turning north into the town and ended up cut off and surrounded in Bakkerstraat and were eventually all taken prisoner early morning on Tuesday 19th.[2]

Still out of radio contact, C Company under Major Dover moved away from the demolished railway bridge in Oosterbeek and in fading light pushed forward into Arnhem at full speed towards its second objective. Leading the way were 8 Platoon under Lieutenant Ian H. Russell, followed by Company HQ, 7 Platoon under Lieutenant D. Russell and rearguard were Lieutenant Peter Barry's 9 Platoon, now weakened by the losses sustained in the abortive assault on the railway bridge. Making their way carefully up the Utrechtseweg incline towards the St Elizabeth Hospital, they surprised a large party of Germans that had just alighted from two vehicles and had formed up in three ranks by the side of the road. Ian Russell's platoon moved under cover of the embankment parallel to the assembled Germans and opened fire, killing and wounding a number and taking several prisoner. The company then moved further up the Utrechtseweg towards Utrechtsestraat. At about 2200 hours, having reached the brow of the hill, the company, still led by Ian Russell's 8 Platoon, began the gradual descent towards their secondary objective, the German HQ building on Nieuwe Plein. In the darkness the two leading scouts moved

---

2   David G. van Buggenum, *B Company Arrived* (Renkum: R.N. Sigmond Publishing, 2003), p.62.

cautiously along the pavement keeping to the shadows. The only sounds were from their hobnailed boots on the stone pavement. The silence was suddenly shattered by bursts of machine gun fire from across the street which killed both scouts. C Company, around 100 strong, immediately took evasive action and occupied several adjacent buildings. They had run into a forward German position from SS Hauptsturmführer Hans Möller's 2nd Pioneer Company in the process of forming a blocking line into Arnhem. Dover's men hastily prepared the buildings for defence, whilst recommending that their Dutch occupants move to the cellars or better still, leave the area entirely as Dover, concerned for their safety, expected the Germans to begin their assault in the morning. During the night Dover made radio contact with B Company and explained his situation to Major Crawley. He told Crawley that he intended to break out in the morning and would attempt to reach the Onderlangs and make his way to join Frost at the bridge. It was during the night, around 0300 hours, that Dover was wounded. He was checking that his sentries were awake when he was hit in the backside probably by a piece of shrapnel leaving an entry and exit wound in both cheeks. Dover had his wound dressed by one of his men who made light of the wound, commenting, 'Sir, you'll get your discharge with this one. You'll be no bloody good in the army, but the navy will have you – you've got five of 'em!' Dover appreciated the crude humour of the British soldier in times of stress.[3]

Before first light at around 0700 hours on Monday 18th, Dover moved his company out of the rear of the buildings and with great difficulty they moved under fire across the back gardens over high brick walls and fences in a westerly direction back towards the museum. They were followed in the road outside by German infantry and half-tracks equipped with 20mm flak guns being used in a ground role with devastating effect. When they reached a side road, the Nachtegalspad, which linked Utrechtsestraat with the railway, they encountered flanking fire from the railway embankment. Taking casualties, Dover's fragmented company crossed Nachtegaalspad and finally ended up with around 25 survivors in houses close to the Gemeente Museum, No. 38 (now No. 72 and known today as 'Airborne House') and No. 40 Utrechtseweg. A number of the company along with Lieutenant Ian Russell managed to break out and cross Utrechtseweg. (Russell eventually linked up with Lieutenant James Cleminson's 5 Platoon, leading 3rd Parachute Battalion on the Onderlangs.) The Germans swiftly brought up their mobile 20mm flak guns to point blank range to engage the buildings and Möller's pioneers assisted with their flamethrowers to force Dover and his men out. Dover had no alternative but to surrender what remained of C Company.

Having accounted for 2nd Parachute Battalion's B and C Companies movements, we can now move back to the Sunday evening and the fighting around the bridge area. With the onset of night came a certain amount of respite. Frost visited his A Company positions and found the men cheerful and confident having reached their objective and expecting XXX Corps to reach them the following day.

Around 2400 hours, C Company, 3rd Parachute Battalion, under command of Major R.P.C. 'Pongo' Lewis, began to arrive in the Arnhem Bridge area having made their way along the railway line from Oosterbeek into Arnhem. Led by Lieutenant G. Infield and his 8 Platoon, the company's leading section destroyed an approaching German armoured car with a Gammon Bomb. Lewis decided rather than fight their way through he would try cunning and initially marched his men through the town avoiding contact using the cloak of darkness to hide their identity meanwhile passing several lorry loads of Germans on the way.

3   Major Victor Dover, *The Silken Canopy* (London: Cassell, 1979), p.101.

Left: Tuesday, 19th September. Utrechtsestraat facing west uphill towards the Municipal Museum. A German squad on the right advances up the incline past the bodies of Private Norman Shipley and Lance Corporal William Loney, 8 Platoon, C Company, 2 Parachute Battalion, killed by machine gun fire on the Sunday night. (Photo: Kriegsberichter Jacobsen; Courtesy Gelders Archive). Below: Comparison (Photo: Author's private collection, 1980)

Nachtegaalspad junction with Utrechtseweg looking north towards the railway. Dover's men crossed from right to left whilst under fire. British POWs from the fighting around the Gemeente Museum were later led down the street into Renssenstraat for processing. (Photo: Author, 1980)

Nearing the bridge the company adopted a more tactical deployment. Advancing south along Eusebius Buitensingel in this order: 8 Platoon, Company HQ, 7 Platoon, with 9 Platoon in the rear. As the company neared its objective it split into two halves; as it approached the beginning of the bridge ramp, 7 and 8 Platoons were on the right of the road and Company HQ and 9 Platoon to the left. On reaching the bridge area, Lewis made contact with Captain P.B. 'Bucky' Boiteux-Buchanan, Intelligence Officer, 2nd Parachute Battalion. Lewis was ordered to join the 1st Parachute Squadron, RE, occupying the Van Limburg Stirum School adjacent to the bridge ramp and also send 8 Platoon to buildings on the opposite corner of the crossroads south of the schoolhouse on the Westervoortsedijk, somewhat east of the position occupied by Lieutenant J.P. Barnett and his 1st Parachute Brigade Defence Platoon. Lieutenant G. Infield and his 8 Platoon moved under the bridge east along the Westervoortsedijk with one section occupying the Camiz Dairy; another moved into the Rijkswerkplaats works offices on de Badhuisstraat junction along with Platoon HQ, whilst the third section took over No. 2 Nieuwe Kade opposite Badhuisstraat.[4] The platoon was out on a limb and spread thinly with little hope of holding off a concerted enemy attack for long.

Major Lewis moved into the schoolhouse with his HQ. It was intended that 7 Platoon, under Lieutenant Peter L. Hibburt, should follow Lewis into the school whilst Lieutenant Len Wright's 9 Platoon held the north end of the approach road temporarily whilst the buildings were being

4   Niall Cherry, *With Nothing Bigger Than a Bren Gun* (Taunton: Brendon Publishing, 2007), p.11.

fortified. The Germans in the vicinity had detected the efforts to reinforce the school, having already attacked and occupied the second building next door in line along the ramp, the Red School. Before 7 Platoon could move they were cut off just 50 yards short from the school and were all taken prisoner. 9 Platoon came under increasingly heavy fire during a series of attacks from the front and both flanks. A fighting withdrawal by 9 Platoon resulted in nine men reaching the schoolhouse, five of them being wounded.

The Van Limburg Stirum School force now consisted of approximately 18 A Troop sappers under Captain Mackay and 25 B Troop sappers under Lieutenant D.J. 'Stiffy' Simpson, in addition to Major R.P.C. 'Pongo' Lewis and his 2i/c Captain W. 'Chippy' Robinson, HQ, C Company and the remnants of Lieutenant Len Wright's 9 Platoon, 3rd Parachute Battalion. Lieutenant D.R. Hindley's HQ Troop of around 10 RE sappers plus around 20 brigade signallers occupied a house 30 yards from the school on the eastern side of Eusebius Buitensingel. In the same area, the corner house on the junction of Eusebius Buitensingel and Westervoortsedijk was occupied by around a dozen men comprised of a six-man section of RAOC under Captain Manley and half a dozen brigade signallers. On arrival at the bridge, the 1st Parachute Brigade Major, Major J.A. Hibbert, had instructed that all non-essential personnel of the Signal Section and Brigade HQ were to come under command of Captain B.N. Briggs, Brigade Staff Captain, assisted by Lieutenant J.B. Cairns, 2i/c Signal Section, and proceed across to the east side of the road bridge and take up defensive positions on the Eusebius Buitensingel.

Monday, 18th September

In the early hours of Monday morning around 0200 hours, 30 men of Captain O'Callaghan's No. 2 Platoon of the 9th Field Company RE arrived at the bridge. O'Callaghan's platoon initially took up positions in an old woodworking factory building which ran alongside the approach ramp to the bridge. During the night German movement could be heard around the bridge area whilst the defenders reinforced their defensive positions.

As a misty dawn broke, four lorries approached the bridge area. The first, unfortunately, was a Dutch refuse lorry which was promptly shot up, followed by three truckloads of Germans which received a similar fate. The wounded were taken care of and a few survivors were taken prisoner. Shortly after, advance elements of German armour from Panzer-Kompanie *Mielke* supported by infantry from Kampfgruppe *Knaust* appeared from the east side of the Rhine and were seen off. A short period of calm followed until around 0900 hours when vehicle engines could be heard on the south side of the bridge approaches. Visible confirmation of a build-up of German vehicles was made by observers high up in the buildings surrounding the bridge and Major Munford of the 1st Airlanding Light Regiment RA brought in some pre-registered interdiction fire from No. 3 Battery at Oosterbeek. The fire was directed at an armoured column forming up from SS Panzer-Aufklärungsabteilung 9, under command of SS Hauptsturmführer Viktor Grabner. The artillery fire did little to deter the leading armoured cars from beginning to move at speed north across the bridge. On approaching the British positions at the north end, the leading reconnaissance vehicle ran over a string of Hawkins mines which had been laid across the road; however, only minor damage was incurred and the multi wheeled vehicle carried on, followed by another four armoured cars which headed off into Arnhem. It was noted at the time that some of the German vehicle crews actually had the cheek to wave at the British defenders as they drove by.

Taken somewhat by surprise at the speed of the advance vehicles of the column, the defenders were quickly alert and prepared for the slower moving open-topped half-tracks, lorries and other vehicles following behind. Every defender at the bridge that was able opened fire on the German column including 6-pounder anti-tank guns, PIATs and small arms. The German convoy was decimated by the intense fire; leading vehicles stopped, others crashed into them and burst into flames, and chaos ensued. Several vehicles made it down a side path in front of the Van Limburg Stirum School and were knocked out by the sappers of 1st Parachute Squadron RE and C Company, 3rd Parachute Battalion throwing grenades and firing from the floors above down into the open rear of the half-tracks. Over 20 German vehicles were knocked out in an action that lasted less than two hours, leaving dozens of Germans dead, including SS Hauptsturmführer Viktor Grabner.

Later that day, following Grabner's unsuccessful attempt to cross the bridge, the Germans brought up more motorised infantry to the approaches to the south end of the bridge. However, the German movement was spotted and their intentions were thwarted by a rapid salvo of 3-inch mortar bombs accompanied by fire from the Vickers machine guns of Support Company. The German infantry fled the area leaving several trucks alight. Shortly after the Germans resumed their shelling and mortaring. One enemy mortar was spotted firing from a concealed position behind a building on the south bank. The tell-tale puffs of smoke from each round fired gave the position away and counter mortar fire from Lieutenant Woods' 3-inch mortars soon silenced the German mortar.

The Van Limburg Stirum School position on the eastern bridge ramp had been under attack since dawn and the battle at the bridge seemed to be now becoming divided, with multi-directional attacks initially from the east. Lieutenant D.J. Simpson, RE writes: 'About lunchtime we began to be heavily mortared and it was some few minutes before we realised that this fire was coming from 2nd Battalion. Mackay put his head out of the window and with some very "fruity" words stopped it in no time.'[5]

At around 1100 hours, preceded by a mortar bombardment, the Germans launched a combined infantry and armoured attack from the east along the Westervoortsedijk and the Nieuwe Kade river road towards Ooststraat and the crossroads of Eusebius Buitensingel and Westervoortsedijk, targeting first the buildings occupied by Lieutenant J.P. Barnett and his 1st Parachute Brigade Defence Platoon and Lieutenant Infield's No. 8 Platoon, C Company, 3rd Parachute Battalion. The intention of the German attack was to secure all the buildings east of the bridge along the river and the houses on the east side of Eusebius Buitensingel. By noon, Panzergrenadiers and tanks of Kampfgruppe *Knaust* had taken control of the Camiz Dairy and pushed further west towards Ooststraat. 8 Platoon, C Company, 3rd Parachute Battalion were overrun and Lieutenant Barnett's Brigade Defence Platoon forced to withdraw.[6] Two of the German tanks, both PzKpfw IVs, were engaged by the No. 4, C Troop, 6-pounder anti-tank gun situated outside the 1st Airlanding Anti-Tank Battery HQ on Markstraat on the west side of the bridge. The first tank to be hit was recorded to have come to a halt slewed across the Westervoortsedijk some 100 yards east of the Camiz Dairy, with the second tank being knocked out directly underneath the Camiz Dairy pipe bridge with three successive hits to the front of the tank.[7] The 6-pounder anti-tank gun commander, Sergeant Cyril Robson, claimed both tank kills. Robson endured constant replacements to his gun crew during the course of the battle until realistically manning the gun due to small arms and mortar fire became impossible. In the course of the battle, Robson had 11 crewmen wounded and one killed.

---

5   CRE British Army of the Rhine, *Royal Engineers Battlefield Tour, The Seine to the Rhine, Vols 1 & 2* (Uckfield: The Naval and Military Press, originally published 1947), p.132.
6   Bob Gerritsen & Scott Revell, *Retake Arnhem Bridge* (Renkum: R.N. Sigmond Publishing, 2014), p.52.
7   Karel Magry, *Operation Market Garden Then and Now, Vols1 & 2* (Barnsley: Pen & Sword, 2002), p.471.

Post-war photo of one of the PzKpfw IVs knocked out at the Camiz Dairy on Westervoortsedijk during the battle. A great deal more destruction to the area was caused after the battle during bombing of the bridge by the USAF in 1945. (Photo: Courtesy Gelders Archive)

Camiz Dairy on Westervoortsedijk in 1945 with the remains of one of the PzKpfw IVs to the right of the picture facing the bridge. At one stage this tank had the collapsed dairy pipe bridge on it. Another PzKpfw IV was disabled just out of the picture to the left. (Photo: Courtesy Gelders Archive)

The impetus of the attack, however, carried the Germans further towards the Ooststraat junction and the building occupied by Lieutenant McDermont's No. 3 Platoon, A Company, 2nd Parachute Battalion situated in the corner building of the office of the Electricity Board and Tram Company on the Ooststraat/Westervoortsedijk junction. In fact, the Germans had succeeded in capturing the Public Works Service Office south of McDermont's position and infiltrated under the bridge itself as far as a house on Rijnkade No. 119, threatening to cut McDermont off.

No. 6 Platoon, B Company, 2nd Parachute Battalion were instructed to first retake Rijnkade 119 on the west side of the bridge and then continue to assault the Public Works Service Office now under German occupation on the east side. Having lost their platoon commanding officer, Lieutenant Peter Cane, who was shot in the head the day before by a sniper, No. 6 Platoon came under command of 2nd Lieutenant J. Flavell, 2nd Parachute Battalion, HQ Liaison Officer. 2nd Lieutenant Flavell received instructions from the A Company Commander, Major Digby Tatham-Warter to recapture the enemy-held buildings and make contact with McDermont's platoon, then under severe pressure from tanks and infantry, No. 6 Platoon was then to come under command of A Company. The first objective west of the bridge was taken with some ease and the 19 members of No. 6 Platoon divided into assault and fire support sections for the attack on the Public Works Service Office. Flavell first made contact with Lieutenant McDermont and his platoon which was still under tank and infantry fire and informed him that the house to his rear in Rijnkade had been cleared of enemy. Flavell's second objective was the Public Works Service Office which was a large building with German defenders ensconced on the first floor. The assault went in against a determined defence with grenades being thrown from upper windows at the assault group. Flavell's men gained entry into the building and room-to-room fighting ensued. As happened so often in house-to-house fighting, at one stage the Germans occupied one floor and the British held another, but eventually the building was cleared of Germans. The German attack from the east continued and shortly after the building was taken, the Germans brought up an artillery piece and proceeded to open fire on the building, firing several rounds until the crew were eliminated or driven off. Later that night, the Public Works Service Office building caught fire and Flavell and his men of No. 6 Platoon withdrew west under the bridge to Rijnkade 119, only to be burnt out of that house by 2245 hours. The platoon then took up positions under the bridge ramp and some smaller outbuildings.

At the Van Limburg Stirum School, the effects of the German attack from the east began to be felt with enemy infiltration into the buildings to the east of Eusebius Buitensingel opposite the school, and by 1400 hours the Germans had set up two machine guns able to fire directly into the eastern facing rooms of the school. With the German occupation of the Red School to the immediate north of the school from which machine gun fire was received earlier in the day, the defenders were now subjected to crossfire from the north and east. Both these threats were eliminated by accurate Bren gun fire from the RE sappers and C Company defenders although it took three hours to clear the houses to the east. The Germans, however, maintained their mortar positions behind the houses. Having already sustained numerous casualties which littered the surrounds of the school, the Germans began to mortar the school and the surrounding buildings in the bridge area occupied by Frost and his men. The biggest concern to the British was ammunition, as only limited amounts remained and any reserves were issued.

Late in the afternoon on the Monday, the Germans deployed a field gun at a crossroads 400 yards north of Brigade HQ and systematically began to shell the building, blasting huge holes in the north end wall. Major Dennis S. Munford, Officer Commanding, 3 Battery, 1st Airlanding

Pre-war photo of the north-eastern side of the bridge ramp. To the immediate right is an outbuilding belonging to the main Public Works Service Office building, which is out of picture further to the right. To the right middle distance on the Westervoortsedijk/Ooststraat junction stands the building occupied by No. 3 Platoon, A Company, 2nd Parachute Battalion under Lieutenant McDermont. (Photo: Courtesy Gelders Archive)

Monday, 18th September, afternoon. Rijnkade 119 just visible to the left of the bridge support. Due to enemy infiltration, No. 6 Platoon, B Company 2nd Parachute Battalion were instructed to first recapture Rijnkade 119 on the west side of the bridge and then continue to assault the Public Works Service Office under German occupation on the east side, visible to the right of the bridge support. Both objectives were retaken until both buildings were burnt out later in the night. Photo taken in 1935. (Photo: Courtesy Gelders Archive)

Light Battery, Royal Artillery was called upon by the brigade major to silence the gun. Munford called in fire from 3 Battery at Oosterbeek which after an initial ranging shot scored a direct hit on the gun, putting its crew out of action. Just as dusk was settling in, the RAOC and Brigade Signallers on the corner of Westervoortsedijk and Eusebius Buitensingel witnessed the arrival of No. 3 gun, B Troop, 1st Airlanding Anti-Tank Battery, RA, under Sergeant W. Kill which was deployed on the corner opposite their house in a small copse to cover the crossroads. The gun was accompanied by a small infantry screen to provide local defence for the gun crew. The gun went into action against enemy targets that evening, but by midnight its position had been spotted and silenced as so many of the anti-tank guns were by mortar and small arms fire, which made the guns untenable. The mortar fire caught the building close by alight, which burnt out by the following morning.

German troops examine Sergeant W. Kill's abandoned 'Bravado II' No. 3 gun, B Troop, 1st Airlanding Anti-Tank Battery, RA, on the corner of Westervoortsedijk and Oostraat. Burnt-out buildings on the Westervoortsedijk in the background testify to the ferocity of the fighting in the area. The firing pin appears to have been removed from the breech before the gun and unused ammunition was abandoned. Private Ted Mordecai, RAOC, was positioned opposite: 'Jerry opened up on us again with long-range stuff and was answered back by the six-pounder which did some good work that night, but was eventually put out of action towards midnight. The Germans had evidently spotted it and had put in a heavy concentration of mortar bombs on its location and the large house alongside. This house was blazing like an inferno and lit up the surrounding area for the rest of the night and eventually petered out towards dawn.' (Photo: Courtesy IWM MH3955)

Arnhem, Monday 18th September. Aerial view from 18,000 feet shows the pontoon bridge with the centre section moored to the north bank, whilst on the road bridge can be seen the wreckage of SS Hauptsturmführer Viktor Grabner's SS Panzer-Aufklärungsabteilung 9. (Photo: Courtesy NCAP:406 US 7GR/3358)

Close-up of the removed pontoon bridge centre section. (Photo: Courtesy NCAP:406 US 7GR/3358)

Arnhem pontoon or 'ship-bridge' looking northwest. Pre-war photo. (Photo: Courtesy Aviodrome Lelystad 2659)

As night drew in, the Germans surrounding the school area set alight the two knocked-out half-tracks, one SdKfz10 and a SdKfz250 which lay beneath the school walls. Using a man-portable flamethrower and firing incendiary shells, the vehicles quickly caught alight illuminating the defenders within the building and threatening to set the school alight. Any useful contents in the half-tracks that may have been valuable and retrievable to the school occupants now perished in the flames. A sapper team crawled out with explosives and blew up the offending vehicles. Shortly after this episode, at around 2000 hours, a German L.gr.W63 light mortar team situated in the Red School began firing 50mm bombs horizontally through the north-facing windows of the Van Limburg Stirum School. This caused a degree of alarm and a hasty withdrawal from the rooms concerned. The Germans continued their attempts to clear the school by first setting fire to the Red School; flames spread rapidly and sparks soon drifted onto the wooden school roof of the Van Limburg Stirum School. RE sapper and C Company firefighting teams used much of the remaining water reserves quenching the flames, which under sporadic machine gun fire proved no easy task. The fire was eventually extinguished just before midnight.

Tuesday, 19th September
The Germans intensified their attacks on the Van Limburg Stirum School during the night. In the early hours of Tuesday morning at 0030 hours, an infantry attack on the north and eastern sides of the school was preceded by a volley of rifle grenades fired through the windows of the ground and first floor. This was rapidly followed up by an infantry assault which reached the outside walls. The Germans then threw hand grenades into the building and pushed a machine gun through the open windows, spraying the rooms and adjacent hallway with fire. The defenders vigorously retaliated and managed to beat off the German assault. Steps were then taken to close off vulnerable rooms and fortify them by knocking out loopholes in internal walls so that each room could be covered by fire from inside. It must be remembered that the school was a large three-storey building and had been prepared for defence by knocking out all glass windows and barricading rooms with school desks and furniture using mattresses to provide blast walls. There were initially around 60 defenders in all, and the building had windows at every level from the basement upwards with at least 25 windows on the east and north sides alone.

At 0200 hours, the Germans switched their direction of attack and infiltrated a Panzerfaust or Panzerschreck to within 150 metres of the south-west corner of the school. Either weapon would have been effective against a building. The Panzerfaust had a handful of variants, the largest of which could penetrate up to 200mm of armour up to 150 metres. Mackay described the weapon as a 'bazooka' so it was probably a Panzerschreck. This 88mm anti-tank weapon could propel a 7.25lb hollow-charged rocket through 100mm of armour and had no trouble penetrating the first-floor walls of the school building, causing extensive damage to the corner of the building and blowing away part of the internal floor whilst concussing the occupants. After this successful rocket attack the Germans apparently considered that they had finally subdued the defenders, and within the hour around a company of Panzergrenadiers had assembled at the south side of the school and casually stood around immediately outside the walls of the building, smoking and deciding on their next move. This golden opportunity proved too much for the defenders to resist and plans were quietly put in place to launch a simultaneous volley of grenades from the first-floor windows down onto the unsuspecting Germans below. The defenders equipped themselves with either Mills 36 grenades or Gammon bombs accompanied by others with Sten or Bren guns and awaited the order to open fire. The ensuing chaos did not fully reveal itself until dawn of the Tuesday morning when the results of the fusillade of grenades became fully apparent, with over 30 German dead sprawled below the school windows.

One important command change took place on the Monday evening at the bridge. It had become apparent through one of the intermittent wireless links with the 1st Parachute Battalion that Brigadier Lathbury was missing and that the likelihood of the remainder of 1st Parachute Brigade group reaching the beleaguered force at the bridge was diminishing. Therefore Major J.A. Hibbert, the 1st Parachute Brigade Major, asked Lieutenant Colonel Frost to take over responsibility for all the forces at the bridge. Frost moved from his Battalion HQ building next door into the larger Brigade HQ situated in the government waterways building which also served as a regimental aid post. Frost handed over command of 2nd Parachute Battalion HQ to his 2i/c, Major D.W. Wallis. Wallis was a popular 'father figure' within the battalion. Later that night, Wallis was making his rounds to the various defensive positions in the houses around the bridge when he approached the building containing A Company HQ and sappers from 9th Field Company RE. The sapper guarding the door into the building challenged the silhouette in the doorway and having failed to hear or recognise the response opened fire, mortally wounding Wallis. Frost later appointed Major Tatham-Warter to take over as OC 2nd Parachute Battalion. Both Frost's new Brigade HQ and his Battalion HQ along with many other buildings on the west side and east side of the bridge were constantly catching alight. Fires were being put out only to start up again through drifting embers from adjacent properties.

At 0700 hours, the Germans intensified their efforts to clear the east side of the bridge. Preceded by an artillery and mortar bombardment a combined infantry and armour attack was launched from the east along the Westervoortsedijk. Lieutenant McDermont's No. 3 Platoon, A Company, 2nd Parachute Battalion were still in possession of their Electricity Board and Tram Company building from the previous day on the corner of Ooststraat and Westervoortsedijk and came under close-range tank fire from the German tanks of Panzer-Kompanie *Mielke*, part of Kampfgruppe *Knaust*. McDermont's men were forced to withdraw around 1030 hours from their building under heavy enemy fire. About midday, having reformed under the bridge, McDermont, with a few additional troops gathered together by Major Tatham-Warter, led a determined counter-attack to retake the building. McDermont's group received fire support from the school during the charge for the building. McDermont was the first to breach the back door and, followed by his men, headed for the first floor where the Germans were gathered. McDermont reached the half-landing where he was met by a burst of automatic fire which mortally wounded him along with the platoon radio operator, Private McAuslan. The German responsible was immediately cut down in a burst of Sten gunfire from a para further down the stairs. The rest of McDermont's group leapt over the bodies of McDermont and McAuslan and recaptured the building.[8]

The German pressure on the east side of the bridge defences continued through the rest of the day with tanks turning their attention on any building thought to contain British troops. The houses on the east side of Eusebius Buitensingel were systematically set alight by the Germans, a tactic now being employed all around the bridge to clear the area of the British. By 1000 hours the tanks, some of which were *PzKpfw* IIIs, pushed far enough forward to engage the south-east face of the Van Limburg Stirum School with armour piercing shot; at the same time shelling Lieutenant Hindley's Squadron HQ building opposite the school. Hindley managed to get close

---

8 Steve Morgan, *With a Machine Gun to Arnhem* (Taunton: Brendon Publishing, 2020), p.15.

enough to one tank to drop a Gammon Bomb on the vehicle from an upstairs window. The Germans persisted with their attacks throughout the day, infiltrating snipers and infantry and tightening their grip around an ever-decreasing bridge perimeter. Many houses on the Eusebius Buitensingel were on fire, and those that were not were either occupied by Germans or the few remaining British. Having lost so many men in infantry assaults, the German tactics were restructured to simply set fire to buildings and burn and blast the defenders out on both the east and west sides of the bridge.

Around 1530 hours, the defenders around the bridge came under a strafing run by a gaggle of German Messerschmitt Bf 109 fighter bombers belonging to Jagdgeschwader 76 based at Stormede. Flying low through the smoke from the burning buildings, one of the aircraft clipped the twin towers of the St Walburgis church, lost control and crashed into an ornamental pond at the northern end of the bridge approach killing the pilot, Unteroffizier Paul Schmidt.

At 1900 hours, two 60-ton PzKpfw VI Tiger I tanks of Schwere Panzer-Kompanie *Hummel* belonging to Kampfgruppe *Brinkmann* appeared from the north end of the bridge ramp and gradually trundled towards the bridge, first engaging buildings on the west side. Firing a mix of high explosive and armour-piercing rounds, they very rapidly began to demolish buildings. They continued to move forward and approached to within 30 yards of the Van Limburg Stirum School and swung their 88mm barrels towards the school. The first two HE rounds blew the north-west corner of the school completely away followed by AP rounds which penetrated the entire building leaving a four-foot hole through eight walls. The RE sappers and men of C Company, 3rd Parachute Battalion, rapidly vacated the upper story of the building to the basement and avoided the remaining fire. The tanks could not depress their barrels below the horizontal as the bridge ramp was level with the upper parts of the schoolhouse. It wasn't long before the defenders around the bridge organised a response to the arrival of the Tiger tanks. Both tanks came under fire from PIATs and 6-pounder anti-tank gun fire. One of the two Tigers was hit at least twice by 6-pounder AP rounds (either APCBC or APDS) which hit the turret and the 88mm gun, causing casualties within the tank. The two tanks then withdrew from the bridge ramp and out of range to await the arrival of the twelve remaining tanks of their unit still making their way to Arnhem from Bocholt.

Fires continued into the night with more buildings in flames, forcing occupants to retire to alternative positions. Lieutenant Hindley and his men of 1st Parachute Squadron, RE, HQ Troop were forced out of their positions and made the hazardous journey over to the west side of the bridge to join Frost's men. The brigade signallers under Lieutenant Cairns, around six in number, were forced to join the evacuation of their building and managed to reach Brigade HQ. Captain Manley and his RAOC group also vacated their building and moved across the Westervoortse Dijk into several buildings and then under the bridge itself, getting split up on the way. There was little resistance now on the east side of the bridge apart from the defenders in the Van Limburg Stirum School. By now most of the area of Arnhem town around the bridge, including two churches, were on fire. Ammunition and water were running low and casualties were mounting with the threat of wounded being trapped and burnt alive. Under the cover of darkness, small groups of German infantry infiltrated into positions around the bridge, making movement extremely dangerous in the light of the fires. It was now becoming apparent that XXX Corps were experiencing problems reaching Frost and that the rest of the 1st Airborne Division were not in a strong enough position to breakthrough and reinforce the bridge defence. The night passed relatively peacefully apart from patrol skirmishes and sniping.

Nieuwe Kade looking west. German infantry move back from the bridge with armoured support from PzKpfw IIIs of Panzer-Kompanie *Mielke*. One tank sits in the middle of the road facing the British positions in the smoke around the bridge whilst in the foreground another tank is parked at the entrance to Jos Pe printing works. Photograph probably taken on Tuesday 19th September. (Photo: Tank gunner Gefreiter Karl-Heinz Kracht. Ed Collection, Courtesy ABM)

Tuesday, 19th September, taken at the height of the fighting around the bridge. Fires can be seen burning from various buildings all around the bridge. Careful examination of the photo will reveal the two S Company, 2nd Parachute Battalion 3-inch mortar positions on the triangular, grassed traffic island along with other slit trenches in the area of the bridge ramp. The wreckage of the German vehicles on the bridge is clear to see. (Photo: Courtesy Gelders Archive)

Wednesday, 20th September

Just after dawn, the Germans commenced their mortar and shelling of the bridge area. Frost finally made radio contact with Divisional HQ and spoke to Major-General Urquhart which confirmed his worst fears. Urquhart knew little more than Frost about the overall situation. At 0915 hours, the Germans launched an attack towards the bridge along the river front from the east and quickly reached the underneath of the bridge supports with the intention of laying demolition charges. Lieutenant J.H. Grayburn, OC 2 Platoon, A Company, 2nd Parachute Battalion supported by Lieutenant Hindley and a handful of his sappers counter-attacked the German demolition party and removed the charges, Grayburn being wounded in the process. Despite defensive fire from the Van Limburg Stirum School, at 1020 hours the Germans themselves counter-attacked with support from a tank and regained a hold on the underside of the bridge, and then attempted to re-lay the fuses, Grayburn led his men into the attack once more only to be cut down by machine gun fire. The charges however were once more removed. Lieutenant J.H. Grayburn was awarded a posthumous Victoria Cross for his actions at the bridge.

The situation around the bridge began to deteriorate rapidly with more buildings alight or already burnt out, leaving little cover for the defenders. Lieutenant J. Flavell and his No. 6 Platoon, B Company group withdrew from their Rijnkade 119 position back towards Battalion HQ where they entered through the rear garden and met with Major Doug Crawley. Shortly after, Crawley met with Frost and whilst they were talking, a mortar bomb landed close by and wounded both men in the legs. Frost was carried off to the RAP to be treated by Captain J.W. Logan RAMC in the cellar of Brigade HQ. Frost handed over command to Major C.F.H. Gough, 1st Airborne Reconnaissance Squadron. There was little Gough could do under the circumstances, but he kept in contact and consulted with Frost particularly regarding the overcrowded conditions of the wounded in the cellars. With so many buildings now ablaze there were grave concerns regarding the continuing safety of those trapped below ground.

It must be pointed out that by this stage of the battle that any anti-tank guns that remained intact were simply unmannable due to the intensity of the mortaring and small arms fire. Each time a crewman was wounded, a replacement was found either from Battery HQ or from the glider pilots that had accompanied the guns to the bridge, until there were simply no available crew left. The battalion mortars were out of ammunition by noon on the Tuesday with the crews thereafter acting as infantry.

The Van Limburg Stirum School came under yet another infantry and tank attack at 1400 hours, which once again resulted in point blank 88mm tank fire, this time directed at the south face of the school resulting in the demolition of the south face and south-east corner of the building. The result of this close-range fire was that the school caught alight again with the resulting inferno burning completely out of control. Casualties increased from the shellfire, and among those were Major Lewis and Lieutenant Wright, both wounded with several others being killed. The decision was made to evacuate the school before it was too late to save the wounded. A plan was devised to move 30 yards next door to the burnt-out 'Red School' and at 1430 hours the wounded began to be carried out. The Germans reacted quickly and began to mortar the area outside the building causing more casualties whilst the Tiger tank turned its attention to buildings on the west side of the bridge. There was little alternative for the school defenders but to surrender. Some of those defenders that remained unscathed chose to stay with the wounded whilst a handful made a break to the east into the burnt-out buildings opposite the school across the Eusebius Buitensingel, but were eventually taken prisoner, having made little progress. Effectively, the fall of the school ended any further realistic hopes of holding the bridge.

German attention now turned to eliminating the remaining defenders around Brigade HQ with its RAP. Efforts were made to remove the wounded from the basement, including Frost, and a truce was called for approximately two hours to enable their safe evacuation. Having been helped out of the burning building, Frost sat on the bridge embankment alongside other wounded and watched as his old 2nd Parachute Battalion HQ collapsed amidst the flames. The Germans inevitably took advantage of the truce and moved themselves into more advantageous positions.

With the resumption of hostilities it became apparent to the remaining defenders, many of whom were dug in in the gardens behind Brigade HQ, that it was nearly all over, yet until the very end most still believed that XXX Corps would arrive. It was decided that the defenders, with very little ammunition remaining, should form into small groups and attempt to evade the Germans. Captain W.J. Marquand, OC, Signals Section at Brigade HQ, along with his 2i/c, Lieutenant Cairns, were ordered by Gough to join Major Crawley's remaining B Company with twelve men, but in the chaos caused by the fire in Brigade HQ he became separated from Lieutenant Cairns and moved to defend another building close by with fifteen men. In less than an hour they were forced to vacate the building and contact with Crawley was lost. Marquand collected twelve men together and moved to yet another building, constantly being hounded by the Germans. With little ammunition, less than ten rounds per man and no grenades, the decision was made to try to escape the immediate area; the group didn't get far and were involved in a brief firefight sustaining further casualties, including Marquand. In common with most of the surviving defenders Marquand had nowhere else to go, and having been wounded, was taken prisoner.[9]

With nightfall and all the buildings alight, the area around the bridge remained eerily illuminated.

By the early hours of Thursday, 21st September, nearly three and a half days after they had captured the north end of the bridge, all resistance at the bridge had ended.

Pre-war close-up of Arnhem Bridge area looking east. Top left, Camiz Dairy and pipe bridge just visible on Westervoortsedijk. Bottom left corner, September 1944, 1st Parachute Brigade HQ. Diagonally facing ramp, 2nd Parachute Battalion HQ. Adjacent to the bridge ramp (middle of photo), the flat-topped roof of the initial HQ, 1st Airlanding Anti-Tank Battery RA and No. 2 Platoon, 9th Field Company, RE (Monday only). The RA Jeep park was in the enclosed garden area, bottom right. (Photo: Courtesy Aviodrome Lelystad 15558)

9   Headquarters, 1st Parachute Brigade Signals Section Report by OC Captain W.J. Marquand, p.3.

1 & 2 PARA BNS, 16 PARA FD AMB   191

Arnhem Bridge, 1st Parachute Brigade and attached unit positions, Sunday, 17th–18th September.
(Photo: Courtesy Gelders Archive)

Arnhem Bridge, 1st Parachute Brigade and attached unit positions, Sunday, 17th–18th September, eastern side of bridge. (Photo: Courtesy Aviodrome Lelystad 16027)

Key to positions:

1. 1st Parachute Brigade HQ and RAP.
2. 2nd Parachute Battalion HQ and RAP.
3. 1st Parachute Brigade HQ Defence Platoon element, occupied until Wednesday morning.
4. A and B Troops, 1st Parachute Squadron, RE elements and 3rd Parachute Battalion, C Company HQ and No. 9 Platoon. Van Limburg Stirum School.
5. A Troop, 1st Parachute Squadron, RE, elements, Sunday night, forced out. Red School.
6. RAOC and 1st Parachute Brigade Signals elements, occupied until Tuesday.
7. HQ Troop, 1st Parachute Squadron RE and 1st Parachute Brigade Signals elements, held until Tuesday.
8. 1st Parachute Brigade HQ, Defence Platoon, held until Monday.
9. No. 3 Platoon, A Company, 2nd Parachute Battalion, forced out Tuesday, retaken Tuesday, finally lost Wednesday. Office of the Electricity board and the Tram Company.
10. No. 6 Platoon, B Company, 2nd Parachute Battalion, Public Works Service Office recaptured Monday afternoon under command of 2nd Lieutenant Flavell, 2nd Parachute Battalion, HQ, Liaison Officer, until burnt out later that night. The platoon then came under command of A Company. At first, the platoon returned to the recaptured Rijnkade 119, No. 28, before that too was set on fire at around 2245 hours. The platoon then moved under the bridge ramp.
11. S Company, Medium Machine Gun Platoon, 2nd Parachute Battalion and No. 1 Platoon, A Company, 2nd Parachute Battalion until late Monday. MMG Platoon provided fire support to No. 6 Platoon, B Company Monday afternoon.
12. S Company, Mortar Platoon, HQ.
13. S Company, Mortar Platoon elements, two 3-inch mortars.
14. 1st Airlanding Anti-Tank Battery, RA, HQ and No. 2 Platoon, 9th (Airborne) Field Company, RE, Monday only. Later elements of A Company, 2nd Parachute Battalion. Wednesday.
15. 1st Airlanding Anti-Tank Battery, RA, occupied after leaving 14.
16. No. 3 Platoon, 250 Composite Light Company, RASC.
17, 18, 19. HQ and S Companies, 2nd Parachute Battalion and Glider Pilots, elements of 19 Flight, B Squadron, Glider Pilot Regiment.
20. No. 1 Platoon, A Company, 2nd Parachute Battalion from Monday night.
21. B Company, HQ, No. 5 Platoon and until Monday afternoon, No. 6 Platoon, 2nd Parachute Battalion.
22. 89th Field Security Section and Military Police, ousted Tuesday evening.
23. No. 2 Platoon, A Company, 2nd Parachute Battalion until Monday afternoon supplanted by No. 2 Platoon, 9th (Airborne) Field Company, RE.
24. HQ, A Company, 2nd Parachute Battalion and 1st Parachute Squadron, HQ, RE. Elements 3 Troop, 1st Parachute Squadron, RE.
25. No. 8 Platoon, C Company, 3rd Parachute Battalion and elements of 1st Parachute Brigade, HQ, Defence Platoon. Lost on Monday. Camiz Dairy.
26. No. 8 Platoon, C Company, 3rd Parachute Battalion, lost Monday. Jos Pe printing firm.
27. No. 8 Platoon, C Company, 3rd Parachute Battalion, lost Monday. Rijkswerkplaats works office.
28. No. 6 Platoon, B Company, 2nd Parachute Battalion, Rijnkade 119, recaptured Monday afternoon under command of 2nd Lieutenant Flavell, 2nd Parachute Battalion, HQ, Liaison Officer, before moving east under the bridge and attacking No. 10, the Public Works Service Office.

Arnhem Bridge Street Key

A. Westervoortsedijk
B. Ooststraat
C. Nieuwe Kade
D. Rijnkade
E. Eusebius Buitensingel
F. Eusebiusplein
G. Eusebius Binnen Singel
H. Markt Straat
I. Kade Straat
J. Hofstraat
K. Badhuisstraat

Arnhem Bridge area looking north, pre-war. (Photo: Courtesy Aviodrome Lelystad 16028)

Sergeant Gwilym Evans, T Company, 1st Parachute Battalion, 1st Parachute Brigade

At the time of the Arnhem operation I was 24 and I'd seen action with the battalion in North Africa and Italy.

Sunday, 17th September

I remember that fateful morning very well indeed. We moved from our camp by lorry and we told jokes along the way. It seemed to me that the further we travelled, the more likely the operation would surely be on. Eventually we arrived at an airfield in Lincolnshire, Barkston Heath, we got off the lorry and we were marched to our particular plane. I'd never seen so many aircraft on the field in my life. I think we had our parachutes issued after we had de-bussed from the lorry. Some of the men were sitting quietly beside the planes and others were making jokes, eating and drinking and smoking. I remember the order being given and we all filed on to the plane. I was fortunate to be sitting in the front of the plane and I had a good view of the countryside.

We were in the air and I remember the hustle and bustle in the plane; people were joking, some were nodding off. I don't remember if I did or not, but I do remember looking at the countryside and thinking how peaceful everything was. As time went by and I looked down and saw large expanses of water, I realised we were over the Dutch coast. We were soon flying over small villages and fields and I noticed a railway and a train, which looked like a toy. One of the aircrew shouted, 'Ten minutes to go, lads, we're on course.' There was quite a lot of movement in the plane. Everyone was checking their parachutes and there was the clanking of steel metal hooks on the rails which ran round the plane. At that moment I glanced down and we were flying over fields and woods and lots of wide expanses of ground. There were lots of gliders down below, then the next thing I remember was being out of the plane and I looked up and saw that the canopy of my parachute had opened well. I glanced around and saw at various heights many other canopies and parachutists dangling beneath them. It was calm and sunny, and I had a very good drop.

I released my parachute and I remember running towards the edge of a thick wood. Not long after that, many others arrived and our company was messed up. It didn't seem long before it appeared we were being surrounded by Dutch civilians with orange arm bands. We were being given refreshments, biscuits, tea and cakes; I know I had some of these. I also saw many parachutes hanging from the trees; some of the civilians were collecting these parachutes. It seemed a long time before the battalion moved off. I can't remember how late in the afternoon it was. It was about this point that I did hear gunfire coming from what appeared to be the right; I know now that that is where the river was. It was getting dark now and I recall moving through dense woods in single file. After what appeared a long time, we emerged from the woods and ahead of us appeared to be a large field. We were told to dig in along the edge of the field; the other companies were on either side and there appeared to be a road separating the field from another company. It all seemed very quiet, and I wondered why we were waiting, but suddenly down that road I heard the tracks of wheeled vehicles approaching.[10] I felt very tense and suddenly all hell was let loose. There were tracer bullets flying through the trees, bursts of machine gun fire – I believe they were Spandaus – and also mortars were raining down. I was surprised that none of this fire was directed at us, but later heard that one of the companies had been heavily attacked and that casualties were high. After this I did meet a sergeant from that company and he had received a bullet wound that had seared his throat. I can't remember how long this attack lasted but suddenly everything was quiet and we were told to advance again. After this we moved on; we must have walked for hours, or so it seemed. I remember crossing the railway and then through more woods. There was a lot of mortar fire and I was glad to get out into the open.

Monday, 18th September
It is difficult to remember what happened in the early hours of Monday morning but I do recall that round about dawn, my section and others of T Company were moving along each side of the road in a built-up area. There was a lot of machine gun fire coming straight down the middle of the road, and I saw tanks and half-tracks edging down the street. I remember blazing away with my Sten with the rest of the section. Mortar bombs were coming down thick and fast and I took shelter behind a stone gate pillar. I remember Sergeant Bert Reid, one of my pals, ran across the road and was hit by a mortar fragment; his arm was taken off by the shoulder and he fell.[11] The next thing I recall is moving through the gardens of the houses off that road, grabbing something to eat, probably apples or pears off the trees. The Dutch houses seemed to be empty; we had no food, so we ate what we could find.

Later that morning, I remember resting with several others in the garden of a house and there was a lot of firing all around and we were told to attack a factory or something which was near the railway. I remember walking with the section towards the objective. It seemed quite far away and there was firing from the windows of the factory. It was early morning and I was going past what looked to me like garden sheds and I remember lifting my left arm head-high to open the door,

10 Amsterdamseweg.
11 Sergeant Herbert G.D. Reid, 4192009, age 29. KIA, 18th September 1944.

and I had a grenade in my right hand. Almost at once I felt a stinging pain in my left forearm. I felt the blood running down my hand, and I couldn't move my fingers. I must have lost a lot of blood because I felt weak. I realised that I had been hit by a sniper and I remember saying to my friend Sergeant Jack Richards, 'Get the bastard, Jack.'

I recall lying in some sort of a building; it could have been the garage of a house. I'd been there for quite a while and I can't remember if I was carried or I walked into a Dutch house. I remember lying on a bed in a small room, and a Dutchmen was asking me questions; he could speak a little English. I remember bullets splintering the glass windows and he told me to keep down. Someone brought me some food and drink. I don't know how long I was in that house but all I can say is that he came into the room and tried to tell me that there was a Red Cross vehicle coming down the road. I went outside and the vehicle stopped, the rear doors of the ambulance were open and on each side sitting down, were wounded soldiers. I asked one soldier to move up, and at that moment, I don't know if it was a stray bullet or a ricochet, he received a bullet right through the back of his head; he just fell out of the rear of the ambulance. I got into the ambulance and what a hair-raising ride it was to the hospital.[12]

The roads were littered with fallen telephone wires and overturned vehicles could be seen everywhere and there were lots of dead soldiers on the roads. It didn't seem a long journey but there were bullets pinging around everywhere. The next thing that I knew we were at the hospital entrance and I was taken into the foyer. I sat on the floor by the entrance and saw British and German medical teams. They were operating and carrying people around. There were many wounded soldiers to be seen, and everything was so confusing I don't know who was in control. I remember a German who tried to grab my watch. I shouted, 'Nein, nein' and just then an officer told him to stop. I don't know what words he used but the soldier, off he went. I was taken to a small darkened room and the sleeve of my jacket was ripped to the shoulder and I felt something very cold being rubbed on my arm. I remember something being cut and tied up, my arm was cleaned and I had plaster of Paris right up to my shoulder. I was taken up some steps to a big room where there were many beds and I got into one, fully clothed, boots on as well. It seemed a pity to soil the beautifully white sheets. My equipment had been taken to another room at the far end of the ward. I got up and went into that room to get my cigarettes. It was dark outside and there was a single light burning in the room. I crawled about looking for my pack, I found it, and took out the cigarettes. I was just leaving when a bullet smashed the window and ricocheted around the room.

The night at the hospital seemed very unreal to me, I remember listening to the sound of fighting outside, the different sounds the machine guns made, the Spandaus and the Brens and the mortar fire and I felt from the noise that the Germans seemed to have guns very near to the hospital.

Tuesday, 19th September
I heard the creaking of tanks on the roads outside and there were several bursts of machine gun fire quite near to the entrance of the hospital. I saw a few soldiers running into the hospital entrance and I could hear someone telling them to leave. I felt very sorry for them. I know now how lucky I was to be in hospital.

During the day time we were told by the nurses not to look out of the windows. I did on one occasion, and outside I saw many Germans, some of them making their weapon pits by the side of the river. I saw tanks and guns and many, many soldiers. We were also warned by the Dutch nurses

---

12   St Elizabeth Hospital.

to get into bed very quickly when the Germans entered the hospital. As the time went by the noise of the battle seemed to get less, and there were many more Germans about. I remember a German officer coming into the ward and saying, 'You are now prisoners of war. All those people who can walk, outside.' We were pushed into open lorries and driven to Apeldoorn. We stayed there for some time and then crowded into cattle trucks. We went to Stalag XIB near Hanover and the journey appeared to take quite a few days. Stalag XIB was a mixed camp of British, Russian and French prisoners. Five weeks later we were moved to Stalag 8C in Silesia where I remember seeing many survivors from Arnhem; not many were able-bodied men, most of them were wounded.

Private George Hill, 1 Platoon, R Company, 1st Parachute Battalion, 1st Parachute Brigade

On return to England from Italy we were stationed at Bulby Hall, near Bourne, Lincolnshire. We endured first of all the agony of 6th Airborne Division and their losses on D-Day and questioned, 'When will our turn come?' Their exploits were followed with pride and envy, and again, 'When will our turn come?' Briefings for airborne operations came and went: Paris, Brussels. Money changed and changed back again with each cancellation and more and more frustration. Training and more training: learn to fire the 2-inch mortar from the hips. No questions about training, just do it and learn from the experts who have done it all and now expect you to do it as well as – no, better – than they can. No mistakes, do it again and better and again until you are exhausted.

The company is now under Major John Timothy of Bruneval Raid fame. An interesting occurrence, this, because he knows me. Why? He was a pre-war subaltern in the Queen's Own Royal West Kent Regiment, my father's regiment, would you believe. He remembers my father teaching him ceremonial sword drill at Maidstone Barracks. Lieutenant Frederick H. Greenhalgh, whose batman I was, suffered severe chest wounds at Arnhem but lived. The batmen live in a bell tent in the grounds and it's great. I attend a wireless course and learn the mysteries of 'netting' the sets, so confident that they will work efficiently when needed.

Sunday, 17th September–Monday, 18th September
And so dawns 17th September 1944, and Market Garden will not be cancelled, so confidently we embus, en route to the airfield, Barkston Heath – no need to worry. The briefing gives us a buoyant hope, little opposition, stomach troops only as the enemy and youngsters. No armour, no problems, events are to prove some slight error or over optimism, but not now, we have great officers and NCOs: Sergeant Barratt, Sergeant Hicks and Sergeant Isherwood have seen it all before and will lead.

After a carefree flight, as we approach the DZ at Wolfheze surrounded by RAF fighters, our aircraft loses about one foot of its port wing to an anti-aircraft gunner, but that's all: one of the fighters quickly sorted that gun out. A few minutes later, about 1330 hours on a beautiful Sunday, with – oddly enough – thoughts of a Sunday dinner, we jump into a foreign land with foreign names, but the only hostile reaction is to come from the Germans.

A perfect landing, can even see the RV point with no problem. Perfect RV, the company is complete and starts to dig in. The other battalions move off and we follow in perfect order; now to use the radios' walkie-talkies, and they do not work. Into the woods towards our first objective, in the woods before the objective, our first casualty, shot by the enemy. A Jeep in a ride, shot straight through the radiator by an 88mm gun, press on, and as evening falls and our first casualties, yes, those 'stomach troops' are determined. They inflict half casualties on our company here.[13]

Joined by those left, we make towards the bridge. Up by the Rhine Hotel, on the lower road, plenty of firing now, plenty of damage, simple orders now apply: *make for the bridge, reinforce 2nd Battalion*. So we press on. Lieutenant Kilmartin leads. Some of those I know are with us. I do not know some of the others, but there is one objective: make for the bridge, my mates around me, yet I am not to know till later exactly where. Into the gardens on the left, sloping gardens, from the back of the houses on the upper road, down to the lower road.[14] At one point I look up. 'What was that sound?' Breaking glass and a German fires at me while I am looking up into the broken window at him. The bullet enters my pack, I slide down feigning injury praying that he believes he has got me.

No further trouble. Back to the path on the left, a machine gunner on the point of grass sward by what now is the Technical School, opens up and hits Lieutenant Kilmartin; he is dead, another dies behind him, another is wounded and crawls into a garden under a rhododendron bush and lies there. I do not know now, but this is my mate, Lieutenant Kilmartin's batman, George Dymott.[15] The German machine gunner stands up. *Why?* He has enough bandoliers of ammunition on him to hold us all up for a long time, but Sergeant Barratt, I believe, sees that he takes no more lives. I duck into a garden and make my way towards the bridge once more. As I am passing the next garden I hear moans, obviously it's someone badly injured. I call in a hoarse voice, 'Who's there?' and there's a strangled reply: 'Is that you, George?' and so the 'terrible twins', the two Georges, meet.

I have morphine, twelve phials; George Dymott has a good dose and is a little relieved. Another batman, Arthur West, is higher up the garden uninjured. A bloody great tank surrounded by German infantry now moves forward and we three are taken prisoner and join many others. George Dymott is carried with us for a little, then put on a trolley and taken away. The uninjured and walking wounded are taken to the square opposite the Musis Sacrum, marching up singing the 'Red Flag'; this does not please the German guards.

Sometime later we are put onto trucks and taken to Zutphen and put in a railway warehouse; aircraft action during the night, plenty of noise, but where are the rest of the 1st Battalion? I do not see any.

Post-Arnhem
Memories fade. The only dates I can remember are Sunday 17th September 1944 and then 8 months in a prisoner-of-war camp at Halle, near Leipzig, working in a German crematorium. During Easter 1945, whilst on the march, we were released by General Patton's American troops. Whether Market Garden was a success or not depends which way one looks at the operation. But the one certain thing is that any failure was not due to any weakness on the part of the men taking part, and in any case perhaps lessons may have been learned. My personal view when I go back to Oosterbeek, Renkum and Arnhem and see the graves and tablet signs of those who died, is the

---

13 Lieutenant Greenhalgh was one of those wounded during this engagement. R Company, unable to extricate themselves, now consisted of less than 40 men. The remainder of the battalion moved off south-east without them. The following day, R Company slipped away and made their way towards Oosterbeek where around 2000 hours, on Monday 18th, along with elements of 2nd Battalion South Staffs, they re-established contact with the 1st Battalion group.
14 Utrechtseweg/Onderlangs.
15 Lieutenant Michael G. Kilmartin, 217467, OC. 2 Platoon, R Company. KIA, Onderlangs area, 19th September. No known grave.

price was too high, and too many lives were wasted to satisfy Higher Command's dreams, without serious consideration of such basics as nearer DZs and better appreciation of intelligence reports.

Looking west. Top left corner, the densely packed houses of the Lombok area with the adjacent St Elizabeth Hospital. The Christelijk Lyceum Grammar School sits further east up the hill on the Utrechtseweg. On the bend in the Utrechtseweg (right centre) the domed roof of the Gemeentemuseum, the extent of the South Staffs advance. The Arnhem railway sidings run along a cutting behind the hospital. To the right, across the railway are the houses on the Noordelijke Parallelweg occupied by the Germans of Kampfgruppe *Gropp*. From these positions the Germans brought flanking fire on the South Staffs. Running parallel to the river (foreground) is the open expanse of Onderlangs along which 3rd and 1st Parachute Battalions initially moved before coming under heavy right flanking fire from the brickworks across the river forcing them into the trees and undergrowth covering the embankment. Once past the left flank support of the stalled South Staffs the two battalions were subjected to enemy flank and frontal fire eventually frustrating any hope of reaching the bridge. (Photo pre-war: Courtesy Aviodrome 35/5)

Private Ron George, Assault Pioneer Platoon, Headquarter Company, 1st Parachute Battalion, 1st Parachute Brigade

The Assault Pioneer Platoon was composed of thirty men, three sections of ten, a sergeant in charge of each and a platoon sergeant overall. Lieutenant John Sutton was platoon officer. There was no specific role planned for Arnhem. We knew we would eventually be called upon to break through rows of terraced houses from one end to the other using explosives, and for this we had been trained, but it did not materialise on this occasion. We were ordinary infantry up to the point where we would be called upon. My role was top dog; I was the platoon runner. (There is a photo of my platoon in the aircraft on our way to Arnhem, No. K7586, available from the Imperial War Museum.)

Sunday, 17th September
The take-off from Barkston Heath was uneventful, as was the flight over and as far as I can remember the landing was A1. It was just after landing that I heard firing in the area. By the by, we had in our stick Captain Leo Heaps, a Canadian. The first contact we had with the enemy was at 1900 hours on the 17th when we were positioned at the crossroads. I had a PIAT at that time, although I wasn't a PIAT gunner. I also had someone with me, I cannot remember who. Tanks did approach within about 80 yards of our position and then turned tail. They must have said to themselves, 'There's old Taffy, let's scarper.' We advanced from this position, after the enemy withdrew. I believe about this time the Assault Pioneer Platoon Officer, Lieutenant John Sutton, was seriously wounded.

Monday, 18th September
On the 18th, 0200 hours, it was heavy going through the woods. We were pinned down with 88mm and particularly sniping and this kept us down for a little while. Then our snipers were sent out to counteract these, and it worked. We did have some very good snipers at that time.

Late afternoon, when we reached a timber yard, we proceeded through the yard; we heard the drum of powerful aeroplane engines. The order came that we should use our yellow recognition triangles and point them towards the enemy. This we did. The aircraft came over, they were not ours, but German Messerschmitts. Our air superiority at that time was so overwhelming it never occurred to anyone that they could be German aircraft. We all dived for cover; you can imagine how the timber was stored, in stacks of different sizes with a gap of about six inches between the timber and the ground. We had our packs on at that time, but we got under that timber; it was hell of a scramble trying to make ourselves as thin as possible.

Tuesday 19th September
It took us a long time before we reached the hospital and then on from there towards the bridge, getting near the railway station. As we were approaching the railway station in Arnhem, a Spandau machine gun opened up on us and hit four of us, Sergeant Harvey, Private Wildman and Private Kinsey. I was the only one left lying on the ground.

A very good friend of mine, Corporal Stan Lunt, ran out from behind cover, grabbed my collar and dragged me back to the safety of a building. By this time my leg was very painful. Two shell dressings were used on my wound and I was given a morphine injection, the time and date written on my forehead. Guardsmen Sam Coster volunteered to carry me on his back to the regimental first aid post. On the way he had to clamber over hedges and fences of a row of houses. My wounded leg took a hammering, I eventually passed out. I awoke lying on a stretcher in the first aid post. On looking up, I saw the padre leaning over me with the Good Book in his hand.

I said, 'I am not going yet, Padre.'

He laughed and asked me would I like some tea. I nodded, and then he asked me if I would like something in it, I said, 'Yes please!' The tea was potent; I then sang a couple of verses of '*Sosban Fach*'.

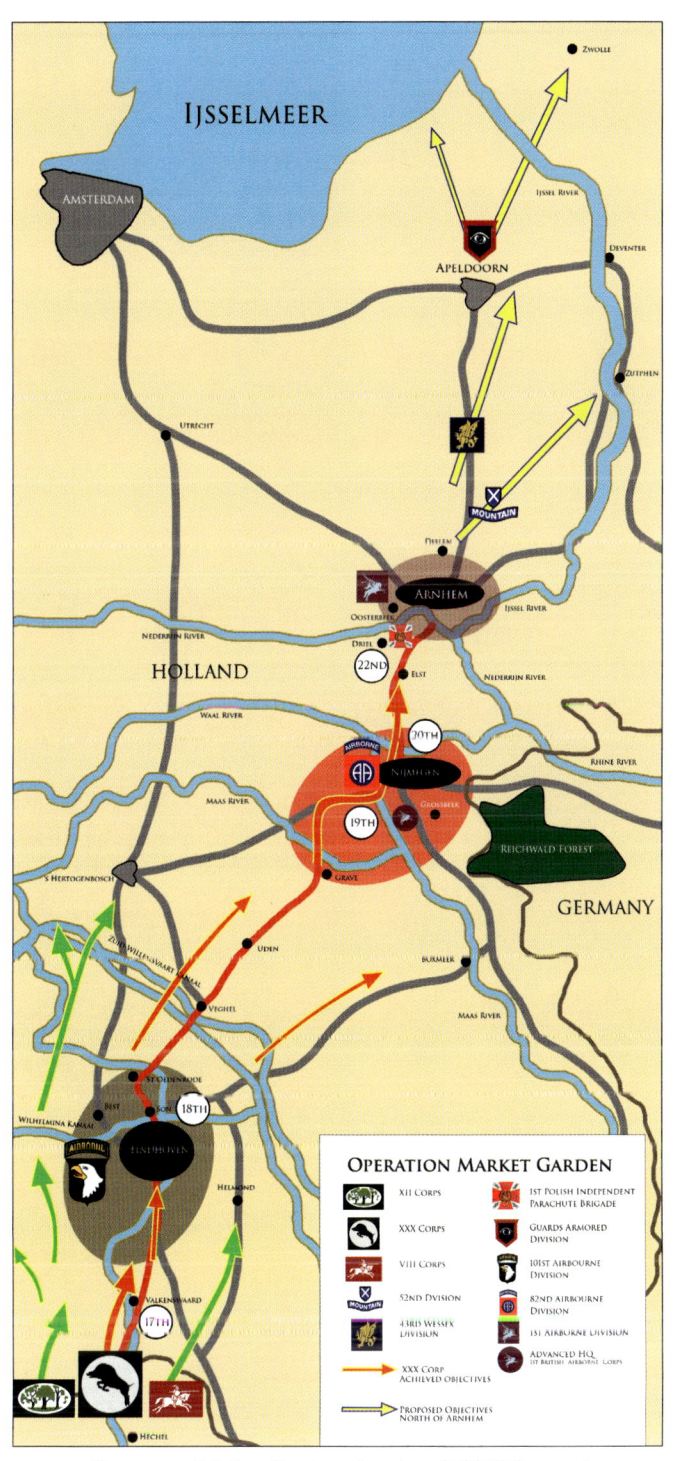

Operation Market Garden, the plan. (SGW Designs)

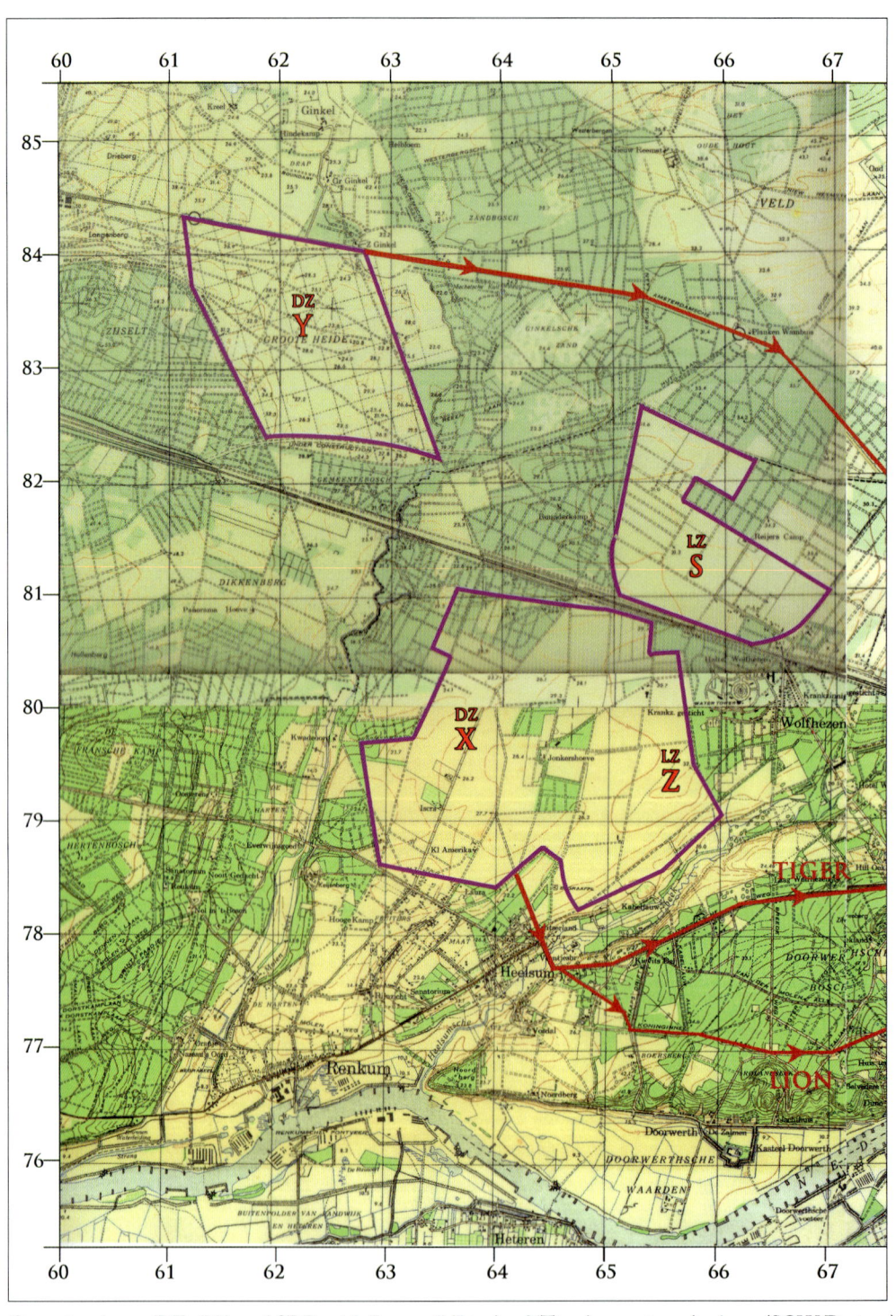

Operational map: DZs, LZs and SDPs with 'Leopard', 'Lion' and 'Tiger' routes into Arnhem. (SGW Designs)

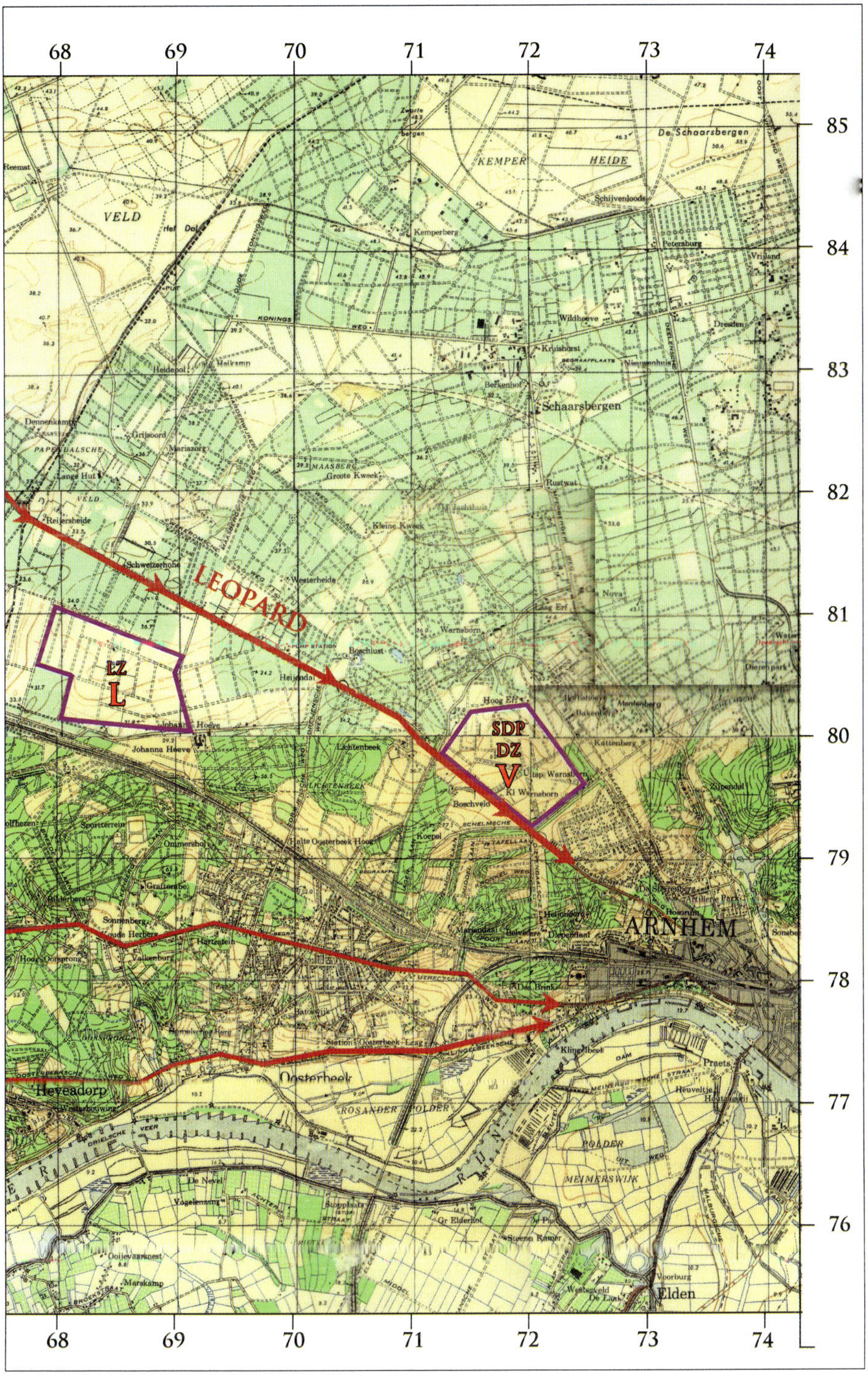
LEOPARD
LZ
L
SDP
DZ
V
ARNHEM
Oosterbeek
Heveadorp
Elden
Schaarsbergen
KEMPER HEIDE
De Schaarsbergen
VELD
68
69
70
71
72
73
74
85
84
83
82
81
80
79
78
77
76

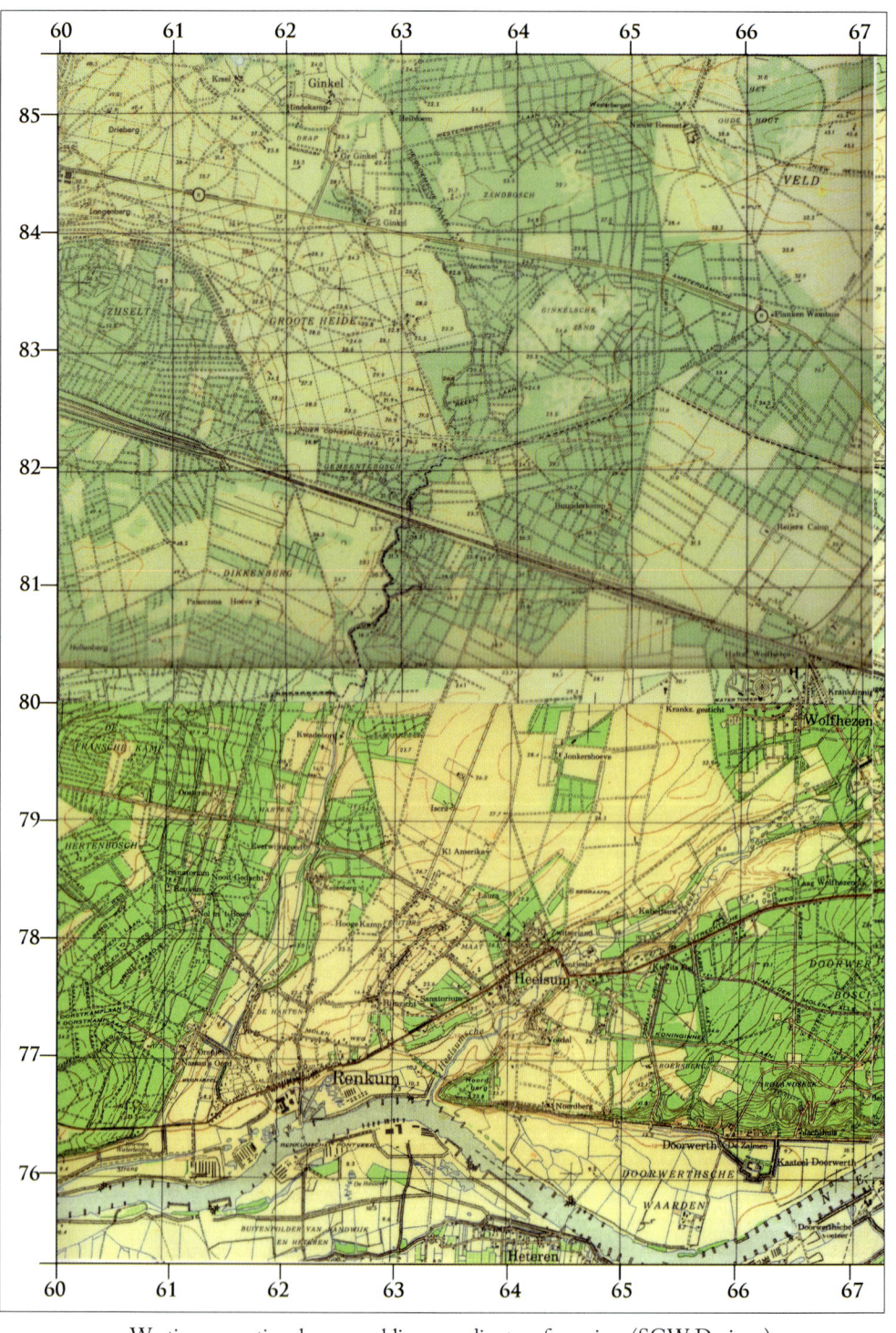

Wartime operational map enabling coordinate referencing. (SGW Designs)

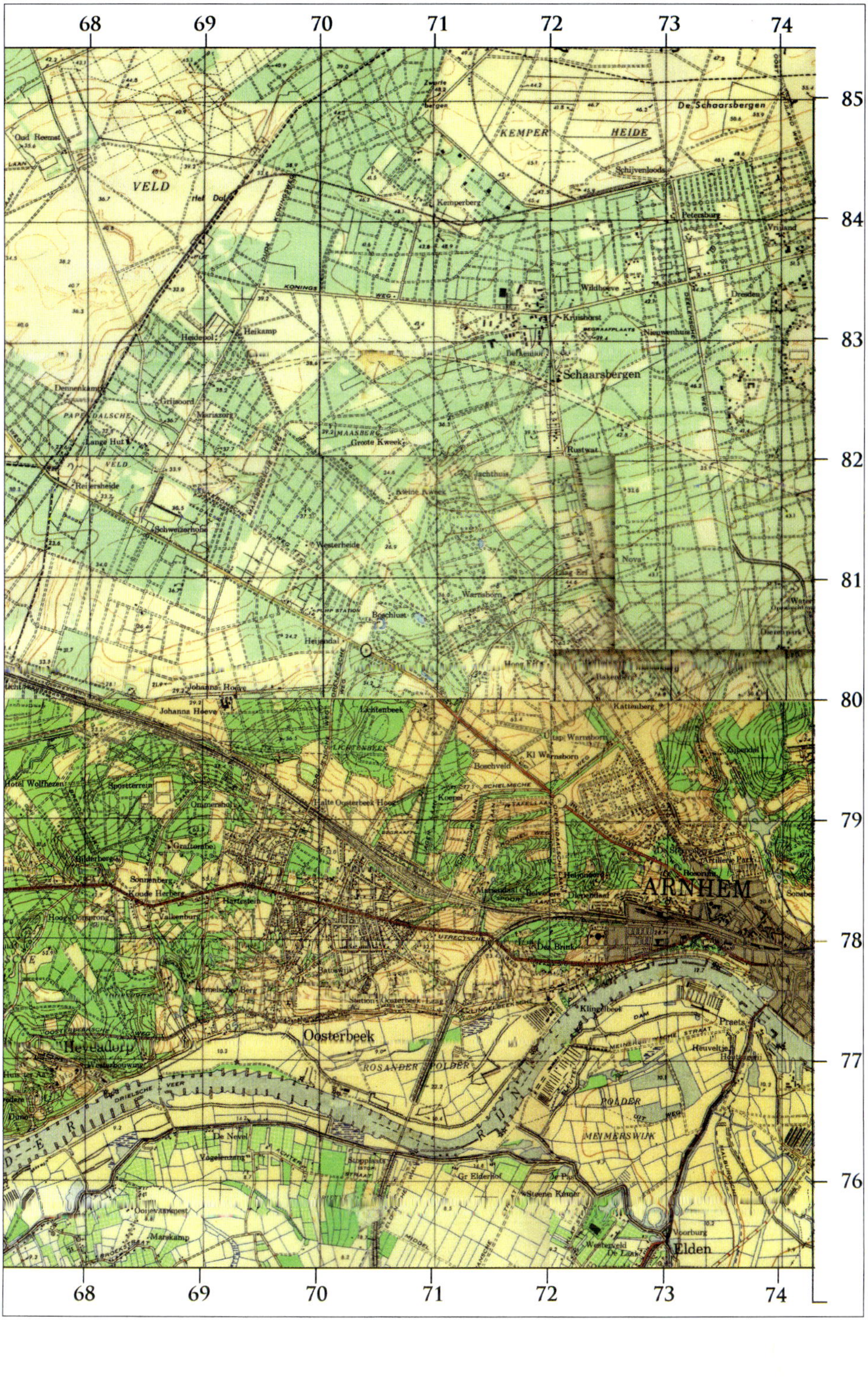

68
69
70
71
72
73
74
85
84
83
82
81
80
79
78
77
76
KEMPER
HEIDE
VELD
De Schaarsbergen
Petersburg
Kemperberg
Schaarsbergen
Wildhoeve
Kruishorst
Nieuwenhuis
Heidepol
Heikamp
Dennenkamp
Lange Hut
Groote Kweek
Rustwat
Nova
Westerheide
Warnsborn
Boschhuis
Heijendal
Johanna Hoeve
Lichtenbeek
Boschveld
Kattenberg
Hotel Wolfhezen
Sportterrein
Bilderberg
Sonnenberg
Hartestein
Valkenburg
ARNHEM
Den Brink
Klingelbeek
Oosterbeek
Heveadorp
ROSANDER POLDER
POLDER
MEINERSWIJK
Praets
Heuveltje
De Nevel
Vogelenzang
Gr Elderhof
Voorburg
Elden

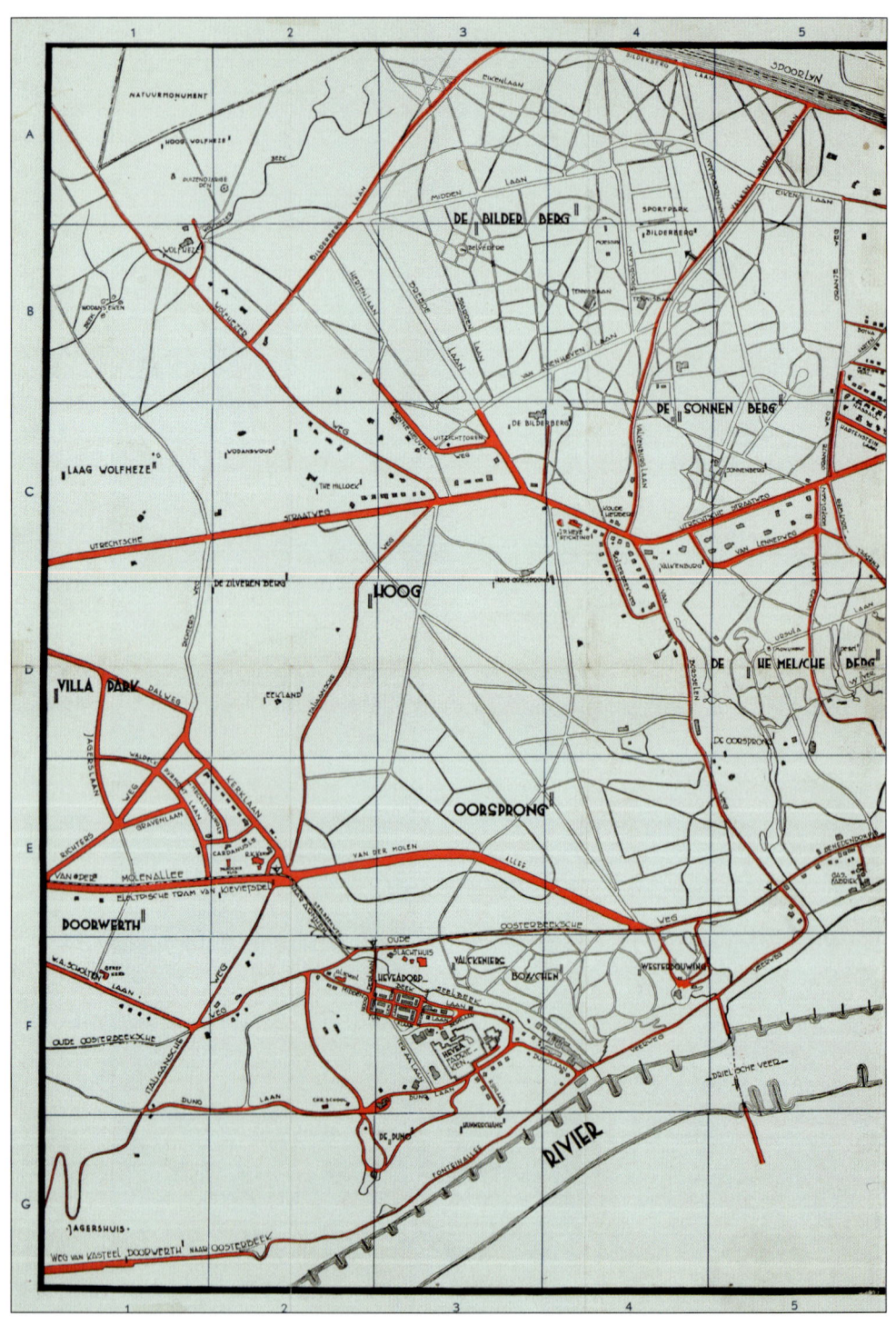

Pre-war street map of Oosterbeek. (Courtesy Gelders Archive)

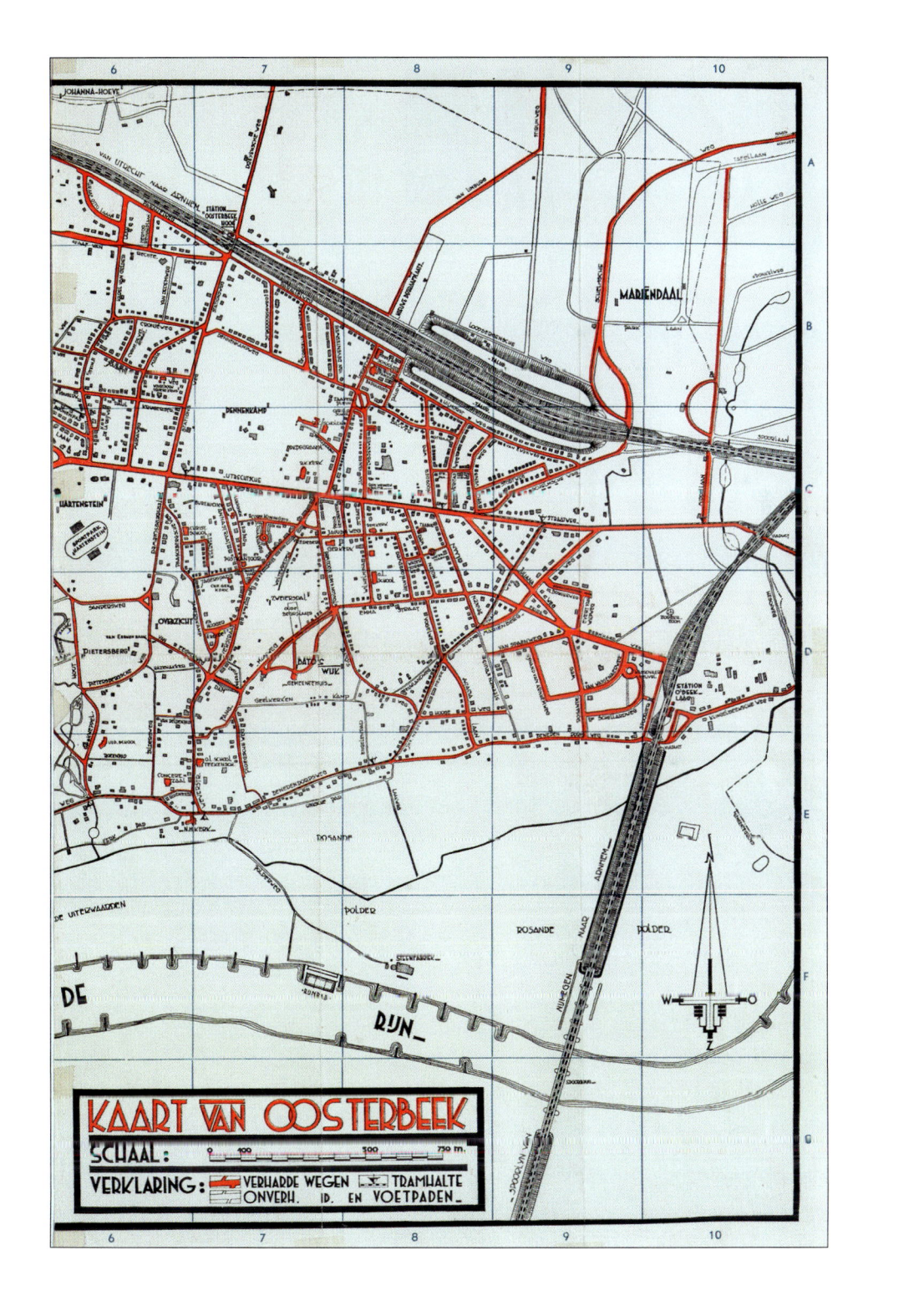

KAART VAN OOSTERBEEK

SCHAAL: 0 100 300 750 m.
VERKLARING: VERHARDE WEGEN — TRAMHALTE
ONVERH. ID. EN VOETPADEN

AIRBORNE FORCES

You are joining the Airborne Forces. They are something new, different and specialized. They are composed of picked troops.

Show by your turn out, saluting, soldierly bearing and efficiency that you belong to a Corps d'Elite. The credit and reputation of the Airborne Forces are in your hands as much as in mine.

Whether you are dropped by parachute or landed by glider, you will normally go into battle by air. That is the difference between your new task and any other you have done in the Army. That is what makes your new work different and intensely interesting.

But do not think that you will be landed in the centre of Germany as a "suicide force." You will not. Airborne Forces will be used in close co-operation with land or air or naval forces. They will always be followed up and reinforced as quickly as possible.

The sort of tasks you may have to do are:—

(I) Capture a line or a particular point in the rear of the enemy, cut his communications, isolate him from reinforcements.
(II) Attack the enemy in his rear, while our main forces attack his front.
(III) Capture airfields in enemy country.
(iv) Assist seaborne landings by attacking coast guns and beach defences in rear.
(v) Be landed close behind our own Armoured Divisions, who have broken through, so providing the infantry, guns and co-operation they require.
(vi) Raid special objectives.
(vii) Assist, by landing with arms, friendly inhabitants of occupied countries in the event of invasions.

Occasions may arise when Airborne Forces will be used in a normal ground role. They are armed and equipped to do so.

In almost every case Airborne Forces will lead the way and be the advanced guard of the attack.

As this advanced guard, the Airborne Forces must be first-class in every way. Every member must be more efficient, more alert and resourceful, and above all more highly disciplined than any other troops in the world.

The following principles are essentials in war and the highest standard in them must be achieved and maintained.

1. **Discipline.**—With this introduction to your membership of the Airborne Forces is given you my views on Discipline. Read them carefully. They are the result of experience on the battlefield and if you take them to heart and practise them, neither the Airborne Forces nor you yourself will fail in battle.

2. **Speed**—In thought and action.—This is the prior requirement in war and all risks will be taken to achieve it.

3. **Alertness and the power to observe.**—Without extreme alertness the soldier is doomed. The man who is alert and sees his enemy first is the one who survives, not only to kill his immediate opponent, but to fight and kill again.

The British are naturally an unobservant people, and it is only by constant training in alertness and the power of observation that these become a habit. It is the habit gained by what you do in training that you will practise in war.

Saluting, especially the flags on Commanders' cars, is one of the best tests of the alertness and discipline of the man or unit. I judge the alertness and discipline, and therefore the efficiency of a unit very largely on its saluting. The test of war invariably confirms this judgment.

4. **Initiative**—Not by leaders alone but by all ranks.—To do nothing when faced with a situation through lack of orders is little short of criminal. To "have a go" and do something, even if it may prove wrong, is infinitely better, mentally, morally and physically. I will never drop on anyone who has a go, even if he is wrong.

5. **Fitness.**—You will be expected to travel by air, to land by parachute or glider, to fight immediately on landing, and to look after yourself on the ground, on compact rations, perhaps for as long as six days at a time. To do this you must be fit. The Airborne Forces only accept A1 fighting men, but you must be the best of the A1 class. Concentrate on building up your staying power, so that you can undergo hardships and think nothing of them. Train also to be capable of short spells of high-speed marching and fighting. If you are not fit you are a drag on your comrades and you will not survive in battle.

6. **Marksmanship**—All weapons.—Airborne troops cannot afford to waste one round of ammunition. All ranks must be expert shots, with all the weapons they are armed with, since the success or failure of any operation will largely depend on the marksmanship of each individual.

7. **Supporting fire**—Both automatic and overwhelming.—No troops, however well trained and dashing, can advance against even minor opposition unsupported by fire. Further, a weapon that is neither shooting nor in a position to shoot is not fulfilling its function. It is essential, therefore, for the majority of weapons to be actually giving, or prepared to give, supporting fire, only those weapons essential to its success being carried in the assault. Therefore, every movement or offensive action will be heavily supported by every weapon available. This principle must become second nature and be automatic.

8. **Security.**—Airborne troops will invariably be given the fullest available details on maps, air photographs, and models of any operation they are called on to carry out. This means that at least 24 hours before the operation every soldier taking part will be in full possession of all the details of the operation. This demands a very high standard in security. In plain words —Keep your mouth shut. The success of the whole operation, your own life and equally, if not more, important, the lives of your comrades, will be jeopardised, if one word is given away.

Now you know what sort of thing you will be required to do; and you know the qualities you will need to take your place worthily in Airborne Forces and to uphold the very high reputation they have already earned.

From now on you will be training hard. Your training will be sound, but you alone can get full value from it. Put all you know into your work.

Never forget that you will be the advanced guard, doing a vital task on which the success of a major attack may depend. Airborne Forces lead the way in battle; so must they lead the way in the whole Army and the world in spirit, bearing, efficiency and discipline.

F. Browning

Lieut.-General
Comd. Airborne Troops.

1944.

Tuesday, 19th September onwards

From the first aid post, I was transferred to St Elizabeth Hospital. Leaving the hospital, I ended up like most of the wounded, in the Caserne William III Barracks at Apeldoorn. It was on a Sunday morning and all the walking wounded had been invited to an open-air service on the barrack square. A few did not return to their rooms. The padre said that during prayers the German troops who were doing the guarding also bowed their heads in prayer. He could see out of the corner of his eye a few khaki behinds slinking away in the distance.

I was then moved from the Caserne William III Barracks to the Juliana Hospital and then to St. Joseph's which was a lunatic asylum. A ward had been emptied and was now occupied by Airborne troops.

Around half of the 1st Parachute Battalion Assault Pioneer Platoon Barkston Heath prior to emplaning for Arnhem, 17th September 1944. *Top row, left to right:* 1. RASC Driver of army truck behind 2. Corporal Albert Osborne, KIA 21st September 44; 3. Private Jack Whitely; 4. Private J.W. Godbold; 5. Private Wildman (WIA, POW); 6. Private 'Jock' Clement (batman to Lieutenant Clarkson); 7. Private Kinsey (WIA); 8. Sergeant H.W. Harvey (WIA); 9. Private Frank Thomas/Thompson?; 10. Sergeant Buck Taylor; 11. Lieutenant Leo Heaps (Canadian, POW, escaped). *Bottom row:* 1. Private Ron George (WIA, POW) ('Sgt Harvey, Ptes Kinsey, Wildman and I were wounded from the same burst from a Spandau machine gun'); 2. Private Kilsby; 3. Private Tommy Davis (POW); 4. Private W. J. King (believed KIA); 5. Lance Corporal Wally Baldock (POW); 6. ?; 7. Lieutenant John Sutton, Platoon CO (WIA); 8. Member of the Signals Platoon; 9. Lieutenant Alastair Clarkson (KIA). (Information supplied by Ron George). (Photo: Courtesy IWM 7590)

Lieutenant Ben S. Lockett, A Troop, 1st Airlanding Anti-Tank Battery, Royal Artillery

6-Pounder Anti-Tank Guns, Attached to 1st Parachute Battalion
I started part-time soldiering at 17 years old in The Duke of Lancaster's Own Yeomanry and was a troop sergeant in 1939. The emphasis was on moving forward at the gallop (we were still horsed in 1940) – we were very much a case of 'Get stuck in and "B" the consequences until afterwards' – the cavalryman's approach, which had been described as 'All dash and no brains!' However, I am extremely proud to have served in such an august regiment. I was never very happy in the artillery; it was much too static for my taste.

I was a newcomer of four months in the unit (1st Airlanding Anti-Tank Battery, RA) and was very proud of being commissioned into such a formation with the reputation of the Airborne Forces. Eric Clapham was the troop commander and had been all the way through North Africa, Sicily and Italy, and was probably the senior junior officer in the battery (if that's not a contradiction in terms). He was used by Major Arnold, Battery Commander (BC), to attend to battery matters on many occasions – as cadets at OCTU, two of us were offered postings to Airborne Forces immediately after commissioning. The BC attached me to A Troop to relieve Eric of some of the routine troop duties and to act as second in command when necessary (with Sergeant Anderson's permission, of course!)

Sunday, 17th September
Apart from instances of small arms fire and the odd corpse, I cannot recall anything of the period immediately after forming up and starting to move east. We crossed a railway line, probably in the region at Wolfhezen. I have vague thoughts of hearing armour in the distance.

Monday, 18th September
The 18th saw us proceeding in fits and starts diagonally into Oosterbeek. I think one of A Troop guns did have a go on the second day, but it was not in my area. To the best of my memory there was no question of deploying the guns; the operation was grinding to a halt, but apart from an occasional alarm, nothing was happening. There were sounds of action away ahead of us but we just waited and slept where we were. Obviously the forward elements of the 1st Parachute Battalion were in close contact with the Germans throughout the night of the 18th, but there was no question of fighting in our area.

Tuesday, 19th September
We spent the night sleeping where we lay, and at first light on the 19th we moved east on Klingelbeekseweg, I say this because I remember watching (German) Bofors on the south bank of the river. We were in the house on Klingelbeekseweg. I suggested we should put a 6-pounder in one of these buildings which, whilst at extreme range, would have given the German artillery something to think about. We did carry some High Explosive (HE) and we could have 'cocked it up a bit'. The idea was greeted with derision, yet I still think anything would have been an improvement on doing nothing. I cannot say who laughed at my suggestion for engaging the flak guns; of course, their reaction may have been due to anticipation of the 'Wrath of God' syndrome. This was my first experience of action and I was therefore quite ignorant of the possible consequences.

About 0630 hours on the 19th, a large bulky figure approached me, unknown to me at first but I quickly learned he was General Urquhart and had been in hiding since Sunday, having been cut off by the Germans; was this the reason we were like a chicken running around without its head?

Whether on the 18th or the 19th, I am uncertain, but at one stage there was a German infantry gun firing west, straight down the road, I think some of the Paras dealt with it. A group of us were discussing mounting a Vickers machine gun (VMG) on a jeep, and were trying to find a VMG just for this purpose; we were going to unload the 6-pounder ammunition from the bonnet of one of our gun-towing Jeeps for this purpose. That must have been about 0630–0700 hours.

The time I was hit, about 0730 hours on the 19th, I was standing talking to one of the paras on the pavement![16] Which begs the question once again: 'Why were we waiting?' This inactivity was not due to lack of enthusiasm for the battle but complete absence of direction and information. The troops were highly skilled and active service experienced; on the approach to where I was hit, we would see 'the bridge' and hear the terrific battle which was going on there but nobody gave the gunners orders. Apart from desultory small arms fire, we really hadn't come up against the enemy, so why were we standing about doing nothing?

Up to the time I was hit, the guns had not been deployed and whilst not in convoy formation, remained grouped together and had been so during the previous afternoon. I do remember great concern because the guns were kept hooked to their towing Jeeps, so were pointing in the opposite direction to the enemy – correct for a quick getaway but useless if needed in a hurry. It depends from which side one is looking at the situation! You have to understand that the [A] Troop, with its guns, was at the rear of the 1st Parachute Battalion.

I have no idea how far ahead there was actual contact with the enemy. There were sounds of battle in the distance, towards the town, but nothing much was happening where I was hit. If there had been, I would have found a safe bolt-hole of some sort; I am not of hero material any more than any other average guy. One moment I was standing up, the next I was on my back with gore all over the front of my smock. Innumerable pieces of shrapnel took up residence, and some are with me still. The largest was identified as a lump of copper from the driving band of an artillery shell. I was hit by a stray piece of shrapnel which was how it had been since we had 'dropped in'. As I write, a picture begins to form of explosions amongst the trees – Eric Clapham returning from taxi-ing the general and taking over again as I was taken into the St Elizabeth Hospital. I think this must have been as far east as the troop managed to get, and the battalion likewise. I would suggest that from that time, it became a rearguard action.

My comments must be read taking into consideration that they are based on 48 years' memory.[17] Also, for most of the 18th and 19th, we were in light to closely built-up areas. There was no question of deploying the guns because the range and field of view was virtually to the nearest building, which most of the time was only one or two hundred yards; I suppose the lateral field of fire was only a few degrees. I had been a gunner for four years, Medium and Anti-Tank, but never did the training include what really amounted to 'Street Fighting'. I suppose I am saying we could not fight the guns. During the period after I was hit, up to the final evacuation of the remains of the division, I have read of them in action in a defensive role and giving a good account of themselves. Given the chance to demonstrate their capabilities, the 6-pounder was a good weapon and the crews very professional; after all, most of them had already been in action at least twice.

---

16 On the north side of Utrechtseweg junction with Onderlangs.
17 Based on conversation with the editor in 1992.

To sum up, it is very evident that the situation on those first two days in my area was very different to that which was being experienced at the front of the 1st Parachute Battalion. The guns could not contribute to the tactical situation in that environment, but did make their presence felt when put into action within the final perimeter. By virtue of what an anti-tank gun is, it can only do its job in a defensive role; it is not a weapon of attack.

A Troop, 6-pounder anti-tank guns (1st Parachute Battalion)
Troop Comd. Lieutenant E.E. Clapham, POW
Lieutenant Ben S. Lockett, POW
Troop Sergeants:
Sergeant G. Anderson [*No. 1 gun*]
Sergeant H. Atkinson POW [*No. 2 gun*]
Sergeant D. Reed [*No. 3 gun*]
Sergeant J.A. Wilkinson POW [*No. 4 gun*]
Sergeant Jock Thomson [*Troop Sergeant*]

Lieutenant G. Ryall, Liaison Officer, 1st Airlanding, Anti-Tank Battery, Royal Artillery

As a liaison officer I did not travel in a glider with our guns but in a Dakota with a stick of parachutists. There is a large photograph of our stick boarding the plane (No. 131) in the museum at the Hartenstein.[18]

Sunday, 17th September
Our landing on the 17th was unopposed. Relieved that my parachute had opened and that all seemed well, I foolishly tried to do a 'stand-up' landing (not recommended!) My head jerked forward onto the cocking handle of my Sten gun and I lost the best part of my front two teeth! I was not able to touch any food for 36 hours!

Following our RV with our battery commander (Major W.F. Arnold), I was sent with a 17-pounder gun (Sergeant Max Rams i/c) to join the 1st Parachute Battalion who were to move off to Arnhem. I should mention here that we had one major problem. The 17-pounder buffer recuperator system worked by a process of oil and air and our gun had no air! This meant that it would probably have fired only one round, a very worrying state of affairs! Whether it had been filled by the air bottle and this had escaped, I can't say. I had not been attached to nor had anything to do with D Troop before landing by parachute at Arnhem.

Monday, 18th September–Tuesday 19th September
We were constantly held up as we made our way through the town and at one such hold up, Sergeant Rams bravely went off in search of a German sniper, was wounded, and we did not see

---

18 Chalk No. 131 comprised of assorted members of HQ, 1st Parachute Brigade and RAOC Recce Party, taking off from Barkston Heath. See Private Ted Mordecai, 1st Airborne Division Ordnance Field Park, RAOC.

him again. He was reported to have died of wounds, but there were grave suspicions about his death as he was Jewish.[19]

Tuesday, 19th September
The next and most important incident involved the loss of our gun. We had taken up a position in front of a house covering a road. Not long afterwards we received a hurried message that the infantry were withdrawing and that we should pull out. In our haste to leave, the wheels of our towing vehicle became embedded in some deep sand and we were stuck. As we were sitting on the top of a rise, I ordered the crew to dismount and we went off in search of a vehicle to tow us out. Some minutes later, I found an infantry Bren carrier which had a tow rope and I managed to persuade the driver to take me back to recover the gun. However, when we were within four hundred yards of it, I was stopped by a captain from the 1st Parachute Battalion (a Captain Williams), who refused to allow me to take the carrier any further.[20] As the carrier belonged to his battalion and he was senior to me in rank, I couldn't argue. He agreed to vouch for the fact that I had attempted to recover the gun. I learnt later that just before this, a German 88mm had blown two Bren carriers to bits.

Somewhat distressed by all this, I left the gun crew with another of our troops (intending to rejoin them) and then hitched a lift to Divisional HQ to report the loss of the 17-pounder. (I had no idea where Battery HQ was). The CRA, Lieutenant Colonel R. Loder-Symonds, ordered me to stay at Divisional HQ and keep an eye on the 6-pounder guns which were covering the roads converging on the Hartenstein. When I arrived on D+2, Divisional HQ was functioning much as one would have expected and there were a small number of German prisoners. It seems that they must have had some idea of the devastating capabilities of their own shelling and mortaring as the slit trenches they dug were deeper and more elaborate than ours. How right they were, for over the next six or seven days the shelling and mortar fire were murderous.[21]

I vividly remember two RAF aircrew whose plane had been shot down arriving at Divisional HQ and sheltering in a slit trench for half a day. (They had been gallantly, if unsuccessfully, trying to re-supply us). So demoralised were they by the constant shelling that they said they were going to try to get across the river. Whether they succeeded or not, I cannot say.

Wednesday, 20th September–Sunday, 24th September
Over the last few days, the Hartenstein area was smashed by artillery fire and the side of my slit trench, about 50 yards from the main building, was blown in by a shell. This was the first of my lucky escapes. On the second occasion I had been standing chatting to Captain N. McLeod (BHQ) by the side of our slit trenches. I then went off to visit one of the guns and as I arrived

---

19 Sergeant Max Rams, 1094468; age 28, D Troop, 1st Airlanding, Anti-Tank Battery, RA. No known grave.
20 Probably Lieutenant John Llewellyn Williams, Motor Transport Officer, 1st Parachute Battalion, liaison officer with 1st Parachute Brigade HQ. Awarded a DSO for actions at Arnhem. The above meeting between Williams and Ryall probably occurred Tuesday 19th in the afternoon. During the morning Williams was still in the divisional area and headed by Jeep into Arnhem to rally 1st Parachute Battalion remnants after learning of the failed attempt to reach the bridge; he then led 1st Battalion remnants back to Oosterbeek.
21 German POWs were kept in the tennis courts at the Park Hotel, Hartenstein, during the battle. After appealing to their captors, they were provided with entrenching tools. German POW casualties during the battle were put at seven killed and twenty wounded; *1st Airborne Division Intelligence Summary*, 27th September 1944.

the shelling started and I jumped into a slit trench. I returned some minutes later to discover that Captain McLeod had been seriously wounded and was in the first aid post, now operating in the cellar of what had been Divisional HQ. By this time a German sniper had his sights on the entrance to the cellar and it was a risky business to go down into it. I managed it and shall always remember the RSM who was hastily removing all those whom he considered to be sheltering in there illegally! Luckily, I managed to get out again having briefly seen Captain McLeod.

Monday, 25th September
It was not long after this, on the night of the 25th, that we were given orders about the withdrawal and I passed these on to the gun crews. Somewhat ironically and very tragically, when visiting the gun crew in whose slit trench I had taken refuge at the time Captain McLeod was wounded, I discovered that the trench had received a direct hit and the crew had all been killed. My last memories are of the dead bodies laid out alongside the first aid post at Divisional HQ – the shelling was too intense to allow us to bury them – and the heavy artillery bombardment of German positions by XXX Corps just before our withdrawal. I came out with a small party at about 2300 hours and, after a wait of several hours on the river bank, I was ferried across the river.

Post-Arnhem
I should like here to pay my own tribute to our CRA, Colonel Loder-Symonds who was an inspiration to us all. Very clever and brave, yet at the same time kind and understanding, he helped me enormously during what was a most severe battle inoculation. What a tragedy it was that he was killed in an air crash just after the end of the war, thus depriving the British Army of one of its finest soldiers!

Gunner E.H. Barnsley, D Troop, 1st Airlanding, Anti-Tank Battery, Royal Artillery

17-Pounder Anti-Tank Gun, Sergeant M. Rams i/c, attached to 1st Parachute Battalion D Troop. 17-pounders. (OC's Command)
Troop Commander: Lieutenant Lloyd.
Troop Sergeants: Sergeant J. Gentles. *[No. 1 gun]*
Sergeant J. Masterson. *[D and P Troop Sergeant]*
Sergeant M. Rams. *[No. 2 gun]*
Sergeant G.E. Thomas. *[No. 3 gun]*
Lance Sergeant S. Fitchett. *[No. 4 gun]*
My gun crew were:
No. 1. Sergeant M. Rams
Bombardier D. Stone
Gunner F. Greeny
Gunner S. Wrightham
That's all I can remember.

Sunday, 17th September
Sunday morning, we took off from Tarrant Rushton Airfield in a Hamilcar Glider with our 17-pounder anti-tank gun and a Morris 'Portee' Tower. An uneventful flight. We had a very heavy and heart-stopping landing at a very crowded landing zone. The glider broke up on landing, the gun was damaged and one of our crew was hurt. We could however tow the gun along despite its damage and have it repaired if all went well. After sorting ourselves out, it seemed like an exercise at first; in fact the most danger came from our gliders coming in all over the place.

The first Germans we saw were out Sunday afternoon strolling with their girlfriends, quite a surprise and shock for them. We moved off towards Arnhem and arrived at the outskirts early Monday morning. We heard our first sounds of tanks in the distance.

Monday, 18th September
As daylight dawned, it seemed all the Underground Movement came out wearing their orange arm-bands. I always felt that we let them down badly. I can imagine how they suffered afterwards. This part is rather confusing; Monday morning we were still going forward in the outskirts of Arnhem. I can remember the infantry chaps cheering as we went by, not knowing of course, that our gun was U/S,[22] but it was good for morale! We saw the second half of our operation arrive from England.

Tuesday, 19th September
I think it was still Monday but we arrived at some crossroads.[23] There was confusion, we were surrounded, told to leave the gun, remove the breech block and return to Oosterbeek. I couldn't understand why we did not unhook the gun and retreat to Oosterbeek in our own vehicle. I recall removing the breech block from our 17-pounder and piling it into a Jeep and haring off to the area around Oosterbeek church. We dug slit trenches outside the church and there we stayed.[24]

Wednesday, 20th September
We were simple riflemen now. I am referring to my own gun crew, D Troop. I can't recall the other guns from the battery. Each day seemed the same, constant shelling from the Germans. We saw the ill-fated Polish Brigade land miles away.

Lack of communication really, any day the relief would arrive or so we thought. Praise for the RAF who flew in low dropping supplies to us. Unfortunately our area around Oosterbeek was getting smaller by the day, so a lot of the supplies dropped in the fields for the Germans to get their hands on. We could actually see them over the fields but couldn't reach them with our rifles. It was dreadful to see some of the planes shot down.

Sunday, 24th September–Monday, 25th September
Due to the intense bombardment, we moved into the church 24th–25th, which was being used as an OP, but were forced to leave and try and cross the road to the house opposite where they had good cellars. It was on the last day but one, and as I ran across the road, I was hit in the leg. I was helped to the nearest dressing station. My wound was attended to and I got back in the cellar and fell asleep.

---

22   Unserviceable.
23   Tuesday, 19th September.
24   Field of fire facing east.

Armeekorps		**Formblatt 5**
Luftgau		zu Wm. San. B. Teil 8, Nr. 46

Krankenblatt

Berichtsjahr 19 44

Kriegslaz. 2/686 (Haupt-) Krankenbuch Nr. 2666 Abt.-Krankenbuch Nr. _____
Enschede-Holl. „ Nr. _____ „ Nr. _____
Leicht. Kr. Lz. d. 7/595 Glanerbrug „ Nr. 392 „ Nr. _____
(Lazarett, Krankenrevier)

Krankheitsbezeichnung: Durchschuss rc. Wade

Krankheitsnummer:

Name	Familien-	Barnslay	Zugang am	28.9.1944
			woher?	
	Ruf-	Ernst	überwiesen verlegt am	5.10.44
			wohin	Laz. Glanerbrug
Dienstgrad		Soldat (Engländer)	überwiesen verlegt am	26.10.44.
Truppenteil			wohin	Kgs.Laz. Enschede
Geburt	Tag, Monat Jahr	23.10.21	überwiesen verlegt am	
	Ort	Coventry	wohin entlassen	
	Kreis		am wie	
Diensteintritt		19.6.41	wohin	
Religion			(Truppenteil)	
Bürgerlicher Beruf		Schreiber	Gesamtzahl der Behandlungstage	

Nächste Angehörige u. deren genauer Wohnort (auch Straße u. Hs.-Nr.): Florence Barnsley, 41 Park Street, Coventry, England

Wehrdienstbeschädigung von dem Kranken behauptet? ja — nein ¹)

Wehrdienstbeschädigung ist gemeldet am _____ an _____ ¹)
nicht gemeldet, da zu geringfügig.

W.D.B.Liste war vor Lazarettaufnahme bereits angelegt ¹)

¹) Nichtzutreffendes ist zu durchstreichen.

Datum	Krankheitsgeschichte
23.9.	Verwundung in Arnheim. B. lag bis zur Gefangennahme am 28.9. versteckt in einem Keller, er wurde von einem Kameraden verbunden. Am 28.9. Einlieferung ins hiesige Lazarett. Befund: Kalibergrosse Ein-u. Ausschusswunde re. Wade. Eitrige Absonderung, Infiltrat. Behandlung: Steriler Verband (Volkmannschiene)
4.10.	An der re. Wade 2 gut kalibergrosse, frische Schusswunden. Das umgebende Gewebe ist scheinbar durch ein tiefes Haematom, welches wenig druckempfindlich ist,verhärtet. Verbandwechsel, MP-Puder.
5.10.	Verlegt nach Laz. Glanerbrug
5.10.	Aufnahme im Leichtkr.-Lazarett Glanerbrug 9.10. MP-Puder, Verband 12.10. dto. — gute Wundheilung 15. und 17.10. Rivanol-Verbände 20.10. Fortschreitende Wundheilung 23.10. MP-Puder - Verband - Wunde reizlos 26.10. Trocken-Verband
26.10.	Dem Kr.-Lazarett Enschede zur Weiterbeförderung mit einem Lazarettzug überwiesen.

Stabsarzt

POW ID, Gunner E.H. Barnsley, D Troop, 1st Airlanding Anti Tank Battery RA. (Photo: E.H. Barnsley)

Tuesday, 26th September–Thursday, 28th September

I awoke the next morning to an eerie silence. All those who could, had left in the night. Investigating upstairs, I saw Germans driving our Jeeps up and down the road. In the cellar with me was Gunner Wrightham, with a head wound received during the move from the church and another wounded chap, can't recall his name. I remained for three days in the cellar. On 28th September a search party of Jerries came along. We were treated quite well; they even found a walking stick for me. Walking down the road, a Dutch lady came out and gave us a drink of water. We were taken to a large house for interrogation, then to hospital run by nuns. By coincidence, on the Red Cross train taking us to Germany, I travelled in the same coach as Captain McLeod, who I believe had his left leg amputated.[25]

---

25 Other gun crew members belonging to D Troop suffered casualties in the church area: Sergeant G.E. Thomas, 794078, age 34, and Bombardier John J. McCullock, 1459052, aged 25, both found buried in RAP of the Ter Horst family garden, Benedendorpsweg. Gunner Purnell, also D Troop was wounded. Sergeant Thomas had his final 17-pounder position situated outside the church, facing east. See the account of Gunner E.T. Burridge, P Troop, 1st Airlanding Anti-Tank Battery, Royal Artillery.

Corporal Geoff Stanners, Royal Army Medical Corps, 16th Parachute Field Ambulance, R Company, 1st Parachute Battalion, 1st Parachute Brigade

I was a corporal in 16th Parachute Field Ambulance on permanent attachment to R Company, 1st Parachute Battalion. My weapon was a .45 automatic pistol.

Sunday, 17th September
The [2nd] Battalion dropped first and we secured the DZ and allowed 2nd and 3rd Parachute Battalions to move off. We then made off for our objective, the aerodrome at Deelen. We were advancing up a slope as it was getting dark when we were cut to pieces by 88s. We then had instructions to help 2nd Parachute Battalion at the bridge.

Monday, 18th September–Monday, 25th September
We moved through the trees to Oosterbeek crossroads and turned left and after about 500 yards ran into two German armoured cars. We moved through the gardens of the houses to the lower road and higher roads where we came to a stop. By then the remnants of the battalion which I was with were so small it did not need the two medics, so we[26] joined up with two medics from the 3rd Parachute Battalion[27] and formed a regimental aid post in a German medical store about 100 yards back from the furthest point forward of where we had got to. After about two hours of tending the wounded and evacuating them, we were obviously spotted by the enemy because eight 88mm shells came through the asbestos roof of the building, killing most of the people in there.

I evacuated four wounded out on one Jeep to the Schoonoord Hotel at Oosterbeek crossroads. The commanding officer[28] there ordered me to open up the Vreewijk Hotel on the opposite side of the road as a post-operative dressing station (this was Tuesday, 19th September) which I did and I stayed there until removed to Stalag XIB on 25th September.

Awards
Corporal Geoff Stanners, 7387144, received the Dutch Bronze Star for his actions as a medic at Arnhem. The citation reads:

> Lance Corporal Stanners dropped with his Field Ambulance at Arnhem on the 17th September and was employed as an orderly at a Main Dressing Station from the 18th to the 25th September. During that period he chose the duty of carrying in casualties and searching for the wounded. Day and night he moved around the lines of both forces, treating German and British wounded alike, often under heavy shell fire, and wearing no equipment other than his uniform, and his first aid bag. On one occasion when mortar fire was causing casualties, he went out to collect a wounded German SS Officer and continued working in the open until he had carried four other wounded as well into his Main Dressing Station. On the night of the 20th/21st September he went through the German front-line to an isolated British position, where he treated the wounded and helped the worst cases back to the MDS. On many of his journeys he received shrapnel wounds of varying severity until by the 24th September

---

26 Corporal Stanners and Private Smith, RAMC.
27 One of whom was Private G. Thompson, RAMC.
28 Lieutenant Colonel Marrable.

he had been hit in thirty-seven different places. He persisted in dressing his own injuries until ordered to have fuller attention, when a dressing of his wounds by a superior Officer lasted for two and a half hours. He could have walked across a road to regain his own lines at any time but remained with his wounded and was evacuated as a prisoner of war into Germany on the 25th September. Despite his wounds he never ceased in the hazardous duty of looking for wounded and many men of both Forces owe their lives to his devotion to duty and his great personal courage.

Lieutenant Tony V. Driver, Troop Leader, E Troop, 3 Battery, 1st Airlanding Light Regiment, Royal Artillery

Sunday, 17th September
Although I was a subaltern in E Troop, 3 Battery, I never saw the guns. I went over in a glider on the Sunday and the arrangement was that I would be the forward observation officer to the 1st Parachute Battalion unless Lieutenant Noel Farrands, who was senior to me, did not arrive to be the gun position officer. Noel arrived safely and my action was entirely with the 1st Battalion. I rendezvoused with their commanding officer, Lieutenant Colonel D.T. Dobie.

Monday, 18th September
I was involved in the fighting in the houses alongside the river in our unsuccessful efforts to get to the bridge. I seem to remember having a successful shoot at a German anti-aircraft gun on the other side of the river on, I believe, the Monday afternoon. Our E Troop captain, Tony Harrison, was with me using a sniper rifle to take pot shots at the Germans who had to leave their anti-aircraft gun pit because I was air bursting shells over them. A German sniper on our side of the river took a shot at me as I lay down behind a wall directing the fire. He missed me and hit Harrison who got a wound in the stomach. He went back to have his injury dressed and later on won the MC for some brave effort.

I went on with David Dobie and took part in the disastrous battalion attack at night.

Tuesday, 19th September
The 1st Battalion, then reduced to about 15 (I believe), went down the tow-path at night. Eventually at daybreak I was holed up in a house on the tow-path with Dobie and my signaller. We were in the basement and the Germans were upstairs. We were taken prisoner and I finished the war in Oflag 79.

How many things apparently impossible have nevertheless been performed by resolute men who had no alternative but death?

Napoleon Bonaparte

Looking across Onderlangs and the Rhine to where German flak guns were engaged by Lieutenant Tony V. Driver, Troop Leader, E Troop, 3 Battery, 1st Airlanding Light Regiment, Royal Artillery. He writes: 'Our E Troop captain, Tony Harrison, was with me using a sniper rifle to take pot shots at the Germans who had to leave their anti-aircraft gun pit because I was air bursting shells over them.' (Photo: Author, 1980)

Morning of Tuesday, 19th September, Utrechtsestraat /Bovenbergstraat crossroads, Arnhem. Seated on the back of a Citroen car, left to right: Lieutenant V.A. Brinev, Intelligence Officer; Major J. Timothy, R Company, both of the 1st Parachute Battalion; and Lieutenant Tony V. Driver, Troop Leader, E Troop, 3 Battery, 1st Airlanding Light Regiment, Royal Artillery attached to the 1st Parachute Battalion. (Photo: Courtesy Gelders Archive)

The three officers leave what was possibly the HQ of Hauptsturmführer Möller, commander of SS Panzer Pionier-Bataillon 9 *Hohenstaufen*, Utrechtsestraat/Bovenbergstraat crossroads, Arnhem, Tuesday, 19th September. (Photo: Courtesy Gelders Archive)

Private V. Boast, 4 Platoon, B Company, 2nd Parachute Battalion, 1st Parachute Brigade

Sunday, 17th September
On Sunday 17 September, I awoke a bit late; we had slept in the open. Went to breakfast and I had kippers … to do battle on kippers! Later on we embarked on the trucks and left Colsterworth village to waving and cheering of villagers, they had treated us so well. We arrived at (Saltby) Airfield, still wondering if it would be cancelled like the others which had been planned; this time no. I was in Lieutenant ('Loopy') Leviens Platoon. On the way over, I saw through the door of the Dakota the flooded fields of Holland. Upon one, which was not under water, a glider had been put down. I saw one of our escorts diving down, shooting up flak-ships on the canals. Time came and we prepared to jump.[29] Having landed and looked around, it was exactly as the sand table at our briefing. I looked for the yellow smoke which denoted the forming up point (RV) for the battalion.

The battalion formed up and we pushed on to Arnhem[30] passing the work done by the Pathfinders – they had done a good job.[31] On the way in, the company had its first casualties, the 'Twins' in the company among them.[32] We pushed on; people were lining the route cheering and laughing and

---

29 1445 hours.
30 Via Heveadorp.
31 21st Independent Parachute Company.
32 Private Claude Gronert, 5511524, and Private Tomas Gronert, 5511523, aged 21. Found buried near Benedendorpsweg/Klingelbeekseweg railway viaduct, Oosterbeek.

they presented us with marigolds. Approaching the bridge, the platoon I was with came under fire again; a sergeant was hit in the crotch. The Jerry machine gun seemed to be firing low. We pushed on, for again we came under fire. With some others, we took cover in a house; as we entered the occupants left. The Germans let us know we were there. Several bursts of machine gun fire came through the window, and everything on the mantelpiece went for 'a burton'; we returned fire and decided to get out. We found that there was no back door, so we all had to drop out the second floor window. Dusk was falling and at nightfall we were in position near a wounded Jerry; his moans started to get on our nerves.

Monday, 18th September–Wednesday, 20th September
The following events I cannot say are in sequence, owing to the length of time. The morning of the second day, about a dozen of us were making our way down a path, when we came under machine gun fire. We returned fire and decided to get out, several of the boys had been hit in the legs. As we passed a house we heard Jerries inside. We gave them something to talk about; we tossed a few 36s through the windows. We had gone several hundred yards when Taffy, who was with me, said he had been hit. He must have just started to feel it. He rolled his trouser leg up, and he had been hit through the shin. I put my shell dressing on it; the medics would be picking him up. Later I saw my mate, Robbo (Private Robbert, B Company), he had been hit in both legs, he was applying a tourniquet to stop the bleeding. Whilst in one house I managed to cook one of the meat blocks out of the ration packs with a few little spuds I found. Having cooked it, one of our wounded needed it more than I did. I don't think many of us bothered about eating. By now, things were beginning to hot up, moving from house to house, street to street. I am sure it was the third night an officer came round with information that the attack from our armies would be coming in that night or first thing in the morning.

The next night the message was the same – before he could finish it we all chorused the remainder. I knew that no help would arrive, but gave no thought to the outcome. I saw some of the chaps carrying a bedridden old lady out of one house. She did not want to go, I believe she would rather have died in her home. I am sure that the most gallant and unhesitating deed performed was by a medic in our company when he leapt out of the house we were in, to go to the aid of one of our chaps laying in the street. Firing was very heavy; he had no sooner reached the casualty, when he was shot. His Red Cross armband could clearly be seen, and an officer in the house gave the order that the German must be got if it was the last thing we did, and the Bren gun got him. This incident is recorded in a book under the heading 'Murder of a Medic'.

Tanks were now the biggest problem together with ammunition getting short. I saw the crew of one 6-pounder dead over their gun, it was apparent that they had been firing to the last. I remember taking over a Bren gun for a short spell. The building I was in at the time I think were offices. Water was coming in through the floor, it was nearly dark and I could hear these Jerries coming, perhaps they got confidence in talking in loud voices at night. I let go with the Bren, but I could still hear them coming. I asked Rossiter who was carrying spare ammunition, for another magazine, which he gave me. I tried to put the magazine on, but it didn't seem to go on. I was really sweating now, and it occurred to me to feel the end of the magazine. I had been trying to put it on upside down! What a relief, the Jerries were getting right near. I sprayed the area from which the voices were coming and after doing so they were silent. I asked Rossiter for another magazine and he said that it was the last one he had. I asked him where the other members of our group were and he said that they must have moved out. I said that we should do the same. Passing someone

Oblique aerial photograph taken on Monday, 18th September clearly shows the destroyed vehicles of SS Panzer Aufklärungsabteilung 9 commanded by SS Hauptsturmführer Viktor Grabner, which attempted to cross the bridge on the Monday morning. (Photo: Courtesy Gelders Archive)

SS Hauptsturmführer Viktor Grabner's view of the north end of the bridge as he would have seen it as his SS Panzer Aufklärungsabteilung 9 raced across on the Monday morning (minus the horse and cart). Pre-war photograph. (Photo: Courtesy Gelders Archive)

who would not want his rifle again, I took it over with some ammunition, what was left. We passed some of A Company under the command of Major Tatham-Warter. He had still got his umbrella. The next time I saw him he was hobbling around with a stick, having been hit in the legs.

After a while the two of us came on a position where quite a few had dug in; this was, I know now, near the end. Jerry was bringing down everything he had got. I started to dig in with Rossiter; he was nearly twice my size. The trench never got big enough to take us both. Throughout the battle, like many more, I had prayed. I believe that without a faith, one has nothing to hang onto. It was on this last night that I believed I could not survive. It was then that I had a great feeling of tranquillity. I had no feeling of fear; I believe I had experienced the feeling you have when the end is near.

It was then that an officer gave the order that small groups from companies would be on their own and to try and break out. I moved out with about four others and two officers who led the way and whom we lost on going through some damaged buildings. We tried all night and found it impossible; we heard some had made it to the river but no further. We entered an office block and we got no further.

Thursday, 21st September
In the morning the Jerries entered the building. It would have been suicide to try anything, one or two of the chaps had no ammunition. We were taken into the street, with our hands behind our heads, when a German officer came up in a vehicle. He told us to take our hands down; we were to 'march as soldiers'. We were taken to a church where there were more like us. It amused me when some of the boys complained to one of our officers that the Jerries had taken their watches. He reported this to a Jerry officer, who then proceeded to get some of the watches back, which he then handed to our officer. It was the turn of the Jerries to get a rollicking, I often thought what would have happened if the shoe had been on the other foot.

Post-Arnhem
I would like to say it was a great honour and privilege to have served with 2nd Parachute Battalion under the Commanding Officer, now General Frost and all the officers, NCOs and the men, all gentlemen.

Private Vince Goodwin, B Company, 2nd Parachute Battalion, 1st Parachute Brigade

Sunday, 17th September
After a very uneventful passage we arrived over Arnhem. Already there was a large farmhouse on fire as we drifted down; that was the first sign we were finally going into action.

I was a private in B Company, 2nd Battalion. I had already served in North Africa, Sicily and Italy, so this jump didn't seem any different from the next.

On grouping as a company, we were ordered to take up positions about 300 yards from the DZ (the danger on leaving the DZ were the canisters, with weapons and ammunition, raining down from the sky. There seemed to be dozens of them falling, mostly without the parachute. One unlucky mate was hit by a canister and badly injured). I think we must have been about twenty minutes in the DZ position, when the platoon sergeant told us to form up into sections. As we were marching to Arnhem, the order of march was: A, C and B Company. At this point we all thought it was going to be a walkover, we hadn't seen one enemy, although we had heard small arms fire. In fact my first sight of a German was seeing five or six of them with their arms in the air, as we passed through the village.

As we continued, the firing was getting heavier, and we knew A and C Companies were coming under fire. From then on we were engaged in small actions until we came to 'Den Brink', a small road bridge with the railway line over it, leading to the railway bridge over the river (this was C Company's objective).We were held up for a while at the road bridge and it was there I met with my first action. We had already lost the Gronert twins, Tom and Claude. I believe one got the beginning of the burst, and the other twin got the end of the burst.

My section was ordered to go to the left flank of the road bridge as a German machine gun post had the under-bridge covered on the other side. We more or less crawled to the left of the road bridge and took up positions on a rise in the ground (by this time it was dark) and as we lay in this position another body dropped down at the side of me. After a while I found out he was from the 3rd Parachute Battalion. He had got mixed up on the DZ, God knows how he got there, at the side of me. About this time, all hell seemed to break out and what the two of us thought was 'advance', was in actual fact 'get out quick' (back to the small bridge).This new found pal and I crept forward as we thought the rest of the section was doing, and found ourselves within this small wood, where in fact I killed my first German. We continued through the wood, and although we heard voices (we thought they sounded like English), we came across this road and small road bridge which we now know was the main road into Arnhem. By this time, we both knew we were completely isolated from my company.

We did in actual fact try to continue under the bridge towards Arnhem but we came under heavy small arms fire from the other side. My pal from the 3rd Battalion received a bullet in the elbow as we tried to run back under the bridge. He said simply that he had been hit in the arm, and remarked that he was going back for his Sten gun that he'd dropped when he was hit. I told him no way were we going back, so we tried to retrace our steps back to where we came from, but by this time we were getting deeper and deeper into more trouble. There seemed to be Jerries everywhere. We eventually came to a small Dutch farmhouse where the farmer was sat outside watching the fireworks (as he put it). We went inside, sat down, whereby his wife made a cup of coffee and offered something to eat. We declined and said we were trying to get back to our battalion and it was at this point that Alf (I never knew his surname) asked me to dress his wound. I did so with my field dressing and noticed that he was holding his fist very tight. When he opened his fist, there was the German bullet in the palm of his hand. The bullet had entered his elbow, travelled down the arm and came out in the palm of his hand. I asked him if he wanted to continue with me or stay in the farmhouse, but he insisted in carrying on.

By this time the Jerries were everywhere and we knew that if we wanted to get to the bridge at Arnhem we somehow had to cross over the railway line, which by this time the Germans had machine guns on a fixed line covering the length of it. We decided to find a quiet spot to cross, and as we lay at the side of the line I noticed a British para was burning. What had happened, his phosphorous grenades had been hit and he had died burning – a terrible death. We managed to get across okay and ran smack into four Germans having a quick smoke behind a house. Alf fired a signal pistol cartridge (red) at them (that he had picked up from the burning para) as it was the only means he had. I killed three of them with my Sten and we took the other prisoner. He was a young man of about 18 and very timid. I managed to get out of him that a British section of troops had passed them about an hour ago. We turned the German over to two brothers who lived in the house and carried on to Arnhem. I was wondering at this moment, that out of a whole division, we seemed to be the only two on the road. After what seemed to be hours and hours we came to the suburbs of Arnhem and by this time we knew we were in the thick of it, and by now we didn't know who was who. We were simply coming face to face with Jerries on every corner. We knew that British lads were in the immediate area, because we could hear English voices, but we also knew the enemy could speak good English too.

About this time we came across four para lads (Royal Engineers), who were guarding some prisoners-of-war in a back garden. We told them where we were trying to get to, so two of them joined us while the other two stayed with the POWs. Quite a few houses were burning by this time and as we came to this particular road junction (which I now know was the St Elizabeth Hospital) where a fair bit of action was going on, we decided as a small group, we would go to the right, which happened to be, luckily, the right choice. We continued along the side of the river, when suddenly we ran onto a German truck with about twenty German troops. We had no alternative but to fire on them. The truck was set on fire, but one of our group was killed while throwing a grenade and my pal Alf was again hit in the leg. I and the other able Royal Engineer managed to get Alf into the house across the way. The old lady and her husband (who owned the house) promised to look after Alf while we carried on, but I saw a very humorous thing while I was in the house. The old man was explaining to me and my new buddy the best way to get to the bridge where the battalion was. Suddenly, there were German voices under the window (which was wide open). The dear old man went to the window, and came back with two fingers up, to indicate there were two Jerries under the window. With a finger to his lips he went into the kitchen and returned staggering under a large bacon machine and very coolly dropped it out of the window. It was like a scene from a Buster Keaton film. We heard a scream outside, and decided the house was too dangerous for us. We ran out of the back door, being fired upon all the time and as dawn was just beginning we could see the large Arnhem bridge against the light sky.

Monday, 18th September–Tuesday, 19th September
Within 20–30 yards, we ran into machine gun fire. Two Germans had taken a couple of flagstones up and dug a slit trench in the pavement and set up an MG 34. Somehow and from somewhere, someone had thrown a hand grenade because there was a sudden explosion and both Germans were killed. As we both ran past I decided to pick up the German MG 34 as it was a far superior weapon to ours. After running down one or two more streets, we eventually arrived in B Company positions. My Royal Engineer pal was told to find his own positions at the other side of the bridge, and that was the last I saw of him. I hope he is still living and well and happy.

I reported to my platoon commander as soon as I could find my platoon, they had been allocated positions, which in fact were two or three houses at the side of the bridge. I noted at this stage that a lot of German vehicles had been knocked out all along the bridge. I settled in with a few mates within the house nearest to the side of the bridge and for the rest of the day, Monday, we were given various tasks to do. One of these tasks I remember very well: I was told to go with another mate, a signaller, to see if there was a way through to Arnhem railway station. We set off and made our way through some very old streets and buildings (it was a terrible shame that within a few hours they would all be in flames). I can't remember very clearly how we managed to get to the railway station, as when we got there it was a mass of flames. Apparently, an advance body of 1st or 3rd Battalion had got *that* near to us on the bridge.

It was whilst coming back from there, that I saw an indescribable situation, whilst sheltering from a salvo of German mortar bombs (or were they our own mortars?) within this cafe (in ruins). We were looking out of the upstairs window, when my mate said, 'Look at this, Vince, it's going to be funny.' What happened was, most of the Dutch street corners more or less came to a point, more or less like a letter 'V' and creeping along the wall was a German with a machine pistol in his hand, and doing the same thing was a British para lad doing the same on the other side of the 'V'. We both realised that given time, they would both meet on the corner. At this point we both wondered whether to shoot the German, but my friend said, 'Leave them, and see what happens.'

Well, the inevitable happened: they both came face to face at the corner of the 'V'-shaped street. The German looked the British lad in the face with their noses practically touching – the German dropped his machine pistol and ran towards our building and the British lad did the same thing, he dropped his Sten gun and ran the other way! We thought it was very humorous at the time. Meanwhile the German soldier (SS) ran into the ruined cafe where we were sheltering. We held him at gunpoint and found he was sixteen-years-old. We couldn't take him with us, and neither of us could shoot him in cold blood, so we did the next best thing and shot him in both legs. I often wonder if he survived or not.

When we arrived back at the bridge, we found our platoon houses on fire. We occupied other positions until the burned-out houses had cooled down, then we reoccupied them. Shortly after we lost our officer; he put his head out of the window and a German sniper shot him in the head. Apparently the bullet entered the side of his helmet, because when his helmet was removed, it was found that the bullet had travelled around his helmet and cut his skull completely in half. It wasn't very pleasant to see the top of his head still in his steel helmet.

Tuesday 19th September

By Tuesday evening, things started to get really uncomfortable and at most times, we didn't know if we were standing on our heads or our feet. We were hunted from house to house, sleep was impossible and food was nearly all finished. We knew at this stage that the enemy was all around us and we knew that the 2nd Army wasn't coming, but still the good old British humour never flagged. For instance, I (and Corporal Chilton) had been detailed to go under the bridge (my heart sank!) with a message for Captain Mackay's lot.[33] I got through okay but on the way back the Jerries started to heavily mortar the road, so I sheltered in the ruins of what had been a blacksmith's forge, and I thought the best protection would be under the forge where the fire was. Underneath the forge was all the small coke for the fire. What I didn't know was that the workmen there, had over the years, done their 'dirt' on a shovel and then thrown it under the forge again, and every time a mortar bomb fell on the forge I sank lower into the coke. By this time the smell of the past human dung had really got to me. I thought, bombs or no bombs, I was getting out of there, but I never realised until I crawled out from under the forge, just how filthy I was. I was covered from head to foot, and when I reported to Major Crawley; he took one look at me and told me to 'bugger off and get a bath.'

Wednesday, 20th September–Thursday 21st September

On the Wednesday morning, we managed to find a house, half burned, and as we sat downstairs, looking filthy, very tired and hungry, a mate of mine saw a telephone under the rubble, and I asked

---

33 Elements of 1st Parachute Squadron, Royal Engineers and C Company, 3rd Parachute Battalion.

him to ring the nearest 'cafe' for more grub. When he lifted the phone a voice asked him what he wanted. To cut a long story short, he was actually in touch with the fire station in Arnhem.

I think Wednesday night was the worst night of my whole life. We had no ammunition and I was just running around with an empty rifle with a bayonet on the end. At some time past midnight, the last house we were in was set on fire. Myself and the company commander and another chap threw our remaining smoke grenades outside in the street (which was as bright as day with the flames), and made a dash for it. At this point I was hit in the legs, but still managed to get across the street into the other house. By this time the German SS were just touring the streets with our own captured Jeeps and it was only the fact that they (SS), were collecting our badly wounded chaps and loading them onto the Jeeps that saved them from being shot.

Thursday, 21st September
At about 0300 hours, the remaining house was set on fire, and all we could do (about 20 of us left by this time), was retreat to the back garden of the house and dig in (I remember using half a mess tin to dig in with). At some time about 0400 hours in the morning, some German SS came up to my slit trench, two of them, and said, 'What a waste of time and lives to carry on and why not give ourselves up?' I could see at least three tanks ready to blast us, but we very calmly said if they didn't get out of the garden we would start firing. Just then a German stick-grenade landed just outside the slit trench, killing the para lad who was in the trench with me and badly wounding another para lad in the eyes, and also killing one of the German SS blokes. Well, for the next 15 or 20 minutes there seemed to be British and Jerry troops all over the area. I remember assisting the chap who was blinded through a gap in the garden wall, and running into another building which was in ruins, but not burnt.[34] In actual fact, it was a cider factory with three very large vats in the floor; they measured about 12 feet deep by 12 feet across and even when all hell seems let loose, you can still see the funny side of things, because in one of the vats was a British para lad struggling to get out, covered from head to foot in what appeared to be rotten apples. I managed to help him out, and as we ran out of the building there was a large explosion and that's all I remember until waking up strapped to a German tank with another British lad who had also been wounded. This was on the Thursday morning, and by now nothing else could be expected from the 2nd Battalion. It was a terrible four and a half days, with nothing to eat, nothing to shoot with, dirty and very, very tired: we just couldn't do any more.

I think that in the four or five days on the bridge at Arnhem, I must have been witness to dozens of very brave acts, each one warranting the VC no less. One brave person I saw, knocked out a Tiger tank with a PIAT gun and then very calmly walked away. He was wearing a large white cook's hat on his head. One very big German, dressed in black (Tanks), gave me a cigarette and a slice of bread and cheese with a hot cup of coffee and informed me it was the hardest battle he had been in, and that, if he was in another one, he hoped it would be against the British paras. He had a lot of respect for them. Then off we went to a POW camp (in my case, hospital first).

---

34 Possibly Private Roy S. Purnell, 5498235, B Coy, 2nd Parachute Btn. Aged 24. Blinded during the fighting in the bridge area, he was taken POW, 20–21st September and moved along with other POWs to 'The Green' slope on the bridge ramp. Subsequently killed, possibly by shellfire.

6 Platoon, B Company, 2nd Parachute Battalion prior to Arnhem. (Photo: Author's private collection)

Private Jack Beeston, Anti-Tank Platoon, Support Company, 2nd Parachute Battalion, 1st Parachute Brigade

In the summer of 1942 at the age of 20 years, I sewed on my Wings. I had become a paratrooper. By the end of the year I had joined the 2nd Battalion. The next year saw us fighting in North Africa, Sicily and Italy. December 1943 saw us back in England stationed at Stoke Rochford in Lincolnshire to prepare for the invasion of Europe. D-Day came and went and where were we? Still at Rochford. From June 6th to the end of August we spent our time 'Standing To' and 'Standing Down' from operations, but early in September we were briefed for a mini invasion of Holland, i.e. one battalion to Eindhoven, one battalion to Nijmegen and the 2nd Battalion to Arnhem. This was postponed for a fortnight, so we went on leave sworn to secrecy. When we returned to camp and the enormity of Market Garden was revealed to us, I don't think anything in the world would have stopped it.

Sunday 17th September
On Sunday 17th September the sun was shining as we scrambled aboard our Dakota, some 20 or more men to a plane. The take-off and forming up in the sky was a sight to behold. Then the armada set sail for Holland. We crossed the Channel surrounded by formations of Dakotas, some towing gliders. Squadrons of fighters above and below us, how can we fail? Down in the Channel a string of Air-Sea Rescue boats stretching almost to Holland, some making for the plane, down in the sea. As we crossed the coast, a few puffs of ack-ack appeared in the sky suddenly reminding

us of what lay ahead. A large area of Holland was flooded, and nestled on a bit of dry ground was a solitary glider which had broken its tow rope and the pilot had managed to bring it down to dry land. The troops standing beside the glider waved up to us.

Shortly after, we stood up and began to prepare for the drop. The officer who was first to go was now hanging out of the plane, suddenly he was screaming, 'I can see the bridge, there's the bridge,' then he was gone and we all spilled out. To this day I can never forget the wonderful sight that greeted me as my chute developed and I slowly floated down. Formations of planes, all unloading paratroopers with masses of different coloured chutes everywhere, containers and cases plummeting straight to earth as the chutes failed, helmets and rifles, not securely fastened during the jump, whistling past you. Planes to the north dive-bombing an airfield, and then touching down to see Dutch civilians with prams and barrows collecting up parachutes and making off with them.

The 2nd Parachute Battalion consisted of three rifle companies and a support company. The support company had three platoons: the Mortar Platoon, the Heavy Machine Gun Platoon and the Assault Anti-Tank Platoon of which I was a member. The Assault Anti-Tank Platoon had three sections and each section had a PIAT gun. We were first introduced to these weapons in North Africa in 1943. We were given a disabled Sherman tank to practice on. For a crude weapon it was very effective. We were also trained to lay mines and lift mines, lay booby-traps and dismantle them. Also we could erect barbed wire and remove it when required. In fact, any 'sticky' job was ours.

Our first job on landing was to make for the north-east corner of the drop zone and ignite huge firework style flares which sent up a column of yellow smoke to guide the battalion together. This worked very well and very soon A Company moved off to start the eight-mile trek to Arnhem and 'The Bridge'. We moved off next and as we started down the cobbled tree lined road we heard a car coming up behind us, as near as I can remember, a camouflaged small Opel, definitely not a military vehicle. Corporal Chalkie White said, 'Leave this to me,' so we all moved behind trees. As the car approached, Chalkie tossed a grenade into its path. The grenade exploded as the car was almost clear, so Chalkie fired his Sten at the rear of the car which veered into the kerb, with the back door coming half open. We hurried to the car; in the front the driver was dead, slumped over the wheel and leaning against the half-opened back door was a badly wounded officer who said to me in perfect English, 'What about the wounded?' I told him the medics were coming along behind us and we moved off.[35]

A few Germans were beginning to surrender to us, so they joined the column carrying some of our equipment. We were making steady progress until we hit the first village where the whole of the population was waiting to greet us. They all wore orange flowers and were threading these through the scrimmage on our helmets, giving us bottles of orange squash, singing, dancing, taking troops into their homes to show their grandparents that the war was over and the British had arrived. The whole situation was ridiculous, until the order came from behind to push on as fast as possible for the bridges. We approached a large hospital and some of our forward troops were driving German ambulances back to the landing area to pick up casualties. So we continued to move nearer our objectives on this hot Sunday afternoon. This did not last very long as machine gun fire came at us. Our main objective was the bridges, not to get held up in a small battle, so we moved out of the village, turned right at the crossroads, which was under fire, and made for a track which ran along the Rhine, leading to the bridge. It was late afternoon and as we moved along this

---

35   This is very similar to the 3rd Battalion ambush of Generalmajor Kussin in his staff car, which may explain confusion between the two events.

track, the odd shots were coming from the other bank of the Rhine. As we veered left, into our view came the railway bridge. This was the objective of C Company. We passed under the bridge[36] and took up defensive positions while C Company prepared to take it.[37] As they got to the bridge and started to cross, there was an explosion and a part of the bridge fell into the Rhine.

It was now dusk and we were told to go hell for leather for the main bridge, so we raced along the last stretch with shots coming in from everywhere. As we passed side turnings we could see the Germans firing at us. We turned left up a long avenue and suddenly we were at the main bridge. From the photographs and models we had seen during the briefings, there was no doubt this was 'The Bridge', the climax, but it was much larger than we had expected and here we were, all opposition removed by A Company. After a short pause, Colonel Frost said we go over to the other side, and we climbed a steep grassy slope on to the road approach and made our way slowly across. When we were about a third of the way and just going under the steel span, shell fire came at us from the German side of the bridge. It looked like armoured vehicles in the road.

We had no choice but to withdraw off the bridge, back down the grassy slope where we took up defensive positions in the front gardens of the houses until told where to go. (When we followed A Company onto the bridge on the Sunday night to cross over, it was dark and we formed columns each side of the road. Civilians were still crossing over both ways and an elderly man driving a horse and cart passed us all, completely unaware who we were. Even a German armoured car came toward us, and we were told to let it go by. I'm sure in the dark the German sitting behind the machine gun mistook us for his own troops.) It was now very dark and a column of troops came up the road almost on our position, and Pete Murray casually challenged them as it had to be one of the other battalions. In fact, they were Germans coming to occupy the positions we were in. There was a quick spate of fire, with the Germans hurriedly retiring and us entering the houses we were at. Sad to say, Pete Murray had stood up to make his challenge and was hit by fire and died,[38] he was the first to die in our platoon and probably the first man killed at the bridge. We occupied the top floor of a large 'H'-shaped building,[39] which had a perfect view down and across the bridge. Later on, we slept fitfully in turns through the night, hearing sounds of battle going on in Arnhem with cries of 'Whoa-Mohamed', which meant the other battalions were striving to reach us. So ended the first day with everyone quite chuffed.

Monday, 18th September

Everyone was on their toes as dawn broke on Monday morning, then the air filled with the sound of breaking glass as windows everywhere were being knocked out to prevent flying splinters during the battle to come. The rest of the division were flying in today and would surely reach us by afternoon, better still the 2nd Army could cross the bridge by evening and I could greet my elder brother who was a sergeant in the 2nd Battalion, The Coldstream Guards, who were leading the advance. I am not sure now, but I thought we were in a large school as the room we were in had a couple of desks and a blackboard. The blackboard had a large piece of drawing paper pinned to it and someone had drawn the bridge exactly as it appeared outside. Sergeant Nick Carter rolled

---

36 Station Oosterbeek Laag, railway bridge, Benedendorpsweg/Klingelbeekseweg.
37 The main Arnhem-Nijmegen railway bridge over the River Rhine.
38 Private Patrick. M. Murray, 886001, Assault Platoon, Support Company, aged 21.
39 1st Parachute Brigade HQ, Rijkswaterstaat building, at the junction of Eusebiusbinnensingel and Marktstraat.

the drawing up and stuck it in his blouse, commenting, 'What a souvenir.' There then followed a lot of inter sniping between houses until we identified each other. We rustled up some breakfast and could hear the battle starting up in the town. Major Wallis was killed last night, we were told he went on a patrol, captured some of the enemy and coming back the prisoners were talking in German rather loud and in the darkness they were shot.[40] Major Wallis was a perfect gentleman, absolutely fearless and knew us all by our first names, in fact he was a father figure to us, and so his sudden death was a bit of a blow.

On the ground floor a couple of rooms had been turned into a first aid post with a few wounded inside and down in the basement every room seemed to be filled with prisoners. Half way through the morning we saw movement the other side of the bridge. Someone shouted, 'Here's the 2nd Army!' but as they came into view we were looking down on a German armoured column. In the lead was a motorcyclist followed by an armoured car then two canvas covered supply trucks and then an endless stream of armoured cars and tanks. Everyone at the windows and down on 'The Green' opened fire, the motorcyclist roared up the road like a rocket, the armoured car was hit by a shell in the side and a large piece of steel fell off and landed in the road. This was a piece of false plating. Anyhow, the vehicle accelerated and also made it up the road. The supply wagons were hit and stopped which in turn halted the column. The next six armoured cars were hit by shells, the crews being shot as they ran to safety, while the remainder of the column withdrew. We were elated. By afternoon, the houses behind us were under attack and some were blazing and the smoke was beginning to obscure the bridge. We could hear a lot of air activity and guessed the rest of the lads were dropping. All we saw was a couple of German fighters. The enemy set up a heavy gun near us and started to shell the building. The shells appeared to be 'solid shot', because when they hit the roof, all the tiles fell off and as dusk fell the battle seemed to die away. So we settled down looking at the stars through the roof at the end of the second day.

Tuesday, 19th September
As Tuesday dawned we were pretty sure that this was the day when it all happened. The 2nd Army had broken through and were racing toward us and the rest of the division were to assault Arnhem and sweep on to us, at least that is what we were told, but being paratroops we had heard it all before in other battles, so nobody seemed bothered anyway. Half of the buildings behind us, nearer the Rhine, were smouldering ruins and our troops had dispersed to other houses. The first aid post now resembled a hospital, filling up fast with wounded and many manning the barricades were now bandaged. Food was running short as the last meal we had was breakfast on Sunday morning. To make matters worse, the enemy had cut off the water, so I decided to collect the section's water bottles and try and fill them. There was a tap on the wall at the top end of our back garden. As I left the back door I was told the whole back area was under German observation, so I hugged the wall and made it to the tap and was in the process of filling the fifth bottle when shells came whistling over churning up the garden, so I grabbed all the bottles and ran like a hare back into the building. When I got back to the top floor, sniping and mortaring was going on and there was six of us in the room having a drink, when a mortar bomb came through the roof and landed on the floor. We just

---

40   Major David W. Wallis, Deputy Commander, 2nd Parachute Battalion, 93375, aged 29. Found buried near Roermondsplein, Arnhem. Major Wallis was shot after Sapper Donoghue from 9th Field Company RE guarding a doorway inside a house heard no response to his 'Who goes there?' challenge and opened fire, tragically mortally wounding Wallis.

looked at it. Our officer, Lieutenant 'Stuttering' Douglas said if we left the room he would pick it up and drop it out of the window. We said 'Don't be daft', then I remembered that on each landing there were sandbags in case of fire, so we collected these bags and stacked them around the bomb, and that was how it remained when we left the room for the last time.

By now, more houses were ablaze and a mortar bomb must have landed on the supply truck on the bridge because it was blazing and exploding ammunition was spreading the fire to the next truck, then the armoured car until all the vehicles were burning. The armoured cars were exploding as their shells were swamped by fire, scattering their pieces all over the bridge, completely blocking it. The column was burning for hours. The sniping continued and all the inner doors were removed because as you opened a door to go in, it was spattered with bullets. Survivors from burnt-out buildings were making for our building which seemed to be the centre of resistance. As the day drew to a close, a huge tank came rumbling down the bridge road, let fly at us with a couple of shells and then bulldozed the wreckage on the bridge to one side and rolled over to the German side. Colonel Frost wasn't having that, so Corporal Rattray, Corporal Tennant and myself armed with a PIAT anti-tank projector and a few grenades, went up The Green slope and alongside of the road and crouched down and waited for another tank to come along. Luckily for us, nothing happened and as the night dragged on, we made our way back to our section and settled down for the third night.[41]

Wednesday, 20th September

Wednesday had arrived and we were looking a bit unshaven and although our numbers were decreasing and quite a few rooms were unmanned, we were in good spirits because we had to be relieved as we only had to hold the bridge for two days and this was the fourth. Ammunition was collected from the wounded as it was becoming scarce and the anti-tank guns on The Green were unmanned due to lack of shells. We were getting a lot more attention from the enemy with increased sniping and the rumble of tracked vehicles to the side of us. It did appear that our building and the one on our left were the only two buildings we now held. The ground floor was full of wounded; names of dead paratroopers were passed among us verbally. On the bottom step of the basement sat a solitary para, guarding the prisoners. We were a bit puzzled by the absence of the rest of the division and also the 2nd Army. In fact these answers were not known to me until May 1945 on returning to England from a prisoner of war camp.

All morning we stayed at our posts expecting something to happen, when we received the news that Colonel Frost and Major Crawley were wounded and in the sick bay. That didn't sound too good for us. Very little happened in the afternoon and dusk settled on the forth night. We were alerted by the sound of heavy tracked vehicles rumbling along in our direction, then the shells hit us, blowing holes into the building with debris falling everywhere. We were told to evacuate the top floor and gather downstairs. By now the area was blazing and shells were still exploding around us. We scrambled downstairs over heaps of rubble to the ground floor. About 30 of us who were still on our feet were told by Major Gough that as the building was alight and collapsing around us they were going to surrender the wounded to the Germans. All able-bodied men were to run through the back door to escape and carry on fighting individually. So it was 'Every man for himself, good luck.' Two of the prisoners were officers and they were screaming out 'Cease fire' in German.

---

41 Corporal Arthur A. Rattray, 2879697, Assault Platoon, Support Company, aged 24. KIA 20th September 1944. Found buried in the Rhine bridge area, Arnhem.

Looking east along the Westervoortsedijk close to the Nieuwe Kade junction. PzKpfw Ausf.L on the left and on the right a PzKpfw Ausf.G with the River Rhine behind. The tanks are facing the British bridge positions, probably taken on the Wednesday, 20th September. (Photo: Tank Gunner Gefreiter Karl-Heinz Kracht; Courtesy ABM)

As the first six men ran through the back door I joined the next six, when the first six came back to say the back of the building was full of Germans, so I went outside and sure enough, there was a group of SS troops talking and driving our Jeeps away. So I went back into the house and made my way to the front door or the hole where the door used to be and stepped out and started down the path, when suddenly a patrol of SS troops came off the road and started up the path. We all stopped dead and they levelled their Schmeissers at me, so I gently lay my rifle on the ground and put my hands up. They came up to me and started thumping me on the back, saying, 'Good soldiers – good battle.' I was taken to The Green to join a group of half a dozen prisoners. The wounded had all been removed from the building and were scattered all over the place. The Germans who had surrendered to us were formed up and marched away by the SS. The building was now smouldering rubble. An armoured car approached us with a very stern-looking German officer with a monocle standing up who conversed with German officers on the ground and they seemed delighted. At this precise moment shells whistled over our heads, bursting on Arnhem. It was the 2nd Army.

Post-Arnhem
Being a paratrooper in World War Two was a risky business as there were many obstacles before you reached your objective i.e. the plane could crash or be shot down, your chute may not open; all the gear you are carrying may result in a bad landing causing broken limbs. When you are in

a plane being fired at, you can only sit there and take it as there is nowhere you can take cover. You can be dropped in the wrong place at night and have to wander around in enemy territory in daylight, so if you can reach your objective and dig in you have a good chance of surviving.

When we left for Arnhem I expected at the worst to be killed or even wounded but to be captured was an unbelievable nightmare, and that was the opinion of everyone. Arnhem was the first time we had fought in a town and buildings. In North Africa, Sicily and Italy it was always in the open, up in the Atlas Mountains or in wooded areas or olive groves, but always in the open where you can advance, withdraw, or change positions in the night safely.

Private George McCarthy, Headquarters Company, 2nd Parachute Battalion, 1st Parachute Brigade

Saturday, 16th September

My story starts on Saturday evening, 16th September 1944, in a large house near Grantham, Lincolnshire, which was headquarters of 2nd Parachute Battalion. The five orderly room staff, of which I was one, rested on our sleeping bags on the floor of the orderly room considering the briefing we had been given for an attack by the 1st Airborne Division on Arnhem Bridge, proposed for the following day. Our orders were clear, to capture and hold the bridge. This was probably the tenth such briefing we had had since D-Day. All of these had been called off. Tomorrow was my birthday. If this fizzled out, perhaps I could wangle a pass home to celebrate. We were in good spirits. Someone was playing our only gramophone record. It didn't do justice to Vera Lynn because it depended on an ordinary sewing needle which I had earlier fixed in a typewriter ribbon tin for its reproduction. We were ragging Corporal Sid Spratt, my particular friend, a re-headed lad from Blackburn. Sid was a King Scout and wrote regular articles for his local paper under the pen name of 'Grey Wolf'.

I checked my compass, which was shaped as a button; it had been sewn as one on the back of my trousers. I fingered the Dutch currency which I had been given and had concealed in my field dressing. We all 'tried on' our maps, which were made of cloth and worn as scarves around our necks. Suddenly, the Regimental Sergeant Major's batman came in confirming this was the real thing. We were the First Lift and would be off in the morning as briefed. Sleep was impossible, but nevertheless chatter died out and we quietly retreated into our own thoughts. I remember wondering if and when I should return to England again. Thus sleepless and thoughtful, we waited for Reveille.

Sunday, 17th September

Early the following morning we emplaned at Saltby airfield, the journey taking considerably longer than usual because of the large number of troops involved. Everyone was talking at the same time, underlining the excitement and tension. Jokes were cracked, speculation abounded. We were 100 percent fit, trained to a high level, and, above all, confident. Soon we were airborne and on our way to what was to become one of the bitterest and most bloody battles of the war. Most of the men on my plane were experienced parachutists and therefore we quickly settled down to conversation and occasional singing. Those near the windows gave commentaries on what was below. We crossed the coast, much speculation where, and then obvious by extensive flooding, into Holland.

Eventually the signal: 'Quarter of an hour to go.'

Tension mounted, the aircraft door was removed, seats folded and weapons carefully checked.

The voice of the Dispatcher: 'Five minutes to go … hooking up drill. Number 20, OK, Number 19, OK…' and finally, 'Number 1, OK.'

Again, the urgent voice of the Dispatcher: 'One minute to go … standby.'

Utter silence, until: 'Red light on, prepare to jump.' We waited. 'Green light on … GO.'

Colonel 'Johnnie' Frost was first to jump, followed by his batman. I followed after Sid Spratt. And so, at approximately 1400 hours on my birthday, I was drifting down to land on Dutch soil. Hundreds of containers (weighing approximately 5cwt), packs, bicycles and canisters hurled through the air. The sky was darkened by hundreds of parachutists, their weapons and kitbags dangling below them, came swinging to land.

Once down, we made our way to the rendezvous. I remember the cheers and embraces of the Dutch people who were running to greet us. Women and children were gleefully gathering our parachutes, helped by us to cut them free of the rigging lines. The rendezvous was, as one might expect, in a state of confusion, but within the hour we were ready to move towards Arnhem, some twelve kilometres away.

A Company was first to move, B and C deploying right, left and rear. Support Company and Battalion Headquarters (my own section) moved in after A Company. Throughout the feverish activities at the dropping zone, spasmodic firing could be heard and isolated skirmishes were fought as we moved on, but at this stage, no strong opposition was encountered. A Company destroyed a German staff car in such a skirmish and a group of Germans was passed through the lines. Shortly after this incident I was to see an old training days pal (serving with A Company), lying dead by the roadside. Regrettably, I was to see many more men die before I was to return to England, but I doubt if I was to experience any deeper emotion than to see Tommy Gibson killed so early in the battle.[42]

It was about 1800 hours when we reached Arnhem and by this time, things were beginning to hot up. We engaged a group of troop-carrying enemy vehicles, concentrating our fire and inflicting very heavy damage and casualties.

Our unit had been carrying pairs of communication pigeons which were in cylindrical containers. I had been detailed to take charge of one of these. The little creatures were to suffer much discomfort during the next few days when the battle intensified and, when of necessity, I was dashing from place to place. In fact I was later to place them with my pack in what I hoped was a comparatively safe place in the house at Arnhem from which at that time I was fighting, but unfortunately I was shot out from the house, being unable to return to release these birds before the house was burnt to the ground. I remember hoping desperately that someone had been able to release them. Two little birds who had remained so calm and seemingly indifferent to the hell breaking loose about them.

By evening on that Sunday, the 17th, we had established Battalion Headquarters in an impressive tall house which faced the north side approaches to the bridge, and subsequently the enemy activity which was to take place there. I remember that the house was attractively furnished. In one of the rooms there was an interesting collection of books containing seals and coats of arms which were etched out in sealing wax. A fine china tea service was laid out on a table, maybe even ready for use. I have a clear recollection of Regimental Sergeant Major Strachan carefully moving

---

42 Thomas A. Gibson, 6856184, A Company, 2nd Battalion, aged 23. KIA, 17th September. Found buried near Oosterbeek Laag station.

a table to the side of the wall uttering threats to anyone who damaged the china. Alas, soon the books were to be essential to us to use as barricades and indeed it was the RSM himself, I was later to see, sweep the china from the table which we now so urgently needed for a window barricade. Fighting became intense throughout the night and continued so into the following day, but we had the initiative.

Monday, 18th September

A large number of enemy armoured vehicles attempted to rush the bridge from the south side during the morning, but were repelled as they reached the north side approach by fire from Royal Artillery anti-tank troops and battalion supporting weapons which were withheld until the vehicles had reached this exact point. Hell was let loose, as we inflicted very heavy damage and casualties to the Germans. This success, and news that we were expected to be relieved by link-up troops the following day, gave us added impetus and despite fatigue, we fought savagely and with high morale. A light enemy truck carrying troops, lost in the confusion at the bridge approaches, charged down the road in front of battalion positions. Fire directed at it was so intense, that the actual fire power stopped it dead, horrifically plucking the occupants from their seats, hurtling them dead to the ground.

Aircraft were spotted during the day, but we were unable to identify them. As they did not fire on us we presumed that they were Allied planes. At the bridgehead we saw no further aircraft activity than this throughout the battle.

Later in the evening a tremendous commotion at the bridge approaches announced enemy Panzer tanks taking up positions. I was on guard outside the house when they started to fire at us. Our anti-tank gun units exchanged fire, but with very little effect. Systematically and with precision the tanks blasted each of the houses in turn, creating havoc. (I have since learned that the German 9th SS Division had been in the area and had been ordered to retake the bridge, I have also learned they were ordered to surround, and annihilate us, and this they came close to doing.) The facing house heaved violently as I dashed back into the 'Headquarters' house in order to be able to give supporting fire. As I did so, a further blast hit us. The middle floor of the house was totally demolished, but the top floor remained uncannily intact. I struggled from the ruins to try and make my way through a hole which led to a flat roof at the rear of the house. As I did so, a further shell hit us. The force of this explosion lifted me right through the window and hurtled me about twenty feet to the ground below. I was undoubtedly saved from injury as I landed on top of Father Egan, our Roman Catholic Padre, who was crouched on the ground below.

Having picked myself up, I dashed for the garden in order to join the remaining Headquarters staff. I was subsequently detailed to contact the anti-tank gun commander to order him to report to Colonel Frost. It was during this dash to reach the gun position that I was hit in the chest on the left side. My whole side became numb and my left arm was limp. The force of the blow had knocked me off my feet, but fortunately I was able to get up and complete my mission and report back to Headquarters, which was still in the garden.

The tanks withdrew but we were then subjected to constant concentrated heavy mortar fire. The whole area around us was totally devastated and casualties were enormous. Everywhere were the dead and wounded, many of the wounded still struggling to fight on, the firing was so concentrated that many could not be taken to the casualty station which was just 'next door' and which was struggling feverishly to cope with what was now a flood of wounded. The constant fire prevented me from seeking attention for my wound and it was some time before I could cope with applying a field dressing. It was quite obvious that the enemy had infiltrated our line and had us at their mercy. Fighting had now become individual, and bitter individual skirmishes were taking place all around the bridge area. Fire had also been started by phosphorous bombs and most buildings were totally ablaze.

Mercifully the withdrawal of the tanks at least enabled us to return to the ruins of what had been the house which afforded a little more cover than the open garden where none existed. We were totally exhausted as well as hungry and thirsty. As we dropped to the ground from complete and utter weariness, in so many cases from pain, we would drop into an uneasy exhausted doze. The battle nevertheless continued.

Tuesday, 19th September
Tuesday morning found us still under constant merciless bombardment. Slightest movements would bring bursts of enemy fire from every direction. Dead and wounded were mounting, yet I heard no complaints. I was getting considerable pain from my side, but was still unable to get to the casualty station. Sid Spratt, unbelievably still uninjured, insisted that I had his field dressing. So typical of a man who displayed so much courage and faith throughout this battle and later as a prisoner of war, but to return home to his beloved family, only to die within a few weeks.[43]

The relentless and vicious bombardment continued until mid-afternoon when a message was received from the commanding officer of the enemy calling on us to surrender. We were completely surrounded, the message said, a fact of which we could hardly be unaware. Colonel Frost's immediate reply was to call on the Germans to surrender to us!

In keeping with our nightmarish situation there ironically followed a short lull in the fighting during which time a white flag was spotted. Unbelievable though it was to us all, for a moment we thought that the enemy had acceded to Colonel Frost's demands. A cheer went up from us all. Regrettably our jubilation was very short-lived as we identified a pathetic band of Dutch civilians desperately trying to reach German lines. These poor Dutch people, who three days earlier had greeted us with joy and gratitude, were seeing our arrival as the beginning of freedom for their country. I prayed that they made it. After this short lull, firing commenced with as little mercy.

It was later in the afternoon we learned that the expected link-up troops had been seriously delayed, and I think we all knew our situation was hopeless, yet we did not share our thoughts.

If possible, now enemy fire became even more concentrated. We were desperately in need of relief, yet I heard no complaints. Supplies of everything were extremely low. It was intended we should hold the bridge for 24 hours. Casualties continued to mount in a horrific way. We were determined to resist the enemy as long as we could and all did whatever they could to do so. But courage was not enough under these desperate circumstances. As night fell, once again we all knew that our situation was hopeless. The whole of the battalion was under ceaseless fire. Paratroopers, once so full of optimism, were being driven out of one position after another with machine-like proficiency. But totally weary and most in pain, we fought on.

I think perhaps the bitterest blow was to come when the casualty station adjoining our positions came under fire in spite of a clearly marked Red Cross. This was no doubt because the long heavy bombardment we had endured had driven remaining troops back into the Battalion Headquarters which was adjacent to the casualty station. Our situation was desperate.

---

43 Corporal Sidney J. Spratt, 213018, aged 31. Died from diphtheria, 24th May 1945, contracted in Stalag XIB, Fallingbostel, whilst a POW.

Word was passed that the colonel was trying to arrange that a ceasefire be agreed in order that casualties could be evacuated to German lines. At about six o'clock we saw below us German medical staff, driving captured British vehicles, drive into the courtyard of the burning remains of the casualty station which was next door. Those of us able, helped to place our own and German wounded on to the trucks. How unreal it all seemed, in the quickly fading light, battered, bloody and mauled by battle and fatigue, we struggled to help the enemy convey all possible wounded to safety, aware that after this short respite, we would again be killing each other.

Was it pity or admiration which made our enemy offer us cigarettes and sweets which was among those supplies dropped by the RAF earlier in the battle, intended for us but unfortunately much too far from our positions for us to be aware of this? I even remember Len Kent, one of our group, being given a weapon by one of the German orderlies which he had taken from a wounded soldier we had placed on a stretcher.

After this short release but so welcome armistice, fighting broke out as ferociously as ever. I later learned that Lieutenant Buchanan was very actively responsible for this evacuation of wounded. Tragically, he was killed by the first salvo of resumed battle.[44]

Wednesday, 20th September

By the Wednesday morning we knew that the relief would never come. Water, food and ammunition were gone! The enemy were merciless, we were flushed from the shell of the building in which we attempted to take cover, into the garden, back to the ruins and into the garden endlessly and constantly. No building remained that was not totally blasted or burnt out. The pathetic group left with me were Sid Spratt, Larry Wainwright and Denny Wicks. We made a desperate attempt to find a way out of our trapped position but it was quite hopeless. We did find some rabbits, terrified, huddled together in a hutch in one of the gardens which we released to enable them to fend for themselves, but for us there was no escape.

By now, reports of any relief had ceased completely and we were resigned to the hopelessness of the situation. It was at this stage that the adjutant, Captain McLean, decided that those who were able to try and make a break for it should attempt to do so. The wounded were to be left to the mercies of the enemy. The word surrender was not mentioned. A young Austrian Jew, who of course spoke German, was serving with us in the Intelligence Section. By the grace of God, he was not wounded but he volunteered to stay behind to try and negotiate the surrender of the wounded to the Germans. There seemed no other way out. Touched by his extreme courage, I volunteered to accompany him and somehow we managed to find a piece of white cloth which we tied to a pole, eventually managing to contact a German who called us to enemy lines.

It was far from easy to persuade the Germans that what we sought was a brief ceasefire to carry our wounded into the safety of their lines. We were thoroughly searched, and there followed a period of negotiation before it was agreed that this young man and I carry our wounded comrades through their lines. With courage, my undoubtedly terrified Jewish friend never faltered in his story or request. His determination to carry out what he had volunteered to do, filled me with the deepest admiration. We were able to carry between us eleven seriously wounded men to safety, among whom was Bobby Blunt, Signals Officer, seriously and painfully wounded who we had no

---

44 Lieutenant Clifford D. 'Bucky' Boiteux-Buchanan, MC., 148629, Intelligence Officer, 2nd Battalion Headquarters. KIA, 20 September 1944, Arnhem Bridge area.

choice but to carry on a wooden plank, because no stretchers were to hand. The journey to the German lines was undoubtedly excruciatingly agonising for him but he did not complain.[45]

It was at this stage that the Germans refused to allow either of us to continue gathering the wounded up; there was nothing more that we could do. My wound was now extremely painful and I knew that I had a fever. I had had nothing to drink for some considerable time and was completely exhausted. I found it hard to believe that for us the battle was lost, and indeed, I together with other wounded comrades, was a prisoner of war.

Utterly dazed and weary, we were sorted out and, with other prisoners taken earlier, moved out of the fighting area. It was at this stage I saw Colonel Frost lying on a stretcher wounded (I understand, in the legs) and recognising me, passed me some English cigarettes.

Those considered able were 'marched' to a church on the outskirts of the town. Even while making this journey we were again subjected to mortar fire, and several of us were wounded again; in my own case, in the foot. It is possible that this mortar fire was from our own weapons, such was the confusion of the battle at this stage. On reaching the church an appeal was made for water. It was promised that we should be given some if we caused no trouble. I don't believe that there was much trouble in any of us at that stage, but the water did not come. We were left weary, in great pain and in many cases burning with fever from neglected wounds until the following morning when we linked up with another party of prisoners (to my real delight) which included Sid Spratt and several more of my pals.

Wednesday, 20th September

Lined up with other prisoners, we limped on our way, having little idea to where we were being taken, but assuming at some stage we would be taken to a special camp. Miraculously someone produced a mouth organ and what we hoped was true British spirit we joined in singing with far more enthusiasm than accuracy. We saw Dutch people peering at us encouragingly from behind their curtains as our pathetic crocodile 'marched' by. After about two hours on the march we reached what appeared to be a cafe and which was being used for an interrogation centre. The procedure which followed was quite pointless as little information was forthcoming from the captured men. In spite of our miserable condition there was suppressed laughter as one by one we were asked to give our peace time occupations, and the range of these stretched from a very unlikely ballet dancer, opera singer and manager, to a lion tamer. The most improbable occupations were being given and as everyone fell into the spirit of the moment, each becoming more improbable than the next. Satisfied or frustrated, the Germans then gave us what was to be our first refreshment of any kind for days, some black bread and a beverage which I understand was made from burnt acorns.

Subsequently we were driven to a dressing station set up by the Germans where, in the crudest of manner, no doubt all that was possible, our wounds were treated. A British doctor was administering the chloroform whilst a seemingly most efficient German doctor carried out the surgery. A tremendous task, as most of the wounds were seriously complicated by the fact that they had been neglected. I remember that when I 'came to' I was swathed in paper bandages obviously underlying the fact that the enemy were short of medical supplies.

---

45   Lieutenant John Bobby G. Blunt, survived the battle, POW, Oflag 79, Braunschweig, Niedersachsen, Germany.

Post-Arnhem

For the paras,[46] this was the end of the bloody battle of Arnhem. What went wrong or what was the strategic outcome, we had no way of knowing, only the tragic and painful repercussions. However, from our point of view, we had not failed. Our objective had been to capture and hold Arnhem Bridge until the arrival of link-up troops, expected twenty-four hours later. We had held it for four horrific days. Field Marshal Montgomery was later to say, 'If you were there you will stand up and say I am proud to have fought at the Battle of Arnhem.' I am proud, not simply to have been there, but to have fought side by side with men of courage and determination, so many of whom did not come back.

2nd Parachute Battalion HQ and RAP in the white building right of centre. On the far right partially out of picture 1st Parachute Brigade HQ and RAP. Middle building in front of Eusebius Church was Support Company Mortar Platoon HQ in September 1944. The small grassed island just visible through the trees to the left of the photograph was the two 3-inch mortar positions. Pre-war photograph taken from the pedestrian steps leading up to the bridge ramp looking northwest. (Photo: Courtesy Gelders Archive)

46 At the bridge.

Private Bert 'Tich' Orrell, Royal Army Medical Corps, 16th Parachute Field Ambulance, 2nd Parachute Battalion, 1st Parachute Brigade

I'd had six weeks training with the East Lancashire Regiment at Blackpool and I was then transferred to the RAMC where I was trained at Boyce Barracks, Aldershot. I didn't want to be a medic until I came into contact with a Sergeant Fearnley, who was a medical officer at Dartmoor Prison before the war. He was a very good instructor; I say this because many men owe their lives to this man, not me, and Fearnley was a very good teacher.

Sunday, 17th September 1944

We had already been briefed and seen the sand table of Arnhem and been told the now well-known story of how easy it was going to be for the 1st Airborne Division to take Arnhem. We were awoke at 0430 hours that morning and had of all things, kippers for breakfast. Tension among the lads was showing. We had our chutes already; we had used them as pillows, although I did not sleep well. We went to the airfield, all the planes lined up ready, had a cuppa and a fag. It seemed ages before we emplaned, this was it, 'butterflies' in the tummy. We took off about 1100 hours and took a long time to form up in the air. I think our pilot found every air-pocket en route to Arnhem. Quite how I thought I was supposed to jump with all the equipment; I carried my Colt pistol and ammunition and in my map pocket I had dozens of syringes of morphia, and strapped to my leg, a sixty-pound kitbag, field dressings and two bottles of plasma in my pouches.

Well, after all, I had a very good landing at 1345 hours. My first thought was, where are all the windmills and tulips? Someone shouted, 'If you don't get your head down, you'll get it shot off.' My pal Ginger Brown was down alright, so we made for the yellow smoke and started off the DZ. I was in a section of nine men, we had a Bren gun and I helped to carry the magazines. Not much action at first, lots of Dutch people around giving us milk and fruit and very glad to see us. Very near the railway bridge we were running into snipers. A Lance Corporal Kirk pushed me into a ditch; the grass was being cut down right in front of my eyes. Suddenly into the ditch appeared a German soldier. Believe it or not he was going on leave; he did not even know we were there. Every street corner they were waiting for us; my sergeant, Bob Priestly, seemed to count the seconds it took the Germans to re-load, he stood on each street corner to see his section got across safely. You begin to feel safe with these men around you.

Around 1930 hours in the evening we were nearing the bridge. I'd learned a lot in a few hours. We passed three Jeeps on fire and kept going in and out of houses, still not so bad for casualties. Once we got to a house at the bridge we had a cup of tea and took it in turns to have a nap.

Monday, 18th September–Wednesday, 20th September

Now all hell was let loose, tanks appeared. Lance Corporal Kirk sent four medics out to look for wounded and Stan Hope, one of my mates, never forget his face, was killed by a sniper on the island by the bridge.[47] Somebody was calling for a medic. I crossed the road and met Corporal Ron Francis, and he had a bullet in his leg. There were no other medics around and he told me later that he did not know how I got to him as I was under very heavy fire. He told me I had eight bullet holes in my small pack. He went on fighting after treatment.

---

47 Private Alfred S. Hope, 7380447. 16 Parachute Field Ambulance. Aged 24. First buried General Cemetery Arnhem.

I then went into a building which happened to be a school occupied by the Royal Engineers; all these men should have got a medal. The building was shelled and set on fire. It was nearly over-run but still they fought on, wounded were everywhere, the building was shaking. We had German wounded as well, one of them was a right moaner, he had a grenade which he rolled along the floor, self-preservation, and I threw it out. I heard somebody say they shot him.

Eventually, the school was really burning and all the walking wounded were ordered out and I was ordered to stay with the wounded. A lad who should have got a medal was Sapper Bob 'Brummie' Jones, RE. He and I carried some of the wounded lads out; we could not get them all. An avenue of trees outside was all on fire, but the only place to go. I had done my job to the best of my ability, I'd no morphia left. The two bottles of plasma were never used, I was not clever enough to use it and I tried very hard to get it to somebody who could, but there were not that many medics about. All the wounded were taken by the Germans to Apeldoorn. Along with Ginger Brown, I ended up in Stalag IVB.

An Sd.Kfz 181 Pz.Kpfw.VI Tiger I of Schwere Panzer-Kompanie *Hummel* and an Sd.Kfz 251/1 half-track, on the corner of Ooststraat and Nieuwe Kade, next to the Office of Public Works. Photo taken from a Dutch wartime newspaper *Het Nationaal Dagblad,* published in October 1944. (Photo: PK Hoppner, Courtesy Gelders Archive)

Major Cedric J. Longland, Specialist Surgeon, Royal Army Medical Corps, 16th Parachute Field Ambulance, 1st Parachute Brigade

Sunday, 17th September
The Field Ambulance HQ and No. 2 Section, commanded by Lieutenant Colonel E. Townsend, MC RAMC, took off from RAF Barkston Heath airfield at 1000 hours with other units of 1st Parachute Brigade and dropped seven miles west of Arnhem at 1415 hours without incident. Within my stick was my own surgical team. We landed on heathland, a fine sunny afternoon with little wind. All personnel and 95 percent of equipment reached the RV. We were all there with all our equipment, like a well-regulated exercise, and quite unlike the excitement of our previous effort at night at the Primasole Bridge in Sicily. I do remember fighter bombers bombing the bomb line shortly afterwards and then flying off, as of course did our transport aircraft. One had the feeling of being entirely on your own.

We certainly set off along the road, I think through Heelsum rather than Wolfhezen, in a long column, which, again like an exercise, progressed steadily and without hindrance past cheering Dutch outside their houses. They had orange colours, were shouting 'Tommy' and offering food and drink. They thought, and we hoped, liberation had come. Their reaction was reassuring, for our briefing had prepared us for the possibility that the Dutch might be pro-German in quite a big way. At least, that was my belief; nothing could have been further from fact. The Dutch that I had to do with were quite magnificent for us at great risk to themselves after. Indeed, I have the highest admiration for them.

It had been decided that the Field Ambulance HQ and No. 2 Section should jointly set up in St Elizabeth Hospital, situated in the western part of Arnhem close to the north bank of the Rhine on the road leading from the DZ to the centre of the town, to receive, treat and retain casualties. As we neared the town we slowed down with a succession of halts. There were some shells landing somewhere around now and again., but we never came under small arms fire. In this way we arrived at St Elizabeth Hospital about 2330 hours and arrangements for accommodation made with the Dutch civilian staff. A few casualties reached the hospital and work was begun about midnight as had been planned. The accommodation included a reception area, two theatres, one large and some smaller wards. Every facility was extended by the Dutch. One surgical team and one nursing shift went on duty, remaining personnel turning in.

Monday, 18th September
Shifts were changed at 0600 hours. A few more casualties had arrived, but one surgical team was considered sufficient to deal with them, and the first shift turned in for their first rest for nearly 24 hours. A number of German casualties that had been brought in were taken over by the Dutch surgeons who were also undertook to treat civilian wounded. At 1100 hours the hospital was recaptured by the Germans. They agreed to leave the two surgical teams, but the commanding officer, all other officers and other ranks were removed and not allowed to continue working. A staff of two surgeons, two anaesthetists, a nursing orderly sergeant and about 16 other ranks were therefore left. The hospital had a capacity of about 300 beds. Fighting continued round the hospital. The Germans rifled all personal kit, and departed leaving no guards. Later an SS officer arrived to take all remaining British staff into safe custody, alleging that grenades had been thrown from the hospital. With the help of a Dutch Red Cross official as interpreter this was avoided, and we were left in the hospital on parole. Numbers of British casualties were brought in by the Dutch

Red Cross workers and the Germans. The Dutch assisted in nursing and provided food for both staff and patients.

Tuesday, 19th September
A further British attack from the west aimed at the Rhine bridge near the centre of the town made progress and passed the hospital during the morning. A number of casualties were brought up in its wake. The ground gained had to be given up however, and from then on the hospital was isolated from the main divisional position Oosterbeek to the west and from the force holding the north end of the bridge to the east, and was in communication with neither. Two medical officers and several other ranks reached the hospital and were added to the staff. During this fighting several hits were made on the hospital with mortars and SP guns. Some small arms fire came through windows, patrols passed through the ground floor, and bursts were even fired up the corridors. A few minor casualties were caused in the hospital by glass, further damage was prevented by the prompt action of the nursing orderly sergeant (Sergeant A. Tennuci) in moving all our cases to corridors and other safe places. Some civilian cases were however killed. There were few civilian cases in the hospital, and the civilian staff except for those on essential duties remained in the cellars.

Brigadier Lathbury had received shrapnel wounds as I remember. He had previously been wounded in Sicily where I operated on him, so it was no great surprise when he was brought in while I was on duty at St Elizabeth, though he apologised profusely for his second appearance. He wisely removed his badges of rank; if he made any mistake it was to put on a music hall type of act as 'the groaning wounded man' when I and the visiting German medical officer went round the patients. He did not wish to be evacuated into Germany, but was worried that my German colleague might wonder at the agonies depicted. He didn't twig.

Wednesday, 20th September–Thursday, 21st September
The neighbourhood became quieter. Cases continued to arrive and were dealt with as far as possible by the two teams under Captain Lipmann-Kessel and myself. General supervision of the cases in the wards was carried out by Captain J.H. Keesey and Reception and Walking Wounded were under Captain J. Lawson (133 Parachute Field Ambulance). Considerable responsibility fell upon Sergeant Tennuci who was responsible for running the wards, carrying out treatment, and obtaining the assistance of the Dutch nurses. These nurses despite the conditions all volunteered to stay on, and as the number of cases grew we could not have managed without their invaluable aid. Catering was carried out entirely by the civilian staff which contained a proportion of German nuns working as sisters. Mains water and lighting had failed. I made a survey of the hospital with Dr Siemens, the hospital steward, earmarking further accommodation, cellars for shelter, etc. Definite feeding times were laid down, and duties allotted to men who had arrived in the preceding two days.

Sunday, 24th September
Two German ADMS visited the hospital, and gave warning of the arrival of several hundred more wounded. Some supplies were asked for (medical), though with the help of supplies in the hospital, particularly of plaster of Paris and wool and gauze, we were in a position to carry on for several days. By this time the civilian cases had been moved to a safe place in the basement corridor.

During the morning I accompanied the German DADMS to Oosterbeek where several British dressing stations had fallen into British hands to make arrangements for the transfer of cases to

St Elizabeth Hospital. I drove there in a Jeep with a British driver and a German soldier with his rifle to the dressing station.[48] The streets were strewn with tree branches from gunfire, rubble, bodies (not many), knocked out anti-tank guns, and lined with shelled buildings, a scene, in fact, of the carnage and litter of war. The dressing station was crowded, with casualties everywhere on the floors of the houses used, little space between individuals. Medical orderlies were bandaged, having been hit, as well as combatants. All seemed remarkably cheerful, though there was an underlying air of strain. The spirit of these wounded, many of whom had been hit several days before, and after having first aid had had to remain in lightly-built houses continuously under fire, further wounds being received by some of them in the dressing station, with both water and food short and with the nursing orderlies in some cases themselves wounded, was beyond all praise. I was thankful for St Elizabeth's.

A local armistice was arranged with the Germans by ADMS. 1st Airborne Division. We made arrangements about evacuation back to St Elizabeth's and departed. Some hundreds of casualties were got back to St Elizabeth's during the course of the day. Owing to the excellence of the Dutch catering it was possible to feed all these cases soon after arrival. The majority of the walking wounded were evacuated further back by the Germans the same evening, but something like 300 lying cases remained.

On our way back we ran into mortar fire (premature I suppose, the truce should have held longer). The Jeep swerved off the road, the young German clapped his hand to his backside and we all jumped out. We found our guard had been hit in the buttock, and applied a field dressing. We then put his rifle back in the Jeep for him, helped him back in again, and took him back into St Elizabeth's where I later operated on him. I've no doubt one of his own mortars got him; the wound was not severe. Such is the fortune of war. Major P. Smith (133 Parachute Field Ambulance) arrived from Oosterbeek to assist with the surgery; we had also received a number of RAMC other ranks, forming a total staff of between 30 and 40. Those from Oosterbeek had been through a very trying period, but they all gave valuable help after a few hours of sleep.

The flow of cases through the hospital continued, cases being evacuated by German ambulance cars and trucks to Apeldoorn. One truck was borrowed from the Germans to collect food from a dump in the town known to the Dutch, since the Germans were apparently incapable of supplying rations. Some of the food obtained was dispatched to Oosterbeek. Some medical supplies arrived from the Germans who also sent up some of our own equipment, such as plasma.

In the evening, Lieutenant Colonel Herford, MC of a XXX Corps Field Ambulance who had been passed into the German lines under a Red Cross flag, arrived at the hospital. He asked for such help as I could give him in the establishment of a hospital at Apeldoorn for British wounded, and to which cases were already being evacuated in large numbers. Major Smith and Captain Keesey, about 20 other ranks and equipment therefore went with him to Apeldoorn that night.

Monday, 25th September–Tuesday, 26th September
A diminishing number of wounded passed through the hospital each day.

After St Elizabeth Hospital was recaptured by the Germans, their medical organisation kept some sort of an eye on us, in the person of one of their senior divisional medical officers. He would go round the patients with me from time to time. One day we had finished the round and he was about to leave the hospital when a terrific British air raid by fighter bombers (Tempests)

---

48   Schoonoord Hotel, Oosterbeek.

started, to be greeted by ack-ack. The street outside was definitely unsafe. So I invited him up to our mess, where there were a number of wounded British officers enjoying a large and remarkably beautiful box of chocolates, brought to us clandestinely by the ever-courageous Dutch. We offered him a chocolate and he sat down while the racket went on outside. He spoke good English and we proceeded to discuss the works of Dickens, a favourite author of his. I could no more have discussed, say, Thomas Mann in German than pigs can fly. The irony was of course, that he was temporarily in effect our prisoner, while technically we were all his prisoners! When the air raid was over we said polite good byes and ushered him out again. Naturally nothing was said about the chocolates!

Wednesday, 27th September
All cases fit to travel were evacuated to Apeldoorn, about 30 being left. Captain Lipmann-Kessel's team, one other MO and a number of other ranks were left to care for these cases, while the rest of the staff accompanied the other cases to Apeldoorn, where we arrived at a barracks which was being formed into a divisional hospital under the command of the ADMS 1st Airborne Division. The remaining cases and staff were evacuated to Apeldoorn about ten days later. A number of other RAMC officers passed through the hospital, including Captain J. Logan, DSO and Captain Graham-Jones.

Summary
Cases dealt with:

> Total numbers estimated at approximately: 700–800
> Total operations estimated: 150
> Deaths before evacuation estimated: 10–20 (many inoperable)

Nearly all these cases were British wounded; very few, if any, sick were admitted. A very few very urgent operations were performed by us on German wounded and Dutch civilian wounded. A small proportion of the cases were received with a few hours of wounding, but the larger part, owing to the peculiar conditions, had wounds of some standing. Among the wounded officers treated were the commanders of 1st and 4th Parachute Brigades. The Dutch staff of the hospital and several outside civilians who came in to help gave us every possible assistance, we were never refused anything we asked, and most was done for us for which we had not asked. With their help we were able to treat the wounded in comparatively good conditions; without it we could have done very little because of our shortage of staff, nearly all of whom would have had to be employed in getting food and water. The Germans, having captured the hospital, stupidly removed most of the British staff and later proceeded to evacuate large numbers of casualties to the hospital. Otherwise, apart from allegations of grenade throwing from the hospital, and some typical Bosch bombast from a warrant officer in charge of ambulance convoys, behaviour was correct and cooperative. A number of patients successfully escaped, usually with the help of the Underground Movement. The parole given early on applied only to the Red Cross personnel then in the hospital.

St Elizabeth Hospital after the battle. Remains of two German vehicles ambushed outside the hospital on the 17th September by Lieutenant Ian Russell's No. 8 Platoon, C Company, 2nd Parachute Battalion on the way into Arnhem. Major Victor Dover, CO, C Company, 2nd Parachute Battalion: 'It was only seconds before PIAT bombs were exploding into the midst of the Germans. There were about eighty of them and by the time five bombs had landed only a few were still interested in the war.'[49] (Photo: Horst Brink; Courtesy Gelders Archive)

49   *The Silken Canopy*, Major V. Dover, MC (London: Cassell, 1979), p.94.

St Elizabeth Hospital, Arnhem. (Photo: Author, 1980)

3

1st Airborne Division Ordnance Field Park, RAOC, 1st Airlanding Light Regiment, RA, 1st Parachute Squadron, RE

Private Ted Mordecai, 1st Airborne Division Ordnance Field Park, RAOC

The 1st Airborne Division Ordnance Field Park RAOC was formulated at or about the same time as the Parachute Regiment and the 1st Airborne Division was formed in 1940. Its function was to supply and equip the various units of the division with everything that would be required, except for food, ammunition and petrol, to maintain the division as an efficient fighting force in an operational or non-operational capacity. To carry out this function it was necessary for the unit to be completely mobile and to travel with the division wherever it went. The Ordnance Field Park strength was approximately 110 officers and other ranks under the command of Major C.C. Chidgey, all of whom were experienced specialist and non-technical storemen and had to be able to drive all types of army vehicles and motorcycles.

Jeeps and trailers were used for airborne operations and travelled in Horsa gliders. The trailers were low with two wheels and could be attached to the Jeeps. They were also fitted with small rows of bins at the front and sides which held the smaller stores whilst the centre of the trailers normally held the bulkier items, and to keep them weather-proof the whole trailer top was covered with a waterproof cover held on with tie ropes. For each airborne operation the storemen and Jeep crews would load the Jeeps and trailers into the gliders by removing the tail sections and, once aboard, secure the wheels to the floor, and then re-secure the tails of the gliders with bolts. The crews would then travel in the gliders and after being cast off from the tug planes would land on the DZ, unbolt the tails, offload the Jeeps and trailers by using a ramp and then drive off to their rendezvous, leaving the gliders where they land. Once the Jeeps and trailers had reached their position slightly to the rear of the parachute battalions, they would form up and wait to receive demands from the units. The demands would then be processed and the stores issued to the bearer of the demand. All things being satisfactory the glider party would then wait for the main body of the Field Park travelling by sea and/or road to join them and set up base.

It was the spring of 1944 that we were informed that the RAOC had to provide a small group of paratroopers as a reconnaissance party to be attached to 1st Parachute Brigade Headquarters in any future operations. Apart from Harry Walker we had no parachutists amongst us, so volunteers were called for. Harry was very persuasive and eventually some of us volunteered and we went to Ringway for our training where we all passed out and received our wings within a week or so. Unbeknown to us, six of the first volunteers were chosen as the recce party and I was amongst these. In late July or early August 1944, we were told that something special was in the offing and that Field Park would shortly be leaving to travel by sea into Belgium. The recce party was to be left behind as we were shortly to be assimilated into the 1st Parachute Brigade Headquarters. We bid our comrades farewell and they moved off by road to the docks. The recce party was left on its own in Spitalgate School and things were very quiet now that all the vehicles and men were gone, so until we received orders to join Brigade HQ, the six of us took things easy as there was nothing to do except wait and see what was in store for us. Towards the end of August 1944 after the Seaborne Element of the unit had left Grantham, Captain Manley paid several visits to Brigade HQ just on the outskirts of Grantham and one day informed us that we were to take part in a special operation and that we would be shortly moving out to join up with the other detachments at Brigade HQ. We travelled out to Brigade HQ each day and on one of these occasions we were informed that the operation was to take place in Holland and to back this up we received as a part of our pay some Dutch guilders and some British invasion money in Deutsch marks as well as sterling. The day finally arrived when we were ordered to assemble in a Nissen hut in order to receive details of the operation we were to take part in. We sat down, and an officer outlined the plan of Operation Market Garden. Providing the operation went as planned, the role of the Ordnance Field Park recce party would be as follows: we were to seek out large garages or vehicle depots, with petrol pumps if available, and to commandeer any vehicles which we thought would be suitable for passengers or equipment. We would then note these and when we had linked up with Major Chidgey and his Jeeps and trailers we would occupy the accommodation, and then set up a stores depot and await the arrival of the main body of the unit coming with XXX Corps. After the officer had imparted all this knowledge to us we were told to keep our mouths shut and keep it to ourselves. He then showed us round the Nissen hut and pointed out several aerial reconnaissance photographs which we were to study, showing the bridge at Arnhem and the D.Z. The piece de resistance was then shown to us and this was a table model of the route we were taking from the D.Z to the bridge. For our part we were also shown a street map and an index listing all the main buildings in Arnhem together with garages and the estimated number of vehicles they were holding. We were informed that providing we kept to a group we could visit the Nissen hut at any time to familiarise ourselves with the information it contained.

Shortly after this, we were issued with maps of the area and our escape kit, consisting of a silk escape map of France, Holland and Germany and a special compass each, which we had to secrete about our persons. We were also issued with our parachutes, ammunition and two 24-hour iron ration packs. The only thing we did not know at this time was the date scheduled for the operation. Because the time for the operation was now near, we were ordered to move out of the school in Grantham and join Brigade HQ where we were accommodated in small tents. We were here for a few days and occupied our time map reading, taking compass bearings, doing target practice and generally taking things easy. We also took the opportunity of hiding our escape map and compass. The map folded up very small and flat, so I undid the grease protector in the top of my red beret, put the map inside and carefully re-stitched the protector back in place. The compass I had been issued with (they were all different) consisted of a set of identical brass buttons, two of which made up the compass. One button had a small point on its back which acted as a base and the other button was magnetised with a small dot of luminous paint which represented the north. When this button was balanced on top of the other one, the luminous dot swung round to the north. I took all my existing buttons off my uniform jacket and stitched the new set with one of the compass buttons at the top of my jacket and the other on one of the cuffs. The weather was fine and we were enjoying the sunshine when towards the 13th or 14th September, Captain Manley told us the operation was due to take place on Sunday the 17th September and that we would be confined to camp until we took off. Now knowing it was imminent, we went to the NAAFI shop and spent some of money on cigarettes and chocolate ration to take with us. Saturday 16th September was spent loafing around, checking our kit, doing some more target practice and generally discussing what might lie ahead of us. We all went to bed fairly early about 2130 hours and the last thing Harry Walker remembered was Kevin Heaney's voice singing '*This is a lovely way to spend an evening*', a popular song at the time and most appropriate for the occasion.

Sunday, 17th September

Sunday, 17th September dawned pleasantly with a hint of being a warm day. We rose out of our beds about 0700 hours and after the normal ablutions went for our breakfast which we collected in our mess tins and returned to our tents where we sat outside and consumed it. It was a good breakfast, consisting of fried bread, sausage, bread, jam and tea. About 0930 hours we had a further mug of sweet tea and 'Scribona' pastries with the cook.

As it was getting near to the time when we should leave our camp we put our equipment on about 0945 hours and checked that we had everything: cigarettes, ammunition and two 24-hour ration packs. We said 'cheerio' to the cook, who wished us well and we all boarded the Jeep where we drove to Brigade HQ, a short distance from our camp. Upon arriving at Brigade HQ we collected our chutes and climbed aboard a three ton truck and drove to the aerodrome at Barkston Heath. The drome was a bustle of activity with paratroopers either chatting away or sitting on the grass near their allotted aircraft. We unloaded from the truck and, having found the number of our Dakota aircraft, sat down on the grass and waited for emplaning orders. The number of our aircraft was chalked on the side, No. 131, and I could not help thinking at the time that this was an omen. No matter which way one looked at the number, back or front, it came to 13. However, this thought was soon dispelled as everyone was in such good spirits.

After sitting for a short while we began to take stock of our surroundings. The aerodrome seemed chock-full of Dakotas nose to tail, some pilots revving their engines and others silent. The place was swarming with parachutists and USAAF staff with the former lounging around or making adjustments to their equipment. About this time the Yanks came around with tea, sandwiches and cake which we ate, not knowing when our next meal would be, and it also provide some substance in case of air sickness. Shortly after about 1100 hours, the groups of paratroopers situated near their aircraft began to put on their parachutes and tighten up their harness, so we guessed that word was beginning to circulate that emplaning time was near. We fitted our parachutes and checked one another's straps etc., and as I was having difficulty in securing my Sten gun I enlisted the aid of an onlooking American who helped to fasten it around my left leg. It would have been too bulky to fasten it across my chest in case of accident when landing. Whilst waiting for the order to emplane we noticed an American officer going round taking photographs of each stick by their aircraft. It appeared that he was an intelligence officer and was taking photos either for his own interest or officially. Several comments were passed such as, 'Say cheese, please,' or 'I'll have a dozen when they're ready.' I often wish I knew who he was, as it is the only photograph that was ever taken of our party and it would have been nice to have had one for the record.

The Dakota aircraft were now warming up and soon afterwards we received the order to emplane in stick order. Our stick comprised the RAOC Recce Party, a couple of RCMPs (Paddy and Jock, whom we knew well), and some of the Defence Platoon. Our order in the stick was as follows, followed on by the remainder of the stick:

No. 1 Captain B. V. Manley
No. 2 Staff Sergeant Walker
No. 3 A chap from HQ (complete with leg kitbag)
No. 4 Ronnie Pugh
No. 5 Myself
No. 6 Kevin Heaney
No. 7 McCarthy

We settled down in the aircraft in the traditional order, even numbers on the port side and odd numbers on the starboard side with the lower numbers one, two, three, etc., nearest to the exit door. The pilots began to push forward the throttles, the engines roared and soon the aircraft began to quiver and shake as if it was eager to take off. The aircraft in front of us began slowly to move away and we in turn followed. We raced down the runway and with a slight bounce our wheels touched and we were airborne and on our way. I was too excited to notice the exact time and although the time in the log book says 1148 hours I thought it was much earlier.

We were part of the First Lift and I believe our route was the northern one which meant crossing the coast at Aldeburgh and heading out across the Channel and over the Frisian Islands to our objective. By this time, it was a fine day, the sun was shining with little or no cloud in the sky and we thought of the population down below just about to sit down to Sunday lunch after a few jars in the pubs. It was a slightly bumpy passage due to air pockets until we reached the English coast, but once we were over the Channel it was a relatively smooth flight. Some of the boys were violently air sick, particularly Paddy the MP who was prostrate on the floor of the aircraft, retching away. I think it was the sight of him and the fact that we shouldn't have had the snack on the airfield that did it, but it affected me too, but to a lesser extent. However, we were prepared for this eventuality as we had been issued with our greaseproof *Bags, Vomit, Mk.I* and we made use of them.

Due to the steady flying and having gotten over the first bout of being sick, we sat up and started taking notice. We were flying about 1,500 feet and down below we could see 'V' shaped trails of white water where the Air-Sea Rescue launches and other maritime craft were darting about in our general direction in case any aircraft should abort and come down in the channel. If this should happen, we were prepared for this as well as we had inflatable life jackets on as well as our parachutes, the idea being that if we had to bail out, our chutes would open, we would float down to about 20 feet above the sea, jettison our chutes, drop into the sea, inflate our lifebelts and wait to be picked up. This was alright in theory, but I never found out if it had been put into practice.

Looking out of the open door of the aircraft, we could see a mighty air armada filling the sky. Sometimes it appeared as if the plane's wing on our port side was coming through the door, it was so near. Very soon after crossing the English coastline we met our fighter plane escort and all we could see in the sky were planes steadily droning on and the escort weaving about above us. This sight was very reassuring and cheered us up considerably, as we would have been sitting ducks for any German fighter that had appeared without our escort. About 1320 hours we approached the Frisian Islands and crossed the Dutch coastline and knew that we couldn't be too far away from Arnhem. As we flew over Holland we could see vast stretches of water with the tops of houses poking above it where the fields had been flooded out deliberately by the Germans or Dutch. Very soon afterwards German flak guns started opening up on us. None of it came too near us, but every now and then there was a slight tinkling of metal from shrapnel on the skin of the aircraft and the plane rocked a bit from the blast. The flak looked a marvellous sight coming up at us; it appeared to come very slowly like a big powder puff floating up. We noticed some flak towers that had been shot up by Typhoons prior to our approach. Very soon the American Despatcher came from the cockpit and told us there was twenty minutes to go, so we all sat up on the alert. Later on, he came again and said, 'Ten minutes to go,' whereupon we all stood up on the order to "Stand up, hook up,' and checked off, which consisted of checking the person's chute in front of you in the order of drop to see if all of the ties and fittings were correct and making sure we were hooked up properly on the static line with the hook safety pin in position. After checking off, we all edged nearer to the door and to one another and watched the little black box with the red and green lights near the exit door. The reason for being so close to one another in exiting ensures that the stick lands near to one another. Any delay in exiting means that the stick becomes separated from one another with the last man landing hundreds of yards away from the first man out.

The red light was now on, warning us that the time to jump was now near and that when the green light came on, it was time to go. The minute interval between lights seemed like an eternity and when it did come on we were startled. There it was, green, and with a mighty shout of 'Go' we moved forward to the exit. Captain Manley as No. 1 stood in the doorway and seemed to hesitate! Harry (Mick) Walker was an experienced ex-jumping instructor and wasting no time, he pushed the captain out and immediately followed him. The rest of the stick exited quickly and the last thing I remember was the despatcher's: 'Best of luck, cheerio.' He was alright; he'd be back home for tea!

Sliding down the slip-stream I felt a slight jerk on my shoulders and looking up I saw that my canopy was filled with air and I was coming down at a rather fast rate due to the weight of equipment that I was carrying. Whilst floating down to earth I looked around me. The sky was filled with planes, parachutes, men, containers and kitbags. The chutes were various colours, lemon for men and bright red, orange and green for the containers. This is so that the containers can be identified and the contents extracted quickly. Looking down I observed a long farm track or road running horizontally to a ploughed field. In the right-hand lower corner was a small barn surrounded by a barbed wire fence. On the right-hand upper corner a farmhouse near some trees and way up ahead a large wood. I noticed that I was being drawn towards the barn and that I was beginning to oscillate whereupon I pulled my rigging lines to avoid landing on the barn or barbed wire.

I landed in the ploughed field with a bump and my chute collapsed ahead of me. I slapped my quick release box to get out of my harness and dumped my lifejacket. Keeping a wary eye open for objects dropping from the sky I looked around for the rest of my companions and took stock of the situation. It was a lovely afternoon, the sun was shining and quite warm and for all the world it seemed like a practice jump in England. The only thing lacking was the mobile canteen! I looked at my watch and found that it had stopped at 1447 hours. I must have nagged it on my QR box when I jumped, as the watch was hanging on its double leather strap by one strap support only. About two miles away we could hear the sound of bombs and see clouds of smoke and dust. Overhead the Dakotas were still spilling out their contents and above them were some Spitfires circling the DZ. It was then that I saw our first casualty. A chap was coming down with a kitbag dangling below him. I think it must have contained mortar bombs already fused up, because as the bag hit the ground it exploded with a mighty bang. As he was only about twenty feet above it, he caught the full blast and there wasn't much left of him. This brought me back to reality, whereupon I put my small pack on my shoulders, took my Sten gun from my leg, fitted a magazine, lit a cigarette and set off towards the rendezvous (RV). On the way over the ploughed field I caught up with Kevin

Heaney and Mac (McCarthy) and we made our way together. It is a far cry from studying the map in England and then dropping into a strange country and finding one's way to a little wood where Brigade HQ had to RV near a football pitch cum tennis court, but we had studied well, and from our maps, we knew which way to go from the DZ at Renkum Heath.

The drop had nearly been completed but there were still supplies dropping above us, so keeping a wary eye open, the three of us made our way towards the wood where we had to branch off towards the RV. Upon reaching the edge of the wood by a crossroad we saw some gunners who had mounted a 6-pounder anti-tank gun to cover the DZ. One of the gunners was named Campbell and we had both met at RAF Ringway where we had done our jumping course. He had been in our training stick and we had nicknamed him 'Candle' due to the fact that on one of his jumps his rigging lines had been partially closed. The resulting effect looks like a candle flame, hence the term 'Candle' – a bad one can prove fatal! He was part of the Royal Artillery, and after having a few words with him we wished each other 'Good luck' and parted. We eventually reached a small wood near a football pitch which was our Brigade HQ's RV. After about 30 minutes our group was complete and we grouped around Captain Manley for further orders. During this time we noticed some Dutch resistance workers giving our HQ staff some information and a trickle of German prisoners started to arrive. They looked like they had been caught on a sick parade, and not too far away we could hear the sound of small arms fire on the outskirts of the DZ.

Round about 1500 hours the order came through to march into Arnhem which was about seven miles away. Our route was to go along a secondary road running close to the north bank of the Lower Rhine whilst the 1st and 3rd Parachute Battalions approached from the north, each from a different direction. Whilst going through some woods shortly after leaving the RV we received an alert that Germans were about so we dropped down into the fern and undergrowth and took up firing positions. About 15 minutes passed and nothing came of it so we resumed the march.

We finally emerged from the wood after crossing a railway line and came out onto a small country road. We passed a few houses in a small village where the occupants came out as we arrived and offered us apples, pears and drinks ranging from water to coffee. This village was either Heelsum or Heveadorp. Nearly all the Dutch civilians were wearing marigolds for patriotic reasons. At one point the landlord of a small village pub was handing out glasses of beer but we were told not to take it. I really could have done with a cool drink as I was hot with all the weight we were carrying. We eventually reached Oosterbeek where we halted as there were Germans snipers ahead and they had to be cleared out. We were sat on garden walls or in the road and whilst we were waiting the civilians came out and gave us some cups of ersatz coffee. They seemed overjoyed to see us and we were treated as liberators. We spent about an hour in Oosterbeek whilst the opposition ahead was dealt with, and then received orders to resume the march. On the outskirts of Arnhem we came across an Opel open-topped armoured car which had been caught with small arms fire. The driver was dead and hanging out of the side of the car with his legs still inside and his arms hanging down nearly touching the road. Up ahead we could hear the sounds of heavy gunfire and word came down the line that the 2nd Parachute Battalion who had preceded us earlier were catching it pretty hot, so the rate of march was stepped up, A Company in front of us and C Company behind us.

By this time, it was getting dusk and as we marched along by the river road we heard an explosion ahead and were told that the railway bridge had been blown by the Germans. We passed by this bridge shortly afterwards and made our way to the pontoon bridge across the river but could not use this as one of the sections had been removed. From now on it was obvious that we had to get to the big span bridge as soon as possible. About half a mile from the bridge we halted outside a house, brightly lit up, and teeming with British troops and Dutch civilians. We went inside whilst Captain Manley went to receive further orders. Outside at the same time a German flak barge was cruising up and down the river but fortunately didn't throw anything our way. When Captain Manley and Harry Walker went into the house they were met by an Airborne officer and a Dutch civilian who evidently informed them that the 2nd Battalion A Company were in the thick of the fighting and that they needed all the help they could get. Our orders were that we should forget our intended role of searching out garages and suitable vehicles and take an active part in securing the bridge. It was now quite dark and the time would be about 1900 hours. In the house at this time were some HQ signallers who were ordered to join us and we set off in about platoon strength with Captain Manley taking command, to link up with the remainder of the 2nd Parachute Battalion and Brigade HQ.

As we moved up the road parallel to the river we could see the span bridge outlined against flashes of gunfire against the sky. At the same time the Germans on the other side of the river were concentrating all their fire in our direction and at the bridge. About two or three hundred yards from the bridge we turned left into a small street running at right angles to the one we were cautiously making our way up. Captain Manley led the way into one building using his torch to guide us, and we went up the stairs and into a large hall filled with stacked wooden chairs.

We followed him along an aisle and he must have decided that this was of no use to take up a position as he suddenly did an about turn and rushed back past us and outside leaving us fumbling about in the dark. I fortunately found my way out to the sound of bodies crashing into chairs and knocking them over. We assembled in a small group outside where we were joined by Kevin Heaney and Ron Pugh. We then had to make our way diagonally across the road to a line of houses which led to the bridge where we had to take up positions in some houses alongside the end of the bridge which was in our possession. Either hugging the walls of the houses or crawling in the gutter, we made our way up to an archway under the bridge ramp. We had no option but to crawl up the road as lead was flying all over the place and we couldn't see who was firing at whom. At this point we lost Ron Pugh who had evidently tagged on to some other troops and I did not see him again until many months later in the POW Camp Stalag XIB at Fallingbostel. Up ahead the bridge was lit up with flames and explosions and it appeared as if our chaps had thrown phosphorous bombs onto it to light it up in case Jerry decided to come across. This way nobody could get across to our end without being seen. The sound of shot and shell was deafening, but we inched our way forward up to the bridge.

We eventually reached the archway and moved singly across the road to turn left into a street where there were some houses facing the bridge embankment; it was our intention to occupy one of these, but suddenly we were scattered by a stream of tracer bullets which came whistling down the street. Diving for cover, we waited a while, then regrouped and made our way to another archway nearer to the end of the ramp. Crouching down, we waited for a lull in the firing and then scooted across to the end house of a block of about five or six houses on the corner of a side street and banged on the door. Captain Manley was the one knocking on the door with Harry Walker and me behind him: the rest of the group were across the road waiting until we gained entry. Eventually, the door was opened by a Dutchman and we tried to explain that we had to occupy the house and it would be safer for them to leave the house and the area.[1]

---

1   Corner house on Eusebiusbuitensingel/Westervoortsedijk.

Shortly afterwards, the man fetched his wife and a small daughter from the cellar, packed a small suitcase and they left, walking down the middle of the street away from the bridge. My thought was, *I hope they don't get shot by the Germans and where on earth could they go to?* We had hardly settled in to the house when we were subjected to mortar fire directed at the bridge approaches. Although I didn't see the incident, Kevin Heaney observed some lorries filled with troops arriving from the south; he thought they were troops returning from a day's leave. However, due to the fires on the bridge the lorries themselves caught fire and some of the occupants surrendered. I saw about half a dozen Germans come forward with their hands up. I don't know why they didn't go back to their side and could only assume they were getting out of crossfire. They were taken prisoner immediately.

Having now occupied the house we took stock of our surroundings and were detailed to take up positions in the lower and upper rooms facing onto the bridge and embankment. The time was now about 2000 hours and it had taken us nearly six hours since we dropped to march seven or eight miles from the DZ and gain possession of the northern end of the bridge. To the best of our knowledge at the time, all the houses near the bridge were occupied by our troops. We had been joined by some six signallers, one of whom was called 'Paddy' Perry, a corporal in the Royal Signals; therefore we numbered about twelve in all. All the lights in the house had been extinguished and when we took up our positions in the windows facing the bridge embankment our first task was to knock out all the window panes to avoid glass splinters from blast waves and to obtain a clearer view. I was in position in the upper room and had a good view of the end of the bridge and the ramp leading up to it.

By this time the fires on the bridge and some houses had really taken hold and lit up the whole area. To avoid the light reflecting off my face I pulled the scrim netting from my helmet over my face, thus avoiding offering the enemy a target. There was a continuous sound of miscellaneous fire, mortars and machine guns going on all around us. Eventually, the flames and the firing died down and it became almost quiet. I don't know how long I sat in position at the window but during a quiet period we observed a figure approaching from the end of the bridge where we had originally been before we entered the house. We stared in amazement as the figure materialised carry a rolled umbrella and in a loud voice called out, 'I say, who is in there?' When we told him he then said, 'I want six of you to come with me and see who is in the large house at the end of the ramp.' At the time we thought it was Brigadier Lathbury but later found out it was Major Digby Tatham-Warter.[2] Captain Manley told six of us to go with this officer, so we went outside with our Sten guns at the ready and walked down the road towards the building he pointed out.

Upon reaching the building we covered the doors and the windows, and again in a loud voice the officer shouted out, 'Who is in there?' Personally, I thought it was stupid, because if Jerry had been in the house we would have been in for a rough time being out in the open without cover. Fortunately for us, the reply came back that it was occupied by some gunners and sappers. This evidently satisfied the officer and he strolled off into the darkness still directing operations with his rolled-up brolly. We started to make our back to the house we had occupied, but Jerry must have heard the voices and spotted us in the half-light as a machine gun opened up from the far end of the street and bullets came whistling at us through the air. We all dived for cover on the roadside and waited for the firing to cease. In between bursts of machine gun fire we made a mad dash across the street to our house in ones and twos. Kevin Heaney was the last to cross and about half

---

2   Officer Commanding, A Company, 2nd Parachute Battalion

way across the road the machine gun opened up again. Kevin put on speed and came through the front door like a Sherman tank in top gear. It certainly was a close call for him. Once inside and having regained our breath we resumed positions at the windows until daybreak. All we had to do now was to keep control of the northern end of the bridge until we were relieved by XXX Corps, hopefully on Monday, 18th September or at the latest Tuesday, 19th September 1944.

Monday, 18th September
Shortly after daybreak we heard the sound of engines revving up and looking towards the other side of the bridge to the south we saw a line of open-topped Opel armoured cars coming across the bridge in 'line astern'. These cars were very small, reinforced with steel and carried between four and six occupants. The cars were about ten yards distant from each other and as the first car across reached the top of the ramp there was an explosion as one of our six-pounder anti-tank guns mounted just below the ramp fired and caught the car in the middle. It immediately slewed round and blocked the bridge as none of the others could get by it. The other cars following pulled up immediately, offering a perfect target for all of us. Our chaps didn't let it pass either. They must have known the old adage, 'Opportunity only knocks once' and everybody took advantage of it because everyone within range immediately opened fire on the cars with Bren guns, Stens, rifles and grenades. As soon as a German soldier tried to get out of a car he was knocked over. It was just like snap shooting, as soon as anything moved every paratrooper who saw it just opened up. It was a hectic ten or twenty minutes and it was soon over. It was also just what we needed to bring us awake and liven us up, as nobody had been able to sleep during the night with keeping watch. We also realised that it was breakfast time and that we had not eaten since leaving England twenty-four hours earlier.

The most anyone had had was a few boiled sweets from our rations with a few sips of water from our bottles. Taking advantage of the respite and the fact that everything was quiet again I went into the kitchen, found a pan and filled it with what water remained in the tap. I tried the gas stove but there was no gas as it had evidently been cut off, so I collected three blocks of solidified spirit which were issued with our little 'Tommy Cookers', lit them and started to boil the water in the pan on top of the cooker. Kevin Heaney produced about eight Oxo cubes which he had brought with him so I proceeded to make a hot drink with these and, finding some cups in the cupboard, I rationed it out to everybody in the house. We then made our own arrangements as to what we ate. I wasn't feeling very hungry and just had two hard-tack biscuits from my 24-hour ration pack. We all felt better after this and more alert than prior to the armoured column attack.

Apart from a few spasmodic shots in the distance it was quiet and around 1000 hours, Captain Manley said that we ought to take advantage of the lull and try and get some sleep. We were detailed off to take watch at the windows whilst those not on watch tried to catch a few winks of sleep. McCarthy and I went into the middle bedroom and we both flopped down onto a feather bed, but sleep wouldn't come. However, we both lay on the bed thankful for a rest. This was short-lived because we had only lain there for about twenty minutes or so when there was a mighty explosion and a large cloud of smoke and dust came gushing through the bedroom door. Mac and I immediately sprang off the bed and dashed out into the passage. We couldn't believe our eyes at what we saw. Either a mortar bomb or an 88mm shell had hit the back of the house and there was a gaping hole where the back wall and roof should have been. This wasn't the worst of it – three of the signals chaps had gone into a small back bedroom to get some rest. One had lain on the bed and the other two had settled down on the floor. The two men on the floor were only stunned and suffering from shock but the one lying on the bed was in a bad way as he was directly against the back wall which had been blown in on top of him. He was covered with bricks and laths from the ceiling. Harry Walker and myself helped the two men with shock down the stairs and into the cellar and went back to see what we could do with the one on the bed.

We took him into another bedroom and laid him on the bed. He was covered with blood and looked to be dead, but in case he wasn't Harry gave him a shot of morphine from one of the little tubes with which we had been issued. There was a terrific din going on all around us and it was obvious that Jerry was plastering us from a distance with everything he could lay his hands on to get rid of us. We, therefore, thought it prudent to retire into the cellar for the time being until it eased off. Once in the cellar we sat down on the floor and looked around. There was a small wine rack with one or two bottles of wine in it, and a large Edam cheese. Some tinned evaporated milk and some jars of fish. We opened some of the tinned milk and had a drink to clear the dust from our throats but this wasn't successful. I thereupon extracted the cork from a bottle of wine and offered it around. We all had about two mouthfuls each as Captain Manley told us not to drink too much because of not having had much food to eat. We had covered a little window at pavement level with a small piece of blanket in case any German patrols noticed the cellar was occupied. It was at this period that I realised I was hungry, so catching hold of the cheese I tried to cut it with my jack-knife, but it was useless as the cheese was like a cannon ball and must have been there for years. Up above, we could still hear explosions and during this time we heard footsteps from above. I realised we should not have been in the cellar as we were, but orders were orders. The captain was clutching his handkerchief whilst we gripped our Stens. If by some chance the Germans were taught the way we had been and realised there were British troops in the cellar we could expect a grenade at any time at all. Fortunately, the footsteps did not come to the stairs and receded, so we assumed it must have been our chaps from nearby seeing if there were any casualties. The time was now about 1400 hours and as the firing and shelling had died down a bit we were ordered back upstairs and resumed our position at the windows. I was in the upstairs front room where I had been earlier on when we fired on the armoured cars. From my position, looking out over the bridge ramp and embankment I could see a clock tower on top of a church about three to four hundred yards away and every now and then the bell in the tower gave a few rings but it had nothing to do with the time. We suspected that some German observers must be in the tower giving signals by the bell to direct patrols, because very shortly afterwards one of our six-pounders started shelling the tower to get them out. About the same time, in the background we had also heard a klaxon horn and whistles sounding at odd intervals and assumed that these were another form of signalling for patrols to advance and take up positions. Later on in the afternoon we saw some Spitfires patrolling over the town, and hearing the sound of heavier engines we guessed that the lift timed for Monday was taking place, but we couldn't see the tug planes and gliders as they were seven miles away on the DZ. Although I didn't actually witness it, Harry Walker and Kevin Heaney saw an armoured car come across the bridge slowly and weave in and out of the vehicles we had put out of action that morning. It reached our end of the bridge, turned around and went back the way it had come. No one fired at it so assuming it to be safe the car did another U-turn and came back again with two Germans hanging onto the side of the car to avoid any shots from the opposite side to us. However, as it came opposite to the buildings on our side, both the Germans hanging onto the side were shot as was the driver and the car careered out of control down the opposite bank.

Things were pretty quiet after that but we still remained vigilant. It was a pleasant sunny afternoon, not too warm and all our troops were quiet with their own thoughts. However, towards evening just as the sun was dipping down we heard the old battle cry of 'Whahoo Mohammed' ring out and going out onto the veranda just in front of the bedroom window we waived our yellow recognition silks which we wore as scarves and returned the battle cry, thinking reinforcements had arrived. Our elation was short-lived as it turned out to be only a small platoon with a six-pounder. Upon arrival they mounted the gun to one side of the bridge by the house which we had gone to on the Sunday night to see who occupied it.

Very soon the sun dropped low and it became dark. Jerry opened up on us again with long range stuff and was answered back by the six-pounder which did some good work that night, but was eventually put out of action towards midnight. The Germans had evidently spotted it and had put in a heavy concentration of mortar bombs on its location and the large house alongside. This house was blazing like an inferno and lit up the surrounding area for the rest of the night and eventually petered out towards dawn. After the barrage, it quietened down with just a little spasmodic firing thereafter, but we still couldn't afford to relax or sleep due to German patrols sneaking up on us.

Tuesday, 19th September

Tuesday dawned with a hint of fine weather and about 0800 hours we decided that it was time for a brew up. I went into the kitchen and after clearing debris out of the sink turned on the tap, but no water was forthcoming as the pipe leading to the tap had been broken. By now I only had a half bottle of water left. I had brought two bottles with me but had used one and a half bottles. The other men were in the same position, so we pooled our water and made a drink. There was no likelihood of obtaining any more; even the toilet cistern was empty, so we had to conserve the remaining water. After having our drink I took up a position in the ground floor window where I was joined by Harry Walker. Suddenly we heard a whistling sound and we both ducked behind a sideboard in front of the window. An explosion followed almost immediately; it was mortar fire and the bombs were landing outside in the road. We lay on the floor for some considerable time whilst splinters of steel came whanging through the window and hitting the outside wall. The barrage then stopped and we resumed our positions, with me on the left and Harry on the right looking out onto the road and the embankment opposite. Whilst we were looking out of the window we observed one of our medical orderlies emerge from the archway under the bridge about twenty-five yards to our left. His white armband with a plain red cross on it was clearly visible and he was escorting three German prisoners. Suddenly a shot rang out and he staggered back towards the arch with two of the Germans with him. The third German prisoner started to run in our direction hoping to make a break for it. This was fatal as one of our chaps with a Bren gun in a house near the archway opened fire and hit the German in the legs. He fell to the ground, but still tried to crawl away and was immediately hit with another burst from the Bren. This finished him off and we could see the tracer bullets going straight through his back and ricocheting off the pavement in front of him. This seemed to be a cold-blooded act but it was also a dirty trick on the part of the German sniper who had shot down an unarmed medic merely to allow the prisoners to escape.

Shortly after this incident a runner came from Brigade HQ with a message for Captain Manley to report to a Captain Briggs for a conference.[3] Captain Manley was away for about half an

---

3 Staff Captain Bernard W. Briggs, 1st Parachute Brigade HQ.

hour and came back with a worried look on his face. He told us that XXX Corps under General Horrocks, who were supposed to relieve us, had been held up by enemy opposition and that it would be some time before they reached us. In the meantime, we had to hang on to the bridge end as long as possible. We had no doubt that we would not be relieved and settled down once again to await the relieving force. The time passed by and Harry and I were still at the ground floor window keeping watch. Directly opposite us was the grass embankment with a few thinly-leaved shrubs about six to eight feet high. Over the embankment the sun was slowly going down and the rays were shining onto the rear of the shrubs. At the same time, Harry and I both noticed a movement behind one of the shrubs and peering at it intently we observed the silhouette of a man standing up. Towards our left we also noticed another movement behind a smaller bush and slowly a German soldier raised his head above the bush. Both Harry and I slowly raised our Sten guns and waited to see if there were any more Jerries about. There weren't, so I whispered to Harry to take out the Jerry on the right behind the tree whilst I attended to the one behind the bush. The Germans must have thought that there were no British troops about because they both stepped out from behind their cover, and Harry and I let them have it from about 15 yards range. Harry dropped his man almost immediately and mine came down the bank on his hands and knees screaming out with pain and fear. I gave him another short burst and he stopped screaming and rolled down the bank to lie perfectly still at the foot of it. Where they had come from we had no idea. We could only assume they had been lying doggo since Monday when we shot up the armoured cars and were probably part of the crews.

Unbeknown to us, some of the houses on our left had caught fire from incendiaries; most of the morning and afternoon we had heard the sound of heavy diesel engines around us and assumed that Jerry was bringing in tanks to get us out of the houses. It was somewhere about this time that some of the chaps in the house near the bridge had spotted a group of Jerries doing something under the bridge span and it was assumed that they were either trying to connect the charges already laid under the bridge to blow it or were disconnecting them. They were kept under observation until it was opportune to catch them all together and when this happened they were all caught in a long burst from a Bren gun.

Towards early evening another runner came from Captain Briggs or Captain Mackay and ordered us to evacuate our house and move further down the street to our left and to take up occupation in another house where some of our troops were. We picked our way out of the wreckage and went out the back door where we found ourselves in a small garden separated from the next house by a high dividing wall and a back gate leading into a narrow alleyway which was blocked by the continuation of the high wall in the garden. Two of us cupped our hands and gave the rest of our lads a leg-up over the wall and then we were hoisted up by the chaps preceding us who sat on top of the wall. We dropped into a garden, hopped over a dividing fence and went in through the back door entrance of the house we had been ordered to. Upon entering we noticed a batch of German prisoners in a room and some of our troops busily engaged in knocking a hole through the dividing wall of the next house in line. We joined in with the other troops in this 'mouse-holing' operation using bayonets, entrenching tools and anything else that came to hand. This was necessary as the houses to our left were ablaze and the flames were spreading along the row and it was safer to 'mouse-hole' our way along the street than go outside and be met by machine gun fire. The heat from the blaze about two houses away was terrific and it was obvious that we had to get out soon or be caught in the fire. This was borne out later as we received orders to make our way towards the river and to join up with Captain Mackay and his sappers under the bridge. Captain

Manley had ordered Harry to send Kevin Heaney to Captain Mackay to ask if we should join him. It was now late evening but still moderately light so we had to be careful.

We all went out of the back door, prisoners as well, where we assembled in the gardens and proceeded to black up our faces with mud. The light was fading rapidly now and we were gradually being choked by the smoke from the burning house we had just vacated. We were then ordered to move out. I have no idea what happened to the German prisoners! We were in no position to shepherd prisoners as they nearly outnumbered us and as I didn't hear any shots behind us I could only guess that they had been released to find their way back to their lines, a matter of a few hundred yards. Forming Indian file we went into the back alley and squeezing between a tall chimney stack and a wall we made our way to a wooden gate at the end of the alley which looked out on to a roadway running parallel to the river, and to our right led to the first archway under the bridge. To our left, which was a street covered by the Germans, we saw a tank which had been knocked out in the middle of the road. It had been a Tiger tank, but was now a heap of charred and twisted metal with its bogie wheels burnt away.[4]

Opposite us we saw a long low building and behind it a large piece of open waste ground leading down to a road running parallel to the river. This piece of waste ground was flanked on the roadside by a large hedge with a road running alongside at right angles down to the river. On the extreme right was the bridge with some ruined houses on the roadside. We cautiously opened the gate and in small groups dashed across the road to the building opposite us. I was amongst the first troops across the road and after we had crossed a German machine gun opened up down the middle of the road and prevented the lads crossing. We fired back at where we had seen the tracers coming from and this enabled the rest of our group to dash across the street and enter the building. We found ourselves in some kind of a workshop, but as Jerry now knew where we were, we decided to get out as quickly as possible. Going out of a side door, we ran across the piece of waste ground and flopped down in a ditch alongside the hedge. It was now quite dark and we could hear the sound of a tank moving towards us from the street we had crossed earlier. The sound came nearer and we could hear tracks clanking away on the road. We all hugged the ground not daring to lift our faces in case some German spotted our faces. The clanking sound came nearer and lifting my head slightly I could see the darker shape of the tank through the hedge about ten feet away. I sincerely hoped and prayed that it wouldn't turn around and come grinding up the ditch. The tank slowly moved down the road towards the river, turned around and came back the way it had come. Every one of our group had lain perfectly still and no one had fired a shot at the tank as we had all realised that Sten guns wouldn't work or have been much use against armour. As soon as we heard the sound of the tank die away in the distance we signalled one another and made a mad dash in groups across the road to the demolished houses near the bridge. On our way across we were silhouetted against the flames from the houses we had vacated earlier and a German machine gunner must have spotted us as he opened fire on us and tracer bullets came through the darkness in our direction. Some of the group dropped flat on their faces but our little unit of five put on a spurt and carried on to one of the demolished houses. We only just made it because as we dived

---

4 Probably one of two PzKpfw IVs of Kampfgruppe Knaust knocked out on Westervoortsedijk. Both attributed to Sergeant Cyril Robson's 6-pounder anti-tank gun situated west of the bridge (C Troop, 1st Airlanding Anti-Tank Battery, Royal Artillery). Another 6-pounder No. 2 'Bravado II' belonging to B Troop, 1st Airlanding Anti-Tank Battery, Royal Artillery under Sergeant W. Kill was positioned in the area east of the bridge near the corner of Westervoortsedijk/Oostraat.

for cover behind a low wall, a stream of bullets started bouncing off the wall opposite to us with intermittent tracers carving a pattern against the sky. This fire was coming at us from across the river which was too far away from us to return the compliment with our Stens. This gunfire was so concentrated it kept us pinned down for what seemed ages but was probably only about ten minutes or so and then it ceased.

During the lull I said to Harry, 'We aren't going to be relieved and I think we should swim across the river and make our way towards our own lines,' but Harry replied, 'I think we should stick together and hope for the best.' By now, we were almost under the bridge, so we ran across the remaining distance and linked up with Captain Mackay's men under the bridge itself, with the span directly above us. Once inside we immediately set to building a perimeter barricade with anything we could find, facing in three directions as far as we could tell in the darkness. Whilst we were erecting the barricades, a party of sappers with an officer went forward about seventy-five yards and planted some mines, whilst another group of REs set about removing fuses from the bridge stanchion against which the Germans had planted demolition charges. The Germans couldn't blow the bridge until they had eliminated us and had advanced across the bridge to our side. Finishing the barricades we then took up positions behind them and waited to see what would happen next. We were all exhausted and were thankful just to lie down on the ground and rest. During the snatches of conversation that went on around us we heard that at the time we were making our way from the burning houses some of the 1st Battalion had tried to get through to us but had been driven back. It was now quite obvious that we were on our own and cut off as the deadline for being relieved had passed some hours earlier. Furthermore, we were completely hemmed in and gradually being compressed into an ever-decreasing circle.

Wednesday, 20th September

Wednesday dawned with a damp drizzle and we could see our surroundings. We were directly underneath the last archway of the bridge in some kind of yard cluttered with old building materials, a steam roller and some heavy planks which looked like railway sleepers, also some barrels of solid tar for road making. To our left was a large wooden door which opened out onto the road running parallel to the river. In front of us were some half built or demolished buildings and slightly to the right, a medium sized brick building with a wooden door. On our extreme right was a wall about seven feet in height behind which were ruined buildings running along the main street leading up to the bridge ramp. Behind us were some houses which protected our backs but there was an opening between this and the stanchion through which we had arrived the night before. Also to our left was the bridge stanchion itself with some stone steps running up the side and the parallel with the bridge. On top of the steps was a blockhouse with twin Oerlikons mounted inside which had been in action against us the previous day. Looking around me I estimated that there were no more than fifty to sixty officers and other ranks and our perimeter was no more than fifty yards across. At the moment, things were quiet, but we all knew that it wouldn't be too long before the fireworks started again. McCarthy, Heaney and I were crouched behind a large iron boiler filled with tar, so we decided to take advantage of the quiet period and have something to eat. There was no chance of making a hot drink so I ate three hard tack biscuits, two bars of fruit chocolate and swilled it down with the remainder of my water. The bottle was now empty so I threw it away as it was excess baggage. At the same time I took my maps out of their case, burnt them and cast the map case aside.

Shortly afterwards we heard the sound of aeroplane engines and thinking they were some of our Spitfires we ventured from behind cover to have a look. We soon dashed back for cover again as the sound came from a flight of six ME109s about 300 feet up and cruising overhead. They were painted light blue and we could distinguish the markings easily. As they flew over one of them peeled off at right angles flying away from us. It turned around and came straight back at us firing short bursts as it came. He was off target though and nothing came near. I don't think the pilot knew we were under bridge end because it flew straight on and we never saw the plane again. We were all thankful and breathed a sigh of relief as we thought we were in for a strafing. Most of the chaps immediately reached for their cigarettes and lit up to steady their nerves a bit. Soon after that incident a patrol came to report to Captain Mackay and before the NCO i/c of the patrol left he was ordered to take back with him to Brigade HQ two German prisoners who had been locked in a hut. We settled down to await events and shortly afterwards we heard the sound of a German armoured car roaring up the road parallel to the river under the bridge. We were adjacent to this road and could get out on to it by opening a large wooden gate which was about fifteen feet away to our left. As the car passed by, an officer asked for two chaps to throw a Gammon bomb at the car if it came back. He gave them one each and taking one himself, the three of them went to the gate and slightly opened it. About five minutes passed and we heard the car coming back, whereupon the gate was opened and as the car flashed by the officer and one trooper threw their stick bombs. The gate was closed and the men came back with a glum look on their faces. It was enough to tell us that they had missed with their aim.

On each side of the bridge at our end and built into the bridge was a blockhouse which afforded a good view across the bridge and surrounding area. One of the officers decided that as our view was very limited some men should take up position in these blockhouses with a Bren gun. Two men went up the steps to the top but were immediately shot. It was then that somebody had the bright idea of barricading the rails on the steps to offer a safe passage up. These stone steps led up the side of the bridge stanchion and then ran parallel to the side of the bridge where the blockhouse was and were in full view of the enemy. Captain Manley detailed Harry Walker, McCarthy, Heaney and I to do this job, so we went to a pile of wooden sleepers and cautiously started wedging them between the rails and the steps. It was hard and heavy work and every moment whilst we were fixing the sleepers in position we expected to receive a hail of bullets, but luckily they didn't arrive. We had reached about two-thirds of the way up the steps when suddenly we were called down as one of the officers had spotted some movement down the road. We were glad to come down!

Jerry had evidently spotted what our intentions were and no doubt had been alerted earlier by the armoured car's crew that we were still in occupation. He had, therefore, decided to put a stop to our activity as he opened up with an 88mm SP gun. There was a terrific explosion as the shell burst on the left-hand blockhouse. Everybody ducked or fell flat on their faces and we had good reason as Jerry kept up a steady fire on the bridge above us. Within five or six shots he had blasted a hole in the blockhouse and we blessed our good fortune that we hadn't carried on with the barricade and the intention to station someone in it permanently. Some chaps had been in it but after the first shell they threw a smoke bomb and as the smoke drifted up to screen them they dashed down the steps for cover. The 88mm gun was still banging away and suddenly I felt a sharp thwack on my right shoulder. I immediately felt my shoulder with my left hand, but apart from a rip in my jumping jacket I was OK. I looked on the ground and picked up a piece of jagged metal about an inch square which was still hot. This piece had evidently ricocheted off the bridge and had hit me. Fortunately for me it must have been spent when it landed on me.

We had all been waiting for an attack since dawn and this was it. It was obvious that Jerry meant to dislodge us and to do so was trying to land his shells under the bridge where we were, where, if they exploded they would soon make mincemeat out of us. The only thing preventing them from doing this was a high wall of a house to our rear which had been gutted by fire. To carry out his plan Jerry had to demolish the wall first and this he proceeded to do with his 88mm gun. Our officers then decided that it was time to move, so we moved further back under the bridge and found cover.

Facing us in the large stockyard where we were, was a large steamroller and behind it a fairly large building. To the left of the building was a path and adjacent to the path butting onto the river road a row of gutted houses. A party of us were detailed off to take cover in the building and both Harry Walker and I were in this party. Climbing over our barricades we made a dash for a pair of small wooden doors in the side of the building. As the first man reached them and tried to open them he found it was jammed, so some of the other fellows gave a yank to the other door and managed to get it half open. As the four men in the front of me tried to get through the opening they became jammed in the doorway. At the time a German machine gun opened up directly on the doorway. I immediately dropped on my face behind a little stone wall by the path.

I saw the man in front of me (the last man trying to get through the door) stagger inside; he had caught a burst right down his left arm and left thigh. The firing stopped and after counting ten seconds I jumped up and flew through the door and dropped on my face inside the building. Jerry must have seen me fly through because he opened up again. The wooden doors were now a mass of splinters and holes and bullets were coming through the doors and windows and ricocheting off the opposite walls.

Lying next to me on the ground was a signaller and strapped to his back was a small cage with a pigeon in it which was cooing away quite contentedly. At that moment I wished I could have felt the same way as the bird.

Harry Walker was the only NCO with us in the building, which was empty and without cover. Harry said we couldn't stay there much longer and when the firing stopped we should get back under the bridge. We waited for a lull in the firing and when it ceased we decided to make a break for it. Crouching on my hands and toes I awaited my turn and when it came I was off my mark and through the doorway like a hare – I was always a good sprinter! I reached the barricade we had left earlier and practically cleared it in one leap to safety. Matters were getting worse now and we were being subjected to LMG fire, mortar fire and shelling. Captain Mackay RE as the senior officer split us into sections and ordered us to occupy some gutted houses to the right of the building we had just vacated. To reach these houses we had to cross a little road, clear a six-foot wall and then dash across an opening into the ruined buildings. The firing was now coming at us from all angles and it was becoming decidedly dicey where we were, so we set off in our little batches singly and in twos between bursts of machine gun fire. It was at this point that I became separated from my pals. Following the chaps who had set off in front of me I dashed across the clearing, up some rubble, jumped on top of the wall and rolled over it on my stomach. As I dropped down on the other side I nearly landed on a dead German who had been roasted, lying at the side of a house that had been burnt out. At first glance I thought it was a tailor's dummy and stopped for a moment trying to make it out. I suddenly realised that the chaps in front of me had disappeared and there was nobody behind me, so I decided to get moving. I reached the gutted buildings alright and turned around to see what was happening at the bridge. The bridge was under mortar bomb fire and whilst I watched I saw a mortar bomb explosion amongst a group of men still under the bridge. I ducked down and started making my way through the ruined houses against which we crawled up on the Sunday night. As I passed by a window I looked into the main street and saw a stream of tracers emerging from some bushes on the embankment opposite to the one we had covered earlier. This tracer fire was directed at our chaps under the bridge so I stopped, and taking steady aim with my Sten let go a full magazine spraying the bushes back and forth. The firing stopped and after observing for a couple of minutes with no answering fire I assumed that I had put the gun out of action.

Upon looking around for the rest of the section that I had followed, I saw they had gone and I was now on my own, so I decided to look for them. Keeping my head down, I went through the building and came to a dead end, so I retraced my steps. On my way back somebody took a shot at me so I crouched low down on a pile of bricks behind the cover of a wall. Not long afterwards I noticed that I was perspiring freely, the sweat was running down my face and my clothes were feeling wet. My feet began to get hot and looking down I saw little wisps of smoke and smelt singeing leather. I suddenly realised that I was crouching down on bricks that were still nearly red hot from a house that had been burnt down earlier and that I was slowly being cooked. Not wishing to be grilled, I made a dash into another ruined house to cool off a bit before setting out to find the rest of my comrades. In the house that I was in, or what was left of it, was a small passageway with the roof still over it. Wedged in the passage were the remains of a bedspring and underneath it was one of our No. 18 wireless sets. I dragged it out and inspected it to see if it was still working, but I was out of luck as the RT battery was burnt as was the flex from the earphones, so I threw it to one side.

Looking out of a window space I discerned that I was looking onto a main street. To the right, about 200 yards away, was the bridge and to my left was an electric tram in the middle of the road. The tram was badly battered and the overhead cables for supplying the power for the trams were dangling down. In the middle of the street was a small green with some pits dug in it which looked like mortar pits, so I assumed that they had been dug by our chaps for a mortar position, but they were now empty. On the other side of the road was a house in which I could see some of our troops and therefore assumed that this was Brigade HQ. I decided that it was of no use hanging about on my own so I decided to join them. At this particular time German patrols with LMGs were infiltrating and surrounding us and were using a series of whistle blasts for giving orders. One of these patrols, an LMG crew, came by on the river road facing the back of the house which I was in. Each man was festooned with ammo belts and as they passed by an open gateway I gave them a burst from my Sten and decided to join our chaps in Brigade HQ, which turned out to be the last house occupied by our troops in strength.

At the same time as I jumped out of the window onto the main street, some more of our chaps from under the bridge emerged from a house on my right and we all headed across the street. Halfway across the street an LMG opened up on us, so putting on an extra spurt I ducked underneath one of the overhead electric cables hanging down and dived into one of the pits in the green facing us. As soon as the firing stopped I dashed across to the house where our troops were and they let me in.

It is at this stage I feel I must record what happened to the rest of my unit after I left them under the bridge, and as told to me by them in later years.

Just after I left them, the Germans poured down a heavy barrage of mortar bombs which I had witnessed. To the troops left under the bridge an attack by infantry seemed imminent and Kevin Heaney remembers being ordered to fix bayonets to their Sten guns to repel the attack. Whilst this was taking place, Harry Walker remembers that he and a lance corporal were ordered to cover an engineer officer who wanted to do something in the lower part of the blockhouse stanchion, possibly to defuse the charges as it was never our intention to blow the bridge. To get to the doorway in the bottom of the stanchion meant crossing an exposed position so the officer crawled forward on his stomach followed by Harry and the corporal. As he entered, Harry and the corporal opened fire with their Stens to draw any fire away from him. After a few minutes, the officer dashed out of the doorway shouting, 'Right!' and was immediately shot in the legs. Harry and the corporal grabbed a leg each and started to drag him back under the bridge arch. They were joined by two other men who took an arm each and the four men carried the officer back. This episode was witnessed by Kevin Heaney before he left the bridge. Harry does not remember much after that incident as another mortar 'stonk' took place and he was either knocked out or blacked out. When he came to, it was dark and there was no firing at the bridge and he was on his own. Leaving the bridge he saw two men in a slit trench and joined them. By a strange coincidence one of the men was a Sergeant Les Phillips in the Royal Engineers whom he had known in North Africa. The two of them were subsequently captured by the Germans in the early hours of Thursday morning.

Kevin Heaney took the same route that I had taken earlier. A bunch of them went over the six-foot wall and survived a grenade which exploded about a yard or so in front of him, but a young soldier nearby was wounded in the throat. The Germans were all around now so he and the rest of the group including the wounded soldier took refuge in the passageway of one of the ruined houses. They then heard the Jerries asking our troops to surrender and after due consideration the six of them decided to accept and searched for something white to surrender with. Kevin reached inside his battle blouse and tore his vest off which he passed up the line. The first four soldiers including the one with the throat wound were shot as they emerged from the hallway, so Kevin decided to remain where he was and to surrender later at a more opportune moment by following the example of some of the paratroopers trapped by falling masonry and calling for help. This he did when some Jerries entered the house, and he put up his hands in surrender and was immediately taken prisoner by a German machine gunner. When Ron Pugh became separated from us on the Sunday night he tagged on to some other chaps and was detailed to defend the schoolhouse in which Colonel John Frost had his HQ. He took part in some street fighting and shooting up German transport on the Tuesday and Wednesday but was shot in the upper left arm by a snipers bullet. He was taken prisoner and transferred to the St Elizabeth Hospital for a time before being sent to Stalag XIB where I met him about three or four months later.

The last anyone saw of Captain Manley was after the mortar attack under the bridge. He was completely deaf and probably suffering from shellshock. Harry Walker said that he appeared to be out of his mind but was sheltering behind a steel sheet. He was captured and served on in the army after the war. No one knows what happened to McCarthy, but he was wounded and taken prisoner. The glider party under Major C.C. Chidgey arrived on the Monday afternoon and were immediately involved in the battle of the 'Witches' Cauldron'. They never linked up with us and were all wounded except for four, two being killed and one making his escape.[5]

5 Corporal Frederick W. Grantham, 10541663, aged 26 and Corporal Kenneth C.W. Andrews, 14216620, aged 28. Both killed night of 25th/26th September 1944, during withdrawal to the river.

To return to my story, after I had entered Brigade HQ I was ushered into a room where a small group of officers were sitting around a table. One of them, a very small chap with a large set of handlebar moustaches handed me a bottle of wine, told me to have a drink and asked where I had come from. I told him I had come from under the bridge and outlined the position as I knew it. He told me to have a rest for a time so I was shown into a room which was filled with some of our troops who were badly wounded. I took off my helmet and sat down on the floor with my back against the wall. I hadn't been sitting there long before I heard someone shouting, 'Does anyone here know anything about Bren guns?' The shouting went on so I went into a front room covering the street and told the officer that I knew something about Brens. There was a gunner manning the Bren in the window with a corporal acting as his No. 2. The gunner said he couldn't fire the Bren as it wouldn't work. I moved into his position and tried the standard procedure of removing the magazine, cocking the gun and squeezing the trigger. I told the corporal that the gun was OK and put the magazine back on and squeezed the trigger again. It didn't work as the bolt would not push the cartridge into the barrel, so removing the magazine I ejected two of the cartridges, put the magazine back on the gun and tried it again. This time it fired! Whoever had loaded the magazine had crammed too many cartridges in it; consequently they were too tight to move. Although the magazine would hold 32 cartridges it was a policy never to put more than 28 in. The officer then asked me if I would take over the gun. I couldn't very well object, so I took it over with the same corporal acting as my No. 2 on my left. I, therefore, became the only Bren gunner at the last bastion.

The room we were in was not very large and contained about six or seven chaps including the little officer with the big moustache. Four of these chaps sat with their backs to the wall to my right. From my position in the window I could see up the main street to my right and looking towards the left I could see the grass embankment leading up to the end of the bridge which had now been vacated by our troops and it appeared that we were completely surrounded.

Somewhere to my left a machine gun had been positioned and every so often fired at our window. I couldn't see from my position so I asked someone on my right side to try and locate it so I could get a shot at it. Keeping careful watch from the right-hand side of the window, one of the chaps spotted the position behind a clump of bushes on the embankment. This was the same position I had fired at earlier from across the street. Taking careful aim, I let go a short burst at the bush but received an answering burst in reply and from then on a short duel took place between myself and the Jerry. He was good and his aim was excellent as every time I pushed the barrel of the Bren out of the window he let fly and bullets spattered off the outside wall. His angle of fire was probably such that he couldn't get a burst through the window. However, by ducking below the window edge and putting the Bren at the right-hand side of the window I managed to silence him. By now, Jerry had infiltrated into the ruined houses at the other end of the street on the opposite side to us and at one point had taken up position in a cellar just below street level. I managed to spot face blobs every so often in the open ground-level window and kept pouring in short bursts of fire, and consequently we did not receive any answering fire from there.

It was now late in the afternoon and somewhere behind the houses to the extreme right on the opposite side Jerry had positioned a mortar and was lobbing bombs over the houses. These bombs were exploding near us and suddenly one exploded right on the corner of the room we were in. There was a small alleyway between the houses and the wall on my right was the outside wall of the alleyway on which the bomb had landed. We didn't know what had happened at the time as we were all in a heap on the floor of the room, covered with dust and bricks and suffering from slight concussion from the explosion. As my head cleared and I struggled to get to my feet I could see a gaping hole in the corner of the room and the four chaps who had been sitting there were either killed or knocked out. My head was ringing and the Bren was under a pile of rubble. The little moustachioed officer in an act of defiance took my Sten and emptied a whole magazine of bullets through the hole in the wall. At the time I thought it was bloody daft as he was just wasting bullets which we would need if we were rushed. He couldn't see anything to aim at as the mortar team were out of sight. Having now zeroed in our position Jerry started opening up with his mortars and 88mm SP guns and the shells started coming our way. We were then ordered to clear out of the houses which were becoming too dangerous to occupy, and to take up positions in the long back garden, in slit trenches which had been dug earlier. The 88s were blasting away quite regularly now and I was in a slit trench trying to clean up the Bren which I had retrieved from the debris. Whilst doing this somebody offered me a tin of pilchards. I opened them with my jack-knife and was just about to eat the first fish when a shell landed nearby. Once again I was covered with earth and when I looked for the pilchards the tin was empty and covered with dirt. I was annoyed because I hadn't had anything to eat for hours, or time to think about eating.

On top of that, I had to set to cleaning the Bren again. Very soon the 88mms got on target and started demolishing the house we had just left. First one shell would hit the outer wall and then the following shells blasted a way through to the rear wall and out. I believe that it was in this house that an old invalid lady who couldn't be moved from one of the upper rooms was killed when one of the shells came through the upper floor. Soon the whole top of the house was demolished and darkness was beginning to fall.

To the rear of the garden we were in, there was a small alleyway leading to a little warehouse containing bottles or jars and to the right a gateway leading into the street. On the opposite side of the street was a long wall behind which was a large orchard garden with some houses at the top end looking out onto the main street. A hole had been made in this long wall and the houses and garden had previously been occupied by our troops. Because mortars and shells were now coming in on top of us we were ordered to vacate our garden and cross into the orchard on the other side of the street. The situation had worsened as Jerry had closed in and was almost on top of us occupying gardens and houses around us, but not coming too close.

We scuttled across the road and through the hole in the wall into the orchard, but Jerry had brought up his 88s fairly close and alternately was firing shells into the house on one side of the street and then into the orchard on the other side. A bunch of us were trying to dodge these by running back and forth across the street from the orchard and into the bottle warehouse in between shell bursts.

On one of these evasive trips a shell blast caught the warehouse roof and we were caught in a shower of glass bottles which crashed down on us. Considering the warehouse to be an unsafe place to be we rushed out into the garden of the first house. This too was unhealthy, so we dashed back down the alleyway and during one of these excursions Jerry lobbed a potato masher grenade over the wall. I was behind three other chaps and the first one caught the full impact as the grenade exploded. Hours after this event I felt a pricking in my ankle and found a small piece of shrapnel which had pierced my gaiter and was stuck in my leg. Jerry then mounted an attack and I was positioned with the Bren gun at the gateway leading onto the street. I kept on firing into the darkness at the flashes of gunfire until my ammunition ran out and then I used my Sten gun. It was very hectic at the time and there was a lot of activity in the orchard, but we beat off the attack. There was a lull in the proceedings and it was during this period that Jerry called upon us to surrender and a truce was called whilst a discussion took place between the Germans and our officers who were left. The truce lasted about an hour during which time Jerry agreed to let us hand over our wounded. After the wounded had been evacuated the Germans again called upon us to surrender as we were completely cut off, surrounded and nearly out of ammunition.

Jerry was told in army fashion to 'Shove off' but much cruder, and when someone threw a grenade at them hostilities commenced once again.

Jerry started shelling once more and again we dashed back and forth across the street as each alternate shell landed. This couldn't go on for long and it was on one of these runs that Jerry changed his order of fire and dropped two in succession at the same place. Four of us had just dashed through the hole in the wall into the orchard and just as we arrived so did a shell. It exploded right in front of us and the three chaps in front of me went flying into the air. I saw this explosion and ducked my head to one side just as the blast reached me. I felt a blow like being hit with a stick on the right side of my face and across my right eye as the blast whipped under my helmet. It lifted me off my feet and knocked me flat out, and when I came round I couldn't see anything! Eventually I could make out things in the darkness with my left eye, but all I could see out of my right eye was a blinding glare. I felt my face but couldn't feel any blood and as the shelling was still taking place decided to try and find some cover. I crawled over the ground and eventually found a slit trench up against the wall and flopped in on top of another chap lying in the bottom. The shelling kept up all night and there was no reply from any of our chaps at all. They were either lying low or there weren't any left.

Thursday, 21st September

Dawn eventually came and everything was quiet. I must have had a cat nap earlier on in between the shellfire as I didn't remember it stopping. I tried testing my eyesight to see how bad it was. I could now see alright out of my left eye but there was still this blinding glare in my right eye. The chap under me stirred, but we both stayed in the trench until it got lighter. It was then that we heard Jerry shouting in English, 'Come on out, Tommy, come out and you will be treated alright' and 'Come on out and surrender.' The chap under me said he was going to surrender and climbed out of the trench, went out of the hole in the wall and up the street with his arms in the air. I stood up in the trench and the first thing that met my sight was an 88mm shell with a bent nose lying half over the edge of the trench. It had evidently hit the wall without exploding and had then fallen on the edge of the trench. Being careful not to disturb it I climbed out of the trench and took stock of the situation. I was blinded in one eye and without any Sten gun ammunition. Everything was still quiet except for Jerry still shouting out to us to surrender. I was out of cigarettes and water and had to decide what I was going to do. It was at this moment that I saw a chap come out of the ground and limp towards me. I knew him by sight, and nicknamed 'Darkie' due to his black hair and moustache, and he belonged to the 4th Independent Brigade. I asked him if he had any cigarettes and he gave me an American cigarette from the few he had left in the packet.

I asked him what he intended to do and he replied, 'I am going to give myself up.' Not knowing what frame of mind the Jerries were in, I said to Darkie, 'Well, I'll wait and see what happens to you before I go out.' He then went out with a handkerchief in the air and I watched him go up the street. There were some Germans at the top of the street and Darkie walked, or rather limped up to them and they took him away round the corner. I waited for a while, but couldn't hear any shooting at all and guessed it was all over, so I decided to give myself up. However, before doing so I dismantled the Bren and Sten guns and threw the parts to all points of the compass so they couldn't be used. There was a Jeep in the orchard and I toyed with the idea of driving it out, but being surrounded knew that I wouldn't get far. I took a white towel out of my small pack, took a deep breath and walked up the street with my arms in the air holding the towel. When I reached the Germans (in actual fact they were Hungarian satellite troops), an officer garbed in black leather breeches, jacket and boots searched me for weapons and then gave me a bottle of wine to have a swig at. It tasted good! I was then led to another group of our chaps, most of whom were wounded, where one I suspected of being an officer, minus his pips, asked if I was from Brigade HQ, and for some reason gave me his pistol lanyard. We were then marched to the town hall where one of our doctors was trying to attend to the wounded. He had a look at my eye but said that he couldn't do much as the pupil was widely dilated. However, he gave me some eye drops and a black eye patch which I put on. Because he was short of medical supplies he asked us all for our morphine tubes and field dressings which we collected and gave to him. We all stayed there for most of the day whilst most of the badly wounded were sent off to the St Elizabeth Hospital. During this time I observed that most of our guards were either Hungarians, Hitler Youth, Luftwaffe personnel or marines, so it looked like Jerry had called upon every unit and organisation to dislodge us.

When night fell, a small group of us, being walking wounded, were herded into the back of a small truck with some German wounded and transported to the hospital. Here, some of our chaps and the Germans were taken into care. Nothing could be done for me, but some of the lightly wounded paras were treated and later on that night we were again put into a truck with some German wounded and taken at speed to a small town called Gronau on the German/Dutch border. The back of the truck was open and I was sitting near the end, I considered jumping out as I knew that the best chance to escape was in the first 24 hours of capture, but the truck was travelling too fast and I decided against it. Eventually we reached Gronau where we were off-loaded into a large hall near a hospital. The hall was fitted out with straw palliasses and blankets and in all there were about 60 of us including some of the Poles. The guard consisted of a German Corporal and about six privates who were also walking wounded. Once inside the hall we chose a palliasse and immediately dropped off to have our first sleep in five days.

We were in this hall for about ten days to a fortnight where our meals were served to us by German nuns. During this period I volunteered to help out one of our MOs at the hospital down the road, but I was placed upon my honour not to escape. This was disappointing as I had volunteered to see what the chances of escape were. It would have been fairly easy to get away as I was allowed to go to the hospital and back without any escort! I assisted in the hospital by attending to simple things, like giving the patients water and helping them to the toilets, etc. It opened my eyes to the aftermath of battle as I was assisting in an amputee ward which had both German and British patients. The bandages were like crêpe toilet paper and were soon soggy and messy. There was even an English pilot in here, who had been burnt all over his face when his Typhoon caught fire. His face was all charred and it was very difficult trying to raise his head to give him sips of water. Another thing that brought home the horrors of war was seeing a pile of discarded odd boots where they had been thrown after legs had been amputated. Some amusing incidents took place in the hall and after my capture, but this would take another account to recall it all. Suffice it to say, that after I had helped out in the hospital for a few days we were all shipped aboard a train whence we were transported to Stalag XIB at Fallingbostel to await the end of the war or release whichever came first. As Jerry had said, 'For you, Tommy, the war is over!'

Looking north along houses on Eusebius Buitensingel. Pre-war and after the battle in 1945. Private Ted Mordecai writes: 'Having now occupied the house we took stock of our surroundings and were detailed to take up positions in the lower and upper rooms facing onto the bridge and embankment.' (Photos: Above: Kramer. Below: Courtesy Gelders Archive)

DIVISIONAL SUPPORT, 1 PARA SQDN RE 265

1st Parachute Brigade elements emplane. Barkston Heath, Sunday, 17th September, Chalk No. 131. 15 and 53 Squadrons, 61 Troop Carrier Group, USAAF. Drop Zone 'X'. From left to right: 1. Private Ted Mordecai, 1st Airborne Division Ordnance Field Park, RAOC with Mk.V Sten butt strapped to right leg; 2. Private McCarthy, 1st Airborne Division Ordnance Field Park, RAOC; 3. Private Kevin Heaney, 1st Airborne Division Ordnance Field Park, RAOC; 4?; 5. Lance Corporal Jock Wright, No. 1 Section, 1st Airborne Provost Company; 6? 7. Lance Corporal Mick 'Paddy' Cox, No. 1 Section, 1st Airborne Provost Company; 8. Lance Corporal Jim Keddie, No. 1 Section, 1st Airborne Provost Company; 9, 10, 11, 12 all unknown.

Private Ted Mordecai writes: 'Whilst waiting for the order to emplane we noticed an American officer going round taking photographs of each stick by their aircraft. It appeared that he was an intelligence officer and was taking photos either for his own interest or officially. Several comments were passed such as, "Say cheese, please" or "I'll have a dozen when they're ready." I often wish I knew who he was, as it is the only photograph that was ever taken of our party and it would have been nice to have had one for the record.' (Photo: Courtesy IWM.K7588)

View from under the bridge looking to the west. On the far right 1st Parachute Brigade HQ, RAP and to its left 2nd Parachute Battalion HQ building. (Photo pre-war: Courtesy Gelders Archive)

Major Dennis S. Munford, Officer Commanding, 3 Battery, 1st Airlanding Light Battery, Royal Artillery

Sunday, 17th September

When I first set off for the bridge I had two forward observation officers and travelled with 3rd Parachute Battalion on the centre route. They first had a skirmish with General Kussin's entourage (Commandant of Arnhem) and later met stiffer resistance at Hartenstein. They made it clear that if I wanted to motor to Arnhem I could expect considerable delay. I decided to retrace my steps and get into the southern route with 2nd Parachute Battalion and travelling briskly westwards almost collided head-on with Freddie Gough (Reconnaissance Squadron CO) hell-bent on his coup de main at the bridge. He decided to join me but I let him take the lead as his Jeep was fairly bristling with machine guns. I think it was here I lost one Forward Observation Unit who must have remained with 3rd Parachute Battalion, because hereafter I only remember Captain Buchanan, our customary forward observation officer (FOO).

Accompanied by Captains Harrison (E Troop CO) and Buchanan (No. 1 Forward Observation Unit Royal Artillery, attached to 2nd Parachute Battalion) I got to the bridge at about 2000 hours on Sunday, 17th September and reported to Brigade HQ. The Brigade major, Tony Hibbert, told me that communications within the division were practically non-existent. I decided to establish an observation post on the roof at the southeast corner of Brigade HQ and another with Tony Harrison in the 2nd Parachute Battalion HQ building. 'Buck', the forward observation officer, would find another east of the road by the river with A Company. Returning to my Jeep to collect my chaps I was informed that none had adequate radio contact; this was embarrassing to say the least of it, all these heavy vehicles and radios and no joy. Freddie Gough was also out of touch. We were fortunate to have Tony Hibbert at Brigade; a good friend, he was also a gunner and understood our problem when I told him I intended to return to the gun area, leaving the Forward Observation Unit (FOU) but taking Tony Harrison in an effort to rectify the radio problems.

We set off at high speed taking the Germans completely by surprise; it was dusk and they were brewing up and parking vehicles, and by the time they had got around to shouting and shooting we had gone. Lance Bombardier J.W. Crook, my driver/signaller, enjoyed himself as we raced westward at illegal speed, Tony Harrison following and checking my navigation as we distanced ourselves from the town and things got quieter. Eventually somewhere southeast of Wolfhezen I spotted the Commander Royal Artillery's tent and Major Philip Tower to whom I gave a report on the situation at the bridge. Meanwhile my crew were changing a shot-up wheel; afterwards I told them to follow Tony Harrison to the gun area, off-load the extra gun ammunition (under our seats), re-net the 22 sets, and check the batteries and return to pick me up.

I did not know where the guns were because when Sherriff and I were looking for a position after leaving the LZ we ran into a cycle patrol.[6] The leader's reaction was quicker than ours, he put his foot down, turned the bike on the rear wheel and vanished into the scrub whence he came with his rifle still slung before we got a round off. As we were following 2nd and 3rd Parachute Battalions he was the last person we were expecting. The cat now being out of the bag, Sherriff said he would bring the guns into action and ordered me to join 1st Parachute Brigade, before I was cut off. My

---

6   Lieutenant Colonel W.F.K. 'Sherriff' Thompson, Commanding Officer, 1st Airlanding Light Regiment, Royal Artillery.

driver returned with a message from Tony Harrison telling me not to wait as he had been ordered by Sherriff to help bring up the guns. Tony had the foresight to put his signaller, Lance Bombardier J.J. Hall into my Jeep and he became indispensable during the next three days. Once again Lance Bombardier Crook took us back through the town with his foot on the floor; this time, almost dark, it was a quieter journey apart from the complaining Jeep engine and the signaller's tuning calls. I had been expecting a road block, but surprisingly the Germans had not thought of it; however, they did seal the road shortly afterwards and thus prevented Tony from re-joining us at the bridge. On arrival I reported to Brigade HQ, re-occupied the observation post, brewed up and got some sleep, once more in radio contact.

Monday, 18th September
At first light we stood-to with 2nd Parachute Battalion and I contacted Buchanan (FOU) telling him that we could contact the guns and that I hoped shortly to see a few ranging rounds on the ground. Brigade HQ sent a message to Divisional HQ via my 22 set and thereby had to accede to my request to open fire on the approach road to the south end of the bridge, which 2nd Parachute Battalion had failed to take after several costly attempts. I promised to hit only Germans and they had nobody south of the river anyway. No. 1 and 3 Batteries were ranged on to the south approaches and much use was made of this target when infantry and armoured columns tried to cross from the south later. In the late afternoon the brigade major came up to look for a field gun which the Germans had sited on crossroads to the north of us. We found it, but Tony said he could not let me have a go at it as they had some troops nearby. Shortly afterwards the gun opened fire and the resulting demolitions were appalling. Tony Hibbert re-appeared and told me to go ahead providing I did not drop a round south of the crossroads. I ordered close target, enemy field gun my position, right-ranging, smoke. The command post queried how a German field gun could be in my position. I explained that I was looking straight down the bore at about 400 yards range, and for God's sake do not hit our chaps. The brigade major told 2nd Battalion to keep their heads down, and I solicited everyone near to help me spot the first round as there were so many fires in the town. True to form and with reference to our first target (which I seem to remember we had called M.1) No. 3 Battery gave me a wonderful first round, about 400 yards over; everyone saw it and we soon put paid to the gun which by now had wrecked the north end of our building. Buchanan (FOU) was helping to break up an attack from the east; Freddie Gough thought I should go to the regimental aid post as I had been hit in the face, fortunately, not seriously. I was startled to see the number of wounded in the basement, testimony to the hard fight 2nd Parachute Battalion were putting up. One of the medical orderlies put on an enormous white turban-like dressing, which my chaps later decided to soil and make less likely to draw fire on the Observation Post (OP).

Tuesday, 19th September
I remember as a day of constant pounding, the Germans shot at us with everything including heavy tanks which were cruising the streets. I think they were loading HE and phosphorous because they were causing so many fires. We collected chunks of masonry and some sandbags we found in the building and built a sangar round the signallers and the set in the corner of the building. Visibility was excellent, as by now we had lost most of the roof and the whole town seemed to be on fire.

Wednesday, 20th September

At first light it all started again, and the Germans seemed determined to eliminate us at the bridge. John Frost spoke to Divisional HQ on my set and told the general that things were getting critical with us, ammunition, medical supplies etc.; he was told they were doing their best to reach us but were themselves being contained. Shortly afterwards John Frost was wounded in both legs by a mortar bomb and Freddie Gough assumed command. The brigade major came to say that arrangements were being made to evacuate the building in the event we were unable to control the fires; we would all help to carry the wounded from the basement. Soon afterwards a tank that had been potting at us hit the corner of the building and pushed our sangar, 22s and most of us down the stairwell. The set was smashed and Lance Bombardier Hall badly hurt; Crook, Lowe, Observation Post Assistant (OPA) and I dug ourselves out of the rubble and carried him down to the regimental aid post, difficult because the stairwell had filled with debris. The cellars were crowded with wounded; we left Hall with the MOs and returned to salvage our gear.

Looking east, the burnt-out remains of the armoured column of SS Panzer-Aufklärungsabteilung 9 under SS Hauptsturmführer Viktor Grabner, destroyed on the morning of the 18th. Oblique photo from Wing Commander 'Sandy' Webb's Spitfire of No. 16 Photo Reconnaissance Squadron, RAF, Monday, 18th September. Major Dennis Munford writes: 'I got to the bridge at about 2000 hours on Sunday, 17th September and reported to Brigade HQ. The brigade major, Tony Hibbert, told me that communications within the division were practically non-existent. I decided to establish an observation post on the roof at the southeast corner of Brigade HQ and another with Tony Harrison in the 2nd Parachute Battalion HQ building. 'Buck', the Forward Observation Officer, would find another east of the road by the river with A Company.' (Photo: Courtesy Gelders Archive)

The 68 set was still functioning but we were unable to contact Captain Buchanan, the FOO east of the road by the river, later, as a POW, I heard that a bomb or shell through the roof of the OP had killed them all but to this day, as far as I know, Buck was never found.[7]

Battalion HQ next door was now burned out and Brigade HQ burning; as everyone else had left the building we clambered down to the ground floor. Shortly afterwards I heard Freddie Gough urgently shouting for me and saw him vanishing up the stairs with the tail of his smock unfastened and smouldering. We called him down and beat out the flames. He told us to cease firing as the Germans had agreed to allow us to remove our wounded to collection points where we should find their medical orderlies. We all helped with this task, not forgetting our own Lance Bombardier Hall, until the indefatigable Freddie ordered us to rendezvous, if possible, in a school on the crossroads north as the truce was broken and 'the bastards are infiltrating our positions.'

Tanks were once again prowling the streets and infantry closing in from all directions, so we had to leave by vaulting boundary walls behind the houses on the main street leading north. We had seen many soldiers killed in the last few days, and I did not think I would be so moved as I was when I came upon Dutch civilians lying dead in their own homes and gardens.

The secret of war lies in the communications.
Napoleon Bonaparte

Bombardier J. Leo Hall, i/c E Troop Signals, 3 Battery, 1st Airlanding Light Regiment, Royal Artillery

For post-D-Day Airborne Operations, I functioned as wireless operator for E Troop Observation Post (OP) in support of 1st Parachute Brigade, dropping with Brigade HQ. The E Troop observation party of three was led by Captain C.A. Harrison, the third member being Gunner 'Jock' R. Morrison; aggressive, brave, the right person to be with in a tight spot.

Sunday, 17th September

Take-off time was to be at about 1000 hours. We expected a first class breakfast such as that cooked for aircrew on an operation day, one that included an egg, a delicacy rare enough in wartime homes and non-existent in army cookhouses. Instead we were greeted as nuisances by the Army Catering Corps of 1st Parachute Brigade who were themselves getting organised for the 1000 hours take-off. We ate unmemorable makeshift food, but once on the airfield, milling around our Dakotas, waiting for the order to board, we were uplifted by an unending supply of dainty boiled ham sandwiches served by motherly members of the Women's Voluntary Service (now WRVS). This was luxury! None of us had seen boiled ham for five years.

The day was a beauty, the flight uneventful. Harrison and Morrison were looking pale and set, so was I, I suppose. Nobody cracked a joke; nobody spoke. For all this none of us would have turned back, for this was it, the day we'd wanted, morale was sky high, determined. I felt like a crusader. Over Holland I saw a burst of flak through the exit doorway; we were flying without the door in position. The three of us were last in the stick, last to exit. I couldn't avoid landing in trees,

---

[7] Captain Henry S. Buchanan, 276993, age 30. 1st Forward Observation Unit, RA. Attached 2nd Parachute Btn. KIA 19th September 1944. No known grave.

but, dangling only six feet from Dutch soil, encountered only a little difficulty. Harrison gave Morrison and me a swig of spirits from his flask then we set off, joining the rest of Brigade HQ on the lower road to the bridge.

It was close country, leafy from the canopy of trees that lined, in my memory, the tracks that led to the narrow, metalled road which was our Lion route to the bridge. The Dutch were ecstatic; the war seemed over to them; well, they knew what the Gestapo was like, but what did they know of the German Army which would fight with unbelievable efficiency – and obey the code of warfare. Did they realise how much havoc the enemy could cause given a couple of snipers, a machine gun and a light field gun? I wanted to tell them that it wasn't over, by any means; there would be killing, devastation, even if all went according to plan. But no; I passed an elderly man, tears streaming down his face as, eyes closed, he sang, 'God Save the King' in English. Young men were urging us on, wanting to help, bringing hijacked trucks, wearing their orange 'Oranje' armbands with patriotic pride that I'd never seen before in my 23 years. *Bang goes number one briefing*, I thought; *I'll trust these people any day; where on earth did that duff 'probably Nazi' rubbish originate?* A theoretical 'play-safe' bit of intelligence, I guessed.

Number two snag was soon known to us; there was to be no coup de main; the gliders had crashed or something. Ah well, never mind; let's get on with it. There were skirmishes ahead, dealt with long before we got to the trouble spot. Soon, at a minor junction, I saw our Jeep – 'RE', the E Troop 'O' party transport. Bombardier M.C. Ogle was at the wheel (Ogle was Harrison's 'Ack', his assistant in the working out details of a shoot from an OP) and Gunner Chrystal, the wireless operator of the 22 set in the Jeep.

'Are you through to the guns?' I asked. Chrystal nodded. *So far so good*, I thought. 'Watch the Dags,' I advised (so called, I think, from the trade name of high quality batteries, 'Dagenite'). 'We don't know when we can get them recharged.' For the same reason I didn't want to open up the 68 set humped along by Morrison, unless told to do so by Harrison. There was also the business of air security. Best to keep the 68 set switched off for the present.

Harrison took the Jeep ahead, with Ogle and Chrystal. For some reason he wanted Morrison and me to carry on with the 68 set on foot. We were on the right-hand side of the road, the river side, although the river must have been, then, several hundred yards away; we couldn't see it. In my memory there were fields, minor roads, hedges, and the canopy of trees having thinned out. To our left were houses, gardens and small buildings, but leisurely placed. Morrison walked in front of me, and as we were passing a minor metalled road which led towards the river I was taken by complete surprise as a German bicycle patrol turned from a parallel road to our advance towards me, up the minor road. They had been cycling against our line of advance. I swung round and walked towards them, my Sten gun pointing at them. But in my surprise there was no aggression; it was a game, in a way. The Germans were quick in their reaction. With rifles slung they were helpless, so off their bikes they tumbled and quickly surrendered to me. Their panniers contained stick grenades. I felt chuffed. Easy! (I have pondered, since about the incident. Surely they must have known that we were there, 500 of us strewn out between Oosterbeek and the bridge. I can only think that they must have been sent from across the river, presumably interrogation found out. Whatever their purpose, they had even less military sense than I had shown in my surprise.) It seemed soon that we came in sight of the Rhine, even now I can't realise that we'd covered three or four miles. We heard a massive explosion to our right rear; it was the German demolition of the railway bridge, one of our secondary objectives. As we approached the built-up waterfront of the town of Arnhem we came to a junction to a major road. (It was the junction of the Lion and Tiger routes, I discovered years later. Tiger was designated to the 3rd Parachute Battalion, but there was no sign of them; of course, I didn't expect any.)

Approaching the Bridge
Several features stay in the mind at the thoughts of this junction (now, 43 years later on, and with a map, I can give its ref as 726777).[8] The Rhine, having negotiated a bend, now swung right as we faced its length upriver, taking the eye to the bridge, the central span high and clear in the far distance. That was an indelible moment in any memory. The broad river-road ran up to our objective, a kind of Strand, promenade-like, well above both water level and the river banks which showed all the accoutrements of river trade. Tall buildings of various sorts lined the road on the town side; it was on the roof of one of these, any one, that I'd had a notion to establish a relay wireless station a few days back, years ago, when we were briefed. As my eyes travelled back towards us along the road from the bridge, and swung to our left, I recall seeing a stationary tram with its passenger trailer, continental fashion, lying abandoned. But most memorable of all was the intermittent call for help from a wounded German a hundred yards, perhaps, down to our right, on the river bank, it seemed. 'Tommy! Help!' he called in a pleading voice. But nobody did. Fortunes of war are cruel; humanity is anaesthetised. *It was probably a trick, anyway,* I comforted myself thinking, *and if not, well, poor sod.* Such is the nature of mental priorities in those conditions that I found myself musing more the oddity of being called 'Tommy'.

Crossing the junction to advance up the road, we on the right moved over to join those on the left, close to the building, the right-hand side being open and too exposed. Nevertheless, I wasn't aware of any German interference of worrying proportions; there was some small arms fire going on most of the time, but nothing close. It seemed an unopposed advance to the bridge. (And indeed it was for us; I had no idea that the other two battalions of 1st Parachute Brigade were being held up by swift and effective German reaction, that we should be the only battalion to reach the divisional objective. There was no military prowess in it, just fortune.)[9]

The Bridge
Darkness had set in by the time we reached the vicinity of the bridge, although the night never proved to be dark particularly to wartime eyes, used to black-out conditions. Here we could see well enough how the river road had to continue under the high bridge. In order to get on the bridge and go over it one had to take a left-hand veer to gain access to a lengthy ramp, embanked on both sides, and overlooked, just by a variety of largish buildings. (That part of the bridge over the river road, the ramp with its embankment, the adjacent buildings with their off-spaces and, to a degree, the centre span over the water was to be our battleground for the next four days, although that centre span was something of a no man's land.)

My next memory is of entering a house with Harrison and Morrison. Why we went there I don't know; as I've remarked, Harrison was a bit like God, moving in mysterious ways; we were used to it; we just followed. It was a large house. Two (I think) prosperous-looking middle-class, middle-aged gentlemen received us without protest. Harrison went through to the back with one of them. I waited with Morrison in a large living room. The place was dark but not gloomy. I had a nasty headache and was able to get a couple of aspirins and a drink of water there. By this time

---

8   Klingelbeekseweg/Utrechtseweg junction.
9   One must not ignore C Company, 3rd Parachute Battalion, plus accompanying troops, REs, RASC, RA etc.

all thoughts of not trusting the Dutch had gone; we were all in this together. We moved out of the house closer to the embankment, closer to where the pillbox and ammo store were brewing up with a marvellous display of HE fireworks. There we waited, now with Chrystal, Ogle and the Jeep. I asked Chrystal if we were through to the guns. He shook his head. I listened; it was as if every snap, crackle and pop in the Milky Way had been captured to the exclusion of any intelligible sound.

'We'll be OK when we get the set out of the Jeep and gain some height,' I said. Chrystal agreed. We weren't worried. We carried on enjoying the fireworks waiting for Harrison's return. He'd be consulting the paras nearby. Harrison joined us once more; we were to establish ourselves with the HQ of 2nd Battalion building. On the uppermost floor the paras had already bashed out the windows with scrupulous care, no fragments of glass to fly around, and erected sandbag firing positions a yard or so back from the gaping windows. Riflemen weighed up their field of fire. I was impressed by the hand-held radios I saw; as clear as a telephone they were; none of the crackling interference dominating our 22. A 2nd Parachute Battalion signaller explained that they were FM sets, I'd never heard of FM before, and outlined the FM principle in a couple of sentences. I marvelled. Why couldn't our own interference troubled FM 22 been a noise-free AM 22? (The FM principle, using a much shorter wave band than that of the AM 22, was more susceptible to screening in the event.) At this stage I can't be sure that we had off-loaded the 22 from the Jeep, nor can I be certain which of the following two decisions came first. I think that it was our patrol along the river road.

The Puzzle of the River Road Trip

It's difficult to put a time on it; few of us carried watches in those days, and fewer still were issued with War Department watches. The sun was fully set; that I well remember. My sure assertion is that it was before midnight, perhaps even an hour or more before. Harrison had come to tell us that we were going to take a trip back along the road, he didn't say how far. We piled into the Jeep, Morrison driving, and Harrison sitting on his right. I stood behind Morrison, Chrystal and Ogle sitting, I think. What of the 22? I just don't remember. But I do recall that near to that time we learned that the brigadier, Lathbury, had gone missing and couldn't be contacted. Everything seemed fairly quiet apart from distant small arms fire; the river road was relatively peaceful. I had no qualms about the trip, so I remained standing, able to see more. Harrison was intent on looking around as well as ahead as we travelled. I think that he, in one of his rare bursts of confidence, told us about Lathbury, and I know that we assumed that the trip, patrol, call it what you will was to look for signs of the missing brigadier. (We Other Ranks in the Jeep knew nothing of the swift German reaction to the advance of the other two battalions making for the bridge. Had we known there may well have been less levity among us as we proceeded. Harrison was well aware of the general situation through the OC Recce group, and Major Munford, our Battery OC, who by that time had arrived at the bridge; both majors, having seen the German reaction, had turned to the Lion river road route for progress to the bridge.) I could see quite well along the road. As we travelled the small arms fire exchanged seemed to be around the bridge, although at the time I thought that much of it was the pillbox and the magazine still brewing-up. More exchanges came from over the river road buildings from somewhere in Arnhem town. But the river road, the river and both north and south embankments were still. Suddenly I saw a figure lying across our path. Morrison bumped the Jeep over it. We stopped, Harrison alert.

'What was that?' he asked.

'A German, Sir,' I said.

'Is he dead?'

'He is now,' I replied. I didn't fancy examining a bloody mess of flesh for signs of life. We pulled Morrison's leg as we drove on, pointing out the effect that his sex life was having on his eyesight. Harrison didn't join in; he wouldn't, of course.

Tommy! Tommy!

Harrison appeared undecided when we reached the end of the river road, the end, that is to say, in the sense that whilst the river continued to bend to the left the road we were on took to the right. A minor road, the 'Lion' route back lay ahead. It was the junction, mentioned above. There was no sign of any divisional conflict, no movement. I wondered what was happening. Where were the Jerries? Small arms fire was continual rather than continuous – but distant. Then, as we paused, above the ticking of the Jeep engine I heard 'Tommy! Tommy!' cry again, the one of a few hours ago, but very much weaker. It was genuine, all right. What to do was decided by Harrison. 'We'll go back,' he told Morrison. The drive back to the bridge was without event.

Again we waited whilst Harrison went to report or consult or something, we were completely in the dark about situation or purpose. He wasn't away long before he returned to say, 'We're joining Major Munford in Brigade HQ.'

Monday 18th September
0001 Hours, D+1

I felt peeved at that decision; no explanation accompanied it, but I'd no intention of letting Battery HQ 'O' party have radio initiative. I think it was the first time that I'd heard that Munford and his lot were at the bridge, or had planned to go to the bridge. They'd no right to be there, of course; this was our spot, our show, E Troop's. What on earth was Harrison thinking about? Or, rather, Munford, since he was OC. Mealy-mouthed, we moved the 22 and all our gear up to the top of Brigade HQ building, up into the attic. Nobody told me to set up there, but we needed height. I seem to have a strong memory that Munford's signallers had much the same idea; they were there fiddling with their own 22. I found some satisfaction in noticing their difficulties in getting in touch with the Command Post Control. I deliberately took notice of them, as if they were the second eleven, and pretty poor stuff at that. I looked for a suitable spot in that attic.

Almost above the open-tread stair which led down was a roof skylight. I set up under it, pushing the fully extended aerial through, several feet above the roof. That wasn't without qualms; I could readily hear Farrands' voice: 'Bombardier, are you not aware that your aerial is the very thing to attract the German mortars when daylight comes?'[10] The aerial stayed as put. The interference, unfortunately, blotted out all other sound when the 22 was switched on. I was tempted to twiddle the dials. The noise in the headset was typical of that caused by unsuppressed electrical machinery or a nearby petrol engine; I wondered even if the set could be faulty. (I thought at the time that the problem was confined to me; I knew nothing of other sets experiencing the same one. A report quoted by Perrett and others says that the radio nets were 'overlaid by a distant but more powerful British transmitter operating on the same frequency.' But the 22 sets at the bridge, and there must have been at least six of them, were on several different frequencies – different nets; to my mind electrical interference was the cause because of its characteristic sound and its spread over the

---

10 Lieutenant N.F. Farrands, 3 Battery, E Troop, Gun Position Officer (GPO).

frequencies. Funnily enough, the German sets must have had the same difficulty. I wonder how it affected their counter-moves. No writer has mentioned that, to my knowledge.)

I don't recall exactly what made me try the 68 set that Morrison had kit-bagged down in the drop and had humped the seven miles from the DZ to Brigade HQ attic. But there it lay, doing nothing, not earning its keep. Well, you try anything in difficulties; at least it would tell me if the interference was just that and not an internal fault of the 22. I set up the 68, the aerial sections, each about a foot or so long, not quite reaching the roof timbers above our heads. Then I switched on.

At first there seemed to be little difference in reception; then it was apparent the noise wasn't quite so strident, not so penetrative, something to expect on an indoor aerial. Using the 22 I called up Control, the Battery Command Post a few miles west with the guns. I didn't know how far away they'd be, five or six was my guess. (Actually it was little more than three.) I sent a standard 'report my signals' request. Back came an immediate reply, garbled on the 22, as clear as one could have hoped for on the 68. It seemed a miracle. So my luck had held. The time was, perhaps, 0100 hours D+1. (I believe the success is simply explained; the height of the 22 aerial beat the screening. It is also likely that the Command Post 22 with its own aerial was, at that stage of the battle, more exposed than it would be when the shooting really got going later on. The interference, muted on the 68 sufficiently for the Command Post signal to make its coherent mark, was surely overcome by the indoor aerial. But it must be remembered that the 68 also had height.)

Next, I ought to have sent one of the other signallers to find Munford or Harrison with a 'wireless through, Sir' message. They couldn't have been far away, either in 2nd Parachute Battalion HQ or below with 1st Parachute Brigade HQ. But I didn't, I expected one of them to come up to see how things were going on. Neither did. Well, there was no air of urgency about the bridge area that I could detect. There was continual exchange of small arms fire which I mistook at the time for the pillbox and the magazine in their death throes. There were two things on my mind; conserving the Dags and the 68 battery, and keeping off the air as much as possible to deny the Germans any listening intelligence. So I switched off both sets, occasionally switching on to ask for a signals report. Strangely, the Command Post asked for no information; there was no 'officer to set' or 'fetch sunray.' I decided to stay with the set throughout the night and see to the registration of the area which there must be at first light. I can't remember how many of our ORs spent the night in the attic, perhaps three of us. I lay back and dozed, content that I'd pulled one over that Battery HQ lot, and was through to the guns.

Sometime during that night, I can't say when, I got the news from the Battery HQ lads that Harrison had gone to look for the missing Lathbury and that Munford would be registering the area at first light. I wondered what sort of planning that was to leave just one artillery officer at the Primary Divisional Objective with four signallers, two OP acks and Morrison!

It was as if both sides had been waiting for the referee's dawn whistle in order for play to begin seriously. I'd wondered what moves had been made during darkness; we'd appeared to be content to sit the whole thing out until XXX Corps came, which they would, of course, any hour now. No point in getting worked up with things; there were few Germans about. I was in comfortable contact with Command Post back at the gun position; daylight had eased the interference. I do believe I was able to carry out two-way traffic without using the 68 set all the time. I had had a fairly comfortable night on the wooden floor, cat-napping most of the time, waiting for dawn and Munford. He came up into the attic and took up a position where, looking south and along the bridge, he could readily see also the approaches to it on the southern side of the river. The attic had generous headroom and was plentifully windowed. I remember vaguely the timbered ceiling with apexes. (Later reading confirms all but for the roof which was flat.) Without any ado or situation reports or what had happened – if anything, during darkness he steadily registered the whole of the observable area south of the bridge, and I transmitted his orders to the battery position. There was no difficulty in transmission.

(Registration normally follows the occupation of artillery positions. The shooting officer selects likely targets, e.g. a crossroads, a high prominence, a set of buildings, etc., anything of use to the enemy or being used by him in an annoying way. The shooting officer uses a single gun to find the range and direction of the target. Once established by him he knows that if all the guns use the same data the target will be smothered with a spread of HE. The data is recorded at the guns and given a number, e.g., 'record as Target Easy One' is a common order for the registration of data with troop (i.e. the four guns of 'Easy' Troop) requirements in mind. Then, sooner or later, the shooting officer at the OP will order, 'Target Easy One, one round gunfire, fire!' to ensure swift response to need from E Troop.)

Munford's targets were registered as 'Mike' targets, i.e. regimental targets, targets for the 24 guns of the regiment to engage. An officer wanting a target to be registered as a regimental one must have good reason for it, and a fair rank. Well, of course, Munford was a major and the targets represented probable threats to the Primary Divisional Objective. The orders were received by 3 Battery CPO and GPOs. Soon enemy activity made for calls on various Mike targets previously registered, and were answered swiftly by the guns – rounds on the ground well within a minute, the time of flight of a shell being no mean item. (I thought that the 24 guns were responding; I'd forgotten that those of 2 Battery were due to arrive later on the second lift. Moreover, 1 Battery had to support the LZs, DZs and the bridge within its range since those zones and the bridge were ten miles apart, allowing a little for target area. The range of the American 75mm Howitzer is, I'm told, five miles, and inaccurate at its extreme.)

That morning, D+1, saw a number of exciting shoots. I recall with yesterday's clarity the one recounted by C. Ryan when a full scale rush of assault vehicles charged over the bridge from the southern end. Somebody shouted, '30 Corps!' but bursts of firing confirmed the opposite. Within minutes everybody was firing off something; not me, of course, concentrating on orders to the guns, or the brigade's 22 set operator nearby, or Munford's own 22 set operator. I don't know which net Munford's operator was concerned with; I do know that it wasn't the battery net. But the success of our aggression against the vehicles raised morale even higher than it had been.

Sometime round this time, late morning, the E Troop 22 had established itself as the reliable one, with its 68 back-up. Perhaps I'd troughed into the battery netting signal more accurately; perhaps it was the position and height of the aerial; whatever it was, I couldn't help feeling an inner wave of smug satisfaction. I ceased to worry about Dags running down when word came to the attic that Brigade HQ, down below, were seeing to all recharging. They wanted, also, our packs of 24-hour rations (each of us had two) and our water-bottles; the ACC lads were going to sort out food and drink in bulk. Well, it couldn't be any blander than that abysmal D-Day breakfast. But I was glad of the arrangements. (Strange, I have no memory whatsoever, not the slightest, of eating drinking, sleeping, washing, shaving or any latrine visits during the four day battle for control of the bridge.)

RA Link to Oosterbeek, Midday, Perhaps

There were two or three officers on one occasion observing through the Brigade HQ attic window. Munford may have been one of them. Another, the brigade major, I think, wanted some words with division, but his 22 was out of touch. With unaccustomed deference Munford, after checking that I was through, offered the facility. (If Frost was one of the group it would account for Munford's humility.) From then on the brigade officers and others used the Royal Artillery 22 regularly; I took no record of the messages; they were usually officer to officer exchanges.

(I had no idea until more than 20 years had passed that the Royal Artillery channel was the only reliable one for much of the four days. I was under the impression that my 22 was being used just because it happened to be there, convenient. I knew that there were R/T difficulties, but no notion of their acuteness. Had I known I could have done something about easing them. It wouldn't of course, have affected the course of the battle.)

There is, however, one important message that I have clear memories of sending. It is a puzzle because no accounts that I know of mention it. It could be, and probably was, the occasion mentioned above when the brigade officers first used the RA set to reach division at Oosterbeek.

Call for Air Support (Monday, 18th September D+1 – About Midday)
The call came from three officers in Brigade HQ attic OP, possibly Frost or Hibbert (brigade major), Gough (recce OC) and Munford. The brigade 22 was out of touch so the artillery 22 took the call. I was the operator. The officers discussed the area to be treated. I think that I transmitted the message given me phrase by phrase, though it might have been Munford who phrased it to Lieutenant Sam Wilkinson, the 3 Battery CPO. Of the message I am certain of the figure 1000, certain of a square to be bombed/strafed and certain that one corner of that square was the southern end of the bridge. The message was rather longer than I give below, but what I give is what I remember. Although I could make it more plausible by a few adjustments, I have resisted that mild temptation. 'A one-thousand bomber raid required on the square mile south-west of the southern end of the bridge.' No map references were given. The message passed, we got on with our ordinary business of artillery support and officer-to-officer chats.

Communications were reasonably clear without resorting to the 68 set. Perhaps an hour elapsed after the air support call when I was contacted by the 3 Battery CPO operator to tell me that the message was through to the Commander Royal Artillery (CRA) at Divisional HQ. (I hadn't realised that the CRA handled air-support until then).[11] I recognised the operator's soft Birmingham slant as that of Lance Bombardier Willis, so the reception must have been quite reasonable. I was friendly with Willis, having been with him in the 169th Field Regiment RA, though he joined the Airborne Forces more than a year before I did. I felt highly chuffed that we, the RA sigs, had got the important brigade-division request through. But the support it asked for never came. (Bombing/strafing support would not be available at the same time as air supplies or lifts were being undertaken, and this was the day of the second lift. Moreover, Air-Marshal Sir Arthur Coningham, the AOC of the 2nd Tactical Air Force, felt that (a) the army asked for destructive raids too readily and (b) it was bad policy to destroy areas of occupied territory being liberated, and (c) the enemy could often use bombed urban areas as effectively as if the buildings had been spared. One surmises that these considerations would not have prevented his positive reaction to

---

11 In fact air support requests were to be provided by two US Air Support Signal Teams attached to 1st Airborne Division. Each team was equipped with a modified Jeep called a 'Veep', fitted with two radios (HF) radio SCR-193 and a (VHF) SCR-542. Situated behind Div HQ, Hartenstein, under command of Lt Col R.G. Loder Symonds, CRA. Communication was virtually non-existent and by the 20th both Veeps had been put out of action by mortar fire.

the request had he only received it, remembering that the southern end of the bridge was far from urban density in 1944. But he didn't receive it; in fact no account that I have read mentions such a call from the bridge; and I must say that I find that amazing. C. Ryan mentions a request for air support on Browning's desk on the 19th; the request that I transmitted was on the 18th, I feel sure.)

Then there was the business of 'The Gun.' The Germans brought a 150mm piece to the south bank and began pounding us with it. Immediate calls for our own guns to respond were unsuccessful; for once, when support was critical to our positions, I couldn't get through. I was particularly relieved when our mortars opened up and neutralised it with a direct hit. Failures like that weigh heavily on a signaller.

Tuesday, 19th September
Was it D+2 when Munford told me to detail a man to join a party to storm the bridge – a suicide mission if ever there was one, but a desperate attempt that may just, just, succeed? Such were my thoughts as I groaned. I was unfitted for the task of detailing anybody to undertake a job with a 50/50 or worse risk of death. It was to be done by an armoured carrier and, perhaps, one of Gough's gun-toting Jeeps. The approach to our end of the bridge was cluttered with the brew-up remnants of the ill-fated German vehicles of the previous day; the armoured carrier would have to weave its lumbering way through helped only by our own covering fire, and surprise. I pitied those in that carrier, a tracked, shallow-slung, open-topped affair with low sides of 3/8ths steel at a guess; its protection was against nothing heavier than small arms fire. As for the Jeep, there was no protection at all. Well, there was only one person for it: Morrison, the truculent, sexy, boozy, god-swearing Glaswegian. But a soldier. 'Sorry, Jock,' I said, 'it's got to be you.' He took it without comment and went straight to report with the rifle I'd dropped with.

A little later I saw him at the back of Brigade HQ, crouching as if ready for the order, bayonet fixed, wearing protective armour – this is my last picture of him. I gave a sigh of relief when the venture was called off. I neither saw nor heard anything of Morrison after that; I felt sure that he'd attach himself to the 2nd Parachute Battalion riflemen for a bit of real soldiering.

Later that day, early afternoon, Munford said that he was going below and that if any officer came up calling for support from the guns I was to order a round of gunfire at Target Mike One. I smiled. *My goodness,* I thought, *what a crazy operation we were on!* One battalion with a few odds and sods holding a Divisional Primary Objective, the business being controlled by a trio of majors with occasional nods from a half-colonel who had his own command to worry about, and here was me, a two-stripe signal bombardier with authority to fire the regimental guns in this laughable cock-up. A good thing that XXX Corps would be soon be with us!

I remember looking out often through the glassless windows and seeing an ever increasing number of blazing buildings. I saw the St Eusebius Church brewing up and shivered a little; we could have had an OP in the steeple. The ring of fire seemed to be the German plan, enclosing us, squeezing us. But none of us ever doubted that XXX Corps was on the way, only an hour or so, perhaps, from the bridge. Morale, never low, surged at hearing a distant 'Woho Mohamed!' battle cry from North Africa.

With Munford below I had to suppress an exciting urge to drop one on Mike One; that would have been worth a paragraph in the *Gunner* magazine! I wondered why we didn't drop a single round there at annoyingly unpredictable intervals; there seemed to be no shortage of 75mm HE rounds. The odd round can cause disruption to a concentration, a worthwhile expenditure at that stage. I pondered about the action I should take if Munford became a casualty. No word had come from him; did he think he was fire-proof? And why on earth did he arrange for Harrison to leave the bridge early on D+1 when there was potential need for even three artillery officers? We had a surplus of signallers; five, in my memory, a couple of OP Acks and Morrison, all to one officer. We had a spare 22 and a spare 68. I'd thought of a probable forward-forward OP at the other end of the bridge; there'd be no screening from there. It was 50/50 that we'd have to move across shortly to meet the forward elements of XXX Corps; we'd have to be ready to spot and correct for their artillery. Did anybody know the frequency? Well, the spare 68 could twiddle for that.

But a big why was the failure of the Germans to do something about the OP I was in. They'd attended to the two churches, St Eusebius and St Walburge's. Surely they knew the nature of the Brigade HQ building; could they still not see my aerial? Probably not; it would be visible but not distinctive only from parts of the northern ramp and the bridge. The southern bank of the Rhine was too distant for them to spot evidence of me but not for Munford and company to see evidence of them and their activities. One was soon woken from any reverie. Explosions and automatic fire was incessant, continuous, above me and all round. I was indeed lucky. I had the advantage of a wireless headset designed to cut down extraneous sound. Moreover my perception had to be tuned into that headset, on its intelligence. Battle noise was thereby attenuated. Again such noise is something that you grow used to tolerating, like speed on a motorway – provided you don't have to cope with the stress of excessive explosions and have to take on too many instances of imminent danger; then of course, shellshock, battle fatigue, takes over. It may have been late on that D+2 Tuesday when Munford wanted a relay running to a floor below. He didn't give a reason. The relay cable was thickish to allow for transmission and reception control by means of a trigger switch on the microphone and two headsets. The 22 in the attic still needed a signaller in attendance to monitor tuning and to deal with routine matters. When on duty I was in the attic. I was never below with the relay.

I recall having the unworthy thought that Munford had abandoned attic observation because it was safer below. In fact it wasn't. Attacks on the building were lateral; the two lower floors more vulnerable, although the northeast corner of the attic had been blown off at an early stage and through the gap came automatic fire from time to time. Two of our signallers were slightly wounded by such a burst (Gunner Bowles and another). It skipped me. So again I was lucky. There were some occasions when I felt some anxiety, but never fear; the burning buildings that surrounded us seemed to be connected with a super Guy Fawkes Night rather than with danger. I felt something of a cheat, tucked away comfortably in the comparative safety of the Brigade HQ attic, seemingly ignored by the Germans, while the lads of 2nd Parachute Battalion and Morrison were battling it out with bullet and bayonet and not much else only yards away from my haven, my place of non-aggression.

I well recall either Gough or Hibbert speaking over the brigade 22 in the attic. The brigade signaller (probably a signalman of the Royal Signals) had picked up a XXX Corps unit. There was no attempt on our part to deal with niceties of security. 'This is the First Airborne Division at Arnhem,' he said. After a good deal of understandable caginess on their part they did say that XXX Corps were to put in an attack at…? I've forgotten the time which they gave us; I could hear their voices quite distinctly through the 22 headset that the major was wearing. None of us believed the promise of attack. You just don't say things like that in clear, not unless you're desperate, which they weren't. Neither were we really, although we had expressed frequent wishes by that time that XXX Corps would take their fingers out. I can't place the time of this of this wireless conversation on that D+3 Tuesday; in my memory it may have been on the D+4 Wednesday, but well before noon.

Wednesday, 20th September

We knew that we were in a tight corner, but faith in XXX Corps never waned. German strength had been unbelievably able, different altogether from what Intelligence had briefed us to expect, yet still we'd coped. When Munford received a 'Sunray to set' call to be warned that 16 tanks (I think it was) were heading our way, he'd exclaimed, 'Sixteen? I didn't think they'd sixteen in the whole of Germany!' There was never any concern shown in Munford's manner; he was calmness itself throughout without displaying any laid-back affectation. This incident happened on the morning of D+4, but it may have been D+3, before the relay was run.

Certainty accompanies the next group of events on that fateful Wednesday. Towards midday I felt that we were losing contact with Oosterbeek; our transmissions were not reaching them and we could only just make out the voice of Control as it spoke to other stations on the net. There was a background of annoying but tolerable interference. I formed the view that their conditions had worsened, as if they were operating on half-charged Dags, whereas our own conditions had realised an easing from interference. It was possible that they too, were under constant attack, affecting the position or function of their aerial. (It didn't occur to me to check my own aerial which may have been shot short, above roof level. I cursed myself afterwards for that omission.) I sent a 'Report my signals' call to Control. No reply. I tried again, several times without result. When Control spoke to another station, very weakly, I twiddled to re-net more keenly, still no result. Then I decided to try Morse. I went below to the Jeeps at the back of the building to get a Royal Artillery Code from the dashboard compartment. No Codes there. The Royal Artillery Code reduces every conceivable gun control order to a list of two-letter groups. For instance, the order 'Fire!' is tapped out as WA; it was the only group that one was permitted to memorise. I asked the E Troop signaller (Chrystal) where the Codes were. They hadn't been told to bring any, nor had the Battery HQ team, and I cursed being away from the troop when the Jeeps were serviced for loading on the gliders. Back at the 22 in the attic I started by tapping out the call-sign (now forgotten). I felt that I could abbreviate orders although I'd have to go easy on the figures, which always caused problems to RA signallers armed only with a basic and largely unpractised skill; it's easier to send Morse than it is to receive it. I did realise that to call for a round of a gun fire on Target Mike One (VE AAA TGT M1 1RD GF WA AR) was just as likely to be received as six rounds of gun fire on Target Mike Six this because the DOT-DASH-DASH-DASH-DASH for *one* was likely to be on our level of proficiency confused with a DASH-DOT-DOT-DOT-DOT for *six*. But it was never put to the test. Tapping out the call sign not only got no reply, it was also interrupted by Control passing an R/T message to another station, showing that the Morse Call Sign meant nothing to the Control Operator. From the situation I inferred that my Morse was just another element in the chaos of interference; it had no relevance to the operator's perception. Again I despaired at my absence from the troop once the call sign had been issued, when I might have had a little influence in imprinting the pattern of the call sign Morse on 3 Battery operators.

Still, my 22 was not being used. I had the impression that German forces were so close that artillery fire, even if I could get through to the guns, might well cause as much havoc to our own forces as to the Germans. Then there came an incident that I can only describe as theatrical. I went below to tell Chrystal that it was time for his stint; I felt that I'd been in the attic long enough without a break.

He refused to go. 'I'm not going up there,' he said. All the signallers were standing at the foot of the attic steps, taking notice. Up the steps the battle noise was increasing.

'It's your turn, Jock; I'm ordering you to go!'

But Chrystal wouldn't budge. 'I dinna care,' he said, quite evenly. 'You can shoot me if you want, but I'm not going up there!'

Well, here it was a test of my soldiering qualities. Chrystal had been shelled in an Italian OP; his back was still heavily scarred where falling masonry had put him in hospital there. The others were gripped, it seemed, by the drama. I knew I couldn't send one of them instead. I was glad that Munford wasn't a witness.

'Don't be bloody silly,' I said, and went back up the steps to monitor the set. I never pretended to be a strong soldier. I think that soon – how soon I don't know – after that, it must have been evening, perhaps an hour before dusk, our 22 the only set in the attic; with the general situation lost on me, no traffic, no messages, no gunfire for hours; lying there by the 22, I felt a hand on my shoulder.

It was Munford. 'Come on,' he said. 'We're evacuating.'

'What about the set, Sir?' I asked.

'Fuck the set!' he replied.

We crept to the stairway, then some discipline made me turn back to switch off the set. For the same reason I didn't spin the dials; there was the possibility of re-occupation. I smiled at the amusing side to this compulsive action. I didn't attempt to raise Oosterbeek; there was no point. (The CO, Lieutenant Colonel Thompson, may well have regarded the closure of Thompson–Munford link as abrupt, but it wasn't; it just faded out, at the Thompson end!).

Last Hours at the Bridge

At the foot of the attic steps stood a group of the Battery HQ party, two or three of them with Munford. They stood in the space between the steps and the regular stairway leading below to the first floor. The din of the battle was almost deafening to me now that I was without a headset for the first time in hours; my perception took in the significance of ambient explosions. A Tiger tank was patrolling up and down outside having a field day, potting at whatever it wanted without any armour-piercing opposition. As I joined the Battery HQ group (there was no sign of Bombardier Ogle or Jock Chrystal from E Troop) I recall with certain clarity reaching for a cigarette from my Bren gun pouch, saying as I did so, 'It's getting bloody hot up there–' when a mighty explosion to my right (the southeast corner of Brigade HQ 2nd floor) hurled me in an instant – literally – some fifteen feet into the stairway crashing me against its far wall, on my back, head down the stair. I felt a complete numbness in my right hip outside of my buttock then I felt the trickle of warm blood beyond the numb part. Several thoughts occurred within a second: *So this is being wounded, it's a kind experience, everything anaesthetised with numbness, I wonder if my buttock's been shot away, and that impact, hurling me bodily so far from a standing start. I'll never believe again how a man can take a Hollywood bullet without at least falling over from the impact. How lucky I was again to be reaching for a fag or my right elbow would have been shattered.*

Munford was the first down; there was a moment's hesitation how to handle me. 'Grab my legs,' I said, 'there's nothing broken.' Well, it felt like that and fortunately it was so. But my right leg was completely paralysed. The fact that nerves vital for movement may have been cut never entered my head. Munford took my feet, and another my shoulders. They carried me down to the place where the medical officer (Logan) was operating on the innards of some unlucky para, and laid

Aerial photograph of the Arnhem bridge area on Friday 22nd September. The full extent of the fire damage can be seen in the burnt-out buildings surrounding the bridge. (Photo: Courtesy NCAP3613 US 7GR/3399)

me nearby, on the floor; there was little room. As a medic was cutting up my trousers to put on a dressing, another para came in, clutching his stomach. Logan glanced to his right and exclaimed 'Morphine!' when the para puked blood and guts over my face and head.

My face roughly wiped, my wound dressed, I was hauled to my feet by a couple of bearers who helped me out to the cellar where other wounded, now treated, were lying. The journey there, now upright, right leg useless, was an ordeal. I passed out twice, one after another, through loss of blood, and underwent the most bizarre fantasies as I was coming round, the same in each case; we were fighting, all of us in that space where I was, hand to hand, anything, when forward elements of XXX Corps infantry came bursting in to our relief, but were they XXX Corps or weren't they, they were, but, as I came round, they weren't.

'How long was I out?' I asked the medics.

'A couple of seconds,' said one. *Heavens!* I thought; *there's an eternity in a second.* But what made the biggest impression on me, now that I was vertical again, was the sight and sound of so many men, officers and ORs, moaning, whimpering for comfort, lining the walls and staircase, wounded, but not in the flesh; in the very depth of their psyches, a shattered hold on reality now regressed to childhood, a revelation to me of battle fatigue. They could take no more, and put me to shame.

They laid me in a small room in the cellar with a few other wounded, all on the floor. A medic was tending to someone in the darkness, cradling his head, giving him sips of water or bathing his face. I heard shouts from outside for an English-speaking German prisoner then, later, for the walking wounded. I sensed that the Germans would soon take over. There were a couple of Mills bombs clipped on my belt. They'd been there for four days. Thinking that I'd be better thought of without them, I put them on a low shelf by my side. The medic, still tending his patient, kept announcing '*Kamerad*!' from time to time until the wounded officer told him to shut up.

A casual German came in, rifle slung, looked around, picked up one of my Mills bombs (silly blighter!), put it back and went. Soon more came to clear us out, gently. Two of them got me to my feet and, with great patience, helped me out of the front of the building, across the courtyard where several dead lay, their ankles relaxed, their jaws jutting upwards. One was German. I was laid on the embankment in front of the Brigade HQ building. It was ablaze, flames leaping from our attic. But I was glad of the fire. I felt cold in the chill of the darkness. A young SS private came to me, gave me a swig of ersatz coffee from his water bottle, stuck a cigarette in my mouth, lit it, and disappeared into the flame- flickered darkness with '*Auf wiedersehen*!'

More came to help a group of us into a nearby half-track, none too gently. When we saw a dead German lying on the half-track floor and one of us pointed it out, the Germans showed some anger. It was a painful ordeal for us to clamber as best we could into the back of the open half-track. Most of us had leg wounds and were not in absolute need of stretchers. The half-track soon got underway, the Germans taking us from the battle zone, as, I understand, the Geneva Convention obliged them to do.

Sergeant Norman Swift, A Troop, 1st Parachute Squadron, Royal Engineers

Sunday, 17th September

The flight to Arnhem was quite uneventful. I think the most memorable thing was the fighter escort, quite amazing and comforting. The drop too was more like an exercise rather than the real thing. I saw our Squadron Sergeant Major, Les Ellis, carrying a dead partridge, on which he had landed. The blue smoke for our RV was clearly visible and in no time we formed up and moved off towards Oosterbeek and Arnhem. The only signs of the enemy were a few German POWs, pressed into service loading gear onto Jeeps and trolleys.

By the time we reached Oosterbeek dusk was falling, and leading my troop, I saw what I thought was a 'Teller mine' in the middle of the road. Halting the lads, I went forward and to my embarrassment, found the Teller mine to be the circular shade of a street lamp. How it came to be there goodness knows, but it wasn't the result of enemy action. In fact, the first time we were fired upon occurred at a road crossing in the outskirts of Arnhem. A burst of machine gun fire ripped down the road we were crossing. No one was hurt but our loaded canvas trolley received a direct hit, the most serious casualty being a demijohn of rum!

Later that evening we occupied the school with members of B Troop, and various odd-bods from the battalions, Captain Mackay was in overall command and I was directed to take charge of two of the upper rooms with members of my troop.[12]

Monday, 18th September
Incidents I remember most clearly from those days in the school are as follows.

Some of the lads thinking I had been wounded when they saw one of my trouser legs soaked with what appeared to be blood. In fact it was rusty water from a fractured radiator.

The defiant German crew-member of the armoured car which ran off the main road and finished up beneath our window. Although obviously badly wounded, he still fired his pistol towards the school.

Sapper 'Ginger' Partridge having the foresight shot off his rifle during the Monday fracas when the German armoured vehicles attempted to cross the bridge.[13]

Tuesday, 19th September
A large group of German infantry gathered in the school grounds under cover of darkness. We were told to hold out fire until ordered, then hit them with all we'd got. I went into a passageway leading from our rooms where an unmanned window, suitably blocked with furniture, faced the gardens. When we received the command to fire, I threw a 36 grenade through the window. At least, that was my intention. Imagine my horror when the grenade hit the wooden cross-piece of the window, bounced back and landed amongst the piled up furniture! Luckily, I was the only one in the passage so, with a yell of 'GRENADE', I dived back into the room. Thank heavens no one was hurt. I also remember cries of the German wounded after this incident: '*Wasser, Tommy, Wasser*' but there was no way we could help.

A pendulum clock hanging on the wall opposite one of the windows lasted until Tuesday morning when a stray shot caused it to fall. We wrapped our boots in torn clothing, pyjamas, found in the school, the idea being to deaden the noise of our movements; Venetian blinds were

---

12 The Van Limburg Stirum School, in the Eusebiusbuitensingel.
13 Sapper F. Ginger Partridge recalls the incident: 'Norman was right, it was my rifle, we were together at the time and both of us were wounded in the incident. I had just left my Bren gun with my No. 2 and went off for something, maybe the call of nature or to try and get a drink; I just can't remember. When the call went up of 'armour attack' I grabbed a rifle and manned a window. I got hit in the head, it knocked me down, and it must have been a piece of masonry as it was not a deep wound. I just put my hand up, got a handful of blood and in fright, put my other hand to the back of my head to see if it had gone through. What a fool. We had many good laughs since.'

Two photographs taken in 1945 of the Red School. Above, looking northwest along Eusebius Buitensingel, the building was occupied briefly on the 17th by Mackay before his withdrawal to the Van Limburg Stirum School next door. (Photo: Courtesy Gelders Archive)

Looking northeast from the lane running parallel to the bridge ramp outside the Van Limburg Stirum School (just off the picture to the right). In the foreground are the remains of one of Grabner's burnt-out half-tracks. (Photo: Courtesy Gelders Archive)

lowered over some of the windows to prevent movement within being seen from outside. Sapper (Poacher) Paine crawled from room to room with welcome mess tins of lukewarm tea from time to time.

Armour-piercing (AP) shells, fired by German tanks, coming straight through the walls of the room and creating so much dust that we thought we had been blinded.[14] Captain Mackay told me to gather any Gammon bombs the lads had left and we would try and get the Tiger tank under one of the school walls. My relief when, with a canvas bucket containing the bombs, we started to go back up that big, wide, main staircase, when the ceiling of the landing collapsed, putting a stop to that idea.[15] By Tuesday night, many buildings round about us were on fire. It seemed as if it were 'snowing' fire.

Wednesday, 20th September

I visited some of the wounded lying in a large landing. In particular, Corporal Bill Hazelwood, one of my corporals, mortally wounded, unconscious and clasping a photograph of his wife and children.[16] The cries of 'Whoa-Mohammed' grew fewer as our positions were overrun. We were fighting fires in the upper part of the school and then prepared to leave the school because the fire had finally won. With three others, we carried a badly wounded Major Lewis on a mattress, whoever was in front of me had half his face blown away and fell without a sound.[17] There was bedlam, shouting and shooting and the stink of smoke; Sapper Butterworth was shot as he went forward with a white cloth on his rifle.[18] I was directed by a Jerry soldier to leave Major Lewis in a cellar. The major asked me for water so I stayed behind to leave him my water bottle and was chased out with my arms raised by another German soldier. From outside the school, I looked back to see Sapper Bretherton emerge from a doorway and fall with a bullet in the head. His wife had been expecting a baby on or about the 17th.[19]

I remember the kind treatment we received from our captors, even to being given cigarettes and drinks of wine. It was only later that the rear echelon troops, who were no doubt more afraid of us than we of them, got a bit nasty. We were marched through the streets of Arnhem singing '*Roll out the Barrel*', whilst our German guards sheltered in doorways from the strafing of British fighter planes overhead. The citizens of Arnhem surreptitiously gave us 'V' signs as we, the soldiers who had come to liberate them, but instead brought so much death and destruction, were marched off to captivity.

---

14 Around 1900 hours, two Panzer VI 'Tiger I' tanks under command of Leutnant Knaack and Feldwebel Barneki fired HE followed by AP shot at the school before withdrawing at dusk. The two tanks, Panzerkampfwagen VI Ausf.E belonged to S.Pz.Kp Hummel had preceded the other twelve Tiger I tanks belonging to the unit and arrived at the bridge early evening. They were immediately placed under command of KGr. Brinkmann and were sent into action.
15 The Gammon bomb was designed by Captain R.S. Gammon MC, 1st Parachute Brigade, whilst in North Africa in 1943. The bomb consisted of a variable amount of plastic explosive contained in an elasticised stockinette bag, a metal cap, and a fuse. Used primarily against armoured vehicles or infantry.
16 Corporal William V. Hazelwood, 1913439, aged 25, A Troop, 1st Parachute Squadron RE. Died of wounds 20 September 1944.
17 Major R. Peter Lewis, Officer Commanding, C Company, 3rd Parachute Battalion.
18 Sapper Norman Butterworth, 2141624, aged 27, B Troop, 1st Parachute Squadron, RE. Wounded in both legs, died of his wounds in Apeldoorn.
19 Sapper John Bretherton, 2196447, aged 27, 'A' Troop, 1st Parachute Squadron RE.

1st Parachute Squadron Royal Engineers being led away from the Van Limburg Stirum School, down Johan van Oldenbarneveltstraat, afternoon of the 20th September. *Left to right:* Sergeant Norman Swift, A Troop; Sapper Charlie Grier, B Troop; supporting Sapper Dick Robb, A Troop. (Photo: author's private collection)

Corporal Dave Thomas, A Troop, 1st Parachute Squadron, Royal Engineers

Sunday, 17th September
The drop on that Sunday in September 1944 was like a scheme back in England, for us anyway, that is 1st Parachute Brigade. I remember Captain Mackay (A Troop Commander) leaving us and moving off with two or three sections (20–30) to recce along the river and into Arnhem. Eventually there may have been 60 or more REs at the bridge.

The rest of A Troop moved off with the 1st Parachute Battalion for the high ground north of Arnhem, there in theory, to take up defensive positions. Reports came back (well, we could hear the heavy firing ourselves) that there was severe resistance, armour, etc. So that move was scotched and we wheeled away in an effort to follow 2nd Parachute Battalion towards the bridge. A great deal of time had been lost now. I remember we tried to rest in a wood that night.

Monday, 18th September
All day Monday, vain efforts were made by the 1st Parachute Battalion to reach the bridge, through the streets, along the riverside. It would appear that communications were fouled up, to say the least. Officers were sending out runners as their wireless sets seemed useless; this meant that movements between groups couldn't be co-ordinated. A 1st Parachute Battalion officer gave me the order to escort one of his sergeants in a Jeep, loaded with food and ammunition. He was going to drive hell for leather for the bridge. I can't remember what my thoughts were at the time, but

looking back, I shudder. Anyway, I sat beside the driver with my Sten gun at the ready as we moved off. We had only gained 50 or 60 yards, probably still in second or third gear (I didn't drive) when the Jeep spun right and mounted a slight embankment between some houses, turned over on its side, throwing me and some of the load clear. Picking myself up, I went to the driver. The sergeant was dead: a sniper, the bullet had been very close to me, yet I felt nothing, except being thrown out of the vehicle.

I returned to my group and my section officer, Lieutenant Robertson, gave me the order to take two sappers and get after the sniper who was thought by now to be using a church spire lancet window. The three of us moved into a house and in no time were in the attic. Removing two roof slates, we had a view of the spire. We didn't have to wait long before we saw a slight puff of smoke from one of the openings. Lance Corporal 'Jock' Wiley, one of the sappers, took aim using the roof timbers as a rest and fired about five rounds at the aperture. Our position was diagonally to spire, so that we could not fire directly into the opening but no sniper would stay put, once detected.

To this day I cannot remember Monday night except that I was under a garden hedge at daybreak. I think fatigue was beginning to tell.

Tuesday, 19th September

On one occasion I saw the bridge with fires and a huge pall of smoke hanging over the town. We were caught (about 40 or 50 of us), when moving along the edge of the river, by crossfire from the other side of the river and tanks ahead and to our left. With orders to use smoke grenades, it was then every man for himself. I followed a track towards the road, reached a wire fence and was about to get through when a burst spewed the earth under my boots. I had to move then and looking to my right, the direction of the enemy, I saw a tank half-hidden by a fallen tree pumping cannon fire at a riverside restaurant to my left.[20] Across the road from me were some trees on a rise leading to another road.[21] I raced across the road, passing under the cannon fire (tracers) that seemed to travel so slowly that I felt I could grasp one out of the air. I only had to wait a few moments, standing to attention behind one of the trees. I wasn't alone, others were doing the same, before the tank reversed away quickly. The smoke was drifting towards it.

Late morning we pulled back to Oosterbeek. It was at this time that I felt most fatigued; it was very difficult, even to keep one's eyes open. I was placed in a building, front room on the first floor, covering an orchard to the front and a length of road to the right. We smashed out all the glass in the bay windows. Myself, Lance Corporal Jock Wiley and another sapper (I can't remember who he was) didn't have long to wait before an enemy tank trundled down the road. Our weapons included two Bren guns and no PIAT, so we kept quiet. Sometime later another one came into sight, this one towing flame-throwing equipment. Before reaching us it opened up with its machine gun, raking our room and making it like the proverbial hornets' nest. Luckily nobody was even scratched. One bullet did knock an incendiary bomb off a table that was in the middle of the room. The tape had been partly unrolled, ready to throw. I watched it roll across the table and about to fall where it would have ignited; catching it before it hit the floor, I lobbed it through the gaping window in the direction of said tank, which didn't stay around but moved off.

It was exactly 2400 hours Tuesday night when I made my way downstairs to a small room where about 12 or 15 troops were trying to rest. I wanted know from a sergeant of C Troop who was to

---

20   The Rhine Pavilion.
21   Utrechtseweg.

be our relief. He was next to my section officer, Lieutenant Robertson. I touched the sergeant's boot – as I did so, it happened. An explosion to my left on the other side of the room, an orange flash, practically filling the room, I felt myself spinning like a top, then hit the wall behind me with a crash, still on my feet. My head was splitting and from a mere pinpoint between my eyes and spreading out into the distance, in an ever-widening band, were the most brilliant coloured stars of all shapes and sizes, moving faster and faster. A few moments of this and my mind began to clear. It was then I realised the full horror of it, the groaning and screaming of those in real agony. The room was thick with dust and acrid smoke. There was dryness in my mouth and throat as I pushed my tongue out to moisten my lips I tasted the unmistakeable salty tang of blood.

My thoughts went immediately to my face: *where was the blood from?* Cupping my face in my hands, all I could feel was thick, sticky congealing blood. It was like jam. My face had received four small nicks under my eyes. My left hand was mashed up, shrapnel in my left elbow and through the right shoulder. (I've been to three hospitals for my elbow since returning as a POW and am glad to say that eventually everything was put right). I can still smell the cordite and see the flash.

Comrades burst into the room and started leading the wounded away. Lance Corporal Jock Wiley came to my help and took me into a corridor. He wanted me to lie on a stretcher. This I would not do at once because if I did, I felt I would never get up. He attended to my wounds and gave me a jab of morphine but could not find a place on my forehead to put the letter 'M' in blood (denoting that morphine had been given). I was taken to the regimental aid post and whilst waiting in the hall of this house, I saw the medical officer amputating the sergeant's leg, just above the knee. He had received the fin of the mortar bomb full in the knee. To keep the sergeant out, an orderly held a swab of cotton wool over his face and allowed small drops of ether to fall onto the wool. After my wounds were attended to, I was put under the stairs with a trooper from 1st Parachute Battalion.

Wednesday, 20th September
On making enquiries in the morning, I was told the sergeant hadn't survived and also Lieutenant Robertson had died of his wounds. The house we were in was the house of Kate Ter Horst.[22]

Sapper F.A. Woods, A Troop, 1st Parachute Squadron, Royal Engineers

Sunday, 17th September
I was a Jeep driver for Captain E. Mackay (OC A Troop). I had a trailer with the Jeep which was filled with PIAT bombs and canisters of petroleum jelly for the squadron's flamethrowers. I glided into the DZ ahead of the squadron, and joined up with them after they had dropped. There was another Jeep in the glider with me but I don't recollect it being B or C Troops as I knew both drivers well.

---

22 Sergeant Frederick J. Hoath, 6398554, aged 27, C Troop, 1st Parachute Squadron RE. Buried in the garden of Kate Ter Horst, Benedendorpsweg. Lieutenant Richard A. Robertson, 264567, aged 22, A Troop, 1st Parachute Squadron, RE, probably buried alongside Sergeant Hoath in the Ter Horst's garden. No known grave.

Arnhem bridge looking south-east. Photographs taken from St Eusebius Church tower, pre-war. (Photo: Courtesy Gelders Archive)

Looking west towards Arnhem city centre. On the left across the bend in the river can be seen the brickworks and in the distance is the dome of Arnhem Prison in the Lombok area. (Photo: Courtesy Gelders Archive)

I drove into Arnhem with A Troop. However, I did not accompany them when they went to take the explosives off the railway bridge, but continued to the road bridge with the Squadron OC, Major Douglas Murray. I was in a house by the western side of the bridge with Major Murray. Colonel Frost was also there during the period that I was in the house. The first night I was with a sortie that went onto the bridge, but was driven back by fire from the pillbox (on the bridge).

Monday, 18th September
During the second day Major Murray took a party under the bridge and we confronted a Tiger tank. We were driven back, having no suitable weapons to dispose of the tank. It was about this time that Lance Sergeant Stanley Halliwell, B Troop, who had been captured by the Germans, was sent back to us to tell Colonel Frost to surrender.

Tuesday, 19th September
On the 19th, the house in which we were staying was no longer tenable and some of us moved to another to the west on a street corner by the river.[23] Lance Sergeant Halliwell and I and some of B Troop were compelled to retreat to the cellar when this house also caught fire. The cellar filled with smoke and we evacuated through a manhole cover onto the pavement. There was a street between us and the river, but also a few yards to the west there were a number of Germans with machine guns. There was no alternative but to give ourselves up.

Corporal John E. Humphreys, B Troop, 1st Parachute Squadron, Royal Engineers

It was late August 1944 when my stick commander sent for me and said that he and I plus two sappers and two drivers would be taking two Jeeps and two trailers loaded with weapons, flame throwers, mine detecting equipment, explosives and sundry other sapper gear down to the transit camp near Bristol. We motored through the night reaching our destination in the early hours of the morning and were shown a couple of tents to put our kit in and where we could rest for a few hours before the briefing started. When we made our way to the briefing area I saw that there were Parachute Regiment people about and also a few glider pilots and not far away a number of Horsa gliders. I started listening to the briefing with only a vague interest; too many had been aborted for me to rouse any great interest, when I was suddenly wide awake and listening intently. We were to load our Jeeps and trailers into two Horsa gliders and travel with them to a place called Arnhem where we were to be crash-landed onto the bridge that crossed the River Rhine. Whilst the infantry engaged the enemy we were to remove the demolition charges from the bridge before the Jerries blew it up. It meant that I would have to move like greased lightening once we had touched down and race for one of the bridge supports where there would almost certainly be an explosive charge and the electrical leads that must be cut before the enemy could connect the ends to a dynamo condenser and blow the charges. The thought of travelling in a flimsy glider terrified me, I was a parachutist and used to flying with one on my back; now I would be completely at the mercy of the pilot.

23 Rijnkade-Kadestraat junction.

Briefing over, we collected the vehicles and spent the afternoon loading them into the Horsa and then listened to Lieutenant Simpson as he outlined in detail what we should do and how we would do it. It was obvious to me that I would lead one of the groups and that he would lead the other, me to take the upstream side and him to clear the downstream charges. As we had been given two gliders I knew that our role must be vital to the operation. If one glider was written off there was still the other and between us we should be able to sever the electrical leads to the charges. As I climbed into my sleeping bag that night, I lay awake with my mind going over all the details and wondering whether I would still be alive in 24 hours, it seemed a very dicey operation but the sheer audacity of it would give us our best chance. The Jerries wouldn't be expecting us and it would be all over before they could mount a stiff resistance.

As it turned out, it would have been far safer for me to have gone on that operation because the enemy was very demoralised at that place at that time; but once again it was cancelled and once again we made our way back to Donnington, one half of me thinking that I had escaped almost certain death and the other half bitterly regretful at not having been allowed to take part in what would have been an Homeric fight. Not much more than a fortnight later and once again we were confined to barracks. It was Friday the 15th September and we would normally have been looking forward to the weekend and the village hop but instead here we were again sorting out our battle kit and packing up the rest, some of which would be left behind and some to travel with the seaborne party who would meet us after the fight was over. Saturday morning was taken up with briefing, most of which went in one ear and out of the other. I had listened to so many that had been cancelled that the thought that we would actually go was quite remote, I gathered that we were to have another go at the bridge over the Rhine at Arnhem but that this time the whole division would be going, led by our brigade, and that the Americans would be assaulting the bridges at Grave and Nijmegen which was necessary to secure the road which leads to Arnhem. We would be the furthest from our own lines and were required to hold the bridge for 36 hours, by which time the British 2nd Army were due to relieve us. The role of my troop was to provide the engineer support to the 2nd Parachute Battalion in the assault on the northern end of the bridge and our route from the Dropping Zone (DZ) at Wolfheze to the bridge would be along the road that ran parallel to the river. The rest of the day was spent drawing ammunition, grenades, explosives, maps, compasses and equipment special to one's role. And so to bed, expecting to be woken with the now familiar cry of 'It's off', but not so.

Sunday, 17th September

Instead we were all out of bed and making for the cookhouse at 0600 hours and the first across the field got the best and biggest mushrooms to go with their bacon and beans. An hour later we climbed into the three-tonner staggering under the weight of a parachute, a kitbag with which we would jump and a weapon. On arrival at Barkston Heath, the Dakotas were loaded and the containers fitted into the bomb bay and eventually we climbed in and sat in our allocated seat trying our best to look nonchalant, some cracking the odd joke, others were fidgeting with their equipment although by now anything that had been forgotten could not be replaced. I had a copy of *Reader's Digest* which took my mind off the impending battle. It was a glorious summer day, England at its best as though it were wishing us 'Good fortune'. As our plane took off and joined the others circling the airfield I could look down and see people coming out of the pubs with a glass of beer in their hand and see all the faces staring up at this armada of aircraft filling the sky with noise until we formed columns in line astern and made our way towards Holland.

As well as our Dakotas there were Stirlings towing Horsa and Hamilcar gliders in which the vehicles, guns and non-parachutists were being airlifted. I saw one glider break loose from its towing aircraft and spiral downwards long before we crossed the water and later I saw one go down in flames; how glad I was to be a parachutist! All was peaceful, apart from those prone to airsickness, until we got over the Scheldt when we were met with our first experience of anti-aircraft fire but these guns, mounted on flakships, were soon taken care of by the accompanying Typhoons who blew them out of the water with rocket fire. And then it was 'action stations' which was the command to stand up, hook up our static lines and to check that the man in front of me was correctly hooked up (that his static line which was hooked to a steel wire strong point had not been inadvertently passed through his parachute harness). The aircraft was now approaching the DZ and standing in the door I could see red flaming balls creeping slowly up only to go past the aircraft with the speed of light: I realised then that they were anti-aircraft shells and wondered what else lay in store but then the red light came on and soon the green and out I went.

The sky seemed full of aircraft and parachutes with my first quick glance around and then my canopy developed, I lowered my kitbag and prepared to land. The last thing that I wanted was a broken limb or back through not paying attention to my landing drill. Head down, shoulders round, feet together and watch the ground and up it came in the usual rush and I made a forward landing and very quickly got out of my parachute harness, took my equipment out of the kitbag and put it on and loaded my Mk.V Sten gun. There were sappers all around me and our containers, which were loaded with radio, flame throwers, explosives etc., were waiting to be collected and carried across to the DZ. Looking across the DZ I saw on the edge of it a farmhouse and a man with two big shire horses harnessed into a flat-bottomed wagon. Running across to him, I explained that I wanted to use the wagon and signing a piece of paper with the name 'B. Montgomery' I jumped onto the wagon and galloped across to my troop who soon loaded all the heavy stuff onto it and off we went to the RV with the 2nd Parachute Battalion; it was marked by yellow smoke, so was easy to find.

As soon as we got there, the wagon was claimed by an officer with the remark, 'Oh! Jolly good idea, I'll have that.' We waited for what seemed a long time and then started on the march to the bridge. The landing had been unopposed; we had caught Jerry having his Sunday lunch but now he was wide awake and starting to show it. Bursts of machine gun fire came ripping through the woods and mortar bombs were falling, here and there men were falling having been hit, but the long, strung-out column was starting and stopping when I thought that we would have to walk-run into the town. The railway bridge which B Troop was supposed to clear of explosives was blown up as we got level with it. It was 1400 hours when we landed and now, four hours later we were moving into the area near the bridge and all hell was let loose.

There was heavy machine gun and rifle fire; mortars were bursting and houses burning as we prepared to capture the bridge. The 2nd Battalion were held up by a pillbox on the end of the bridge and could not move until that was destroyed. It was overlooked from a three storey house built near the end of the bridge and so it was easy to take a flamethrower up to one of the windows and give the pillbox a good squirt before igniting the fuel; that end of the bridge was soon ours but not the other end. That too had a pillbox but we could not get near it and so the southern end of the bridge remained in German hands but they could not blow it as we had removed the charges. From there we went to a school which overlooked the north end of the bridge and prepared it for defence; it was supposed to be the site for brigade headquarters but they never got that far.[24] The first task was to ensure that all the glass was removed from the windows; it would be bad enough getting mortar fragments through the window but a lot worse when accompanied by flying glass and we needed to see without the handicap of dirty windows. All the containers that could hold water were filled and obstacles placed at the foot of the stairs. We were then assigned to defensive positions covering areas around the school. My first position was at a circular window overlooking a park and as the window was quite high I pushed a school desk up against the wall and rested my Bren gun on the window ledge and prepared myself for whatever was about to happen. Sid Gueran, my number two on the Bren gun, did likewise so that he was close to me and could pass the magazines as I needed them.

There was a lot of noise, rifle fire, machine guns, and explosions and in the early hours a very loud bang as the house next door to us was blown up. It had been occupied by most of A Troop of our squadron and what was left of them came into our building lead by Captain Mackay, their troop commander. Our troop commander[25] had been wounded early in the battle and we had been commanded by my stick officer, Lieutenant Simpson known as 'Stiffy', but he now handed over to Mackay.[26]

Monday, 18th September

As dawn broke, the enemy attacks started with offensive patrols, no doubt to gauge the strength of the opposition. The school was situated beside the ramp that led up to the bridge, the ramp actually being level with the second floor, so we had a good view of and could cover the approach to the bridge from the top floor where most of us were. The north side of the building covered the park. The rear looked on to a grass play area that was dotted with trees and the south looked across a lawn towards the bridge. It was not long before the Jerries started attacking in earnest and they came across the park in armoured half-tracks heading for us but were stopped by the volume of fire poured at them from mine and other Bren guns and rifles. This firefight went on for what seemed a long time but eventually the half-tracks pulled back out of sight and there was time to reload the magazines and get ready for the next scrap. I turned to Sid to ask him to help with loading the mags and saw that he was still kneeling on the desk but with his head down as though he had fallen asleep; it had certainly been a long night but when I shook him to waken him up his head fell towards me and blood poured out of his mouth over my parachute smock. He had been shot in the head and chest and had died instantly.[27]

Monday, 18th September was another long day as were all the others that we spent there. The second action came as the Jerries tried to rush the bridge from the other side with half-tracks but although they were armoured they had no roof to the vehicle so we, who could look down on them, shot up the first vehicles which slewed across the road and blocked it leaving us plenty of time to deal with the remainder. Those burnt out half-tracks were still there at the end of the battle. The rest of the day was spent fighting off attacks by small enemy forces and getting used to the incessant din of small arms fire and mortars bursting around the school. There was no time to think of food or any other bodily function other than surviving. Day went into night, lit by burning houses with no let up from the noise.

24   The Van Limburg Stirum School.
25   Captain Trevor J. Livesey.
26   Lieutenant Dennis J. Simpson.
27   Sapper Sidney F. Gueran, 1989425, B Troop, 1st Parachute Squadron, RE, aged 27, no known grave.

Tuesday, 19th September

Tuesday saw the attacks getting stronger. We knew now that we were up against two armoured SS Panzer divisions that had been regrouping near Arnhem and that they also were elite troops. The attacks that they put in were of company size but luckily for us they had to cover open ground to get into an attacking position, so we let them get quite close, about 15 to 20 yards away, then clobbered them with all that we had. By the end of that day there were an awful lot of dead Germans around the school. During the afternoon they brought up a Tiger tank and positioned it on the road leading up to the bridge and stopped when they were opposite us. The gun slowly turned until it pointed straight at the top floor of the school, so we quickly nipped down the stairs to the second floor and waited for the tank to open fire, which it did. Tanks can only depress their gun to an angle parallel with the road, so he couldn't shoot at the second floor and the ceiling of the second floor was like standing on an underground rail platform as a train goes through, plus a helluva lot of dust and flying brickwork. After he had fired a half a dozen rounds at us he packed up and went away whilst we trudged back up to what was left of the top floor. I had my first and last meal that night: a meat block, dehydrated, was put into a mess tin with some water and left to cook whilst I took a shot at any Jerry stupid enough to get too close. We had been told to hold the bridge for thirty-six hours when we would be relieved by the Second Army but forty-eight hours had passed and there was no sign of relief. Of the forty odd that we had started with, half were now killed or wounded and although we had taken their ammunition stocks we were desperately low and another day's hard fighting would see us without any. The town was still burning and one of our resupply Dakotas had been hit by anti-aircraft fire and had hit the steeple of the church opposite our street which resulted in more fire and debris.[28]

Wednesday, 20th September

Wednesday dawned wet with drizzling rain but that was the least of our discomfiture. The Jerries were still active, even more so as they had wiped out most of the pockets of resistance around the bridge and it looked to us as though only we and a few others around the bridge were left. It was fairly obvious that they were taking on one position at a time and only moving on when they had wiped out that one. But it was difficult for them to get at us and so they began mortaring us and dropping high explosive mixed with incendiary bombs in the hope that they could burn us out. In the early afternoon, we could see some distance away the enemy were forming up with infantry and tanks and it was obvious who their target was.

Mackay got the few of us that were left together and he said, 'We will let them get very close before opening fire, then if they succeed in breaking in we will go up to the first floor and fight from there, moving up until we are on the top floor when we will fight to the last man and the last round.'

The thought came into my mind that he too must have read 'Beau Geste' and standing in that window I wondered who would tell Brenda what had happened to me. She was not my official next of kin and as far as I knew, she did not know where I was because I had written a number of letters and given them to the NAAFI girl to post at intervals whilst we were away. I didn't want Brenda worrying about me. And then the tanks and infantry started moving towards us but the tanks

---

28 In fact the plane was a German fighter bomber and had attempted to bomb the school. Whilst evading ground fire and dense smoke it hit the steeple of St Walburgis church and crashed in a square 400 yards away.

were baulked by the trees and the infantry came on only to be decimated at point blank range. Then a rifle grenade came through the window and killed Jock Grey and two others. By now there were about a dozen left fit to fight but with only a few rounds amongst us, there was no way we could hold off another determined attack but it seemed as though they had had enough and were going to mortar us out.[29] The mortar bombs were dropping around the house and on the roof with hardly a break in the intensity. It got so that when there was a lull in the noise we automatically got ready for the next attack but it was probably that they had run out of mortar bombs and were waiting for resupply; they certainly did not seem very keen to get close to us again. The first fire broke out in the early afternoon and that was extinguished with most of the water that was left, but by late afternoon the school roof was a blazing inferno and it was obvious that we were going to have to get out. Mackay ordered those of us who had automatic weapons to go out first and to try and keep the Jerries' heads down whilst the badly wounded were brought out and laid amongst the ruins of the next-door house.

By now we were all filthy with not having washed for four days, being covered in dust when the tank shelled the school and like me, most had bloodstains on their smock – no wonder the Jerries were reluctant to get close to us! I lay on the patio of the ruined house with a Sten gun and one half-empty magazine and knew that we would be damned lucky to get out of it but I wasn't ready to pack up yet; the memories of the prisoner of war camp in Italy were too fresh in my mind and I didn't want to go into another one. In a short while everybody was out, the school was collapsing as the inferno raged and cremated the dead and we lay there waiting for the next event.

It was not long in coming. The Jerries started mortaring again but now they were dropping around us and the wounded, so Mackay said that we would have to surrender. It seemed such an anti-climax to that long desperate fight and I had no wish to just pack it in when there was still a chance of making it across the Rhine, so I told the four in my stick that I was going to make a break for it and that they were welcome to follow me.

When Mackay said he would surrender I shouted, 'Not bloody likely, I'm off!' and waited for the enemy machine gun to finish firing a long burst, and then raced across the road to the shelter of the ruins opposite followed by the other four. As with most continental houses these had cellars and the gutted windows were level with the pavement, allowing me to dive through one and land amongst the still-hot bricks inside what was left of what had been a row of houses. The houses ran in the direction of the river and were separated by gardens at the back, all of which had walls over which it was necessary to climb. There were four of us now; one had been hit crossing the road, all scrambling madly over each wall accompanied by odd bursts of fire which cracked as they flew over our heads.

All was going well and I thought that we would make it to the river when I heard Joe Malley shout, 'Help, I'm stuck.' I looked back to see him caught up in the barbed wire on top of the wall and unable to move back or forwards. I raced back to him and reaching grasped his webbing at the shoulders and started to pull him down when, much quicker than I can tell, there was a chattering rasp of an MG42 (an efficient German machine gun) and a rash of bright pink bullet holes appeared in the brickwork less than one inch from my left eye. I thrust Joe back over the wall and dived to my right into a flower bed and had a quick pee, without standing up, and then flew over the remaining walls catching up with the other two on the edge of the tram depot only a few hundred yards from the river. The depot was large but so was the number of Germans there. I came

---

29   Sapper David Gray, 2077436, B Troop, 1st Parachute Squadron, R. aged 22, no known grave.

around the corner of a building going fast and almost ran into a group of enemy soldiers who saw me and ran even faster, away from me. Before any shooting could start I led the other two to a tram under which we crawled and got behind the big iron wheel or steel wheel, knowing the Jerries would have to come at us without cover and in thirty minutes it would be dark enough to make a run for it. We lay there and the minutes ticked by and my hopes were rising when once again I heard the noise of enemy tank tracks and a self-propelled 105mm gun clanked up towards us. They were certainly taking us seriously. It stopped about thirty or forty yards away and the barrel was depressed so that I could see the rifling inside the barrel and then a voice said, in Oxford-accented English, 'If you don't come out, I will blow you out.'

Well, I wasn't going to argue with that bloody great gun, so I said that we were coming out but before I did, I stripped my Sten and threw the bits every which way, took my jack-knife and lanyard off my shoulder and slipped it around my waist under my trousers with the knife between my legs. My silk map and button compass were already in the lining of my smock. The one thought in my mind was *how long will it be before I get a chance to escape?*

I walked towards the SP gun with my hands up and the other two behind me. Two SS troopers came from behind the gun with Luger pistols in their hands and one pushed the barrel into my navel and the other stuck his in my back. My anus popped out like a flute player's lip and I thought that this was it; we had, after all, killed rather a lot of their friends and comrades, and the school had been surrounded by dead German SS troops. The one facing me took my AB64 (it stated who I was and complied with the Geneva Convention) and then told me to take off my equipment. He then reached out to take my beret and I knocked his hand away and told him to leave it alone; it was then that I realised that he was more scared of me than I was of him. We were then marched to their headquarters where an officer tried to interrogate me but all I would say in reply to his questions was '1877368, Corporal J. E. Humphreys', and then he proceeded to tell me who my squadron commander was, the names of my troop officers and a whole lot of things that a corporal never bothered to know, after which we were made to wait in a courtyard and given a tin of meat and a packet of biscuits, and how I enjoyed it.

Sitting in the courtyard watching the antics of the opposition, it became more obvious that we had given them a hard fight. Whenever there was a burst of fire that was from a British weapon, and they had a very different sound from the German weapons, a party of SS troops were sent out to deal with it but the group of soldiers was always accompanied by a half-tracked vehicle and quite often by a soldier who carried a flamethrower and from the remarks he made and the look on his face, he was not keen on the idea; but then a tracer bullet through the pressurised fuel container would not have done him any good, so I could understand his fear! Night fell and we were ordered to climb into the back of a lorry guarded by two soldiers armed with machine pistols, so there was no chance of escaping.

Thursday, 21st September
Sometime in the early hours of the morning we stopped and were told to move into a disused roadside cafe where we slept for a few hours, then back into the truck until reaching our destination which was a transit POW cage at Emmerich. The cage was an 'L' shaped building with a double barbed wire fence, ten feet tall across the apex and the familiar sentry boxes on stilts at intervals along the wire, each manned by a sentry with a machine gun and a searchlight. The long part of the 'L' was an empty room into which all the POWs had gone; the cage already contained a lot of captured British soldiers when we got there, but I wanted to find out if I could get away from this

place, knowing full well that it was going to get more difficult the further we got into Germany. Looking into the short part of the 'L' there was only one room that was open and that was the kitchen. It contained two Soya stoves and what was more important, there were two windows. Admittedly they each had three bars running vertically in the window space but at least I could now start thinking positively. I immediately made myself the cook and nipped inside, wedging the door closed. The next step was to look closely at the bars and see how I could loosen them. Using the jack-knife which I had hidden inside my trousers with the lanyard around my waist and the knife hanging behind the fly buttons, I picked at the cement and found that I could remove it with the marlin spike.

Working with haste and hoping that a Jerry wouldn't try and open the door, I picked the cement completely away from the bottom of the bar and knew that if I could do that to all three it was possible, with the knowledge of what lay before me, to bend the bars and get out through the window. One long dose of prisoner of war life had been enough for me. In two hours I had cleared the cement from the other two bars then made a mix of ash from the stove and the cement chippings and covered the window sill so that it was not obvious what I had done. Whilst freeing the bars I had seen that the building backed onto a slope leading down to a country lane with hedges so it should not be difficult to get away from the cage without being spotted as the sentries were on the other side of the building. All that I had to do was bend up the bars, climb out, and then walk to the Rhine and swim it or steal a boat, but first I wanted to let Joe Malley know as I needed a second person to be in the kitchen whilst I looked around the rest of the cage. The difficult part was to leave the kitchen, a place where I had a certain way of escaping, not knowing what would happen in my absence. However, I slipped out of the door unobtrusively and quickly made my way to the main building where I found Joe and explained to him what I was going to do and did he want to come. Somewhat to my surprise he was not at all keen but I should have realised that having been captured once, my morale was not affected the way theirs was. Most of them were still in a state of shock but then I saw 'Chick' Weir who was a corporal in A Troop. He was keen, so I led him to the kitchen and showed him what I had done. I also explained that the reason that I had not let everybody know what I was doing was that there could be an informer amongst the prisoners whose task it was to listen to the conversation and report back to his masters, and that would have stopped me getting out and there was no way that I was going to let that happen.

The next task was to look around that part of the cage that I had not yet seen and to look closely at the sentry boxes to determine what their field of view was. Whilst I was doing this, a German NCO called to me and told me to follow him. We went up to their headquarters where I was given a sack of potatoes and told to take them back to the cookhouse and cook them for the POWs. It must have been late in the evening by this time as no sooner had the water started to boil in the Soya stoves than there was a great hullaballoo outside as another batch of prisoners entered the camp. They were making their way to the main building looking for their friends, and for me it was the ideal time to go as the Jerries were more interested in watching what was happening than looking at the kitchen.

I asked Chick Weir if he would let Lieutenant Simpson, my stick commander, know what we were doing so that he could come with us. He came back with Simpson and his troop commander, Captain E. Mackay. As soon as they were inside, I grasped one of the bars with both hands, put both my feet against the wall and with all my strength born of desperation, I pulled. I was surprised at how easy the bar bent and lost no time in bending up the other two and climbing out. There was a drop onto a grassy bank down which I quickly slid to hide in the lee of the hedge which bordered the lane. Mackay came out followed by Simpson and we watched with horror as Chick Weir got stuck in the window and a German soldier was seen coming down the lane with a girl on his arm; thank goodness he was more interested in her than what was going on around him. Weir had the sense to keep still until I ran back up the bank and freed him. There was enough light to see by as we started walking towards the Rhine, making our way across fields where we could and avoiding the roads and tracks.

The only incidents that stick in my mind were crossing a field with a bull in it; we all broke the 100 metres sprint record, and coming out of a wood to cross the road only to see the dim shape of a soldier trying his utmost to persuade a girl to surrender her virginity. I don't know what the others were thinking but I was wishing that she would give in and quickly. It seemed ages before it was safe to cross the road and carry on.

Friday, 22nd September

Dawn broke to find us on very flat and open ground with the Rhine in sight but nowhere to lay up. We followed the river until we saw a small wooden hut on the river bank and quickly got inside knowing that it was not the best of places as there was no way out if we were unfortunate enough to have a Jerry look in.

It was a long day. About 0800 hours a van delivering bread stopped on the road that ran parallel to the river and was just below us. The smell of the newly baked bread was so appetising to us that had eaten very little for the last few days that I was almost tempted to run out and steal a loaf. The day wore on with the odd alarm; a policeman cycled by and then there were children playing on the river bank and the occasional pedestrian but eventually night fell and with the dusk came a Rhine barge which moored up almost opposite us. The crew scrambled ashore and no sooner were they out of sight than we were on board. In the cabin was the remains of their supper, a stew, which we quickly scoffed together with the loaf that was there, but the best of all was the row boat that was tied up alongside. Grabbing a few blankets we settled into it and I took the oars whilst the others made themselves comfortable and cast off. Mackay told me to keep to the far bank and to make certain that I took the left fork when the river split farther downstream.

Saturday, 23rd September

The current ran fast so all I had to do was keep the boat pointing in the right direction and not too far from the far bank. The journey was uneventful apart from the odd burst of machine gun fire which went over the top of us and then as the false dawn was breaking I saw over my shoulder a bridge that looked like the one at Arnhem. I woke the others up and they looked, and they then started to accuse me of taking the wrong direction when clearly a voice called, 'Halt. Who goes there?' It was obviously a British sentry on the bridge. We did not know that the bridge at Nijmegen was identical to the one at Arnhem.

The sentry had not seen us and was challenging someone on the bridge and so we went into the bank, moored up the boat and climbed out to find that we had landed in a gunner defensive position, all of whom were in slit trenches facing away from the water. When I touched one on the shoulder he turned and looked at me and I thought he was going to faint. I didn't realise what I looked like covered in dried blood and grime and to see an apparition like that at five o'clock in the morning was enough to frighten anybody. After he had calmed down and we had located his battery officer – we did not want to get shot by our own troops at that stage – we moved out of their perimeter and made our way towards 1st Airborne Division Headquarters where the officers went to report and get debriefed whilst Chick and I sat on the grass and waited. Sometime later we were told to find our seaborne element where our spare clothing was and where we could get cleaned up. All four of us were later interviewed by the press and photographed with the bridge in the background. Chick and I were not allowed to say anything about the escape.

Saturday, 23rd September onwards and post-Arnhem
Many years were to elapse before I read an article by an officer describing his experiences at Arnhem in which he stated that he secreted a hacksaw blade up his anus and used this to free himself from the POW cage at Emmerich. His physical courage and leadership during the battle impressed me very much and made it all the more difficult to understand why he had not given to me the credit due to me for planning the escape.

Recreating their escape. *Left to right*: Corporal J.E. Humphreys, Corporal C. Weir, Lieutenant D. Simpson and Captain E. Mackay. Nijmegen, 23rd September. Corporal John Humphreys writes: 'The sentry had not seen us and was challenging someone on the bridge and so we went into the bank, moored up the boat and climbed out to find that we had landed in a gunner defensive position, all of whom were in slit trenches facing away from the water.' (Photo. J. Eston, Daily Herald. Courtesy IWM)

Nijmegen, Saturday, 23rd September. *Left to right:* Corporal Charles 'Chick' Weir, Corporal John E. Humphreys, Lieutenant Dennis 'Stiffy' Simpson and Captain Eric Mackay. Corporal John Humphreys writes: 'All four of us were later interviewed by the press and photographed with the bridge in the background. Chick and I were not allowed to say anything about the escape.' (Photo: Courtesy IWM)

I think it was the next day that the survivors from the battle broke out of the encirclement and made their way back across the Rhine and all of us were moved back to Nijmegen. Most of this period is a bit vague but I do remember the remains of the 1st Airborne Division standing on a crossroads with the 1st Parachute Brigade on one corner, the 4th Parachute Brigade on another, the Airlanding Brigade on the third corner and what remained of the Polish Brigade on the fourth. It didn't seem possible that this was all that was left of a division but then there were only ten left out of the 153 that had jumped in of my squadron. Not long after we were all ferried down to Louvain and spent the night in a school there before moving to Brussels airport and flying back to the UK. We didn't go to our former camp but to a different village in Lincolnshire, some twenty miles from Donnington. Leave was not granted to any of us; we were kept out of the public eye for a few weeks until the war moved on and Arnhem was no longer hot news. During this period we were employed building Nissen huts, although I was given the job of going to the Land Army Camp and telling the many girls who were courting or friends of those in my squadron what had happened to them. Not an enviable task!

Lance Sergeant Harold Padfield, B Troop, 1st Parachute Squadron, Royal Engineers

We had stood by to drop the week before, which would have been very adventurous, using the three brigades to take the three bridges, Maas, Waal and Neder Rijn. This was cancelled owing to the 2nd Army meeting fierce resistance at the Albert Canal, so the mission would have been suicidal. General Montgomery decided that more planes and more parachute troops were needed. Hence the 82nd and 101st (US Airborne) Paras took the lower bridges and the 1st Airborne were to take the bridge at Arnhem.

Sunday, 17th September
We loaded the containers on the Friday and set off in the early hours of Sunday morning to Barkston Heath Airfield. My stick commander and I checked straps and hooks on the plane and that the door opening was taped and that the bomb rack switches worked before getting the stick to fit up the containers. It was a lovely sunny day and we laid around until we were told to emplane at around eleven o'clock. The plane eventually taxied into position at the head of the runway lining up for take-off, which in our case was around midday. The flight was quite smooth and we had plenty of fighter escort. When we had crossed the North Sea we heard some gunfire, but nothing to worry about. When we saw the dykes and windmills of Holland, we knew that time was getting close, and the butterflies had risen from their slumbers and were playing havoc with my stomach. Lieutenant Simpson told us to us to hook up and it was then red on – 'action stations', green on – and 'go!' Time was 1407 hours, or to the uninitiated, seven minutes past two.

A good exit, no twists, not a lot of oscillation, but there was a tree in my way; I could see that I wasn't going to miss it, so I took evasive action to cover my face. The chute was caught in the trees and I just hung there. I hit my release box, pulled out the leg straps, and lowered myself on to a branch and climbed down. The scene was bewildering; gliders were coming in thick and fast, many with a horrible 'crunch', and there were hundreds of parachutists. At any other time it would have been a sight to behold. I spotted the blue smoke for my rendezvous, and ran over to join the rest of the stick. We collected our weapons and stores and moved off in the direction of Wolfheze. In battle we carried our explosives and grenades on our person, so you made sure that the detonators were stored where you wouldn't fall on them.

As we moved off the dropping zone, we came across a German vehicle and a German general and his driver who had been killed, which bought you to the reality of the situation we were in. We marched in single file with rifles at the alert, but it was all quiet. Then we were welcomed by the Dutch people like conquering heroes. As we left Wolfheze, and came to the outskirts of Oosterbeek, we saw a lot of men dressed in white; they were quite strange-looking and eerie and they were apparently from an asylum down the lane.

In Oosterbeek, we were once again greeted by hundreds of Dutch with flags and bunting, it was like a victory parade, when all of a sudden the action came to life. We quickly dispersed, went into back gardens, took up defensive positions and local skirmishes developed. The railway bridge was across the fields from these back gardens and we knew that 9th Field Company, who had come in by glider, were to take the bridge and demolish is it. As we were having our little battles they were making their way across the field to the bridge. As they arrived on the bridge, about twenty in number, the Germans blew it up. These were the first casualties we saw.[30]

30 In all probability, the infantry that Harold Padfield witnessed attacking the railway bridge were C Company, 2nd Parachute Battalion. A degree of elaboration might explain some of the confusion over the allotted roles in the attempted capture of the railway bridge (codename: CHARING X). Frost's 2nd Parachute Battalion had allocated Major Victor Dover's C Company to capture the railway bridge and if successful, to then delegate a platoon to approach the Arnhem road bridge (codename: WATERLOO) from the southern bank. If this was not possible, the company was to enter Arnhem town centre and take over the German Headquarters building. It would seem that a degree of duplication, consciously or unconsciously, had been incorporated into the plan to guarantee capture of the railway bridge. Not only had C Company, 2nd Parachute Battalion with support from elements of B Troop, 1st Parachute Squadron RE led by Lieutenant Peter Stainforth RE been given the task, but No. 2 Platoon, 9th (Airborne) Field Company, Royal Engineers, under Captain O'Callaghan had also been given the task to neutralise and remove enemy demolition charges by seizing and holding the railway bridge of the River Neder Rhine and make a temporary cut of the railway from the south. No demolitions of the railway bridge were planned. (Ref: Operation Market, CRE 1 Airborne Div Op Instructions No. 1. Provisional Notes on CREs Verbal Orders.) According to a personal account of the operation by Lt Col. J.C. Winchester, MC, RE, Officer Commanding 9th (Airborne) Field Company RE: 'No infantry had been detailed for this task, so I ordered the whole of 2 Platoon to take it on.'

Captain O'Callaghan's No. 2 Platoon, 9th Field Company RE, advanced alongside 2nd Parachute Battalion on the southern (Lion) route through lower Oosterbeek, tucked in-between A and B Companies. At approximately 1700 hours, the column reached the concrete archway that carried the railway line over the Benedendorpsweg and O'Callaghan's No. 2 Platoon departed towards the railway bridge. Stealthily working their way parallel to the railway embankment, they crossed unseen over to the other (eastern) blind side of the embankment. They succeeded in reaching within 20 yards of the first span undetected. The twenty or so German defenders were on the south side of the bridge, some 150 yards away situated in a pillbox and several houses. As the sappers carefully moved forward they were surprised by the appearance on the other side of the embankment of paratroopers from 9 Platoon, C Company 2nd Parachute Battalion, led by Lieutenant Peter Barry. As Barry's 9 Platoon stormed onto the bridge, fire rapidly intensified from the German defenders at the opposite end on the bridge. Captain O'Callaghan's group continued forward some fifty yards, now themselves under fire from the alerted Germans, and started to remove charges from the first span. Meanwhile, Lieutenant Barry with one rifle section rushed the bridge under cover of a smoke grenade whilst supported by fire from his two remaining sections. The remainder of HQ, C Company with 8 and 7 Platoons followed by elements of B Troop, 1st Parachute Squadron, RE providing covering fire from the area of some wrecked brickworks off the Polderweg some 200 yards from the bridge.

Lieutenant Barry and his assault section reached the first span of the bridge when the German defenders detonated the explosive charges under the centre and southern sections of the bridge. The first span remained intact, the charges having been neutralised by Captain O'Callaghan and his men. The blown third span descended into the Rhine, and Barry, now wounded and unable to proceed any further, withdrew his men under machine gun and accurate rifle fire, back towards the north bank, losing one man, Private Sadler of 9 Platoon, killed on the way down the embankment. (Private Leslie D. Sadler, 14529484, C Company, aged 20. No known grave.) Evidence would suggest that the assault on the railway bridge whilst simultaneous, was in fact uncoordinated between 9th Field Company RE and C Company, 2nd Parachute Battalion.

Major Dover stated that the attack was not accompanied by 9th Field Company RE. In the book *By Air To Battle*, it is stated that Lieutenant Peter Barry and his platoon were accompanied to the railway bridge by a section of Royal Engineers of the 9th Field Company under command of Captain E. O'Callaghan. This was not so; Lieut. Peter Stainforth, RE was in command of the sappers attached to C Company, and they did not take part in the assault on the bridge. Peter Stainforth's own account in *Wings of the Wind* makes the position clear: his job was to stand by and 'clear the bridge of demolition charges after it had been captured'. (Major Victor Dover, MC, *The Silken Canopy*, Cassell, London 1979, page 90.)

In fact it would seem that not everyone was aware that 9th Field Company were involved or indeed had already removed charges from the north end of the railway bridge which is understandable in the circumstances. Following the blowing of the bridge, just as it was getting dark, C Coy were ordered to

As the afternoon wore on, the battles were beginning to rage around Oosterbeek and we had to get to the bridge at Arnhem, which was quite a few miles ahead. It was, I suppose, about 2100 hours when we got into Arnhem, and things were pretty lively with fires lighting up the place. I had to get down to the river, to find the pontoon bridge and check its suitability for use at a later stage. I took Danny Neville and Frank Navin with me. We found it about a mile downstream, minus its centre section. We carried on for a further half mile and found the centre section. On inspection, we found that it had explosive charges fixed to it, so we cut them away and dumped them in the river. We then made our way back to the main section, which also had explosive charges fixed, so we did the same with those. As we were coming away a German soldier must have mistook us for one of his own, poor chap. We made our way back to the bridge area and hoped to find the rest of them there. As luck would have it they weren't far from where we had left them. They had just finished being briefed on the situation. Our stick was detailed to go under the bridge and take up a position on its north end. There seemed to be all hell being let loose at the bridge itself; apparently a shed at the side of the bridge containing ammunition and explosives had been hit and this was causing the extra fireworks.

We managed to get under and round the back with no bother. We came to a building which Lieutenant Simpson told me to break into and search. It didn't need a lot to break in, I just broke the glass in the door and turned the handle from the inside. I asked Joe Malley and Arthur Hendy to give me covering fire as I searched around. I went upstairs and realised it was a school, there were desks and chairs and a blackboard and blasted great picture windows on one side of the main classroom and porthole windows on the opposite side, but other rooms weren't too bad. There was a good view of the bridge from the room at the end of the passage. I went out and reported back and we then took over the building; this must have been around 2230 hours.

Everyone was told to be as quiet as possible whilst we used the desks to make barricades, etc. We had the advantage of fires all around the place to see what we were doing, and then we settled down to watch. I positioned myself on the stairway, so that I was available for any occurrence. I sent Arthur Hendy to have a scout around the basement to see if there was anything of use in the way of clothing that we could use to muffle the sound of our boots, and just as important to see if there was any food. Our luck was in as he came up with pullovers, slips and skirts – obviously a girls' school. We passed them around and he cleared off again as he said, 'There were some vegetables down there.' After a while he came back with some hot soup, which went down well. Sometime later we heard movement down below and it was some of A Troop, though how they came to be in the area I don't know. Anyway, we could do with some extra hands up top to cover the area properly.

Monday, 18th September
Daylight came and I went around and sorted out the arcs of fire I wanted each man to cover. I went to Sid Gueran and set him up on a desk so that he could comfortably sit and cover a vital

> continue their advance into Arnhem. Half a mile down the road, Lieutenant Stainforth RE along with four sappers was ordered to return to the bridge to check for any remaining demolitions, which unknown to him, had already been removed. By this time Captain O'Callaghan had moved his No. 2 Platoon, 9th Field Company RE and was on his way into Arnhem where he arrived finally at the bridge early the next morning. Much of the confusion at the time would have been avoided had all those involved had working communications. Neither Captain O'Callaghan nor Major Dover had any working radios. According to Dover, 'We were out of touch with everyone, except the Germans.'

area to the west through his porthole window. I was telling him the area I wanted him to cover and couldn't understand why I wasn't getting a response. When I turned towards him, he was sat upright, and my first loss. He had been shot through the mouth; it must have been a stray bullet because I certainly didn't hear anything. I got hold of Joe Malley, whom I had put in charge of this particular area, and we laid him out on the floor, and made sure that his identity tag was round his neck. I then continued round the other areas, but they were well engaged and our defence of this vital bridge had begun. Among the A Troop contingent, who came in during the night, was a signaller from the 3rd Parachute Battalion. He was trying to get information locally and further afield from XXX Corps, who were pushing through to take over from 1st Airborne Division, but he wasn't having a great deal of success.

Three lorries approached the bridge from the south. We waited until they were well inside the net of troops around the bridge, and opened fire. Grenade and PIAT guns opened up from other areas and those who got out were mown down. Later that day a convoy of tanks and half-tracks came from the same direction and met the same fate. There must have been a dozen or more – three went over the embankment, others were burnt out and four came towards the school, all guns blazing. They were successfully put out of action and laid to rest at the side of the building. We had a lull of almost an hour except for the odd sniper and Tommy Gray was our next to be killed. The Germans then opened up with mortar and artillery, and life was getting difficult. 'Twiggy' Hazlewood was badly wounded and 'Ginger' Partridge had the sights shot off his Bren gun, but miraculously he wasn't touched. Houses round about were set on fire from the constant barrage of shells, and we just waited. You could hear battles going on all around, but at this particular time shelling was our main worry.

Night time came and with it an attack from grenades and spasmodic raids from outside, which were always successfully beaten off, but this meant that you couldn't have a well-earned doze. At midnight I decided it was time to take one of my Benzedrine tablets, as I hadn't had any sleep since Saturday and we were now entering the early hours of Tuesday.

Tuesday, 19th September

We had a watchful period from midnight till dawn, when all of a sudden a grenade came through a window, Sapper Butterworth immediately picked it up and threw it back out. I don't know what damage it caused outside, but he certainly saved us from disaster inside. In one of the rooms off the landing were about a dozen mattresses which we had stacked up to give a decent protection from splintered glass. During the afternoon there was an explosion and one of the mattresses was on fire. I went in to pull it off the pile and put it out and was hurled back to the doorway by another explosion. 'What the hell was that?' I asked, and someone thought it might have been a rifle grenade from a sniper across the road. I crawled back and there was another explosion with the same result. The third time was lucky and the fire extinguished.

I got a couple of sappers – Charlie Grier and Billy Marr with their Bren gun – and we watched for any movement in the house opposite. After a nerve-racking thirty minutes, the Bren gunner said, 'Got him, Sarge,' and let go a burst, followed by two more which silenced our menace from that quarter.

The shelling was continuing and our own ammunition was getting dangerously low. In fact my own was spent except for a few rounds in my 9mm Browning pistol. During the afternoon the signaller had got through to XXX Corps; they were held up with fierce fighting thirty-odd miles away and prospects of our being relieved in the foreseeable future were fading fast.

Wednesday, 20th September

Two German tanks were brought up on to the bridge and started to blast away with their 88mm guns. They had a direct hit on the front of the school and the roof was set alight. Joe Simpson and 'Paddy' Neville were killed, the rest were okay and we went to the basement.[31] It was becoming obvious that we should have to move out. Twiggy Hazlewood was getting worse by the hour, and sure enough there was another direct hit, and the school was well alight. We got the wounded downstairs and I went round all the rooms to be sure everyone was out. Joe and Paddy were limbless bodies; otherwise, everyone was out. We tore down doors to put the wounded on, and went out the way we came in. As we made our way across to a wall we came under fire and John Bretherton was killed as he was getting over it. Twiggy got a machine gun burst up the side of his body as we were lifting him over the wall, but he was still clinging on to life. We were all eventually over and the bank gave a little protection.[32]

One of the wounded was Major Lewis; he must have come into the school with the signaller on the first night. When he got wounded I don't know but he was the company commander of C Company, 3rd Parachute Battalion.[33] The next twenty minutes were phenomenal, we were caught in an enfilade of fire, and air bursts. Charlie Grier was hit by a stray bullet; it made a hole in his helmet but didn't mark his head. Billy Marr had his pack severed from his back but with no injury. Major Lew told us that we should surrender, and that we should all take pride in our performance. We took the bolts out of our weapons and threw them away; we left the weapons where they were. Sapper Butterworth put a white handkerchief on the end of his rifle and went forward waving it. As he was walking forward a machine gunner opened up and hit him in the legs and his German officer drew his pistol and shot the machine gunner. He then told us to come forward, saying, 'You are very brave, but foolish.' We considered we were unfortunate. We were then led off with our hands up, through the streets of Arnhem and held in the basement of some houses; we were prisoners of war. Our wounded had been taken away from us when we were captured. That night we had a few snatches of sleep. I say snatches because just as you were nicely off, they wanted you moved to another room or another house, just to be bloody minded.

Thursday, 21st September

The next morning all the prisoners were formed up. I was surprised and pleased to see Norman Swift, so we fell-in together. We marched off singing all the old songs, 'Tipperary', 'Pack Up Your Troubles' etc, until about a mile up the road we came to a halt at a memorial. To our amazement it had '17th September 1944' emblazoned in beautiful flowers, it was really something. The reason for the halt wasn't to admire the memorial, but to be loaded on to lorries and transported to Apeldoorn. Here we were herded into a big railway shed, told to take our boots off, tie them together and mark them. We were then given one black loaf of bread between five of us; the date indentation on it was 16th September. I got my knife out of my haversack and commenced trying to cut it into equal portions, but the blade snapped. Anyway we did eventually get it cut and that was all we were getting. As time went on more and more were arriving, including familiar faces from the squadron who had their own stories to tell. It appeared that it had been gruesome everywhere.

---

31 Corporal William L.G. Simpson, 1919427, A Troop, 1st Parachute Squadron RE MiD, age 29 and Lance Corporal Daniel Neville, 1911650, B Troop, 1st Parachute Squadron, RE, age 29. First buried near the Rhine Bridge.
32 Corporal William V. Hazlewood, 1913439, A Troop, 1st Parachute Squadron, RE, aged 25. No known grave. Sapper John Bretherton, 2196447, A Troop, 1st Parachute Squadron, RE, age 27. First buried Moscowa Cemetery, Arnhem.
33 Major R.P.C. 'Pongo' Lewis and Lieutenant Len Wright, C Company, 3rd Parachute Battalion, both wounded by the same artillery blast on Wednesday, 20th September.

Right: Johan van Oldenbarneveltstraat, Arnhem, Wednesday, 20th September. *Left to right:* Lance Sergeant Harold Padfield, B Troop, 1st Parachute Squadron RE, along with Corporal Gerald Withers, RAMC, attached to C Company, 3rd Parachute Battalion form the front pair of a stretcher party carrying severely wounded Sergeant Geoffrey Lawson of No. 19 Flight, B Squadron, Glider Pilot Regiment, who later died of wounds. Rear right visible stretcher bearer is Private J.O. Withers, C Company, 3rd Parachute Battalion. (Photo: Author's private collection)

Below: 1st Parachute Squadron Royal Engineers and C Company, 3rd Parachute Battalion survivors from the Van Limburg Stirum School make their way to the Klugkist timber yard at No. 15 for processing. Johan van Oldenbarneveltstraat, Arnhem, Wednesday, 20th September. (Photo: Courtesy Gelders Archive)

Sapper Les 'Curly' Plummer, C Troop, 1st Parachute Squadron, Royal Engineers

Sunday, 17th September
I was a member of C Troop; we embarked on our planes from Barkston Heath aerodrome in Lincolnshire. It was a lovely sunny Sunday morning and we were all very pleased to be going into action at last after being briefed and 'stood-to' about 18 times since the invasion of Normandy. We took off about midday – a great sight as we were going three planes abreast down the runway. We were lucky as we didn't meet any opposition except a small amount of flak. I jumped out No. 2 after the officer and we had a good landing. It wasn't long before we had gathered up our containers etc., on our trolleys and formed up with the 3rd Parachute Battalion with whom we were attached, then out of the stick of ten men we were detailed to stay on the dropping zone (DZ) to help collect any ammunition etc and put it in a small barn at the farm Klien-Amerika and stay there to guard it.[34] By this time there were a lot of Dutch people on the dropping zone collecting parachutes, etc. There wasn't any opposition at that time although the Germans were soon in position in the woods facing us; we had to be careful as we were being shot at if we moved about the farm. During Sunday afternoon a party of soldiers and some Dutchmen came with a coach and loaded it with ammunition and shells and escorted it away. I don't know how far they got! During the evening we were shelled and the barn at the back was destroyed and two horses were killed.

Monday, 18th September
I think a battalion of the Border Regiment were left at the DZ to keep the woods clear of the Germans but they must have got back in as later when the gliders landed on the Monday they were under heavy fire and lots of them crashed on landing and were soon on fire. There was nothing we could do to help them as we came under fire and took up positions to reply. We couldn't see anything as the Germans were hidden in the woods about 500 metres away! Our Corporal Cossadinas decided that we should move with the glider troops, so we went under a railway bridge I think at Wolfheze and marched into Oosterbeek. It was another lovely sunny day with no opposition until we dug our trenches on the green opposite the Hartenstein. It wasn't long before we were attacked by enemy fighters, there was also quite a lot of sniping going on but they were well hidden.

Tuesday, 19th September
We were then told to take up positions in the narrow road leading up to the Sonnenberg where we stayed the whole time on the right side under the trees. We had a Bren gun position up forward near a wood where we took turns to watch. We only had food and water for 48 hours and were soon short of water. Sapper Campbell volunteered to go and fill some bottles up at a well behind the Hartenstein; unfortunately, he never came back and we were told he was killed at the well as it was under fire from snipers, that was probably on the Tuesday?[35] From that day we were heavily shelled from morning until night, not able to move from our trenches.

---

34 Half of C Troop, DZ clearance under command of Captain Stephen George, 2i/c 1st Parachute Squadron RE.
35 Sapper John Campbell, 3189332, C Troop, 1st Parachute Squadron RE, aged 24. Found buried near Hartenstein sports ground.

Wednesday, 20th September

We had our second casualty on the Wednesday when Sapper Henry Sherwood had a shell land in his trench, so it was rather messy. We were under so much bombardment that we couldn't get out to bury him for some hours later.[36]

Thursday, 21st September–Monday, 25th September

Next day we had two flame-throwing tanks come along the road and could hear the shrieks of people being burnt alive in their trenches. There was an anti-tank gun dug in at the end of the drive, so I went back and warned them to get ready. They did, and hit the first tank and set it on fire and I think they may have damaged the other one as it soon went off the road into the edge of a wood. An officer of the 9th Field Company RE came and asked me to help carry some bombs to attack this tank which was in the woods, which we did. I think he hit the tracks and did further damage and as he had used up the bombs I made to go back to my unit. He went behind some bushes and was never seen again, I think he was killed by a sniper nearby as I was fired on whilst I was crawling back. I heard several shots fired at me. I was behind some fallen trees, so I was a difficult target and a very lucky person. Afterwards I went to try and locate this German who was causing the trouble. I went forward and threw a smoke canister to cover my approach but the wind took it the wrong way. Whilst I was there I saw three soldiers come nearby carrying an anti-tank PIAT and they lodged it on a tree trunk ready to fire. I shouted to warn them that a sniper was close but they carried on and the soldier with the PIAT was killed instantly with a bullet right between the eyes. He just stayed leaning on the tree as if nothing had happened. We were getting rather tired and dirty and hungry but still in good spirits. Unfortunately we were not getting any information on how things were going. We were surrounded and being heavily bombarded day and night although we managed to get a little rest at night. I remember going to a house over the main road to try for some water and all the family were in the cellar, I believe they had a new-born baby there. I told them things would soon get better but they didn't and later the Dutch civilians were allowed to leave under escorts.

Every night there were houses being set alight all round and I remember the Germans bringing up a speaker into the woods nearby telling us to surrender. Two more of my friends were killed near the main road, Lance Corporal Shaw[37] and Sapper Jeb Taylor together in a trench.[38] Also, Tommy Hicks got hit with some shrapnel which temporarily paralysed him. I was able to pick some of the metal from his neck and helped him to the first aid house. Another boy with us was blinded by a shell burst and we were able to take him to the medics but I never heard of him again. One night, Captain Storrs[39] took Tommy Hicks and another. They went down to where the ferry was to see if it would be able to be used again, but I don't think it was of any use.[40] At one time the 9th Field Company boys went through the wood with fixed bayonets to clear it.

---

36   Sapper Henry M. Sherwood, 2094357, C Troop, 1st Parachute Squadron, RE, aged 26. No known grave.
37   Possibly. Instead of Lance Corporal Shaw, it could have been Lance Corporal William C. Kill, 1911649, C Troop, as he was wounded, apparently in the same trench as Taylor. Lance Corporal C. Kill, aged 29, died of wounds in Apeldoorn 28th September 1944.
38   Sapper Gilbert Taylor, 1880946; C Troop, 1st Parachute Squadron RE, aged 24. KIA, 21.9.44. No known grave.
39   Captain David V. Storrs, Field Engineer, HQ, Royal Engineers.
40   See Sapper Tom Hicks' account. According to Tom Hicks, the officer who led the successful patrol to the ferry was Lieutenant Tim Hall, C Troop, 1st Parachute Squadron, RE.

We didn't have any information about the 2nd Army who were to relieve us in two days and none of the wirelesses were working. Therefore things went from bad to worse. My best friend was killed by a mortar bomb landing on his head about the eighth day, although I didn't see him killed. His name was Tom Brooks.[41]

Monday, 25th September
On the evening of the ninth day we were informed that we were going to try and escape over the river. It was a wet and windy night; we were gathered together in various units under Captain George of the 1st Parachute Squadron RE. We were told to wrap rag round our feet to make no noise as we had to go near the German lines. We started off about 2130 hours that evening. There were about 50 people; we crossed the main road and walked up the garden of one of the houses, and at the end of the garden we went right. I think we should have gone left! We had gone about 100 metres when we were halted, not knowing by who. After a few minutes we moved on, we were then fired at by an automatic close by, hitting my friend Doug Chiltern in the eye and arm. I was next to him in the rear. It appeared that it was our own people who were guarding the rear who thought we were Germans. We had to pass my friend over to them; he survived and was a prisoner.

We carried on to a junction where we came under machine gun fire. I had a Bren gun and with Sergeant Smith's Sten gun we returned the fire but were unable to see anything. My Bren gun jammed; I suppose it was full of sand etc., so I threw it away. We marched on for a few miles and were lost. We went down a small track and at the bottom we were again stopped by the Germans. As we went on, my friend Joe Davies was hit in the knee by a bullet, so us four at the rear of the group retreated and I bandaged my friend's leg up and helped him across a field where we were machine gunned once again. We rolled under a wire fence and laid in a gulley until things quietened down. After about fifteen minutes I whispered to my friend that we would be going back. I didn't get a reply and thought he was dead. It appears afterwards that he couldn't walk, so he would not hold us back. He laid there until daybreak then gave himself up.

My friend Alec Johnstone had got by the Germans and walked to the river and swam over to freedom. That left me and Driver Whitehouse. We went back the way we came and had some near escapes. We went to rest in a school but when we went to sit down there were about fifty pairs of boots lined up, so we got out very quickly. Carrying on up the road, my mate wanted to give himself up. I persuaded him to carry on, saying we would have a rest in one of the houses. We came to a bungalow on a corner and walked in, we got halfway down to the basement stairs to find about twelve Germans resting there. Imagine the surprise (and shock) for us and them because we quickly retreated, and they rushed after us chasing us up the garden. It was like daylight with the Very lights that they let off. We went through the bushes at the end of the garden into a field; we walked along a path on the edge of some trees. A German soldier passed on the narrow path, not realising who we were, then I saw a party of Germans sitting around a fire only about 60 feet away. They didn't see us as we carried on. Seeing some lights at the end of a narrow road, we kept to one side and walked towards them. We came to a hill with trees right along. I told my friend that I would go forward and see what was happening. I had crawled about 20 metres when I came across some trenches, then I heard somebody snoring. I went back for my mate and we crawled through and down the other side of the bank through a wire fence, over a road and then we were only about 100 metres to the river.

---

41   Sapper Thomas Brooks, 2189799, C Troop, 1st Parachute Squadron RE, aged 24. No known grave.

What a relief. We must have been walking five to six hours in the pouring rain. I was a good swimmer but my friend could not swim. I wouldn't leave him, so we walked along the riverside until we saw a building, either a gasworks or a brickworks. It was very dark, then we turned the other way and to our surprise we found two boats that had washed up. I think they had been used in the evacuation and were sunk. Using some wood for oars, I pushed the boat out until I was up to my neck in the water then jumped in. The tide was very strong and twisted us round in the water but we managed to get to the other bank safely, we thought. But to our surprise against the skyline we saw a soldier. It was a few minutes of tension as it could have been a German. It was an officer from the Dorset Regiment. He enquired if we had seen any of his men. He had sent 200 men over to help relieve us – I think they had all been captured.

Tuesday, 26th September
In the morning we went to a school in Nijmegen, then the next day to Brussels and a flight home.

Sapper Tom Hicks, C Troop, 1st Parachute Squadron, Royal Engineers

The 1st Parachute Squadron Royal Engineers was only a small unit in the 1st Parachute Brigade but an important one. The men of the brigade, 1st, 2nd and 3rd Parachute Battalions were very protective towards us; the cry of 'Send in the Sappers' was quite common amongst the Djebels in North Africa and the mountains of Sicily. So we did not fight as a unit very often, A Troop, B Troop and C Troop, with the 1st, 2nd and 3rd Battalions.

Sunday, 17th September
Good take-off. I ate a cheese sandwich and drank a bottle of beer on the plane. Over the Dutch coast whole villages were under water, I could see the red roofs peeping out, and a few gliders that had forced landed in a few dry fields, also a flak ship burning in a river. When I landed on the heath on that Sunday afternoon with the 1st Parachute Brigade, there were about six sappers with me in the Dakota. On the DZ we joined an officer and some more of our lads of C Troop. There was a farm alongside our DZ named 'Klien-Amerika'. We dug our slit trenches in the garden facing the DZ. We then began to collect the containers lying around making a dump in the garden. We used the farm horse and cart (and also the farmer). Germans in the woods opposite started to mortar us and also fire MG42s into our position. It was here we received our first casualty when one of the lads, Geordie, had several toes shot off. They hit and set fire to the barn killing the horse. We thought it was rather callous of the farmer when he came out of the burning barn with a huge chunk of horse flesh; little did we know that in a few short weeks how welcome that meat would have been.

Monday, 18th September
We kept our part of the DZ clear until the gliders arrived, and what a sight it was. They landed all around us, some crashing into the woods, and a few overturning, but plenty made good if bumpy landings. I remember the chalked slogans on the sides of the gliders – 'The Vestal Virgins', 'Up Yours Hitler' etc. It was like watching a giant cinema screen and the quiet DZ erupted with the noise of battle. The lads had just cleared the DZ when a gaggle of Messerschmitts strafed the now-deserted gliders.

We loaded our airborne trollies and set out for, as we thought, Arnhem Bridge. We passed the staff car all shot up with the bodies of the two German officers with their driver all dead, hanging out of the doors. Several Dutch ladies were sweeping the broken glass from the road; we had seen our first dead Germans.

Tuesday, 19th September
I think we reached Oosterbeek crossroads and dug-in around the Castle Sonnenberg, nearly opposite the Hartenstein. (The castle has been demolished and a home for old people now stands nearby, also named 'Sonnenberg'.) We fought our own battle in the houses and woods around, helped by anyone who came along, glider boys, paras, whatever. The MG42s, mortar and air bursts never stopped. I remember running through the trees and across the road draped in flapping water bottles, past the prisoner of war cage, i.e. the tennis courts, to the water point and thinking, *Hell, I have to go back now,* to the yells of the boys in their slit trenches shouting encouragement. I was wounded in the woods later on, or rather I was wounded twice in my neck in the woods.

Wednesday, 20th September
The highlight of the battle for me was our 'Sapper Patrol'. Lieutenant Tim Hall, George 'Cosy' Cossadinas and I set off on the Wednesday night to carry out a recce across the river to the now-blown railway bridge. It was very dark as we dashed through the streets and lanes; everyone had shot at us, friend and foe. We parked the Jeep in the trees and an old Dutch ferryman took us across the river to the Driel side; he said he would wait for us. The Dutch ferryman was sat in a small hut when we arrived, the ferry was shown on our map as 'Driel Veer' and it wasn't very far from the old church.[42] There must have been a few Germans roaming around because there were plenty of slit trenches around the river bank. We called at a Dutch house for information (I think they made cider here). They told us that German patrols were wandering with no set pattern, so we must have been lucky.

We walked to the bridge; our job was to examine the bank seats, the speed of the current and depth of the river. We did this by tying a hand grenade to a length of parachute rigging line, with a knot at every foot and dunking it in the river. Our information was to be sent to the sappers of the relieving troops. The Dutchman was waiting and we arrived back at the Hartenstein in good heart, and strangely enough, we all enjoyed it. Lieutenant Hall hadn't been with us for long. I know he was a Catholic and me being the same, I was asked if I would 'bat' for him (or bodyguard as we called them) but I was 'one of the boys' and batman was not for me. He went to Arnhem by glider. He was wounded later on and I think I spoke to him in the German barracks used for a hospital at Apeldoorn. (It was here that the Dutch nurses refused to treat German wounded, so they were not allowed to treat us).

Thursday, 21st September–Saturday, 23rd September
We were dug-in a hundred yards or so from the Utrechtseweg. We could hear the tanks but they kept to the road and didn't venture into the woods. There was no need, they just lobbed shells and airburst at us.

We did have one 'brewing up'. There was a self-propelled gun (SP) not far from us, somewhere in the lane behind us (where the Airborne Monument now stands). Curly came up with one of our anti-tank guns pulled by a Jeep and we went to cover him and the gun. The anti-tank gun and

---

42 Pieter Hensen.

the Jeep came up the lane from the main road to our position, and then we guided it to our left, not far from the area where the SP gun had been tormenting us. The lane was quite bushy and we had to break down some bushes so the gun could be sighted. We manhandled the gun into the shrubbery, the gunnery sergeant took aim and hit the SP first round, he then hitched up and away he went, leaving us to the anger of the burning SP crew's comrades; they gave us a real plastering for a couple of hours.[43]

We could also hear the German broadcasting van, asking us to surrender and playing 'Pistol Packing Mama, Lay Your Pistol Down'.

I told you I used to trot down to the water point with a cargo of water bottles, well, later on in the week this was denied to us, but we found in the woods near Sonnenberg a stone shrine, like an altar, and in front a stone font full of water and several families of frogs. This helped us along when the green slime had been skimmed off. My No. 2 on the Bren was killed here when he jumped into my slit trench instead of his own. (I have often since searched for the mausoleum, to once more take of the water, but it must have gone the way of all good mausoleums).

There was another incident in these woods, something I have never told anyone about. I think I was a little ashamed, I don't know why, because all soldiers have to retire some time. I think it was the sheer panic on some of the young lads' faces. The group of Borderers came running through the woods towards us through our positions. I remember so clear, a young officer (he was wearing horn-rimmed glasses), shouting, 'Back! Get bloody back, there's a platoon driving a bloody company back!' I wonder why, after 48 years, a small incident like this (which was no big deal) should stick in my mind. There were a good number of men in our division who had not been in the army very long. Some in our squadron about six months, most of us had seen action in North Africa, Sicily and Italy. It takes a couple of days to settle down to battle conditions.

Sunday, 24th September

Back in the woods things were getting worse. I was already wounded once, hit with a small piece of shrapnel in the back of the neck, drew blood, nothing much, and a few days later, on the Sunday, wounded again and this time it put me out of the battle. I don't know what hit me, a mortar landed well-nigh on top of me; there was so much 'iron' flying around, and there was only my head poking out of the ground. It hit me in the neck in the same place and I felt the blood running down my neck. Curly helped me up, Lucky dashed across the field for a Jeep, bombs were bursting all over the place. There were Red Cross Jeeps running around on bare rims with stretchers on the back and that is how Curly took care of me. I was with or near Curly Plummer most of the time, and it was he who took me to the field dressing station, 'Gelders Hoff', when I was wounded. Things were very hazy, lying on a floor next to a wounded SS man. Heavy shell fire in the night, hit the house several times. A Dutchmen and his wife were with us, both wounded.

Monday, 25th September

The MO told us that the division were retiring across the river and couldn't take us with them. My mate came to take me across the river but I couldn't move. Curly Plummer was one of the few who crossed the river and came home in one piece. I had to wait for the Jerries to move in. Of course I ended up a POW like hundreds of others, and like the SS men told us, 'For you the war is over.'

---

43   The anti-tank gun was manhandled into position just off Oranjeweg near the Nassau Laan junction. The SP gun was on the edge of the open field to the northern edge of the wood.

4

261 Field Park Company, RE Defence Platoon, Headquarters 1st Airborne Division. Advance Workshop Detachment, REME

Introduction

261 Field Park Company Royal Engineers (Airborne)

261 Field Park Company Royal Engineers (Airborne) came under command of Major J.N. Chivers. Although Chivers did not take part in the airborne operation he led the Seaborne Tail along with the company heavy equipment.

261 Field Park Company were split into three separate detachments for the operation.

No. 1 Detachment of five men under command of Lieutenant W.H. Skinner, attached to 4th Parachute Squadron RE. One Jeep and Airborne Trailer. Lance Corporal Roff, Lance Corporal Trim, Driver Witmore, Driver Day and Sapper Connolly.

No. 2 Detachment of five men under command of Sergeant E. Flower, attached to 1st Parachute Squadron RE. One Jeep and Airborne Trailer. Sapper L.T. Anderson, Sapper Battersby, Sapper Collins, Sapper Bryant and Sapper Cooksley.

No. 3 Detachment of nine men under command of Lance Sergeant M.J. Potter, attached to 9th Field Company Royal Engineers including one Airborne Trailer, 1one Matchless motorcycle and one Clark Air Tractor (Bulldozer). Sapper Anderson, Sapper Greenwood, Sapper Cheetham, Sapper Boden, Sapper Page, Sapper McFarlane, Driver Clarke, Sapper Diamond and Sapper Belcher.

Each Jeep/Trailer contained:

25 Anti-Tank mines or 100 Hawkins Grenades
300 lbs explosives
General field engineering stores

The company role on joining up with the unit to which it was attached was to provide assistance in organising an RE dump from captured equipment with the Clark Air Tractor unit to assist clearing the landing zone (LZ) of stuck vehicles, earth moving and to provide the ability to construct (or clear an existing) airstrip. First and foremost as skilled engineers they were to provide any engineering roles such as the removal of demolition charges from bridges or other functions that the Parachute Squadron were unable to fulfil because of their lack of tools and equipment. Because of the way the battle developed, 261 Field Park Company RE were unable to fulfil any of their highly trained specialist roles and ended up like most of the other Royal Engineers being used as infantry, a role which they performed admirably.

Commander Royal Engineers 1st Airborne Divisional Operational Instruction No. 1 dated 12 September 1944[1]

Glider Allotment:

> 9th Field Park Company RE were allotted 14 gliders on the 1st Lift
> 261 Field Company RE were allotted one glider on the 1st Lift
> 261 Field Company RE were allotted one glider on the 2nd Lift
> HQRE were allotted one glider on the 1st Lift. (HQRE will arrange resupply with 261 Fd Pk Coy RE)
> 1st Parachute Squadron RE were allotted three gliders on the 1st Lift
> 261 Field Park Company RE were allotted one glider on the 2nd Lift
> 4th Parachute Squadron RE were allotted three gliders on the 1st Lift
> 261 Field Park Company RE were allotted one glider on the 2nd Lift. (1) Detachment

Det 261 Fd Pk Coy RE (less Clark Crawler Det)
Operation of RE Stores (Resupply and captured stores) in area FMC. All Dets will concentrate at RE Stores Dump area FMC.

According to the Commander Royal Engineers 1st Airborne Divisional Operational Instruction No. 1 dated 12 September 1944.

Glider Allotment:

> 261 Field Company RE allotted 1 glider on the 1st Lift.

I can find no further details of this 1st Lift glider or the contents, however it would make sense that No. 2 Detachment attached to 1st Parachute Squadron RE would land on the first day alongside 1st Parachute Brigade.

---

1   Sources: Air 37/1217 Air Movement Table Operation Market
    WO 171/1515 War Diary 9th Field Company RE
    WO 171/1609 War Diary 261 Field Park Company RE (Airborne)
    Operation Instructions Royal Engineers, 1st Airborne Division
    Report by CRE, 1st Airborne Division

Monday, 18th September
Tarrant Rushton 2nd Lift

Hamilcar Glider. Engineer Stores. One of three bulk-loaded Hamilcars containing ammunition, ordnance stores and engineers stores. Chalk numbers 913–915. '12 troops of 261 Field Park Company RE accompanied this mission'.[2]

As only 22 men from the company went on the operation I am unsure about the number of men (twelve) attributed to this sortie. However, I believe that not all detachments flew together in the same designated Chalk numbers. See No. 3 Detachment.

Out of three bulk loaded Hamilcars which landed on the 2nd Lift, the contents of two were successfully recovered; the remaining one the Germans captured before it could be emptied.

Hamilcar Loads

Glider No. 1 75mm HE Fuse M54 20 Panniers
6-pdr A Tk APCBC 15 (Panniers)
3-inch Mortar HE 5 (Panniers)
17-pdr AP 60 Rounds

Glider No. 2 RE 10 16 Panniers
75mm HE Fuse M54 10 (Panniers)
6-pdr A Tk APCBC 10 (Panniers)
3-inch Mortar HE 6 (Panniers)
17-pdr AP 30 Rounds
Barbed Wire 4 Rolls
Mines A Tk Mk5 40
Tape Mine 4 Rolls
Shafts, Pick 4
Heads, Pick 2
Signs, Mine 4
Pickets, Screw 16

Glider No. 3 RE10 9 Panniers
6-pdr A Tk APCBC 5 (Panniers)
3-inch Mortar HE 4 (Panniers)
Ord Stores 30 (Panniers)

Keevil 2nd Lift

No. 1 Detachment, 5 Personnel under command of Lieutenant W. Skinner.
Horsa Glider, Chalk No. 968.[3]
Contents: Jeep, Trailer, Motorcycle.

---

2   Arie-Jan van Hees, *Tugs and Gliders To Arnhem* (A.J. van Hees, 2000), page 161.
3   John Silz, *A Token Force: The 261 Field Park Company RE (Airborne) at Arnhem* (Toronto: Travelogue 219, 2015), page 19.

1 AIRBORNE DIVISIONAL SUPPORT 317

Down Ampney 2nd Lift (maybe 1st Lift?)
No. 2 Detachment, 5 Personnel under command of Sergeant E. Flower.
Horsa Glider, Chalk No. 852,[4] listed under Admin.
Contents: Jeep, Trailer, Motorcycle.

Down Ampney 2nd Lift
No. 3 Detachment. 9 Personnel under command of Lance Sergeant M.J. Potter.
Horsa Glider Chalk No. 848, listed under 9th Field Company RE.
Contents: Clark Air Tractor, Trailer, Motorcycle.
All detachments arrived safely on the LZ at approximately 1430 hours.

No. 3 Detachment under Lance Sergeant Potter could not immediately make contact with 9th Field Company RE so Lance Sergeant Potter decided to make his way to Oosterbeek riding on his Matchless motorcycle with the rest of the detachment sitting on the Clark Air Tractor driven by Sapper Tommy Cheetham or on the airborne trailer in tow.[5] When they reached Divisional HQ at the Hartenstein at around 1800 hours they linked up with 9th Field Company RE and were deployed in an infantry role to the west of Divisional HQ north of Utrechtseweg to the Huize de Sonnenberg estate. The Clark Air Tractor was parked close to the Utrechtseweg and saw no more action. The Sonnenberg area had park-like woodland interspersed with open field areas intersected by tracks and the diagonally running Sonnenberglaan which ran from the Utrechtseweg/Hoofdlaan junction in a north-westerly direction towards Valkenberglaan intersecting the Sonnenberg estate.

Detachment No. 2 were unable to make contact with 1st Parachute Squadron RE. (There were, however, a small party of the RE 1st Parachute Squadron in the Sonnenberg area.)

Tuesday, 19th September
Detachment No. 1 were attached to 4th Parachute Squadron RE. Early Tuesday morning, along with the 4th Parachute Squadron RE, they moved to the Wolfheze Station, dug-in and were placed in reserve for 4th Parachute Brigade. At 1130 hours along with 4th Parachute Squadron RE they moved eastwards parallel to the railway line towards LZ 'L' along Johannahoeveweg. Around 1600 hours, the detachment got caught up in the withdrawal of Hackett's 4th Parachute Brigade across the railway line and Wolfheze crossing. Some of 4th Parachute Brigade that could, climbed the steep embankment and crossed over the railway line into the woods beyond whilst others headed back towards Wolfheze to cross the railway level crossing there. Many of 4th Parachute Brigade made their way through a culvert east of Wolfheze underneath the railway embankment with the aid of Royal Engineers. Members of No. 1 Detachment were last seen withdrawing through the railway culvert. It is believed that Lieutenant Skinner and three of his men were taken prisoner after crossing under the railway and entering the woods, with another two of the detachment taken prisoner shortly afterwards. Lieutenant Skinner was subsequently murdered by the Germans whilst marching at the head of a column of British prisoners on Wednesday 20th along the Dreijenseweg probably towards the German HQ at the Leeren Doedal Inn at the top of the road at the junction with the Amsterdamseweg. A German

---

4   *Tugs and Gliders To Arnhem*, page 174.
5   Lance Sergeant Mervyn J. Potter, 261 Field Park Company, Royal Engineers. Correspondence with editor, 1992.

SS Rottenführer armed with a captured 9mm Sten gun climbed out of his trench and opened fire on the column headed by three officers, Captain Ian Muir, 'D' Squadron, Glider Pilot Regiment, Lieutenant Skinner, 261 Field Park Company RE and Lieutenant George Paull, OC 'X' Troop, 2nd (Oban) Airlanding Anti-Tank Battery, RA. Tragically, Skinner and Muir were both killed in the burst. A nearby German SS officer immediately shot the offending German dead, but it was too late for Skinner and Muir.

No. 2 Detachment arrived in Oosterbeek on the Tuesday morning and reported into Divisional HQ at 0900 hours. They were then attached to 9th Field Company RE and deployed as infantry on the Sonnenberg estate. Both No. 2 and No. 3 detachments were moved by 9th Field Company RE into a secondary defensive line position giving greater depth to the defence. Around 1100 hours the area was strafed by German fighter aircraft causing no casualties to the detachments.

Wednesday, 20th September
Both detachments were now dug-in on the north side of Utrechtseweg in the grounds of the Sonnenberg estate facing German infantry and armour threats from the west and north. This area formed the north western section of the divisional defensive perimeter and was held by a mixed force of 261 Field Park Company RE, 9th Field Company RE, elements of 1st Parachute Squadron, 4th Parachute Squadron RE, A Company, 1st Battalion The Border Regiment, 'E' and 'F' Squadrons, Glider Pilot Regiment and to the north up until Thursday night, the 21st Independent Parachute Company. The Germans started shelling and mortaring the area early on and probed the western defences with infantry from SS-Bataillon Eberwein supported by PzKpfw B2(f) tanks from Panzer-Kompanie 224. One such tank was knocked out around 1500 hours as it crossed the Sonnenberglaan by a 17-pounder anti-tank gun of X Troop 2nd (Oban) Anti-Tank Battery RA situated on the road junction with the Utrechtseweg.

Thursday, 21st September–Sunday, 24th September
Thursday at 0600 hours, a heavy mortar bombardment began and continued throughout the rest of the day. The remaining days were filled enduring mortar bombardments and shelling which resulted in several of the company being wounded by fragments. Trips to refill water bottles were fraught with danger but nonetheless successful. On several occasion members of the company were called forward to reinforce forward positions.

Monday, 25th September
At 2115 hours the two detachments began to withdraw down to the river having previously destroyed and made unserviceable any items of equipment. Further casualties were sustained during the evacuation with one fatality incurred during a particularly heavy mortar bombardment of the polder resulting in the death of Sapper Lennox 'Todd' Anderson, whose body was later recovered from the Rhine. On arriving at the south bank the men made their way towards Nijmegen, many getting lifts on DUKWs or Jeeps, some walking. On arrival they met up with the Seaborne Party under Major J.N. Chivers. After a couple of days the Arnhem men were flown back to the UK.

Out of the twenty-two men that went on the operation, twelve escaped across the river including two wounded. Nine were taken POW, three of whom were wounded. One was murdered whilst a POW and one KIA.

1 AIRBORNE DIVISIONAL SUPPORT 319

1st Airborne Division Headquarters Defence Platoon[6]

The 1st Airborne Divisional Defence Platoon was formed around a nucleus of men from the Oxfordshire and Buckinghamshire Light Infantry (43rd and 52nd). By the time of the Arnhem operation the platoon had been joined by members of other regiments and was commanded by Lieutenant A.D. Butterworth, Parachute Regiment.

The Defence Platoon along with the HQ, RASC, were based at Leadenham High House a few miles north of the 1st Airborne Divisional, HQ, at Fulbeck Hall, Lincolnshire. The surrounding area contained the divisional support units such as the RAOC and REME HQ at Fulbeck Manor and the HQ for the divisional artillery and engineers situated at Fulbeck House.

Sunday, 17th September, LZ 'Z'

HQ 1st Airborne Division including Major General Urquhart along with personnel of the Divisional Headquarters Defence Platoon, CRE, AA & QMG, ADMS, A, B, C and G Section Divisional Signals and a PR team took off in ten Horsa gliders (Chalk Nos. 431–440) flown by glider pilots from HQ 1 Wing, 24 Flight 'G' Squadron Glider Pilot Regiment towed by Stirlings of 190 Squadron and 620 Squadron from RAF Fairford.[7]

General Urquhart's personal glider was piloted by the CO of No. 1 Wing, Glider Pilot Regiment, Colonel Ian Murray and his co-pilot Lieutenant Brian Bottomley.[8] Urquhart's glider had on board his batman, Private Hancock; aide-de-camp Captain G. Chatfield-Roberts; Captain, Reverend George A. Pare; two MPs, Lance Corporals Jackie Mole and 'Paddy' Breen from No. 4 Section, Provost Company; along with their Police Matchless 350cc motorcycles.[9] Urquhart also had on board his personal Jeep along with two members of the HQ Defence Platoon, Privates 'Nobby' Clark and Vic Holden, seated at the rear of the glider.

One of the HQ 1st Airborne Division gliders, flown by Staff Sergeants Ken L. Bryant and George Duns, took off at 0930 hours carrying signals equipment including a Jeep and trailer and four personnel plus Major H. Maguire, GSOII Div HQ, Intelligence Branch. The glider had a tow rope failure in low cloud at about 2,000 feet and was forced to ditch in a farmer's field on the Wiltshire/Gloucestershire border. They successfully landed with the 2nd Lift on the 18th September and made their way to the Divisional HQ at the Hartenstein where they dug-in, with Bryant sharing the slit trench for most of the battle with Sergeant Bill Briggs, GPR. The two glider pilots occupied the area to the southwest of the Hartenstein Divisional HQ perimeter close by to the tennis courts where the German POWs were kept until the withdrawal.[10]

Lieutenant Alfred D. Butterworth and his 1st Airborne Division Headquarters Defence Platoon deployed in the Divisional HQ perimeter close to the Hartenstein alongside all the other attached divisional units. These units included REME, RASC, Provost Company, Royal Signals, GHQ Signal Liaison Regiment (Phantom, ten men), 6080 and 6341 Light Warning Units RAF, two US Air Support Signal Teams of the 306th Fighter Control Squadron and Glider Pilot elements.

---

6   Sources: War Diary: HQ 1st Airborne Division Operation Instructions 1st Airborne Division.
7   *Tugs and Gliders To Arnhem*, p.60.
8   Urquhart, *Arnhem*, p.27.
9   Jack Turnbull & John Hamblett, *The Pegasus Patrol* (Jack Turnbull, 1994), p.120.
10   Staff Sergeant Ken L. Bryant, correspondence with editor, 1991.

The Defence Platoon slit trenches were dug along the south side of Utrechtseweg in front of the Hartenstein, in some cases burrowing under the road surface to provide extra cover. Other members of the Defence Platoon occupied a small lodge next to the nearby fire station and a small force were sent to defend the house 'West End' on the corner of Utrechtseweg and Steynweg. The platoon remained in its divisional protective role until the evacuation when it was one of the last units to reach the riverbank during the night and early morning of the 25th/26th September. The platoon suffered six killed during the battle mainly from mortar and shellfire.

1st (Airborne) Divisional Workshops Royal Electrical and Mechanical Engineers

In June 1944 plans were drawn up for an Airborne REME element. The workshop of 1st Airborne Division at full strength consisted of 220 men and six independent Light Aid Detachments (LAD) with each detachment composed of 10–15 men, under a warrant officer class 1 (Artificer Sergeant Major – ASM). The role of the Light Aid Detachments was to provide each individual unit, battalion etc., with a repair facility or to forward major repairs to the workshops. No. 3 LAD and No. 6 LAD were short in numbers for the Arnhem operation and were made up to strength by workshop personnel.[11]

> No. 1 LAD attached to 1st Airlanding Brigade, i/c ASM T. Dunlop
> No. 2 LAD attached to 261 Field Park Company, RE i/c ASM Mathewick
> No. 3 LAD attached to 1st Parachute Brigade, i/c ASM 'Jaspar' Jaboor
> No. 5 LAD attached to 1st Airlanding Light Regiment RA, i/c ASM L. Short
> No. 6 LAD attached to 4th Parachute Brigade, CO Lieutenant A.M. Brodie
> No. 13 LAD attached to 1st Airborne Division Signals, i/c ASM A.H. Roles

HQ REME consisted of the adjutant to HQ REME, Captain A.F. Ewens in the absence of Comd REME plus 3 ORs (batman/driver, clerk and driver) with one Jeep and trailer. Between 60–70 REME men in total formed the divisional content split between the HQ REME, REME workshops and LAD units with various men attached to either glider or parachute units. REME Advance Workshops Detachment equipment strength comprised two Jeeps, one welding trailer, one wireless trailer, nine motorcycles, eighteen folding bicycles and two handcarts.

Advance Workshop Detachment REME

The month before the Arnhem operation, REME formed an Advance Workshop Detachment comprised of 37 men with Lieutenant G. Manning in command, based at Sleaford, Lincolnshire. As with many of the divisional units, REME had a Seaborne Tail which would accompany XXX Corps with heavier workshop equipment which would join the airborne element on successfully linking up, or at least that was the intention.

---

11   Joe Roberts, *With Spanners Descending* (Liverpool: Bluecoat Press, 1996), p.38. Joe and I kept in contact for over eight years and it was after he had contributed his reminiscences to me in 1983 that he decided to continue his research into REME at Arnhem which resulted in his fine account which he eventually published in 1996.

In the planning stage of the operation it was considered that the main role of REME would probably be the maintenance of wireless sets and weapons and that there would be no time or opportunity during the operation for major repairs to vehicles. All Jeeps for the operation were supplied with spares in order that drivers could carry out any repairs.[12] As things turned out, during the static perimeter phase of the battle, Advance Workshop Detachment REME carried out numerous repairs on Jeeps which proved very vulnerable to mortar shrapnel, particularly Jeep tyres which were susceptible to splinters. Jeep petrol tanks were often punctured and in at least eight cases Jeeps were damaged in this way. With the increasing intensity of mortar and shell fire it became difficult to carry out any movement for any period of time above ground, although one deep REME slit trench in the grounds of the Hartenstein was put to good use providing an inspection pit for Jeeps. One such repair to a Jeep clutch was being carried out when a particularly heavy barrage descended, leaving one mechanic underneath a suspended engine; fortunately the remaining mechanics remained above ground supporting the engine throughout the barrage. Weapon maintenance certainly kept the Advance Workshop Detachment armourers busy, with the harsh conditions of house to house fighting taking a toll on weapons. Sten gun magazine springs proved a great problem (throughout the division) due to the poor quality of the springs. This problem was encountered numerous times especially at the most inopportune moments as has been mentioned many times by the combatants themselves. The sandy conditions around Oosterbeek did not help matters, requiring constant weapon cleaning and maintenance of magazines. Magazine springs left fully loaded for more than a few days became fatigued and became extremely unreliable. Armourers were required to replace overheated Bren gun barrels and provide replacement Brens from the few supplies that were recovered. Three Bren guns recovered from containers were covered with thick packing grease and required several hours of de-greasing before it was discovered that they were missing breech blocks and were useless. Unfortunately the Workshop Wireless Trailer was destroyed on the LZ; nevertheless the wireless mechanics of the Advance Workshops Detachment REME carried out 36 wireless repairs during the operation.

Sunday, 17th September

Sixteen REME men would take part in the 1st Lift. Nine from the workshops, two of whom were general fitter, Craftsman Terry Criddle and one vehicle mechanic, Craftsmen Frank Dudley. Both were attached to 1st Parachute Battalion and took off from Barkston Heath to parachute onto LZ 'X'. The other seven REME personnel were attached to 1st Parachute Brigade HQ. Four men from No. 3 Light Aid Detachment were attached to 1st Parachute Brigade. 3rd Parachute Battalion had two men attached from No. 13 LAD each allocated a Horsa glider with a Jeep. The Jeeps were allocated to provide 3rd Parachute Battalion with transport but in the event one Jeep was lost in a crash landing, although both REME men joined up with the one remaining Jeep. The 2nd Parachute Battalion also had two No. 3 LAD men attached, Lieutenant A.S.M. Jaboor and Craftsman Gillet. In total, five REME personnel made it to the bridge accompanying 2nd Parachute Battalion,[13] three of those were Lieutenant A.S.M. Jaboor, Craftsman Ducker and Craftsman Gillet. Craftsman Ducker was actually attached to the 3rd Parachute Battalion HQ Company along with Craftsman Frank Pilbeam but after landing they got separated, Ducker still managed to reach the bridge. Two REME personnel, Sergeant D.

---

12   1st Airborne Division Report on Operation Market.
13   Martin Middlebrook, *Arnhem 1944: The Airborne Battle* (Viking Books, 1994), p.288

Ferguson and Craftsman Vehicle Mechanic, G. York, MM were attached to the 1st Airborne Reconnaissance Squadron and one REME man, Sergeant Nick Carter, accompanied HQ 21st Independent Parachute Company.

On landing two of the REME men along with the 1st Parachute Brigade Transport Officer, two Provost Company MPs and battalion guides were detailed to gather at the RV and direct transport to their respective units.

Monday, 18th September
HQ REME

At 1100 hours the HQ REME glider took off from RAF Fairford. Onboard was the adjutant to HQ REME, Captain A.F. Ewens plus one OR and two other personnel, Sergeant Barraclough, clerk, and Driver Mechanic Mick Harger with one Jeep and trailer. Captain Ewens' glider came under fire on landing but the party still managed to unload the Jeep and trailer. Both glider pilots remained with HQ REME accompanying it to Divisional HQ.

Advance Workshop Detachment REME

REME gliders (Chalk Nos. 849–851) also took off from RAF Down Ampney towed by Dakotas of 271 Squadron RAF. All REME gliders landed on DZ 'X' used the previous day by 1st Parachute Brigade as their drop zone. The landings along with those of the 4th Parachute Brigade also arriving on the 18th were not entirely unopposed; in fact some gliders came under fire upon hitting the ground, although the four gliders of the Advance Workshop Detachment landed safely. One glider, Chalk No. 850, containing a Jeep and the Workshop Wireless trailer along with passengers Lieutenant H. Roberts and three ORs did come under heavy machine gun fire when it touched down. Driver Kenneth Gould, HQ REME, accompanying the Workshop Detachment in the glider was unfortunately killed whilst Lieutenant Roberts was badly wounded along with one of the glider pilots, Staff Sergeant Sydney Bland, 'E' Squadron, GPR. The remaining pilot and two REME mechanics survived. The remaining three gliders carried the rest of the Advance Workshop Detachment. One glider carried Lieutenant G. Manning along with thirteen personnel with three motorcycles, two handcarts and ten folding cycles. Another glider carried ASM A.E. Reed with thirteen personnel along with seven folding cycles and six motorcycles. The fourth glider contained AQMS R.A. Turner with the workshop Jeep and welding trailer, one folding cycle and three personnel.

It must be remembered that the REME Light Aid Detachments were accompanying their respective battalion and subsidiary units and had either parachuted in or landed by glider.

The initial REME LZ RV was on the corner of a wood on DZ 'X'. The main RV was situated at the Wolfheze railway crossing and some, but not all members arrived at 1600 hours. Some failed to arrive until 1700 hours due to problems extricating vehicles and equipment under fire. By 1635 hours those that had arrived moved off towards the Divisional HQ at Oosterbeek, Lieutenant Manning arriving at Divisional HQ around 1830 hours. As the day was drawing to a close, the Advance Workshop Detachment set up under trees along the Oranjeweg, close to the junction of Hartensteinlaan digging-in facing across a large open field into woodland to the west. These positions were adjacent to the 1st Airborne Reconnaissance Squadron HQ which had only just been set up at 1800 hours on the corner of Oranjeweg and Utrechtseweg, almost directly across from the recently established Divisional HQ at the Hartenstein Hotel.

1 AIRBORNE DIVISIONAL SUPPORT 323

Tuesday, 19th September
The German reaction to the landings had been swift and unexpected and already German infiltration had begun. The REME positions on the Oranjeweg came under sniper fire from the woods to the north-west of their trenches causing some alarm although no casualties. On the Tuesday afternoon orders came through to move out of their positions and make for the Divisional HQ and set-up the Advance Workshop behind the Hartenstein. This they did under sniper fire and found their new positions outside the tennis courts which had already begun to fill with German POWs. Trenches were dug and overhead cover was provided by earth-filled panniers and resupply containers, whilst preparations were made to receive equipment that might need REME attention. Three vehicles were requisitioned from a local garage during the afternoon and were repaired and made available along with two captured German vehicles which were put into running order and were used for ferrying ammunition supplies to the initial Divisional Maintenance Area (DMA) set up on the triangular green in front of the Hartenstein. These vehicles were later used to transport vital 75mm Howitzer ammunition from the DMA down to the 1st Airlanding Light Regiment gun positions in the church area. Such was the increase in the intensity of the mortaring and shelling the DMA was moved the following day closer to Divisional HQ. By the afternoon of the 19th, German mortars including multi-barrelled Nebelwerfer had found their range and began to mortar the Divisional HQ area.

Wednesday, 20th September
On the Wednesday, units of the 4th Parachute Brigade began to arrive in Oosterbeek after their advance north of the railway was halted along the Dreijenseweg. Amongst those that turned up at the REME Advance Workshop Detachment were the remnants of No. 6 LAD attached to 4th Parachute Brigade, under Lieutenant A.M. Brodie; the LAD unit had suffered several wounded on the way. Apparently Lieutenant Brodie was placed under field arrest upon his arrival by Artificer Quartermaster Sergeant Ron Turner and Artificer Sergeant Major Matty Reed.[14]

Thursday, 21st September–Sunday 24th September
Shortages of men in the vicinity of the Divisional HQ led to personnel of the Advance Workshop Detachment being commandeered by officers or NCOs of other units to go out on patrol or to fill gaps left in the perimeter frontline without first seeking permission from either CREME or the OC workshops. This resulted in two casualties on the first occasion with a further nine men removed on the second, none of whom made it back to the workshop, depleting the capabilities of the unit. Whilst the REME men were more than willing combatants and were first and foremost infantry-trained, their official role was one of highly skilled and valuable craftsmen.[15]

The shelling and mortaring became a daily pattern and it was during one of these mortar bombardments on Thursday, that Captain Ewens was badly wounded being caught above ground whilst making his way to Divisional HQ. Ewens was taken to the aid post underneath Divisional HQ.[16] It wasn't just men that were being put out of action; Jeeps and equipment began to suffer

---

14 Karel Magry, *Operation Market Garden Then and Now, Vols 1 & 2* (Battle of Britain International Ltd, 2002), p.666. 5
15 Report on Operation Market. Airborne Element, 1st Airborne Div. W/Shop. REME WO171/405.
16 War Diary HQ CREME 1st Airborne Division. WO171/404. Signed by Lt Col Kinvig, Comd REME (not at Arnhem). According to the War Diary, after Captain Ewens was wounded Lieutenant Brodie took

from the effects of the constant mortaring, including the welding trailer and Jeep which were destroyed. By Thursday, rations such as they were, were restricted to one-third.

As the week went by and German pressure mounted, so the perimeter decreased and German infantry could be seen infiltrating through the woodland to the south of the Hartenstein between the Divisional HQ and the river. Sniper fire became an increasing problem to contend with along with the shelling and mortaring, all of which contributed the overall feeling of exhaustion exacerbated by lack of sleep, food and water. Water supply proved precarious and was provided by a nearby well in the grounds of the Hartenstein but retrieval involved a certain amount of risk filling water bottles in daylight due to the well being covered by a German sniper.

Monday, 25th September
Orders for the withdrawal were received quite late in the day at around 2100 hours and after an hour to prepare, the Advance Workshop Detachment REME moved off towards the river at around 2200 hours, divided into two fifteen-man sections. Lieutenant Manning led with one section followed by Lieutenant Brodie with the other section. Making their way in the pouring rain, avoiding German patrols and machine guns firing on fixed lines, the two sections got split up. Coming under machine gun fire, three of Brodie's party were wounded and taken prisoner. Subsequently Lieutenant Brodie was also taken prisoner. Most of the remnants of the Advance Workshop Detachment REME made it to safety across the Rhine, some by boat and some swimming. In all, twelve were taken prisoner during the course of the battle and the evacuation, eight of those being wounded. Three were killed: Craftsmen Vincent Harvey on the 21st, wounded near the tennis courts and succumbed to his wounds whilst being carried to the Divisional HQ aid post; Corporal James Murphy was killed during the evacuation near the gas works on the Benedendorpsweg; and Craftsman Ivor Brewster died of wounds in Apeldoorn.[17]

LAD and Workshop Personnel
The LAD units and workshop personnel attached to the various brigades and battalions suffered as much as, if not a higher proportion, of POWs, wounded and killed. Not all of the exact details are available. Those that are available are reproduced below.

> **No. 1 LAD attached to 1st Airlanding Brigade, i/c ASM T. Dunlop**
> Nineteen personnel
> **No. 2 LAD attached to 261 Field Park Company, RE i/c ASM Mathewick**
> Four personnel
> **No. 3 LAD attached to 1st Parachute Brigade, i/c ASM 'Jaspar' Jaboor**
> Four POW (three wounded)
> **No. 5 LAD attached to 1st Airlanding Light Regiment RA, i/c ASM L. Short**
> Seventeen personnel

---

command of the Advance Workshop Detachment. In correspondence with the editor, Joe Roberts wrote in 1983: 'I was *most surprised* to read that Lieutenant Brodie had assumed command of our detachment. He certainly didn't give me any orders…'

17 Craftsman Vincent J. Harvey, 5990037. No known grave. Corporal James W.Murphy, 10591137, age 34. First buried near the gas works. Craftsman Ivor J. Brewster, 7590648, age 20. Treated at St Elizabeth Hospital, then moved to Apeldoorn.

No. 6 LAD attached to 4th Parachute Brigade, CO Lieutenant A.M. Brodie
    Eight attached:
    Six POW (two wounded)
    Two returned across the river
No. 13 LAD attached to 1st Airborne Division Signals, i/c ASM A.H. Roles
    One wounded returned across the river
Workshop personnel attached to 1st Parachute Brigade: 9 personnel attached
    Seven were made POW
    One KIA
    One returned across the river
Workshop personnel attached to 4th Parachute Brigade: 4 personnel attached
    One KIA
    Three returned across the river
HQ CREME: 4 personnel
    One wounded – POW
    Two returned across the river (one wounded)
    One KIA
HQ RA: One officer attached, Captain R. Hayward
    One returned across the river
1st Parachute Battalion
    One POW (wounded)
21st Independent Parachute Company
    One returned across the river
1st Airborne Reconnaissance Squadron: two attached
    One POW (wounded)
    One returned across the river
10th Parachute Battalion: two attached
    One POW
    One KIA
11 Parachute Battalion
    One POW
HQ Airlanding Brigade
    One POW
2nd Battalion South Staffordshire Regiment
    One KIA
7th Battalion The Kings Own Scottish Borderers
    One POW
1st Battalion The Border Regiment
    Two returned across the river

Lance Sergeant Mervyn J. Potter, 261 Field Park Company, Royal Engineers

261 Field Park Company RE consisted of 4 sections (troops):

> HQ Section
> Workshop Section
> Stores Section
> Mechanical Equipment/Bridging Section

HQ Section, as its name implies, was the office and transport section of the unit.

Workshop Section was made up of skilled tradesmen of all trades, such as plumbers, carpenters, painters, tinsmiths, welders, electricians, etc., and their equipment such as circular saws, welding equipment, lighting equipment were capable of being carried by Horsa glider.

Stores Section were responsible for holding and looking after field engineering stores, picks, shovels, etc.; everything which might be required for field engineering and again was transportable by Horsa glider.

Mechanical Equipment and Bridging Section – held under their wing was Bailey bridging, (demolition equipment explosives) earth moving equipment, which included TD 18 bulldozer, D4 bulldozers (both these models were originally only transportable by road/sea. I understand plans were made for the model D4 to be flown by Hamilcar glider, but I cannot confirm this. Many trial loadings were made and flown of Bailey bridging and finally established that it was a feasible proposition, should it be required.)

After D-Day in June 1944 we were continually going to airfields to take part in an operation, only to have the operation cancelled, mostly at reasonably short notice until finally Operation Market Garden went ahead. From our company went:

Lieutenant Skinner and five men. Lance Corporal Roff, Drivers Whitmore and Day, Lance Corporal Trim, Sapper Connelly (by glider). To be attached to the 4th Parachute Squadron RE for whatever work was required. I have no knowledge of what equipment they took or what airfield they flew from, but the whole party according to my information were captured very early on and Lieutenant Skinner was (I was told later by one of the released prisoners) shot by a German soldier after capture and this German soldier was immediately shot by a German officer who had witnessed the incident.[18]

Sergeant Flower and five men. Sappers Bryant, Anderson, Battersby, Collins, and Driver Cooksley (by glider). They were intended to be attached to 1st Parachute Squadron RE but I believe there was a problem in contacting them and they joined me and were attached to the 9th Field Company RE (Airborne). I know that on the night of escape, Sapper Anderson was killed, but apparently this was not witnessed.[19]

My party. Lance Sergeant M.J. Potter and nine men. Lance Corporal Underwood, Sappers Diamond, Belcher, Greenwood, Cheetham, Boden, McFarlane, Page and Driver Clarke. Our equipment was:

A Clark Air Tractor Crawler (small bulldozer of USA make), airborne trailer, Matchless motorcycle (for me) and we were attached to and under orders to the 9th Field Company RE (Airborne) and went on day two. Our trailer contained a large quantity of explosives and general field engineering

---

18 Lieutenant William H. Skinner, 258862, aged 24. Shot whilst POW, 20th September 1944.
19 Sapper Lennox T. Anderson, 1886002, aged 25. Anderson's body was later recovered from the Rhine in October 1944.

stores. I was given to understand at the pre-take-off briefing that the role my party might be expected to play was demolition or earth moving, or any other field engineering as required, with whatever tools and equipment we had or could find, with extra labour from the 9th Field Company. In order to load the bulldozer into a Horsa glider (Mk.2) a special ramp was required and this was taken around with us in a three-tonne lorry, but obviously could not be taken on an operation. It was only just possible to get it round the corner of the side entrance of the glider without causing damage and this was a continual headache to me as each time an operation was planned and cancelled we had to unload, change airfields (they told us to relieve boredom) and reload when ordered. On the last occasion, I obtained permission to fly my loaded glider to the next airfield. This fact has been disputed by some, but was a fact. It was not a popular arrangement with the glider pilots, for some reason or other, but it did save me a lot of anxiety in possibly damaging the glider. Since there would not be a special ramp to unload when we arrived (hopefully) at the landing zone, the only way to get the bulldozer out was to blow the legs off the glider with explosives so that she settled on her belly. Start up the engine; put her in gear and 'stand clear', which is exactly what we did. Since the bulldozer was stronger than the glider, there was no damage to the bulldozer.

Monday, 18th September

> Glider serial no. (British) B-27, airborne block No. 88
> Glider pilots: Lieutenant P. Brazier (KIA 23/24.9.44); Sergeant M. Hibbert, 'E' Squadron
> Chalk numbers: allocated to the 9th Squadron (to which I was attached)[20] 843 to 848 inclusive. My exact number: not known.[21]
> Tug squadron: 271 Squadron RAF, Dakota.
> Airfield of departure: Down Ampney. LZ believed to be 'X'

We left on day two and my orders were, immediately after unloading, to make contact with the 9th Field Company RE by radio (our sets having been 'netted' on D-1) and receive orders. It is well known that radio, for some reason, proved to be useless and no contact could be made. There was plenty of rifle fire coming across the LZ so I decided to move off in the direction of all the others who had landed and seemed to know what they were doing. I was on my motorcycle and the rest of my party on the bulldozer and trailer. Eventually, we came to a main road and proceeded in the direction of Arnhem and about 200 metres before the Hartenstein Hotel, we found the 9th Field Company RE and reported and were told to dig-in and wait for orders.

Tuesday, 19th September; Wednesday, 20th September
Orders to stay put (still in the same position as previous day).

Thursday, 21st September
Being heavily mortared with no chance of doing anything, I requested permission to go forward with some of my detachment and take up a frontline position between the château and the road on its left.[22] I was given permission to do this, but after several hours told to retire to original posi-

---

20   Fd Coy RE.
21   CN848.
22   Sonnenberg and Utrechtseweg.

tion with the rest of my detachment as we might be needed for some engineering. About this time, I was told to take a PIAT gun and take up a defensive position by the side of the road about 100 metres forward to our left as a German armoured vehicle had driven straight through our lines. I did this, but later was told to withdraw to original position with the rest.

Friday, 22nd September
Nothing for us to do but take the heavy mortaring and wait for orders. During a lull in the mortaring, with one of my men, took water bottles and went in the direction of Oosterbeek to try and get them filled, as the water had been cut off in our immediate area. We dodged in and out of houses, and eventually succeeded and returned to our slit trenches.

Saturday, 23rd September
I requested to go forward again as sitting in the bottom of a slit trench was becoming unbearable and I wanted to become active, but permission was refused. During this day, one of my drivers (Driver Clarke, in the next slit trench) was seriously wounded in the head with mortar shrapnel and bleeding heavily. I got him out of the slit trench and carried him over to the first aid post, a cottage or small house about 100 metres to our rear.[23]

Sunday, 24th September
Lance Corporal Underwood, Sappers Page and McFarlane were sent forward as instructed with a Bren gun and they came under orders of 4th Parachute Squadron RE. The position was forward and to the right of us. Later they were told to return.

Monday, 25th September
Sometime during the afternoon I was called to a briefing in 'the cottage' (first aid post). We were told that we were going to break out and return across the river that night and during the meantime do as much damage to our Jeeps, etc., as we could. My personal orders were that I should, together with my men, cross the river as quickly as possible after the starting time and report to the Canadian engineers who had an HQ in an orchard below the river bank on the far side and render what help we could with the manning of the boats in the evacuation.

At the appointed hour, we retreated to 'the cottage' (first aid post) in order to cross the road and on reaching the other side, I found one of my men missing, so I told the others to go on and recrossed the road, returned to the slit trenches to look for him, but did not find him. It was at this time, the Germans must have guessed there was something happening, as the mortaring became very heavy and after I recrossed the road, I consumed the whole contents of a brandy flask, thinking, *No b***** German is going to get this.* I continued on down through to the church, passing a lot of wounded men on the way and out on to the river bank, where we were instructed to lie down until called, as men were arriving faster than boats could cope. At this time, a mortar bomb fell on a man next but one to me (there wasn't much left, it severely wounded the next man, but I was untouched).

I crossed the river eventually and spent about an hour looking around the area of the orchard for the Canadian Engineers HQ without success. Wondering what to do, I was standing by a large tree when a mortar bomb exploded the other side of the tree and I must have been having a charmed life, as I was not touched. It was then I decided my luck might run out, so I set off in the direction

---

23 The cottage was the De Sonnenberg gate lodge on the corner of Sonnenberglaan.

the other chaps were taking, until we came to a mobile kitchen where we were given a hot drink, put on DUKWs and taken to Nijmegen where we received a large issue of rum, some food and sleep.

Post-Arnhem

The remainder of our company under Major J.N. Chivers arrived at Nijmegen as part of the 'Seaborne' element and we joined them for one or two days. The Arnhem men went on back to Louvain and flown home back to England and leave.

Lieutenant Skinner killed. Five men were taken prisoner.

Sergeant Flower and his men escaped except Sapper Anderson who was killed.[24]

Lance Sergeant Potter and his men escaped, except Driver Clarke who was wounded and taken prisoner. Sapper McFarlane wounded but escaped.

Specialist troops such as signals, engineers, and REME, etc., have a primary role to apply their knowledge and skills in battle as and when required, but in unforeseen circumstances, that always seem to occur in war, they are called upon to fight as infantrymen. As I see it, higher powers have to decide as and when these 'specialists troops' are used alongside the infantrymen and hope that their skills will not be needed, should they have been lost in battle. On our return to England, neither Sergeant Flower nor I were asked for a report on our Arnhem activities and it was only in 1991 that I saw a photocopy of a report made by our CO who was with the Seaborne Element. The report contained inaccuracies.

Lance Corporal Ken L. Underwood, No. 3 Detachment, 261 Field Park Company, Royal Engineers

The average soldier's view of a static battle such as around Arnhem and Oosterbeek is almost zero. 50 or 100 yards from his position is almost like a foreign country.

Monday, 18th September–Saturday, 23rd September

When we had dropped at our DZ and contacted our parties we started towards Arnhem, all at foot pace. There was some difficulty extracting the Clarke Crawler, but that was due to wrong procedure of detaching the tail from the Horsa glider, but once detached it was driven in the proper manner.

The first thing that stood out in my mind was, as we were passing what I took to be a farmhouse, the occupants, standing at the side of the lane, offered glasses of water and a few very small wizened apples. The looks on their faces were ones of welcome, yet rather scared of how we would react to them, us being foreign soldiers. I really felt rather humble, yet very glad I was there giving them a spark of hope. The next incident also involved the Dutch people. Coming into the outskirts of Oosterbeek, along the Utrecht road, we were passing a crossroads with crowds of people waving, cheering and clapping, but at the side of the road, half on the verge, was a German military vehicle with the two occupants both half in and half out, both dead. It appeared to me that the local crowds treated the dead men as just trash, which looking back in retrospect I can understand, but it stands out in my mind as 'happiness to see us and ignorance to death'.

---

24 According to Lance Corporal Ken Underwood, 261 Field Company RE, Sapper Anderson was killed on the evening of the withdrawal in the company of Sapper Battersby. He nevertheless ended up dead in the Rhine where his body was recovered in October 1944.

Pre-war postcard of the Kasteel de Sonnenberg from Sonnenberglaan. (Photo: Courtesy Gelders Archive)

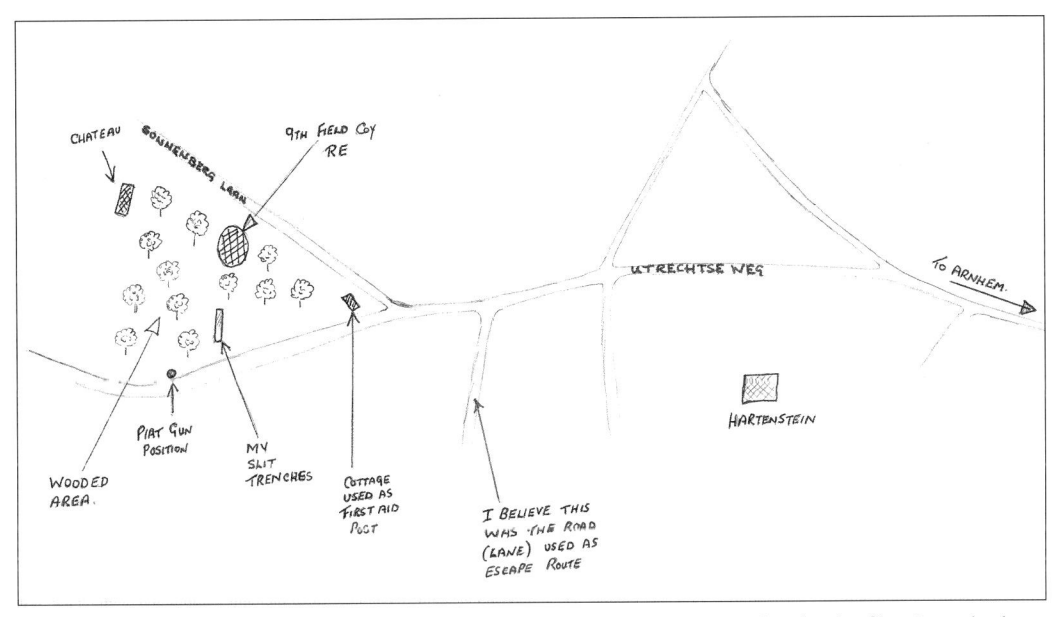

1 AIRBORNE DIVISIONAL SUPPORT 331

Lance Sergeant Mervyn J. Potter, 261 Field Park Company, Royal Engineers – his sketch of his Oosterbeek positions. The small cottage or gate lodge was, and still is, on the eastern corner of Sonnenberglaan. Kasteel de Sonnenberg, the 'château' top left of sketch.

Kasteel de Sonnenberg, pre-war. (Photo: Courtesy Gelders Archive)

Whilst entrenched in the grounds of a rather large house, Sonnenberg I believe, I heard the sound of approaching aircraft and looking up saw a Dakota transport dropping supplies in pannier baskets. The despatchers were calmly going about their job, but the thing that stuck in my mind was that the plane was on fire, blazing from the port engine, almost as far back as the doors. The heroes in that aircraft were doing their job. There were literally thousands of heroes, but only too few were recognised.

Sunday, 24th September
Sappers McFarlane and Page and I were sent forward to assist a mixed force of 9th Field Company RE, 4th Para Squadron RE and a few men from 261 Field Park Company. Detachment i/c was Sergeant Flowers, with number two Sapper McFarlane. We were ordered to take over a field of fire by Bren gun.[25] We covered a field and a lane, not a great deal of activity, just gradually losing men. I was number one on the Bren and McFarlane was number two until he got wounded, then Sapper Page took over. Sergeant McFarlane was wounded in the right hand. I cannot be sure whether by rifle, machine gun, or mortar fire, but I know he lost at least one finger. I slapped a dressing on it and I took him to the nearest first aid station situated in De Sonnenberg, and then went back to our positions where we stayed until the withdrawal.

Monday, 25th September
On the night of the withdrawal we had got to a few hundred yards from the river when I heard a rather plaintive cry of 'Don't leave me fellows.' Looking towards the sound I saw a hand waving. I said to a few of the lads, 'Come on,' so four of us grabbed him, one on each arm and one each leg. One of us said, 'Blimey, he got this far, we'll get him the rest of the way.' We went to where a queue of men were waiting patiently for boats. When one came in, we waded out and put our wounded mate on board and turned to join the queue, but those queuing yelled, 'Get in, you brought him, you take him all the way.' Grand bunch of lads.

When we got across the river we went to a farmhouse or barn, I can't quite remember. We had a snack, not much, we couldn't take too much. We embarked on a DUKW, given a dry blanket and because it was raining, stuffed them up our smocks to keep them dry. When we got to Nijmegen, we had those same blankets taken from us and given two to bed down with. Just goes to show our minds weren't working 100 percent, that single blanket was to protect us on our trip to Nijmegen.

Post-Arnhem
As to the role of our small detachment I do not think that anyone of us knew anything. The only exception to this might be our detachment i/c, Lance Sergeant Potter. This was most strange, for any previous engagement we were briefed pretty well. The Clarke Crawler tractor in fact was a small bulldozer, hydraulically operated with a five to six foot blade in front and a winch at the rear. The operator was Sapper Cheetham, and the tractor was left about twenty yards from the main road under a few trees in the grounds of the Sonnenberg, almost opposite a small road now signposted as 'Airborne Walk'.

> *There are no bad soldiers, only bad officers*
> Napoleon Bonaparte

---

25   Facing north-east.

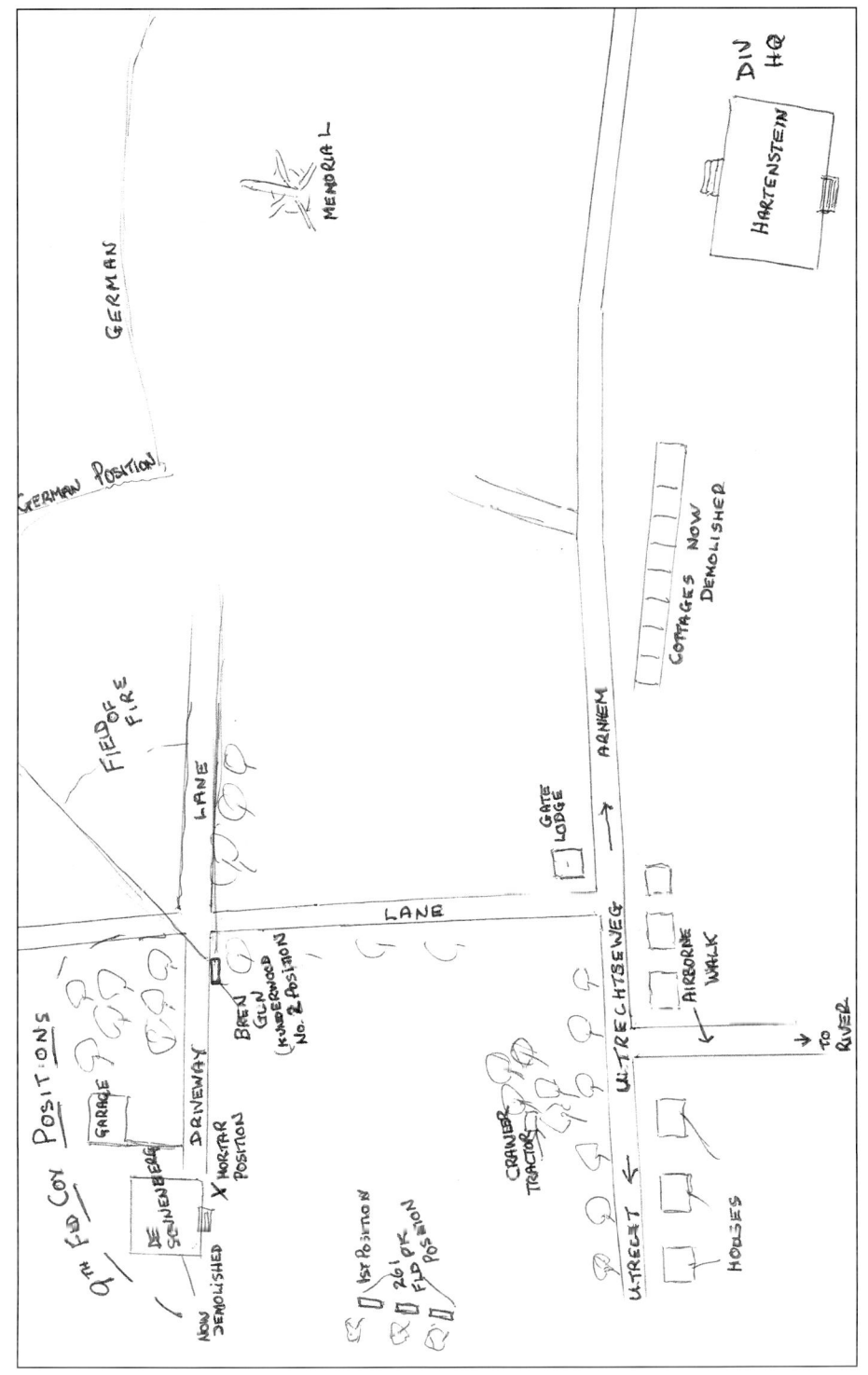

Lance Corporal Ken L. Underwood, No. 3 Detachment, 261 Field Park Company, Royal Engineers' sketch map of positions in the Utrechtseweg/Sonnenberg-glaan area.

Private Vic Holden, Defence Platoon, Headquarters, 1st Airborne Division

For weeks we waited in tents a few miles from Down Ampney Aerodrome.[26] We were seldom allowed out apart from the occasional night by lorry into Stroud under heavy warnings of no talking in the pubs. Every week we were briefed for landings somewhere! Evreux outside Paris, Maastricht near the borders of France and Germany, all duly cancelled as no longer necessary. Boredom increased; when we went on the liberty lorry we got very drunk.

Then another briefing – we have to take Arnhem Bridge in this town in Holland. The whole division is going and the army is going to meet us at Arnhem. Dutch money is given to us – this one is the real thing. We have heard that before! We are going in a week's time so everybody can have some leave; sounds crazy, not like the army at all. We have been stuck here for so long that we are being issued with tins of de-lousing powder to sprinkle on our clothes and the hairs on our bodies, and now we are assured we are going into action and we are having a 48 hours' leave. Obviously it will be cancelled before we leave on Sunday. However, two days at home is something!

I go on leave for my two days; what a pleasure to be out of those tents. The two days are soon over and back to camp we go and await the cancellation of the Arnhem attack. On the way home I wonder, *will we go this Sunday?* The war is being won in France and Belgium and nobody seems to need the best division in the British Army. The cancellation is not announced yet. More briefings on what we are supposed to do! The officers seem to have a new air of importance and seem to swagger more. Our Lieutenant Butterworth briefs us time after time on various aspects of the attack. I have no confidence in him at all. He tells us that we must not take prisoners as we have no facilities for prisoners and we are taking no food to feed them. This puzzles me; I thought that we obeyed the rules of war. What do we do if and when German soldiers surrender? Just shoot them? He is vague on this point but reiterates no facilities and no food for any prisoners. This bothers me!

Still no cancellation announced on the boards between the tent lines! It appears that we land on the outskirts of Arnhem, march in and take the bridge and the British Army meets us the next day or two. Simple enough. The Germans in the area are all stragglers from units from their 15th Army or officers' cadres or low medical category units used on supply, no match for the 1st Airborne Division, The Red Devils.

Saturday, 16th September
The Saturday arrives and still no cancellation; perhaps we shall be in action tomorrow, we hope. We draw supplies and ammunition, bandoliers of bullets and our choice of hand grenades. I choose three grenades (two Mills and one plastic fire grenade). We are given a fly button to sew on our trousers which is actually a compass in disguise. It shows true north, our 'Escape Kit!' A morphine syringe to inject into a wounded man, with instructions to mark 'M' on their forehead, so they don't get a double dose. A yellow scarf of silk and a silk map of Europe complete our battle order. All our letters and personal effects are taken away so that we cannot be easily identified if captured or dead. We clean our rifles and chat. We laugh at our mate Private Sainty, who in the NAAFI and in the billets is always going to parachute down with his fighting knife in his teeth and kill Germans: let's hope he leaves some for us!

One man is looking sad and worried and insists he will not come back. Most of us cannot imagine that we will be killed or injured; it is going to be a walk-over, the Germans won't know

26 RAF Fairford.

what has hit them. As night approaches we get quieter and everything is ready. What do we do now until tomorrow morning? The padre is giving a service for soldiers of all denominations in the big tent at the top of the field. He can get stuffed; then shouting down the lines of tents: 'Rum is being issued to all blokes who attend the service, bring your mugs and you get rum as you leave at the end of the service.' We all decide to attend the service, singing 'Onward Christian Soldiers' we await the end of the service and the rum issue. Afterwards we sit in the tent drinking our rum, chatting occasionally but thinking more of the next morning. Rise at 0400 hours and then to Down Ampney Aerodrome. Surely they can't cancel the operation now?

Sunday, 17th September

It's before dawn, dark and bloody cold. Everybody is shouting as usual, plenty of orders from all directions, it's like a beehive. Surely they can get organised without everybody shouting orders to everybody else. I am shivering with cold and I find it difficult to get my straps done up properly. Am I shaking with cold or am I nervous as to what is to come? We wait as usual, shivering. Christ, it's cold. I check and re-check the pins in the grenades I have stuck on my webbing belt, and wonder if I should have taken another bandolier of bullets. I wish I had a Sten gun or Bren gun instead of a rifle.

At long last with, of course, much shouting, we move off and arrive at the aerodrome. We are dumped in batches by the side of the runway and as dawn comes we can see masses of aeroplanes and gliders, some moving into position.

Dawn breaks. It's very cold and we are waiting. Tea is being issued off a van travelling around the files of men. We don't get any! Time goes by and the day gets better. There is now a plane and a glider quite near awaiting its passengers being loaded, and at last Nobby Clark and I are ordered on to the rear of the glider in front of us. I feel nervous and excited. This is it.

The glider is full at the back, military police with motorbikes in front of the rear of the glider and a Jeep right in front of us. Can we smoke? No, the general and his officers are up at the front of the glider; definitely no smoking! We wait, thinking, *what is going to happen? Are the Germans going to get a shock when we arrive amongst them?* From the briefing this could be virtually the end of the war; there is nothing to stop the British Army once they are over the bridges in Holland. I have been twenty-one years old for five days now. Years of training have culminated in this moment arriving, going into action with the finest troops in the world. I feel flushed and a little nervous, my usual fear beginning to worry me again. As always, I am afraid of being afraid. *Will I make the grade? Will I be a coward?* I reassure myself that I am as tough as any.

We are a long time getting airborne. Suddenly we feel a tug and we are moving, I think we are the first glider in the air! The ground is rushing past by the window beside me and then the ground is falling away beneath us. No other planes or gliders are with us. I hope we are not going on our own.

We all have a red beret neatly laid in the top of our battle order packs and round our necks we have a yellow silk recognition scarf. In full battle order we look a tough crowd with our flying smocks and airborne helmets, loaded up with grenades and ammunition. Lots of fields rushing beneath us and I wonder what part of England we are flying over. Suddenly the sea is beneath us and the sky is full of planes, 'millions' of them, everywhere the sky is thick with planes and gliders. A tow rope breaks and a glider is going down into the sea, but a large fast launch races across the water to meet it, so they are OK. Fighter planes are whipping about high above us. I've never seen so many aeroplanes, it's fantastic. We are certainly not alone!

We near the coast of Holland and it looks as if rivers run off into the land with lots of sand. There are shells bursting round us, the Germans are firing anti-aircraft. I wish I had a parachute and was going with the rest of my platoon! The explosions soon stop and we are going across very green countryside. It seems so quiet in the glider; all conversation has stopped. We must be near our destination.

The plane has let us go! This is it! Below us are large expanses of ploughed fields with small woods on the edge of the fields. To the right is a small white building with a large wall around. We are now bouncing across the field and are on our own again. Nobby and I get ready to get the tail off the glider so that they can get the Jeep out. We stop and Nobby and I dive to the stops that hold the tail on but they won't come away. I grab the axe which is fixed by them and smash the stops out. Then Nobby and I dive out and place ourselves on the ground facing the edge of the field. Nobody is shooting at us! We were on our own; now there are gliders landing everywhere all around us. We wait, but still no Germans and no shooting! The Jeeps are coming out of the gliders, soldiers and officers all over the place. Our Jeep is out and the motorbikes. Platoons are forming up with, of course, much shouting, and moving to the edge of the fields. Still no Germans!

Nobby and I shoulder our rifles and start walking to the white building. There are civilians there, standing by the wall looking at us. They look very strange. I wonder what the building can be with such a high wall around it. A lunatic asylum, they say! The 1st Parachute Brigade is jumping near the trees, a fantastic sight; the sky is full of planes and parachutes of all colours. Soon they will be joining us. That's comforting, another 1,500 men. There are civilians acting excited, wearing bands on their arms, and trying to talk to the officers but nobody seems to want to know them. Lieutenant Butterworth rushes up looking very harassed and excited. 'You two get on the general's Jeep and stay with it; keep your eyes open.' Sixty miles behind the German lines – does he think we will go to sleep? We curse him quietly and stand by the nearby Jeep.

It is the first time I have seen our new General Urquhart. Compared with our original general who got himself shot at Taranto he is a very large, tough looking man.[27] Talk has it that he has been out in the desert with the infantry. He certainly impresses me! My stomach says it must be getting near dinner time, and I fancy a fag. Better not, only a couple of yards from the general, I will be in trouble again!

I start admiring a huge German artillery gun which is parked and see a keen young officer go and check that the breech block has been removed to make it useless. The general is issuing orders to various high ranking officers; the colonel of the 2nd Parachute Battalion is ready to move off. He is going a different way to the rest of us. The 1st Parachute Battalion is going to lead, with the 3rd Parachute Battalion behind in support. The men are going up each side of the tree-lined lane pulling the handcarts that carry their ammunition and stores. They are very quiet for so many, no NCOs shouting!

It's now lunchtime and gone, no grub, no fags. Perhaps later we shall get something to eat. Where are the Germans? Not a shot has been fired yet. They must know we are here! Perhaps they have run away; I don't blame them. The general seems to be ready to move off. There is a driver in the Jeep and a corporal signaller in the centre of the back with a large wireless set. He has his earphones on and seems to be trying to 'net' into the sets of the moving battalions. Nobby Clark jumps on behind the driver and I clamber on behind the general.

---

27   Major General G.F. Hopkinson.

We're off! Slowly down the road the column of marching men, have we got a cushy number! Lots of soldiers look at the general with interest; probably they had not seen him before either. It's a nice day for going for a drive. The sun is shining, what a smashing Sunday.

Corporal Brown, the general's signaller, is trying all the time to 'net' with the other battalions wireless sets. He keeps on: 'Sunray here' – 'Sunray here.' This must be the general's personal call sign. No luck! He doesn't seem to be able to contact anybody and the general keeps looking at him with an enquiring look, sort of, 'Haven't you got them yet?' The general seems to be getting angry at the wireless set not working, and keeps looking at Corporal Brown, which the signaller obviously finds embarrassing; non-stop, 'Sunray here!'

Suddenly we are in a mass of explosions; everywhere around us are noise, smoke, pieces of metal flying about. The Jeep stops and General Urquhart and the driver hurry off into the trees on the right-hand side of the road. We are in between two groups of soldiers, but none are near us or have been hit by the shells. Nobby and I throw ourselves down a trench beside the left of the Jeep. It's nice and deep and seems to have been dug quite recently. Very kind of the Germans! I wonder what had happened to the signaller and look up over the top; he is still sitting there, saying his 'Sunray here' no doubt.

Heavy shells are still bursting in the road with masses of flame and smoke. The signaller, Corporal Brown, has slumped sideways. I yell to Nobby, 'Let's get him out,' and we rush through the noise and smoke to the Jeep. Between us we drag him out of the Jeep, cart him to the trench and throw him in, jumping in with him. Christ, its murder on the road. I can see the corporal is hit in the upper leg, so I tear his trousers further and feel weak and sick; he has a large hole right through the thick part of his upper left leg coming out the other side. He doesn't say anything, just looks at me. I am not a bloody doctor. What do I do? It doesn't seem to be bleeding much, but the hole is very large, with veins and so on hanging out. We get our field dressings out, one over each end of the hole, and tie it up. He still says nothing and makes no sound.

We know we will move soon and the orders are: *not to wait for wounded but leave them where they are.* Some branches of the trees have been blown in on our trench and we cover him with these; perhaps the leaves will help to keep him warm. The explosions on the road are easing slightly and again I look over the top to see the road deserted except for the general standing waving a walking stick in the trees by the side of the road. I get out of the trench and go towards him; the shells are still hitting the road. The general shouts, 'Get that Jeep up the road,' and I reply, 'I don't know how to drive it, Sir.' He then strides up to the Jeep to drive himself, and Nobby and I jump on the back as he moves off. This shelling can be nasty! There are some Germans around somewhere but I haven't seen one yet.

The general makes a good chauffeur! We drive slowly along the centre of the lines of soldiers. As we near a few houses there is a man screaming in a garden somewhere and somebody shouts he has been shot in the knee. Rifle and machine gun fire is now heard every few minutes and the general starts getting angry. A few rifle shots and the soldiers stop, there does not appear to be any urgency to get to the bridge and the general wants to get on. Another flurry of shots and the soldiers stop again. The general drives furiously up to some officers and shouts at them, *not to keep stopping, but get on!* Another burst of firing and the soldiers stop again. It seems only snipers are shooting at us and we keep stopping to get them before we move on again, so one sniper is stopping 1,500 men. General Urquhart is now looking furious, driving madly up the lines shouting at officers to get their men moving. I wouldn't like his anger to turn to me, he sure looks tough. Suddenly, he stops. He has seen a window with broken glass in the bedroom of a house from which he is sure sniper fire has been coming. He points to the window and shouts to me, 'Get a grenade in there.' The soldiers have stopped again and are sheltering under a low wall running along the front of the gardens.

I jump off the Jeep and run to the low wall. My fumbling fingers pull off a Mills grenade from my belt, out comes the pin, I let the arm up and wait a second and throw it. It misses the window, hits the wall and explodes. Christ, it would. Do I feel exposed, the only man standing up! I had to miss when the general is watching. I pull out the next Mills grenade, out with the pin, let the handle go, one second then throw again. It misses and hits the wall and explodes, and pieces are flying everywhere. I'm more dangerous to our soldiers than the Germans. My face is brilliant; I dare not look in the direction of the general. My last grenade, a phosphorous fire grenade. Out comes the pin and up it goes straight into the window, the tape falling away just as it goes in; a burst of flame and the room is on fire. I jump back on the Jeep and as we go by I see soldiers going into the ground floor, so any Germans there have had it!

The general is still driving away and seems to be intent on seeing that everybody is moving on towards the bridge. There is still shooting but not heavy and the battalions are moving on. We are now going into a large area of houses and the civilians are out on the pavements, cheering and smiling at us and offering the marching soldiers lemonade and fruit. The women are waving handkerchiefs and seen deliriously happy. I feel proud!

The Germans must be on the run! We come out on to a larger road and there are Germans! – German Women ATS, all walking on the pavement back to way we are coming from. The general orders Nobby Clark to go with them as escort. (I never saw Nobby Clark again.) So we are taking prisoners. I suddenly feel much more comfortable. A very large German SS officer comes along with his hands up and a small paratrooper is kicking him up the arse as he goes along in front of him. As I expected the Germans are surrendering!

We are now in a really built-up area and in front is a car with two dead Germans. As we get up to it I see that the German hanging out of the car is an officer and the top of his head has been shot off. There are a lot of pieces of grey stuff and some yellow bits, and I wonder if the grey stuff is his brains. The general has slowed right down and I see he is having a good look. Off we go again, just the general and me, and I am really alert for trouble; around any corner we could run into Germans, but we have been lucky so far! It is beginning to get dark now. I have no idea where we are but the general seems to know. He pulls up outside a house with a high hedge across the front and gets out and speaks to a young second lieutenant at the gate. Turning to me he says, 'Look after the Jeep' and walks into the house. The tall young second lieutenant standing by the entrance and I sit in the Jeep. No chance of grub again, better not have a fag, bound to be choked off by the officer. There is a lot of firing going on in the distance; it seems like half a mile away. I relax and feel hungry and tired and I want a fag. The young officer gives me a dirty look, obviously not a friendly type. You would think he couldn't see me sitting two yards away. Perhaps he is something to do with the other high ranking officer that is in the house with the general. I have had enough war today; a cup of tea would do me a treat. I bet the general's having some grub.

It is nearly dark and a full lieutenant is coming towards the Jeep; he has 'Canada' written on his arm. He starts to talk to the other officer. Running footsteps and two second lieutenants are running towards us, one with tears running down his face. They know the 'Canadian' lieutenant and are agitatedly telling him that their company is being cut to pieces. Anti-aircraft guns are firing on the soldiers from a factory area, their troops are practically out of ammunition and most of the troops are wounded or dead! Lieutenant Fraser, the Canadian officer, comes over to me. 'Get that wireless set out of the back of the Jeep, we will get the ammunition.' The tall young second lieutenant protests that it is General Urquhart's Jeep and he cannot do that. I hesitate. 'Get that wireless set out and dump it on the pavement.' I don't argue!

A young officer, this Canadian, with dark wavy hair, he looks very strong and hard, no nonsense with him! The young second lieutenant is still protesting but Lieutenant Fraser ignores him completely, so out goes the general's radio set onto the pavement. The 3rd Battalion's two officers hurry off back to where they came from. 'Let's get some ammunition,' so off we go looking for handcarts that have ammunition in them and seem to have been left abandoned by the side of the road. We fill up with all the good things, cases of bullets, mortar bombs, Mills grenades, soldiers for the use of; if a shell hits this lot we really are going to be buried in a matchbox. Lieutenant Fraser drives rather fast, I think, but the firing has died down and we can't find anyone who wants our wares; in fact you can't find anyone.

Monday, 18th September
It should be dawn soon and then things will start up again. I could do with some food, a cup of tea and a fag – no chance. As dawn breaks we head up the main road; there is already firing ahead. When do we sleep and eat?

We go up to the furthest troops we can find and give them the contents of the Jeep. There is a lot of shooting going on, and Lieutenant Fraser decides to chat to a large sergeant who is shooting a two-inch mortar virtually straight up in the air, so that the bombs land on the other side of the house where the Germans are stopping the soldiers advance. I stand by the side of Lieutenant Fraser as he chats unconcerned at the concentrated rifle fire, you'd think he was on Salisbury Plain manoeuvres. Into the Jeep and off looking for more mortar bombs and Mills grenades, bullets not required. We have our shopping list! We tear along the road, looking for handcarts. No good, bullets; and then one with Mills grenades and another with mortar bombs. We load up and back up the road to deliver the supplies. Now we have got to find .303 bullets and 9mm for Sten guns. The forward troops are in a dense housing area, then we have about a mile of open country to get back to the village where the handcarts are. These trips of ours are not unnoticed by the Germans and as we speed out of the housing area into open country they really are trying to get us, bullets in front and behind. I am glad Lieutenant Fraser drives fast. My boot suddenly rises in front of me, I had left my left leg hanging over the side of the Jeep and a bullet had hit the heel and knocked my leg up. It's unhealthy; the Germans are getting really nasty.

We load up again and taking our shopping to the forward troops. Lieutenant Fraser insists upon walking on the dead Germans. I try to avoid walking on the bodies or even looking at them, but if they are in front of him he just walks on them. I am interested to see some of the dead Germans are wearing camouflage flying smocks similar to those we wear. Lieutenant Fraser seems to be familiar with some of the NCOs and will have a chat to see if there is any help he can give; I do not feel very helpful. The excitement, the noise, the explosions, the dead, no food, no sleep, no fags, I feel irritable and decidedly anti-German, and I don't like officers much (as usual). Lieutenant Fraser amazes me, nothing bothers him. He doesn't duck when something explodes, bullets leave him unconcerned: has he got guts!

Lieutenant Fraser points out that there are fighter planes about, several of them coming straight towards us. 'Quick, get your yellow scarves off so they know we are British in this part of the road.' About ten of us lay our yellow scarves in the middle of the road and as they come close we start to wave; unfortunately they are German planes, so we take our scarves back. They turn and come back overhead but do not shoot at us; we are too close to the German, they dare not shoot.

Off we go again for more shopping; bullets and Mills grenades seem to be favourite. When we return it must be dinnertime. I feel very hungry and the soldiers are further into Arnhem. Things are really bad; the mortar bombs don't stop falling, bullets are flying everywhere. We can't see any of our soldiers and there is a tram burning in the middle of the street, smoke everywhere. Lieutenant Fraser stops the Jeep and we dive for the side of the road. Can't see and anything much for smoke and explosions. It's really dangerous! You feel if you move a muscle you're dead. We try to move forward, but it's impossible, a quick run for a few yards and then into a doorway.

A large paratrooper comes out of the smoke with his hands held out in front of him. He's shouting, 'I'm blind.' Neither of us moves. Standing up, he can't live for more than a few yards. There is a hospital about 200 yards behind us on the left, but he will be very lucky to reach there. As the smoke from the tram lifts we see our dead all over the place. Lieutenant Fraser decides to check the general's Jeep, so I stay where I am and watch him examine it.

He walks back in disgust and says, 'A bomb has hit the engine.' The Jeep looks sad. We move on very carefully and a sergeant is moving in front. Lieutenant Fraser asks if he can help and the sergeant replies that they are short of everything. A Bren carrier is abandoned nearby and Lieutenant Fraser goes and checks it. 'Hop in,' he says and off we go again. This time we are slower but you can get down behind the metal plating on the carrier and bullets just thud. When we get back, the soldiers have moved on again and it is difficult to find anybody except the dead, so we leave the Bren gun carrier and start walking up the road; the mortar bombs start dropping again! Suddenly I see a British mortar team on an open piece of ground, all dead, lying around the mortar. (The grass area in front of the Arnhem Museum in Arnhem Town). Lieutenant Fraser says, 'Where you going?' I point to the Sten guns, and say I want one. He says, 'You bloody fool, the Germans have that open ground covered, how do you think they were all killed!' I immediately lose interest in the new Sten submachine guns!

It is now getting dusk again and we can't find any British troops alive. Where are the 1st and 3rd Parachute Battalions? Lieutenant Fraser decides to find a cellar to rest for a while, and we go in a convenient door and soon find a likely cellar. It's dark in there and we wait; there are marching boots in the road above our heads – and German voices! Where are the paratroopers?

We wait and everywhere is silence. It won't be long before the paras come this way again. They're probably in other houses in the area. So we wait! It worries me in a way, I haven't seen any officers among the soldiers; they seem to be in the charge of sergeants. Funny that! I still feel hungry. How long is it now since I ate or drank anything? It's only two days but it seems ages. I wish Lieutenant Fraser smoked then he would light a fag and so could I. Lieutenant Fraser has decided that we must do something. We must go out separately and try and find soldiers and bring them back to the cellar to form a group and find where there is a unit. He will go in one direction and I another. I must crawl around in the dark and where there is movement stop and listen, make sure they are English voices and then if they are stragglers bring them back to the cellar; if they should be a unit come back to the cellar and wait for him. Anything is better than sitting in the cellar.

I make my way up and to the back of the house, lie down by the back door and look out. It's a clear moonlight night, which I decide is dodgy; I will only be able to crawl about. I start crawling towards the low hedge separating the next garden, over that and then crawling to the next hedge, stopping and looking around so that when I come back shall know where our cellar is. Over the next hedge and there are several dead bodies to crawl over, and then a British para officer is looking at me over the next hedge, his yellow scarf easy to spot. I crawl quickly towards him and as I get near I look up to speak and I see he is kneeling up looking over the hedge but he is dead, with a bullet hole in the centre of his forehead. I immediately feel very nervous, it seems I am in the land of the dead. We can't be the only British soldiers left alive; over 1000 men came this way! I can't go over the hedge by the officer so I crawl to the end of the garden and look over that hedge. No sound, so I decide to rest a while. My nerves are jumping, dead bodies seem to move when you crawl over them. After a while I crawl across a few more gardens without any luck, but I make sure I have my bearings – that cellar is now very important to me and I am longing to be back there in the dark.

Sometime later I get back to the cellar and there is a lot of breathing and movement. Lieutenant Fraser has found some men somewhere in the house up the street. I lean against a wall and rest, but before long Lieutenant Fraser is telling everybody he is taking us somewhere else down by the river. We should take off our boots, tie the laces together and hang them round our necks, and we should check everything to make sure nothing rattles.

As we come out of the house Lieutenant Fraser leads us quietly along a road into another one and then we have to wait. A German searchlight is sweeping the roads and a machine gun is shooting at intervals down the road. He tells us to wait and as the searchlight goes past our road four of us run across to the other side and wait for the next four. I soon realise that there are now about twenty-five of us, and we seem to go a long way until eventually we go into another house and down into the cellar. Lieutenant Fraser sent some men to various rooms, and to me in the cellar he said, 'Make me a cup of tea.'

Tuesday, 19th September

It is dawn and there is some light to see the cellar, so I unpack my mess tin and start to brew up, and light my first fag. As the water is heating I look around at my companions. Lieutenant Fraser looks as assured and unafraid as ever. Opposite me is a major from, I think, the 1st Battalion. He sits with his back to the wall and his arms clasped around his legs. He just stares in front as if he is not with us and does not speak at all. There is a sergeant PTI, 1st Battalion, and another sergeant and two other soldiers, one with a PIAT gun, about the same age as me. In ten minutes I have a cup of tea and have smoked two fags. Daylight is here and Lieutenant Fraser goes about organising the defence of the house. The PIAT gunner and a Bren gunner are in the front door, various other soldiers in the windows of the rooms. He tells me, 'You stay with me.'

The house has no front garden, but has a small back garden with a low fence on each side. It is a substantially built house in a long street all the same with between every two houses a small alleyway. We seem to have the area well covered if Germans should come this way. But where are we? I look out of the back window and see this house backs onto the River Rhine and I can see people on the opposite bank but it is too far to see if they are German soldiers. I get my favourite order again: 'Make me a cup of tea.' He seems friendlier now so I ask him, 'Where do you come from, Sir?' He says his family come from Inverness but have gone out to Canada. He also says he is with the 3rd Parachute Battalion.

About mid-morning trouble starts again. The Germans seem to be looking for us and seem to know we are in one of the houses, but they obviously don't know which one. Lieutenant Fraser instructs us not to give our position away, not to open fire until we have to. There is a terrific grinding and rattling noise and a huge German tank has arrived at the corner of the road about 100 yards away. All we have got is a bloody PIAT gun. I look at the young man in charge of it in the doorway; he looks very white and tense. The German tank starts firing into the houses coming down the street one house at a time and shooting into them.

Lieutenant Fraser runs down into the cellar. The major and the two sergeants are still down there; the PTI sergeant is looking very nervous – he obviously wants to live forever. Lieutenant Fraser gets out two Gammon bombs for throwing at tanks, big balls of plastic high explosive that stick on a tank and then explode. They are not primed and he asks the sergeants if they know how to prime these. They shake their heads, they obviously don't want to know. I do, so I put the detonators in them. Lieutenant Fraser runs up the stairs and looks to see how close the tank has got to our house; it is still 50 yards away, but the noise is terrific.

Down the other end of the street an organised unit comes round the corner, pulling an anti-tank gun – *Help, thank God! No!* They are going, tugging their gun with them, they must have seen the bloody tank. Could it have been imagination? No, Lieutenant Fraser is wondering which battalion it could be but he says he is only guessing. They have gone off to find an easier way to the bridge. We wait and the tank is just shooting straight into each house one after the other. After a while, Lieutenant Fraser goes out with one of the Gammon bombs into the back garden. He is gone a little time and comes back running, without the Gammon bomb. He says to me, 'Take the other Gammon bomb, jump over the hedges of the next two gardens, run up the alley and by that time the tank should be by the head of the alley, and then throw the thing.' This is what he had already done, no luck. I go out, thinking, *nobody lives forever,* run like mad jumping the hedges like a hurdler, up the alley – no tank in front of me, so I throw it anyway and run back.

So both our Gammon bombs have gone and the huge tank is getting very close now. Lieutenant Fraser gives the order for everybody to get out into the back garden away from the gun of that tank. We crowd into the back garden and it is very cramped. The German infantry with the tank are coming over the back gardens towards us. Now they know where we are, and hand grenades are landing amongst us, but the Germans aren't waiting before they throw them. One egg grenade lands by my side and I throw it back; another egg grenade, and back over the fence I throw it. The other soldiers are doing the same and the German officers are shouting at their men, they don't seem happy either!

Suddenly some of our men jump over the wall at the bottom of the garden and the rest follow. Lieutenant Fraser holds my arm and says, 'Wait.' I wait. When they have all gone, he says, 'Now' and we run and throw ourselves over the wall, to land on top of a mass of struggling bodies and then roll clear. This is what Lieutenant Fraser had foreseen.

We are on a narrow tow-path alongside the river, which seems very wide. Lieutenant Fraser and I start running away from the attacking Germans, this is one thing that I can do. We run neck and neck for about 400 yards and in the way is a barbed wire entanglement across the tow-path. I see there is a hole in the centre just enough for one man to get through, so I dive for it and receive a heavy blow on my helmet – the lieutenant has hit me over the head with his revolver butt. Turning back I say, 'It's me, Sir' and he says, 'Get through.' He follows me, the wire getting entangled with our small packs. Once on the other side of the wire we start running again until we reach the end of the tow-path. We are quite puffed out and looking back we see all our colleagues with their hands above their heads surrounded by Germans. Two or three Germans are standing by them shooting at us two, the bullets whistling by, but we ignore the bullets and start walking. We are now in a cabbage field and they are still shooting at us. The bullets whistle through the air and make a strange noise when they hit the cabbage leaves, but I am past caring about bullets! I hope if one hits me it will hit a soft spot and not my head.

We walk on through the cabbages and after 100 yards a German soldier comes up out of a hole immediately to our left. He was dressed in an unusual uniform with a black peaked cap. He has not seen us and is looking intently towards the other Germans to see why they are firing in his direction. The shock of him suddenly coming up out of the cabbages causes me to freeze up and when Lieutenant Fraser says, 'Shoot him' my reaction is slow, so he takes the rifle out of my hands and shoots the German soldier. He falls, obviously dead, and we walk on in silence. The German shooting is very poor if they can't hit us. We are making no attempt to avoid the bullets, I don't think either of us cares anymore! I am glad that we did not surrender with the others; while we are free we might meet some more of the 1st Airborne, but there is no sign of life anywhere now. Everything is very quiet here. Can we be the last alive out of the 1st and 3rd Parachute Battalions, the Recce Company, divisional troops, 2nd Parachute Battalion? We haven't seen them at all.

The lieutenant stops on a piece of open ground and says, 'We have run far enough and we will run no more; you will go on and try to find members of the 3rd Battalion or any other troops and you will bring them back to me here.' I said, 'Yes, Sir,' and walked on. When I have walked some way and he cannot see me, I go to the river bank and sit down. It is mid-afternoon I would guess and I work out that it must be Tuesday, and I have last eaten anything on Saturday; I am very hungry. I have not slept since Sunday and am very tired.

Not far away is a small bridge over the river which has been blown up in the centre. I decide to eat half the chocolate bar that all soldiers carry which is supposed to sustain you for 48 hours; better not eat the whole bar, perhaps there won't be any food available for a few days. I dangle my feet over the river and eat half of the chocolate. There is a noise of aeroplanes to my right and, looking towards the way we had come from, I can see hundreds of parachutes coming down, a long way away but I immediately feel better. My best friend, Stan Clitheroe, is jumping with the second wave – perhaps we shall meet up again soon? I wonder if they realise that there can't be anybody left out of the 1st Parachute Brigade. It's only two and a half days since we landed – they can't have killed us all. What has happened? I decide there must be another answer. Where is the bridge? It must be to my left but so far I have not seen it, and I am sure no one else has!

I've eaten my half of chocolate and decide to start walking and try to carry out my order – that lieutenant is a smashing bloke! I walk away from the river, over the fields; perhaps I shall find a road with our soldiers. I will ask them if they are 3rd Parachute Battalion and if they are, take them back to Lieutenant Fraser. If they are not 3rd Parachute Battalion I will still try to get them to come back with me. Obviously Lieutenant Fraser intends to hold a position there, perhaps he wants to attack back into Arnhem again. It's about time we taught these German bastards a lesson, and Fraser gives you confidence, a smashing bloke to lead us. I walk faster with the new hope that we can have another go!

There's a road in front of me, it's the main road into Arnhem, I recognise the railway bridge across it. I have been under that bridge often in the Jeep. The road is empty; a few abandoned handcarts and no sign of life! I will walk under the bridge back the way we had come and see what I can find.

An airborne Jeep is coming with a solitary officer in it; he is a captain. He asks what my unit is and I tell him, 'Divisional Defence Platoon, Sir.' He says, 'Get in.' I point out that I have left Lieutenant Fraser of the 3rd Parachute Battalion on some high ground by the river with orders to bring soldiers to him. He says, 'Get in.'

I hesitate. 'But Sir, what about the lieutenant; shall I go back to him?' He shouts, 'Get in,' and I get in. He swings the Jeep round and heads towards the way I was walking back, to where we had started from on Sunday. Civilians are still standing outside some of the doorways, but they are very quiet. There are no cheers and smiles now; they look very worried and sad. It is almost as if they think we are beaten already!

I can't understand what I see; in front coming towards us, is a twin column of soldiers, each side of the road in single file, armed only with rifles. They are glider pilots, all sergeants and warrant officers, moving up towards the Arnhem road obviously to hold the Germans. They must be all we have left! No airborne division is going to send up their glider pilots when troops are available. I doubt if they are trained as much as the ordinary soldiers. They look very grim, and are practically silent except for the noise of their boots. They must know there is nothing in front of them but the Germans. Can they know what has happened to us in Arnhem? They look as if they do! Those that see me looking at them just stare back, what the hell can they do with just rifles?

We get to the village of Oosterbeek. There are a few shops and houses we pass but the civilians have disappeared. The captain says, 'We are all coming back here to hold this area.' He stops the Jeep in the middle of a small crossroads surrounded by an area of small trees, with a few small bungalows in a row, some large houses and standing separately amongst the small trees a very large hotel building, the Park Hotel.[28] I see several familiar faces; our Lance Corporal 'Judy' Wright, and Private Cohen have a small trench a yard off the main road and others of my platoon are around a small lodge nearby with a fire station next door. Wright and Cohen's trench looks most inviting, so I jump in. We discuss what is happening and I learn that the general and his senior officers are in the Park Hotel, with the medical officers in the cellars. Our platoon is spread about the area. By the side of the Park Hotel is a large tennis court where we have been collecting the German prisoners, and to the side of this there is a well where we can get water.

Our Sergeant Chapman has just been killed with another of the platoon, Private Barton, in a trench, a mortar bomb landed right in it.[29] As we are talking bullets are whistling overhead. I am told we are plagued with German snipers but they don't seem to be much to worry about. I think I will go for a walk and see if I can find my friend, Stan Clitheroe, so I stroll about looking into trenches and saying, 'Hello' to people I know. An officer shouts for me, and going across I see he is a padre. Bearing in mind my philosophy that all officers are trouble, I wonder what a padre can want with me. I soon find out! A Polish soldier has been shot about fifty yards to the right of the Park Hotel and he wants to bury him in a nearby trench; he has also recruited another soldier to help put the Pole down the trench. The padre begins to fuss about. He takes the items out of the pockets of the dead soldier and gives them to us – ten cigarettes, a box of matches, a small hair comb and a small pair of scissors.

The German snipers are now taking an interest in us three and bullets are coming uncomfortably close. Let's chuck him in and get out of it! The padre has other ideas. Out comes his Bible and he starts muttering; I think, *soon there will be another body for a share out*. The padre talking to his God does not seem to hear the bullets hitting all around us; at last he nods to us and with a 'Gently, boys,' the Pole goes to the bottom of the trench. I walk off hurriedly, deciding to avoid padres – they can get you killed easily.

We seem to have a strong position here. There are lots of soldiers in trenches all around and in some of the houses. The Park Hotel is the most substantial place around, reserved of course for 'officers only'. I find our Lieutenant Butterworth in a trench well back from the road. He does not seem to want to chat; the strong feeling of dislike is mutual. By the time I get back to Wright's and Cohen's trench, Cohen has brewed up and I decide to eat my other half bar of chocolate. It is now

---

28 Hartenstein.
29 Corporal Arthur Chapman, 4622104, aged 24 and Private Lawrence J Barton, 5683257, aged 21. Both found buried near the Hartenstein Sports Ground.

about three days since I ate a meal but I do not feel too hungry, just a little tired, so I have a kip and the night is soon over.

Wednesday, 20th September
This is a better life. The trench is most comforting, two excellent companions, and a large water container and we have some type of Oxo cube which when heated with water swells up and makes a small meal. There are shells continuously landing on the road above and in the tree area in front of the Park Hotel, and bullets are whistling about overhead, but we are OK. Here I could stay for a long time!

About 1100 hours a soldier comes to say we three are wanted to go on patrol work with Lieutenant Butterworth. This, we agree, could be dodgy! However, we join him by the fire station and head up the road. We are soon at the back of the shops and there is a large pile of abandoned guns and ammunition of all types, mostly German. I spot my favourite, a new Sten gun with a butt, so I swop it for my rifle and fill my pouches up with 9mm and Sten gun magazines and also a long-barrelled German revolver which is a real smasher. Lieutenant Butterworth tries to hurry us along. We reach the end of the shops and now we are going through the back gardens of big houses. There are some explosions going up and bits are flying through the air, dust and smoke and noise. The patrol stops and Lieutenant Butterworth tells me to go round the front of the house to see what is going on the other side! I don't like that man!

Very gingerly, I edge round the house which has a very big garden surrounded by trees and bushes; the noise of explosions is intense and the smoke and flashes are unnerving. I peep round the corner as a tremendous explosion goes off. The smoke and flame is right in front of me and I see through the smoke that it is a group of German soldiers firing a large gun in the direction of the Park Hotel. I run back fast! Lieutenant Butterworth immediately decides to return to the Hartenstein area and report. We all think this is an excellent idea!

Back in our trench, Wright and Cohen and myself are quite happy to let the war go on over our heads; we are content! To keep ourselves amused, we decide to deepen our trench and take it under the main road a little so that the shells and mortar bombs will explode harmlessly on the road above us. There is an added bonus for as we dig deeper and sideways, the earth we are digging out is thrown on top, and makes the trench even deeper. We are proud of our comfortable trench.

The general is looking down at us. I smile in recognition, but he looks very angry, then says, 'You have not washed or shaved; every man in my division will wash and shave every day,' and then strides off. We discuss his likely parentage and the parentage of all his officers. Cleaning the cold tea out of our mess tins, we fill them with clean water and, getting out our shaving kits, have our first wash and shave. We feel far better afterwards! It is best to keep an eye out for officers in future; they are, next to Germans, a great source of trouble to us soldiers! They never leave you in peace.

The day is going by; you would think the Germans would get fed up or run out of ammunition, but they never stop. In front of us is a very nice, large house on the corner, 'West End'. It looks very substantial and I wonder if there are civilians in there or food, perhaps. A few yards away in the centre of the small crossroads is a 17-pounder anti-tank gun of ours, no crew, no ammunition but it looks impressive, pointing in the direction of Arnhem. If the Germans see it, they won't rush a tank down here! We have good weather all the time we have been here; it's very nice for September. While one keeps awake the other two pass the daylight and night hours sleeping.

Thursday, 21st September

Dawn comes with the usual brew up, but the Germans have obviously got this lined up because as soon as we start heating the water in the mess tin, a barrage of mortar bombs hits the general area. The bombs hitting the road cause dirt to fall in the mess tin, the water overspills on to the small candle and out it goes. This is intended to shatter our morale; we find it very irritating.

Today is going to be a bad day for us. We can't brew up because of the continuous mortar fire, we don't want to get out of the trench because of the shrapnel and bullets to get more water, and our plastic water can has a large hole in it where we left it on top of the trench and some sniper has decided to cut off our water supply. We must wait till dark to go to the well. There is a lot of shouting from the tennis courts where the German prisoners are, they have no trenches and no means of digging them; we think this is funny! They say there are German women soldiers there but that we have let the women go into trenches outside the tennis court. I do not go to this area; in fact it is not healthy to go for a stroll anywhere in daylight.

We notice that the lodge next to the fire station that is held by other members of our platoon appears to be empty. It did have a Bren gun sticking out of the window. I stroll over as dusk falls to see what has happened. There is nobody on the ground floor but I hear voices from the cellar so I go down and ask what is happening. They say, 'It is safer down here and anyway there are no Germans around.' I point out that they should be covering the area with their machine gun, but they are not interested so I tell them if they don't man the gun I will go and get an officer to make them. Corporal ********, *******, *******[30] and several others tell me to get lost, so I go in search of Lieutenant Butterworth. After examining the contents of lots of trenches I finally find him, but he looks as if he would have been glad if I had not found him. I tell him the situation, that the platoon main building is not manned at all; the corporal and soldiers are in the cellar and refuse to come out.

He says, 'I will see about this,' and I wait as he climbs out of the trench and strides across to the lodge with me. Drawing his revolver in front of the soldiers, he tells them to get upstairs and stay there. They go and take up their positions again and Lieutenant Butterworth is gone! I feel utter contempt for these men; they had done nothing, seen nothing, but were happy to loiter safely in a cellar. For the first time in battle I am really angry and not with the Germans but some of my own platoon, and to think some of these men were regular soldiers who had boasted about their spell in India. Gutless bastards, I concluded, and went back to my comrades in the trench.

It is really dark now and 'Judy' Wright has gone off to get some water for the morning, and we can relieve ourselves near the top of the trench. The Germans are quiet so far at night – perhaps they like to go to sleep, too! I sleep well in the trench; the three of us in such a tiny area, all cramped up, keep each other warm.

Friday, 22nd September

And so a new day breaks and we start to brew up; the Germans immediately hammer the whole area with their mortars and shells and our water is spoiled again. It's a beautiful sunny day. I don't even feel hungry, what day is it? We landed Sunday, Monday and Tuesday in Arnhem, two days here – I think it is Friday. In five days I have eaten a chocolate bar and two Oxo cubes and yet I am not feeling hungry all that much! Mind you, a Sunday dinner would be nice, but I am not all that bothered. Fags are very short and this is far more serious than food; we must take steps shortly to get some fags somehow.

---

30 Names withheld for obvious reasons.

The trees around us are now getting denuded of branches and leaves and the ground is getting churned up by the continuous German shelling. I would guess that the Germans are about two hundred yards away, but somehow our chaps are holding the strategic houses at the crossroads. We are obviously in a very small area and unless the British Army gets here soon we are going to be in some difficulty. We are told by a soldier that the 2nd Parachute Battalion was holding the bridge but nothing has been heard from them lately; that the British Army will be up to us soon. He tells us that we may wear our red berets if we wish; it is the general's order that we may, but it is up to each soldier. We unpack our red berets and throw away the uncomfortable airborne helmet. This is the best tonic of all, we now feel that things aren't that bad and when the British Army comes through us we will be proudly wearing our red berets. The cream of the British Army!

There is a new spirit abroad now; I am sure wearing their red berets has cheered all the soldiers no end. As I wander about the trenches seeing if I can scrounge some fags, the blokes seem happy and friendly and smiling again. A lot of activity is taking place in front of the Hartenstein, lots of yellow recognition scarves are being laid out on the flat ground, and officers have appeared again. Something must be up!

I am right! There are planes coming over. The Germans are shooting everything at them, and they are coming straight in over the top of the Hartenstein. An officer is lighting flares which send off a blue smoke and others that let off yellow smoke; they are obviously to show the planes where we are. The side doors of the planes open as they get over us and I can see men struggling to push out very large wicker baskets. Can it be food and fags? This is great. The planes are going through the most terrible German barrage of gunfire but they keep straight in line. Suicidal, they will all be blown out of the sky! But what courage, fantastic, 'Up the RAF'.

One of the first planes is on fire but the men at the side door are still pushing out the wicker baskets. What's happening? One of the men has a parachute and has jumped with his mate holding on to him. I watch, a dreadful cold feeling comes over me; the man holding on has lost his grip and he is screaming as he crashes to his death. The planes are still coming in. I would rather do without food than this! Another plane is on fire, another has gone down beyond the trees, and still they come on.

Then there is silence and the planes have gone. What about the wicker baskets? As far as I can see only one has come down in our area; the rest have landed in the German territory. What a waste – still no food or fags!

I go for a walk – perhaps there may be some fags or food about now – and I walk into my friend, Stan Clitheroe. We are both very pleased to see each other; for two years we had been inseparable, except when I was in hospital in Africa. We decide to find ourselves a comfortable billet and wander over to the small bungalows directly opposite the Hartenstein. We do not hang about as there is the usual heavy mortar fire and choose a small bungalow. In the doorway lying on his back is a lieutenant who has obviously been dead for several days; he has a watch on his wrist which I feel like pinching but think perhaps some officer is bound to catch me with it later on.

We investigate the bungalow and in the cellar are lots of glass jars on shelves. We sample them and they are some kind of small fruit in sugar. We cannot eat them. This will be our bungalow, but we must go out and look for food. Over the back gardens into another house – no food; over the road and into another house – no food. The thought of food had now made us feel really hungry. We continue to investigate the houses. As we peer into a doorway, kneeling, heads close together, guns ready to fire, a bullet smacks right into the woodwork between our two heads! Christ, that was close! Stan and I hurtle into the hall, realising that the Germans are now behind us – between us and our soldiers. We sit in the hall looking at each other and thinking how lucky we are to be alive. Two inches either way and one of us would have been dead.

After a little while we agree to rush over the road, from a window, and hope we get across before the Germans start shooting. We jump out of the window and run across the road, but as we run my revolver falls out into the middle of the road and we are in a German-held row of houses. I am not going back without my revolver, so we agree that Stan and I run out together and while I get my revolver, Stan will blast the immediate windows with machine gun fire. He calmly stands in the middle of the road shooting into windows while I pick up my revolver and we make our way back to the Hartenstein area over the gardens.

The German fire is intense again; the RAF are trying to drop supplies to us again, and this gets the Germans excited. The Dakotas are overhead in the most awful anti-aircraft fire and the planes are coming in as if they do not care! The planes are being hit and again I can see the soldiers in the aeroplanes pushing out their wicker baskets, but we are in so small an area that their efforts are in vain and the supplies are floating down into the German-held area.

We have found a trench by the road in front of the Hartenstein which is unoccupied and we stay there in the hope that if any baskets have landed we can see if there is any food being given out. It is the usual heavy shelling and suddenly Stan, Jeff and I hit the bottom of the trench together – a terrible noise has gone on over our heads, like an express train. When we look over the top of the trench again, there is a huge German shell that looks six feet long, stopped about five yards from the centre of the Hartenstein. What sort of a gun shoots a shell as big as that? We have never seen anything of such a size; we wonder if it is explosive or just to knock a house down. The noise we had heard was this thing coming down through the trees over our heads. If the Germans are trying for the Hartenstein and our officers, they are right on target. An explosive shell of that size must have knocked the Park Hotel down completely if it had hit!

There is a peaceful lull in the shelling and suddenly the general walks out of the Park Hotel with another officer and an Airborne flag on a stick. The two officers look at the huge shell and the junior officer bends down as if to lift it. It is obvious the general has told him to leave the thing alone. The officer then sticks the stick with the Airborne pennant on it in the ground and the general stands by it while the other officer takes a photograph. I think the general looks embarrassed.

The pile of British dead is now getting very large and the whole area has a sweet, sickly smell in the air. No dead have been buried since the first few days; it is quite impossible to live long above ground, let alone bury dead. At the front of the Park Hotel to the left of the main steps going into the building, is a small flight of stairs leading to the cellars and underneath here our wounded are being attended by our medical officers. As they die they are being put on a heap at the left side of the Park Hotel, and the pile of dead now looks six feet high. They appear to move when hit by shrapnel. I think the medical officers must be busy in the cellars. I guess there must be a hundred soldiers now on the pile, probably far more; it is best not to look at the pile of dead.

I am not afraid and I have not been afraid at all during these days; my nerves are very good. Stan is alright, but Judy Wright shows signs of nerves; he jumps out of his trench when the machine guns stop, runs into the road and jumps up and down waving his arms and cursing the Germans, and then throws himself back into the trench again; I guess this helps him to relieve the his tensions. When I have nothing else to think about, I try to remember the lines of a poem I learnt in Tunisia. I believe it was found on a soldier's body and it goes:

> I am but the son my Mother bore

> A simple man and nothing more
> But God of strength and gentleness
> Be pleased to make me nothing less.
> You stilled the water at Dunkirk.
> All your work is wonderful.
> You led us down that dreadful road…

And then I can't remember any more and Stan speaks to me and we laugh and joke again. A soldier comes up with some orders: Stan, Jeff and I are to take over the large house on the corner, 'West End', and there will be some others to join us if they can be found. We are to hold it until relieved. This is smashing; it is a large substantial house that we have admired from our trench. There could be water, toilets, food. We set off to West End immediately.

The main door is on the side of the house. There is a very large front room with many large windows (not so healthy), going back across a hall to the kitchen which has a long window, and so to the back garden. Very rich people live here; the furniture is most expensive and there are silk tablecloths – I am taking one of those home with me. I look for cellars and there is one near the kitchen with a sort of trap door; under this I hear women and children. What can we do? Nothing. We decide that the cellar will not be entered. There is another large cellar down some wooden stairs under the front half of the house; it is empty. Magnificent bedrooms above which are spoilt by the roof having received many direct hits from German shells. The rear bedroom: in the corner the rafters are intact and with slates of the roof missing, gives us a first class machine gun post. We need a Bren machine gun for there. I decide that the points to defend immediately are the kitchen and the large front room; there are no windows left and the front room window areas are low so a soldier could just step in. The toilet does not work, but we use it just the same, it's better than a field at night. There is no food. But this is the last thing in comfort, after trenches. We take it in turns to have a nap; sitting against the wall in the hall it is easy to sleep.

Saturday, 23rd September

I am sure today is Saturday, but who can be sure? The British Army was supposed to have arrived at least five days ago. Sometimes when it is quiet we think we can hear very heavy guns firing to the south of us; perhaps they will come today or tomorrow. We all hope that they will hurry up! No doubt they have their difficulties too. The news here is grim. Odd soldiers popping about the area tell us what they have heard; the Germans have finished off the 2nd Parachute Battalion that took the bridge and nothing more is known of them. All that is left of the 1st Airborne Division is in this small area. This doesn't seem possible – 10,000 men gone in a week?

We are told that the Germans have been calling upon us to surrender and we have refused. We discuss this amongst us and decide that whatever happens we will not surrender but will try to make our own way north; although we have only linen maps from our escape kits, we will go north on our own. We three will not surrender! I think we can hold out easily until the British Army gets here, they can't be far away now. And what about the two American Airborne Divisions that dropped between us and the British Army, what's happened to them? We joke about the briefing we were given at Down Ampney, 'second-rate' German troops, stragglers being re-grouped. I told my friends of the first class German soldiers with Tiger tanks in Arnhem. It's a typical army cock-up again! Still, we are still together, what is left, and we are still holding an area on the north bank of the Rhine which the army could find useful when they get here.

I am sure I can hear heavy guns to the south at intervals; the army is definitely coming up. It is unthinkable that the army would let us be wiped out, so they are late, but they will come.

It is now dark and we move upstairs. Germans have nasty habits and one is to creep about at night and throw grenades into ground floor windows. The other thing that interests me is the way when they are holding a row of terraced houses, as in Arnhem, they burrow a hole between the walls of the bedrooms so they can go from house to house without going out of doors. This is disconcerting – Germans in one house and appearing again halfway down the street. I am living and learning.

Stan decides to go looking for fags and goes off to see what he can find, so we go downstairs again to await his return. Suddenly a leg comes over a windowsill followed by a body. I hold my fire; who is it? He is a glider pilot who tells us that the Germans came with tanks and flame-throwers and burnt the glider pilots out of the trenches. He is obviously in a bad way – his nerves are gone. I show him the cellar and ask him if he would like to join us, but he says he would prefer to stay in the cellar. Perhaps he can be useful to us by making tea and that sort of thing. I like him; he makes no pretence, his nerve has gone and he knows it. He is a sergeant glider pilot but offers to do what I ask him. Our defending force is now three and one non-combatant. Stan returns from his prowl. He has found what we call the 'jackpot', a dead glider pilot. They are obvious because they have a very large pack on their backs and they invariably have plenty of fags. In his pack Stan had found two hundred Marlborough cigarettes and a packet of biscuits. We share the spoils between us and settle down to one awake and two asleep. Lieutenant Butterworth visits us, walking efficiency! He asks if everything is alright and looks out of our windows. After a few minutes he goes.

Sunday, 24th September
Dawn comes again with the usual German stonk, but now our tea, with water from the lavatory cistern, is brewed safely in the cellar. The only safe place is sitting under windowsills in the front room where you can keep an eye on the outside and still keep your head down.

About mid-morning, another soldier comes through one of our side windows. He is a Polish sergeant major and he doesn't speak English; looks a tough bloke, but completely lost with nobody to speak his language. He makes it obvious he wants to know who is in charge and I say I am. He then makes it plain that I tell him what to do and he will do it! I give him our most dangerous window to look after, and feel comfortable that I have no need to worry further about that area.

Surveying my house I feel very lucky. I now have three bloody good soldiers with me, hot tea coming up at regular intervals in the cellar, and plenty of fags in my pocket; what more can I want? The army will be here soon but until then I am in good company. I wonder why they accept me as in charge. There is no reason at all and yet everything I ask is done immediately, and nothing I say is questioned!

Stan is shouting for me and I tear up the stairs with a Bren gun that we have won; he has spotted a German patrol going behind a tall hedge on the opposite side of the road. He thinks there are five of them. I dive into the roof, into a corner I have previously lined up. There appears to be some movement behind this hedge, and Stan is yelling at me, 'Get those bastards.' I fire a burst of bullets along the hedge; the movement stops. To be sure, I empty the magazine's thirty-two bullets into the length of hedge and I wait. Nothing moves, and after a few minutes we go downstairs again. Some Germans won't be going back to their Fatherland.

The Polish parachute sergeant major never leaves his window; he just smiles at us, doesn't smoke cigarettes, but seems to like a cup of tea.

A German barrage of mortar shells is coming down all around us. There is shouting in the kitchen and I run through to see what is happening.

I have been hit. I am lying on my face and I can't breathe. Funny feeling! My body won't move and I can't breathe. I see Stan's boots and gaiters come through the door to me and pull me along the floor by my arms. He has opened up the door to the cellar and is saying something. Soon I am down in the cellar with several women and children and the women are taking off my flying smock.

Later I can breathe again alright and feel strong again, and the women help me to get my uniform on. I return to the boys upstairs who are obviously worried as to my injuries, but all that happened was that a lump of paving stone had been blown through the kitchen window by the explosion and had hit me in the middle of my pack. Stan shows me the lump of concrete which was as big as my hand. After an hour, I am as good as new.

The night is coming and we have had a visitor with pills; they are supposed to keep you awake at night. I bet an officer got a pat on the back for thinking of sending all soldiers two pills each. The officers in the Park Hotel are on the ball today.

Every soldier you speak to has heard the army is getting to us tomorrow. Each day it is definitely *tomorrow*; somebody must eventually be right. We have been here now eight days, so the army is six days overdue. I get the feeling that the shells going over our heads are going both ways now! Perhaps it is not possible, it's just what I am beginning to believe. I have been sitting listening to the shells whining overhead and I feel sure some shells are coming from the south where the army should be coming from. I am convinced I am right and discuss it with my friends; they seem to be relieved and brighten up no end at the thought that our own guns have started to fire over our heads. Even if I am wrong, it's done the world of good for our morale. Perhaps in a few days we can stand and be thrilled to watch the British Army go on through us to Germany and the end of the war. I will not allow my mind to go further than this; I do not think of home, wife, children, this would be bad and weakening. Just the army going through and we would all say this has been worthwhile, and so would our dead and wounded. Tomorrow will be the 25th September, the day my brother died in 1936. A fleeting thought, *perhaps it's my turn on the anniversary date – not so likely, he doesn't want me up there!*

From the Polish sergeant major's window you can see the pile of dead; it grows bigger and higher every day. Every one was a young soldier like me!

There is little movement now between the houses and nobody has been in to try and scrounge a fag. I don't feel hungry anymore. It's funny, isn't it, a bar of chocolate, two Oxo cubes, three biscuits in eight days and I do not feel hungry. Nobody does. I ask the others and they say they are not bothered either. We cannot ask the Polish NCO but he looks from his window position and smiles; friendly bloke.

The glider pilot sergeant is very cheerful and smiles all the time, looking for anything to make tea with. He always seems pleased if I talk to him for a little while. He has spoken before of the attack where the Germans came with flamethrowers on their tanks and burnt the pilots out of their trenches. He ran and ran and arrived at 'West End'. I think of the men I saw several days ago when I was in a trench on the crossroads in front of the Park Hotel; about six of them came from woods over to our left shouting, 'The Germans are coming.' Officers dashed out of the Park Hotel and shouted and carried on at them and they ran back to the trees from where they had come. For a short time they had lost their nerve. What a fragile barrier there is to cross to let your nerve go! I realise that when my nerve could have gone in the first two days I had the example and steadying influence, the calm courage, of Lieutenant Fraser to bolster me, to lead me. Having got through the first two days, the rest has seemed easy to me, but I will never forget him; what an officer for any soldier to have! I wonder what he thinks of me not coming back to him with some soldiers? Perhaps he thinks I double-crossed him! I would like to think he knows I couldn't get back there.

Monday, 25th September
The night has gone and it's Monday, 25th September, 1944. Lovely weather, the Germans are firing and the bombs are dropping all over as usual. The lodge in the driveway leading to the Park Hotel is on fire and members of my platoon are moving out. I see with sinking spirits that Corporal ******** and ******* are going to join us in 'West End'. They come in and we glare silently at them. Thick-skinned as ever, they try to seem friendly and can't hear Stan's, 'Yellow bastards' muttering. Corporal ******** asks where I would like them and I say, 'You are the corporal, it's up to you.' He says, 'Come on, where do you want us?' and I think quickly. 'The main door on the side of the house needs guarding.' It doesn't; it is a very strong, thick door and has never been opened, but it gets them out of the way.

A soldier comes over and says that an NCO from each house has to report to the Park Hotel for orders and as I am only a private soldier and cannot go we suggest Corporal ******** goes. He returns with our orders. At 2200 hours we must leave our house and report behind the Park Hotel. What is left of the division is going to break out of the trap we are in; the code word is 'Operation Berlin'. Some glider pilots have marked trees through the forest down to the River Rhine with white tape to show the way, and all the soldiers will put their spare socks over their boots to deaden noise whilst going through the German lines. We are to watch the sky for tracer shells; the British gunners are going to fire tracer shells, which light up in the sky, over the river at spots where some small boats will be waiting to take us across the river. When we get across the river we are to make for a small village called Driel and when we get there, there will be food and blankets. While this is going on the British guns, which are still miles away, will put heavy fire over our heads to keep the Germans occupied.

We are told that it has been found impossible to get help across the river to us and that rather than surrender, the general has ordered that we will break out through the German lines tonight. Different lots of troops are going at different times, so it is essential that each batch keeps to its time. Before leaving their position all soldiers will shoot and throw grenades, if any, to try and give the impression to the Germans that we are going to attack! The medical officers will stay behind with the wounded; they have volunteered to do this. Good show for them. The military police will stay behind with the prisoners and will kick up a noise to try to convince the Germans we are still in position. My sympathies have never been with the military police, I hate their guts!

I begin to chew over this plan in my mind. It sounds alright, but how many miles away is the British Army now? It doesn't sound as if they are at Driel, they just say that there is food and blankets there; if the army was there wouldn't they say so? So where is the army now? If they can't get soldiers over to us, how do they get us back over there? It seems confused, but at least we will be moving and that is more exciting than defending a house. Although I am not hungry, this talk of food and blankets sounds good; anyway we need some fags again.

So that is the plan. We can only wait and see.

The day goes by without anything interesting occurring and the dusk comes down. As we are going to leave at 2200 hours we are all interested in the time and the corporal has a watch.

It is dark and we are waiting for another hour and a half to go by. There is some movement, troops can be seen occasionally nipping about, the German mortar fire is very heavy and the area is a mass of explosions, smoke, flame and noise. Suddenly there is machine gun fire from the side of the house and I rush to the main door, which is shut. Corporals ******** and ******** are leaning against the wall looking like terrified children. What has happened? They say the Germans are trying to get in the door! This can't be right, the kitchen window and the side front room window overlook the main side door and Germans would have been seen by Stan and Jeff Whitehouse. I open the main door. Oh my God, two young paratroopers in their red berets and flying smocks are lying terribly wounded in the doorway. Stan and I look at them; they seem still alive but both seem to have about five bullets through each of them. They make no sound. I am demented with anger that two good soldiers had been shot by two cowards who hadn't even looked before they fired their machine guns. For a fleeting second I want to kill both cowards as they stand shivering in the hall, but there is a greater urgency. Perhaps we can save their lives. Stan runs off towards the Park Hotel looking for a stretcher; I hold their arms and tell them they will be alright. I have never felt anger like this; the lives of two men of my platoon hang by a thread as I look at these two young paratroopers riddled with bullets shot by their own soldiers. They seem conscious and their eyes are looking at me but they do not speak or groan or anything.

Stan is back with a ladder, this is all he can find. We have a hundred and fifty yards to go to the cellar under the Park Hotel: the mortar fire is very heavy, but we have to get these soldiers there somehow. We put the first soldier on the ladder, pick it up and start running. Jeff comes with us carrying all our guns around his neck just in case we run into a German patrol. The bombs are bursting all around us and it is difficult to keep the ladder balanced and the soldier on it. Crash, we are all blown over by an explosion, the soldier is off the ladder and rolled away a yard or so. Jeff is in a hell of a state with the bandoliers of the guns wrapped around his shoulders, he is blown over, all the guns hanging in different directions, most awkward. Again, we put the soldier on the ladder and start running again. The ground is all churned up, worse than a ploughed field, and there are trenches in the way, handcarts upended, Jeeps, everything in the way. At the steps to the Park Hotel we take the soldier off the ladder and carry him down the steps. There is a queue of wounded sitting in a small corridor and a room off to the left where the doctors are working. We leave the soldier on the end of the queue of about six men and go back for the other soldier. We load him on our ladder and start to run again, but we can't, our strength seems to be leaving us; we fall down and again the soldier rolls off the ladder. Christ, this is dreadful. We load him on again and press on through the rough ground. Crash and we are blown over by another explosion. We load the soldier on again; I hope he can't feel anything. We are doing our best, God knows we are doing our best!

Through the smoke is the Park Hotel again and once more we carry a soldier down and dump him on the queue. We feel exhausted and lean against the wall. Out comes the medical officer: 'You men get upstairs, no loitering down here.' Stan and I go up the stairs and now we don't care anymore and we walk back to 'West End' through the trees, the explosions and the smoke, and we are not interested. When we get to the window of 'West End' we sink against the wall and I feel that I could cry. I seem to be getting weaker; my legs feel like lead, my arms ache and my head aches, and I rest against the wall. My back is just one big bruise from the paving stone.

We have no fags!

It is 2145 hours so we shake ourselves out of the feeling of 'don't care anymore' and go to the windows, firing our machine guns up into the air. With the German mortar bombs and our machine gun fire the noise is enough to convince anyone that there is somebody attacking someone.

At 2150 hours I go across to the Polish parachute sergeant major and thank him for helping us; I shake his hand and wish him luck. He smiles at me as I explain he must follow me, and he shakes my hand and says something in Polish which I can tell is sentimental by the expression on his face. He seems near to tears. The sergeant glider pilot is ready and he is in tears; as he shakes my hand the tears are coming down his cheeks and he thanks me. It is most embarrassing; I have been able to do so little, and yet he is thanking me! I can't bear to look at Corporals ******** and ******** and ignore them. They wait at the back on their own.

We go out through the window and make our way to the Park Hotel around the back as our orders. Out of somewhere springs who? Our own Lieutenant Butterworth: 'Now line up, men, look like soldiers.' As I stand in line and look at him, my thoughts are murderous.

We put our socks over our boots and soon the sprightly little lieutenant says, 'Move off, follow me,' and we head off into the trees, going south-west, I reckon. We don't get along very fast. It is pitch black and the white tape we have to follow is obvious in some places but not so in others. We are ordered to hold the flying smock of the soldier in front so that we keep together. Progress is very slow. We are stopped again; the Germans are calling out to each other on either side of us. It seems amazing that we can hear every word they say and yet they do not know we are going through in batches right by their positions. It is raining, the first rain since we came here, and heavy rain at that; this will help us to get through unobserved. We seem to have been going slowly through the trees for hours, it is difficult to judge. There is a commotion on our right: a man is screaming and banging. The man ahead says it's a Polish soldier who has caught a German and is chopping him into pieces; he's got him over a tree trunk and has gone mad. He's just chopping him to pieces.

We move on and out of the trees and there is grassland in front of us, sloping down to the river. We can't see the river yet, but lying in the rain in a great queue are our soldiers, about five men wide and as far as one can see. There are lots of glider pilots, easily distinguishable by the packs on their backs. We join the queue, which does not move, lying in the rain. In thick mud we wait for the queue to move. I look around for Stan but I don't recognise anybody around me except Jeff Whitehouse; he has kept with me. It was easy to lose the people around you in the trees. Still, Whitehouse is a good mate!

The line wriggles forward in the mud. Lying on my back, I watch for the tracer shells and they are going over our heads slightly to the right of where I am laying. All you can hear is the whine of the shells going over us towards the Germans; now it is their turn to get a pasting. Not before time! The Germans are firing machine guns along the fields about four feet off the ground. I don't think they know where we are, but they are shooting over our heads and if you stand up you could get hit. I am quite happy to rest in the mud and let the rain come down on my face. The queue moves very slowly and we have arrived at the top of a rise in the ground and can see the queue going down a hundred yards to the river. There is a colonel walking along the river bank with a walking stick shouting out orders and there seems to be two small boats going backwards and forwards across the river. They only seem to hold about eight men at a time. With this queue we could be here forever.

When a boat reaches the shore there is a shout for walking wounded, but there doesn't seem many with us. Whitehouse says, 'Look, you're wounded; put your arm around my shoulder and we will stagger down and get on the first boat.' Although my back hurts, I do not consider I am 'walking wounded' and I am sure an officer wouldn't think so; if caught as 'walking wounded' I do not care to think of the consequences.

Tuesday, 26th September

The first signs of dawn are beginning to appear and I realise that we cannot wait much longer; when the dawn comes and the Germans see us we have no chance. When daylight comes, we are dead! I say to Whitehouse, 'We must try it,' and we both get up. I put my arm around his shoulders and we walk to the river bank past all the other soldiers still lying in the queue. As we near the river an officer is shouting, 'Walking wounded' and Whitehouse shouts, 'Here, Sir.' A small boat is waiting and we are the last two to get in. A soldier pulls the rope on the outboard motor and this little boat loaded with soldiers and equipment chugs slowly across the Rhine. There are plenty of waves and the river seems rough. There are bullets flying about so the Germans have not given up: they seem to be just shooting and hoping to hit something. When we are in the middle of the Rhine I think that it would be nasty if the boat sinks now. There are many men in the water, boats are sinking, there are Very lights shooting up, lighting the targets for the German guns, screaming, shouting; hell.

We get to the other side eventually, and there are Canadian soldiers there helping us off the boat. Near the river bank there is a large dyke and I try hard to climb it, but I have little strength left. A large Canadian soldier picks me up in his arms and carries me up the side of the dyke; at the top he sits me down and gives me a push and I slide down to a small pathway.

Whitehouse is still with me! We look ahead and see some buildings in the distance. Dawn will be breaking soon; the village ahead should be Driel and there is food and blankets.

We reach the village and at a crossroads is a large Canadian soldier. We enquire where we can get food and blankets, and he says, 'None here, mate; all gone. You got to go to Nijmegen, about five miles down the road.' He might have said five hundred miles; the thought of five miles through the dawn to Nijmegen seems a very difficult task. Still, we want to live and it's only five miles; we can make it, and we start walking.

There is only Whitehouse and myself, no sign of other troops and we walk on and on. As dawn breaks we see a British soldier over by a hedge; going over to him for a likely fag we find a British tank hidden in the bushes. A lieutenant is in charge. He asks us if we are alright and we assure him we are OK. Has he got any fags to spare, and how far is Nijmegen? He says Nijmegen is only about a mile, gives us some fags and then says, 'Stay there.' We wait. What have we done wrong now? The officer comes back with two mugs half full of rum and says, 'Have a drink.' This is a good officer! We drink the rum and light up a cigarette and the world has become a better place. When we finish the rum we say, 'Thanks a lot,' and continue our walk to Nijmegen.

This is a nice day again and the rain has stopped a long time ago. We are now on the outskirts of a big city. There are Airborne signs with arrows for us to follow and eventually we see in front of us a large building which looks like a German Sandhurst Military College. There are a lot of Airborne types walking about, some in uniform, some in part uniform and civilian trousers, some very smart and clean shaven, but all with red berets. This is going to be where we will form up again into units to go back over the river and have another go at the Germans. Let's hope we have some tanks on our side next time. Perhaps the rest of our platoon, who were not on the operation, have got up this far with our kitbags so that we can change our clothes. At least it is nice to be able to stroll along feeling safe.

There is the noise of a plane overhead but it must be British or American so we do not even look up; there is food and fags! Up the stone steps towards the entrance of this imposing building, and there is a terrible crash; two men fall down and then there is smoke. The plane has dropped a bomb. I run, I don't know where I am going but it is terribly urgent to run as fast as I can. I am tearing down one road after another.

A sergeant of the King's Royal Rifle Corps is bending over me, bathing my head with water; we are in a cellar. He is saying to me, 'You are alright, son. You are going to be alright; just relax and I will get you a cup of tea.' He soon brings in a cup of tea and I ask him for a fag. A woman is standing by the cellar door looking worried. I ask him what happened. He says, 'I was in the doorway of the house and saw you running along like mad, so as you got to the doorway I grabbed you and dragged you in here. You were a bit of a handful but you fell unconscious.'

I smoke a fag and drink the tea. He must be about 35 years old, this sergeant, and he is treating me like a son. I am embarrassed and get to my feet, quite shakily. There are now two younger Dutch women with the older woman by the door. I sort of smile awkwardly, thank the sergeant and he shows me the road I came down. I walk back wondering why I lost my nerve, it had not happened before. After a while I see the large building again, walk up the steps and then I am in; it must be a barracks or a very large school. There are long corridors and very large rooms. Some officers have swum the Rhine and are walking about with towels around the waist. There are Red Cross signs up for wounded personnel, but although my back is painful I will look for grub first thing.

I am sitting down and eating a meal and it is very friendly; the atmosphere is all very jolly and happy. A very smart sergeant keeps smiling and asking us, 'Do you want any more? Is everything alright?' This won't last for long, I am sure! A tin of fifty fags is given to any soldier who smokes, so I am happy, food and fags. I am going to find my equipment and have a nap. There are hooks on the walls of the big rooms to hang your guns and equipment and three palliasse, of horsehair I would think, to lay on. I lay back, smoke a fag and wonder who else I know got back here. After a nap I go for a walk outside this building and in the grounds at the back I run into my friends, Judy Wright and Cohen. They are chatting to the seaborne element of our platoon; amongst these is my friend Bechervaise and we lay on the grass and chat.

Another meal, and to bed to sleep all night. This seems very strange, to be able to sleep all night!

Wednesday, 27th September

During the night a man has died; he was just found dead this morning, for no apparent reason.

I have had a shower, changed my clothes, cleaned my boots, and hidden my revolver in my kitbag. There is a high-ranking officer coming to talk to us this afternoon in the main hall; can't imagine what it is he has to say, but it can't be good for us. There must be something nasty afoot. We all have to go to the main hall. I am not interested at all, so I stand at the back with Bechervaise and hope he will say what he has to say and then leave us in peace for a few more days. There are some officers up on the stage and the front of the hall and then the important officer steps up. It is a face not known to me but other soldiers say it is General Browning, the boss of all Airborne troops. Difficult to understand what he is saying but he seems to be thanking us for our efforts in Arnhem. He is saying that we will not be used again in the war, which will soon be over; we have done our bit! As soon as possible we will be flown home to England. This sounds very nice, but I am not impressed. However, he should know better than me! We are given small cards to fill in. On the front you have to put the name and address of your wife, and on the back is written, 'I am wounded, I am not wounded (cross out incorrect)' This is our communication to our wives. I smile as I fill this card and think of Joan with the baby; perhaps she will be glad to get even this card.

As Bechervaise's wife has been living with Joan since we went away, I ask him if he has had the chance to drop his wife a line. He says they have had a smashing time coming up with the Jeeps and equipment behind the main British forces. They had a wonderful time in Brussels with women and wine as they came through with the liberating forces. He had, however, managed to write to his wife every day. I think perhaps Joan will understand that this was not possible with me and be pleased to get her little card, 'I am not wounded'. The time is passed very comfortably. We are all waiting to hear when we will be flown home. The orders are that tomorrow all men who were at Arnhem are to be ready for a convoy to go down 'the corridor' the next morning, down to Belgium, and planes will be ready to fly us home from Brussels aerodrome. The men who have not been in the fighting will return by land and ship back across the Channel. This presents a problem as Bechervaise wants to come back by plane with me. How can we wangle this? Very difficult one! We can't see a way because Bechervaise is on the sea list of men. He can't just line up with us because they have lists.

An officer is walking about asking if anybody would like to be his batman. Nobody is interested until, 'My batman will fly back with me tomorrow.' Bechervaise is there like lightning and the officer is happy. Bechervaise is looking like the cat that ate the cream.

Thursday, 28th September

The next morning is here and we are on the lorries to go down the 'corridor'. The corridor is explained to us. The British Army has been trying like hell to get to us in Arnhem; it has taken a road from Belgium and so as not to waste time has left the Germans on both sides of it. These Germans and their tanks keep cutting the road and the road is then out of action until it is cleared of Germans again. This road goes from Nijmegen to Louvain in Belgium – about fifty miles. The road is at the moment reported clear, but could be retaken in places by the Germans at any time. We must hope for the best.

We set out down the road and do not take a great deal of interest in our surroundings. England and Joan is occupying my mind, and the miles roll by. Occasionally there is a German tank burning in a field just off the road; at one place there are several Germans standing up in a hedge on the side of the road, but they are all dead, just held up by the branches of the hedge.

What I can see of the British soldiers going up to Nijmegen they seem very fit and healthy-looking types, and wave and smile to us on the lorry. It's a nice day but the wind is blowing across the airfield and I am in a queue to get on a plane. So many get on and then the plane goes; another few on a plane and off it goes. Chatting together we are quite sure that they are flying to England and then the same two or three are coming back for more. The middle of the afternoon, and I am finally on the plane with Bechervaise and we are heading towards England. We don't even trouble to look out but have a nap.

We have landed and out we get. Three Jeeps are coming towards us. In the front of the first Jeep is one of our platoon; he has no hair at all, having been burned in a bombing raid on London, so is distinctive. He pulls the Jeep up in front of us and says, 'All Defence Platoon get on.' Four of us immediately embark. He seems puzzled. 'Where are the rest?'

We say, 'There is no rest,' and watch the tears run down his cheeks. He seems terribly shattered to think we may be all that is left of his mates. He revs up and off we go to a large aeroplane hangar. In we go! Now I am shaken.

The whole hangar has tables in lines running down the entire length, all laid with tablecloths, knives and forks, plates and glasses for water. Laid fit for a King! On a small stage at one end there is a little RAF band, playing music. An RAF sergeant asks us which unit, so we tell him and he shows us to some seats at the tables. We sit and wait, speechless. I think we have come into the wrong place, that this is for officers only. I feel very uncomfortable; we should be sitting on the ground outside eating out of our mess tins. We smoke, and the time is going by. Everybody, including the RAF staff, looks uncomfortable. More soldiers have come in; we must have a long time to wait because there are only about sixty to eighty of us and the tables are laid for three hundred or more.

The band stops and an RAF warrant officer, his face strained, says, 'Would you all come up to the near ends of your tables; we had been expecting (hiccup), hoping there would be more of you.' I look at the endless empty tables and the silence is oppressive. I now realise the extent of our casualties, the many good blokes who never made it. I do not enjoy the meal and I am sure my friends do not either, but we are making a show of cheerfulness, and thanks for the good food, in front of the RAF men who have gone to all this trouble.

We are glad to leave, and embark in lorries back to our original billets in Leadenham. Our huts are as we left them; our beds still in position. We throw our equipment down, lay on our original beds, light fags and survey the ceiling. We have not seen any officers or NCOs so we are happy.

Bechervaise and I decide to walk up to the NAAFI at Fulbeck, the next village, and have a 'char and wad'. We walk along an English lane and the world is good. We discuss the chances of disembarkation leave, which is automatic on soldiers coming back to England, and decide it will no doubt be given to us next week, give them a chance to sort things out.

I phone my mother to tell her I am home safe, and I break into a telephone call my father is having with my wife. He gets the operator to put the call through him to my wife. She sounds excited that I am back safely, and how lucky to call my father at the same time she was calling him. She says she will come up to Leadenham to see me.

The NAAFI is empty. We walk up to the tea bar, and the friendly, familiar faces of the girls behind the bar appear; their faces light up with joy at the sight of 'their' soldiers. 'They're back!' they shout. 'Where are the rest?' We don't know! 'Where's Sainty?' (Their favourite!). 'Dead.' One girl bursts into tears, and they all look sad. The good-looking one who was always chatting them up and who was always going to kill all the Germans? 'Dead.' They ask about different members of the platoon and the recce squadron, the transport chaps, but we can only say, 'We honestly don't know.' We have our 'char and wad' and it doesn't taste as good as usual, and we walk back to the billets.

Stan Clitheroe is back! That's great! Judy Wright and Cohen and Lieutenant Butterworth are back! Corporals ********, ******* and ******* are back. Old familiar faces seem to be reappearing every each day! The place is beginning to look regimental again. Nobody seems to know about any leave. We spend most time lying on our beds and eating. Very few officers about, but I can feel that we are soon going to be an organised unit again.

The padre stops me and says he is pleased to tell me that I have been recommended for a Military Medal, and congratulates me. Perhaps he is mad, or perhaps he has me mixed up with somebody else. I can't imagine that anybody would dream that my antics deserve such an honour, unless you get it for scrounging fags! No, there is a mistake.

My wife is in the village and we are spending our evenings and nights together for a few days. She liked Sainty also; *wasn't he good-looking*, she says! Lieutenant Butterworth stops Joan and tells her, 'I have recommended your husband for the Military Medal,' and Joan wants to know what it is! We are so happy together, and we each know that it can't last for long.

There is a big dinner being given by 'Quaglinos' in the West End of London for survivors of Arnhem and two people from each unit are selected to go: Stan Clitheroe and I are to represent our unit. This should be a good night out.

It is, and I end up sitting on an underground platform with an iron rubbish basket jammed on my head. Sloshed to the wide!

1 AIRBORNE DIVISIONAL SUPPORT   359

Utrechtseweg/Onderlangs, Tuesday 19th. The alleyway on the right (behind the garden bench) is where Holden and Lieutenant Fraser threw their Gammon bombs hoping to knock out a Sturmgeschütz in the street. An SS infantryman checks the alleyway for anymore surrendering Airborne, one having just emerged with his hands raised holding a piece of white material, seen in the middle of the photo. By this time, Holden and Fraser had made good their escape out the back. Any remaining Airborne were rounded up and Dutch civilians removed from their houses. (Photo: Courtesy Gelders Archive)

Two photographs of 'West End' on the corner of Steijnweg and Utrechtseweg, looking north and to the west. Private Vic Holden writes about Friday, 22nd September: 'A soldier comes up with some orders. Stan, Jeff and I are to take over the large house on the corner, 'West End' and there will be some others to join us if they can be found. We are to hold it until relieved. This is smashing; it is a large substantial house that we have admired from our trench. There could be water, toilets, food. We set off to 'West End' immediately.' (Photo: Author, 1984)

Arnhem. Rear view of the houses along Utrechtseweg backing on to the river tow-path. On the right is the Rhine Pavilion. These houses were initially occupied by the remains of the battalions that withdrew after their abortive attempts to reach Frost. Off picture to the left is the house that was defended by Vic Holden and Lieutenant Fraser with around 25 other men of 1st and 3rd Parachute Battalions in the early hours of Tuesday 19th until forced out later that morning by German self-propelled guns and SS infantry of Kampfgruppe *Harder*. Holden and Fraser narrowly escaped running along the tow-path making their way westwards.

Private Vic Holden, Tuesday 19th September, writes: 'Suddenly some of our men jump over the wall at the bottom of the garden and the rest follow. Lieutenant Fraser holds my arm and says 'Wait.' I wait. When they have all gone he says, 'Now' and we run and throw ourselves over the wall, to land on top of a mass of struggling bodies and then roll clear. This is what Lieutenant Fraser had foreseen. We are on a narrow tow-path alongside the river, which seems very wide. Lieutenant Fraser and I start running away from the attacking Germans; this is one thing that I can do.' (Photo: Author, 1980)

Lieutenant William Annfred Fraser, Liaison Officer, 3rd Parachute Battalion, Oosterbeek Airborne Cemetery. Private Vic Holden writes about 20th September: 'Lieutenant Fraser amazes me, nothing bothers him. He doesn't duck when something explodes, bullets leave him unconcerned; has he got guts! I get my favourite order again: 'Make me a cup of tea.' He seems friendlier now so I ask him, 'Where do you come from, Sir?' He says his family come from Inverness but have gone out to Canada. He also says he is with the 3rd Parachute Battalion.' (Photo: Author, 1984)

Craftsman Joe R. Roberts, Advance Workshop Detachment, Royal Electrical and Mechanical Engineers

My story begins at an army camp in Boston Road, Sleaford, a small country town in the county of Lincolnshire, in August, 1944, where I was a clerk stationed with the 1st Airborne Division Workshops, REME.

During the preceding months it was obvious that we were going to take part in some sort of action, because we as a unit of tradesmen were being trained to become fighting soldiers as well; and, I might add, not very much to our liking. The route marches to the rifle range some ten miles away, field firing on Glossop Hills in Derbyshire, sleeping under stone walls in the open, map reading and all the other duties one would imagine an infantryman would be trained to do. We as a REME workshop consisted of men such as armament artificers, instrument mechanics, vehicle mechanics and most other trades that one could imagine and all very skilled men. I was a clerk, and one day whilst I was preparing Company Orders for the following day, it fell my lot to type out a list of names of thirty-three men and two officers who were to be formed as an Advance Workshop Detachment, myself included, to perform the clerical duties. In the short time that followed much activity took place preparing the equipment necessary for the forthcoming operation. Mobility appeared to be the order of the day, for in addition to the Jeeps and machinery trailers, nine motorcycles and eighteen folding cycles were provided. Upon landing at our intended destination it was decided that each two cyclists should be towed by one motorcyclist. The cyclists, of which I was one, were provided with a piece of parachute cord by which to attach to the motorcycle.

Craftsman Joe R. Roberts.
(Photo: Courtesy Joe Roberts)

The barrack square provided the testing ground for this intricate operation, it not being as simple as it sounds. The sight of twenty-seven men going around and around in circles on the square caused much amusement to the rest of the men in the unit, and we too could see the funny side of it. Shortly afterwards, we as a unit, set off for an unknown destination which turned out to be Harwell and from the 1st of September it was a series of moves from one airfield to another. After a while I was instructed to issue the men with francs, so it was obvious then that we were to be dropped somewhere in France, but in the time that followed, operation after operation was cancelled, and eventually francs were exchanged for guilders. The time for departure was obviously imminent for a voluntary religious service was arranged for the Saturday evening, and much to my surprise it was attended by what appeared to me to be nearly every soldier in the camp. Our church was a tent, which up to that evening, services been attended by only a handful of us, still it was gratifying to know that all those men had enough faith to hope that their prayers might be answered, and that they would be granted protection in their hour of peril.

Sunday, 17th September; Monday, 18th September

On the Sunday morning the first of the troops made their way to the airfields and we watched them fly overhead on a journey to somewhere in Holland. The following day we arrived at Down Ampney, an airfield near Swindon, and loaded our equipment into the gliders. Soon we were to be airborne and on our way. For the benefit of those who have never travelled in a glider being towed, I can assure them that it is not the most comfortable means of travel, it being extremely noisy and bumpy, and not at all recommended for those who suffer from travel sickness. Immediately after take-off the man opposite me took out his false teeth, opened his brown paper bag, and took no further interest in the journey.

When we crossed the coast of Holland we were greeted with anti-aircraft fire and the bursting of the shells around us caused our glider to rock about, which did little to improve my nervous system. Eventually we arrived over the Landing Zone and very soon afterwards we found ourselves hitting 'mother earth'. Here our training stood us in good stead, for we quickly unloaded the glider and made our way to the assembly point. Our unique transport system was then put into effect and the motorcycles and cycles in tow were heading their way into battle. A short while afterwards we were held up and I came into contact with another REME soldier who had a Jeep and empty trailer; being a man of initiative I decided that the Jeep and trailer would provide a more comfortable means of transport. I put my cycle on the trailer and we set out on our way following many other vehicles and my detachment following behind. After a while the convoy in front stopped and the driver of the Jeep said, 'this is as far as I go', but much to my alarm my unit carried on. I quickly unloaded my cycle from the trailer, and head down, made off in the direction of the motorcycles. What I hadn't realised was that they had turned left opposite the Hartenstein and I was pedalling on my way to Arnhem. The sight of the lone cyclist must have affected the aim of the German machine gunner for a burst of tracer bullets shot across in front of me. I thought, my God, *this is the real thing* and I did a very quick U-turn and headed back from whence I had come, only twice as fast. A short way up the road, I turned into a driveway which proved to be the Hartenstein and our Divisional Headquarters. I reported to my adjutant, explaining that I had lost my unit and the circumstances which had led thereto.[31]

A few hours later two men of my unit arrived and reported me as being missing and were quite surprised to see my smiling face. I returned with them to my unit and was greeted warmly by my lieutenant,[32] who was more than a little concerned that he might have lost his clerk, and requested of me that I should not leave his sight again.

Tuesday, 19th September (REME Workshop Area Positions, Oranjeweg, Oosterbeek)

The positions we took before moving to the Hartenstein Hotel were about a quarter of a mile directly opposite the front of the hotel in some trees by the roadside (Oranjeweg) and some houses nearby. The people from the houses gave us some milk and water to drink. We were only there

---

31 A Captain A.F. Ewens, HQ, REME.
32 Lieutenant G. Manning, REME.

overnight and the morning of the following day (19th). The following day, Tuesday, things began to get very unpleasant. A sniper was causing a lot of trouble and had us pinned down for quite a time. The sniper causing the trouble was in a wood directly opposite to us; fortunately he didn't hit any of the men.

Wednesday, 20th September
We were ordered to make our way, at intervals, up the road and into the grounds of the Hartenstein. My turn arrived, and for the speed of movement the cycle was again brought into use; a shell burst in the road about a hundred yards away in front of me and I charged through a cloud of dust and across the main road into the grounds of Divisional Headquarters.

We made our way to the tennis courts which had been turned into a prisoner of war camp for the Germans, and proceeded to dig ourselves in. Our trenches were made deep enough just to pop our heads over the top, and we covered most of the trench with empty containers and baskets, which had previously dropped, and filled them with soil in the hope that they would give us further protection. Alan Wood, the reporter, was dug-in close by and we used to have a chat to him. I was armed with a .303 rifle but I also spent some time on the Bren gun which was covering the far side of the tennis courts. We could see the Germans moving about some distance away but too far to engage.

Thursday, 21st September
From then on our position appeared hopeless. Our motorcycles were blown up by a direct hit from a shell and burnt themselves out and the cycles suffered a similar fate. The men of the unit carried out the duties of their applicable trades and busied themselves in many other ways, such as going out on patrol. In fact on one such patrol one of our staff sergeants shot a German sniper. I never went out on patrol myself because as I have already explained, my duties were mainly of a clerical nature and Lieutenant Manning had bid me to keep at my post. My time was spent mainly in the region of my trench, which was also my office, and receiving information regarding the active strength of the unit. I had to give a daily return of those killed, wounded or missing and write it on the form provided and then take it along to the adjutant, and he in turn would take it along to HQ. On one such visit to him with the daily returns, heavy shelling commenced, and I quickly made use of his trench for safety, much to his amusement. He assured me that I had nothing to worry about, and during this time he stood at the top of his trench totally oblivious of what was happening around him. When things quietened down a little, I returned to my trench, but a short while later all hell broke loose, containers were falling through the trees and shells were bursting around us. I saw one of our men fall to the ground and heard someone shout for a stretcher.[33] Four of us dashed forward and placed the wounded man on a stretcher and hastened to the casualty post, but unfortunately the wounded man died as we reached the cellar. On our return I saw my adjutant lying under a tree beside the path, quite badly wounded, and being attended to. He had been taking the return I had just previously taken to him to HQ, when he had been hit by shrapnel. The loss of the adjutant meant that my daily return ceased and I think that my most important job after that, other than on the Bren gun, was the responsibility of issuing the cigarette ration to the men, which if I remember rightly, was one per man per day, plus mine, because I was a non-smoker, which made me very popular.

---

33   Craftsmen Vincent John Harvey, 5990037. No known grave.

What happened in the days that followed have been related many times before, but I do recall that during one very heavy shell attack and I was in the safety of my trench, hoping that it would soon cease, when suddenly there appeared a German sniper at the foot of my trench, his left arm hanging off from the shoulder and pointing desperately to his wound and obviously appealing for help. My rifle not being handy, I pointed in the direction of the casualty post and he quickly disappeared in the direction to which I had pointed. He had obviously been hit by one of his own shells whilst sniping at us from the trees.

Monday, 25th September

I now move on to the night we were to retreat and were told to blacken our faces with mud, cover our boots with socks and to take our rifles with ten rounds of ammunition and to bury everything else. Personally, I filled my pockets with fifty rounds of ammunition, for having survived so far, nothing was going to stop me crossing the river that night without a fight. I also brought out papers which I thought should not be left behind.

We set off at 2200 hours each holding on to the flap of the smock of the man in front. I can remember coming to a narrow road and all of us diving into a ditch whilst a German patrol passed a few yards away on the other side of the road. Very slowly we carried onwards, much of the time on our stomachs on the wet ground, being held up from time to time by machine gun fire and flares exploding above us and lighting up everywhere. Eventually I could smell gas, and it appears that we were somewhere near the gasworks.[34] We then arrived at a wide ditch and one by one we leapt over it, that is except for me, for being only 5 feet 5 inches tall, my legs were not long enough to reach the other side and I landed up to my waist in water and was to find out later, tar, which was running down the stream from the gasworks.

After what seemed like hours we eventually arrived at the riverbank. I will remind you that I stated at the beginning of this story that we were tradesmen and not really fighting soldiers as such, because it would appear that our leader, who shall be nameless, had misread his compass and we were too far down the river to get to the ferry before daylight.

After much searching of the riverbank we found a rowing boat attached to a post with a chain and after much effort we got the post out of the ground and put the boat into the water complete with post and chain. Our leader then asked for volunteers to cross the river and get help for the others. I think I was the first in the boat, my determination to get out being uppermost in my mind, and not through bravery. Having no oars by which to row, we used our rifle butts and baled the water out of the boat with our helmets. Upon leaving the bank the current was so strong it turned the boat around immediately and we found ourselves heading for the bank we had just left. I can recall a rather fat sergeant sitting in the middle of the boat who then took charge and got us heading in the right direction, and all the way across saying to us, 'row, your lives depend upon it.' He, by the way enjoying a free ride – for he had nothing by which to help us row.

On nearing the opposite bank I remember hearing strange voices and thinking to myself, *they must be Germans*; my fear was short-lived for they turned out to be Canadian soldiers, who helped us out of the water. We explained that the rest of our unit were on the other side of the river and they promised to go and bring them across. We were to find out later that they had found a raft and had crossed the river on that. The Canadians gave us a cup of tea and set us off in the right direction to join the rest of the column of men, a bedraggled lot, and none so more than me, for the tar on my

---

34   The gasworks stood south of the Benedendorpsweg on the most western edge of the perimeter at the time.

trousers from the ditch by the gasworks had now begun to set and my face was also covered in tar, which was later removed by the use of a penknife, the scars remaining for many days afterwards. As we walked on tired, but free men, I am sure that the thoughts of all of us were those of thankfulness and my mind went back to the service which had been held some ten days before in England and the realisation that our prayers had been answered. My greatest regret was for the wonderful Dutch people who would now have to face the wrath of the Germans for helping us.[35]

Advance Workshop Detachment, Royal Electrical and Mechanical Engineers, Div HQ Hartenstein. German POWs confined in tennis courts in background. Left to right: 1. Looking down the Bren gun barrel, Artificer Quartermaster Sergeant Ron Turner. 2. In trench, Lieutenant A.M. Brodie. No. 6 Light Aid Detachment REME. 3. In trench, Artificer Sergeant Major Matty Reed. 4. 'Cooking the last tin of "Date Pudding" which AQMS Turner had found somewhere, and he and I shared it between us,' – Craftsmen Joe R. Roberts. Craftsman Joe R. Roberts writes about Wednesday, 20th September: 'We made our way to the tennis courts which had been turned into a prisoner of war camp for the Germans, and proceeded to dig ourselves in. Our trenches were made deep enough just to pop our heads over the top, and we covered most of the trench with empty containers and baskets, which had previously dropped, and filled them with soil in the hope that they would give us further protection.' (Photo: Courtesy Gelders Archive)

35   In 1983 during the course of my research I came into contact with Staff Sergeant R.S. 'Dick' Wade, 25 Flight, 'E' Squadron, Glider Pilot Regiment who kindly contributed his account of the operation. It became apparent that Dick Wade was one of the two glider pilots that carried Joe Roberts into battle in his Horsa Glider, Chalk No. 852. The other pilot was Lieutenant Ron Johnson. I managed to put Joe and Dick into contact with each other after 39 years.

5

1st Airlanding Anti-Tank Battery, RA, Polish 1st Independent Parachute Brigade Anti-Tank Battery, 'B' Squadron, The Glider Pilot Regiment

Introduction[1]

1st Airlanding Anti-Tank Battery, Royal Artillery, and the 1st Polish Independent Parachute Brigade Anti-Tank Battery

UBIQUE

This introduction concentrates primarily on the 1st Airlanding Anti-Tank Battery, RA, and the 1st Polish Independent Parachute Brigade Anti-Tank Battery. The 2nd (Oban) Airlanding Anti-Tank Battery RA along with the anti-tank units of the 1st Airlanding Brigade will be covered in later chapters although as paths crossed during the battle, some re-referencing may be encountered.

The 1st Airlanding Anti-Tank Battery, RA, had a short but illustrious career. Formed in 1941 and stood down in 1946, it began life as a pre-war territorial unit, the 4th Battalion, The King's Own Royal Regiment (Lancaster) in Barrow-in-Furness and in 1938 became the 56th Anti-Tank Regiment. As part of the British Expeditionary Force to France it was evacuated from Dunkirk in 1940 after which it became 223 (Independent) Anti-Tank Battery RA, part of the 56th Anti-Tank Regiment, 31st Independent Brigade Group. In December 1941 it was absorbed into its airborne role. It can claim to be the first airborne artillery unit to take its guns in the air. It took part in the invasion of Sicily in 1943 as part of the 1st Airborne Division and then into Italy in September 1943. After Arnhem, the unit returned to its spiritual home of Heckington and reformed, before taking part in the liberation of Norway.

1st Airlanding Anti-Tank Battery RA was commanded for the Arnhem operation by Major W.F. Arnold and formed part of the 1st Airborne Divisional anti-tank complement along with the 2nd (Oban) Airlanding Anti-Tank Battery RA, under Major A.F. Haynes attached to the 4th Parachute

---

[1] Sources: Air Movement Table, Operation Market. Air 37/1217. Doug Colls, *As You Were. September 1944, 1st Airlanding Anti-Tank Battery RA* (Redcar, 1985).

Brigade. The 1st Airlanding Brigade were self-contained with their own integral Battalion Support Companies each of eight 6-pounder anti-tank guns. In addition, the 1st Polish Independent Parachute Brigade Group had their own Brigade Anti-Tank Battery commanded by Captain J.K. Wardzala.

The 1st Airlanding Anti-Tank Battery RA was composed of primarily four 6-pounder anti-tank gun troops, A, B, C and Z, with two additional 17-pounder anti-tank gun troops, D and P.

A Troop was attached to 1st Parachute Battalion, B Troop the 2nd Parachute Battalion and C Troop the 3rd Parachute Battalion, all under command of the 1st Parachute Brigade. Z Troop and the four 17-pounder anti-tank guns of D Troop were to be deployed in the divisional area whilst P Troop was to be split with two 17-pounders attached to the 1st Parachute Battalion and the remaining two guns to be held as the divisional reserve. Z Troop was not formed until June of 1944 having previously been part of the anti-tank defence of the 1st Airlanding Light Regiment RA. It was born out of necessity to provide Divisional HQ with a reserve anti-tank capability and was commanded by Lieutenant Eustace McNaught, RA. Medical facilities within the battery were provided by a team led by Lieutenant Derrick Randall, RAMC.

1st Airborne Operational Instruction No. 10 [1st Parachute Brigade]
Anti-Tank
(a) troop (6-pdr) under command each battalion
(b) sec (17-pdr) under command 1st Parachute Battalion [2 guns]
(c) sec (17-pdr) remains in reserve; moves with 1st Parachute Brigade HQ and is available for engaging flak barges and flak positions as required.

RAF Manston 1st Lift. LZ 'Z'
17 Horsa gliders: Chalk Nos. 327, 328, 330, 332, 334, 336–347. Minus 329, 331, 333, 335. 19 Flight, 'B' Squadron, Glider Pilot Regiment
Abortive glider: Chalk No. 336
Towed by 296 Squadron RAF
Loads:
1st Airlanding Anti-Tank Battery RA Headquarters
A, B and C Troops
Twenty-one Jeeps, five trailers, twelve 6-pdr anti-tank guns and four motorcycles
(Because of tug aircraft shortages, C Troop had one gun, No. 2 gun, i/c Sergeant Shaw, deferred to the Second Lift which placed the 3rd Parachute Battalion in the initial part of the operation one gun short).

Sunday, 17th September. Failures and Crash Landings
There were numerous reasons for gliders and their loads failing to arrive safely. In earlier Airborne operations such as the invasion of Sicily in 1943, many gliders were cast off prematurely because of naval and ground fire and the inexperience of the USAF tug crews resulting in 68 gliders landing in the Mediterranean sea; losses of 326 men, missing, presumed drowned are recorded.[2]

On the Arnhem operation, four gliders did land in the sea; two of these were due to tug rope failures and two due to tug aircraft engine problems. Cast-off gliders were rapidly picked up in the Channel by Air-Sea Recue launches. Glider failures were due in the main to lack of visibility between the glider

---

2   Alan Lloyd, *The Gliders* (Leo Cooper, 1982), p.42.

pilots and the tug in thick cloud resulting in the tow rope breaking. There were instances of the tug aircraft experiencing engine problems, forcing the release of the glider. Finally, anti-aircraft flak en route in varying intensity resulted in damage to the glider or its tug and their crews. In the case of the Polish glider Third Lift, some losses were due to German fighter interception over the LZ. For the 1st Airborne Division on the First Lift alone there were 161 parachute aircraft, 149 of those belonging to the US IX Troop Carrier Command and another 12 belonging to 38 Group RAF carrying the parachute elements of the division. There were 297 glider and tug aircraft combinations courtesy of 38 Group RAF making a total of 755 aircraft and gliders involved in the First Lift.[3] With the huge numbers of aircraft involved in the operation and with columns of aircraft stretching miles, a great deal of air turbulence could be encountered further back along the stream. This in itself caused some problems with glider control which at the best of times could be difficult. There were communication cables between tug and glider pilots of variable quality but this was susceptible to breakage.

A Troop, 1st Airlanding Anti-Tank Battery RA, attached to 1st Parachute Battalion arrived on LZ 'Z' one gun short. Horsa Glider Chalk No. 336 containing a 6-pounder anti-tank gun, Jeep and three gunners had to release early because its tug aircraft was experiencing engine problems. The glider flown by Sergeant Rupert Goldsack and Sergeant Laurie Foster 'B' Squadron, 19 Flight, GPR, landed near the villages of Macharen and Megen in the Dutch Province of Brabant. The gun, 'A1', named 'Aurora' was part of A Troop and commanded by Sergeant Herbie Atkinson. Upon landing, Atkinson and his crew, Bombardier W. Cotteral and Gunner F. White, proceeded to remove as much as they could in the way of small arms and equipment and then blew up the gilder and its contents, setting it all on fire. The Dutch Underground hid the crew until they met up later with US forces at Grave.[4] Both glider pilots were evacuated and swiftly returned to base at Brize Norton by the 23rd September.[5] One Horsa glider carrying the Z Troop Commander, Lieutenant McNaught, cast off prematurely 20 miles west of Nijmegen. McNaught was subsequently sheltered by the Dutch and joined up with the US 82nd Airborne. Another Horsa glider containing a Z Troop 6-pounder anti-tank gun, Jeep and crew was forced to land on Walcheren Island off the Dutch coast.[6]

Sunday, 17th September Onwards

To sum up, upon landing, C Troop were one gun short (under Sergeant 'Doc' Proctor to follow in the 2nd Lift), A Troop had lost Sergeant Herbie Atkinson's 'Aurora' A1 gun and D Troop had lost half its strength with two 17-pounder guns lost in crashed gliders. (Chalk No. 318, Gun No. 1 under Sergeant N.S. Gentles, and Chalk No. 319, Gun No. 4 under Sergeant S. Fitchett). As the parachute battalions moved off, Major W.F. Arnold CO,1st Airlanding Anti-Tank Battery, RA, ordered C Troop's Sergeant Cyril Robson and his 6-pounder No. 4 gun to follow Arnold and the Battery HQ behind Frost's 2nd Parachute Battalion's advance on the lower road or Lion route. Frost was accompanied by a full complement of B Troop 6-pounder guns under their troop commander Lieutenant P. McFarlane and was now reinforced with Sergeant Robson's C Troop gun.

3rd Parachute Battalion moved off the DZ around 1500 hours having linked up with their glider transport and the two remaining 6-pounder guns of C Troop under Lieutenant E. Shaw. As

---

3   Report on Market Garden by 38 and 46 Groups RAF.
4   *Tugs and Gliders To Arnhem*, p.94.
5   War Diary, B Squadron, 1 Wing, Glider Pilot Regiment.
6   War Diary, HQRA.WO171/957.

mentioned earlier, Lieutenant Shaw accompanied Sergeant L. Garnsworthy's No. 1 gun 'Deceased' which was supporting B Company close to the front of the column, whilst further back in the line of march Sergeant F. Shaw with his gun followed between the remaining rifle companies. Advancing in an extended column along the Utrechtseweg towards Oosterbeek, B Company suddenly came under fire from a German armoured car emerging from the Sonnenberg estate. The infantry immediately deployed, leaving Sergeant Garnsworthy and his gun in full view. In the ensuing burst of machine gun fire two of the gun crew were hit; the driver, Gunner George Robson was killed and Gunner Fail wounded. The Jeep was immobilised but the gun remained intact. After the departure of the armoured car, another Jeep was commandeered to tow the gun and the advance continued. Further back down the column, the other C Troop gun under Sergeant Shaw came under machine gun fire from their left flank. The Jeep towing the gun was damaged by the machine gun fire and exchanged with a Jeep towing a trailer. The 3rd Parachute Battalion settled down for the Sunday night in Oosterbeek to resume their advance in the early hours of the following day (See Chapter1).

1st Parachute Battalion left the DZ at around 1530 hours and made their way north-east towards the Amsterdamseweg and the Leopard route accompanied by the three remaining 6-pounder guns of A Troop under command of Lieutenant Eric Clapham. Due to the losses suffered by D Troop, Lieutenant Geoff Ryall was ordered to join Sergeant Rams and accompany him and his D Troop 17-pounder anti-tank gun into Arnhem in support of the 1st Parachute Battalion. It is worth pointing out at this stage that there was a serious terminal fault with this particular 17-pounder gun. The 17-pounder buffer recuperator system worked by a process of oil and air and possibly due to damage incurred during the glider landing Sergeant Rams' gun had no air and it would probably have only fired only one round, having no means of absorbing the recoil of the gun.

The progress of the 1st Parachute Brigade and its parachute battalions has already been covered earlier in detail but to keep some form of context and continuity with the supporting units I will endeavour to keep any repetition to a minimum. Having been halted in their advance on the Sunday night and early hours of Monday morning along the Amsterdamseweg, the 1st Parachute Battalion side-stepped the opposition on the Dreijenseweg and made their way in a south-easterly direction to the lower 'Lion' route. It was on the Klingelbeekseweg that a 6-pounder anti-tank gun was brought forward into action to successfully deal with a German strong point in a factory which was threatening to stall the advance (possibly Sergeant Shaw's C Troop gun attached to the rear of A Company, 3rd Parachute Battalion). A German armoured car was also destroyed in the attack. Progress on the Monday was slow and the battalion column extended, often with the anti-tank gun support well in the rear and only being called forward when required. At this stage the battalion was still on the offensive and anti-tank guns are not best suited to offensive action, being designed to be static, well concealed and to await targets to come into their field of fire. The Royal Artillery anti-tank guns were not always deployed in the most efficient manner during the battle and criticism of their use by the infantry was made by the HQRA after the operation, in particular the misuse of 17-pounders being used as mobile anti-tank guns in the forward areas. Often the infantry would fail to realise that the tank must come to the gun, not the gun to the tank; there were instances when a gun and crew had gone forward and then were left behind by its protective screen of infantry.[7]

1st Parachute Battalion spent Monday fighting and working its way into the western outskirts of Arnhem and were preceded by the 3rd Parachute Battalion, although uncoordinated at that time. Sergeant Max Rams' D Troop 17-pounder gun, under the overall command of Lieutenant

[7] War Diary, HQRA.WO171/957.

Ryall, accompanied the 1st Parachute Battalion. En route the gun-crew came under sniper fire and Sergeant Rams decided to go single-handedly after the sniper. Subsequently wounded, he was never seen again, and as a result crewman Bombardier D. Stone took command of the gun.

With the 1st Parachute Battalion up ahead along the Utrechtseweg, A Troop, 1st Airlanding Anti-Tank Battery, RA deployed two of their 6-pounder guns as an anti-tank screen on the junction of Utrechtseweg and Klingelbeekseweg with Sergeant J. Anderson on the south side of the junction and Sergeant D. Reed facing north up Diependalstraat. Sergeant J. Wilkinson remained limbered up as reserve on Klingelbeekseweg. On the Tuesday, Lieutenant Ryall took the Bombardier Stone's 17-pounder gun forward in support of Dobie's battalion and took up a gun position. With German resistance proving too much for the battalions moving towards the bridge and the subsequent withdrawal, Ryall found himself and his gun too far forward with airborne infantry rapidly passing his position in a rearward direction towards Oosterbeek. In trying to turn the gun around, the Morris Portee became bogged down in soft soil and Ryall was reluctantly forced to abandon the gun (considered a heinous crime in the Royal Artillery). Leaving the crew to join the exodus to Oosterbeek where they dug-in, Ryall returned by Jeep to Div HQ to report the gun loss to the CRA. Ryall was then ordered by the CRA to take command of the defence of Div HQ along with Z Troop which then consisted of three 6-pounders, one on each end of the driveway facing east and west along Utrechtseweg with the third gun behind the Hartenstein.[8]

In the afternoon of Monday 18th September with the late arrival of the Second Lift due to poor weather in the UK came the remaining No. 2 C Troop 6-pounder gun under Sergeant Proctor and all the remaining gun crew members (two crew out of every gun team) plus additional Jeeps and ammunition trailers that were unable to accompany their guns on the First Lift due to space restrictions. Sergeant Proctor made for Ooosterbeek and reported to the CRA at Divisional HQ and was ordered to deploy his gun near the tennis courts (close by was the trench of the Canadian reporter, Stanley Maxted) where the gun remained overnight. The following day it was moved to the east side of the Hartenstein entrance driveway pointing in a westerly direction along the Utrechtseweg.[9] The gun was responsible for knocking out at least one German half-track.[10] On the opposite side of the road, camouflaged in some bushes, sat a 17-pounder gun facing east towards Arnhem (This was a 17-pounder belonging to the 2nd (Oban) Airlanding Battery RA. See the account given by Gunner F. John Winser, D Troop, 1st Airlanding, Anti-Tank Battery, Royal Artillery. John Winser became a spare crew member, having lost his own D Troop 17-pounder in his crashed Hamilcars.)

On the Wednesday, Sergeant Proctor was ordered to move his gun to just past the Oosterbeek crossroads to a position on the eastern side of Stationsweg to the Huise Berghege garden with the gun able to engage targets along Utrechtseweg and Annastraat. Opposite the gun position on the other side of Utrechtseweg a number of paratroopers appeared. Sergeant Proctor was ordered to fire at the German-occupied houses opposite and then ordered to leave the gun in position by Lieutenant Colonel Smyth, CO, 10th Parachute Battalion who along with a number of his men was retiring at the time. The gun-crew returned to the area of Div HQ where they were counter-ordered to retrieve the gun by Brigadier Hackett, which they duly did. On the Thursday the gun was moved into a position on the south side of Utrechtseweg opposite Mariaweg facing north with a field of fire approximately 600 yards long up the street. The whole area was now under intense

---

8   John C. Howe, *Point Blank Open Sights* (Hough Publishing, 1999), p.61.
9   Gunner W. Shilleto, Sgt Proctor's Bren gunner. Correspondence with the editor, 1992.
10 See Gunner Ralph Cook's account. Correspondence with the editor, 1992.

mortar and shellfire which made manning the gun very dangerous. Close to midnight on the Thursday 21st the gun was moved yet again into its final position onto the green in front of the Hartenstein which the 17-pounder of 2nd (Oban) Airlanding Battery RA had previously occupied. The 6-pounder gun faced east and now came under command of the troop sergeant, Sergeant Jack Davis, where it remained until the withdrawal.

Also amongst the Second Lift were the remaining crew of No. 1 gun, C Troop of Sergeant Garnsworthy. Gunner J. Disdel brought in additional ammunition in his Jeep and trailer for the gun but could not get forward far enough to replenish the gun. One Jeep and ammunition trailer went forward to Arnhem but never returned and it was not until the Thursday that Disdel was ordered to take his Jeep and trailer down to the church. Prevented from travelling any further by a parachute battalion major, Gunner Disdel was ordered to off-load some of his 6-pounder ammunition which he did before being ordered to return to Div HQ. Coming under small-arms fire en route, Disdel returned to the grounds of the Hartenstein and dug-in next to his Jeep and ammunition trailer. Within a couple of days, German mortar fire eventually hit the Jeep and trailer causing the remaining ammunition to blow up. Fortunately Disdel was unhurt in the blast and he remained as an infantryman defending the Div HQ until the withdrawal across the river.[11]

It was around midday on the Monday that Sergeant Garnsworthy's C Troop 6-pounder gun was lost due to mortar fire whilst supporting the 3rd Parachute Battalion close to the Rhine Pavilion. Garnsworthy's gun had engaged enemy targets on the south side of the river and had consequently attracted enemy mortar fire. German infantry and armour overran the area on the Tuesday forcing Sergeants S.L.G. 'Gus' Garnsworthy, D.G. Strong and their troop commander, Lieutenant Ted Shaw, to take shelter in the nearby Rhine Pavilion. Vacating the Rhine Pavilion because of enemy pressure, Lieutenant Shaw led his party into a house further west. German infantry approached their building and were engaged by Garnsworthy; two enemy entered the front door and were shot by Lieutenant Shaw, and the gunners then made a hasty 'tactical withdrawal' out of a back window but came under small arms fire from the rear along the tow-path. The gunners made their way back into the house and worked their way along the street to eventually meet up with Sergeant Shaw's gun at the Hulkesteinseweg/Klingelbeekseweg junction.

C Troop's driver/gunner Eric Milner drove Sergeant Shaw's No. 4 gun towards the rear of the 3rd Parachute Battalion column and on the Tuesday morning reached the side of St Elizabeth Hospital. Close by Lieutenant Colonel Dobie was holding an 'O' Group in a nearby house on the corner of Utrechtseweg/Oranjestraat attended by A Troop's Lieutenant Clapham. A Troop's 6-pounder No. 4 gun and Jeep under Sergeant Wilkinson had been limbered up and parked outside the building when a shell exploded close by, wounding Bombardier Lambert, and Gunners Broomhead and Batley; the remaining crew took shelter in a nearby building. A shell from an approaching StuG hit the building in which the 'O' Group was being held which called a halt to the meeting. Clapham ran outside and commandeered C Troop's Driver Eric Milner to extricate the jeep and gun from the approaching StuG which Milner, under fire, successfully achieved. Milner then rejoined Sergeant Shaw's gun team and joined the withdrawal back to Oosterbeek via Klingelbeekseweg. It was during this withdrawal that the Jeep and gun came under small arms fire and the crew dismounted; Milner was wounded in the left arm in the subsequent fire fight.

Lieutenant Ted Shaw directed Sergeant F. Shaw's gun driven by the wounded Driver Eric Milner back towards Oosterbeek. On reaching the church, one of the battery officers directed Milner to

---

11   Gunner J.M. Disdel. Correspondence with the editor, 1992.

a position in the Weverstraat-Fangmanweg area. Having unlimbered Sergeant Shaw's gun, Milner went off to seek medical attention at the Schoonoord dressing station. Milner believed the gun position in the Weverstraat/Fangmanweg area covered both avenues.[12] Late afternoon early evening, two StuGs approached down Fangmanweg from the Bato's Wijk. Sergeant Shaw scored a hit on one but the second knocked the 6-pounder out, killing Gunner Mitchell and wounding Sergeant Shaw. Lieutenant Shaw arrived in the church area on the Benedendorpsweg and put Sergeant Garnsworthy's gun into a garage near the church, possibly that of F.W. Klaassen. Lieutenant Shaw brought the gun into action on the Thursday against enemy infantry and armour; however, the garage was subsequently hit by enemy shellfire setting the garage on fire with the gun inside. C Troop lost four gunners: Bombardier George Robson; Sergeant Garnsworthy's driver, Gunner Mitchell; Gunner Leonard Underwood died of injuries in the RAP of the Ter Horst family next to the church, and Gunner Ogden was killed near to Div HQ at the Hartenstein.

The A Troop 6-pounder guns of Sergeant Anderson and Reed had been moved forward to the junction of Zwarteweg and Utrechtseweg to support the 1st Parachute Battalion's Tuesday morning advance. Anderson's gun was actually successfully deployed outside the hospital to engage enemy guns across the river. When the 1st Parachute Battalion and the other battalions began their withdrawal from Arnhem, Sergeants Anderson, Wilkinson and Reed withdrew also to form an anti-tank screen in the area between Oranjestraat/Alexanderstraat and Utrechtseweg/Hulksteinseweg. (Wilkinson either regained control of his original gun or took command of another gun with a makeshift crew, having previously lost three of his gun crew.) All guns engaged with the advancing enemy StuGs. Wilkinson had his gun at the gates of the KEMA/Den Brink area at the end of Alexanderstraat. Wilkinson's gun, although it had a good field of fire down Alexanderstraat, was taken by surprise by enemy armour advancing down Diependalstraat to its flank; the gun's line of sight was blocked by retreating airborne infantry and could not fire for fear of hitting friendly forces. The German StuG, not constrained by such reservations, opened fire on the anti-tank gun and knocked the gun out and killed several of the crew. Sergeant Wilkinson managed to escape and rejoined the battery. Both Reed and Anderson moved back to their previous evening's positions on the Utrechtseweg/Klingelbeekseweg junction and again were in action with Reed facing the oncoming threat down Diependalstraat and Anderson facing along Utrechtseweg. The guns successfully halted the enemy armour, albeit temporarily, during which time the two remaining A Troop guns were given the order to withdraw to Oosterbeek where they initially deployed close to the MDS crossroads. On Wednesday morning, Sergeant Reed was ordered to take position on the Annastraat/Jagerspad junction whilst Sergeant Anderson took up position on the Annastraat/Weverstraat junction, with both guns now covering north, north-east and southern approaches. By the afternoon, enemy infantry were creating problems for the gun crews and a decision was made to withdraw Anderson and Reed. Sergeant Anderson was deployed on Pietersbergseweg with Sergeant Reed on the junction of Paasberg and Jagerspad with Battery HQ personnel acting as an infantry screen. Both guns remained in position under mortar and sniper fire using up their remaining ammunition until on the Monday the crews disabled their guns and moved into an infantry role.

Down by Oosterbeek Laag church, Private Fred Radley, 3rd Parachute Battalion recalls one 6-pounder gun being sited behind a small house which contained Major Lonsdale's HQ, just a few yards north of the then RHQ of the 1st Airlanding Light Regiment RA (Oosterbeek concert hall area). Lonsdale's HQ was not situated in the church as folklore would have it; the location of his

---

12 Driver Eric Milner. Correspondence with the editor, 1991–1992.

The Rhine Pavilion, Onderlangs, after the battle, 1945. (Photo: Courtesy Gelders Archive)

Arnhem bridge, Monday, 18th September, afternoon. Vehicles of SS-Panzer-Aufklärungs-Abteilung 9 destroyed earlier that morning litter the north side of the bridge. (Photo: Courtesy Gelders Archive)

HQ was in close proximity with the Command Post of A Troop,1st Airlanding Light Regiment RA. Besides the gunners dug-in locally, the 6-pounder had a small group of 3rd Parachute Battalion and mixed infantry acting as close protection.

Arnhem, Anti-Tank Guns and the Battle at the Bridge

We must now catch up with the B Troop guns and the one C Troop gun accompanying the 2nd Parachute Battalion heading towards the bridge and arriving around 2000–2030 hours on Sunday evening along with the 1st Airlanding Anti-Tank Battery, RA, HQ which had followed the 1st Parachute Brigade HQ. The Battery HQ first established itself to the west side in a square flat-roofed building right alongside the bridge, sharing the building with members of the 9th Field Company RE. The HQ consisted of the battery commander, Major W.F. Arnold; battery captain 'O', A.D. Llewellyn-Jones; and liaison officers Lieutenants A. Cox and H.W. Whittaker. The battery officers were accompanied by the battery clerk, Sergeant D. Colls; acting battery sergeant major, Sergeant L. Doughty; and despatch rider Gunner Hartley, along with several other Battery HQ staff. As described earlier, several of the 1st Airlanding Anti-Tank Battery 6-pounder guns initially moved into cover under the bridge tunnel before being deployed. However, Sergeant Shelswell's No. 3 gun 'Blighty 2' was called into action soon after arriving at the bridge by Major Arnold to deal with a strongpoint and pillbox on the north-western end of the bridge which was preventing any attempts at getting men across to capture the south side of the bridge. The gun and its Jeep were skilfully reversed up a bridge approach footpath then the gun was manhandled the last few yards into position on the edge of the bridge approach. Three well-placed SABOT shots later with some assistance from an RE flamethrower team, the strongpoint and pillbox and its occupants were silenced or taken prisoner. Sergeant Shelswell then moved his gun back behind Brigade HQ where he and his crew dug-in for the night to be joined by Sergeant Doig and his crew who left their gun and Jeep in Hofstraat. Before Sergeant Doig had time to deploy his gun on Hofstraat, the Jeep sustained damage from a mortar bomb which punctured tires, making driving dangerous.[13] Doig's crew were uninjured, having been dug-in. Shelswell and his gun later moved out onto the corner of Kadestraat where he and his crew spent the Monday night inside an adjacent house.

Meanwhile on Sunday evening, Sergeant Kill and his gun arrived on the corner of Westervoortsedijk and Oostraat and deployed in a small copse to cover the crossroads with what would appear to be a somewhat restricted field of fire both north along Eusebiusbuitensingel and east along the Westervoortsedijk. It is possible that Sergeant Kill may have manhandled his gun so as to cover Oostraat, providing a better field of fire on Nieuwe Kade. Kill must have relied on an interlocking field of fire with that of the guns on the west side of the bridge. This assumption is based on photographic evidence of Sergeant Kill's abandoned gun position with a photograph taken by the Germans immediately after the fighting at the bridge had ceased and also of RAF aerial reconnaissance photographs. Kill's gun position was made untenable by midnight Monday by enemy mortar fire and encroachment, as witnessed by the RAOC occupants of the house opposite.[14]

Sergeant Robson's C Troop gun arrived a little later than B Troop having spent half an hour on the LZ helping to try and extricate Sergeant Gentles' D Troop 17-pounder gun and the occupants of one of the overturned Hamilcars. As a consequence Robson failed to link up with all his gun crew. When he did arrive at the bridge, Major W.F. Arnold deployed Robson on the

---

13 Sergeant Ernie Shelswell. Correspondence with the editor, 1991–1992.
14 Private Ted Mordecai. Correspondence with the editor, 1983.

north side of Markstraat about 100 yards from the bridge facing east, where he could cover the Westervoortsedijk road under the road bridge. Robson successfully halted a German Mk.III tank approaching under the bridge from the east at around 0700 hours on Monday morning. After initially failing to dig the trail spades in, which resulted in recoil injuring several of the crew, a substitute crew from Battery HQ were found. With the spades dug in, the gun resumed engaging the tank, resulting in the vehicle being immobilised.

Expecting further enemy movement across the bridge, under instruction from Lieutenant A. Cox situated in a window overlooking the bridge, Robson's gun fired several shots at the bridge knocking a large gap in the two foot six inches-high parapet which had slightly obscured his view of the road over the bridge. Robson now had a clear view down his gun-sight of the road bridge.

Sergeant J. O'Neil's No. 4 B Troop gun was moved initially into the tunnel entrance of the Van Eeuwen garage adjacent to Brigade HQ. Later that day, O'Neil moved his gun to a gap between 2nd Parachute Battalion and Brigade HQs which would prove to be its final position. Both guns now covered the bridge.

Around 0900 hours, vehicle engines could be heard on the south side of the bridge approaches signalling the arrival of an armoured column from SS-Panzer-Aufklärungs-Abteilung 9, under command of SS-Hauptsturmführer Viktor Grabner, the destruction of which has been described earlier. Both Sergeant Robson and Sergeant O'Neil both played a prominent role in the destruction of the German column.

Later on that morning, the intensity of the mortaring and shelling of the Battery HQ had caught not just the building alight but hit several vehicles in the yard outside. Lieutenant Cox dashed out of the Battery HQ and personally removed containers of 6-pounder ammunition from one of the Jeeps. Lieutenant Harry Whittaker was seen attempting to drive a Jeep and gun out onto Markstraat, most likely the Jeep and gun of Sergeant Doig's which had earlier been damaged by mortar splinters. Captain A.D. Llewellyn-Jones witnessed the event. 'One unit driven by a very brave young officer made it out into the road by the HQ, but here the blast from a mortar killed him, though this was not known until later. What was seen, was a Jeep and a gun in tow, careering round the wide road by the bridge until it finally drove itself into a wall.' In fact, Whittaker was badly wounded by the mortar blast and died on the 23rd September in the St Joseph Psychiatric Hospital in Apeldoorn. Doig's salvaged gun was later moved near the bridge concrete pillar not far from the steps leading up the bridge ramp.[15]

1st Airlanding Anti-Tank Battery HQ moved to a large building to the west of the bridge perimeter on the northern side close to the Markstraat/Eusebiusplein junction, some hundred yards from the 2nd Parachute Battalion HQ. Robson's gun was deployed on the street close to the new Battery HQ enabling the gun to cover both east and west approaches. This was to be Robson's final gun position and it was from here that Robson engaged and knocked out two German Pz.Kpfw. IVs in the afternoon advancing from the east along the Westervoortsedijk past the Camiz dairy in support of a German advance on the east side of the bridge.

Late on Monday around 1730 hours, Sergeant O'Neil's position came under heavy shellfire with the building behind his gun taking hits. The whole of the side of the building collapsed on top of the gun. O'Neil and his crew sheltering in the house were all injured in the blast and the subsequent collapse.

---

15 Nigel Simpson, Secander Raisani, Philip Reinders, Geert Massen, *Standby-Steady-Fire!* (NL Books, 2020), p.79.

ANTI-TANK BATTERIES 377

The two Pz.Kpfw.IVs of Pz.Kp Mielke knocked out by Sergeant Robson's C Troop gun. The first, above, was hit on the Westervoortsedijk and slewed across the road with a broken track presenting its rear end to Robson. A subsequent round penetrated the side skirt. The tank then received a hit in the rear from a PIAT bomb fired from behind a ruined wall by Captain Tony Frank, A Company, 2nd Parachute Battalion. Below, another 100 yards further along the Westervoortsedijk the second tank was hit under the Camiz dairy pipe bridge which later collapsed on top of the tank. 6-pounder hits can be seen on the lower front hull plate. (Photographs: P.J. de Booys, October 1944. Courtesy Gelders Archive)

Tuesday, 19th September–Wednesday, 20th September
Sergeant Shelswell and his gun were situated on the corner of Kadestraat and Markstraat where he and his crew had spent the Monday night inside a house. Early on Tuesday morning, Shelswell turned the gun to the south, facing down Kadestraat to engage German vehicles that were moving along the Rijnkade close to the river. The gun was moved again early Tuesday morning westwards opposite Robson's second position on Markstraat. Shelswell was then wounded in the foot by a stray bullet that ricocheted off the wall of a nearby house. Shelswell was left with a Bren gun whilst Major Arnold placed Sergeant Harold Doig in command of Shelswell's gun and crew which then moved into a position in the corner of the 1st Parachute Brigade HQ garden next to the end wall of the Van Eeuwen garage. Doig was killed later that day from a direct hit by a mortar, whilst at the same time mortally wounding Shelswell's gun layer, Gunner Lock and wounding gun layer Gunner J.J. Connelly.

From Tuesday onwards, pressure increased with heavy mortaring and determined German attacks from the east and north during the day. These attacks culminated at around 1900 hours with the appearance of two Pz.Kpfw.VI Tiger I tanks of Schwere Panzer-Ersatz und Ausbildungs-Abteilung 500 supported by German SS Panzer grenadiers approaching from the north ramp. The tanks caused a great deal of damage and fired at will into any buildings they suspected of harbouring airborne defenders.

After the death of Sergeant Doig, Major Arnold led a make shift gun crew, comprising Captain Llewellyn-Jones, Lance Sergeant Cools and Lieutenant McFarlane along with two gunners, to retrieve the salvaged gun of Sergeant Doig's No. 1 gun left by the bridge ramp. Major Arnold organised the manhandling of Doig's salvaged gun into a position in front of Brigade HQ to counter the threat from the Tiger tanks. Major Arnold's gun engaged one of the Tiger tanks, scoring two hits resulting in several of the tank crew being badly injured. Unable to depress their 88mm gun sufficiently to hit the 6-pounder, the tank sent several rounds into the wall above Arnold's gun. Both tanks reversed out of the line of sight of O'Neil's gun and away from the bridge, much to the relief of all those around him. Major Arnold left the gun to head back to Battery HQ leaving Captain Llewellyn-Jones in command of the gun. Llewellyn-Jones then moved the gun onto the grass embankment where the crew dug the gun in and then dug their own slit trenches. Later in the night, Lieutenant McFarlane took over command when Captain Llewellyn-Jones went off to check on the remaining battery members who were now acting as infantry in various buildings.

The culmination of the battle at the bridge has already been described in detail earlier. From the Wednesday onwards the gun crews that remained, many of whom were wounded, were unable to effectively man the few remaining guns. Resistance realistically finished at the bridge on the Wednesday apart from small groups of men that attempted to fight or evade the Germans through the night and the early hours of Thursday morning.

The Royal Artillery gun crews deserve special recognition for their outstanding bravery, not just at the bridge but throughout the battle. In time of need, gun crews left the comparative 'safety' of their slit trenches and buildings to venture out and man their guns often out in the open with nothing but a gun shield to protect them, and engaged enemy armoured vehicles whilst not only coming under direct fire from the armoured vehicle itself but also attracting small arms, mortar and shellfire.

1st Airlanding Anti-Tank Battery Royal Artillery, Arnhem Bridge Positions. (Photo: Courtesy Gelders Archive)

Key to 1st Airlanding Anti-Tank Battery Royal Artillery, Arnhem Bridge Positions

Battery HQ Major W.F. Arnold
H1. Initial HQ position Sunday to Monday Jewish School (Joods Lyceum).
H2. Second HQ position early morning Monday onwards north side of Eusebiusplein.

B Troop
Sergeant H.E. Doig No. 1 Gun
D1. Initial position 2100 hours Sunday night, deployed Kadestraat facing Rijnkade.
D2. 2230 hours. Second position Sunday, overnight gun limbered and standing in Hofstraat, crew dug-in behind 2nd Parachute Battalion and Brigade HQ alongside Sergeant Shellswell's gun crew. Mortar fire damaged gun and Jeep tires. Crew uninjured, still dug-in behind Brigade HQ.

D3. Monday 1230 hours Hofstraat, gun salvaged by Lieutenant Whittaker, who was mortally wounded by mortar fire in the process. Gun moved to road tunnel concrete support pillar. (There is some conjecture as to whether the gun was then moved to 'M' Jeep and Gun park before later being re-positioned by road tunnel concrete support pillar).

Early Tuesday, Sergeant Doig was ordered to take command of the wounded Sergeant Shelswell's No. 2 Gun and moved the gun to the front garden of Brigade HQ north end, next to the end wall of the Van Eeuwen garage. By 1700 hours Sergeant Doig had been killed with Gunner Connelly wounded and Gunner Lock mortally wounded by shrapnel and falling masonry.

After the death of Sergeant Doig, and the loss of No. 2 gun, Major Arnold led a make-shift gun-crew to retrieve the salvaged gun of Sergeant Doig's No. 1 gun left by the bridge ramp (D3). Major Arnold organised the manhandling of Doig's salvaged gun into a position in front of Brigade HQ to counter the threat from two Tiger tanks (D4). Major Arnold left the gun to head back to Battery HQ leaving Captain Llewellyn-Jones in command of the gun. Llewellyn-Jones then moved the gun a few yards onto the grass embankment where the crew dug the gun in (D5). Later in the night, Lieutenant McFarlane took over command.

Sergeant E. Shelswell No. 3 Gun 'Blighty II'

S1. Sunday, 2230 hours. First position on bridge ramp path, engaged enemy strongpoint and pillbox on bridge Sunday evening. After this action the gun reported back to the Joiners' Yard and joined Sergeant Doig. Both guns were ordered to the rear of Battalion and Brigade HQ. Doig was then ordered to move his gun into Hofstraat. Shelswell and Doig's crews both dug-in for the night.(S2)

S3. Late Monday, moved to corner of Markstraat opposite Battery HQ on the opposite side of the road from Sergeant Robson's gun; both guns faced towards the bridge tunnel.

Tuesday morning, Shelswell turned his gun to face down Kadestraat to counter enemy vehicles on Rijnkade.

S4. Gun moved early Tuesday morning westwards opposite Robson's second position on Markstraat. Shelswell wounded in the foot by stray bullet.

S4. Sergeant Doig takes over command of the gun from Shelswell. Gun moved to the front garden of Brigade HQ. Doig later killed and gun lost.

Sergeant W. Kill No. 2 Gun 'Bravado II'

K1. Sunday evening, took up position close to corner of Westervoortsedijk/Oostraat. Gun manhandled to engage enemy on Oostraat and Nieuwe Kade.

K2. Monday, midnight gun position abandoned as untenable.

Sergeant J. O'Neil No. 4 Gun

O1. Sunday night moved into undercover entrance to Van Eeuwen Garage adjacent to 1st Parachute Brigade HQ building. Brigade Defence Platoon occupied the building above.

O2. Monday, 1200 hours. Moved position to gap between 2nd Parachute Battalion HQ and 1st Parachute Brigade HQ covering the bridge tunnel. Shellfire collapsed section of wall behind gun rendering gun inoperable.

C Troop

Sergeant C. Robson No. 3 Gun

R1. Sunday, initially took up position 100 yards west of the bridge on Markstraat on the other side of the street from Kadestraat. Monday engaged enemy armour under the bridge (Mk.III). Directed by Lieutenant Cox, battery liaison officer, Robson blew a gap in the bridge road wall to gain a line of sight onto the road bridge so that enemy vehicles could be engaged.

ANTI-TANK BATTERIES 381

R2. Final position. Monday afternoon moved further west to outside new Battery HQ Markstraat covering east and west, engaged enemy armour east of bridge on the Westervoortsedijk (MkIVs). By 1530 hours on Tuesday, Robson's gun had been put out of action.

Street Key
A. Westervoortsedijk
B. Ooststraat
C. Nieuwe Kade
D. Rijnkade
E. Eusebius Buitensingel
F. Eusebiusplein
G. Eusebius Binnensingel
H. Markt Straat
I. Kade Straat
J. Hofstraat
K. Badhuisstraat
L. Joiners' Yard
M. Jeep and Gun Park

Pre-war looking west. Camiz Dairy and pipe bridge visible centre right of photo. It was under this bridge that the second PzKpfw.IV was knocked out; the first was stopped about 100 yards further east (bottom right) along Westervoortsedijk. Sergeant Robson, C Troop, knocked both of these tanks out from his gun position outside 1st Airlanding Anti-Tank Battery, RA second HQ (extreme top left). Elements of 1st Parachute Brigade HQ Defence Platoon occupied the Camiz Dairy on the northern side of Westervoortsedijk until the 18th, whilst No. 8 Platoon, C Company, 3rd Parachute Battalion and elements of 1st Parachute Brigade HQ Defence Platoon occupied the dairy buildings across the road on the south side (lost on the 19th). No. 3 Platoon, A Company, 2nd Parachute Battalion under Lieutenant McDermont held the building centre lower left (with the sun awnings) until forced out on the 19th. Later that day, McDermont led a force of around twenty men and reoccupied the building during which McDermont was mortally wounded. The building was finally lost on the 20th. Sergeant Kill's B Troop gun was positioned opposite McDermont's building in the trees on the corner of Westervoortsedijk and Oostraat and lost during the night of the 18th. (Photo: Courtesy Aviodrome Lelystad 16027)

The Second and Third Lifts and the Oosterbeek Perimeter
RAF Manston Second Lift. LZ 'X'
    4 Horsa gliders: Chalk Nos. 886-889. 19 Flight, 'B' Squadron, Glider Pilot Regiment
    Towed by 297 Squadron RAF
    Loads:
    1st Airlanding Anti-Tank Battery, RA
    Four Jeeps, eight trailers, four motorcycles
    Twenty-three troops of the 1st Airlanding Anti-Tank Battery, RA

    Polish 1st Independent Parachute Brigade Anti-Tank Battery
    7 Horsa gliders: Chalk Nos. 890-896. 3 and 4 Flight, 'B' Squadron, Glider Pilot Regiment
    Towed by 297 Squadron RAF
    Load:
    No. 3 Troop Anti-Tank Battery under command of Lieutenant Mleczko
    Five 6-pounder anti-tank guns Jeeps, trailers and personnel

The five guns, two ammunition trailers, seven Jeeps, several motorcycles and seventeen men provided the advance party of the Polish 1st Independent Parachute Brigade Anti-Tank Battery, the main part of which would arrive with the Third Lift. (Each gun was allocated enough room per glider for one Jeep driver and two gun crew per gun. The remaining gun crews were to parachute in on the south side of the river.) All guns successfully landed and Mleczko led his troop to Div HQ at the Hartenstein where he was met by a colonel (probably the CRA, Lieutenant Colonel R.G. Loder-Symonds) who informed him that Mleczko would come under his command. Ordered to set up his 6-pounder anti-tank guns to protect Div HQ, Lieutenant Mleczko deployed his guns around the road junction of Utrechtseweg/Oranjeweg covering all approaches.[16]

RAF Fairford Second Lift. LZ 'X'
    6 Horsa gliders: Chalk Nos. 1004-1009. 10 Flight, 'G' Squadron, Glider Pilot Regiment
    Towed by 190 Squadron RAF
    Load:
    1st Airlanding Anti-Tank Battery, RA
    Z Troop
    Four 6-pounder anti-tank guns

Chalk No. 1007 ran into trouble whilst avoiding another aircraft during the flight over the coast of Holland. The tow rope broke during the manoeuvring forcing the glider containing a Z Troop 6-pounder gun and three gun crew to land at Overflakkee. The glider was torched and the gun firing pin removed. The two glider pilots and the three gun crew of Z Troop were later taken prisoner.

    Chalk No. 1005, containing Z Troop CO, Lieutenant McNaught, RA, dropped just short on the south side of the Rhine due to tow rope failure. The party unloaded and managed to cross the Rhine via the Driel ferry, still in operation.

16   George. F. Cholewczynski, *Poles Apart* (Greenhill Books, 1993), p.99.

RAF Tarrant Rushton Third Lift. LZ 'L'
   20 Horsa gliders: Chalk Nos: 129–139. Composite Flight, Glider Pilot Regiment
   Abortive gliders: Chalk Nos. 126, 130, 133.
   Towed by 298(10) 644(10) Squadrons RAF
   Load:
   1st Polish Independent Parachute Brigade Anti-Tank Battery
   Ten 6-pounder anti-tank guns
   HQ Troop (Chalk Nos. 120–123)
   Twenty Jeeps, ten trailers, sixteen motorcycles and seventy-four personnel

No. 1 and No. 2 Troop Anti-Tank Battery (Chalk Nos. 124–130 and 131–137). Under temporary command of Lieutenant Jerzy Halpert until the battery commander, Captain Jan Kanty Wardzala would attempt to join the battery after parachuting in with the remaining gun crews. The British glider pilots would remain temporarily attached as gun crew until the arrival of the Polish crews (in reality many of the glider pilots remained with the guns throughout). Having landed with the parachute element of the Polish Brigade south of the river, Captain Wardzala was taken prisoner when he finally crossed the Rhine with other Polish troops on the night of the 23/24th.[17]

1st Polish Independent Parachute Brigade Anti-Tank Battery

Tuesday, 19th September Onwards
The 1st Polish Independent Parachute Brigade Anti-Tank Battery suffered two tow rope failures, one over Ostend where the Horsa glider landed safely along with its load of a 6-pounder anti-tank gun, Jeep and two Polish gun crew. The other tow rope failure occurred when the glider came under ground fire and the rope was cut by flak. The glider landed near the village of Retie where both pilots, 6-pounder gun and crew were taken prisoner by the Germans. Flak was responsible for the loss of another Polish glider, Chalk No. 126, with its 6-pounder anti-tank gun, Jeep and crew of Ognm. Piotr Maslorz and Kan. Kazimierz Nowak along with both glider pilots, Staff Sergeant Ronald Osborn and Sergeant Norman Whitehouse, A Squadron GPR, when it was shot down over St. Michielsgestel in Holland, killing all those on board.[18]

Following close behind the Polish gliders came a flight of German Messerschmitts which engaged the defenceless gliders as they approached their Landing Zone ('L'). Over the LZ one glider was seen to completely disintegrate under fire disgorging its load of 6-pounder gun, Jeep and crew.[19] German infantry and armour then counter-attacked the elements of the KOSBs who were trying to defend the LZ and the 4th Parachute Brigade that were still withdrawing from the area towards Wolfheze. Chaos ensued with the Polish gun crews attempting to unload their equipment under fire from the Germans and mistaking the airborne troops in the locality for Germans; instances of friendly fire occurred. British 1st Airborne Division veterans recalled the difficulty in communicating on the LZ with Polish gun crews and later within the perimeter as to gun positioning etc because of language barriers. The Polish gliders on the Third Lift had great difficulty

---

17   *Poles Apart*, p.203.
18   *Tugs and Gliders to Arnhem*, p.199.
19   Marek Swiecicki, *With The Red Devils At Arnhem* (Maxlove Publishing, 1945), p.26.

extracting their anti-tank guns. Three of its guns were lost on the approach as detailed above before reaching the LZ. Out of the remaining seven guns only three were successfully extricated under fire; one was immediately commandeered by a passing British officer who needed the gun and its crew. It would appear that this gun and its ammunition Jeep were dug-in close to the Wolfheze crossing to cover the 4th Parachute Brigade withdrawal and was manned by two Polish gunners and one wounded gunner, Bombardier Józef Oprych. This gun remained in position covering the withdrawal until the Germans closed in on the crossing later that day. The gun crew opened fire on a German Sturmgeschütz which appeared from behind the Wolfheze station; the StuG retaliated knocking out the gun's Jeep and the StuG then withdrew. The Polish crew decided that it was time to leave before the StuG and German infantry returned, and hastily removed the breech block and disposed of it before heading over the railway embankment carrying the wounded Oprych with them. Oprych was captured the following day and made a POW.[20]

Remains of one of the Polish Anti-Tank Battery gliders on LZ 'L' containing a Jeep, trailer and motorcycle. The trailer and motorcycle can be seen in the Horsa wreckage along with ammunition containers for the 6-pounder anti-tank gun. (Photos: Courtesy Gelders Archive)

Only two of the remaining Polish guns reached the Wolfheze railway crossing and made their way down Wolfhezerweg and onto Utrechtseweg where they were directed towards the Hartenstein. On reaching the Oosterbeek perimeter they were ordered to join the other five Polish 6-pounder anti-tank guns that had arrived with the Second Lift. They passed No. 3 Troop and Lieutenant Mleczko's guns at the bottom end of Oranjeweg and headed north 300 metres up Oranjeweg where they deployed, covering a long rectangular field which ran in a north/south axis that had until 1600 hours that day contained No. 2 Battery, 1st Airlanding Light Regiment RA

20   *Poles Apart,* p.116.

ANTI-TANK BATTERIES   385

LZ 'L', Johannahoeve, 1600 hours, 19th September. Horsa gliders containing the Polish Brigade Anti-Tank Battery coming into land. (Photo: Staff Captain H.B 'Jasper' Booty, 4th Parachute Brigade HQ. Courtesy ABM)

LZ 'L', Johannahoeve, 1600 hours, 19th September. Horsa gliders containing the Polish Brigade Anti-Tank Battery coming into land under fire from German forces on the far side of the LZ. (Photo: Staff Captain H.B 'Jasper' Booty, 4th Parachute Brigade HQ. Courtesy ABM)

who had departed heading for their final positions down at Oosterbeek Laag Church (Oude Kerk). Lieutenant Halpert set up his two 6-pounder guns with a good field of fire towards Ommershol to cover not only the field which ran up to Eikenlaan but would also cover the remainder of Oranjeweg in front of the positions of the 21st Independent Parachute Company and the glider pilots of 'E' and 'F' Squadrons, GPR.[21] Staff Sergeant Tommy R. Moore, MM, 14 Flight, 'F' Squadron, No. 2 Wing, Glider Pilot Regiment recalls two 6-pounder guns situated either side of his then-squadron positions at the bottom of the rectangular field facing north. A German Sturmgeschütz SP gun eased its way out of Bothaweg across Oranjeweg and into the field and began to traverse towards the glider pilot positions. The two 6-pounders opened fire and after several rounds knocked out the SP gun. The German crew bailed out and were dealt with by the glider pilots. Whether the two 6-pounders were Polish is unclear but probable.

The following day, Wednesday 20th, German infantry began to infiltrate from the north across the railway and from the northwest from the Bilderberg area, and began to engage Halpert's gunners with small arms and mortar fire. Halpert and two gunners were wounded as a result of the mortar fire and were carried off to the aid post at the Hartenstein. Pressure also increased from the west along the Utrechtseweg towards the positions of C and A Companies Border Regiment astride the Utrechtseweg and Sonnenberg. Mleczko was ordered to get one of his Polish 6-pounder guns limbered up and deal with the oncoming German tank. The result was a 'tragic misuse of an anti-tank gun resulting in the destruction of the gun, the loss of its crew and that of the British officer directing them'. The gun was unable to deploy fast enough to get a shot off before the tank or infantry knocked it out.[22]

Lieutenant Mleczko was ordered to prepare to move his No. 3 Battery and by 1730 hours led his battery down towards the Oosterbeek Laag church. Coming under shellfire during the journey, one gun crew member was killed. On arriving at the church Mleczko discussed gun deployment and the requirements of a Royal Artillery officer concerned about anti-tank defence for the 75mm Howitzers of the 1st Airlanding Light Regiment RA situated around the church. Mleczko agreed to deploy two guns facing north and the remainder facing west along the Benedendorpsweg one of which was on the corner of Kneppelhoutweg with another some 100 metres further west along the Benedendorpsweg near the gasworks.[23]

With the delayed 1st Polish Independent Parachute Brigade's arrival on the Thursday around Driel it became apparent that the Polish Brigade's anti-tank defence was now on the north bank of the Rhine whilst the brigade was on the south bank relying on hand-held PIATs for their defence against armour. Meanwhile, earlier in the morning in lower Oosterbeek, German armour probed the perimeter from the west and knocked out one of Lieutenant Mleczko's guns at the junction of Kneppelhoutweg under command of Lance Sergeant Stanislaw Horodeczny. Simultaneously the other gun further west deterred German infantry from deploying in woodland and buildings near the gasworks by placing HE shells into the woodland and AP shells through the buildings. Although wounded, Horodeczny took command of the other gun on the Benedendorpsweg and concentrated on the Kneppelhoutweg. The German incursions must have been made by infiltrating between B Company and D Company Border Regiment, both of which were experiencing German attacks from the west through the day and had an overextended frontage resulting in a

---

21 *Poles Apart*, p.115.
22 Report by CRA 1 Airborne Division on Operation Market, Annexure 'C' p.4.
23 *Poles Apart*, p.124.

ANTI-TANK BATTERIES 387

Utrechtseweg, looking west and north, 100 yards west of the Koude Herberg at Wolterbeekweg. A knocked-out 6-pounder anti-tank gun in the towed position with the muzzle facing back towards the C Company, Border positions. Two dead, one of the gun crew under the barrel of the gun possibly killed whilst in the process of unhitching the gun and attempting to manhandle/traverse the gun 180 degrees to face west towards an oncoming threat; the other body is probably that of a glider pilot captain. 6-pounder anti-tank guns were notoriously 'trail heavy' and required one of the gun crew to straddle the muzzle-end to counter-balance the trail whilst the rest of the crew moved the trail into its firing position. The 6-pounder guns of the Border Regiment were some 80 yards to the east of this photograph. There is evidence in the photographs of a towing Jeep showing the gun was limbered when these crewmen were killed. This gun is probably that sent by Lieutenant Mleczko of the Polish Anti-Tank Battery on Wednesday 20th in an attempt to engage a German tank along the Utrechtseweg approaching the positions of C Company, Border Regiment. (Photo stills from a German '*Wochenschau*' propaganda newsreel; author's private collection)

lack of mutual fire support and flank vulnerability. B Company Border Regiment lost the high ground on the Westerbouwing this day resulting in a 'reining in' of the airborne perimeter along the river. Further German progress was only halted by the forming of 'Breeseforce' (covered later). On the 23rd, the Germans continued probing the defences along river. Corporal Pawalczyk's 6-pounder gun at the corner of Kneppelhoutweg and Benedendorpsweg came under tank fire and returned fire, forcing the German tank to retire.

Fifty-two Poles crossed to the north bank of the Rhine on the Friday night and again on the Saturday night to Sunday morning some 95 men[24] of the Polish 3rd Battalion crossed along with thirty-seven Polish anti-tank gunners.[25] Apart from two men, the anti-tank gunners were assigned infantry roles as they were not needed on the guns. Only four guns remained in action by then and were still manned by a mix of Polish gunners and British glider pilots that had remained with the crews. The Polish anti-tank guns in lower Oosterbeek around the church were subjected, along with everyone else in the area, to the shelling and mortaring. The Germans had identified the 75mm gun positions of the 1st Airlanding Light Regiment RA situated around the church and blanketed the area with fire. Journeying above ground level and lingering for any amount of time invited the risk of being wounded or worse. One of the Polish 6-pounder guns was situated just a few yards east of the church on the south side of Benedendorpsweg facing north up Weverstraat crewed by Corporals Waldemar Gasior, Waclaw Kajduk and Bombardier Nosecki and one other. Nosecki's gun was hit and put out of action with damage to the elevating gear which rendered the gun useless. The crew stayed in their trenches and took on the role of infantry.[26] Across the road behind the Bremans' house at 119 Benedendorpsweg, the Poles had another 6-pounder anti-tank gun dug-in supporting the British 3rd Parachute Battalion, facing north across the open ground towards the end of Ploegseweg. At dawn on the Saturday 23rd, artillery from XXX Corps in Nijmegen opened a barrage on the previous day's target of German mortar positions in the Bato's Wijk. However, several shells dropped short around the South Staffs positions at the Van Hofwegen Laundry causing casualties and the 3rd Parachute Battalion trenches behind the Bremans' house and one shell landed on the Polish 6-pounder gun, killing two of the Polish crew.[27] The two Polish anti-tank gunners, Bombardiers Josef Skaczko and Kazimierz Chartonowicz were buried alongside each other in the garden behind No. 119 Benedendorpsweg.[28]

One by one, Lieutenant Mleczko's anti-tank guns were knocked out and by the afternoon of the Monday 25th, all guns had been lost. One of the last to be lost was the gun on the corner of Bildersweg facing west along the Benedendorpsweg. The remaining crew withdrew towards the church armed with a PIAT and fought on for the rest of the day and withdrew across the Rhine with the rest of the division that night.

---

24 *Arnhem 1944: The Airborne Battle.*
25 *Poles Apart*, p.212.
26 *Poles Apart*, p.239.
27 Private F. Radley. Correspondence with the editor, 1983–1991.
28 Bomb. Josef Skaczko, 24030, age 38. Bomb. Kazimierz Chartonowicz, 30451, age 22.

… ANTI-TANK BATTERIES   389

17-Pounder Anti-Tank Guns of D and P Troops, 1st Airlanding Anti-Tank Battery, RA

RAF Tarrant Rushton First Lift. LZ 'Z'
3 Horsa gliders: Chalk Nos.376–378.[29] Flown by 'C' Squadron, Glider Pilot Regiment
Towed by 298 (1) 644(2) Squadrons, RAF.
Loads:
1st Airlanding Anti-Tank Battery RA HQ elements
D and P Troop elements
Six Jeeps
8 Hamilcar gliders: Chalk Nos.314–321. Flown by 'C' Squadron, Glider Pilot Regiment
Towed by 298 (4) 644 (4) Squadrons, RAF.
Loads:
D and P Troops
Eight 17-pounder anti-tank guns
Eight Morris commercial artillery tractors (Quad/Portee)

Two Hamilcar gliders, Chalk No. 318, containing No. 1 gun, D Troop, under Sergeant N.S. Gentles and Chalk No. 319, carrying No. 4 gun, D Troop, under Lance Sergeant S. Fitchett, both turned over on landing in the soft sandy soil. Each glider carried a 17-pounder anti-tank gun plus its Morris commercial artillery tractor (or Portee, as it was commonly known) and gun crews of eight men. Unfortunately with the pilots cockpit on the Hamilcar sitting high above the fuselage, when the glider turned over, both pilots were crushed and trapped by the load. Pilots of Chalk No. 318, Staff Sergeant David A. White and Sergeant Charles W. Winkworth, C Squadron, GPR, were both seriously injured. Winkworth died on the LZ whilst Staff Sergeant White died of his injuries in the Schoonoord dressing station in Oosterbeek. The other Hamilcar glider that turned somersault was flown by Staff Sergeant Jack Shaw and Sergeant Charles T. Brackstone and both suffered similar injuries. Trapped beneath the combined weight of the gun and Morris truck, Sergeant Brackstone succumbed to his injuries and died. Staff Sergeant Jack Shaw survived the crash although badly injured and became a POW.[30] Several members of both gun crews were injured including Lance Sergeant S. Fitchett who sustained a broken foot, and both loads were lost.

No. 1 17-pounder gun and the crew of P Troop under command of Sergeant T.H. Hughes landed safely in their Hamilcar glider Chalk No. 316, and deployed in defensive positions around the LZ. The following day after stand-to and a brew, they remained in position awaiting the arrival of the Second Lift. Later they made their way off the LZ towards the lower road along the river. Lieutenant Casey, the troop commander, initially deployed No. 1 gun close to the Oosterbeek gasworks facing west along the Benedendorpsweg. The gun was subsequently temporarily moved to outside the house 'de Lindenhoet', No. 151 on the junction of Benedendorpsweg and Bildersweg before moving on Monday further into the western outskirts of Arnhem. Early on Tuesday morning the gun moved as far as the Rhine Pavilion in support of 1st Parachute Brigade where it engaged an enemy flak barge on the river before being ordered to fall back to Oosterbeek via the railway viaduct at Oosterbeek Laag station on the Benedendorpsweg. The gun then took up position

---

29 *Tugs and Gliders to Arnhem*, p.97.
30 *Tugs and Gliders to Arnhem*, p.100.

covering the railway viaduct until coming under mortar fire. A hasty withdrawal was made back to the Veerweg facing west where it remained in support of B Company 1st Battalion Border Regiment until Thursday 21st. Sergeant Hughes moved his gun back along Benedendorpsweg to a position near the gasworks before moving further east to the apple orchard between E and F Troop, 1st Airlanding Light Regiment, RA behind Oosterbeek Laag church.[31] (Whilst Gunner Burridge's account of the movements of No. 1 gun do not mention travelling further east than Oosterbeek, it would appear from different sources that the gun did indeed travel into Arnhem and engaged targets on the river before pulling back to Oosterbeek).[32] As with many of the anti-tank guns deployed in the battle, the gun was eventually put out of action by enemy fire; in Burridge's case, the blast cracked the recoil buffer making the gun inoperative. No. 1 gun formed part of the anti-tank defence of the Lonsdale Force area, in particular the 1st Airlanding Light Regiment RA positions around the church with No. 3 Battery, 1st Airlanding Light Regiment, RA, south of the church. (See Chapter 14's account by Battery Sergeant Major Tom Kent, F Troop, 3 Battery, 1st Airlanding Light Regiment, RA regarding this 17-pounder gun.)

No. 3, P Troop, 17-pounder anti-tank gun of Lance Sergeant T. Neary was flown into battle by C Squadron pilots, Sergeant Geoff Higgins and first pilot Staff Sergeant John Bonome, Chalk No. 317. Their landing on the Sunday had been relatively straightforward although they did witness another Hamilcar turn over on landing in front of them. Once safely unloaded, the glider pilots had been ordered to accompany the gun and crew for 48 hours before rejoining their squadron. Remaining on the LZ until the Second Lift, the gun, Morris Portee tractor and crew along with the two glider pilots moved off to Oosterbeek. There being no sign that they would rejoin their squadron, the two pilots decided to stay with the gun crew and act as local defence of the gun. The gun was deployed for Divisional HQ defence on the corner of Hoofdlaan and Utrechtseweg and set up facing west with the gun's Bren gun dug-in on the opposite side of the Utrechtseweg. Over the coming days, the gun crew, like everyone else in the vicinity, were subjected to heavy mortaring and shelling. On Saturday 23rd, the Morris tractor containing the ammunition for the gun along with all its equipment received a direct hit and caught fire, cooking off all the 17-pounder ammunition. Staff Sergeant John Bonome was severely concussed, and Higgins guided his first pilot to the RAP having previously taken Lance Sergeant Neary there for treatment. On returning to the gun position Higgins found another of the gun crew incoherent and dazed, having been wounded in the head. Dressing the wounds, Higgins then accompanied the gunner to the RAP.

On returning again to the gun position, Bombardier Haslam, one of the remaining crew, informed Higgins that another of the crew had been killed during the bombardment. It is possible that three crew were killed. The crew that died were probably 21-year-old Gunner L.G. Larkin and 24-yearold Gunner A.C. Richardson both previously of D Troop (Sergeant S. Fitchett's Gun No. 4 which was lost in its overturned Hamilcar glider on the LZ and assigned to assist the P Troop gun crew,) and P Troop Gunner T.S. Warwick. This unfortunately, is a typical example of the fate of many of the anti-tank and artillery gunners of the Royal Artillery during the battle, particularly during action stations. Uninformed of the withdrawal on the night of the evacuation, the glider pilots and the few remaining gun crew only discovered the evacuation had been carried out in the

---

31   Gunner E.T. Burridge. Correspondence with the editor, 1992.
32   Nigel Simpson, Secander Raisani, Philip Reinders, Marcel Zwarts, *Battery D Troop, The First Airlanding Anti-Tank Battery at Arnhem* (NL Books, 2021), p.70.

ANTI-TANK BATTERIES 391

Troop 17-pounder No. 2 gun under Sergeant J. Bower moved into its final position on Monday 18th opposite the 'ice factory' facing east along Benedendorpsweg. P Troop's Sergeant Bower and Sergeant Thomas of D Troop would provide anti-tank cover in the church area screening the 75mm guns of No. 3 Battery, 1st Airlanding Light Regiment, RA. (Photo: Courtesy Gelders Archive)

Sonnenberglaan, Oosterbeek. After the Airborne withdrawal. a German Fallschirmjäger inspects Sergeant Horace 'Nobby' Gee's No. 1 gun, X Troop 17-pounder gun. Notice the shrapnel-punctured tyre which would have prevented the gun being manoeuvred by the gun crew. The gun in this photo is often confused with another nearby 17-pounder No. 3 gun of P Troop deployed on Hoofdlaan which sustained an 88mm hit on its gun shield which left it fractured and bent. (Photo: Courtesy Gelders Archive)

early hours on the Tuesday morning. They arrived at the river just as it was getting light and were shortly thereafter taken prisoner.[33]

One of the other 17-pounder anti-tank guns in the area forming the Lonsdale Force anti-tank screen was that of No. 3 gun, D Troop, 1st Airlanding Anti-Tank Battery RA under command of 34-year-old Sergeant G.E. 'Taffy' Thomas. On landing the glider came to a sudden halt in the soft soil, resulting in the Morris Portee breaking free of its shackles and being propelled through the front of the glider. The Portee was badly damaged in the process which left Thomas without any means to tow the gun. The crew removed the ammunition from the Portee and manhandled the gun out of the glider whilst Thomas engaged the services of an infantry Bren gun carrier to tow the gun – consequently the gun was late in leaving the LZ.

Eventually Lieutenant Lloyd, D Troop CO, deployed Sergeant G.E. Thomas' No. 3 gun immediately in front of the north-east corner of the church on the Benedendorpsweg in support of 3 Battery, 1st Airlanding Light Regiment, RA, where it remained engaging enemy targets until knocked out on Friday 22nd by shell and mortar fire resulting in the death of Bombardier John McCullock, Sergeant Thomas and Lance Bombardier L.G. Ryden. Thomas and McCullock were both buried in the garden of the Ter Horst family which acted as the RAP for the Light Regiment guns in the area. The remaining crew ended up being treated in the RAP where they were eventually taken prisoner. Before his gun was put out of action, Thomas was requested to deal with a sniper some 400 yards away in houses on the south side of Benedendorpsweg opposite the 1st Parachute Battalion positions. This request was made by Private Fred Radley, 3rd Parachute Battalion, having seen the 17-pounder gun in position after returning from a signal line repair. Fred Radley recalls: 'Jock and I ran through the backs of the houses, onto the footpath and down to the church, saw our 'friend' the sergeant and explained the situation to him. We had no sooner finished than WHAM – a 17-pounder shell went streaking up the road, straight through the top floor of the house.'

No. 3 gun, like several other 17-pounders, appears to have suffered buffer recoil problems due to blast or a rough glider landing. The gun, preserved outside the Hartenstein Airborne Museum in Oosterbeek, still has its barrel stuck in its recoil position. The storage of volatile anti-tank ammunition close to anti-tank guns could apparently be susceptible to blast causing secondary explosions as a result of nearby mortar or shell detonation. Battery Sergeant Major Tom W. Kent of F Troop, 3 Battery, 1st Airlanding Light Regiment RA, noted that, 'Both anti-tank guns and most of their crews on our position went out of action as a result of their own ammunition.'

Both 6- and 17-pounder guns carried APCBC (Armour-Piercing Capped, Ballistic Capped) and APDS (Armour-Piercing Discarding Sabot or SABOT) rounds. The 6-pounder carried 42 rounds into battle, 15 APCBC and 27 APDS, whilst the 17-pounder carried 27 APCBC and 10 APDS (Mk 1T) rounds.[34] The newly developed SABOT rounds, even under the short ranges usually encountered at Arnhem of between 300–400 yards, were difficult to observe but proved highly effective against German armour. A small proportion of 6-pounder HE (Mk10T) was received in re-supply. There was, however, a reluctance to use HE due to the possible disclosure of the gun's position due to its ferocious signature.

C Squadron glider pilots Sergeant H.H. Rathband and Staff Sergeant G.T. Jenks carried P Troop's 17-pounder No. 1 gun and Morris Portee in their Hamilcar glider Chalk No. 316.

33 Mike Peters & Luuk Buist, *Glider Pilots at Arnhem* (Barnsley: Pen & Sword, 2009), p248.
34 Peter Wilkinson, p.23.

17-pounder anti-tank gun of D Troop, 1st Airlanding Anti-Tank Battery RA under command of Sergeant George Thomas stands facing east in front of Oosterbeek Laag church. Knocked out on Friday 22nd September. Photo taken after the battle. (Photo: Courtesy ABM)

Rathband recalled, 'Our Hamilcar was third in line and our excellent ground crew had, as usual, painted our crest and name on the fuselage. The crest was a girl, three darts and a foaming pint. The name "Bun House" is the name of a famous East End London pub. From the cockpit window fluttered our ensign, an article of ladies' underclothing presented by the landlady of the pub, plus a bottle of champagne.' Onboard apart from the gun and Portee, Rathband carried the gun crew of seven who had only flown with Rathband once before. The passengers would have to rely on the glider pilots to keep them informed of the flight, being ensconced in the bowels of the glider. Rathband had been out drinking on the Saturday night in Bournemouth and had only an hour's sleep before being dragged out of bed and being told that the operation was on. Rathband recalls: 'I rolled out of bed and staggered into the cold shower where, after a few moments. I began to feel a little better. Back in the billet I got dressed, checked my kit and arms and got down to the mess just in time for 0730 hours.'

The take-off was at 1044 hours, described by Rathband: 'The slack in the tow rope was taken up, and we were moving. What a take-off. If our past instructors had seen it they would have passed out. She came unstuck off the runway at about 100mph but for a long time or so it seemed, we could not get the starboard wing up and had gone down the runway at an acute angle. At last we straightened up and were on our way, nothing wrong with the aircraft, just pilot error due to the mess party.' The glider flew over Hatfield, the assembly area and then headed to the east coast over Clacton and across the North sea. On approaching the Dutch coast enemy flak was encountered, but 'nothing really serious' although one red-hot piece of shrapnel penetrated the floor of the glider causing some concern to the gun crew. As the shrapnel was still smoking the gun crew were worried that it might set the glider alight. Asking Rathband what they should (no fire extinguishers were carried on board) he suggested that they urinate on the red-hot metal which they duly did and put out the fire whilst at the same time causing some laughter amongst the gunners. On approaching LZ 'Z' Rathband saw two Hamilcar gliders in front of him. One was flown by Major R. Dale DFC which landed safely, and the other turned over on landing (probably Sergeant Gentles No. 1 gun, D Troop, Chalk No. 318). Rathband skipped the hedge and landed in the next field adjacent to the Wolfheze Psychiatric Hospital. Rathband: 'We decided to come in low, go through the top of the hedge and into the next field. This we did at about 90mph. We held her off and she settled like a bird. The "Bun House" had arrived at Arnhem. It was September 17th 1944, 1300 hours. Her last flight. What a wonderful aircraft she was.'

Rathband continues: 'We unloaded our load of a Portee truck and 17-pounder gun and followed the track alongside the mental hospital to its junction with another road going towards Wolfheze. We brewed up here awaiting orders; gun was placed in action. Orders were received to proceed to the bridge by the southern route. We crossed the road [through] Heelsum and into Oosterbeek. Unlike the rest of the forces that day who were going to the left, we were ordered straight across and except for Dutch people we never saw another airborne member. We arrived at the end of the tram lines and put the gun in position at the end of the bank dividing the road.[35] [We] stayed all night, despatched two of the enemy next morning on what we found out later was the road to the ferry. We saw no other troops around the junction of the road to the ferry. Again ordered to proceed to the bridge, passed another 17-pounder by the concert hall and another on the corner by petrol pumps, carried on till in sight and range of the railway bridge, [the] gun placed in position right of the road, a number of airborne troops were about but not 'dug-in'. We got as far as the approach to the railway bridge when we came under fairly heavy fire and had to stop and take up a defensive position, one armoured vehicle was destroyed under an arch of the railway on the southern side. Our position on the side of the road towards the bridge was so exposed, that under orders we returned back to the final position in the orchard south of the church, again a position with limited arc of fire, it was in this position that the gun was finally put out of action. (On Tuesday we came under fire and troops were coming back up the road, the gun was hitched up to the Portee and we went back to the gasworks, I considered this position hopeless and although not in charge, as an ex-anti-tank gun troop commander I persuaded the No. 1 of the gun to move, we went as far as the church and the gun was positioned in the orchard, the Portee by the north side of the church, this was destroyed by mortar fire two days later). We received two direct hits and all the crew were killed or severely wounded. Sergeant Jenks was an infantryman so he took up a position with members of the South Staffs.

We witnessed a Typhoon (only appearance) destroy a tank with rockets which was underneath a small arch on the south side of the Rhine.

As an ex-anti-tank gunner I considered all the positions badly sighted and we had complete lack of information. I consider the capture of the ferry could have had a great impact on the battle. Although I was a troop sergeant second i/c of an anti-tank troop, once on the ground [we] came under control of Lieutenant Price [Casey] Troop Commander and the sergeant i/c of the

---

35 Junction of Oude Oosterbeekse Weg/Benedendorpsweg and Veerweg near to the Van Daalen house and nearby farm where the crew were given milk and sausage.

17-pounder, [Sergeant T. Hughes] although as a gunner from 1938 I did not agree with the positions chosen, my opinions were not asked for and I had no authority, my late co-pilot and myself carried out any duties allocated to us mostly as infantry protection. Staff Sergeant Jenks and myself were taken prisoner on the Tuesday [26th] but did not meet up, he did not overcome his spell in POW camp and passed away a few years later.'[36]

D Troop Driver/Gunner William H. Cameron never managed to join his troop. 'From the time I touched down until we escaped across the river, I fought as an infantryman with different units. The only anti-tank guns I saw were two from possibly the second battery. That was on the Thursday night, we were ordered to give infantry protection to these guns who were sighted just short of the railway bridge on the Arnhem/Oosterbeek road. As the full might of the German tanks were expected, as they were not needed at the bridge. We were to wait until the tanks came under the bridge, engage both sides of the road hoping to knock out any tank under the bridge therefore blocking the road.[37] We were ordered away just before midnight, to report to defend Div HQ. I never saw any other guns, and the men on this patrol were lost in the next few days.'[38]

Sergeant Ernie Shelswell, i/c 6 pounder 'Blighty' No. 2, B Troop, 1st Airlanding Anti-Tank Battery, Royal Artillery 6-pounder anti-tank gun, attached to 2nd Parachute Battalion

Sunday, 17th September
Airfield: RAF Manston; **Tug Aircraft:** Albemarle Mk I, V.1391; **Pilot:** W.O.C. Barlow RAF
Horsa Glider: 1st Pilot, Sergeant A. Rigby, 2nd Pilot, Staff Sergeant E. Healey; 19 Flight, 'B' Squadron, The Glider Pilot Regiment
Chalk Number: 343; 'Droop', 'Old Faithfull'. Landing Zone 'Z'

A perfect take-off at about 1116 hours. Just before the east coast I remember seeing people going to church, they were walking up the path, something I will never forget. Soon after the east coast I saw a Horsa down in the drink with Airborne chaps out on the wing; not far away was an RAF pick up and as far as the eye could see was the American Airborne off to Nijmegen, a stirring sight. At about 1330 hours the pilot pointed to the destination and I went to the door to lift it up ready to land. One thing we lost was the flask of tea that went out with the suction. One thing I shall never forget at the LZ, the big drop chutes of every colour, hundreds like petals from the sky. Perfect landing with easy tail off-load, and joined up with the rest of B Troop and moved to the bridge area slowly, arriving at approximately 2030 hours.

Sometime after, my troop officer[39] detailed me to take the gun up a ramp walk to the end of the bridge and deal with a pillbox, so with my driver, gun team, glider pilots and paras we slowly reversed the Jeep and finally near the top it was manhandled into position. Light lorries and vans were using the bridge, and when we started to operate the Germans bailed out and it appeared they were coming from all directions. We fired several shots at the pillbox using SABOT rounds and then a flamethrower moved in – it was rough stuff.

---

36   Sergeant Harry H. Rathband. Correspondence with the editor, 1991.
37   Benedendorpsweg viaduct Oosterbeek Laag station.
38   Driver/Gunner William Cameron. Correspondence with the editor, 1992.
39   Lieutenant P. McFarlane.

Monday, 18th September

During the night I withdrew from that position and parked up in a street behind HQ,[40] but during the morning of Monday the mortaring was merciless, and we lost our first gun there. It was a direct hit, just across the road from me, it was Sergeant Doig's gun and it was still attached to the Jeep; no loss of life. During that morning my gun was not in a position, we were dug-in in the garden behind HQ. I was then detailed to take some ammunition to a gun out on the road. I went on my own with as many 6-pounder rounds as I could carry and when I arrived at the bottom of the street I looked left and saw an anti-tank gun about 50 yards away and about 150 yards beyond that was a Tiger tank, the tanks came under the river bridge.[41] The tank fired and took down a three-storey building behind me. I arrived at the gun position, dropped the rounds and it was then I found it was a C Troop Gun with Sergeant Robson firing it.[42] The first tank had stopped but from behind it appeared another, and I can assure you I moved very fast back to my slit trench. Shortly after this my driver, Driver Hodges, was wounded in the back from mortar shellfire. I was then given a gun position across the road and I was glad to get out of that garden and get some cover from a house.[43]

Tuesday, 19th September

We stayed there all night and during the early morning of Tuesday with my layer, Gunner Lock, I decided to turn the gun and take on some light vehicles crossing the bottom of the road (no more did) and it was at that point I was wounded by a bullet. It came off the wall of the house and went sideways through my boot. At first I thought I had dropped the trail of the gun on my foot, but not so. (41 years later I pulled it out of my foot at home; it had passed from the top and came out at the bottom). Later on Tuesday they took my gun and team to a new position, leaving me to man a Bren gun. After dark, 2nd Parachute Battalion lads came through the house, I stopped them and asked if they could get me to a dressing station which they did. I was put in a cellar along with a lot more wounded and shortly afterwards they brought Gunner Lock in on a stretcher and he was able to tell me that Sergeant Doig had taken over my gun and was killed, and he died shortly afterwards.[44]

Wednesday, 20th September

It was during Wednesday a ceasefire was arranged to shift the wounded out; the house was burning. I was able to hop out with some help and sat on the grass waiting to be moved; a German soldier came up to me and said 'Cig, Tommy, we have met before – North Africa,' of course he was talking of the unit, not me personally. Then to hospital in Apeldoorn.

Gun Team. 'Blighty' No. 2 B Troop, 6-pounders (2nd Parachute Battalion)

Sergeant E. Shelswell, POW. Troop Commander: Lieutenant P Mc Farlane, POW
Bombardier C. Coughlan. Troop Sergeant, Sergeant W. McCarner, POW
Driver S Hodges. Sergeant H.E. Doig, KIA
Gunner A. Lock, KIA. Sergeant W. Kill, POW
Gunner D. McNeil. Sergeant E. Shelswell. POW
Gunner Allwood. Sergeant F. Shaw, POW

---

40 Hofstraat off Marktstraat.
41 Panzerkampfwagen IV.
42 Troop attached to 3rd Parachute Battalion.
43 Late Monday, gun position on Markstraat corner of Kadestraat, facing east.
44 Gunner Arthur F. Lock, 875607, age 24. Died of wounds. No known grave. Sergeant Harold E. Doig, 614509, age 29. KIA. First buried in the Moscowa General Cemetery, Arnhem.

Sergeant Arthur Rigby, 19 Flight, B Squadron, No. 1 Wing, The Glider Pilot Regiment

At the briefing we learned that our Albemarle tugs had not sufficient range to reach the Dropping and Landing Zones around Arnhem, so we were moving lock, stock and barrel to a south coast resort, which turned out to be Manston, and we (19 Flight) were billeted in a vacated girls' school at Birchington-on-Sea. We were there about a week before the operation was timed to take place, and I think everyone had a whale of a time, the weather was excellent, and one would never have guessed there was a war on (apart from the occasional shell warnings), and I don't think any of us bought any beer. I know our little lot didn't; we spent most of our time in Birchington, keeping out of Margate, and found a much better type of pub, and far superior clientele who insisted on keeping our glasses full without any expense on our part. It was a very enjoyable run-up to the major event. The date set for the operation was Sunday, 17th September. First Lift take off 1030 hours. On Saturday morning, 16th September, about 0830 hours I received a signal from the RAF Signal Office telling of the birth of my daughter, Josephine! The drill was that after the briefing for an operation, everyone was confined to camp, but on the receipt of this signal I decided to take a chance, went along to see the OC, told him of the event, and surprise surprise, he gave me ten hours' leave to get home and back again, and I did it with a half hour to spare.

Sergeant Arthur Rigby, 19 Flight, B Squadron, No. 1 Wing, The Glider Pilot Regiment. Sketch by Staff Sergeant Alan Richards, B Squadron. (Courtesy Alan Richards)

Sunday, 17th September

The day was a little misty at first, but cleared as the sun got up, and rapidly became warm and sunny. We breakfasted at 0530 hours, and collected big flasks of tea or coffee as required, and huge doorstep corned beef sandwiches as the day's rations, and by 0830 hours, we loaded on to trucks, our rucksacks and weapons altogether. Ted Healey and I had a Bren gun and rifle, four boxes of Bren magazines, 400 rounds of .303 in bandoliers.[45] When we arrived on the perimeter track, all the squadron's gliders were lined up one behind the other, and our anti-tank gun crew were already awaiting our coming. We had to do the usual checks to make sure everything was working: 'Controls OK?' (me in the cab working the column and rudder, Ted calling the instructions). 'Left-right-OK, up-down-OK!' Then compression bottles, etc., and finally the head lashings and fixtures.

We were carrying a 6 pounder anti-tank gun, all the gun crews' gear and personal weapons, plus 20 rounds of ammunition for the gun, and a Jeep to tow the whole she-bang. The gun crew consisted of three men: Sergeant E. Shelswell, Gunner A. Lock and a driver named Hodges. We

---

45 Staff Sergeant E. Healey, co-pilot.

knew them quite well, having spent some time with them at Brize Norton, and we had knocked around Birchington during the time before take-off and found they were quite a good bunch.

When everything was checked and found to be OK, we walked across and had a chat with our tug-crew who were standing in line on a parallel perimeter track in their take-off position ready to swing on to the main runway in turn.[46] Everyone was in high spirits, jokes being bandied about, and general mickey-taking on various characters' flying capabilities. On return to the glider formation, we found two of our particular mates standing by our glider, Staff Sergeant 'Paddy' Clenaghan and Staff Sergeant Charlie Thackeray. Poor old Charles was a bit apprehensive, but I hope we managed to josh him enough to take his mind off possibilities.

Word came along the lines, by way of assembly marshals, to mount up and prepare for movement. Soon everyone was in position, though by this time it was too hot to close the doors, so we left them both open, and also the door in the rear of the cockpit.

At 1000 hours we started to move and the first of the stream started to move down the runway on their take-off runs. We were pretty well down the running order and it was around 1040 hours before our tug swung onto the runway and went forward to tow rope length, the hawser was attached and secured to the tail end, and then we were towed on to the take-off line and the tow rope was fixed to the underside of our main-plane; this is when the butterflies start to flutter in one's tummy. The send-off marshal started to signal to the tug to 'take-up the slack' and then to us to prepare to roll, and as the brakes came off, the glider started to roll gently forward and to rapidly gain momentum, 20-40-60-80-85-95, ease back on the column, and the 'Droop' came off the deck as smoothly as she always did and we rose about 50 feet and settled down at that height until the tug got airborne, and she did just that, so we started to gently climb ahead of her rise, all very smoothly and gracefully. As we gained height and started to circle and join the main stream, the whole formation was in its various stages, some at assembly height, some still climbing, some taking off, and still more awaiting take-off. It was not long before the head of the stream settled down and turned out to sea, to head towards the enemy coastline.

It was extremely bumpy flying in the formation of the stream, both for tug and glider and already our gun crew in the body of the glider were feeling sick, and I was very relieved when our tug pilot called up on the R/T saying he was going to try to get on to the outside edge of the stream. With some very pretty flying, he gradually worked his way with me following him, right onto the extreme left flank of the formation and the ride suddenly became very smooth. We stuck there for the rest of the crossing. As we approached the Dutch coast, we speculated on whether or not we should meet any opposition, either aerial or ground fire. I was fully occupied flying the kite, but I must admit that it was with some trepidation that I looked down for the first time on enemy occupied territory, but nothing happened, and the stream sailed majestically on. Looking around now, one could see that the sky was literally full of aircraft as far as the eye could see either side. There seemed to be thousands of planes and gliders all heading in one direction: Dakotas, Stirlings, Albemarles, Horsa and Hamilcar gliders. Here and there Typhoon and Thunderbolt fighters were sliding around like black and white minnows in a pool of pike.

The noise of our passage must have been awe-inspiring, but still no opposition. We passed Nijmegen away to starboard and it was here that we encountered our first flak, but as we were bearing round to port toward Arnhem, I was so concentrating that I didn't even notice it. I don't

---

46 296 Squadron, RAF: Albemarle MkI, V.1391: WO C. Barlow; F/SGT E. Edeyvean; F/SGT H. Rogers; WO R.B. Wood; F/SGT. B.A.J. Brown.

think there were any casualties; at least no one reported seeing any aircraft going down. We were passing rapidly over the countryside toward the allotted LZs. We began to recognise landmarks on the run-up, and there below us and way ahead was our LZ 'Z' and just as we recognised the area, our tug pilot warned us of our approach run, I acknowledged and handed the controls over to Ted, pretty gladly too, having flown the whole of the crossing from rendezvous point over Manston to Arnhem, and I was pretty tired.

I took over the casting-off gear and when Ted called the time, I pulled the lever to release the tow rope. It came away quite smoothly, and we were in free flight and heading straight toward the LZ, everything was quiet, not a sound other than the rushing sound of the wind as we swept on, no gunfire, nothing. Ted called for 'half flap' and I set the flap-lever to the required position. The glider began to lose height as the nose sank, 'full flap' called Ted and again I moved to the new requirement, and the gliding angle stretched. Our air-speed settled at 90mph, the LZ was right beneath us and rushing toward us as tidy fast. Ted started an S-turn to put us further toward the railway embankment which was the extreme boundary of our area. On the first part of the turn I glanced back into the body of the aircraft and saw that the artillery boys had slid the door back open, which was OK except that our two flasks of tea were standing close by the open door, and before I could warn the boys about them, Ted was banking to port and it was too late. Our two flasks fell out their sides and rolled out of the door and away into space. There was no time to bewail the loss for already we were levelling out to land, and we touched down in what appeared to be a potato-filled, absolutely bone-dry ground, and as we touched down the cockpit and the whole aircraft was enveloped in clouds of dust, from which we all emerged coughing and spluttering. Ted and I threw off our seat belts and jumped down to join Sergeant Shelswell and his crew. We were right on the edge of the LZ, safely out of the way of succeeding landing aircraft, which by now were coming in thick and fast and very safely too. We did witness two tragic landings though.

The first was a Hamilcar. For some reason he came in cross-wind, and much too fast for safety, and the moment he touched down, his wheels sank into the soft earth, and he turned tail over nose and finished upside down. No one escaped that crash, and the other crash was a Horsa that overshot, leapt over the railway embankment, and ended up in some trees on the other side.

We started to prepare to off-load and the whole system worked like a dream. As we undid the last couple of bolts, Sergeant Shelswell and his lads stuck the trestle under the tail section and as the last bolt was released, the tail came off and rolled safely to one side out of the way. The ramps were got into position, and as we undid the chains holding the Jeep and gun in place, Driver Hodges started the Jeep engine, and slowly rolled down the ramps onto ground level. Our gear and weapons were loaded onto the Jeep and we left the 'Droop' – 'Old Faithfull' – and started off toward our flight rendezvous point. As we started to roll, thousands of parachute troops were floating down on the DZ; the sky was full of them as far as the eye could see, and the strange thing was that there was not a sound, beyond the noise of aircraft engines, no gunfire of any description. It was almost as if we had come and landed in Holland completely unnoticed.

The time of our arrival was around 1330 hours, and it was a perfect Sunday afternoon, sunny and warm and very suburban-like, very quiet. We passed some houses on our way, and there were men digging their gardens and mowing their lawns just as though it was quite usual to have an entire Airborne division drop in on a Sunday afternoon and not to cause too much fuss. We arrived at our RV and sorted ourselves into a column; we were the last vehicle in the line, sort of tail-end Charlies.

There was hardly time to settle, when coming down the road toward us was Staff Sergeant Clenaghan, herding about 25 German prisoners along with him. Apparently he had landed close to the railway line on the LZ, and had found these Jerries in a little hut drinking their midday bevies and they surrendered to him without a murmur. First blood to us!

Around 1630 hours we were starting to move off toward Arnhem, some 8 to 10 miles away but before we left, 20 Flight glider pilots were detailed off to take over a sort of hospital; it was a bit confused, and as it didn't concern us, we didn't bother too much. We learned later it was something of a German ATS barracks, with something like 200 girl soldiers, that they had to guard. It sounded alright at the time, but we later learned that it was not so good later. The column started off down the road toward Arnhem. It transpired that of the two routes into the town, we were taking the road closest to the River Rhine, which led through Oosterbeek. It wasn't long before we started to travel into populated areas; it was like a royal progress. Men women and children were standing along the pavements and in their front gardens, throwing posies of marigolds to us, giving us apples and bottles of wine, shouting, 'Welcome! Welcome! Four year we have waited!' Shaking our hands, little boys running along with us, their faces shining. We stopped at a road junction, and a young woman came up to me. She was carrying a little girl, about two-years-old in her arms; she spoke a little English and asked me if the war was nearly over, and how were things in England. I told her it wouldn't be long before peace returned and she cried. The little girl was somewhat scared by my appearance and she did not respond to my friendly approaches.

The column did not stop again until we arrived in the village of Oosterbeek, quite a pretty little place, with nicely-situated well-built houses mostly of bungalow type. The village stood raised above the fields which sloped down to the river. Away across the fields we could see where the railway, on an embankment, crossed the Rhine by way of a large iron cantilever bridge. It was still Sunday quiet, no opposition had been met, and not a shot had been fired at us so far. Quite a number of cattle were grazing in the fields around the village. Some REs and infantry were sent off to the bridge to neutralise any explosives that might have been planted on the bridge and railway, but after a very short time a sharp fight developed. We could hear rifle and machine gun fire for the first time since our arrival and suddenly there was a tremendous roar of explosives, and the railway bridge began to collapse in a pall of dust and smoke. No doubt some of our chaps went up with it if they had made the distance to the bridge as was intended. The strange thing was the effect the explosion had on the cattle and horses which had been grazing around the area of the bridge. They appeared to collapse, and were all lying on their sides as though dead.

Immediately after this occurrence there was quite a dangerous delay. Quite obviously the officers in the column were taken by surprise by the sudden appearance of enemy resistance after the quiet start of the operation. It was some little time before there was any forward movement. Various members of the column, including Ted and I, were sent to the outer fringes of the area to take up defensive positions. Ted and I lay up under a hedgerow with our Bren gun and ammunition, all ready for action. There was a broad field of fire across some 300 yards of open country to a wooded area in the distance; the hedgerow was at the foot of the gardens belonging to a neat little house, and not a sound was to be heard except the song of birds and the quiet murmur of vehicle s from the road.

After about twenty minutes I felt a tap on the shoulder and when I looked round there was a pleasant-looking motherly lady, and in perfect English she said, 'We are just about to have tea. If you have time, perhaps you and your friend could join us, you would be most welcome.' I was pretty taken aback by this, perhaps we were not being taken very seriously, it seemed that our arrival on the back doorstep was not so dramatic after all; well, it certainly had not upset the daily routine. However, we weren't able to take up the invitation, but did accept some lovely tomatoes which the family offered us as we rejoined the column a little later.

I think that delay caused us quite a bit of trouble, for we had not gone more than a couple or three miles, when we ran onto some real trouble at the place called 'Den Brink'. Being at the rear of the column, perhaps our view was distorted, but the impression was that we were ambushed by some mobile troops who probably had been alerted by the fire-fight at the railway bridge followed by the explosion. Anyway, whatever it was, we were held up by some brisk opposition but there did not seem to be any casualties on our side, at least I saw no evidence, but I did get involved in a little action later on in an area of woodland at a road junction. A German Army ambulance clearly marked with Red Crosses came racing down the road and crossed our path. We were ordered not to open fire as it approached, but to our surprise, following closely behind the ambulance tucked in tight to its rear, was a staff car, and we were ordered to stop it, which together, almost in unison, we did, in no uncertain terms. (I have seen pictures since the event showing a car of similar appearance with bodies hanging half out, much the same as this vehicle I speak of, with a caption saying that this was General Kussin the Arnhem Commander, but whether this was the same car that I encountered I would not be sure).[47] However, I do know the car; I fired at it with my Bren gun, it skewed off the road and the occupants were very dead and that was the end of any further actions before our column arrived in the outskirts of Arnhem city.

By the time we got this far it was already becoming dusk and it was surprising how quiet it was, like a ghost town. For some miles back we had noticed the absence of people as we approached the suburbs, whereas in the country, people had lined the road to welcome us with flowers and fruit and wine, making no doubt about their loyalty to the Queen of Holland by throwing marigolds to us and wearing orange armbands or orange scarves at their necks. Here in the town, at approaching 2000 to 2030 hours it was all quiet and still as we crept through the streets towards our target: 'The Bridge'.

We stopped for a short while under some trees at the side of a wide street or square, no lights showing, and to our surprise two German army lorries pulled up and off-loaded some German soldiers at what appeared to be some sort of billet. There was lots of shouting and laughing and they never saw us or even realised we were there. No attempt was made to eliminate them and we quietly moved out of the square through an archway on to a road running along the side of the Lower Rhine, a sort of esplanade with the river on our right and houses on our left and there in front of us stood 'The Bridge', gauntly silhouetted against the night sky. It was now quite dark and again we stopped under the trees which lined the road. Ted and I were sat on the anti tank gun talking, I thought quite quietly, when suddenly the window of the house we stood by went flying up, and we ducked a bit smartly expecting to be shot at, thinking we had driven into a fire-trap, but we couldn't have been more mistaken. It was an irate householder who mistook us for German troops and proceeded to dress us down in the ripest of terms because we had woken his children up and that he was heartily sick and tired of these nightly disturbances and so on, ad infinitum. I don't speak German, but one of the Airborne troops close by did, and translated for us. We let the poor Dutchman finish his tirade and then told him of our true identity. The change in his attitude was remarkable; he almost burst into tears, then called his wife and elder children to the window, fetched two smaller children from their bed, still in their night clothes, and held them out so that

---

47   Not the same vehicle.

they could kiss us. He and his wife almost fell out of the window in their excited efforts to shake everyone within reach by the hand.

During this episode, word came down the column for all personnel other than drivers and personnel responsible to guns and loads, to dismount and wait by the roadside. Some of our flight officers including Captain D.A. Simpson and Lieutenant H.C.L. Cole were in evidence, and they took us glider pilots over. The column moved off down toward the bridge area. After their departure, we moved off on foot, together with some paratroopers, and we eventually arrived in front of what appeared to be some sort of ornamental gardens on a sloping bank intersected by pathways leading from road level up to the roadway approaches to the bridge. We waited on the pavements for a short while and quite suddenly rifle and automatic fire began to erupt from both ends of the bridge, heavy automatic fire from the south side, two heavy machine guns pouring tracer shells across the bridge. The sound was like 20mm Oerlikons, and it proved to be so. Out of nowhere and whether it was chance or not, I wouldn't know, but directly in front of Ted and I, a Jeep towing an anti-tank gun pulled up, and it was 'our gun'. Sergeant Shelswell told us that he was to get the gun up on to the ramp at the entrance to the bridge and knock out a strongpoint. However, he couldn't take the Jeep up, therefore the gun had to be man-handled up the path through this park affair, and would we give a hand? Captain Simpson gave us three additional troops, making eight all told and off we went.

As we got to the start of the path we could see that it was quite a distance to where we had to go, so the driver turned the vehicle around and very skilfully backed the gun and Jeep almost two-thirds of the way up the slope, and that was as far as he could take it; from there up it was our pigeon. We placed chocks under the gun wheels and un-hooked the Jeep, off-loaded the ammunition, sent two men to the ramp gun-site, and the remaining six of us started up the slope. It was certainly heavy, but we eventually got it up and into position. By this time, the firing from sides, ours and the enemy was terrific, tracers looping over, or travelling in various straight lines sometimes too close for comfort. As soon as the gun was in position, Sergeant Shelswell sent the remaining helpers back down the path to rejoin their unit, retaining Ted and myself as gun crew. Ted took the Bren and got himself into a vacant slit trench, whilst I stayed with Sergeant Shelswell, I was loader, he was the layer and No. 1. The noise around was terrific, cracks and bangs and enormous explosions, rifles and machine guns clattering away. Our target was a concrete pillbox about halfway up the approach ramp to the bridge from which quite a lot of opposition was emanating, and we had to either knock it out or quieten the occupants down, whilst a flamethrower party could get in close enough to deal with it. We pumped three shells into it, and the firing died down. I didn't see the flamethrower brought up, but we were told to hold our fire, and quite suddenly, there was an enormous burst of flame and black smoke around the strongpoint, followed by the most terrifying screams I have ever heard, and then no sound at all, except for the unearthly din of the opposing forces. I guess the entire garrison inside the pillbox had been destroyed, in a very nasty way.

The gun was withdrawn, but Ted and I were told to stay where we were to assist with our extra firepower in any way possible. Then in amongst all this racket, we could see vehicles approaching at quite a rapid pace from the south side of the bridge, and the firing stopped (I thought that XXX Corps, the troops that were to link up with us from Nijmegen, had arrived) but before there was time to settle back, someone shouted, 'They're Jerries', and there was no doubt that they were. Every machine gun and rifle opened fire, and absolutely chopped the vehicles to pieces. The leading wagon turned off the road and crashed into the parapet of the bridge, the ones behind either collided into each others' rear or stopped any way they could. One very brave German soldier leapt out of the cab of a crashed vehicle and dashed across the road through this hail of fire and jumped up on the parapet wall about twenty yards from where I lay and with a revolver in either hand proceeded to pump bullets in every direction. Fortunately, he didn't last for very long before he was cut down or he might have inflicted quite a lot of damage. One of his victims was a young lad, who lost his nerve and dashed across to my slit trench and promptly fell in on top of me shouting, 'I've been bloody hit,' over and over again. He had, too, a rather nasty wound in the upper arm. Ted and I placed his field dressing on it and sent him off to find the RAP (Regimental Aid Post).

Very soon the whole scene at our end (the north end) of the bridge was like an inferno, and a firework display as the lorries which had which had tried to cross the bridge caught fire and blazed away, with the ammunition they had been carrying exploding and sailing up into the night sky like so many rockets, but in general, the firing between the opposing forces died down considerably. Around midnight we heard a voice calling for 'Glider pilots to reform over here.' Ted and I quickly made our way toward the direction of the voice and found Lieutenant Cole at the end of the path with two or three others of our Flight, including Charlie Watson. It seems we were detailed to stand as sentries at Battalion HQ which had been established in what appeared to be some sort of municipal buildings.

When we arrived in the forecourt of this place, we found our Jeep standing close to the main doorway, with Driver Hodges in the driver's seat munching away at his sandwiches which suddenly reminded me that I hadn't eaten since breakfast, and that was way back at RAF Manston, and I was somewhat peckish. So both Ted and I found our rucksacks, and dug our doorstep sandwiches out – corned beef, my favourite, and we sat on the tail-board of the Jeep, and chewed away. The only regret was the loss of those two flasks of tea which had fallen from our 'kite' just before our landing. But those sandwiches certainly went down well, and I had just finished chewing when an officer appeared through the door and very civilly enquired if we were the chaps detailed for 'stag duty', if so he would take charge of us and place us in the most advantageous positions – 'What!' – just like someone out of P.G. Wodehouse. Well, I was placed by the entrance gate, and now it all seemed unreal, dreamlike, for it was quiet again, very little firing at all, an occasional burst of machine gun fire, sometimes the enemy and then our boys. You could tell which was which; the German MG34 had a much faster rate of fire than the Brens.

I had only been on sentry about an hour when I was relieved, and was told to report back to the Jeep, and on arrival there found Ted and Charlie and all our gun crew still intact. Nobody seemed to want our services for about an hour, so I had a little kip and was woken up to find Captain Simpson and about a dozen blokes from our Flight, and his news was that we were to carry out a patrol of the area and try and find out what was going on, mainly because there was little or no radio contact with neighbouring elements. By this time it was just starting to get toward dawn and it was possible to see one's way around.

Monday, 18th September

There was still quite a lot of light from the burning lorries on the bridge, but this didn't throw light into the streets away from that area, so it was with a certain amount of apprehension we set off down the street. We hadn't gone far before I saw my first dead soldier, one of our boys, lying on the pavement in a huge pool of blood, not really to be recommended in the early hours of the morning I can assure you. We arrived at the edge of a small factory area, and for some reason, our patrol leader decided it would be a good idea to search it and make sure the enemy were not in possession. Well, they weren't, but they might have been had I personally not captured the entire garrison single-handed.

It happened like this. We had searched the buildings and yards (it was a sort of furniture factory), and found nothing and in one, we were just on our way out, I was tail-end Charlie again, and some yards behind the main party. On passing some wooden screens I suddenly heard a faint clatter, and looked behind these screens, and there was the oldest soldier I have ever seen. He must have been 70-years-old and he quite obviously had no intentions of getting involved in any warlike proceedings, for as I approached him, he had already laid his rifle on the ground (that was probably the clatter that I'd first heard) and he immediately made signs that he was surrendering, and promptly got busy taking his equipment off and laying it on the ground alongside his rifle, and then he walked up to me with tears in his eyes and said very quietly, '*Kamerad*,' and I took him prisoner. I *didn't* get the VC for that.

There were no other incidents during the patrol, and we returned to the HQ in broad daylight. Lieutenant Simpson went inside to make his report and to hand *my* prisoner over for interrogation. On his return he collected about a dozen glider pilots who were in the HQ. This made our party up to about 25, and then he told us that we were to man a house on a strategic corner, and off we went to find this place. By this time, about 0600 to 0700 hours, heavy fighting was in progress in the town away from the bridge, and in the bridge area particularly, quite a number of the buildings were on fire. The heat was intense, heavy smoke which came from the fires made the throat very dry and the eyes to smart very badly. We arrived at the house we were to hold, and gained entry by breaking the window and climbing over the cills. It was a gorgeous house, beautifully furnished and carpeted, fine glass and china in cabinets, heavily upholstered chairs and settees and great soft cushions. All was smashed up to strengthen the defences; cabinets and furniture were pushed up to the windows to the sound of breaking glassware, cushions were emptied of their soft contents and filled with earth from the garden to make sandbags and when the ground floor was completed, we moved upstairs to carry out the same work. On moving from room to room we were surprised to find an old lady lying in bed, apparently too old or too ill to be moved, and for the next couple of days we looked after her. Ted and I took over the windows facing out toward the bridge, with strict instructions not to fire on any troops coming over the bridge from the south, for 'they would be Canadians from 30 Corps.'

We came under fire immediately from small arms, and were able to return equal stuff when we could locate the source; some of these were particularly nasty ones being snipers hiding among the chimneys surrounding the house. Ted called my attention to one of these 'gentlemen' and I could just see the top of his helmet and part of one shoulder, so I got my Bren gun round to get a good aim. I said to Ted to fire a round just to the left and as close as he could to the sniper to see whether he would duck or move enough to expose himself long enough to allow me to get a burst off. He did, and it worked. As Ted fired, I was already aimed, and let go about five rounds, and saw the sniper tumble down the roof to fall into the street. But what I didn't know was that another sniper had *me* lined up – luckily his aim was not so good, for as I fired there was a spurt of stone-dust from the window frame and I found the distinct mark of a bullet smacked into the crack between the frame and brickwork.

In the afternoon Jerry began to bring up his heavy stuff, mobile 88mm guns, and huge tanks, and they started to shell the streets row by row with high explosive and incendiary shells and very soon huge areas of the town were in flames and ruins. Our house seemed to bear a charmed life for despite the fact that practically all the houses around us were hit and in ruins or on fire, we were virtually unscathed. I was in dire need of a toilet, so decided to try to find one downstairs. I found one and did what was necessary, and was on my way back upstairs, when there was a terrific crash in the upper part of the house, and clouds of dust came pouring down the stairs. I rushed back to our room to find a great hole in the outside wall, and the place full of dust and rubble. In the midst of all this stood a chap named Carter, and his left arm was almost severed just above the elbow. He was repeating over and over, 'Look at my bloody arm.' He was taken off to the RAP, I helped him down the stairs, and left him in charge of a couple of other blokes with directions with which to find their way. When I returned to my post all the dust and smoke had died down or blown away, and it was surprising to find that Carter was the only casualty. Ted was shaken a bit but otherwise OK and two other chaps on the north side were quite unconcerned, apart from being covered in dust. On looking around a bit closer I was horrified to see a huge unexploded shell lying in the middle of the room, partly covered by brick rubble. Obviously the one that had hit and penetrated the wall. At almost that precise moment a young paratrooper officer appeared in the doorway. I called his attention to the 'dud' shell. He said quite unconcernedly, 'Take it downstairs and lose it, there's a good chap.' So there was me, picking up this brute in my arms, carrying it downstairs out of the front door to lay it in the gutter at the side of the road. I *didn't* get the VC for that either.

All the houses in our immediate vicinity were on fire, and the roar of the flames was a bit frightening, but the worst part was the thirst. Fortunately, some bright spark had found that the water was available from the taps when we first occupied the house, and had filled the bath, so water was there but over the period of time it had become very dusty and coloured by brick dust and smoky wood chips from flying sparks but it was still drinkable. We made tea using our ration packs; that didn't include Ted and I, our rations were still on the Jeep wherever that might be, but the other lads shared theirs with us, positive nectar! We had hardly finished our drink when Charlie Watson yelled up the stairs for Ted and I to rejoin the blokes below. So off we went. On arrival in the downstairs hallway we found Captain Simpson gathering all the glider pilots together in order to take us elsewhere where our presence was required, and we had to leave the house by the windows. Hardly had he given us our instructions and directions than Jerry mounted an attack by infantry, preceded by a tank which came round the corner into our street, Marktstraat, from the shelter of the arches under the bridge ramp. It was huge, must have been a Tiger, it seemed to fill the street; it rumbled down the middle of the road, firing its shells into each side as it advanced – again our house wasn't hit. As the tank went on past us, we could hear men shouting in German, and we had to beat off a very determined attack. Firing came at us from houses on the opposite side of the street and from the gardens surrounding, but we rarely saw anyone for long, just a quick glimpse as the men came forward towards our positions.

I suppose we must have put up sufficient firepower to stop them for the attack didn't develop and we were left in peace for a while. Lieutenant Simpson said to hang on until it was certain Jerry had withdrawn, and it was reasonably safe to move, so Ted and I left our Bren downstairs and went back upstairs to see how the old lady was getting on. She was still in her bed, very dusty, but still chatty though we could not fully understand her. She did get through to us that she would like to wash; imagine it, us black and grimy with brick dust and smoke and sweat, trying to find a washbasin and sponge or flannel and soap, and not least a towel, in order to wash a sick old lady in a ruined house. We did find all these except soap, and took them to her, and helped her to wash, but she complained the water was cold, but thanked us just the same, and then we had to leave. When we rejoined our lot downstairs they were watching the efforts of a couple of stretcher parties trying to get some wounded men out of a blazing house across the street. They succeeded in getting four blokes out, and four stretcher bearers set off with the first man. They had hardly gone twenty yards when there was a terrific burst of automatic fire from further down the street and three of the four carrier men went down; the fourth tried to drag the stretcher case to the side of the road, but another burst of fire cut him down. There was no excuse for this scandalous conduct, for all the men wore conspicuous arm-bands with clear Red Crosses, and their lower packs were clearly marked too.

Very shortly we climbed out through the windows and dashed away through a couple of streets to arrive in a small park over-hung with trees, and once again we found our Jeep parked under the trees. All my cigarettes which I carried in my smock pockets had been smoked, but I still had another 200 and some chocolate in my rucksack on the Jeep. I went across and retrieved two packets of twenty and a bar of chocolate together with two packs of 'K' Rations and brought them back to the place where Ted was now busy digging a slit trench. I learned we were to stay the night in this park.

Being a bit peckish by this time, not having eaten since our sandwiches in the early hours of the morning, and it now being early evening (Monday, 18th September) we decided to make the most of this lull, and got stuck into our 'K' Rations. On seeing I had two packs and some chocolate, Ted decided he would fetch two from his rucksack and also some chocolate, then we should be alright for a while, even if we did get separated from the Jeep again. Well, hardly had we decided all this when we were suddenly and devastatingly subjected to a diabolical mortar attack. They bombed us from just a couple of streets away and deadly accurate too. I looked up through the trees and I could see the bombs reaching the apex of their flight before turning downward toward our positions. Unfortunately one of the first ones to land dropped smack onto our Jeep and all our belongings disappeared in a blinding flash and explosion followed by fire as petrol caught alight and burned the lot. Gone our remaining food, all our chocolate and our cigarettes! All we could do was keep our heads down and hope that we would be overlooked and we were; despite a large number of bombs which did considerable damage to our equipment, we were not hit and our weapons and carried ammunition were intact.

Anyway, there were slit trenches to be dug and holes to be cut through the walls to enable us to fire through to the street if need be. So we were kept busy for a while. I suddenly realised in the middle of all this, that it was my birthday, and called across to Ted with the news. Before he answered, a lugubrious voice from a nearby 'funk hole' said, 'Hard bleeding luck, chum, save us a bit of cake!' Typical!

Around 2200 hours, Jerry tried another infantry attack through the gardens, bags of shouting and yelling as they came, and presently they came into view, and we opened fire. Now, just on the other side of the wall from my slit trench there was a sort of garden shed with a single pitch roof sloping toward the top of the wall. The intensity of our firepower drove the Germans to ground, and from cover, they began to lob stick grenades at us, most of which fell short. One particularly strong bloke dropped his grenade slap onto the roof of this shed, and it started to roll down the sloping pitch toward the wall. I started to think, *does that roof overhang the top of the wall onto our side?* Believe me, that bomb took half an hour to roll the length of the roof, before it fell between the shed and the wall on the other side, and exploded harmlessly, and soon after that all became quiet again as Jerry withdrew.

Towards midnight, all us glider pilots were again moved out to another house about a hundred yards from the entrance to the park, a sort of first floor flat over a greengrocer's shop, and the windows overlooked a large square to our left.

Tuesday, 19th September
Apart from a small raiding party of Jerries who tried their luck in the early hours of the morning, we spent a quiet night, but no sleep was obtained by any of us, and strangely enough I didn't feel fatigued at all despite the fact that apart from the short nap in the early hours on Monday, I had not slept since Saturday night (16th September).

Tuesday morning dawned a bit misty but not sufficiently to obscure the view around our flat, all quiet, and the sun began to shine weakly. I now noticed that my boots had suffered rather badly from burning debris I had walked through and they were in very poor shape, but there was nothing I could do, so forget about them. We were hungry again, and we had only one 'K' Ration each – ten 'K' Rations between eleven of us. Ted and I had eaten one of ours the night before, so Ted had a scout round the cupboards in the flat, and came up with potatoes, carrots, onions, and a tin of 'something' (no label). We got a fire going (the smoke from the chimney would not show against the fires and smoke which still hung over the town), and after finding a large saucepan, and mug, I managed to bale enough water from the lavatory cistern to provide cooking liquid, and Ted got cracking on the vegetables and the dehydrated meat cubes from the 'K' Rations. The rest of us returned to our posts, taking turns to wash and shave with water from an outside water butt.

The stew which Ted prepared was good, hot and tasty, but the tin without a label which he found had been punctured, and the meat inside was off. But the dehydrated cubes made a very meaty flavour, well enough to be able to call it 'beef stew'. For dessert we found some apples in a dish on the sideboard. We discovered later, that had we been on the ground floor, we would have had quite a choice of fruits, for in a sort of coach house in the yard there was a cart loaded with all kinds of local fruit, all laid out as if on a market stall ready for sale, but we didn't find this until we were leaving the house later. By the time the meal was over, and we had all cleaned ourselves up a little, it was around eight a.m. and we were all back at our respective positions, when Jerry again tried to dislodge us by putting in another attack with infantry and tanks supported by mobile 88mm guns, a really full-blooded attempt, which got quite hectic as they pressed everything into the attempt to get us to vacate the area around the bridge. We were told that a flamethrower had been used against one part of our defences, but I hoped that this was rumour, having witnessed the appalling effect of our attack on the bridge strongpoint with such a weapon. Anyway, after about an hour the attack again died away, and apart from mortar bombs arriving fairly frequently and noisily, the firing dropped off.

It was then noticed that the house we had previously occupied was now on fire and blazing away, and I thought of the old lady in bed – had our lads moved her? But we learned later that she had been killed by a bomb fragment which hit her in the back of the neck, and she had a Viking funeral when the house was demolished by fire.

Across the rooftops, visible from the window from which we observed, was a tall cathedral belfry quite clearly to be seen through the smoke and it seemed as though the bells were chiming, softly at times and quite loudly at others. Some of the boys reckoned that Jerry had some spotters up in the tower, and they were signalling our whereabouts to their mortar teams, so that they could pinpoint us fairly accurately. In time we realised that the soft tinkles, and the loud clangs, coincided with the intensity of their mortar attacks, and concluded that the bells were being struck by bomb fragments causing the illusion of 'signals'. Later in the morning, the Luftwaffe had a go at us; a gaggle of Messerschmitts came in low over the houses with their cannon and machine guns blazing away, going like the clappers, unfortunately for one of the pilots, the smoke was a little denser at that moment, and he didn't notice the cathedral spire until it was too late to avoid it. He banked steeply to try and get past but his starboard main plane hit the tower and the impact broke it off, the aircraft flipped over onto its back and dived into houses about a mile from us – they didn't try any more strafes after that. About this time, word was passed around, allegedly from Brigade HQ, that XXX Corps were only a few miles away, and if we could hold on for another six to twelve hours, the link up would be accomplished, and the operation would be a huge success. Radio contact was a bit uncertain, and the distance between us and the advancing Guards Division was not very clear. Some reports said seven miles, others thirteen miles, still others as much as thirty, so it was difficult to judge whether any of the reports were genuine, but whatever, we were still highly confident and in good spirits.

Coming up for midday, we were told to prepare to move out, just Ted and myself together with our Bren and ammunition. Captain Simpson arrived and off we went into the garden of the house, over the wall at the bottom, and up on to the roof of an outbuilding and through the back window of a house whose front windows overlooked the orchard at the back of what appeared to be a nursing home or hospital. I noticed that smoke was curling up through the tiles on the roof of this building, and shortly afterwards it erupted into flames. We were presently joined by Clenaghan, Higginbottom and Miller, and as the fire grew in intensity it became increasingly hot in our house. In fact the paintwork was peeling and smouldering, but it didn't spread, and apart from the anxiety of this danger, the night passed fairly quietly, and we were able to catch a few winks of sleep, taking turns to keep watch.

Wednesday, 20th September
In the early hours of the morning, another attack was started against us, but it didn't seem to get to our position, and although there was a lot of firing and shouting, we saw no one. As Wednesday dawned, we could see that the tower of the cathedral had been on fire during the night. No doubt the place immediately in front of us, blazing away, had obscured the tower, but now that the flames had died down, it was possible to look around, and indeed the town was a sorry spectacle; all around the bridge area was in smoking ruins, but our troops were obviously still holding their positions and the northern end of the bridge was still in our possession. Although we never had achieved the southern end, we still hoped that the Second and Third Lifts which were due to arrive on Monday and Tuesday (18th/19th September) would be able to reinforce our sadly depleted numbers, for it was apparent that we had suffered appalling casualties. From where I sat, I could see bodies of our troops lying in the orchard grass, and in the street below.

Ted decided around eight-ish, that he would try to rustle up some food, and started a search through the cupboards of the house, and again came up with vegetables of various sorts, and we still had a few meat cubes left, so he was able to get a 'stewy' breakfast ready whilst we took it in turns to get a wash and shave, using an old bathtub of rainwater for the purpose. Ted used lavatory cistern water for his cooking (all the taps were now dry). Before it was ready, Captain Simpson arrived, and together we went outside into an alleyway to the left of the house, from where it was possible to look across the top of the Market Square to what seemed to be troops milling about, and through his binoculars, Captain Simpson identified them as German. I fired a couple of bursts from my Bren gun, and he reckoned that I had brought three or four soldiers down. I couldn't tell really, anyway they scattered, and after about a half an hour, I was sent off to get some food, leaving my gun with Captain Simpson, and a paratrooper.

After a quick meal, I returned to the alley, and word was passed round that the British forces were only two and a quarter miles away south of the river, and if we could hold on for another three hours, we would be relieved. I got the impression that things were not going well. We had lost a lot of our troops, and we were quite obviously hemmed in on all sides and our ammunition was getting very short, and no re-supply had come our way, as had been expected. A little later we were told that XXX Corps would attack the bridge at 1800 hours in the evening, which was considerably longer than three hours away, and almost immediately after this information, was were ordered to evacuate the house and gather in the gun-park (the place we had started from). Well, all except Ted and I; we were left behind to engage some machine gunners who were firing from the windows of the local jail into the gun-park, found our target and pumped two or three magazines into the windows and the opposition died down, and we withdrew into the gun-park, and joined Clenaghan, Miller, Higginbottom and Watson who were busy digging in. We joined in with gusto, for by this time Jerry was really getting cracking with everything he had. Self-propelled guns and tanks were shelling the area, and mortar bombs were raining down, together with a considerable volume of small arms fire. I saw Captain Simpson talking to an artillery officer on the corner of the street opposite the gate to the park, and after a few moments, the artillery bloke came into the park and spoke to another artillery officer then they dashed off down the road to our left. Meanwhile, this other artillery chap was organising a patrol of paratroopers about seven blokes and a sergeant, and he sent them off down the street away toward the Square, where I'd had a go at some Jerries earlier on. They didn't get very far. As soon as they got to the corner of the road, they must have come into full view of a machine gun, for there was a quick burst of fire and they went down in a heap and lay quite still. After a few minutes, someone noticed that one of the fallen patrol was moving, and the artillery officer who had organised the patrol ran out to fetch him back. I followed him and together we brought him back to the park. He was terribly wounded in the legs, and when we cut his trousers open to dress his wounds, the blood simply poured out all over the ground in a large pool. Several field dressings were placed over the wounds, and he was taken to the RAP by some of his mates, and I went back to our crowd (No VC for that, either).

When I got back, I found that quite a lot of the ammunition had been used up, and things were really desperate. The houses and buildings around us were all on fire again, and the heat was intense, and still we were getting fired on from all sides; our casualties were mounting, dead and wounded men were everywhere. The artillery officer who had gone off with Captain Simpson suddenly came into the street out of a little alleyway, and started to walk down to the park gate, but when he was only about twenty yards from us, he was hit by a sniper, and flung right across the road into the opposite gutter, hit clean through the head, and he was dead before we got to him. Hardly had I got back into the park when I found our Jeep driver, Hodges, and told him to come and join us, and was pointing the way for him to go, when he was hit in the back, and he was taken off by some first aid men.

When I got back to our Bren, we were under very heavy fire from a couple of machine guns, and tracer rounds were flying in all directions, quite a hairy situation, and what was worse, we couldn't locate them to return the fire, which makes one feel a bit helpless. Ted and Miller went off to another area, to try and get a better view, and came back to say they reckoned that one of the MGs was situated at the road junction about 400 yards to our right, behind the corner of the building. I couldn't get a direct shot at the position, so in desperation, I tried a few bursts into the wall just short of the place and ricocheted the rounds on to the area. It seemed to work as well – anyway, the fire stopped coming in our direction from that particular gun.

By this time it was late afternoon and things were beginning to get really hectic. There seemed to be an enormous amount of small arms fire concentrated into our area, and looking up through the trees I could again see mortar bombs reaching their apex in flight and turning over to descend onto us, a decidedly frightening sight, yet so far, neither Ted or I had a scratch, but my boots were so badly charred they were falling rapidly to pieces. A paratrooper noticed my forlorn state, and told me that at the far end of the park, standing in the road outside the entrance there was a German lorry loaded with all kinds of loot, including army boots. So I handed my Bren to Ted, and Charlie Watson, borrowed Charlie's rifle, and set off to try to find this treasure trove. Sure enough, there it was, just as the man had said. I had a quick look round and it was somewhat quieter in this area, so I ran smartly over and climbed into the back of the lorry, and there were literally dozens of pairs of boots, beside other army gear. I reckon it was a QM wagon abandoned for some reason, or perhaps had been parked there on Sunday afternoon before we arrived. Anyway, I got myself a new pair of boots to replace my burned-up ones, very nice ones they were too, soft brown leather uppers and hob-nailed soles; the only snag was they were a wee bit tight but in view of the fact that we would probably be relieved during the next day or so, I thought they would serve their purpose.

When I got back to our battle area things were still pretty hot, if not more so. The strongpoint house which we had recently evacuated was blazing fiercely, flames going high into the air, roof tiles sliding into the street below, and a constant roar as the flames took hold on the roof timbers. I saw a dead German soldier lying on the pavement, and burning debris was showering down onto him, so that he was gradually buried under it, probably lost without trace and posted as 'missing'.

During this period, Allied fighter planes began to appear over the town, and this put some heart into us. Surely XXX Corps couldn't be far away, it would be handy if they were to get to us soon, because ammunition was desperately short; I only had two magazines left, and nothing to replenish them when they were exhausted, and Ted had nothing at all except ten rounds in his rifle magazine. It was now dusk, and the expected and promised attack by XXX Corps from the south side of the river had not materialised, though it was rumoured that 25-pounder shells from XXX Corps artillery were falling on the houses in the areas held by Jerry, but rumours were always flying around.

From somewhere in the rear of our positions I heard a voice shouting, 'Glider pilots – this way' repeatedly, and on looking around I saw that I was practically alone, so gathering my Bren, and the remaining bit of ammo, I started to make my way through the debris toward the voice, falling over a pile of bicycles onto a dead soldier in the process. Eventually I located the voice of Lieutenant Cole, and found about a dozen glider pilots gathered round him including Ted Healey and George Miller – the rest I didn't know. As soon as I arrived Lieutenant Cole set off down an alleyway. We passed Lieutenant Meakin standing at a junction of two alleys pointing the direction to follow, saying quite calmly, 'Pass right down the car please, don't hang about,' and we finally arrived outside what appeared to be a school or technical college, and found the doors locked. Lieutenant Cole stepped forward to do his 'cowboy act' by shooting the lock open. It didn't work. Five rounds from his .45 automatic and the door stayed firm; however, a chap came along and said he had found a basement door open, and we followed his directions and guidance into the building. Quite a large number of troops were gathered in the basement rooms, so we were sent upstairs and told to get rid of our fighting knives, and then lie low and keep quiet in the upper rooms (which appeared to be classrooms) and wait for XXX Corps to arrive in the night.

Thursday, 21st September
So we settled down, whilst outside we could hear the clatter of AFVs and Jerry troops shouting about in the street, and finally fell asleep for a short while. In the early hours of the morning

(around 0200 hours), we were again called into the corridor, and shepherded back down into the cellar, and there we found upwards of a hundred troops, various regiments altogether. We stayed together about an hour and were then split up into small parties of five or six, and told to set off and hide up in the town, to try to better our chances of not being discovered. Our party consisted of Ted, George Miller, an artillery officer, a paratrooper and me. It all seemed dreamlike, we were all dog-tired, and the setting was eerie. The area was still burning fiercely, and among the roar of the flames, we could hear voices shouting in German, and there we were, a little group of blokes, tired out, thirsty and red-eyed from the smoke which swirled around us, looking for shelter. I suggested we make for the river, and as we were still wearing our air life-jackets (deflated), we could possibly slip into the water and inflate the jackets, and drift downstream and join the main body around Oosterbeek. Hoping the artillery officer knew in which direction the river lay, we turned to consult him but he had disappeared, off on his own I guess. The other three thought the idea was sound, but as we didn't know which way to go, why not lay up for the rest of the night, possibly get some sleep, gather strength for the next day, and try the river stunt on Thursday night.

So this was settled, and we found a garden in the rear of a house which included a shrubbery. I got myself well under the bushes, spread my camouflage net scarf over myself, laid down and went sound asleep. Whilst I was doing this, Ted and George found a huge pile of garden refuse, grass cuttings and leaves and dug themselves into this and buried themselves and slept; the paratrooper bedded down in the outside WC.

I awoke in broad daylight to the sound of crackling, burning timber, and saw with horror that the house that Ted and George had bedded down against was ablaze and burning debris showering down onto them, and they were sound asleep! I got them around, and away from the danger, and fortunately no harm or injury had been sustained, but there was no sign of the paratrooper. He must have scarpered during the night. The problem was, where to go? Daylight, danger of being seen, and probably shot at, so we decided to each take a look at possibilities, and rendezvous back in the garden in thirty minutes. George set off to look out of the front of the house, I was going over the wall into an alleyway, and Ted was going opposite ways to me. It all went disastrously awry. George had hardly got into the front part of the house, when there was a terrific burst of firing, automatic pistol and rifles. We heard George shout, 'Not this way,' and then silence, except for German voices shouting to each other. Ted went to the rear of the house, and shouted to George but the only reply he got was Schmeisser pistol fire down the passageway. Ted didn't stand on ceremony, he dashed across to my side of the garden, and together we cleared the wall almost in one bound, and dropped into the alleyway (I had dismantled my Bren gun and dropped it into a water-butt, Ted still had a machine pistol which he had acquired sometime over the previous days). So we could move pretty easily now unencumbered. The German voices seemed to fade away, and at least we were not being pursued. As we were travelling along this alley, we noticed a small cottage standing alone, behind the other houses and decided to make for it, over the fence and into the back door. We were astonished to find about twenty other blokes inside, and one young officer. Most of them had weapons but no ammunition. I spoke to the officer and asked him what he planned to do, and he said he thought we could lie up till night fall, and then get down to the river and possibly escape.

As we had the same mind, we decided to stay with them at least until they moved off, and then go our own way. Thirst was the most urgent thought in our minds; we were parched, and found to our delight that water came out of the taps in one of the bedrooms, a bit brackish, but drinkable. Having quenched our thirst, food was next, there was none to be had in the larder and cupboards

Arnhem bridge area ablaze during the fighting. (Photo: Courtesy Gelders Archive)

downstairs, except for about eight pounds of butter. However Ted opened a wardrobe in the bedroom and of all things to find, there was about 3lbs of grapes; these we devoured with gusto. Having got rid of those we decided to get some more sleep in, ready for the night adventures, and laid ourselves out on the bed.

I hardly seemed to have closed my eyes (though in fact this was over two hours later) when I was awakened by raucous German voices shouting outside, 'Ve know you are in there, Tommy. Are you coming out or do ve haf to fetch you!' … Dead silence … a sudden burst of machine gun fire and the same question asked. This time, I heard the young officer say that he was coming out, and they were not to shoot. Ted and I decided to stay put, and hope that we would be forgotten, but there was no such luck.

Having got the main body outside, the Germans decided to search the house and we had no time to hide. We were marched downstairs, and out through a window to join the others in the courtyard. We were surrounded by German soldiers, all young lads, Panzergrenadiers, 18 to 20 years of age. They were laughing and joking, slapping us on the back, congratulating us on the fine battle we had put up. Then followed the search through our pockets for valuables, I had pushed my service wristwatch up to my elbow, and it wasn't found, to my delight. It seemed to hold that personal possessions like wedding rings, signet rings, and watches were not taken but all service stuff, like binoculars, compasses and service wristwatches were fair game. These young soldiers were obviously very highly trained and well-disciplined troops; there were no recriminations, and we were treated very courteously, and when I was searched I had some photographs of my family and a good luck charm – these were all examined, commented upon and returned to me. I also had 1,800 French Francs hidden on my person, these were not found either. We were then lined up and marched off toward the centre of the town. On the way we saw Sergeant Higginbottom and Staff

Sergeant Clenaghan carrying a wounded officer into a German RAP, and when we arrived in the square by the cathedral, George Bayliss joined us, also Frank Dennis. We were all searched again, but again I was able to retain my valuables, and after this 'going-over' we were told to sit on the pavement. After about an hour we were moved into the cathedral, and by this time our numbers had swelled enormously, various Airborne units all mixed up. Thus began captivity.

Sergeant Cyril Robson, No. 4 Gun, C Troop, 1st Airlanding Anti-Tank Battery, Royal Artillery 6-pounder anti-tank gun, attached to 3rd Parachute Battalion

Sunday, 17th September

The flight to Holland was quite pleasant except when an ack-ack shell burst between our tug and ourselves, and we heard shrapnel sounding like hail on the sides of the glider. The sky seemed to be full of aircraft, gliders, tug-aircraft and paratrooper aircraft. Also our escort of many fighter planes; it was a wonderful sight. Then came the signal to cast off, the slight lift to the nose to lose speed, everything went quiet as we seemed to hover in the air. Then at this point, the small doors of the glider had to be opened in case they stuck during landing. By now the nose was down and we were going in. With a last glance through the cockpit window before getting into my seat and fastening in, I saw some gliders had already landed in the field to which we were heading. When we touched down we were well up the field and heading for the embankment of the electric railway. Suddenly we swung round and came to a standstill, broadside to the embankment. We had landed and only a few shots were being fired. To unload the glider, we had to remove the tail. This was done and we were ready to move off in less than two minutes. It was then we witnessed the first mishap. One of the largest gliders, a Hamilcar, loaded with a three ton truck, a 17-pounder anti-tank gun, stores and men, about three tons in all, came in to land. It made a perfect touch-down, but suddenly the tail came over and it landed on its back spilling out some of the men. On instructions from my battery captain, we spent half an hour helping these men, also one of the glider pilots who was trapped at his controls. Owing to this delay, I did not meet the remainder of my C Troop, or the other three men of my gun-team who had jumped with the paratroops.

I reported to Major W.F. Arnold, my OC, who instructed me to follow on behind B Troop and BHQ, who were attached to 2nd Parachute Battalion. Of the three roads leading into Arnhem seven miles away, the 2nd Battalion advanced along the road nearest the river. We met little opposition on the way and arrived at the Arnhem Bridge after dark. The northern end of the bridge was cleared, and the surrounding area was then occupied by the 600 troops who had arrived at the bridge on this late Sunday evening, September 17th. We did not know at that time that the road behind us had been blocked, or that we would be isolated from the rest of the division for the duration of the battle. We were deployed in defensive positions, and waited for the counter attack which we knew would come. My gun was situated on a street corner about 100 yards from the bridge. From here I was able to cover the road running under the bridge and also a short section of the bridge itself.[48]

---

48   Initially on corner of Kadestraat then moved further west probably between 2nd Parachute Battalion HQ and 1st Airlanding Anti-Tank Bty HQ, Markstraat, facing east. Robson says it was outside 1st Airlanding Anti-Tank Bty HQ.

Monday, 18th September
Things became very lively on the Monday morning, and by noon we had destroyed an armoured column which had tried to cross the bridge from the south. I had also knocked out two tanks which had come up the road under the bridge on the north side of the river.[49] As there were only three of us on the gun, I was firing the gun myself; one of the gunners was loading for me while the other was on the Bren gun.

It was later in the day that the enemy began to saturate our area with shell and mortar fire which was to prove so disastrous for us. By evening, our casualties were mounting and there was no news of the 1st and 3rd Parachute Battalions, or XXX Corps who were to relieve us.[50]

Tuesday, 19th September
All day Tuesday, with casualties increasing, the shell and mortar fire grew heavier. My two gunners had been wounded, and a replacement from Battery HQ had been killed. Houses inside our perimeter had been set on fire and our area was becoming smaller. All this time we were asking, 'Where is the rest of the division?'

Wednesday, 20th September
On Wednesday evening, we at the bridge were in very poor shape. There had been no sleep for over 72 hours, very little food or water left, and ammunition was very low. All the houses we still held were on fire, and there was literally nowhere to lay the wounded. The casualties on my gun alone had been eleven wounded and one killed. My own gunners had returned and been wounded for the second time.

Thursday, 21st September
Those few of us that were left were split up into small groups to try and break out, to hide, to avoid capture. I was picked up by an enemy patrol in the ruins of Arnhem church near the bridge at 0900 hours on Thursday 21st September, and taken to where a party of about 35 officers and men had already been gathered. This was the beginning of seven months as a POW.

---

49 Pz.Kpfw.IVs of Panzer-Kompanie Mielke, Westervoortsedijk, Camiz dairy area.
50 Captain A.D. Llewellyn-Jones, BHQ, 1st Airlanding Anti-Tank Battery, Royal Artillery, commented on the engagement of German armour: 'Deploying anti-tank guns in paved areas has a major problem. The muzzle velocity is such that the recoil is vicious. The spades at the end of the trail arms need a good grip. From under the bridge a light tank was spotted, and the gun outside Bty HQ was ideally placed. The gun spades were not into the pavement edge, nor firm against any strong barrier. The gun was laid, order to fire given, and through the anticipatory excitement, the gun ran back about 50 yards, injuring two of the crew. There was no visible damage to the tank. It remained hidden in part of the gloom of the underpass of the bridge. The gun was recovered, with some difficulty. The two injured became extra inmates of the local dressing station. This time the gun was firmly wedged. The battery office clerk, who had never fired a gun in his life being much happier typing nominal roles on an old typewriter, was taken out of Battery HQ to help man the gun. This time the tank under the bridge had advanced into full view, and looked to be deploying its gun straight at the 6-pounder. The aim was true, as the tank was hit, it slewed and blocked the road.' Account by Captain A.D. Llewellyn-Jones, *Return to Arnhem 40 Years On, Sept 1984*, Airborne Museum Oosterbeek.

Sergeant Cyril Robson's 6-pounder anti-tank gun view under the bridge looking east. In 1945 one remaining Pz.Kpfw.IV can still be seen facing the camera just behind a steamroller being used to clear rubble. Below, close up of the tank above, the collapsed Camiz Dairy pipe bridge having been cleared away. The other Pz.Kpfw.IV which was knocked out by Robson was about 100 yards further east. (Photos: Courtesy Gelders Archive)

Driver Eric Milner, No. 1 Gun, C Troop, 1st Airlanding Anti-Tank Battery, Royal Artillery 6-pounder anti-tank gun, attached to 3rd Parachute Battalion

Sunday, 17th September

We took off from Manston, Kent. Because I was a vehicle driver, instead of parachuting I had to make the trip by glider. With me were the two glider pilots, Sergeant F. Shaw i/c, 'Paddy' Morgan (Bren gunner) and Gunner John Mitchell, who fired the gun. John and I sat in the tail of the aircraft, the safest place in a crash landing. The crossing to Holland was uneventful, though we did observe two or three gliders go down in the sea, with Air-Sea Recue heading towards them.

We made a good landing at Wolfheze in a stubble field, unloaded quickly, and made for our meeting place at the corner of a wood. It was a beautiful afternoon, and peaceful. It was very difficult driving as the paras were dropping all around. My gun-team was attached to the 3rd Parachute Battalion for this operation. We were in the middle of three advances on Arnhem, along the main Utrecht–Arnhem road. As we made our way through woods to the road, we came across a building, fenced, with some very pale, thin people holding out their hands to us; they were dressed in what looked like a blue and white uniform made of very thin material. Political prisoners, we decided, and used wire cutters to release them. It was sometime later we learned that it was a mental hospital, but we did think they acted strangely as they went through the woods.

Shortly after this we came under fire from a flamethrower. We took cover and attacked with rifle fire until the flames stopped going over our heads, not very pleasant, then I noticed my cover was a stack of logs, not the best of places. We reached the main road leading to Oosterbeek and pushed on as fast as possible as the main idea was to reach the main road bridge at Arnhem quickly. I was stopped by an officer saying that a machine gun was firing down a side road at anything crossing, very difficult with a vehicle and gun to pass, and suggested to the others that they went through the gardens for cover. There was a sandy track between a row of trees and houses by the side of the road, just wide enough for a Jeep, so I decided to pick up as much speed as possible and travel up the sandy track. Sergeant Shaw stayed with me, and just as I thought I was safely across, holes appeared in the bonnet of the Jeep just in front of me, and I lost power and found the accelerator pedal had been cut, under my foot. I carried on using the hand throttle. I told Lieutenant E. Shaw of the damage to the vehicle and he told me to exchange with another driver towing a trailer, as the gun was most important. Sadly that driver, Len Underwood, was killed in action.[51] We proceeded along the road, meeting stronger opposition all the time, and had to join the paras with our rifle and Bren fire. We didn't have any gun positions on the way into Arnhem. We encountered a few armoured cars, our leading gun in C Troop was attacked and some crew wounded Sunday evening, but mainly we were engaged in fighting off German infantry. When advancing along a main road as we were, and you suddenly meet a tank, there is little can be done by the time the gun has been un-hooked, turned around, aimed, and loaded – the crew would be wounded or dead. The tank must always come to the gun, already in position.

Monday, 18th September–Tuesday, 19th September

We entered the outskirts of Arnhem and early Tuesday morning we reached the side of the St Elizabeth Hospital. An officer came looking for a driver and took me with him to the front of the

---

51 Gunner Leonard C. Underwood, 900688; C Troop, age 23. Found buried in the grounds of the RAP, Ter Horst family, Benedendorpsweg.

building and showed me a Jeep and 6-pounder with no sign of the crew. A German tank was firing down the road and any moment we could lose a very valuable anti-tank gun. I got into the driving seat to turn the Jeep and gun around, the road was narrow, and so I had to manoeuvre; by this time shells from the German tank were passing over my head. Looking backwards, I saw the rounds were glancing off a rise in the road, deflecting just over me. One more surprise was in store, driving over power cables lying on the road. Blue flashes went everywhere, but I managed to get the gun out of the line of fire. I immediately rejoined Sergeant Shaw's team, I've no idea what happened to the 6-pounder, and I'd like to know how it came to be there and what happened to it.[52]

Tuesday, 19th September–Thursday, 21st September
By Tuesday we advanced further into Arnhem towards the bridge. By this time very few men were left, and we were ordered back to Oosterbeek. On our return via the lower road, no other C Troop was seen. During this operation I received my first wound in my forearm. We ran into heavy small arms fire, forcing us to take cover and return fire. With Sergeant Shaw, I took up position at the side of a house and was firing a rifle when I received a bullet wound. Sergeant Shaw dressed the arm with my field dressing. I drove the gun into position, and went to the dressing station in the Schoonoord Hotel for the wound to be dressed properly. I walked in through the side door and as I did, a corporal took hold of me and asked if I was trying to have them all shot, carrying a gun, when they were in German hands, indicating two Germans guarding the doors. I hid my rifle and my wound was dressed. All the wounded were then ordered outside and searched, then we returned. I didn't intend being a POW, so when a German walked through the door, I followed a pace behind as if he was taking me somewhere – so many people were going in and out, it was fairly easy. As I made my way to rejoin my gun-team, an NCO stopped me, looked at my arm in a sling and asked if I could hold a rifle. When I replied 'Yes' he directed me into the area of the old church to assist some glider pilots who were rather thin on the ground. (I learned later whilst in the dressing station, our gun received a direct hit and John Mitchell was killed.[53] Some years later, John's inscribed ring was found in the garden and returned to his parents in England by Chris van Roekel.)

Friday, 21st September
About Friday all the ammunition was nearly gone, we were overrun. Along with two glider pilots, and we decided to make our way back to Arnhem bridge, as we expected the 2nd Army any time. Going down a street in Arnhem, a tank came around a corner. Opening the nearest door, with others pushing me to escape the tank, I saw Germans inside; I shouted a warning but before I could get out of the way, an officer shot me with his pistol in the same arm. We carried on past the hospital on Utrechtseweg/Bovenover to the top of the hill near the museum, and here we were taken prisoner. I was taken to St Elizabeth Hospital for treatment, then later to a camp in Germany.

---

52   The A Troop 6-pounder anti-tank gun had been positioned outside a house being occupied by Lt Col Dobie, 1st Parachute Battalion, for an 'O' Group when the building was hit by shellfire and the gun crew outside were all killed or wounded. The officer that commandeered Eric Milner to move the 6-pounder and Jeep was Lieutenant Eric Clapham, A Troop, 1st Air Landing Anti-Tank Battery, RA.
53   Gunner John Mitchell, 14277569, age 31. Found buried in the garden, Benedendorpsweg 119, 20th September 1944.

Driver Eric Milner on the right being searched in front of the Berghege house, Oosterbeek. Middle of the photo also with his arm in a sling is Tom Harding, 10th Parachute Battalion. Driver Eric Milner: 'With Sergeant Shaw, I took up position at the side of a house and was firing a rifle when I received a bullet wound. Sergeant Shaw dressed the arm with my field dressing. I drove the gun into position, and went to the dressing station in the Schoonoord Hotel for the wound to be dressed properly. I walked in through the side door and as I did, a corporal took hold of me and asked if I was trying to have them all shot, carrying a gun, when they were in German hands, indicating two Germans guarding the doors. I hid my rifle and my wound was dressed. All the wounded were then ordered outside and searched, then we returned. I didn't intend being a POW, so when a German walked through the door, I followed a pace behind as if he was taking me somewhere – so many people were going in and out, it was fairly easy.' (Photo: Courtesy Gelders Archive)

Lieutenant E.E. 'Ted' Shaw, Officer Commanding, C Troop, 1st Airlanding Anti-Tank Battery, Royal Artillery

Sunday, 17th September
I had taken Sergeant L. Garnsworthy's gun and detachment with me in support of B Company, 3rd Parachute Battalion, leaving the other guns in charge of my second officer, Lieutenant G. Royall. Whilst traversing the roads towards the bridge, we approached a crossroads, two German armoured vehicles nosed out from either side and the infantry (3rd Parachute Battalion) went to ground and left my Jeep, driver and crew completely exposed. The infantry had PIATs with them to deal with soft armour but were surprised by the enemy at this point. Machine gun fire from the armoured vehicles killed the driver, Gunner (Geordie) Robson and wounded Gunner Fail.[54] The

---

54 Gunner George Robson, 1491471, C Troop, age 26. No known grave.

Jeep was also put out of action. The gun was undamaged, so I commandeered another vehicle and continued with B Company.[55] The reason that the gun appeared to be facing the wrong way was because it was being towed. The towing hitch is situated at the tail end; therefore the muzzle must be facing rearward.

Wednesday, 20th September[56]

Brigadier R.S. Loder-Symonds, CRA, 1st Airborne Division: 'Lieutenant Shaw was a Troop Comd of 1 A/L A.Tk Bty RA. On the afternoon of 20th September 1944 at ARNHEM his gun positions in support of 1 Parachute Brigade were heavily attacked by enemy tanks and infantry. During that afternoon Lieut. Shaw gave an almost superhuman display of persistent gallantry. His gun detachments were almost all killed or wounded but he himself continued to man a gun until his last companion was killed. On at least three occasions that afternoon he returned to one or other of the guns and manned them with a single companion only leaving them on each occasion when his assistants had all been killed. Lieut. Shaw's heroism on this most difficult occasion continued for several hours. His consistent and utter disregard of all considerations of personal safety was quite exceptional.'

Thursday, 21st September

On Thursday 21st September I was again with one of the 6-pounders, and we were being heavily mortared. The detachment and I were in a trench at the rear of the gun, and were certainly having to keep our heads down. After a lull in the proceedings I took stock. Sergeant Shaw was wounded and went to the RAP. Those killed were Bombardier Ryden and Gunner Underwood (wireless operator).[57]

Gunner Ralph Cook, No. 3 Gun, C Troop, 1st Airlanding Anti-Tank Battery, Royal Artillery 6-pounder anti-tank gun, attached to 3rd Parachute Battalion

Because of the shortage of aircraft, the battery could not be transported to Arnhem in one complete lift, and I was ordered for the Second Lift on Monday, 18th September 1944. I vaguely remember that my glider was loaded with a Jeep and trailer containing reserve ammunition, and can only recall that the other occupants were Sergeant J. Davis, Gunner J. Disdel and Gunner W. (Bill) Shiletto, so there must have been two others. I should say that my main concern at this time was to get back with my gun team, which I did at the Hartenstein Hotel on Tuesday morning. The entire

---

55 For a 3rd Parachute Battalion infantryman's perspective of this action, see Sergeant Harry Callaghan, HQ Coy, 3rd Parachute Battalion, which contradicts somewhat the official 3rd Parachute Battalion War Diary in respect of availability of PIATs during the action. Also a quote from the 3rd Parachute Battalion War Diary: '…because 6-pounder attached to this (B Coy) was facing wrong way when cars appeared and was knocked out when trying to face right way.' Ted Shaw was quite understandably rather aggrieved regarding the implication that it was the fault of the artillery crew.

56 It was on the Wednesday, following the previous day's withdrawal from Arnhem, that Lieutenant E.E. Shaw's actions earned him a recommendation for a DSO from Brigadier R.S. Loder-Symonds, CRA, 1st Airborne Division, seconded by Major General R.E. Urquhart, CO, 1st Airborne Division. This was subsequently altered to an MC.

57 Lieutenant Shaw continued to fight on as an infantryman around the Oosterbeek church.

action was so confusing and scattered, that my experience is only of my gun crew, and I cannot recall seeing or hearing of any other members of the battery during the action.

My gun-team were:
No. 1 Sergeant 'Doc' Proctor
No. 2 Gunner Sid Turner (aimer)
No. 3 Gunner Vic Haslam (loader)
No. 4 Bombardier Bill Jones
No. 5 Driver Jack Crane
No. 6 Gunner R. Cook (Bren Gunner)

Saturday, 16th September
At Manston Aerodrome and briefed in our billets for the forthcoming operation for the capture of the Arnhem Bridge, Holland. My troop was to be attached to the 3rd Parachute Battalion, and the route of advance would be from the Landing Zone, through Oosterbeek and along the Utrechtseweg and into Arnhem. We were told that the enemy had a few tanks, and their resistance would be slight. Because of aircraft shortage, complete gun-teams could not be taken on the First Lift, and I was delegated to go on the Second Lift, Monday. Sergeant Robson of No. 4 gun requested to take me as his No. 2, but after some discussion with his crew, the request was not allowed. (In retrospect, my luck was certainly in, as this team was not seen again except for Sergeant Robson who was wounded and captured). Of course we were all confined to the airfield, but that night Paddy Morgan and I skipped over the wire and spent a couple of hours in the nearest pub playing shove ha'penny. We didn't have much to drink at all, but as he was going on the First Lift, it was our way of saying cheerio.

Sunday, 17th September
Assisted the loading of gliders and waved the lads off on the First Lift. We felt very lonely as we went back to our billets waiting for tomorrow.

Monday, 18th September. 2nd Lift
We received the first reports of the initial attack which were said to be a success, and completed the loading of our gliders with a lot of enthusiasm. I remember that the weather was very good and visibility was excellent. We took off at about 1300 hours, it was a marvellous sight to see so many aircraft in the air at one time. The flight itself was uneventful until we arrived over the Landing Zone at Wolfheze. The fields below us were literally covered with parachutes and gliders from the previous landing the day before. We were met by enemy machine-gun, ack-ack and heavy flak, which was signalled by black smoke from air bursts. Our glider pilot warned us to brace ourselves, as he was going to go in on a steep dive and would land at some speed. The ground rushed to meet us, and the glider made an excellent landing being helped to pull up by the soft earth.

There was some difficulty in off-loading the glider at first as the tail appeared to be stuck, but with some mighty swipes with the emergency axe, the tail dropped off. The tail actually struck me on the head, but I was assured that I had not been mortared, which was my first thought as the Landing Zone was still under mortar attack. We landed at about 1500 hours, and the glider was off-loaded in good time. We made our way over the Landing Zone, passing a farm on our right which had been set on fire by enemy mortars. Our route took us through an avenue of trees and onto a road from Wolfheze towards Oosterbeek. We passed houses on our right with all the residents out waving orange flags and cheering us on. Just past this point was a road junction to our left, with a German staff car and its four occupants completely riddled with bullets. This had been dealt with by the 3rd Parachute Battalion, and lying half out of the front passenger seat was the Arnhem Town Commander, General Kussin.

Our journey continued slowly along the Utrechtseweg until we were directed into the grounds of the Hartenstein Hotel, which was to be Divisional HQ. We dug slit trenches for ourselves between the tennis courts and the hotel, and found immediately to our rear in their own dug-outs were Alan Wood, Stanley Maxted and other media correspondents. It was interesting at times to hear them chattering away into their microphones.

At about 1800 hours we were buzzed by three Messerschmitt planes, but the damage they caused was negligible. Apart from sentry duty during the night, we were quite comfortable.

Tuesday, 19th September

After the pre-dawn stand-to and brew-up, our two glider pilots left us. They had remained with us since we landed, and now went to find their own units. It was still early when my gun-team arrived intact, and we gathered all the information of the previous day's happenings. I must say that I felt good to be back with my own crew. Apparently Jack Crane had knocked out a German personnel carrier with one 6-pounder shell, and was thereafter called 'Killer Crane'. The confiscated fags were shared out, but they didn't save any for us. The news of the rest of the battery was very vague; although we knew our OC Bill Arnold was at Arnhem Bridge. We were immediately ordered to load the Jeep with maximum ammunition. Our initial order was to force our way along the Utrechtseweg (main road) and make for Arnhem Bridge to reinforce the units there. After some time waiting for the order to go, it was finally decided that the plan was impossible, and the gun was prepared for action in the defence of Div HQ. The Hartenstein area was now under intermittent mortar bombardment, which was to grow increasingly in intensity, and we spent most of the time improving our slit trenches.

At about 1600 hours we were spectators to a re-supply drop by our C47 Aircraft which was completely disastrous. Everyone displayed as many identifying yellow cloths that they had, but the planes continued to their pre-arranged Drop Zones which were still in German hands. Hardly any of the much-needed supplies were recovered by our troops. The enemy flak was terrific, and everyone was amazed at the courage shown by the pilots and crews trying to re-supply us.

Our gun was then ordered into position at the side of a tree, immediately to the east side of the drive to the entrance of the hotel grounds, pointing in the direction west on the Utrechtseweg. Directly to the front of the Hartenstein was a grassed area with several bushes and trees. (This area is now where the memorial stands). Partly hidden amongst the bushes was a 17-pounder anti-tank gun pointing along the Utrechtseweg towards Arnhem.[58] We were in fact covering one another in our defence of Div HQ, but we never did find out who that particular gun-team was. Enemy activity slackened in the late evening, which allowed us valuable time to get well dug in, and our only grumble during the night was when it was one's turn for sentry duty.

---

58 See Gunner F. John Winser, D Troop, 1st Airlanding, Anti-Tank Battery, Royal Artillery.

Wednesday, 20th September

From dawn onwards the whole area came under constant severe mortar and shell attack, and there were occasions when our slit trenches were commandeered by staff officers during their tour of the area. A self-propelled gun or tank kept firing along the main road to our front from the direction of Oosterbeek. We thought that the target was the 17-pounder, but no hits were registered. During the mid-morning, a crowd of men (believed to be RASC), came rushing towards us across the Hartenstein lawns from the west, shouting, 'The Jerries are coming.' We called on them to get out of the way, and staff officers came out of the Hartenstein to order them back. An RASC Jeep drove to the entrance of the drive, and was hit immediately in front of us by the gun firing along the road. The shot took the driver's right arm off at the shoulder, and we made some prisoners take his body into the hotel grounds.[59] A little time after this, the CRA with others of his staff ran over to the houses on the opposite side of the road, and took up position on the upper floor facing the 17-pounder. He ordered and directed the gun to fire along the main road towards Oosterbeek. I'm sure that no more than three rounds were fired, but the enemy gun was not heard of again. Shortly after this, we were ordered to go along the main road towards Arnhem, and take up a position at the side of a house on the left-hand side of the road.[60] The gun was pointed along a side road[61] leading to Oosterbeek church and also covering the main road.[62] Directly opposite us, and just in the side road, was a Tiger tank which had been put out of action.[63] We dug the gun in and awaited developments. Apart from the incessant mortar bombardment and sporadic enemy small arms fire, we did not see any other enemy movement.

In the afternoon we were alerted by movement in the house opposite on the corner of which the Tiger tank lay. The door burst open, and we could see a group of paras; one of them threw a smoke bomb into the centre of the road, and all six dashed across the road and joined us. We were surprised to find that they were led by the CO of the 10th Parachute Battalion (Lieutenant-Colonel K. Smyth), with his right arm in a sling. Without any ado, he ordered Sergeant Proctor to fire several rounds into the houses on the opposite side of the road junction and to abandon our gun and go with him. His explanation was that enemy troops were following his depleted force. We did not take kindly to this, but we had to comply with his order.

After obeying these orders, Sid Turner took out the gun's firing mechanism and we all made our way along the front gardens of houses to the front of the Hartenstein. The paras disappeared into the hotel grounds.

We moved to the shoulder of the road on the same side as the hotel. The shoulder at this time was constructed of shale and pebbles. We stood in a group discussing how to retrieve our gun, when we suddenly realised we were under fire from an enemy MG – little holes were being drilled into the shale at our feet, but the firing must have been from a distance because there was no sound. We moved smartly away and went into the cellar of the nearest house. We found it to be full of civilians, so after excusing ourselves, we went back onto the main road. After a few minutes

---

59 This incident has striking similarities to that involving Lieutenant John Christie, Officer Commanding, Support Troop, 1st Airborne Reconnaissance Squadron. See *Remember Arnhem* by John Fairley (Pegasus Journal, 1978), p. 118.
60 Huise Bergehege.
61 Lukassenpad/Annastraat.
62 Utrechtseweg.
63 StuG on Lukassenpad.

we were joined by Brigadier Hackett, resplendent in his red beret. He asked what we were doing there, and after an explanation of our events, he told us to go back to our previous position in his company. We were walking back along the shoulder of the road, when Bombardier Jones drove up from the rear in a Jeep, and shouted for help to get the gun hitched up, but Hackett told us to keep moving. A sudden burst of enemy machine gun fire hit the jeep and wounded Jones. Jack Crane ran to the Jeep and with Jones, hitched up the gun, and drove it back towards the Hartenstein. Jones was later awarded the Military Medal for this action. We did not see Jones again as he went to a first aid post and was later taken prisoner. (I saw him after the war in Heckington and he was happily married to a local girl). Keeping to the right-hand side of the road, we continued on our way by the rear of houses to the last garden of a house before the road junction. There were a good number of paras in the area who we heard quite clearly. A tank's engine was heard, and firing exchanges were made causing us to take avoiding action by deploying ourselves amidst the bushes and other plants in the garden. Suddenly we heard a disembodied voice broadcast from the tank, demanding everyone in the area to surrender. This was answered by a fusillade of shots and very choice language, and the tank moved away.

At this time, our gun-team were being used as infantry and had been supplemented by Sergeant Davis, Jack Disdel and Bill Shiletto. It was now about 1600-1700 hours and we were ordered to enter the corner house and defend the road junction.[64] The floorboards were taken out, and my particular task with Sid Turner was to defend the rear door. Two others were at the front door, and Sergeant Proctor with the remaining men went upstairs. When kneeling down, I found that my head just came above the floor, and I was reasonably comfortable in this defensive position. I was equipped with a rifle, several Mills bombs and a .38 revolver. (My Bren gun was on the Jeep with the 6-pounder).

After darkness set in, there was a lot of enemy activity in and around the nearby houses. They could be heard distinctly as the Germans seemed to draw some comfort in shouting at the top of their voices to one another. There were definite sounds of roaring flames, and Sergeant Proctor from upstairs said that houses were being set alight by the enemy. We did not need to be reminded to keep fully alert.

Shortly after midnight, the door in front of me suddenly opened and a man stepped in, closing the door behind him. My rifle was loaded with the safety catch off, and I just do not know why I didn't shoot him. I challenged him with, 'Who the hell are you?' and it must have startled him to be so addressed from the direction of the floor. His reply was, 'FOP one' with which someone upstairs shouted, 'Shoot the bastard.' It transpired that he was Forward Observation for an artillery unit on the other side of the river. He was made very welcome by our crew upstairs, but I have often wondered since if he has ever realised how lucky he was. I do not know what happened for the rest of the night, for unknowingly I fell asleep. Perhaps I should say here that before we left England, we were all given two tablets to help us to keep awake for 48 hours, but I still do not know anyone who took them.

Thursday, 21st September

On waking at daylight, I realised I was alone, but I heard movement coming from a room to my right. Without moving my position, I shouted and asked who they were. They were actually brewing up, and said that they were the remnants of the 156 Parachute Battalion and had relieved

---

64 Pietersbergseweg/Utrechtseweg junction, western corner.

us during the night. They did not know where my team had gone, but thought it was towards the Hartenstein area, so I picked up my equipment and left hurriedly. I made my way along the rear gardens and found my team with the 6-pounder in position at the side of the last building which was thought to be a first aid post. From the remarks that were made, I'm quite sure that they had left me for dead. The gun was pointing across the main road directly up a side street to the north.[65] This street was about 600 yards long, and was crossed at the end by another street which ran parallel to the main road.[66] Houses were along both sides of the street and ran the full length. Occasionally, paras were seen to cross the end junction.

We were under sniper fire, and the shell and mortar bombardment kept increasing with intensity. Although we were well dug-in, we took it in turns to do thirty minutes each observing at the gun sight. During mid-morning and my second spell at the gun sight, I saw a Tiger tank beginning to cross the end junction and shouted a warning.[67] Sergeant Proctor screamed back, 'Don't fire.' (Nobody could have missed hitting it even with their eyes shut, as the tank filled the whole road). As the tank progressed across the junction it was clearly seen that our paras were stalking it from the side and rear. I distinctly saw one man wearing a kilt, but the chance of a 'kill' passed and some very choice words were exchanged between us.

In the afternoon, I was in a slit trench with Vic Haslam sheltering from the continuous mortar bombardment. We were conversing and I suddenly realised that Vic was killed from the blast of a salvo. This rather shook me as he was only a few feet from me. At this time I was on the Bren gun, and a couple of the lads took him away to the first aid post.[68] Later in the afternoon there was a lull in the enemy bombardment. A captured Jeep arrived with German officers under a white flag, and they went into the FAP building which was also Brigadier Hackett's HQ. They delivered an ultimatum for our troops to vacate the area by midnight or they would bombard the FAP area. This demand was really laughable, as the entire vicinity had been under continuous severe fire for the past three days.

Anyway, at 2355 hours, we took the gun out of position, and made our way along paths and over the main road, and took up a position where the 17-pounder had been on the green in front of the Hartenstein Hotel. The gun was pointed along Utrechtseweg towards Arnhem, and my position with the Bren gun was in a slit trench facing to the rear, and also covering the front of the hotel. Sergeant Jack Davis (troop sergeant) was now in command, and he handed me a two-inch mortar with orders to fire parachute flares if there were any enemy activities through the night. There were several stand-to's, and plenty of enemy movement was heard, but the night passed uneventfully.

Friday, 22nd September

From dawn onwards our whole area was saturated with intense mortar and shell fire that never ceased at all. At times I was joined by Bill Shiletto in my slit trench, and I think it was just to keep me company for a spell. The weather was not kind at all. Light rain was now falling, and continued to do so until we were finally evacuated.

---

65 The gun position was on the south side of Utrechtseweg facing across the road north up Mariaweg.
66 Paul Krugerstraat.
67 Paul Krugerstraat/Mariaweg.
68 Gunner Vic Haslam, C Troop, 1st Airlanding, Anti-Tank Battery, Royal Artillery. I have found no mention in burial records of Vic Haslam. There is mention however in the 1st Airlanding Anti-Tank Battery, Royal Artillery, *As You Were – September 1944* publication by Doug Colls, privately published in 1985, page 11, of a Gunner Haslam being taken POW. Reference to a Bombardier R.A. Haslam being incarcerated in Stalag XIIA and Stalag IV appears in the book 'Captured at Arnhem', Peter Green, Pen & Sword, 2022. p.81, 236.

Saturday, 23rd September

The day was heralded with the usual bombardment, and we made many remarks about our lack of support aircraft. I remember 'resting' in my trench when I saw much small light dropping towards me. I was really frightened at the time, but felt very silly when they turned out to be pieces of burning paper fragments. Apparently, the Div Ammo Dump, which was nearby, had received direct hits from a mortar attack and was ablaze. Sergeant Davis organised the fire-fight for which he later received the MM (on our return to England, Sergeant Davis also received a Dutch award, but I cannot remember the reason for this). The rest of the day was spent sheltering and maintaining look-out.

Sunday, 24th September

Normal shelling, but the afternoon was made very exciting, as I observed and counted 64 Boston Bombers in formation drop their bomb load to the north east of our position. They were more than welcome, for as long as these aircraft were seen, the enemy bombardment ceased completely. Otherwise a shell-full day.

Monday, 25th September

'Stand-to' in the drizzling rain. Not long to wait for the 'hate' attack. During the afternoon, Sergeant Davis arrived and told me that we were going to retire across the Rhine that night. I do remember that observations were made that we could last a lot longer yet. All equipment that couldn't be carried was to be destroyed. Sergeant Davis gave me two tins of unlabelled food to prepare for the team. I must say here that as far as I knew, our gun-team had nothing to eat or drink after they had disposed of their initial 24-hour ration pack, but I never heard of any complaint.

From 2200 hours onwards we were busy sabotaging the gun and laying booby traps. I have to admit that I lost our two tins of food whilst covering our tracks, but no one even mentioned them. Perhaps the team were too intent on the job in hand. Our boots had to be muffled with rags or torn clothing, and we had to remain in contact with each other by holding the tail of the smock of the man in front.

We departed our position at about 2300 hours, and of course it was still drizzling with rain. A red tracer shell was fired every minute from the other side of the Rhine, to give us some indication of the direction we must travel. We made our way through the grounds of the Hartenstein, and then through woods, the paths of which had been marked with white tape by the glider pilots. Our progress was marked by several alarms, small arms fire and loud German exhortations. Then we passed through open fields strewn with discarded parachutes and dead cattle and so on to the banks of the Rhine. We felt very exposed, and came under more mortar fire as the enemy must have suspected something. The total distance from our original position to the Rhine was probably about 1,500 yards, but it seemed a lot further. We were now waiting for a promised boat to take us across to the other side, in preference to swimming the river. There were a few hundred other men waiting to be taken over, and I must say that discipline reigned supreme.

Eventually a boat did arrive and our team clambered in except for Bill Shiletto. The boat's engine started up and Bill waded into the water and grabbed the side of the boat. He was told by the boatman to clear off, and Bill replied, 'I've been with them all the time and I'm not leaving them now!' We dragged him aboard and made the other side with the help of our rifle butts used as oars. On arrival, we climbed up a slippery muddy bank, and slid down the other side. We were welcomed by Canadian REs who offered us cigarettes. We walked along the road together to a farm house near Driel, where we were given a rum ration and two biscuits. I remember that this repast made me quite ill.

Tuesday, 26th September
Dawn was now beginning to break, and we were taken by ambulance to a field ambulance unit to be screened for injuries. It was here that Sergeant Gentles, unknown to him, was found to have shrapnel wounds and was detained. The remainder of us boarded a 3-ton truck and we were taken to Nijmegen. The route was littered with burnt-out tanks and trucks, which reminded us that someone did really try and relieve us at Arnhem. At Nijmegen we de-trucked at a schoolhouse, where we were given a sumptuous meal by our Battery Sea Party, and a roll call was made. Our small arms were discarded onto a pile, and we were bedded down. I slept for 24 hours, and I don't think that I moved an inch. We were wakened next day in the middle of an air-raid that was aimed for Nijmegen Bridge. The remnants of the battery were now together, and we were taken by lorry to another school in Nijmegen where beds had been placed in the rooms. The beds opposite me were occupied by Doug Stone and 'Badgie' Cameron, and I was flanked on each side by John Disdel and Jack Crane. It was not a happy time, as everyone was re-living the trauma of the past ten days and remembering our lost comrades. Our time was spent resting on the beds, and Doug and Badgie tried raising our spirits by leading us in a sing-along, and before we knew it, we were raising the roof.

The next day we were heartened by a visit from Major Toler, who had come to see how his old battery had fared.[69] We were then taken to a large barn just outside the town, where all the division survivors had gathered to be addressed by General Browning. He congratulated everyone on the Arnhem operation, and said that we would all be evacuated to England as soon as possible.

Gunner E.T. Burridge, P Troop, 1st Airlanding Anti-Tank Battery, Royal Artillery

I was with the 1st Airlanding Anti-Tank Battery, P Troop, 17-pounders. Our 17-pounder was named the 'Pathfinder', Lieutenant Casey was the troop commander, Sergeant T.H. Hughes was No. 1, Gunner Oldfield was loader, No. 2 Gunner Kendall, myself Bren gunner, and the driver I think was named Taylor.

Sunday, 17th September
We took off from RAF Tarrant Rushton. Before leaving the camp for the airfield, Major W.F. Arnold had me on a charge, giving me 14 days CB, 14 days' pay stopped and 14 days Royal Warrant for leaving camp on the Friday.

We landed at Wolfheze; the Hamilcar we were in came to a stop in the trees. The wing was ripped off and we had to get the gun and the truck out.

Monday, 18th September–Wednesday, 27th September
Monday we moved off the Landing Zone and our first gun position was near some gasworks, we did not engage any armour at this position.[70] Then we moved to the road junction near Oosterbeek

---

69   Major T.I.J. Toler, Commanding Officer, B Squadron, Glider Pilot Regt, ex-Royal Artillery.
70   Gun facing west along Benedendorpsweg.

ANTI-TANK BATTERIES 427

P Troop 17-pounder gun 'Pathfinder'. The gun faces east along the Benedendorpsweg. Behind the gun, House De Parre, Cafe De Vergulde Ploeg and opposite, the Ijsfabriek (ice factory). Post-war 1945. (Photos: Courtesy Gelders Archive)

Second position of No. 1 gun. Junction Bildersweg/Benedendorpsweg, No. 151, 'de Lindenhoet', gun facing left, west along Benedendorpsweg. Post-war winter photo. Gunner E.T. Burridge: 'Monday we moved off the Landing Zone and our first gun position was near some gasworks, we did not engage any armour at this position. Then we moved to the road junction near Oosterbeek concert hall, where a Jeep with two paras were wounded. The gun was in front of the house and I was in position upstairs on the front bedroom balcony.' (Photo: Author's private collection)

concert hall, where a Jeep with two paras were wounded. The gun was in front of the house and I was in position upstairs on the front bedroom balcony.[71] After some time there, we moved to our last gun position.[72]

We passed the church and halfway along this road we stopped. We came under heavy fire. We did knock out some German vehicles, and one was a troop carrier. We opened fire when it came

---

71 Bildersweg/Benedendorpsweg, No. 151, de Lindenhoet.
72 No. 1 gun first moved into the outskirts of Arnhem Monday night and then Tuesday morning moved as far as the Rhine Pavilion engaging flak barges on the river before withdrawing west of Oosterbeek Laag station and taking up a temporary position covering the viaduct over Benedendorpsweg. The gun then withdrew to Veerweg until Thursday 21st. No. 1 gun then moved into position by the gasworks before it was ordered into its final position in the orchard near the Oosterbeek Laag church between E and F Troop, 1st Airlanding Light Regiment Royal Artillery. Both accounts of Burridge and Rathband are somewhat confused and contradictory. In particular Rathband's comment: 'Again ordered to proceed to the bridge, passed another 17-pounder by the concert hall and another on the corner by petrol pumps, carried on till in sight and range of the railway bridge.' Sergeant Hughes' No. 1 gun deployed near the concert hall, so what other gun did Rathband see at the concert hall and by petrol pumps?

down the road at about 200–300 yards, the shot knocked out the engine, some of the troops in the back jumped out going to each side of the road. The machine gun opened fire as I did. After this, Sergeant Hughes sent me with the Bren gun to the back of the houses.[73] On the left of me was a 6-pounder anti-tank gun near a farmhouse, to the right of the gun was a machine gun. When the Germans opened up, they fired at the farm house and the 6-pounder. The tanks were concealed by some trees which the tanks came through.

There was some mortar fire coming in as well, the blast from the fire cracked the buffer, the recoil would not work as the gun barrel would fly off the gun carriage. When the fire stopped, I went to see where the crew were. On making my way back I came across our driver and he was in shock. Leaving him with the family Breman to look after him, I went outside after seeing him alright, and there was ordered by a para sergeant who told me to look for mortar bombs and carry them to the mortar crew in the back garden.[74] After getting all the mortar bombs I could find, I was told to make my way back to the church; there was another 17-pounder.[75] On going around the concert hall I was ordered to join an infantry group, and I did infantry work until I was taken prisoner on the 27th September.

Gunner F. John Winser, No. 1 Gun, D Troop, 1st Airlanding, Anti-Tank Battery, Royal Artillery 17-pounder anti-tank gun, under Sergeant N.S. Gentles

Tarrant Rushton; Hamilcar Glider, Chalk No. 318
When we started getting ready for Market Garden we were locked up in the aerodrome and we were not allowed out. We were briefed, looking at maps and aerial maps of Arnhem. Our gun was to go through Arnhem down by the bridge; we would be near to the barracks, and sited out towards the bridge.

Sunday, 17th September
The 17th September arrived, a beautiful summer's morning, we all had breakfast and when we'd finished breakfast we got all our kit ready and all piled into the trucks and were then taken down to the aerodrome. All the gliders were lined up and all the tow ropes laid out. They started revving up and we all thought 'Hello, this is it, looks like we're going to take off.' We hooked up, we all piled into the gliders and away we went. We went across the North Sea, it was a lovely trip, apart from when we got over the coast of Holland we started to get a bit of flak, but the rocket-firing Typhoons were underneath the gliders and whenever the flak opened up they'd go down and sort them out, so we were okay.

When we eventually got over Arnhem, we cast off from the tug and we started coming down but unfortunately for us, whether we came down too fast or not I don't know, we came down and dug in and over we went. The whole glider went over on its back, up on its nose and over on its back, everything came down from the floor, the truck, the gun and I was actually on the gun shield, that was my position on the gun, me one side and my mate the other. We'd got the seat belts around us and funny enough, I taken my airborne smock and all my equipment off and hung it up because

---

73   119, Benedendorpsweg.
74   Almost certainly Sergeant Dick Whittingham, 1st Parachute Battalion.
75   Sergeant George Thomas i/c 17-pounder No. 3 Gun, D Troop, 1st Airlanding Anti-Tank Battery RA.

what with so much ammunition, 36 grenades and ammunition pouches, we couldn't get the belts around. So we took it all off my mate and I, and when the glider went over, my smock and everything went underneath it; I lost it, I was very sorry to lose my airborne smock; anyway, we sorted ourselves out and gradually crawled out. Our driver, Georgie Cook, he'd hurt his neck, but apart from that we were okay. We crawled out of the glider and when we got outside, we looked, and one glider pilot, poor chap, was dead,[76] and the other one was very badly injured.[77] The truck had come down on top of them; in the Hamilcar glider the cabin for the pilots, you go through the body of the glider and up some steps and their cabin was on the roof, so they took the full force of the truck coming down on top of them. All we could see was two boots sticking out, he was dead and the other one was very badly injured. Anyway, we got some shovels and we made a trench and we dug through to him, he was yelling out because he was in so much pain and we gave him morphine – we all carried morphine, we gave him a shot and then a colonel in the medics came over and he said, 'I think we can get him out. If I can get hold of a Bren carrier, and we can get some chains and we'll lash it round and lift the truck off. I'll crawl under and ease him out.'[78] Anyway, we got him out, the colonel got him out, and off he went to hospital. I found out he died that night, it was very sad because we were going to congratulate the pilots on what a wonderful flight we'd had, one of the best we'd had in gliders. It was such a shame that it ended up like that, because we lost our gun and truck and all the gear and us not being able to do the job we were supposed to. This is half the trouble I think of the way the battle went, we weren't the only 17-pounder I don't think that went over, which they lost. It made a lot of difference later on when we ran into the remnants of the SS division reforming at Arnhem itself. (That never came out in the briefing at all. All we were supposed to have met was light resistance from 'boy soldiers' and old men, just a few soldiers in the barracks, not an SS division! Anyway we did quite well when you think what we dropped into.)

Our part of the battle was finished, our role, so they decided we would use our gun-team, they said if you dig yourselves in at the side of the Landing Zone, wait for the next Lift to come in, in the morning, and we'd probably get on to another gun. Anyway, we went over to the edge of the Landing Zone and dug slit trenches and had a brew up and a bit of food, we'd got emergency rations and little tablets of fuel which we put on a little frame, our Dixie, and we could boil the water. We had little cubes of tea, milk and sugar all together. It looked a bit slimy at times and you had to scoop the tea leaves off the top, anyway, it all went down well. We had our meal and drop of tea and then got ready for the night. There wasn't a lot of noise around us, most of the noise was coming from Oosterbeek and Arnhem. Fortunately for us it was quiet, so we put a guard out and took it in turns, the rest of us had a bit of sleep.

Monday, 18th September
First light next morning we stood-to; I think we had a drop more tea, and then we had the job of then waiting for the Second Lift to come in. We were standing-to and then we heard the drone of aircraft and we looked up and thought, 'Hello, is this them coming in?' The weather had changed then, it wasn't so good and they'd had some bad weather in England, mist and fog which had delayed them getting away. Anyway, it was a good job they were late because the aircraft that came

---

76   Sergeant Charles W. Winkworth, 5110811, C Squadron, Glider Pilot Regt, age 22. No known grave.
77   Sergeant David A. White, 421356, C Squadron, Glider Pilot Regt, age 22. Died of injuries, buried near Schoonoord Hotel, 18th September 1944.
78   Colonel Graeme Warrack, Assistant Director of Medical Services (ADMS).

over, that wasn't the Second Lift. We'd got a bombardier with us that was very good on aircraft recognition, and he looked up and said, 'That isn't the Second Lift coming in, you'd better get your backsides in that trench, they're Focke Wolf 190s and ME109s!' They came in and played hell for a while, they were shooting up gliders and all the equipment on the Landing Zone. All the shells and machine gun fire was going over the tops of our heads, we could hear the trees and all the bark being stripped off the trees with the machine gun and cannon shells. Eventually they flew off and after a while the Second Lift starting moving in. We put out markers and most of them got down okay.

We were detailed then to go on a gun of the 2nd Battery, so we all piled on as best we could onto the 15-cwt and we then made our way down to Oosterbeek. From then on, they tried then to get the gun into Arnhem, to the bridge. We got about halfway down the Arnhem road from Oosterbeek and they were meeting pretty stiff resistance. I thought I heard the officer say that they didn't want to lose the gun. The South Staffs who were round about us were getting a hell of a bashing from the SS.

Monday, 18th September–Sunday, 24th September

We decided then to take the gun back to Oosterbeek and it was dug-in then on 'the Green',[79] firing down the Arnhem road from Oosterbeek. We dug it in on the Green, and being that we were 'spare' gunners (the full gun crew were there from the 2nd Battery) we dug the slit trenches at the back of the gun. We used to go out with the paratroopers fighting in the houses opposite and doing duties on the gun when we were needed. The first day wasn't too bad, they started shelling and mortaring our positions but not too bad.

The next day, when we stood-to at first light we could hear a tank engine revving up on the Arnhem road, and we thought, 'Hello, they're getting ready to attack.' We stood-to on the gun, the crew were on the gun, and we were in the trenches at the back waiting if we were needed. The colonel, Loder-Symonds,[80] he came out of Div HQ when these tanks started coming up the road. He lay down in the road and started giving Fire Orders and we opened up, and two or three of the tanks and armoured personnel carriers were knocked out. I was firing the Bren down the road onto personnel. We blocked the road with these tanks which was a good thing because we'd knocked them out. I think they were shaken up a bit when they must have realised that we'd got a 17-pounder that they were coming at. Anyway, the tanks were knocked out and they were slewed across the road blocking it, and we never got any more coming up the road. They used to come so far up the road and fire at us, but we never had a breakthrough from that direction.

Then after a while it settled down again and we had a bit of a brew up. By then the shelling was getting quite hellish, the 88s were training on us (that was a marvellous gun, the 88, they could do anything with that, field gun, anti-tank gun, the lot. Later on when the Dakotas were coming over trying to get supplies to us, they were using the 88s to fire up at them and it was pretty grim to see those poor chaps chucking hampers and containers out of the Dakotas. All but a few went into enemy lines even though we were putting our yellow triangles out to try and attract their attention.)

The battle by then was getting a bit lively and we were taking quite a bashing. The next day, the biggest thing that happened was a breakthrough at the back of us, the back of the gun on the other

---

79   Opposite Div HQ, Hartenstein, Hartensteinlaan/Utrechtseweg, facing east, along Utrechtseweg.
80   CRA.

side, not on the Arnhem side. We had a breakthrough, the Germans broke through and Loder-Symonds again came out from Div HQ in a Bren carrier and we all followed him. He said, 'Come on, let's go get the buggers,' and he was yelling out as he stood up on the Bren carrier and we all chased down after him and we sorted the Germans out, and we stopped them, we killed quite a few and it stopped them breaking through.

We managed to get back then to the gun and it was all quiet except for the shelling and the mortaring which was pretty grim, one or two of the boys were getting hit. We saw a Jeep roll up one day at Div HQ. The driver just got out and he was just unlucky, an 88 shell landed near his Jeep and off came his arm, we saw his arm come off. We rushed him, the medics were in Div HQ, and we left him there, poor devil.[81] We then settled down again for another night, that's the way the battle went. One day my mate and I decided to go to the toilet and have a smoke, we got hold of our shovel and off we went, we were going over to the houses and back of the gardens to do our business. We had our smoke and that, and when got back to our trench, it wasn't there. An 88mm shell had landed right in it which just goes to show you, if your number is on it. If we'd had stayed we wouldn't have been here. The boys were saying, 'Where have you been? You were damn lucky!'

We were going out then with the paras, all the fighting was in the houses, the Germans were trying to get us out of the houses which were all around the Green at Oosterbeek. They were shelling with phosphorous shells which were setting the houses alight, a lot of beautiful houses, and a lot of them were burnt out through the shells. By this time our food was getting short, I can't remember having many meals. Most of the meals we had were when we were scrounging around the houses. We used to get into the houses and go down the cellars; they usually had preserves in the basements of these houses and we used to get the bottled fruits and have some of that, I think that's just about all we lived on.

Monday, 25th September

It was funny, on the last day that we were there, we were out with the paras and one of them saw a deer because there were some woods at the back. This deer ran along and they shot it and got it back to the houses and we found a butcher that was in the cellars. He skinned it and got it ready for the pot, because them poor devils that were in the cellars of the houses, I don't know what they were living on. All we saw was a pot that used to go on and I think all they had was probably a bit of potatoes and a bit of greens if they could get their hands on them. When they saw this deer, they must have thought 'We're going to have a feast' but unfortunately for us, we never got any of it. That was the night we got the orders to pull out.

We were told we were going to pull out and we had to make our way over to Div HQ and leave most of our kit, we had to travel light. We put socks over our boots so we didn't make a noise and when it got dark we started then getting ready to pull out. We put the injured, the walking wounded who could hold a rifle and what ammunition we'd got left, we left propped up at the windows of the houses and they carried on firing while we crawled out the houses and made our way to Div HQ at the Hartenstein Hotel across the road. We got underneath the balcony of the hotel and formed little groups and then we'd got to make our way down to the river. I met up with a Polish chap, and it wasn't until we'd got across the river that I found out that he was a Polish sergeant major. He'd come over from Driel and he said to me, 'You stick with me; I've been this way once!'

---

81 See account by Gunner Ralph Cook, No. 3 Gun, C Troop, 1st Airlanding Anti-Tank Battery, Royal Artillery.

Anyway, we went down in small groups to the river, making our way down we followed little white tapes which marked out the route. There was a Bofors gun on the other side of the river, from the 2nd Army, firing exactly from the spot we'd got to make for; they were firing tracer shells across the exact spot we had to make for. We got down eventually after some of the lads had been shot up with a machine gun on the way down, but we got down on the bank river okay. We were down there a while, then the Germans started shelling the banks of the river; one or two of the lads were hit. The Royal Engineers had flat-bottomed boats and were ferrying the men across the river. I was very lucky with my Polish sergeant major, we managed to get in one of the boats and we made it across to the other side, it was a very fast moving river and it was also bucketing down with rain.

Monday, 25th September–Tuesday, 26th September Onwards

What with being soaked through with the rain and wading through the water from the river. It was a terrible night, absolutely pouring down.

We got off the boat the other side, and we were very thankful, we crawled up the bank and when we got to the top of the bank, the Royal Engineers and the Canadian Engineers were dishing out rum and it was one of the loveliest drinks I've ever had in my life, it went right through your body and right down to your boots, just like somebody turning the fire on, absolutely beautiful.

All the engineers did a marvellous job that night, because they lost a lot of men and boats going backwards and forewords across that river. We'd got across and it was absolutely wonderful being able to walk and stand up again even, because we'd been crawling about for so many days, dodging this and dodging that, keeping your head down and it was wonderful being able to walk down this road. They said just carry on down the road; there were infantry units down the road which were dishing out more rum which went down very well. Finally we got to Nijmegen, and had our first sleep and started recognising one another, that's when I found my Polish sergeant major. He looked at me, he couldn't believe it, seeing me after we'd got rid of our beards and dirt and grime, we'd had a shave, and it was absolutely wonderful to have a wash and a meal.

Then they said we'd got to get to Brussels. They said that we may, because the Germans had been breaking through the road, we might have to fight our way down. We thought, 'Bugger that, we've done enough!' We got our rifles again and some more ammunition and got ready then if they did break through, we'd fight our way down if they got through on the road. It didn't happen and we got through okay to Brussels. We were there a couple of days, and then went by Dakotas from an American airfield and landed back near Grantham and then we went back to Heckington. There was only sixteen of us actually got back to Heckington that day, and a couple of officers. Captain Henry Bear, he'd swum across the river; when we were at Nijmegen he had nothing but a blanket round him, he'd stripped everything off and got into the river naked. Anyway, he'd made it; he was one of our captains.

When we got back to Heckington it was very sad, the people of the village had taken us in, they were like mothers and uncles, every bloke in the battery always had somewhere to go at night for a meal. The people of the village were very sad when they knew there were so many missing because we didn't know who was dead or been taken prisoner, it was so confused. We lost such a lot of good men.

Appendix:
Tigers and Snipers

It may be worth pointing out that many veterans commonly refer to all German tanks as 'Tiger' tanks. This is obviously not entirely accurate but in the circumstances of the heat of battle may be perfectly understandable. During the fighting around the Arnhem Bridge certainly Tiger tanks were encountered. Tiger Is (Sd. Kfz.181 Panzerkampfwagen VI Ausf. E) belonging to Schwere Panzer-Kompanie *Hummel* (equipped with 14 tanks) elements of which arrived at the bridge late on Tuesday, 19th September. Initially only two tanks arrived; due to mechanical and other problems, the remaining tanks arrived on subsequent days. After the end of the fighting at the bridge on the 21st September the unit was deployed near Elst to engage the advancing XXX Corps.

Tiger IIs or Konigstiger (Sd. Kfz.182 Panzerkampfwagen VI) of Schwere Panzer-Abteilung 506, equipped with 45 tanks arrived in Zevenaar on the night of the 23/24th September and immediately two companies (each of 14 tanks) were sent to Arnhem. One company (No. 3) went to Oosterbeek, under command of Kampfgruppe *Von Allwörden*, 9.SS Panzer Division, the other to Elst under the 10 SS Panzer Division.

The German forces encountered at Arnhem employed a variety of tanks and self-propelled guns often from numerous sources and units that were available. These ranged from Sd.Kfz.141/1 Pz.Kpfw.III Ausf.G and Sd. Kfz.161/1 Pz.Kpfw.IV Ausf.H to captured French Char B2 tanks of Panzer-Kompanie 224. The Germans also employed amongst others, ten self-propelled guns from Sturmgeschütz-Brigade 280, which actively took part in the Tuesday 19th actions and after. This unit was made up of *Sd.Kfz.142/1* Sturmgeschütz III Ausf.G and Sd.Kfz 142/2 Sturmhaubitze 42G. The StuGs were deployed between three platoons (Zugs), two with three StuGs, one with three StuHs with one StuG allocated to the CO, Major Kurt Kuhme.[1]

Rather like describing all German tanks as 'Tigers', many veterans recall being shot at by snipers, when in fact more likely describing being shot at by an infantry rifleman. Trained German Scharfschützen or sharpshooters usually existed at company or platoon level having received specialised training in marksmanship and fieldcraft. Genuine German snipers armed with scoped rifles normally deployed in pairs, one shooting and one acting as observer (see the account by Corporal Alex Whitelaw, HQ Company, 3rd Parachute Battalion,1st Parachute Brigade on dealing with such a team of snipers). There simply were not that many riflemen so equipped and trained, so it would be fair to say that although genuine snipers would have been encountered at Arnhem, by far the most incoming 'sniping' would have been from regular infantry squad riflemen (albeit possibly 'marksman'), armed with the same Mauser K98K 7.92mm rifle without a telescopic sight.

---

1   Zwarts, Marcel, *German Armoured Units at Arnhem, Sept 1944* (Concord Publications, 2001), p.27.

Veteran Acknowledgements

With the amount of time that it has taken to conclude my research, in many cases, my contributors, truly a very special generation, have passed on. However, I would still wish to express my sincere thanks not only to them but their families for sharing their experiences. Whilst I thanked them all during our meetings and correspondence, I would like to formally record my gratitude in print.

1st Airborne Division

1st Airborne Division Headquarters: Major M. Willcock. 1st Airborne Division Defence Platoon: Private Vic Holden. 1st Airborne Reconnaissance Squadron: Trooper Stan Hatton. 1st Parachute Battalion: Sgt G. Evans, Pte G. Hill, Private R. George, Pte R. Croudace, Pte D. Morgans. 16th Parachute Field Ambulance: Corporal G. Stanners, Pte. B. Orrell. 2nd Parachute Battalion: Pte R. C. Holt, Pte A. Dennis, Pte V. Boast, Pte V. Goodwin, Pte J. Beeston, Pte G. McCarthy, Pte D. Brooks, Pte C.A.Cardale. 3rd Parachute Battalion: Pte F. Radley, Cpl A. Whitelaw, L/Cpl B.J.G. Stidson, L/Cpl T. Halley-Frame, Pte W. Collard, Pte. L. Harrison, Lt L. Wright, Sgt T. Battle, Sgt H. Callaghan, Pte A. Watson, Pte W. A. Chiddington, Maj M. Dennison, Pte J. Ward.

1st Parachute Squadron, Royal Engineers: Sgt N. Swift, Cpl D. Thomas, Spr F. A. Woods, Cpl J.E. Humphreys, L/Sgt H. Padfield, Spr L. Plummer, Spr T. Hicks, Spr G. Spicer, Spr A. Hackney, Spr F. Partridge, Spr E. Booth, Spr A. Hendy, Spr B. Joynson, Spr J. Simpkins. 261 Field Park Company, Royal Engineers: L/Sgt M. J. Potter, L/Cpl K. L. Underwood. Advance Workshop Detachment, Royal Electrical and Mechanical Engineers: Cfn J. R. Roberts. 1st Airborne Division Ordnance Field Park, Royal Army Ordnance Corps: Pte E. Mordecai, Pte K. Heaney.

1st Airlanding Anti-Tank Battery, Royal Artillery: Lt B. Lockett, Sgt E. Shelswell, Sgt C. Robson, Dvr E. Milner, Lt E. E. Shaw, Gnr R. Cook, Gnr E. T. Burridge, Lt G. Ryall, Gnr E.H. Barnsley, Gnr F. J. Winser. Dvr W. Cameron.

1st Airlanding Light Regiment, Royal Artillery: Lt T. V. Driver, Maj D. S. Munford, Bdr J. L. Hall, Cpt J.W. Walker, Lt R. Staddon, Sgt R. McLeod, Gnr F. Bird, Gnr E. W. Mills, Lt N. F. Farrands, Sgt D. C. Hardie, BSM T. W. Kent, Lt T. R. Barron, Lt D.S. Erskine, Gnr H. Drinkwater, Capt J.H.D. Lee, Gnr R. Allen, Bdr K. Borley, Gnr V. Waite, Bdr J. Noble, Sgt L. Turner, Gnr F. Baker, Gnr L. Newham, L/Bdr J. Jones, Gnr A.D. Rodgers, Bdr V. Jones, Lt P.W. Wilkinson, L/Bdr R. Webb, Bdr J. Briggs, Bdr H. Trinder, Gnr R. Tebbutt, Gnr R. Benthall, Bdr R. Harper, Bdr R. Green, RSM J. Siely, Bdr E.E. Clack, L/Sgt J.A. Scott.

1st Forward Observation Unit, Royal Artillery: Sgt N.S. Patten, Gnr A. Brearton, Bdr W.F. Wrigley, Gnr R.C. Kift, Capt C.W. Ikin, Bdr F.C. Mardell,

1st Airlanding Brigade: 2nd Battalion, South Staffordshire Regiment: Lt H. H. L. Cartwright, Pte A. Harvey, Sgt A. Cook, Lt C. J. MacDonnell, Pte D. White, L/Cpl H. Smith, Sgt N. Howes, Pte M. Faulkner, Pte R. Tyrer, Sgt H. Dalton, L/Sgt J. Gaunt, Pte R. Bagguley, Pte A. Lawson, QMS F. Bluff, Pte N. Gilberts, Pte K. Woodward, Pte G. A. Kite, Pte L. G. Ratley, Pte G. R. Brown, Pte F. A. Bluff, Pte C. Gullick, Pte G. Ashington. 1st Battalion, The Border Regiment: Lt J. S. D. Hardy, Cpl I. Hunter, Lt A. R. Royall, Lt W. P. Stott, Pte E. J. Peters, Cpl C. Crickett, Pte J. Ranger, Pte F. A. Hodges, Pte R. Graydon, Pte L. Powell, Lt A. Roberts, Sgt D. Payne, Cpl W. J. Collings, Pte W. Lewis, Cpl A. Fisher, Pte D. Goulding, Pte T. Northgraves, Sgt G. T. Smith, Pte J. Rainford, Pte S. Black, Pte W. Oldham, Sgt S. Masterton, Pte K. Park, Pte E. Newport. 7th (Galloway) Battalion King's Own Scottish Borderers: L/Cpl T. Lester, Lt. C. Doig, L/Cpl F. Berry, Lt M.L. Kaufmann, Maj G. M. Dinwiddie, Cpl F. P. Rhodes. Capt G. C. Gourlay, L/Cpl S. Livesey, Sgt G. Barton, Pte J. McNaught, Cpl E. Standring, Pte H. W. Turner, Sgt G. Nattrass, L/Cpl S. R. G. Nunn, Maj G. W. Steer, Cpl A. H. Brown.

The Glider Pilot Regiment, A Squadron: S/Sgt D.G. Houghton, S/Sgt W. Blanthorn. B Squadron: Sgt A. Rigby, S/Sgt C.R. Watkinson. S/Sgt R.A. Howard, Sgt G. Freeman, Sgt R.C. Long, Sgt B. Renard, S/Sgt A. Richards, S/Sgt A. Baldwin, C Squadron: Sgt S. Dadd, S/Sgt L. Wright, Sgt J. Taziker. S/Sgt M.W. Wicks, G Squadron; S/Sgt P.B. Withnall, S/Sgt C.E. King, Sgt H.H. Rathband, S/Sgt N. Brown, S/Sgt L.J. Minall, Lt M.D.K. Dauncey, Sgt P. Bryant, Sgt K. Travis-Davidson. D Squadron: Sgt T. Pearce. Sgt R. Hatch, E Squadron: S/Sgt H.N.I. Andrews, Sgt P. Senior, S/Sgt R.S. Wade, Sgt B.A. Tomblin, F Squadron; S/Sgt W. Holcroft, Sgt P. Gammon, S/Sgt T.R. Moore, Sgt A.R. Williams, S/Sgt F. Sullivan, WOII SSM I.J. Blackwood.

4th Parachute Brigade HQ: L/Cpl J. Hughes RASC. 11th Parachute Battalion: Maj D.R.W. Webber, Pte R.G. Baldwin, Pte A. Newell, Pte J.J. Bosley, Pte D.J. Ford, WOII RQMS D.B. Morris. Lt K.F. Bell, CQMS E.E. Cox, Pte A. McQuillian. 10th Parachute Battalion: Pte A.E. Wilmott, Pte R. O'Dwyer, Lt B. Carr, Pte L.W. Baal, Pte N.H. Dicken, Cpl F.A.V. Jenkins, Pte J. Stillwell, Pte F.D. Jackson, Pte P. Banks, Sgt A. Spring. Sgt J. Sunley, Rev R. Bowers, Pte P. Ashberry. Pte T. Barnett, Pte R.A. Anderson, Lt M.H. Broadway, Capt B.B. Clegg, Pte R. Cockayne, Pte J. Fennah, L/Cpl W.R. Newman. 156 Parachute Battalion: Sgt J.B. Borthwick, Pte D.N. Dagwell, L/Cpl K. Scott-Phillips, Rev A.C.V. Menzies, Maj R.L.J. Pott, Capt T. Wainwright, Pte W. Grounsell, Lt J.F. Noble, Pte R.A. Atkinson, Pte H. Boardman, L/Cpl J.J. O'Reiley, Lt Hon P. St. Aubyn, Pte C.B. Budibent, Sgt S.H. Cooper, L/Cpl P.J. McAlindon, CQMS W.G. Fillingham, Pte N. Rawlings, Lt R. Adams, Cpl F. Thompson, Cpl J.T. Keenan, Pte G.F.G. Jessop, Pte J.N. Green, L/Cpl K. Gibbings, Lt M.A. Wenner, Cpl W. Moorcroft, Pte F. Eggleton, Capt J.E. Buck, Sgt G.A. Humphreys.

2nd (Oban) Airlanding Anti-Tank Battery, Royal Artillery: Maj A.F. Haynes. Lt G.A. Paull, Gnr T. Henney. Lt Bill MacInnes, Gnr L. Clarke, Gnr C. Pavey. 250 (Airborne) Light Composite Company RASC: Dvr J.W. Prime, Dvr K.W. Clarke, Dvr J. Staples, Dvr J.A. Taylor, Dvr S. Brown, Dvr W.H. Chedgey, Dvr H.E. Roscorla, Dvr. G. Hutchinson, Dvr K. Barnard.

4th Parachute Squadron, Royal Engineers: Spr J. O'Donnell. 9th Field Company, Royal Engineers: Sgt J.W. Denning. Polish 1st Independent Parachute Brigade: 3rd Battalion: Sgt L.A. Kurzweil.

United States Army Air Force
315th Troop Carrier Group: 2nd Lt E.S. Fulmer, 2nd Lt R.L. Cloer, Lt C.D. Dawkins, Col W.L. Brinson.

Royal Air Force

75 NZ Squadron: J. Glendenning. 19 Squadron: F/L E.S. Hughes. 315 (Polish)Squadron: F/L S.J. Blok. 64 Squadron: F/Lt A.G.H. Cooper. 80,274,501 Squadrons: W/Ldr J. Wray. 165 Squadron: F/Lt S.R. Chambers. 196 Squadron: F/Sgt M.D. Stimson, Sgt E.F. Chandler, F/Sgt J.P. Averill. F/Sgt J.W.Hill.299 Squadron: F/O H. Reek, F/Sgt L.W. Brock. 575 Squadron: F/O W.T. Player, F/O E.F. Brown. 512 Squadron: F/O R.J. Cole, F/Lt J.C.P. Thomas. 295 Squadron: F/O D.W. Thomas, 190 Squadron: F/O R. Lawton. 298 Squadron: F/Sgt W.R.Florence.644 Squadron: F/Sgt J.P. Grant.

XXX Corps Ground Forces

43 Wessex Division, 130 Infantry Brigade:4th Battalion, Dorset Regiment: Captain R.F. Hall. 260 Field Company, Royal Engineers: Sgt R. Hunt, Spr C. Hulbert, L/Sgt J. Wood, L/Sgt S.C.S. Helsdon. 553 Field Company, Royal Engineers: Sgt F.J. Petrie. 64th Medium Regiment, Royal Artillery: Colonel H.S. Hunt.

Primary Contributory Account Sources

Correspondence with the editor (CWE) date
Audio recording (AR) date

Volume 1

Chapter 1

Major Martin Willcock, Parachute Regiment, Airborne Control Officer, RAF Station Harwell, (CWE 1987)
Private Fred 'Rad' Radley, Signaller, A Coy, 3rd Parachute Battalion, 1st Parachute Brigade, (CWE 1983–1991)
Corporal Alex Whitelaw, HQ Company, 3rd Parachute Battalion, 1st Parachute Brigade, (CWE 1985)
Lance Corporal B.J.G. 'Bert' Stidson, B Company, 3rd Parachute Battalion, 1st Parachute Brigade, (CWE 1983)
Lance Corporal Tom Halley-Frame, B Company, 3rd Parachute Battalion, 1st Parachute Brigade, (CWE 1983)
Private Bill Collard, 5 Platoon, B Company, 3rd Parachute Battalion, 1st Parachute Brigade, (CWE 1983)
Private Les Harrison, Intelligence Section, HQ, 3rd Parachute Battalion, 1st Parachute Brigade, (CWE 1983)
Lieutenant Len Wright, Commanding Officer, 9 Platoon, C Company, 3rd Parachute Battalion, 1st Parachute Brigade, (CWE 1992)
Sergeant Tommy Battle, Mortar Platoon, HQ Company, 3rd Parachute Battalion, 1st Parachute Brigade, (AR 1983)
Sergeant Harry Callaghan, HQ Company, 3rd Parachute Battalion, 1st Parachute Brigade, (AR 1983)
Private Arthur Watson, Signaller, C Company, 3rd Parachute Battalion, 1st Parachute Brigade, (AR 1990)

Chapter 2

Sergeant Gwilym Evans, T Company, 1st Parachute Battalion, 1st Parachute Brigade, (AR 1983)
Private George Hill, 1 Platoon, R Company, 1st Parachute Battalion, 1st Parachute Brigade
Private Ron George, Assault Pioneer Platoon, Headquarter Company, 1st Parachute Battalion, 1st Parachute Brigade, (CWE 1985)
Lieutenant Ben S. Lockett, A Troop, 1st Airlanding Anti-Tank Battery, Royal Artillery, (CWE 1992)
Lieutenant G. Ryall, Liaison Officer, 1st Airlanding Anti-Tank Battery, Royal Artillery, (CWE 1991)
Gunner E.H. Barnsley, D Troop, 1st Airlanding, Anti-Tank Battery, Royal Artillery, (CWE 1992)
Corporal Geoff Stanners, Royal Army Medical Corps, 16th Parachute Field Ambulance, R Company, 1st Parachute Battalion, 1st Parachute Brigade, (CWE 1983)
Lieutenant Tony V. Driver, Troop Leader, E Troop, 3 Battery, 1st Airlanding Light Regiment, Royal Artillery, (CWE 1989)
Private V. Boast, 4 Platoon, B Company, 2nd Parachute Battalion, 1st Parachute Brigade, (CWE 1987)
Private Vince Goodwin, B Company, 2nd Parachute Battalion, 1st Parachute Brigade, (CWE 1986)
Private Jack Beeston, Anti-Tank Platoon, Support Company, 2nd Parachute Battalion, 1st Parachute Brigade, (CWE 1986)
Private George McCarthy, Headquarters Company, 2nd Parachute Battalion, 1st Parachute Brigade, (CWE 1986)
Private Bert 'Tich' Orrell, Royal Army Medical Corps, 16th Parachute Field Ambulance, 2nd Parachute Battalion, 1st Parachute Brigade, (CWE 1986)
Major Cedric J. Longland, Specialist Surgeon, Royal Army Medical Corps, 16th Parachute Field Ambulance, 1st Parachute Brigade, (CWE 1985)

Chapter 3

Private Ted Mordecai, 1st Airborne Division Ordnance Field Park, Royal Army Ordnance Corps, (CWE 1983)
Major Dennis S. Munford, Commanding Officer, 3 Battery, 1st Airlanding Light Regiment, Royal Artillery, (CWE 1989)
Bombardier J. Leo Hall, i/c E Troop Signals, 3 Battery, 1st Airlanding Light Regiment, Royal Artillery, (CWE 1992)
Sergeant Norman Swift, A Troop, 1st Parachute Squadron, Royal Engineers, (CWE 1992)
Corporal Dave Thomas, A Troop, 1st Parachute Squadron, Royal Engineers, (CWE 1992)
Sapper F.A. Woods, A Troop, 1st Parachute Squadron, Royal Engineers, (CWE 1992)
Corporal John F. Humphreys, B Troop, 1st Parachute Squadron, Royal Engineers, (CWE 1992)
Lance Sergeant Harold Padfield, B Troop, 1st Parachute Squadron, Royal Engineers, (CWE 1992)
Sapper Les Plummer, C Troop, 1st Parachute Squadron, Royal Engineers, (CWE 1992)
Sapper Tom Hicks, C Troop, 1st Parachute Squadron, Royal Engineers, (CWE 1992)

Chapter 4

Lance Sergeant Mervyn J. Potter, 261 Field Park Company, Royal Engineers, (CWE 1992)
Lance Corporal Ken L. Underwood, No. 3 Detachment, 261 Field Park Company, Royal Engineers, (CWE 1992)
Private Vic Holden, Defence Platoon, Headquarters, 1st Airborne Division, (CWE 1983)
Craftsmen Joe R. Roberts, Advance Workshop Detachment, Royal Electrical and Mechanical Engineers, (CWE 1983)

Chapter 5

Sergeant Ernie Shelswell, i/c 6-pdr 'Blighty' No. 2, B Troop, 1st Airlanding Anti-Tank Battery, Royal Artillery, (CWE 1992)
Sergeant Arthur Rigby, 19 Flight, B Squadron, No. 1 Wing, The Glider Pilot Regiment, (CWE 1991)
Sergeant Cyril Robson, No. 4 Gun, C Troop, 1st Airlanding Anti-Tank Battery, Royal Artillery, (CWE Permission R. Cook 1992)
Driver Eric Milner, No. 1 Gun, C Troop, 1st Airlanding Anti-Tank Battery, Royal Artillery, (CWE 1991)
Lieutenant E.E. 'Ted' Shaw, Commanding Officer, C Troop, 1st Airlanding Anti-Tank Battery, Royal Artillery, (CWE 1992)
Gunner Ralph Cook, No. 3 Gun, C Troop, 1st Airlanding Anti-Tank Battery, Royal Artillery, (CWE 1992)
Gunner E.T. Burridge, P Troop, 1st Airlanding Anti-Tank Battery, Royal Artillery, (CWE 1992)
Gunner F. John Winser, D Troop, 1st Airlanding, Anti-Tank Battery, Royal Artillery, (CWE, AR 1992)

Volume 2

Chapter 6

Lieutenant Hugh H.L. Cartwright, Commanding Officer, Signals Platoon, HQ Company, 2nd Battalion, South Staffordshire Regiment, 1st Airlanding Brigade, (AR 1989)
Private Arthur Harvey, Signals Platoon, 2nd Battalion, South Staffordshire Regiment,1st Airlanding Brigade, (CWE 1989)
Sergeant Albert Cook, 20 Platoon, D Company, 2nd Battalion, South Staffordshire Regiment, 1st Airlanding Brigade, (CWE 1989)
Lieutenant Charles J. MacDonnell, No. 1 Medium Machine Gun Platoon, S Company, 2nd Battalion, South Staffordshire Regiment, 1st Airlanding Brigade, (CWE 1989)
Private Daniel White, No. 2 Medium Machine Gun Platoon, S Company, 2nd Battalion, South Staffordshire Regiment, 1st Airlanding Brigade, (CWE 1989)
Lance Corporal Harry Smith, S Company, 2nd Battalion, South Staffordshire Regiment, 1st Airlanding Brigade, (CWE 1990)
Sergeant Norman Howes, 10 Platoon, A Company, 2nd Battalion, South Staffordshire Regiment, 1st Airlanding Brigade, (CWE 1989)

PRIMARY CONTRIBUTORY ACCOUNT SOURCES 441

Private 'Monty' Faulkner, Signaller, D Company, 2nd Battalion, South Staffordshire Regiment, 1st Airlanding Brigade, (CWE 1989)
Private Reg Tyrer, M.M., 15 Platoon, C Company, 2nd Battalion, South Staffordshire Regiment, 1st Airlanding Brigade, (CWE 1989)
Sergeant Harry Dalton, 11 Platoon, B Company. 2nd Battalion, South Staffordshire Regiment, 1st Airlanding Brigade, (CWE 1989)
Lance Sergeant Jim Gaunt, Signaller, Battalion HQ, 2nd Battalion, South Staffordshire Regiment, 1st Airlanding Brigade, (AR 1989)
Corporal George Aldred, Royal Army Medical Corps, HQ Surgical Team, 181 Airlanding Field Ambulance, 1st Airlanding Brigade, (AR 1991)

Chapter 7

Lieutenant Joe S.D. Hardy, Commanding Officer, Signals Platoon, 1st Battalion The Border Regiment, 1st Airlanding Brigade, (CWE 1990)
Corporal Ian Hunter, No. 1 Section, 14 Platoon, B Company, 1st Battalion The Border Regiment, 1st Airlanding Brigade, (CWE 1985)
Lieutenant Arthur R. Royall, Commanding Officer,12 Platoon, B Company, 1st Battalion The Border Regiment, 1st Airlanding Brigade, (CWE 1991)
Lieutenant W. P. 'Pat' Stott, Second in Command, B Company, 1st Battalion, The Border Regiment, 1st Airlanding Brigade, (CWE 1991)
Private E.J. 'Johnny' Peters, Sniper, 14 Platoon, B Company, 1st Battalion, The Border Regiment, 1st Airlanding Brigade, (CWE 1990)
Corporal Cyril Crickett, Scout Section, 13 Platoon, B Company, 1st Battalion, The Border Regiment, 1st Airlanding Brigade, (CWE 1983)
Private John Ranger, 20 Platoon, D Company. 1st Battalion, The Border Regiment, 1st Airlanding Brigade, (CWE 1990)
Private Fred A. Hodges, 20 Platoon, D Company,1st Battalion, The Border Regiment, 1st Airlanding Brigade, (CWE 1990)
Private Ron Graydon, Signaller, HQ Company, Attached to 19 Platoon, D Company, 1st Battalion, The Border Regiment, 1st Airlanding Brigade, (CWE 1990)
Private Len Powell, Batman, 20 Platoon, D Company, 1st Battalion, The Border Regiment, 1st Airlanding Brigade, (CWE 1990)
Lieutenant Alan Roberts, Commanding Officer, 15 Platoon, C Company, 1st Battalion, The Border Regiment, 1st Airlanding Brigade, (CWE 1990)
Sergeant Dougie Payne, 17 Platoon, C Company, 1st Battalion, The Border Regiment, 1st Airlanding Brigade, (CWE 1991)
Corporal Walter J. Collings, 1 Section, 10 Platoon, A Company, 1st Battalion, The Border Regiment, 1st Airlanding Brigade, (CWE 1990)
Private Bill Lewis, Scout Section, 8 Platoon, A Company, 1st Battalion, The Border Regiment, 1st Airlanding Brigade, (CWE 1990)
Lieutenant Tom R. Barron, Gun Position Officer, A Troop, 1 Battery, 1st Airlanding Light Regiment, Royal Artillery, (CWE 1989)

Chapter 8

Staff Sergeant 'Wally' Holcroft, 14 Flight, F Squadron, No. 2 Wing, The Glider Pilot Regiment, (CWE Permission J. Concannon 1991)
Sergeant Peter Gammon, 14 Flight, F Squadron, No. 2 Wing, The Glider Pilot Regiment, (CWE 1991)
Staff Sergeant Tommy R. Moore, MM, 14 Flight, F Squadron, No. 2 Wing, The Glider Pilot Regiment, (AR 1991)
Private Tom Lester, A Company, 7th (Galloway) Battalion, The King's Own Scottish Borderers, 1st Airlanding Brigade, (CWE 1991)
Lieutenant Charles Doig, Commanding Officer, 7 Platoon, B Company, 7th (Galloway) Battalion, The King's Own Scottish Borderers, 1st Airlanding Brigade, (CWE 1991)
Lance Corporal O'Neill F. Berry, 7 Platoon, B Company, 7th (Galloway) Battalion, The King's Own Scottish Borderers, 1st Airlanding Brigade, (CWE 1991)
Lieutenant Martin. L. Kaufmann, CDN 167, Commanding Officer, 11 Platoon, C Company, 7th (Galloway) Battalion, The King's Own Scottish Borderers, 1st Airlanding Brigade, (CWE 1991)
Major Gordon M. Dinwiddie, Commanding Officer, C Company, 7th (Galloway) Battalion, The King's Own Scottish Borderers, 1st Airlanding Brigade, (CWE 1991)
Corporal Fred P. Rhodes, 10 Platoon, C Company, 7th (Galloway) Battalion, The King's Own Scottish Borderers, 1st Airlanding Brigade, (CWE 1991)
Captain George C. Gourlay, Second in Command, D Company, 7th (Galloway) Battalion, The King's Own Scottish Borderers, 1st Airlanding Brigade, (CWE 1991)
Lance Corporal Stan Livesey, No. 1 Detachment, No. 1 Platoon, S Company, 7th (Galloway) Battalion, The King's Own Scottish Borderers, 1st Airlanding Brigade, (CWE 1991)
Sergeant George Barton, No. 2 Anti-Tank Platoon, S Company, 7th (Galloway) Battalion, The King's Own Scottish Borderers, 1st Airlanding Brigade, (CWE 1991)
Captain J.W. Walker, Troop Commander, B Troop, 1 Battery, 1st Airlanding Light Regiment, Royal Artillery, (CWE 1988)
Staff Sergeant H.N.I. 'Andy' Andrews, 11 Flight, E Squadron, No. 2 Wing, The Glider Pilot Regiment, (CWE 1991)
Sergeant Paddy Senior, 11 Flight, E Squadron, No. 2 Wing, The Glider Pilot Regiment, (CWE 1991)

Chapter 9

Major Dan R.W. Webber, Headquarters Company, 11th Parachute Battalion, 4th Parachute Brigade, (CWE 1991)
Private Ron 'Taffy' Baldwin, Mortar Platoon, S Company, 11th Parachute Battalion, 4th Parachute Brigade, (CWE 1989)
Private Albert Newell, 8 Platoon, B Company, 11th Parachute Battalion, 4th Parachute Brigade, (CWE 1989)
Private John Bosley, Intelligence Section, Headquarters Company, 11th Parachute Battalion, 4th Parachute Brigade, (CWE 1989)

PRIMARY CONTRIBUTORY ACCOUNT SOURCES 443

Private Douglas Ford, No. 1 Section, No. 1 Platoon, A Company, 11th Parachute Battalion, 4th Parachute Brigade, (CWE 1989)
Regimental Quartermaster Sergeant David B. Morris, Headquarters Company, 11th Parachute Battalion, 4th Parachute Brigade, (CWE 1989)

Chapter 10

Lieutenant Brian Carr, Transport Officer (M.T.O.), Headquarters Company, 10th Parachute Battalion, 4th Parachute Brigade, (CWE 1990)
Private Lloyd W. 'Busty' Baal, Intelligence Section, Headquarters Company, 10th Parachute Battalion, 4th Parachute Brigade, (CWE 1990)
Private Norman H. 'Lofty' Dicken, Intelligence Section, Headquarters Company, 10th Parachute Battalion, 4th Parachute Brigade, (CWE 1991)
Corporal Fred A.V. 'Jenks' Jenkins, Intelligence Section, Headquarters Company, 10th Parachute Battalion, 4th Parachute Brigade, (CWE 1990)
Private John Stillwell, Bren Gunner, No. 1 Section, No. 3 Platoon, A Company, 10th Parachute Battalion, 4th Parachute Brigade, (CWE 1990)
Private Fred D. 'Jacko' Jackson, No. 3 Platoon, A Company, 10th Parachute Battalion, 4th Parachute Brigade, (CWE 1990)
Private Philip Banks, Signaller HQ Company, Attached S Company, 10th Parachute Battalion, 4th Parachute Brigade, (AR 1990)
Private Richard O'Dwyer, A Company, 10th Parachute Battalion, 4th Parachute Brigade, (AR 1991)
2nd Lieutenant Edward S. Fulmer, 43rd Troop Carrier Squadron, 315th Troop Carrier Group, United States Army Air Corps, (CWE 1991)
Sergeant Albert Spring, B Company, 10th Parachute Battalion, 4th Parachute Brigade, (CWE, AR 1991)
Staff Sergeant Arthur Russell, Royal Army Medical Corps, B Section, 133 Parachute Field Ambulance, 4th Parachute Brigade, (CWE 1992)
Private Ken Webster, Royal Army Medical Corps, B Section, 133 Parachute Field Ambulance, 4th Parachute Brigade, (CWE 1983)

Chapter 11

Major A.F. Haynes, Commanding Officer, 2nd (Oban) Airlanding Anti-Tank Battery, Royal Artillery, (AR 1983)
Lieutenant G. A. Paull, Commanding Officer, X Troop 2nd (Oban) Airlanding Anti-Tank Battery, Royal Artillery, (CWE 1983)
Gunner/Driver Tom Henney, X Troop, 2nd (Oban) Airlanding Anti-Tank Battery, Royal Artillery, (CWE 1983)
Staff Sergeant Sid T. Dadd, 14 Flight, C Squadron, No. 2 Wing, The Glider Pilot Regiment, (AR 1991)
Sergeant Tom W. Pearce, 5 Flight, D Squadron, No. 1 Wing, The Glider Pilot Regiment, (CWE 1991)

Volume 3

Chapter 12

Driver John W. Prime, Number 2 Parachute Platoon, 250 (Airborne) Light Composite Company, Royal Army Service Corps Attached 4th Parachute Brigade, (CWE 1991)

Driver K.W. Clarke, Number 2 Parachute Platoon, 250 (Airborne) Light Composite Company, Royal Army Service Corps Attached 4th Parachute Brigade, (CWE 1990)

Driver John Staples, Number 1 Parachute Platoon, Jeep Section, 250 (Airborne) Light Composite Company, Royal Army Service Corps, (CWE 1990)

Driver J.A. Taylor, Number 1 Parachute Platoon, 250 (Airborne) Light Composite Company, Royal Army Service Corps, (CWE 1990)

Lance Corporal John Hughes, Royal Army Service Corps, BRASCO's Clerk, 4th Parachute Brigade HQ, (CWE G. Lamb-Hughes 1990–2018)

Chapter 13

Sergeant Jock Borthwick, 11 Platoon, C Company, 156 Parachute Battalion, 4th Parachute Brigade, (AR CWE 1990)

Private David N. Dagwell, Quartermasters Section, Headquarters Company, 156 Parachute Battalion, 4th Parachute Brigade, (CWE 1990)

Lance Corporal Ken Scott-Phillips, Headquarters Company, 156 Parachute Battalion, 4th Parachute Brigade, (CWE 1983)

Reverend Alistair C.V. Menzies, Royal Army Chaplains Department, Headquarters Company, 156 Parachute Battalion, 4th Parachute Brigade, (CWE 1990)

Major R.L. John Pott, Commanding Officer, A Company, 156 Parachute Battalion, 4th Parachute Brigade, (CWE 1990)

Captain Tom Wainwright, Commanding Officer, S Company, 156 Parachute Battalion, 4th Parachute Brigade, (CWE 1990)

Lieutenant Ronald Adams, Commanding Officer, Mortar Platoon, S Company, 156 Parachute Battalion, 4th Parachute Brigade, (CWE, AR 1990)

Private Bill Grounsell, No. 1 Section, Medium Machine Gun Platoon, S Company, 156 Parachute Battalion, 4th Parachute Brigade, (CWE 1990)

Lieutenant Jeff F. Noble, Commanding Officer, Medium Machine Gun Platoon, S Company, 156 Parachute Battalion, 4th Parachute Brigade, (CWE 1989)

Private Ronald A. Atkinson, 8 Platoon, B Company, 156 Parachute Battalion, 4th Parachute Brigade, (CWE 1990)

Sapper J. O'Donnell, 4th Parachute Squadron, Royal Engineers, 4th Parachute Brigade, (CWE 1992)

PRIMARY CONTRIBUTORY ACCOUNT SOURCES

Chapter 14

Lieutenant Roy Staddon, Troop Leader, A Troop, 1 Battery, 1st Airlanding Light Regiment, Royal Artillery, (CWE 1990)

Sergeant Bob McLeod, C Sub, A Troop, 1 Battery, 1st Airlanding Light Regiment, Royal Artillery, (CWE 1989)

Gunner Frederick (Dicky) Bird, D Troop Observation Post, 2 Battery, 1st Airlanding Light Regiment, Royal Artillery, (CWE 1994)

Gunner Driver Eric W. Mills, D Troop, 2 Battery, 1st Airlanding Light Regiment, Royal Artillery, (CWE 1988)

Lieutenant Noel F. Farrands, Gun Position Officer, E Troop, 3 Battery, 1st Airlanding Light Regiment, Royal Artillery, (CWE 1989)

Sergeant David C. Hardie, No. 4 Gun, E Troop, 3 Battery, 1st Airlanding Light Regiment, Royal Artillery, (CWE 1993)

Battery Sergeant Major Tom W. Kent, F Troop, 3 Battery, 1st Airlanding Light Regiment, Royal Artillery, (CWE Mrs E. Kent 1989)

Staff Sergeant C. Ron Watkinson, B Squadron, No. 1 Wing, The Glider Pilot Regiment, (CWE 1991)

Chapter 15

Sergeant Norman S. Patten, Signals Operator, No. 1 Forward Observation Unit, Royal Artillery, (CWE 1989)

Gunner (Driver/Operator) Austin 'Pat' Brearton, No. 1 Forward Observation Unit, Royal Artillery, (CRE 1991)

Bombardier (Driver/Operator) W.F. Wrigley, No. 1 Forward Observation Unit, Royal Artillery, (CWE 1988)

Gunner (Driver/Operator) Rupert C. Kift, No. 1 Forward Observation Unit, Royal Artillery, (CWE 1988)

Captain C.W. Ikin, No. 1 Forward Observation Unit, Royal Artillery, (CWE 1989)

Staff Sergeant Len Wright, C Squadron, No. 2 Wing, Glider Pilot Regiment, (CWE 1991)

Sergeant John 'Jack' Taziker, C Squadron, No. 2 Wing, Glider Pilot Regiment, (CWE Permission Mrs V. Taziker 1991)

Colonel H.S. Hunt, CO, 64th Medium Regiment, Royal Artillery, 43rd Wessex Division, XXX Corps, (CWE J. Jordan, 64 Med Regt RA Regt Association, 1989)

Chapter 16

Sergeant Kenneth Travis Davison, 10 Flight, G Squadron, No. 1 Wing, The Glider Pilot Regiment, (CWE 1991)

Staff Sergeant William 'Bill' Blanthorn, A Squadron, No. 1 Wing, The Glider Pilot Regiment, (CWE 1991)

Sergeant L.A. Kurzweil, 3rd Polish Parachute Battalion, Polish 1st Independent Parachute Brigade, (CWE 1983)

Lieutenant Cecil Dawkins, 310th Troop Carrier Squadron, 315th Troop Carrier Group, United States Army Air Corps, (CWE R.L. Cloer 1990)

Captain R.F. Hall MC, Second in Command, C Company, 4th Battalion, The Dorset Regiment, 130 Infantry Brigade, 43rd Wessex Division, XXX Corps, (CWE 1989)

Chapter 17

Flight Lieutenant Tony G.H. Cooper, Deputy Squadron Commander, 64 Squadron, 11 Group, Royal Air Force, (CWE 1991)
Wing Leader John Wray, Nos. 80, 274 and 501 Squadrons, 11 Group, Royal Air Force, (CWE 1990)
Flight Sergeant Mike 'Taff' D. Stimson, Wireless Operator, 196 Squadron, 38 Group, Royal Air Force, (CWE 1991)
Sergeant E.F. 'Ted' Chandler, Flight Engineer, 196 Squadron, 38 Group, Royal Air Force, (CWE 1990)
Flight Sergeant J. Peter Averill, Pilot, 196 Squadron, 38 Group, Royal Air Force, (AR M.D. Stimson 1991, Averill 2018)
Flying Officer Harry Reek, Observer, 299 Squadron, 38 Group, Royal Air Force, (CWE 1987)
Flying Officer W.T. Player, Pilot, 575 Squadron, 46 Group, Royal Air Force, (CWE 1990)
Flying Officer Edwin F. Brown, Pilot, 575 Squadron, 46 Group, Royal Air Force, (CWE 1987)
Flying Officer Reg J. Cole, Navigator, 512 Squadron, 46 Group, Royal Air Force, (CWE 1991)
Flight Lieutenant J. Courtenay P. Thomas, Pilot, 512 Squadron, 46 Group, Royal Air Force, (CWE 1991)
Flying Officer David W. Thomas, Navigator, 295 Squadron, 38 Group, Royal Air Force, (CWE 1990)

Chapter 18

Sergeant Fred J. Petrie, No. 1 Platoon, 553 Field Company, Royal Engineers, 43rd Wessex Division, XXX Corps, (CWE 1992)
Sergeant Rex Hunt, No. 1 Platoon, 260 Field Company, Royal Engineers, 43rd Wessex Division, XXX Corps, (CWE 1992)
Lance Sergeant S.C.S. Helsdon, No. 2 Platoon, 260 Field Company, Royal Engineers, 43rd Wessex Division, XXX Corps, (CWE 1992)

Bibliography

Published Sources

Aalbers, P.G., *Slag Om Arnhem* (Bibliografie van Gedrukte Werken, Bibliotheek Arnhem, 1975)
Air Ministry, January 1944, *Pilot's Notes for Horsa I Glider* (Air Data Publications)
Alford, Richard, *To Revel in God's Sunshine, The Story of RSM J.C. Lord, MVO, MBE* (Cumbria: Richard Alford, 1981)
Angus, Tom, *Men at Arnhem* (London: Leo Cooper, 1976)
Anker, Marcel, *The Lost Company, C Company 2nd Parachute Battalion in Oosterbeek & Arnhem September 1944* (Maca Publishing, 2017)
Arnhem September 1944 (Arnhem: Gemeentearchief, 1969)
Arthur, Max, *Men of the Red Beret*, (London: Hutchinson & Co Ltd, 1990)
Ayrton, Maj. M. McI, *6th Field Force Headquarters & Signal Squadron, 1941–1979* (Fleet, Hampshire: Mayfleet Printers, 1980)
Badsey, Stephen, *Arnhem 1944 Operation Market Garden* (Oxford: Osprey Military, 1993)
Bankhead, Harry, *Salute To The Steadfast* (Ramsay Press, 1998)
Bauer, Cornelis, *The Battle of Arnhem* (New York: Stein and Day, 1967)
Baynes, John, *Urquhart of Arnhem* (London: Brassey's, 1993)
Bennett, David, *A Magnificent Disaster* (Oxford: Casemate, 2008)
Bernage, Georges, *Le Pont D'Arnhem* (Bayeux: Heimdal, 1977)
Boeree, Lt Col Theodoor Alexander, *Een Libellus Amicorum* (Zutphen: Walburg Pers, 1967)
Boersma, Wybo & Reinders, Philip, *US Air Support Signal Teams* (2016)
Brammall, R, *The Tenth* (Ipswich: Eastgate Press Ltd, 1965)
Brinson, W.L., *Three One Five Group* (Copple House, 1984)
By Air To Battle: The Official Account of the British First and Sixth Airborne Divisions (London: HMSO 1945)
Buggenum, David G. van, *B Company Arrived* (Renkum, The Netherlands: R.N. Sigmond Publishing, 2003)
Buggenum, David G. van, *B Company Arrived The Men* (D. van Buggenum Publishing, 2016)
Buist, Luuk; Reinders, Philip; Maassen, Geert, *The Royal Air Force at Arnhem* (Society of Friends of the Airborne Museum, 2005)
Buxton, David, *Honour to the Airborne* (Solihull: Elmdon, 1985)
Carling, Hugh, *Not Many Of Us Left* (Hailsham: J & K H Publishing, 1997)
Chatterton, Brig. George, *The Wings of Pegasus* (London: Macdonald, 1962)
Cherry, Niall, *With Nothing Bigger Than a Bren Gun* (Taunton: Brendon Publishing, 2007)
Cherry, Niall, *Red Berets and Red Crosses* (Taunton: Brendon Publishing, 1998)

Cherry, Niall, *Arnhem Surgeon* (Taunton: Brendon Publishing, 2010)
Colls, Doug, *As You Were–September 1944, 1st Airlanding Anti-Tank Battery RA* (Redcar, 1989)
Cole, Howard, *On Wings of Healing, The Story of the Airborne Medical Services 1940–1960* (London: W. Blackwood & Sons, 1963)
Cooper, Alan, *Air Battle For Arnhem* (London: Leo Cooper, 2012)
Cholewczynski, George. F., *Poles Apart* (Sarpedon, New York: Greenhill Books, 1993)
Cholewczynski, George. F., *De Polen van Driel* (Narden, The Netherlands: Lunet, 1989)
CRE British Army of the Rhine, Royal Engineers Battlefield Tour, The Seine to the Rhine. Vols 1 & 2. (Uckfield, Sussex: The Naval and Military Press, originally published 1947)
Cummings, Colin, *Arnhem Sacrifice* (Halifax, Nova Scotia: Nimbus Publishing, 1998)
Curtis, Reg, *Churchill's Volunteer* (London: Avon Books, 1994)
Curtis, Simon; Cherry, Niall & Howes, John, *Four Days At Arnhem* (Taunton: Brendon Publishing, 2016)
Dank, Milton, *The Glider Gang* (London: Cassell Ltd, 1977)
Deane-Drummond, Anthony, *Return Ticket* (London: Collins 1953
Deane-Drummond, Anthony, *Arrows of Fortune* (London: Leo Cooper, 1992)
Dear, Ian, *Ten Commando 1942–1945* (London: Leo Cooper, 1987)
Dicken, Harry, with Niall Cherry and Arjan Vrieze, *An Arnhem Diary* (Taunton: Brendon Publishing, 2018)
Dover, Maj. Victor, *The Sky Generals*, (London: Cassell, 1981)
Dover, Maj. Victor, *The Silken Canopy*, (London: Cassell, 1979)
Duyts, W.J.M., & Groeneweg, A, *The Harvest of Ten Years* (Airborne Museum Hartenstein, 1988)
Eastwood, Stuart; Gray, Charles & Green, Alan, *When Dragons Flew, An Illustrated History of the 1st Battalion The Border Regiment 1939–45,* (Horncastle: Silver Link Publishing, 1994)
Ellis, Major L.F., *Victory in the West* (London: HMSO, 1962)
Essame, Maj-Gen. H, *The 43rd Wessex Division At War 1944–1945* (London: William Clowes & Sons, 1952)
Evans, Martin Marix; Boersma, Wybo & Groeneweg, Adrian, *The Battle for Arnhem* (London: Pitkin Guide, 1998)
Fairley, John, *Remember Arnhem, The Story of the Airborne Reconnaissance Squadron at Arnhem* (Bearsden, Glasgow: Peaton Press, 1978)
Faulkner-Brown, Harry, *A Sapper at Arnhem* (H. Faulkner-Brown, 2006)
Farrar-Hockley, Anthony, *Airborne Carpet – Operation Market Garden* (London: Macdonald, 1970)
Firbank, Thomas, *I Bought A Star* (White Lion, 1973)
Florentin, Eddy, *The Battle of the Falaise Gap* (Elek Books, 1965)
Franks, Norman, *Typhoon Attack* (Pennsylvania, USA: Stackpole Books, 2010)
Frost, Maj-Gen, John, *A Drop Too Many* (London: Cassell, 1980)
Frost, Maj-Gen, John, *Nearly There* (London: Leo Cooper, 1991)
Frost, Maj-Gen, John,' Arnhem: Where the Blame Lay' (*Soldier Magazine*, July 1990)
Furbringer, Herbert, *9.SS Panzer Division Hohenstaufen, 1944; Normandie, Tarnopol-Arnhem* (Bayeux: Heimdal, 1984)
Gale, General Richard, *Call to Arms* (London: Hutchinson & Co Ltd, 1968)
Gerritsen, Bob, *For No Apparent Reason* (Renkum, The Netherlands: R.N. Sigmond Publishing, 2000)
Gerritsen, Bob, & Revell, Scott, *Retake Arnhem Bridge* (Renkum, The Netherlands: R.N. Sigmond Publishing, 2014)

Gerritsen, Bob, *Fighting The British At Arnhem, The SS Unterführerschule Arnheim* (Renkum, The Netherlands: R.N. Sigmond Publishing, 2018)
Gibson, Ronald, *Nine Days* (A.H. Stockwell, 1956)
Harlan, Glenn & Spezzano, Remy, *Kampfraum Arnheim* (RZM Publishing, 2013)
Golden, Lewis, *Echoes From Arnhem* (London: William Kimber, 1984)
Green, Alan, *1st Battalion The Border Regiment Arnhem* (Kendal: Titus Wilson & Son, 1991)
Green, Peter, *Captured at Arnhem* (Barnsley: Pen & Sword, 2022)
Gunning, Hugh, *Borderers In Battle* (Martins Printing Works, 1948)
Halteren, Paul van, *Roll of Honour, Dedicated to the Memory of the Men of 48 & 49 Air Despatch Groups, R.A.S.C, Who Gave Their Lives During Operation Market Garden 17–26 September 1944* (2008)
Hamilton, Nigel, *Monty. The Field Marshal 1944–1976* (London: Hamish Hamilton, 1986)
Harclerode, Peter, *Arnhem A Tragedy of Errors* (London: Arms & Armour Press, 1994)
Harclerode, Peter, *Para! Fifty Years of the Parachute Regiment* (BCA, 1992)
Hackett, Gen Sir John, *I was a Stranger* (London: Chatto and Windus, 1977)
Hagen, Louis, *Arnhem Lift* (Hammond & Co, 1945)
Have, Jan ten, *The Shutters Were Closed* (Have J. ten, 2018)
Hawston, Peter, *WW2 Allied Gliders* (ISO Publications, 1987)
Heaps, Leo, *The Grey Goose of Arnhem* (London: Weidenfeld & Nicolson, 1976)
Heaps, Leo, *Escape From Arnhem* (London: Macmillan, 1945)
Hees, Arie-Jan van, *Tugs and Gliders To Arnhem* (A.J. van Hees, 2000)
Henniker, Mark, *An Image of War* (London: Leo Cooper, 1987)
Hey, J.A.; Maassen, Geert & Reinders, Philip, *Battle of Arnhem Roll of Honour, 5th Edition* (Oosterbeek: Society of Friends of the Airborne Museum, 2011)
Hibbert, Christopher, *The Battle of Arnhem* (London: Batsford, 1945)
Hilton, Robert, *Freddie Gough's Specials At Arnhem, An Illustrated History of the 1st Airborne Reconnaissance Squadron* (Renkum, The Netherlands: R.N. Sigmond Publishing, 2017)
History of The 2nd Battalion The Parachute Regiment From Its Formation to The Battle Of Arnhem (Aldershot: Gale & Polden, 1946)
Hogg, Ian V, *British and American Artillery of World War Two* (London: Greenhill Books, 2002)
Horrocks, Brian, *Corps Commander* (London: Sidgwick and Jackson, 1977)
Horst, H.B. van der, *Fury Over Arnhem* (Arnhem, 1946)
Howe, John C., *Point Blank Open Sights* (Hough Publishing, 1999)
Iddekinge, P.R.A., *Arnhem September 1944* (Arnhem: Gemeentearchief, 1969)
Jackson, Robert, *Arnhem, The Battle Remembered* (Airlife, 1994)
Jeffson, Maj. J.J., *Operation Market Garden, Ultra Intelligence Ignored* (Buxton: MLRS, 2002)
Johnstone, Ian, *The Arnhem Report* (London: Allen & Co, 1977)
Junier, Alexander; Smulders, Bart & Korsloot, Jaap, *By Land and Sea and Air An Illustrated History of The 2nd Battalion The South Staffordshire Regiment 1940–45* (Renkum, The Netherlands: R.N. Sigmond Publishing, 2003)
Kelly, Frank, *Private Kelly* (London: Evan Brothers Ltd, 1954)
Kent, Ron, *Arnhem Venture* (Derek Duncan, 1996)
Kent, Ron, *First In! Parachute Pathfinder Company* (London: Batsford, 1979)
Kershaw, Robert, *It Never Snows In September* (Crowood Press, 1990)
Kershaw, Robert, *A Street In Arnhem* (London: Ian Allan, 2014)

Kessel, Lipmann, *Surgeon At Arms* (London: Leo Cooper, 1976)
Korthals Altes, A; Margry, K; Thuring, G; Voskuil, Robert, *September 1944 Operation Market Garden* (Fibula-Van Dishoeck, 1984)
Leleu, Jean-Luc, *10.SS Panzer Division Frundsberg* (Bayeux: Heimdal, 1999)
Longson, Jim & Taylor, Christine, *An Arnhem Odyssey* (London: Leo Cooper, 1991)
Lloyd, Alan, *The Gliders*, (London: Leo Cooper, 1982)
Maanen, Anje van, *Tafelberg Field Hospital Diary* (Uitgeverij Kontrast, 2015)
Magry, Karel, *Operation Market Garden Then and Now, Volumes 1 & 2* (London: Battle of Britain International Ltd, 2002)
Macdonald, Charles, *By Air To Battle* (London: Macdonald, 1969)
Mackenzie, Charles, *It Was Like This, 10th Edition* (Oosterbeek: Linders-Adremo, 1977)
Mawson, Stuart, *Arnhem Doctor* (London: Orbis, 1981)
Meel, Rob van, *British Airborne Jeeps 1942–1945 Modifications & Markings* (Groucho Publishing, 2002)
Michie, Allan, *Honour For All* (London: Allen & Unwin, 1946)
Middlebrook, Martin, *Arnhem 1944; The Airborne Battle* (London: Viking Books, 1994)
Miller, Victor, *Nothing Is Impossible* (Staplehurst: Spellmount, 1994)
Milbourne, Andrew, *Lease of Life* (London: Museum Press, 1952)
Mrazek, James E, *The Glider War* (London: Robert Hale & Co, 1975)
Nichol, J.& Rennell, T., *Arnhem The Battle for Survival* (London: Penguin, 2012)
Norton, Geoffrey G, *The Red Devils* (London: Leo Cooper, 1971)
O'Reilly, John, *156 Parachute Battalion From Delhi To Arnhem* (Thoroton Publishing, 2009)
Otway, Lt-Col T.B.H., *Airborne Forces* (London: IWM, 1990)
Packe, Michael, *First Airborne* (London: Secker and Warburg, 1948)
Peatling, Robert, *Without Tradition 2 Para 1941–45* (Robert Peatling, 1994)
Peelen, Th & van Vliet, A.L.J., *Zwevend naar de Dood Arnhem 1944* (Van Holkema & Warendorf, 1977)
Pelkman-Bongers, M.M.H.; van Roekel, C; van Damme-de Groot, A.J., translated by A.G. Meeuwsen, *The Tommies Are Coming* (Oosterbeek: Friends of the Airborne Museum, 1988)
Peters, Martin; Cherry, Niall; Howes, John & Francis, Graham, *Desert Rise-Arnhem Descent, The 10th Parachute Battalion in The Second World War* (Taunton: Brendon Publishing, 2016)
Peters, Mike & Buist, Luuk, *Glider Pilots at Arnhem* (Barnsley: Pen & Sword, 2009)
Piekalkiewicz, Janusz, *Arnhem1944* (London: Ian Allen, 1977)
Pijpers, Gerrit & Truesdale, David, *Arnhem Their Final Battle, The 11thParachute Battalion 1943–44* (Renkum, The Netherlands: R.N. Sigmond Publishing, 2012)
Pinto, Lt. Col. Oreste, *Spycatcher, The Traitor of Arnhem By The Man Who Trapped Him* (T. Werner Laurie, 1955)
Pirt, Asher C.J., *1st British Airborne Division Phantom* (Walmer, 2011)
Powell, Geoffrey, *The Devil's Birthday* (London: Buchan & Enright, 1984)
Pronk, Patrick, *Airborne Engineers, The Shiny 9th* (Renkum, The Netherlands: R.N. Sigmond Publishing, 2001)
Purves, Tom, *The 9th* (T. Purves, 1998)
Ramsey, Winston, *After The Battle, The Battle of Arnhem* (London: Battle of Britain Prints International, 1973)
Reinders, Philip, *Get at Them With The Bayonet. The Story of The 4th Battalion The Dorset Regiment During The Battle of Arnhem September 1944* (NL Books, 2021)
Reinders, Philip, *The 250 (Airborne) Light Composite Company RASC During the Battle of Arnhem September 1944*, (NL Books, 2020)

Revell, Scott, with Niall Cherry, & Bob Gerritson, *Arnhem A Few Vital Hours* (Renkum, The Netherlands: R.N. Sigmond Publishing, 2013)
Reynolds, Michael, *Sons of The Reich II SS Panzer Corps* (Staplehurst: Spellmount, 2002)
Ritchie, Sebastian Dr, Arnhem The Air Reconnaissance Story, Air Historical Branch (RAF) 2015
Roberts, Harry, *Capture at Arnhem* (Windrush Press, 1999)
Roberts, Joe, *With Spanners Descending* (Liverpool: Bluecoat Press, 1996)
Roekel, Chris van, *The Torn Horizon* (Jan & Wendela Ter Horst & C. van Roekel, 1998)
Roekel, Chris van, *Who Was Who During the Battle of Arnhem*, (Oosterbeek: Society of Friends of the Airborne Museum,1992)
Rossiter, Mike, *We Fought At Arnhem* (London: Corgi Books, 2011)
Royal Engineers Battlefield Tour, The Seine to the Rhine (originally published 1947, reprinted by The Naval & Military Press Ltd)
Ryan, Cornelius, *A Bridge Too Far* (London: Hamish Hamilton, 1974)
Saunders, Hilary St G., *The Red Beret* (London: Michael Joseph, 1950)
Saunders, Hilary St G., *By Air To Battle* (London: HMSO, 1945)
Shears, Philip, *The Story of The Border Regiment 1939–1945* (London: Nisbet & Co, 1948)
Sherin, C.H, *Airborne Assault on Holland*, HQ (Army Air Forces, Washington D.C., 1946)
Silz, John, *A Token Force The 261 Field Park Company RE (Airborne) at Arnhem* (Toronto: Travelogue 219, 2015)
Silz, John, *The Storm Boat Kings, The 23rd RCE at Arnhem 1944* (Vanwell Publishing, 2009)
Sims, James, *Arnhem Spearhead* (London: IWM, 1978)
Sigmond, R.N., *Escape Across The Rhine* (Oosterbeek: Airborne Museum, Ooosterbeek, 1999)
Sigmond, R.N., *Nine Days At Arnhem*, (Renkum, The Netherlands: R.N. Sigmond Publishing, 2004)
Sigmond, R.N, *Off At Last*, (Renkum, The Netherlands: R.N. Sigmond Publishing, 1997)
Simpson, Nigel; Raisani, Secander; Reinders, Philip, *Battery A Troop, The First Airlanding Anti-Tank Battery at Arnhem* (NL Books, 2020)
Simpson, Nigel, Raisani, Secander, Reinders, Philip, *Battery B Troop, The First Airlanding Anti-Tank Battery at Arnhem* (NL Books, 2020.)
Simpson, Nigel, Raisani, Secander, Reinders, Philip, *Battery C Troop, The First Airlanding Anti-Tank Battery at Arnhem* (NL Books, 2021)
Simpson, Nigel, Raisani, Secander, Reinders, Philip, Zwarts, Marcel, *Battery D Troop, The First Airlanding Anti-Tank Battery at Arnhem* (NL Books, 2021)
Smyth, Jack, *Five Days In Hell* (London: Kimber, 1956)
Sosabowski, Maj-Gen Stanislaw, *Freely I Served* (London: Kimber, 1960)
Stainforth, Peter, *Wings of the Wind* (London: Falcon, 1954)
Steer, Frank, *Battleground Europe, Market Garden, Arnhem The Landing Grounds & Oosterbeek* (London: Leo Cooper, 2002)
Swiecicki, Marek, *With The Red Devils At Arnhem* (London: Maxlove Publishing, 1945)
Ter Horst, Kate A. *Cloud Over Arnhem* (London: Alan Wingate, 1959)
Thompson, Julian, *Ready for Anything* (London: Weidenfeld & Nicolson, 1989)
Tieke, Wilhelm, Translated from German by Steinhardt, Frederick, *In The Firestorm of The Last Years of The War, II SS PanzerKorps with the 9 & 10 SS Divisions 'Hohenstaufen' & 'Frundsberg'* (J.J. Fedorowicz, 1999)
Toler, I.&.C., *Gliding into War* (Horseshoe Publications, 1998)
Tout, Ken, *In The Shadow of Arnhem* (Stroud: Sutton, 2003)

Truesdale, David, *Brotherhood of the Cauldron* (Redcoat, 2002)
Truesdale, David, & Gijbels, Peter, *Leading The Way To Arnhem, An Illustrated History of the 21st Independent Parachute Company 1942–46* (Renkum, The Netherlands: R.N. Sigmond Publishing, 2008)
Truesdale, David; Cornelissen, Martijn & Gerritsen, Bob, *Arnhem Bridge Target Mike One, An Illustrated History of the 1st Airlanding Light Regiment RA 1942–45* (Renkum, The Netherlands: R.N. Sigmond Publishing, 2015)
Truesdale, David, *Steel Wall, The Destruction of 4 Parachute Brigade 19 September 1944* (Warwick: Helion & Co, 2016)
Truesdale, David; Rea, Paul, P & Barlow, Joseph, *Just Ordinary Men* (Airborne Battle Study Group, 1990)
Tugwell, Maurice, *Airborne to Battle: A History of Airborne Warfare 1918–1971* (London: Kimber, 1971)
Tugwell, Maurice, *Arnhem: A Case Study* (Thornton Cox, 1975)
Turnbull, Jack & Hamblett, John, *The Pegasus Patrol* (Jack Turnbull, 1994)
Urquhart, Brian, *A Life in Peace and War* (London: Weidenfeld & Nicolson, 1987)
Urquhart, Roy, *Arnhem* (London: White Lion, 1973)
Verhoef, C.E.H.J., *The Battle For Ginkel Heath Near Ede* (Aspekt, 2003)
Verhoeff, Wim, Vroemen, Paul, *Arnhem Voorjaar 1945* (CIP-Gegevans Koninklijke Bibliotheek Den Haag 1989)
Vlist, Hendrika van der, *Oosterbeek 1944* (Oosterbeek: Society of Friends of the Airborne Museum, 1992)
Waddy, John, *A Tour of the Arnhem Battlefields* (Barnsley: Pen & Sword Books, 1999)
Waddy, John, *Arnhem Battlefield Map* (Barnsley: Pen & Sword Books, 1999)
Watkins, G.J.B., *From Normandy To The Weser, The War History of the 4th Battalion, The Dorset Regiment, June 1944–May 1945* (Dorchester: Dorset Press, 1947)
Warrack, Graeme, *Travel By Dark, After Arnhem* (London: Harvill Press, 1963)
Weeks, John, *Airborne Equipment* (Newton Abbott: David & Charles, 1976)
Whiting, Charles, *A Bridge At Arnhem* (Futura Publications, 1974)
Wilkinson, Peter, *The Gunners at Arnhem* (Spurwing, 1999)
Williams, Dennis, *Stirlings In Action With The Airborne Forces* (Barnsley: Pen & Sword, 2008)
Wood, Alan, *History of the World's Glider Forces* (London: Patrick Stephens Ltd, 1990)
Woolacott, Robert, *Winged Gunners* (Quote Publishers Ltd, 1994)
Zeno, *The Cauldron* (London: Pan, 1966)
Zwarts, Marcel, *German Armoured Units at Arnhem* (Hong Kong: Concord Publications, 2001)

Unpublished and Archival Sources

Tatham Warter, Maj. Digby, *Dutch Courage and Pegasus*, 1991
Account of the [2nd] Battalion's Operations at Arnhem 17th September 1944
Operatierapporten RAF Operatie Market Garden Headquarters Group 2
Report On The British Airborne Operation MARKET GARDEN By 38 & 46 Groups, RAF
1 Airborne Division Report on Operation Market
Part I – General Outline of Operation

Part II – Administrative Aspects of the Operation
Part III – The Lessons of the Operation
1 Airborne Division Report on Operation 'Market'; Part IV Annexures:
Order of Battle 1st Airborne Division
Directive from Commander, British Airborne Corps to Divisional Commander
Operation Instructions 1st Airborne Division
Operation Instructions 1st Parachute Brigade
Operation Instructions 4th Parachute Brigade
Operation Instructions 1st Airlanding Brigade
Operation Instructions Polish 1st Independent Parachute Brigade Group
Operation Instructions Royal Artillery, 1st Airborne Division
Operation Instructions Royal Engineers, 1st Airborne Division
Operation Instructions 1st Airborne Divisional Signals
Operation Instructions Medical Services, 1st Airborne Division
Operation Instructions 2nd Parachute Battalion WO171/1237

War Diary: HQ 1st Airborne Division
War Diary: 1st Parachute Brigade
War Diary: 4th Parachute Brigade
War Diary: 1st Airlanding Brigade
Copies of Important Letters and Messages

1st Airborne Division Report on Operation Market; Part V Annexures
Report by G (Int), 1st Airborne Division
Report by CRA, 1st Airborne Division
Report by CRE, 1st Airborne Division
Report by OC, 1st Airborne Divisional Signals
Report by ADMS, 1st Airborne Division
Operation Market; Diary of Events: 1st Parachute Brigade HQ
War Diary 1st Airborne Reconnaissance Squadron
War Diary 1st Parachute Battalion
War Diary 2nd Parachute Battalion
War Diary 3rd Parachute Battalion
War Diary 10th Parachute Battalion
War Diary 11th Parachute Battalion
War Diary 156th Parachute Battalion
War Diary 7th Battalion King's Own Scottish Borderers
War Diary 2nd Battalion South Staffordshire Regiment
War Diary 21st Independent Parachute Company
War Diary No. 1 Wing Glider Pilot Regiment
War Diary No. 2 Wing Glider Pilot Regiment
Operation Market Air: WO205/1123XC143173

Maps

Map References taken from:
1:25,000 A.M.S. M831 (G.S.G.S.4427)
First edition 1944 Arnhem Sheet 6 N.W.
First edition 1943 Ginkel
'Kaart van Oosterbeek' ca 1939. (Wamelink G.F. and Romjin) Courtesy Gelders Archief.
Graphics by SGW Design.

Photographic Sources

Imperial War Museum (IWM). In particular thanks to Sophie Fisher and Dave McCall for all their help and diligence.
Gelders Archief photographs courtesy of Photo Collection, Gelders Archief, Arnhem. My sincere thanks to all the Gelders Archief team, especially Marissa van de Vrede.
Utrecht Archief.
Aerocarto Aviodrome, Lelystad. My sincere thanks to Martin Smit for all his help.
National Center Aerial Photography (NCAP). Formerly Keele University.
Bundesarchiv Koblenz (BA).
Heemkunde Renkum.
Airborne Museum, Hartenstein, Oosterbeek (ABM). With particular help from my good friend, the late Dr Adrian Groeneweg for making many museum photographs available.
Remaining photographs from the editor's personal archives or private collections. With thanks to G. Lombardi, M.D. Stimson, F. Radley, R. Kift, T. Battle, P.Stott, A.R. Royall, D.W.Thomas, R.F. Hall, P. Pariso.

Societies and Fellowships
Anyone with a serious interest in the Battle of Arnhem would be well advised to take a look at both of these groups.
'The Society of Friends of The Airborne Museum'. (SFAM) Oosterbeek, Holland, have published several books on the battle. The society is Dutch based and organises battlefield tours and walks.
Website: www.vriendenairbornemuseum.nl
Email address: info@vriendenairbornemuseum.nl

'The Arnhem 1944 Fellowship' is a registered charity in the UK. Members receive around six digital newsletters per year and have the opportunity to attend battlefield tours and receive preferential prices on certain Arnhem battle related publications and booklets.
Website: www.arnhem1944fellowship.org
Email address: info@arnhem1944fellowship.org

The Battle of Arnhem was lost at Nijmegen, for the bridge there was a key point – a huge great obstacle – and the fantastic thing was that there had been no plans made by Browning (Lieutenant General Frederick Browning, Commander 1st British Airborne Corps) to take that bridge on the first day when it was there for the taking. – Major General John Frost
Soldier Magazine, July 1990

Index

PEOPLE

Allsop, Captain, D, 172
Anderson, Sapper, Lennox 'Todd', 314, 318, 326, 329
Anderson, Sergeant, J, 371, 373
Arnold, Major, W F, 202, 204, 375, 378, 380
Atkinson, Sergeant, E H, 369

Barnett, Lieutenant J P, 169, 176, 178
Barnsley, Gunner E H, 206, 209
Barry, Lieutenant, P H, 170, 173, 178, 303
Baskeyfield, Lance Sergeant John, 52, 70
Battle, Sergeant, Tommy, 103, 137–141
Bear, Captain, H, 433
Bechervaise, Private, 356
Beeston, Private, J, 221–227
Blakely, Sergeant, Ivor, 106, 109
Boast, Private, V, 213
Bonome, Staff Sergeant, J, 390
Bower, Sergeant, J, 391
Breman, B, 20, 97, 108, 109
Brinkmann, SS–Sturmbannführer, H, 187
Brodie, Lieutenant, A M, 323–324
Bryant, Staff Sergeants, Ken L, 319
Buchanan, Captain, H S, 169, 266–267, 269
Bune, Major, J C, 156
Burridge, Gunner, E T, 390, 426, 429
Burwash, Lieutenant, B, 44, 51
Bush, Major, A, 78, 79, 81, 82, 88, 107, 144, 167
Butterworth, Lieutenant, A D, 334, 336, 344–46, 350, 354, 358
Buttlar, SS–Sturmmann, H, 171

Cain, Major, R H, 53, 94, 118–119
Caird, Captain, W S, 167
Cairns, Lieutenant, J B, 187, 190
Callaghan, CSM, Harry, 72, 76, 78, 82, 93, 103, 107, 109, 109, 118, 120, 125, 142–146

Cameron, Driver/Gunner, William H., 395
Cane, Lieutenant, P, 171, 180
Casey, Lieutenant, J T, 389, 426
Chandler, Sergeant, Jimmy, 84, 88, 90
Chartonowicz, Bombardier, K, 388
Clapham, Lieutenant, E E, 49, 202–204, 370, 372
Clarke, Driver, K W 'Nobby', 314, 326, 328–329
Clarkson, Lieutenant, A D, 53, 166
Cleminson, Lieutenant, J, 42, 44, 49, 118-119, 144
Cole, Lieutenant, H C L, 403, 410
Collard, Private, W, 126–128,
Collins, Private, Dennis 'Colly', 57, 60, 62, 65, 72–73, 75, 77, 89
Cook, Gunner, R, 419–426
Cox, Captain, L G, 41, 51
Crawley, Major, D E, 225

Dale, Major, R, 394
Davies, Sergeant, D J, 53
Davis, Sergeant, Jack, 423, 425
Dennison, Major, M W, 42, 57, 60, 61, 65, 67, 142–144, 157, 158
Dickson, Lieutenant, J, 141
Dobie, Lieutenant Colonel, D T, 38, 50–51, 155–158, 162–163, 211
Doig, Sergeant Harold, 375, 376, 378–380, 396
Dorrien-Smith, Captain, G R (Dolly), 46, 50, 51, 72-73, 76-77, 98, 100, 104–106, 118, 125, 143, 146, 163, 166
Dover, Major, V, 170, 173–174, 176, 240, 203
Driver, Lieutenant, Tony V, 157, 211–212

Ewens, Captain, A F, 322–323
Evans, Sergeant, G, 194, 273

Farrands, Lieutenant, N F, 211, 274

Fitch, Lieutenant-Colonel, J A C, 38, 43–44, 46, 50–51, 103, 128, 130, 142
Fitchett, Lance-Sergeant, S, 206, 369, 390
Flavell, Colonel Edward, 36, 180, 189, 193
Flavell, Lieutenant, J, 18
Flower, Sergeant, E, 326, 329, 332
Frank, Captain, T, 377
Fraser, Lieutenant, W A, 53, 338–343, 352, 359, 360–361
French, Lance Corporal, Bert 57, 60, 65, 67, 68, 73, 77, 79, 86–88
Frost, Lieutenant Colonel John, 36, 38, 43, 51, 169, 170–174, 180, 186–187, 189–190, 276, 369

Garnsworthy, Sergeant, L, 42–44, 372–373
Gillespie, Lieutenant, Stanley, 138–139
Gough, Major, C F H, 'Freddie', 155, 170, 172, 189–190, 266–269, 276–278, 266, 268–269
Grayburn, Lieutenant, J H, 171–172, 189
Gasior, Corporal, W, 388
George, Private, R, 199
Gell, Captain, W V A, 169, 172
Gentles, Sergeant, N S, 369, 389, 394, 426, 429
Gillespie, Lieutenant, S, 138, 139
Goodwin, Private, V, 216–220
Gough, Major, F, 155, 170, 172, 189–190, 225, 266–269, 276–278
Grabner, SS-Hauptsturmführer, V 177–178, 183, 215, 268, 285, 376
Gronert, Private, C 171, 217
Gronert, Private, T 171, 217

Harrison, Captain, C A 'Tony', 128, 131, 157, 211, 269–274, 278,
Heaney, Private, Kevin, 244–45, 248–251, 254, 259
Hibbert, Major, Tony, 266–268
Hodges, Driver, H, 396, 399, 403
Holden, Private, Vic, 319, 334, 359–361
Hughes, Sergeant, T H, 390, 428–429
Hackett, Brigadier, J W, 85, 86, 106
Halpert, Lieutenant, J, 383
Hall, Lance-Bombardier, J L, 268, 269–282
Halley-Frame, Lance Corporal, T, 121–125
Hardman, Private, D, 59, 81, 83, 84, 87
Harrison, Captain, C A, 157, 211–212, 266–274, 278
Harrison, Private, L, 128–131
Harzer, Obersturmbannführer, W, 59
Haynes, Major, A F, 367
Heaps, Lieutenant, L J, Canloan 162, 200–201

Hibbert, Brigade Major, J A, 169, 278
Hibburt, Lieutenant, P L, 176
Hicks, Brigadier, P H W, 76, 155, 162
Hicks, Sapper, T 311–313
Higgins, Sergeant, G, 390
Hill, Private, G, 197
Hill, Lieutenant, G T, 121
Hindley, Lieutenant, D R, 173, 177
Holden, Private, V, 334–361
Horodeczny, Lance Sergeant, S, 386
Horrocks, Lieutenant General, B G, 253
Humphreys, Corporal, J E, 291–301
Hughes, Sergeant, T H, 389, 390

Infield, Lieutenant, G, 174, 176, 178
James, Lieutenant, E A, 122
Jenks, Staff Sergeant, G T, 392
Jones, Private, 'Jock', 57, 65, 70, 73, 77–81, 85, 87–89

Kennedy, Captain, C O, 169
Kent, Battery Sergeant Major, T, 392
Kill, Sergeant, W, 182, 375, 381
Killick, Captain, J E, 170
Kume, Major, K, 434
Kussin, General Major, F, 42, 59, 126, 129, 266, 401, 421

Larkin, Gunner, L G, 390
Lathbury, Brigadier, G W, 36, 42–44, 128, 142, 155, 186, 237, 249
Lea, Lieutenant Colonel, G H, 50
Leviens, Lieutenant R H, 213
Lewis, Major, R P C, 42, 43, 133, 134, 147, 149, 150
Liversey, Captain, T J, 172
Llewellyn-Jones, Captain, A D, 205, 375, 376, 378–380
Lloyd, Lieutenant, 206, 392
Lockett, Lieutenant, B S, 202–204
Loder-Symonds, Lieutenant Colonel, R G 205–206, 382, 419, 431–432
Logan, Captain, J W, 169, 189, 239, 280, 282
Loney, Lance Corporal, W, 175
Longland, Major, C J, 236–239
Lonsdale, Major, R T H, 52–53, 77, 79–81, 84–85, 87, 89, 106–107, 109, 118, 123, 144, 166, 373
Lord, Flight Lieutenant, D, 12
Lord, RSM, J C, 97, 98, 105, 130, 131

MacFarlane, Lieutenant, P, 369

INDEX

Mackay, Captain, F M, 172, 178, 185, 284, 289, 294–96, 298–300
Manley, Captain, B V, 169, 172–173, 177, 187, 243–244, 246–252, 256, 259
Marquand, Captain, W J, 190
Marsh, Private, G, 57, 60, 81, 83, 87
Masterson, Sergeant, J H, 206
McCardie, Lieutenant Colonel, W D H, 50, 158, 162, 164
McCarthy, Private, G, 227–233
McCullock, Bombardier, J, 392
McDermont, Lieutenant, A J, 170, 180, 181, 186, 381
McFarlane, Lance Corporal, Reg, 159–160
McFarlane, Lieutenant, P, 369, 378, 380
McFarlane, Sapper, 314, 326, 328–329, 332
McLeod, Captain, N, 205–206, 209
McNaught, Lieutenant, E, 382
Meagher, Sergeant, S, 157
Milner, Driver Eric, 372–373, 416–418
Mleczko Lieutenant, W, 382
Mleczko, Lieutenant, 382, 384, 386–388
Möller, SS-Hauptsturmführer, H, 153, 174, 213
Monsell, Lieutenant, J H A, 172
Moore, Staff Sergeant, T, 386
Mordecai, Private, E, 182, 242–265
Morrison, Gunner, R, 'Jock' 269–274, 277–278
Munford, Major, D S, 169, 177, 180, 182, 266–269, 272–280
Murray, Major, D C, 172, 291

Neary, Sergeant, T, 390
Nosecki, Bombardier, S, 388

O'Callaghan, Captain E 173, 177, 303–304
O'Neill, Sergeant, J, 380
Oprych, Bombardier, J, 384
Orrell, Private, B, 234

Padfield, Lance Sergeant, H, 302–307
Panter, Major, S C, 170, 172
Perrin-Brown, Major, C, 156–158
Perryman, Sergeant Dennis W, 138–139
Plummer, Sapper, L, 308–311
Potter, Lance Sergeant, Mervyn, J, 317, 329, 332
Potter, Lance Sergeant, M J, 326, 329, 331
Proctor, Sergeant, L E, 'Doc', 42, 369, 371, 423–424

Radley, Private, F, 56–96, 104, 143
Rams, Sergeant, M, 157, 204, 206, 370, 371
Rathband, Sergeant, Harry, 392–394, 428

Reed, Sergeant, D, 371, 373
Reed, Sergeant Major, M, 366
Reimann, Luftnachrichtenhelferinnen, I, 59
Richardson, Gunner, A C, 390
Richey, Captain, J A D, 158
Rigby, Sergeant, A, 395, 397–413
Roberts, Craftsmen, J R, 362–366
Robson, Sergeant, C, 178, 369, 375–377, 380, 413–415
Royall, Lieutenant, A R, 418
Russell, Lieutenant, D, 173
Russell, Lieutenant, I H, 173–174, 240
Ryall, Lieutenant, G, 204–206, 371–371
Ryden, Bombardier, L G, 392

Shaw, Lieutenant, E E, 157, 369–370, 396, 416, 418–419
Shaw, Sergeant, F, 43, 368, 370, 372–373,
Shelswell, Sergeant, E, 375, 378, 380, 395–397, 399, 402
Shipley, Private, N, 175
Simpson, Captain, D A, 403–405, 408–409
Simpson, Lieutenant, D J, 'Stiffy', 172, 178, 298–300, 306, 402
Skaczko, Bombardier, J, 388
Skinner, Lieutenant, W H, 314, 316–318, 326, 329
Stanley, Lance Corporal, W H, 53, 118
Stanners, Corporal, G, 210
Stark, Major, R L, 50, 156–157
Stidson, Lance Corporal, B J G, 113–120, 123
Sutton, Lieutenant, John, 199–201
Swift, Sergeant, N, 282, 283, 287, 306

Tatham-Warter, Major, A D, 170, 180, 186, 216, 249
Taylor, Captain, W E, 44, 49
Thessiger, Captain, R, 58
Thomas, Corporal, D, 287, 288, 289
Thomas, Sergeant, G E, 'Taffy', 206, 209, 391–393,
Thompson, Lieutenant Colonel, W F K 'Sheriff' 52, 56, 76, 77, 280
Timothy, Major, J, 155–156, 158, 197, 212
Toler, Major, T I J, 426
Towhey, Private, J, 58
Turner, AQMS, R, 366
Turrell, Lieutenant, J, 162, 168

Underwood, Lance Sergeant, K L, 326, 328–329, 333
Urquhart, Major-General, R E 'Roy', 43–44, 46, 48, 49, 115, 127, 189, 319, 419

Vedeniapine, Lieutenant, Alexis, 128, 130–131

Waddy, Major, A P H, 41, 44, 76, 115, 126–127, 130
Wade, Staff Sergeant, R S, 366
Walker, Sergeant, Harry 'Busty', 242, 244, 248, 251–252, 256–257, 259
Wallis, Major, D W, 135, 186, 224
Wardzala, Captain, J K, 383
Warwick, Gunner, T S, 390
Watson, Private, A, 147–151
Weir, Sergeant Chick, 298–299, 301
Whitehouse, Driver, Jeff, 354–355
Whitelaw, Corporal, Alex, 85, 97–113, 435

Whittaker, Captain, H, 376
Whittingham, Sergeant, D, 54, 82, 93, 167
Wilkinson, Sergeant, J A, 204, 371–373
Willcock, Major, M, 35
Willeke Gefreiter Josef, 59, 129
Williams, Lieutenant, J L, 163
Wilson, Major, B A, 38
Winchester, Major, J C, 303
Winser, Gunner, F J, 371, 429–433
Woods, Lieutenant, R B, 178
Woods, Sapper, F A, 289, 291
Wright, Lieutenant, L, 133–135, 147, 176–177, 306, 438

PLACES

Acacialaan, 25, 51–52, 166–167
Amsterdamseweg, 155–156, 195, 317, 370
Apeldoorn, 93, 131, 139–140, 197, 201, 235, 238–39, 306, 309, 312, 324
Arnhem Bridge, 38, 42–43. 99, 128, 133, 138, 165, 171, 174, 190–192, 194, 218, 227, 233, 281, 290, 312, 334, 374, 379, 412–413, 417, 420–421
Arnhem Garage, 162, 164, 243
Arnhem Pontoon Bridge, 38, 49–50, 102, 163, 170, 173, 183, 247, 304
Arnhem Prison, 51
Arnhem Railway Station, 100, 149, 170, 218

Badhuisstraat, 176, 193, 381
Bakkerstraat, 173
Bato's Wijk, 54, 168, 373, 388
Bechervaise, 356–358
Belgium, 243, 334, 357
Benedendorpsweg, 51–54, 68, 71–72, 82, 90, 93, 96–97, 114, 140, 157, 166–169, 386, 388–392, 416–417, 426–429
Bilderberg, 42, 386
Bovenover, 417
Bremans' House, 388
Bun House, 393–394

Camiz Dairy, 176, 178, 381

Den Brink, 132, 156–157, 161, 217, 273, 401
Diependalstraat, 163, 371, 373
Dreijenseweg, 156, 317, 323, 370
Driel, 112–113, 352, 355, 382, 386, 426, 432

Eusebius Binnen Singel, 193, 381
Eusebius Buitensingel, 152, 171, 173, 176–178, 180, 182, 186–187, 189, 193, 264, 284
Eusebiusplein, 193, 376, 379, 381

Fangmanweg, 373

Gas Works, 311, 365–366, 389–390, 394, 426, 428
Gemeente Museum, 174, 176, 199

Hartenstein, 43, 204–205, 308, 317, 319–321, 323–324, 347–348, 363–364, 371–373, 382, 384, 386, 421–423, 425
Heelsum, 98, 121, 169–170, 236, 247, 394
Heveadorp, 170, 247
Hofstraat, 193, 375, 379–381, 396
Hoofdlaan, 99, 317, 390–391
Hotel Wolfheze, 42
Hulkesteinseweg, 51, 66, 158, 160, 372

Jospe printing works, 193

Kade Straat, 193, 381
KEMA, 51, 132, 160, 163, 373
Klein Zwitserland Hotel, 169
Klingelbeeksewe, 51, 66, 140, 147, 157–158, 163, 171, 202, 370–372
Klingelbeekseweg, 51, 63, 66, 140, 157–158, 160–161, 163, 171, 202, 370–372
Koude Herber, 42–43, 387

Lombok, 44–49, 51, 132, 158, 163, 199

INDEX 459

London, 116, 123, 174, 240, 303, 357–358,

Markstrat, 178, 376, 378, 380, 413
Markt Straat, 193, 381

Nachtegalspad, 174, 176
Nieuwe Kade, 176, 178, 188, 193, 226, 235, 375, 380–381
Nieuwe Plein, 170, 173
Nijmegen, 38, 54–56, 64, 113, 157, 167–169, 221, 292, 299–301, 311, 318, 329, 332, 355, 357, 369, 388, 395, 398, 402, 426, 433
Noordelijke Parallelweg, 46–48, 199

Onderlangs, 44, 49–50, 122, 131, 133, 165, 174, 199, 203, 212, 374
Oosterbeek, 51–52, 66–68, 71, 96, 137–40, 155–56, 158, 170, 173–74, 207, 237–38, 321–23, 328–29, 370–73, 389–92, 416–18, 420–22, 430–32, 449–52, 454
Oosterbeek Laag, 43–44, 51–55, 140, 157, 164, 166–167, 170–171, 373, 386, 389–390, 393
Ooststraat, 178, 180–181, 186, 193, 235, 381
Oranjestraat, 50–51, 162, 164, 372–373
Oranjeweg, 313, 322–23, 363, 384, 386
Oude Oosterbeekseweg, 170

Park Hotel, 205, 344–345, 348, 351–354
Ploegseweg, 53, 77, 88, 93–94, 168, 388
Polderweg, 53, 71–72, 76–77, 82, 96, 104, 114, 117, 120, 122, 125, 143, 156, 170, 303
Primasole Bridge, 37, 236

Red School, 172, 177, 180, 185, 189, 193, 284
Renkum, 173, 178, 198, 447–52
Rhine, 53–55, 57, 68, 71, 87, 90, 95–97, 122–123, 145, 168–170, 177–178, 222–224, 226, 270–271, 291, 298–299, 341, 352, 355–356, 382–383, 388, 400, 425
Rhine Pavilion, 50–51, 101–103, 130–131, 133, 162–163, 372, 374, 389
Rijnkade, 173, 180–181, 189, 193, 378, 380–381
Rosande Polder, 71, 96, 104, 114, 117, 120, 122, 125, 143

Schoonoord, 127, 210, 373, 389, 417–418
Sluice Gate, 74, 106, 118, 120, 122, 125, 143
Sonnenberg, 308, 312–313, 317–318, 330–333, 370, 386, 391
St Elizabeth Hospital, 44–46, 49, 92, 100, 105, 121–122, 128, 158–159, 163, 169, 199, 201, 203, 218, 236, 238, 240–241, 263, 372, 416–417

Tafelberg, 100

Utrechtsestraat, 49, 165, 173–175, 212–213
Utrechtseweg, 41–47, 49–51, 65–66, 98, 121–122, 130–131, 155–159, 161–164, 173–174, 199, 317–318, 320, 359–360, 370–371, 373, 386–387, 390, 420–422, 424

Van Hofwegen Laundry, 53, 166, 388
Van Limburg Stirum School, 134, 152, 172, 176–178, 180, 185–187, 189, 283–285, 287, 294, 307
Vreewijk, 210

Westerbouwing, 388
Westervoortsedijk, 176–79, 182, 186, 190, 193, 226, 254, 375–77, 381, 414
Weverstraat, 54, 373, 388
Wolfhezerweg, 42–43, 155

Zuidelijke Parallelweg, 47–48
Zwarteweg, 44, 46, 48–49, 373

MILITARY FORMATIONS & UNITS

British & Polish
Advance Workshop Detachment, REME, 320–325, 362–366
1st Airborne Division, 36–39, 54–55, 59, 95, 106, 154–155, 167–170, 187, 189, 227, 234, 238–239, 242, 265, 299, 301–302, 305, 314–315, 319–320, 322, 325, 334, 343, 349, 362, 65, 368, 383, 419
6th Airborne Division, 37–38, 197
1st Airborne Reconnaissance Squadron, 39, 155, 170, 189, 322, 325

1st Airlanding Anti-Tank Battery RA, 41–42, 49, 154–155, 157, 160, 163, 169, 172, 182, 190, 202, 209, 318, 367, 381–382, 389, 392–393, 395, 413, 416, 419, 426
1st Airlanding Brigade, 36–37, 39, 155, 169, 301, 320, 324, 367–68, 436, 440–42, 453
1st Airlanding Light Regiment RA, 54–55, 168–169, 320, 324–325, 367–368

Border Regiment, 85, 87, 308, 318, 325, 387, 436, 441, 448, 451
Breese Force, 388

261 Field Park Company RE, 169, 204, 242–265, 314–316, 318, 320, 324, 326–333
Forward Observation Unit (FOU), Royal Artillery, 166–67, 266–67, 269

Glider Pilot Regiment, 36, 39–40, 84, 168, 193, 307, 318–319, 322, 367–369, 382–383, 389, 395, 397

King's Own Scottish Borderers (KOSB), 109, 112, 313, 325, 383

Lonsdale Force, 52–54, 106–107, 118, 148, 168, 390, 392

64th Medium Regiment, RA 55, 78, 167–168

1st Parachute Battalion, 38–41, 49–51, 53–55, 57, 67, 75, 78, 82, 84, 93, 100, 102, 125, 154–157, 162–164, 166–169, 194, 197, 199, 201–206, 210, 212, 287, 321, 325, 356, 368–373
2nd Parachute Battalion, 36, 38, 40–42, 44, 54, 58, 100, 154–155, 157, 169–171, 174, 176, 180–181, 186, 189–190, 193, 210, 213, 216, 221–222, 227, 233–234, 240, 247, 266–268, 272, 274, 277–278, 287, 292–293, 303, 321, 336, 343, 347, 349, 367, 369, 375, 377, 379–381, 396, 423
3rd Parachute Battalion, 35–36, 38–51, 53–54, 56, 59, 61, 63–65, 67–68, 70, 72, 76, 78, 81, 95–97, 100, 102–103, 105, 110, 113–114, 120, –121, 124–126, 128–129, 135–136, 140, 142, 146–148, 155, 157–159, 162–169, 170, 174, 177–178, 187, 193, 210, 217, 247, 266, 271, 305–308, 311, 321, 336, 340–341, 343, 360–361, 367, 369–370, 372–374, 381, 388, 412, 414, 416, 418–421, 434
1st Parachute Brigade, 35–42, 53, 57, 74, 76–77, 80, 95–96, 98, 107, 114, 120–121, 125, 131, 133, 137, 154–155, 158, 166–167, 169–170, 176, 178, 186, 190–193, 199, 210, 221, 227, 233, 236, 241, 265–266, 269, 271, 274, 287, 301, 311, 315, 320–326, 343, 368, 370, 378, 381, 389, 433
4th Parachute Brigade, 37, 77, 156, 239, 301, 317, 320, 322–323, 325, 383, 385
1st Parachute Squadron Royal Engineers, 287, 307, 311

Polish 1st Independent Parachute Brigade, 55, 367, 382–383, 386
Polish 1st Independent Parachute Company, 38, 112, 318, 322, 325, 386

Royal Artillery (RA), 202, 204, 206, 209, 211–212, 254, 266, 269, 276, 370–371, 424, 426
Royal Air Force (RAF), 36, 39–41, 55, 110, 207, 348, 358, 389, 395, 398
Royal Army Medical Corps (RAMC), 41,169, 189, 210, 234, 236, 238–239, 307, 368
Royal Army Ordnance Corps (RAOC), 169, 172–173, 177, 182, 193, 204, 242, 265, 319
Royal Engineers (RE), 41, 43–44, 218–219, 287, 289, 291, 302–303, 308–309, 311, 315, 317, 433
Royal Electrical and Mechanical Engineers (REME), 314, 319–23, 329, 362–63

South Staffordshire Regiment, 92, 436, 440–41, 449

Thompson Force, 52
XXX Corps, 54–55, 68, 72, 78–79, 84–85, 87, 90, 101, 119, 167–168, 174, 187, 190, 206, 238, 243, 250, 253, 274–275, 278–279, 282, 305, 388, 402, 408–410, 413

United States
82nd Airborne Division, 302, 369
101st Airborne Division, 302

German Units
Bataillon Eberwein, 318
Bataillon Kraft (SS-Panzer -Ausbildungs-und Ersatz- Bataillon 16), 42, 170,
Jagdgeschwader 76, 187
Kampfgruppe Allwörden, 55, 156, 168
Kampfgruppe Harder, 50, 55, 153, 166, 360
Kampfgruppe Möller, 153, 174, 213
Kampfgruppe Brinkmann, 187
Kampfgruppe Weber, 155
Kampfgruppe Knaust, 186
213 Nachrichten Regiment, 155
Panzer-Kompanie Mielke, 177, 186, 188, 377
9th SS Panzer Division, 59, 156, 229
SS-Panzer-Flak-Abteilung, 10 171
SS-Panzer-Aufklärungs-Abteilung, 9 177, 183, 215, 268, 374, 376
SS-Panzer-Pioniere- Bataillon, 9 168, 213
schwere Panzer-Kompanie Hummel, 187, 235
2./Schwere Panzer-Abteilung 506, 55

GENERAL & MISCELLANEOUS TERMS

Bruneval Raid, 36, 197

Clark Air Tractor, 314–315, 317, 326
CRA (Commander Royal Artillery), 154, 205–206, 266, 276, 314, 371, 382, 386

DZ (Drop Zone), 37–41, 56–57, 97–98, 137, 155, 169–70, 216–17, 234, 246–47, 274–75, 292–93, 308, 311, 322, 369–70

First Lift, 42, 154, 227, 245, 369, 371, 397, 420

GEE, 169
German POWs, 160, 205, 283, 319, 323, 366
Glider Pilots, 39–40, 53–54, 87, 112, 119, 172, 189, 291, 322, 327, 344, 350, 352, 354, 369, 382, 383, 386, 392, 393, 395, 400, 403, 406, 410, 413, 416–417, 421, 425

Hamilcar Glider, 40, 207, 293, 316, 326, 371, 375, 389–390, 392–394, 398–399, 413, 426, 429–430
Horsa Glider, 291, 316–17, 319, 321, 326–327, 329, 366, 368–69, 382–383, 385, 389

LZ (Landing Zone), 37–41, 98, 157, 162, 266, 275, 311, 317, 319, 321–322, 327, 363, 368–369, 382–385, 389–390, 392, 394–395, 397, 399–400, 420, 426, 428, 430–431

Second Lift, 41–42, 50, 162–163, 275–276, 368, 371–372, 382, 384, 389–390, 419–420, 430–431

Third Lift, 40–41, 369, 382–383, 408

Rebecca-Eureka, 169

The late Dr Adrian Groeneweg OBE stands in one of 1st Battalion Border Regiment 3-inch mortar positions behind 1st Airborne Divisional HQ, Hartenstein.
Dr A Groeneweg OBE 6th June 1944–25th July 2010 (Photo: Author, 1984)